10-6-76

THE PROBLEMS OF PHILOSOPHY

THE PROBLEMS OF PHILOSOPHY

CLASSICAL AND CONTEMPORARY SOURCES

Edited with introductions by
C. F. DELANEY
GARY GUTTING
MICHAEL J. LOUX
HAROLD MOORE

UNIVERSITY OF NOTRE DAME PRESS
NOTRE DAME LONDON

Library of Congress Cataloging in Publication Data

Main entry under title:

The problems of philosophy.

1. Philosophy--Addresses, essays, lectures.
I. Delaney, Cornelius F.
B21.P94 108 76-643
ISBN 0-268-01521-X

Manufactured in the United States of America

Contents

Preface

This book derives directly from the editors' experience in teaching the required Introduction to Philosophy course at Notre Dame. The general problems treated and almost all the individual selections have been chosen because of their success in our teaching. Accordingly, this book is primarily a collection of materials that have worked well; and its primary justification is simply this practical fact.

However, practical successes appear, at least in retrospect, to be based on general principles; and this introduction is the place to formulate and briefly comment on what we now see as having been our principles of selection.

First—and generally overriding—is the principle that beginning philosophy students should be presented with readings that meet very high standards of clarity and logical cogency. Here a first consideration is the simple fact that a successful course requires material that is sufficiently free from technicalities and obscurities to be read with understanding (and, we can hope, intellectual pleasure) by ordinary undergraduates. But a further and even more important consideration is the need to provide students with exemplars of the virtues of clear thought and expression to which we hope to lead them.

Secondly, the student should be brought into contact with a good number of the major figures and main trends of thought in Western philosophy. Accordingly, well over half of our selections are by "great philosophers" in the classical tradition; and all the selections deal with central themes of this tradition. However, we have not made the vain effort of including all major figures and themes. Further, with one or two exceptions, we have not let this second principle interfere with the first principle's demand for clarity.

Thirdly (and finally), this book's structure derives from our conviction that a successful introduction to philosophy must focus primarily on philosophical *problems*, and more particularly, on problems that are both classic and of concrete interest to most students. Here we see ourselves as walking a narrow line between the puritan and the panderer; i.e., between an uncompromising insistence on professional, technical philosophy and a genial attempt to present philosophy as directly relevant to current social and political debates. With regard to the former, we think that technical issues such as the ground of induction, the nature of perception, and the mind/body problem are best postponed until the student has seen how these issues are indeed essential for an ultimately satisfactory discussion of more immediately compelling problems like those of God, freedom, and immortality. With regard to the latter, we think that a course which focuses primarily on "topics of the day" (like abortion, feminism, and drugs) is unlikely to go far beyond the level of a good dormitory bull-session and, by overemphasizing what *is* relevant to the student, will likely fail to bring the student to an awareness of what *should be* relevant.

We owe special thanks first to the students whose reactions to our courses largely determined the content of this text; and to Ryan Welsh and Cathy McInerny for their clerical assistance.

PART ONE

Religious Belief

Introduction

MICHAEL LOUX

I

In this section, we shall consider the question of the rationality of religious belief. There are, of course, any number of different forms of religious belief. Our concern will be with religious belief as it has dominated the Western tradition. In that tradition religious belief has tended to focus on an unsurpassable being, a God who is said to be supremely perfect in every way—to be all-good, all-powerful, all-knowing, and so on. In asking whether religious belief of the Western sort is rational, then, we shall be asking whether it is rational to believe in the existence of a being who is unsurpassable in this way.

Now, many philosophers have held that belief of this sort is rational in the strong sense that it can be supported by a *sound proof* for the existence of a supremely perfect being. The notion of proof that is at work here is fairly straightforward. A proof is an attempt to establish some proposition or statement, an attempt to show that the proposition is true given certain evidence. In a proof, then, we try to show that a proposition follows from other propositions which express our evidence. Logicians call the proposition we seek to establish in a proof the *conclusion* of the proof and the propositions which express the evidence at work in the proof its *premises*. Thus, a proof moves from premises to conclusion. The aim, of course, is a good proof; and to be good, a proof must, first of all, be *valid*. In rough terms, a valid proof is one whose conclusion does, in fact, follow from its premises. More accurately, a proof is valid if it is impossible for its premises to be true and its conclusion false. Validity is a property a proof has because of its structure of "logical form." Thus, any proof that has the following structure will be valid, i.e., will be such that it is impossible for its premises to be true and its conclusion false:

Every *A* is *B*
Every *B* is *C*
Therefore: Every *A* is *C*.

Both of the following arguments, for example, exhibit this structure:

Every Collie is a dog
Every dog is an animal
Therefore: Every Collie is an animal

Every petunia is a dog
Every dog is an animal
Therefore: Every petunia is an animal,

so that both are valid. Only the former, however, is a good argument; and that means that validity by itself does not make an argument good. In addition, a proof must have true premises. A valid proof with true premises is said to be *sound*; in a sound proof we succeed in establishing what we set out to establish; we actually prove the conclusion. But, then, when they have claimed that religious belief is rational in the sense that it can be supported by a sound proof for the existence of God, philosophers have been claiming that there is at least one valid proof which derives the proposition that God exists from true premises.

II

Perhaps the most intriguing proof philosophers have presented in this context is the *Ontological Argument*.[1] This argument has been formulated in a number of ways; but it typically takes as its starting point the apparently definitional truth that God is a being possessing all perfections infinitely. Proponents of this argument have insisted, however, that existence is a perfection and have concluded that God exists. Schematically, their reasoning goes as follows:

(1) God has all perfections infinitely
(2) Existence is a perfection

Therefore: (3) God has existence; i.e., God exists.

Now, critics of the Ontological Argument have generally been willing to grant that this form of reasoning is valid; they have conceded, that is, that if (1) and (2) are true, then God exists. For the most part, their criticisms have focused on (2); and although they have been variously stated, their criticisms of (2) have come to much the same thing. The standard criticism of (2) was first presented by a medieval monk named Gaunilo, who was responding to the use of (2) (or better: to the use of a near relative of (2)) by St. Anselm.[2] Towards capturing the point of Gaunilo's criticism, let us suppose that someone introduces into English the expression 'Insulissima' and defines it by saying that Insulissima is the most perfect possible island. According to Gaunilo, (2) enables us to establish the existence of Insulissima for if Insulissima is to be the most perfect possible island, it must have all the properties that make islands perfect. (2) tells us that existence is one of these, so that Insulissima must have it—Insulissima exists. Now, Gaunilo's point here is perfectly general: the sort of reasoning employed to show the existence of Insulissima enables us to show, for every kind of thing whatever, that a most perfect possible exemplar of that kind exists. It is, of course, difficult to believe that such objects exist; their nonexistence, we want to say, shows us that (2) is false; and what that means is that although valid, the Ontological argument is unsound.

Although this line of argument appears compelling, proponents of the Ontological Argument have insisted that it fails to show (2) false. Gaunilo's attack on (2) works only if the concept of a most perfect conceivable island is coherent. Its coherence, however, presupposes the possibility of specifying a determinate set of features which Insulissima would exhibit. But what would these be? Would Insulissima have a constant temperature of 72°? 73°? Would it have no constant temperature at all, but a temperature that fluctuates from sunrise to sunset? What exactly would the dimensions of Insulissima be? Six square miles? Seven? How many species of animals would inhabit this island? One hundred and thirty three? One hundred and thirty four? How many species of plants would be native to Insulissima? Five thousand? Five thousand and one? It is, of course, unclear *how* these questions are to be answered, and it is equally unclear that any *one* set of answers must be *the* correct set of answers. Unlike the case of the most perfect possible being, the notion of a most perfect possible island does not dictate a unique set of properties. What that suggests is that perhaps there could be no such thing as *the* most perfect possible island; and if that is true, then, of course, Gaunilo's refutation of (2) fails.

But if the proponent of the Ontological Argument can handle the criticism raised against (2), it is less obvious that he can find an interpretation of (1) according to which (1) comes out true and, in conjunction with (2), entails (3). To see the difficulty here, we need only ask for an explanation of (1). At first glance, (1) appears to be a proposition that picks out some object and ascribes a property to it—the property of having all perfections infinitely. The difficulty, however, is that when (1) is interpreted in this way, its use as a premise in an argument for God's existence can be only question-begging; for on this interpretation (1) comes out true only if God does, in fact, exist. After all, the proposition can succeed in picking out the relevant object—God—and ascribing a property to him only if he exists. We need, then, some other interpretation of (1). The fact that (1) presents itself as a definitional truth suggests that we construe it as an implicitly general claim, the claim that if anything is God, it has all perfections infinitely. This claim is true; but it too is useless for the proponent of the Ontological Argument; for on this interpretation, (1) and (2) do not yield (3). They yield only the weaker claim that *if* anything is God, it has the property of existence. That claim, however, is not the outright assertion that God exists. It is a hypothetical claim that is perfectly compatible with the nonexistence of God.

III

But if there are difficulties with the Ontological Argument, there are other forms of argument that present themselves as sound proofs of the proposition that God exists. One of these is the *Cosmological Proof*.[3] Underlying this argument is a distinction between two kinds of objects, *contingent* and *necessary* objects. The former are objects which exist but whose nonexistence is possible; whereas, the latter are existing objects whose nonexistence is impossible or inconceivable. Now, although the Cosmological Argument has been formulated in a variety of ways, these different formulations all agree in accepting the thesis (usually called the *Principle of Sufficient Reason*) that for every contingent entity, there is some other entity that is responsible for its existence. Given that principle, the proponent of the Cosmological Proof chooses some contingent being and argues that its existence presupposes a chain of beings that ultimately terminates in God. Frequently, the chosen object is the universe itself. We are told that the universe as a whole is a contingent being and that, consequently, it must have a cause. The cause of the universe, of course, is either a contingent or necessary being. Now, according to the proponent of the Cosmological Proof, if the cause of the universe is a necessary being, then God exists; for on that assumption, the cause of the universe is a self-caused cause of all that there is, "the Creator of heaven and earth"; and only God fits that characterization. On the other hand, if the cause of the universe is contingent, a second application of the Principle of Sufficient Reason establishes that it too has a cause. The proponent of the Cosmological Argument insists, however, that we cannot go on to infinity positing one contingent cause after another. As he puts it, such a procedure "does not render a sufficient reason why anything should exist in the first place. Instead of supplying a reason why any world should exist, it repeatedly begs off giving a reason."[4] After a finite number of applications of the Principle of Sufficient Reason, then, we reach a necessary being, a self-caused cause of all that there is; that is to say, we reach God.

Although many philosophers have found this line of argument compelling, critics have challenged every one of its premises; and with good reason, I think. It is not clear, for example, why we *have* to say that the universe as a whole is a contingent being; isn't it possible that while all the objects in the world are contingent, the totality of those objects is necessary? But even if the world is contingent, why *must* we accept the Principle of Sufficient Reason? Perhaps, the principle holds for all the objects in the universe, but what *forces* us to say that the principle holds in the case of the universe as well? What is incoherent in the suggestion that while contingent, the universe just exists, exists without any cause, without any explanation? But, again, if we grant that the world has a cause, what *compels* us to say that the sequence of causes preceding it is finite in length? Why is it impossible that there be an infinite series of contingent causes?

Proponents of the Cosmological Argument are seldom very successful in answering these questions; but even if they could establish the premises in question, it is unclear that the Cosmological Argument would have the consequences they claim it has. At the most, their argument establishes the existence of a self-caused cause of the universe; but while traditional religion does associate the property of being self-caused and the property of being the cause of the universe with God, the religious believer will insist that more than these two properties are required of a being if it is to qualify as an object of religious aspiration. To be God, a being must, for example, be all-good and all-knowing; and it is simply not clear that, as a matter of necessity, a self-caused cause of the universe must have these additional properties.

IV

A rather different line of argument in support of traditional religion is the *Teleological Argument,* which seeks to show that the existence of God is required to explain the order or structure of the universe.[5] Towards characterizing the order on which this argument hinges, the proponent of the Teleological Argument appeals to an analogy, telling us that the structure of the universe is, in essential respects, like that of a machine. He wants to insist, however, that it is necessarily true that objects with a machine-like structure are the design of some creative intelligence and, so, concludes that the universe is caused by some intelligent being, who, he insists, is God.

Critics, however, have argued that if the Teleological Argument succeeds in establishing the existence of some intelligent designer of our "world-machine," it fails to establish the divinity of that designer. To establish this, the proponent of the Teleological Argument would have to point to some property exhibited by the universe which entails that an infinitely perfect being was its designer, but the critic of this proof contends that there is no such property. Indeed, he frequently contends that there is much about our universe—its needless pain and suffering, for example—which suggests that an infinitely perfect being *could not* have designed it.

If it is sound, then, the Teleological Argument establishes only the existence of a finite designer of our universe. But does it establish even that much? Well, that depends on whether (1) the concept of a machine-like structure presupposes the existence of a creative intelligence and (2) the world is machine-like in structure. Now, it is clear that most, if not all, of the things we call machines were designed by an intelligent being; but the question is whether this is a matter of necessity. Critics of the Teleological Argument have insisted that it is not and have concluded that even if the universe is machine-like in structure, it is possible that it lacks a designing intelligence.

But is (2) true? Is the universe machine-like in structure? Well, if we focus on the inner workings of the universe, it is not difficult to convince ourselves that it is. As one of the characters in Hume's *Dialogues on Natural Religion* puts it:

> Look around the world, contemplate the whole and every part of it: you will find it to be nothing but one great machine, subdivided into an infinite number of lesser machines, which again admit of subdivisions to a degree beyond what human senses and faculties can trace and explain. All these various machines, and even their most minute parts, are adjusted to each other with an accuracy that ravishes into admiration all men who have ever contemplated them.[6]

Thus, the harmonious interplay of the various systems making up our universe suggests that the universe as a whole is a machine. Unfortunately, the harmonious interplay of its parts is not sufficient to make something a machine. Those parts must be so organized that the whole they constitute produces some effect. Automobiles, for example, run; toasters toast; and wash machines wash. If (2) is to be true, then, there must be some effect we can attribute to the universe as a whole, some effect that results from the harmonious interplay of its parts. But what is this effect? The difficulty, of course, is that being inside the "world-machine," we cannot know the answer to this question; we cannot even be certain it has an answer. To be sure, we can believe that it has an answer; we can believe, that is, that there is some point or purpose to the universe as a whole. But notoriously that belief is one which is held by the believer and rejected by the nonbeliever. It could hardly serve, then, as a premise in any argument purporting to *justify* belief in God.

V

There have been other kinds of proofs for God's existence. For example, some philosophers have argued that we can establish God's existence by reflecting on the introspective data of religious experience; whereas, others have argued that God's existence is presupposed by the objective validity of the moral law; but while these attempts at proving the existence of an unsurpassable being are not without their interest, they have seldom been presented in terms that are as convincing as the traditional formulations of the Ontological, Cosmological, and Teleological Proofs for God's existence. Unfortunately, the difficulties associated with those proofs suggest that it is unlikely that religious belief can be shown to be rational in the strong sense of being supported by a sound proof of God's existence. Indeed, if we recall a point made in our examination of the Teleological Argument, we are likely to think that it is possible to show that religious belief is irrational in the strong sense that there is a sound proof for the proposition that God does not exist. After pointing to the fact that there is little if anything about our world that shows it to be the product of a divine intelligence, we noted that the apparently needless pain and suffering we meet suggests that our world could not have been the product of a being having all the properties traditional religion associates with God. Atheists have seized upon this suggestion and have developed it into what has come to be known as the *Argument from Evil*.[7] This argument for atheism takes as its starting-point a series of what appear to be harmless definitional truths. These include the claims that an all-knowing being would know what a world without evil would be like, that an all-good being would want to create such a world and, finally, that an all-powerful being would be able to do this. Now, the atheist insists that it is a consequence of these three truths that if some being has all three of these properties—omniscience, omnibenevolence, and omnipotence—there is no evil in the world. By definition, however, God is such a being, so that if God does, in fact, exist, there is no evil in the world. But, of course, there is evil in the world; one needs merely to point to the needless pain and suffering in the world to show that this is so, so that, the atheist concludes, God does not exist.

This is a formidable piece of reasoning; one calling for a decisive critique from the believer. Unfortunately, his responses to the argument have all too often been unsuccessful. He sometimes responds by arguing that there is, all in all, more good than evil in the world; he apparently fails to recognize that the proponent of the Argument from Evil needs just a solitary instance of evil. That, he claims, is sufficient to show the nonexistence of God as traditionally conceived. The believer who sees the force of this point sometimes responds by denying that there is any evil in the universe at all. The Christian Scientist, for example, insists that pain and suffering are not *real* phenomena, but only distortions of reality produced by our modes of representing the world. Apparently the Christian Scientist fails to see that even if correct, his analysis leaves us with at least one evil state of affairs—the state of affairs consisting in human beings' being so constructed as to represent reality in the distorted way they do. Yet another response to the Argument from Evil involves the denial that pain and suffering are pointless; the claim here is that they play an essential role in the divine economy. Thus, some believers claim that evil is God's punishment for sin; whereas, others insist that it is God's warning to man. Believers who make the former claim, however, apparently overlook the fact that the pain and suffering individuals experience is in no obvious way proportionate to the moral evil they perpetrate; whereas those who make the latter claim fail to see that so far from providing man with the appropriate warning to "make straight the way of the Lord," evil has been a major factor in leading people to reject the framework of traditional religion. It is, after all, evil in the world that lies at the core of the argument for atheism that we are now considering!

A more sophisticated response to the Argument from Evil hinges on the claim that when we apply expressions like 'knows', 'good', and 'powerful' to God, we are not using these expressions in their ordinary senses. Given the meanings these expressions have when applied to human beings, their use does have the kinds of consequences it is alleged to have by the proponent of the Argument from Evil; but this is not so with respect to the meanings they have when applied to God. If it is to be satisfactory, however, this response has to be supplemented with some sort of account of the meaning of religious language. Just how, we want to ask, are the meanings of the relevant words related to their ordinary meanings? We are typically told here that the meanings they exhibit within the context of talk about God are built upon their ordinary meanings; there is supposedly an analogy here. But how close is this analogy? If it is relatively close, then it would seem that the Argument from Evil goes through after all. If, however, the analogy is not close, then it is unclear that we understand what we are saying when we talk about God; and that presumably is a consequence as disastrous for traditional religion as the Argument from Evil!

A rather different response to the Argument from Evil challenges the claim that an all-powerful being could have created a world with less evil in it than our own. Both theist and atheist agree that an omnipotent being can do only what is not impossible; the theist, however, wants to argue that it is at least conceivable that a world with less evil in it than our own would have involved a contradiction. As the point is usually put, our world could be the "best of all possible worlds." Now, at first glance, this appears to be a promising line of response to the atheist's argument; but if we recall our discussion of Insulissima, we are likely to become suspicious of talk of "*the* best of all possible worlds." In that context, we argued that the concept of *the* best possible island may well not be coherent; but our doubts about that notion would seem to apply here as well.

But while problematic, there is something insightful in this reply to the Argument from Evil; for the theist who makes the response seems to realize that what is required to block the argument is the identification of a *possible* state of affairs in which the propositions 'God exists' and 'Evil exists' are both true. The atheist is contending that these two propositions are inconsistent; to rebut that claim, the theist has only to sketch out a possible or conceivable situation where both come out true. This insight lies at the center of the so-called *Free Will Defense*.[8] Central to this response to the Argument from Evil is the contention that we must distinguish between two kinds of evil—moral and physical or natural evil. The former is evil resulting from the exercise of some finite will; whereas, the latter is evil that is not moral. Now, the proponent of the Free Will Defense insists that no reference to moral evil can legitimately figure in the Argument from Evil; for, after all, its existence is not caused or produced by God, but by the free beings he created.

Underlying this response is the contention that freedom is a value sufficient to justify any moral evil that might result from it. The proponent of the Free Will Defense, that is, holds that a world with free agents who on some occasions perpetrate moral evil is a "better world" than one in which programmed robots invariably do what is right. If he is correct on this point, the proponent of the Free Will Defense still has natural or physical evil to contend with; and here he fastens on the insight just noted and argues that it is at least *possible* or *conceivable* that there is no natural or physical evil, that the evil we take to be physical evil is the product of some powerful, but evil, free being. In this connection, the theist can appeal to the traditional teaching about Satan, arguing that while perhaps false, that teaching is at least coherent, so that the propositions 'God exists' and 'Evil exists' are not, as the atheist claims, inconsistent.

VI

But if the theist is successful here, he has to face an even stronger indictment of religious belief—the claim that the sentences characteristically employed by the believer are not just false, but meaningless or unintelligible. In recent years, this claim has been associated with a certain theory of meaningfulness or significance—the *Empiricist Theory of Meaningfulness*.[9] According to this theory, a declarative sentence comes out meaningful only if it is possible to point to experiences, whether introspective or perceptual, which would enable us to determine its truth value. The claim is that the sentences espoused by the theist (sentences like 'God exists') do not satisfy this criterion and, so, do not even qualify as false; they turn out to be meaningless or nonsensical.

We have so far specified the Empiricist Theory of Meaningfulness in general terms. To count as a real theory, however, it needs to be stated more precisely. Unfortunately, empiricists have disagreed among themselves about how this is to be done. Some have wanted to formulate the theory as follows:

(1) A declarative sentence, *S*, is meaningful if and only if it is possible to verify *S* conclusively on the basis of experience (whether perceptual or introspective).

Now, (1) does have the desired consequence; given (1), religious claims turn out to be meaningless since it is impossible to point to any experience or set of experiences that could conclusively verify sentences like 'God exists'. Unfortunately, the same is true for many other declarative sentences whose meaningfulness is beyond doubt. All universal sentences (sentences of the form 'Every *A* is *B*' and 'No *A* is *B*'), for example, turn out to be nonsense on (1). To verify conclusively a sentence like 'Every man is an animal', one would have to show that there is no object that is both a man and a nonanimal; but to do that, one would have to examine each object that there is. Given the infinity of objects, it is not difficult to be convinced that such an examination is not possible.

To handle this difficulty, empiricists have suggested that we substitute for (1) the following:

(2) A declarative sentence, *S*, is meaningful if and only if it is possible to falsify *S* conclusively on the basis of experience.

Now, on (2) universal sentences can come out meaningful since one counter-instance is sufficient to falsify a universal claim. It seems impossible, on the other hand, to falsify conclusively religious claims like 'God exists'. They can be held true come what may, so that in (2) the empiricist seems to have what he needs. But does he really? No; for like (1), (2) makes sentences whose meaningfulness is incontestable come out nonsense. All particular sentences (sentences of the form 'Some *A* is *B*' and 'Some *A* is not *B*') come out meaningless on (2); for to show such sentences false, one would once again have to consult all the objects that there are; and that, we have seen is impossible.

What the atheist needs here is a more modest version of the Empiricist Theory of Meaningfulness. The notions of conclusive verification and conclusive falsification are simply too restrictive. The following weaker principle is sometimes suggested as a plausible alternative to (1) and (2):

(3) A sentence, *S*, is meaningful if and only if it is possible that there be some empirical evidence for the truth of *S*.

On (3), universal and particular sentences can come out meaningful; for while it may be impossible for the former to be conclusively verified and for the latter to be conclusively falsified, it is possible to find *some evidence* for the truth of sentences of both kinds. But is there any empirical evidence for the truth of 'God exists'? The atheist insists that there is none and concludes that the sentences uttered by the believer are meaningless. Unfortunately, (3) too has its difficulties, difficulties that are shared by (1); for on (3) all sentences that are necessarily false turn out meaningless. 'All bachelors are married' is false and could not be true, so that presumably there would be no *possible* evidence for its truth; but, of course, 'All bachelors are married' is meaningful. (3), then, won't accomplish what the opponent of traditional religion wants it to accomplish.

As a last-ditch effort the empiricist suggests the following formulation of his account of meaningfulness:

(4) A sentence, *S*, is meaningful if and only if it is possible that there be some empirical evidence for the falsity of *S*.

Unfortunately, (4) won't do either, since all necessary truths come out meaningless on (4). '2 + 2 = 4', for example, is a sentence expressing a necessary truth; it is true and cannot be false, so that presumably no empirical evidence for its falsity is possible. Now, the fact that (4) is false as an account of meaningfulness is important. It is necessary truths that show (4) inadequate; and the believer will surely claim that many of the sentences characteristic of the language of religion are necessary truths. 'God exists', for example, is true and necessarily true on the theist's account; and the same is true of sentences like 'God is all-good' and 'God is all-powerful'.

VII

But if he is unsuccessful in showing the theist's characteristic claims to be without sense, the atheist locates what appears to be a genuine difficulty for the theist. If the atheist is correct, then there is no evidence whatsoever for the claims making up the substance of religious belief. But, then, the theist's acceptance of claims like 'God exists' seems to be totally unfounded. At this juncture, the atheist may agree that religious belief is not irrational in the strong sense that propositions like 'God exists' are demonstrably false or meaningless; but he will insist that it is irrational in the weaker sense that given the totality of empirical evidence at our disposal, the beliefs of the theist are wildly improbable, so improbable that no truly rational man would accept them.[10]

Theists have recognized the challenge presented here and have responded in a variety of ways. Perhaps the most radical response comes from theists who insist that the atheist simply misunderstands the characteristic claims of the believer. He takes them to be *statements about transcendental objects* (i.e., objects beyond the realm of experience); but, in fact, they are something quite different. Theists who take this line of defense have provided a variety of analyses of religious discourse. Some have insisted that the claims of the believer are disguised moral propositions, that they are ethical statements cast in a system of images that highlights their ultimate significance for human beings. Thus, when the theist says, "God is love," he is not making any mysterious claim about an ethereal object beyond the reach of perception and introspection; he is simply making the claim that bonds of love and charity among human beings constitute essential conditions of the virtuous life. On this view, then, the atheist is just wrong in maintaining that religious claims are lacking in evidential support; they are based on evidence, the same evidence which supports the more familiar propositions of ethics.

Other theists, however, deny that the concept of evidence has any meaningful application in the case of sentences making up religious discourse. The notion of evidence, they insist, applies only where we have true or false statements; but the sentences uttered by the believer have no truth-value at all. They are not fact-stating sentences, but rather linguistic vehicles for the expression of certain attitudes, feelings, and emotions. Thus, the proponent of this view would deny that the sentence 'God is good' is a claim, even an implicitly moral claim. He would insist that it functions as a means of expressing the believer's utter contentment with his situation in the universe or something of that sort; and, consequently, he would deny that there is any sense in which we can coherently be said to have or lack evidence for it.

A rather different response to the atheist's challenge is provided by the believer who simply agrees that religious belief is, in the weak sense outlined, irrational. He agrees, that is, that the content of religious belief is expressed by a system of fact-stating sentences and that the scientific evidence at our disposal makes the truth of these sentences extremely improbable. He fails, however, to find any indictment of religious belief here; for as he sees it, the believer does not embrace religion because it constitutes a system of well-confirmed hypotheses; the believer's concern is the more practical one of finding eternal salvation and in the interests of that goal, he is perfectly willing to reject the canons of inductive rationality.

This sort of response is sometimes coupled with an appeal to the notion of a *conceptual framework*. Here, the claims of the believer are taken to constitute a way of representing reality, a picture of the world. We are told that associated with this picture is a concept of rationality which is peculiar to and definitive of the framework of religious belief. Given that notion of rationality, the believer's views are said to be coherent and even warranted. The proponent of this view concedes that there are alternative frameworks with their own standards of rationality. According to those standards, he will agree, religious belief is irrational; but the theist who takes the notion of a conceptual framework seriously will deny that this represents any problem for the theist. In adopting the conceptual framework of traditional religion, the believer eschews other frameworks and other canons of rationality; nor, we are told, can his choice of the religious framework in any coherent way be called irrational; for the choice of a framework cannot be either rational or irrational. Canons of rationality are not independent of conceptual frameworks; they presuppose rather than support frameworks.

A more direct response to the atheist is provided by those theists who demand that the atheist himself present evidence for his view.

The theist who assumes this line of defense may concede that there is no empirical evidence for the proposition 'God exists', but he wants to insist that precisely the same point holds for the denial of the proposition: no empirical evidence supports the atheist's characteristic claim 'There is no God', so that if we make evidential support the criterion theism is no less preferable than atheism.

Now, these responses are not without their difficulties. The attempt to reinterpret the language of the believer in ethical or purely expressive terms is likely to be rejected by the believer himself. He will insist that his claims have just the force they appear to have. They aren't disguised moral claims or mere expressions of feeling; they are statements about God and God's relationship to his creation. On the other hand, the attempt to construe religious belief as constitutive of an autonomous conceptual framework runs up against the difficulty that people do come to embrace the framework of religious belief and frequently for what they take to be good reasons. In making the notion of good reasons depend upon the prior acceptance of a conceptual framework, the proponent of this sort of response makes it impossible to explain "reasoned conversion." Finally, the defender of religious belief who attacks the evidential basis of atheism fails to see that it is he who is making the positive claim about the nature of reality and that, consequently, it is he who has to establish his position. He may reply by claiming that the atheist too is making an affirmative claim about the world and that he too must establish his position; but while the defender of belief may be right here what seems to follow is not the rationality of theism, but only the conclusion that one ought to accept some position other than theism and atheism—a critical agnosticism which makes no judgment at all about the theistic hypothesis.

But while these different responses have their difficulties, they all strike a theme that it is difficult not to be sympathetic with. The critic of traditional religion is attacking religious belief on the grounds that it fails to measure up to the standards of acceptability laid down by the scientist. Now, although he does not always formulate his response in satisfactory terms, the defender of traditional religion is effectively challenging the assumption that the evidential standards of science are adequate as *general* canons for the acceptability of propositions. Now, it may be that the defender of religious belief has not succeeded in making the nature of religious belief entirely clear, but his challenge of this crucial assumption is surely to the point. It is simply not obvious that religion is a branch of science or anything like science, thus, unless the defender of science can succeed in showing us that science provides a complete account of the nature of reality (and that is an extremely difficult task), it is not clear that the believer needs to be troubled by the fact that his beliefs fail to meet the criteria of rationality operative in science.

NOTES

1. Cf. the selection by St. Anselm reprinted here for an example of a proof of this sort.

2. Cf. the criticisms of Gaunilo immediately following the initial selection from St. Anselm. St. Anselm's response to the criticism is also reprinted here.

3. The selection from Richard Taylor's *Metaphysics* that is reprinted in this section provides a remarkably clear version of this kind of proof.

4. From the selection from Taylor, p. 19.

5. The first selection from Hume in this section presents a formulation and criticism of the Teleological Argument.

6. From the selection from Hume, p. 31.

7. The second selection from Hume in this section presents a discussion of the problem of evil.

8. The paper by Alvin Plantinga presents one version of this defense.

9. Issues central to the meaning of religious language are discussed in the papers by A.G.N. Flew, R. M. Hare, and Basil Mitchell in this section.

10. The papers (cited earlier) by Flew, Hare, and Mitchell bear on this topic, as well as the selections from Kierkegaard and Russell which are found in this section.

The Ontological Argument

ST. ANSELM'S PRESENTATION

Truly there is a God, although the fool hath said in his heart, There is no God.

And so, Lord, do thou, who dost give understanding to faith, give me, so far as thou knowest it to be profitable, to understand that thou art as we believe; and that thou art that which we believe. And, indeed, we believe that thou art a being than which nothing greater can be conceived. Or is there no such nature, since the fool hath said in his heart, there is no God? (Psalms xiii, 1). But, at any rate, this very fool, when he hears of this being of which I speak—a being than which nothing greater can be conceived—understands what he hears, and what he understands is in his understanding; although he does not understand it to exist.

For, it is one thing for an object to be in the understanding, and another to understand that the object exists. When a painter first conceives of what he will afterwards perform, he has it in his understanding, but he does not yet understand it to be, because he has not yet performed it. But after he has made the painting, he both has it in his understanding, and he understands that it exists, because he has made it.

Hence, even the fool is convinced that something exists in the understanding, at least, than which nothing greater can be conceived. For, when he hears of this, he understands it. And whatever is understood, exists in the understanding. And assuredly that, than which nothing greater can be conceived, cannot exist in the understanding alone. For, suppose it exists in the understanding alone: then it can be conceived to exist in reality; which is greater.

Therefore, if that, than which nothing greater can be conceived, exists in the understanding alone, the very being, than which nothing greater can be conceived, is one, than which a greater can be conceived. But obviously this is impossible. Hence, there is no doubt that there exists a being, than which nothing greater can be conceived, and it exists both in the understanding and in reality.

God cannot be conceived not to exist.–God is that, than which nothing greater can be conceived.–That which can be conceived not to exist is not God.

And it assuredly exists so truly, that it cannot be conceived not to exist. For, it is possible to conceive of a being which cannot be conceived not to exist; and this is greater than one which can be conceived not to exist. Hence, if that, than which nothing greater can be conceived, can be conceived not to exist, it is not that, than which nothing greater can be

---

St. Anselm (1033-1109) was the Archbishop of Canterbury and an influential medieval philosopher and theologian.

These extracts are from Anselm's *Proslogium*, Gaunilo's *In Behalf of the Fool*, and Anselm's "Apologetic." Reprinted from St. Anselm, *Basic Writings*, trans. S. W. Deane, by permission of The Open Court Publishing Company.

conceived. But this is an irreconcilable contradiction. There is, then, so truly a being than which nothing greater can be conceived to exist, that it cannot even be conceived not to exist; and this being thou art, O Lord, our God.

So truly, therefore, dost thou exist, O Lord, my God, that thou canst not be conceived not to exist; and rightly. For, if a mind could conceive of a being better than thee, the creature would rise above the Creator; and this is most absurd. And, indeed, whatever else there is, except thee alone, can be conceived not to exist. To thee alone, therefore, it belongs to exist more truly than all other beings, and hence in a higher degree than all others. For, whatever else exists does not exist so truly, and hence in a less degree it belongs to it to exist. Why, then, has the fool said in his heart, there is no God (Psalms xiii, 1), since it is so evident, to a rational mind, that thou dost exist in the highest degree of all? Why, except that he is dull and a fool?

How the fool has said in his heart what cannot be conceived.–A thing may be conceived in two ways: (1) when the word signifying it is conceived; (2) when the thing itself is understood. As far as the word goes, God can be conceived not to exist; in reality he cannot.

But how has the fool said in his heart what he could not conceive; or how is it that he could not conceive what he said in his heart? since it is the same to say in the heart, and to conceive.

But, if really, nay, since really, he both conceived, because he said in his heart; and did not say in his heart, because he could not conceive; there is more than one way in which a thing is said in the heart or conceived. For, in one sense, an object is conceived, when the word signifying it is conceived; and in another, when the very entity, which the object is, is understood.

In the former sense, then, God can be conceived not to exist; but in the latter, not at all. For no one who understands what fire and water are can conceive fire to be water, in accordance with the nature of the facts themselves, although this is possible according to the words. So, then, no one who understands what God is can conceive that God does not exist; although he says these words in his heart, either without any or with some foreign, signification. For, God is that than which a greater cannot be conceived. And he who thoroughly understands this, assuredly understands that this being so truly exists, that not even in concept can it be non-existent. Therefore, he who understands that God so exists, cannot conceive that he does not exist.

I thank thee, gracious Lord, I thank thee; because what I formerly believed by thy bounty, I now so understand by thine illumination, that if I were unwilling to believe that thou dost exist, I should not be able not to understand this to be true.

GAUNILO'S CRITICISM

For example: it is said that somewhere in the ocean is an island, which, because of the difficulty, or rather the impossibility, of discovering what does not exist, is called the lost island. And they say that this island has an inestimable wealth of all manner of riches and delicacies in greater abundance than is told of the Islands of the Blest; and that having no owner or inhabitant, it is more excellent than all other countries, which are inhabited by mankind, in the abundance with which it is stored.

Now if some one should tell me that there is such an island, I should easily understand his words, in which there is no difficulty. But suppose that he went on to say, as if by a logical inference: "You can no longer doubt that this island which is more excellent than all lands exists somewhere, since you have no doubt that it is in your understanding. And since it is more excellent not to be in the

---

Gaunilo, a monk, was a contemporary of St. Anselm's.

understanding alone, but to exist both in the understanding and in reality, for this reason it must exist. For if it does not exist, any land which really exists will be more excellent than it; and so the island already understood by you to be more excellent will not be more excellent."

If a man should try to prove to me by such reasoning that this island truly exists, and that its existence should no longer be doubted, either I should believe that he was jesting, or I know not which I ought to regard as the greater fool: myself, supposing that I should allow this proof; or him, if he should suppose that he had established with any certainty the existence of this island. For he ought to show first that the hypothetical excellence of this island exists as a real and indubitable fact, and in no wise as any unreal object, or one whose existence is uncertain, in my understanding.

ST. ANSELM'S REJOINDER

A criticism of Gaunilo's example, in which he tries to show that in this way the real existence of a lost island might be inferred from the fact of its being conceived.

But, you say, it is as if one should suppose an island in the ocean, which surpasses all lands in its fertility, and which, because of the difficulty, or rather the impossibility, of discovering what does not exist, is called a lost island; and should say that there can be no doubt that this island truly exists in reality, for this reason, that one who hears it described easily understands what he hears.

Now I promise confidently that if any man shall devise anything existing either in reality or in concept alone (except that than which a greater cannot be conceived) to which he can adapt the sequence of my reasoning, I will discover that thing, and will give him his lost island, not to be lost again.

But it now appears that this being than which a greater is inconceivable cannot be conceived not to be, because it exists on so assured a ground of truth; for otherwise it would not exist at all.

Hence, if any one says that he conceives this being not to exist, I say that at the time when he conceives of this either he conceives of a being than which a greater is inconceivable, or he does not conceive at all. If he does not conceive, he does not conceive of the non-existence of that of which he does not conceive. But if he does conceive, he certainly conceives of a being which cannot be even conceived not to exist. For if it could be conceived not to exist, it could be conceived to have a beginning and an end. But this is impossible.

He, then, who conceives of this being conceives of a being which cannot be even conceived not to exist; but he who conceives of this being does not conceive that it does not exist; else he conceives what is inconceivable. The non-existence, then, of that than which a greater cannot be conceived is inconceivable.

The Cosmological Argument

RICHARD TAYLOR

Suppose you were strolling in the woods and, in addition to the sticks, stones, and other accustomed litter of the forest floor, you one day came upon some quite unaccustomed object, something not quite like what you had ever seen before and would never expect to find in such a place. Suppose, for example, that it is a large ball, about your own height, perfectly smooth and translucent. You would deem this puzzling and mysterious, certainly, but if one considers the matter, it is no more inherently mysterious that such a thing should exist than that anything else should exist. If you were quite accustomed to finding such objects of various sizes around you most of the time, but had never seen an ordinary rock, then upon finding a large rock in the woods one day you would be just as puzzled and mystified. This illustrates the fact that something that is mysterious ceases to seem so simply by its accustomed presence. It is strange indeed, for example, that a world such as ours should exist; yet few men are very often struck by this strangeness, but simply take it for granted.

Suppose, then, that you have found this translucent ball and are mystified by it. Now whatever else you might wonder about it, there is one thing you would hardly question; namely, that it did not appear there all by itself, that it owes its existence to something. You might not have the remotest idea whence and how it came to be there, but you would hardly doubt that there was an explanation. The idea that it might have come from nothing at all, that it might exist without there being any explanation of its existence, is one that few people would consider worthy of entertaining.

This illustrates a metaphysical belief that seems to be almost a part of reason itself, even though few men ever think upon it; the belief, namely, that there is some explanation for the existence of anything whatever, some reason why it should exist rather than not. The sheer nonexistence of anything, which is not to be confused with the passing out of existence of something, never requires a reason; but existence does. That there should never have been any such ball in the forest does not require any explanation or reason, but that there should ever be such a ball does. If one were to look upon a barren plain and ask why there is not and never has been any large translucent ball there, the natural response would be to ask why there should be; but if one finds such a ball, and wonders why it is there, it is not quite so natural to ask why it should *not* be, as though existence should simply be taken for granted. That anything should not exist, then, and that, for instance, no such ball should exist in the forest, or that there should be no forest for it to occupy, or no continent containing a forest, or no earth, nor any world at all, do not seem to be things for which there needs to be any explanation or reason; but that such things should be, does seem to require a reason.

Richard Taylor is professor of philosophy at the University of Rochester.

From Richard Taylor, *Metaphysics*, 2nd ed. © 1974, pp. 84-95. Reprinted by permission of Prentice Hall, Inc., Englewood Cliffs, New Jersey.

The principle involved here has been called the principle of sufficient reason. Actually, it is a very general principle, and is best expressed by saying that, in the case of any positive truth, there is some sufficient reason for it, something which, in this sense, makes it true—in short, that there is some sort of explanation, known or unknown, for everything.

Now some truths depend on something else, and are accordingly called *contingent,* while others depend only upon themselves, that is, are true by their very natures and are accordingly called *necessary*. There is, for example, a reason why the stone on my window sill is warm; namely, that the sun is shining upon it. This happens to be true, but not by its very nature. Hence, it is contingent, and depends upon something other than itself. It is also true that all the points of a circle are equidistant from the center, but this truth depends upon nothing but itself. No matter what happens, nothing can make it false. Similarly, it is a truth, and a necessary one, that if the stone on my window sill is a body, as it is, then it has a form, since this fact depends upon nothing but itself for its confirmation. Untruths are also, of course, either contingent or necessary, it being contingently false, for example, that the stone on my window sill is cold, and necessarily false that it is both a body and formless, since this is by its very nature impossible.

The principle of sufficient reason can be illustrated in various ways, as we have done, and if one thinks about it, he is apt to find that he presupposes it in his thinking about reality, but it cannot be proved. It does not appear to be itself a necessary truth, and at the same time it would be most odd to say it is contingent. If one were to try proving it, he would sooner or later have to appeal to considerations that are less plausible than the principle itself. Indeed, it is hard to see how one could even make an argument for it, without already assuming it. For this reason it might properly be called a presupposition of reason itself. One can deny that it is true, without embarrassment or fear of refutation, but one is then apt to find that what he is denying is not really what the principle asserts. We shall, then, treat it here as a datum—not something that is provably true, but as something which all men, whether they ever reflect upon it or not, seem more or less to presuppose.

It happens to be true that something exists, that there is, for example, a world, and while no one ever seriously supposes that this might not be so, that there might exist nothing at all, there still seems to be nothing the least necessary in this, considering it just by itself. That no world should ever exist at all is perfectly comprehensible and seems to express not the slightest absurdity. Considering any particular item in the world it seems not at all necessary in itself that it should ever have existed, nor does it appear any more necessary that the totality of these things, or any totality of things, should ever exist.

From the principle of sufficient reason it follows, of course, that there must be a reason, not only for the existence of everything in the world but for the world itself, meaning by "the world" simply everything that ever does exist, except God, in case there is a god. This principle does not imply that there must be some purpose or goal for everything, or for the totality of all things; for explanations need not, and in fact seldom are, teleological or purposeful. All the principle requires is that there be some sort of reason for everything. And it would certainly be odd to maintain that everything in the world owes its existence to something, that nothing in the world is either purely accidental, or such that it just bestows its own being upon itself, and then to deny this of the world itself. One can indeed *say* that the world is in some sense a pure accident, that there simply is no reason at all why this or any world should exist, and one can equally say that the world exists by its very nature, or is an inherently necessary being. But it is at least very odd and arbitrary to deny of this existing world the need for any sufficient reason, whether independent of itself or not, while presupposing that there is a reason for every other thing that ever exists.

Consider again the strange ball that we imagine has been found in the forest. Now we can hardly doubt that there must be an explanation for the existence of such a thing, though we may have no notion what that explanation is. It is not, moreover, the fact of its having been found in the forest rather than elsewhere that renders an explanation necessary. It matters not in the least where it happens to be, for our question is not how it happens to be *there* but how it happens to exist at all. If we in our imagination annihilate the forest, leaving only this ball in an open field, our conviction that it is a contingent thing and owes its existence to something other than itself is not reduced in the least. If we now imagine the field to be annihilated, and in fact everything else as well to vanish into nothingness, leaving only this ball to constitute the entire physical universe, then we cannot for a moment suppose that its existence has thereby been explained, or the need of any explanation eliminated, or that its existence is suddenly rendered self-explanatory. If we now carry this thought one step further and suppose that no other reality ever has existed or ever will exist, that this ball forever constitutes the entire physical universe, then we must still insist on there being some reason independent of itself why it should exist rather than not. If there must be a reason for the existence of any particular thing, then the necessity of such a reason is not eliminated by the mere supposition that certain other things do *not* exist. And again, it matters not at all what the thing in question is, whether it be large and complex, such as the world we actually find ourselves in, or whether it be something small, simple and insignificant, such as a ball, a bacterium, or the merest grain of sand. We do not avoid the necessity of a reason for the existence of something merely by describing it in this way or that. And it would, in any event, seem quite plainly absurd to say that if the world were comprised entirely of a single ball about six feet in diameter, or of a single grain of sand, then it would be contingent and there would have to be some explanation other than itself why such a thing exists, but that, since the actual world is vastly more complex than this, there is no need for an explanation of its existence, independent of itself.

It should now be noted that it is no answer to the question, why a thing exists, to state *how long* it has existed. A geologist does not suppose that he has explained why there should be rivers and mountains merely by pointing out that they are old. Similarly, if one were to ask, concerning the ball of which we have spoken, for some sufficient reason for its being, he would not receive any answer upon being told that it had been there since yesterday. Nor would it be any better answer to say that it had existed since before anyone could remember, or even that it had always existed; for the question was not one concerning its age but its existence. If, to be sure, one were to ask where a given thing came from, or how it came into being, then upon learning that it had always existed he would learn that it never really *came* into being at all; but he could still reasonably wonder why it should exist at all. If, accordingly, the world—that is, the totality of all things excepting God, in case there is a god—had really no beginning at all, but has always existed in some form or other, then there is clearly no answer to the question, where it came from and when; it did not, on this supposition, *come* from anything at all, at any time. But still, it can be asked why there is a world, why indeed there is a beginningless world, why there should have perhaps always been something rather than nothing. And, if the principle of sufficient reason is a good principle, there must be an answer to that question, an answer that is by no means supplied by giving the world an age, or even an infinite age.

This brings out an important point with respect to the concept of creation that is often misunderstood, particularly by those whose thinking has been influenced by Christian ideas. People tend to think that creation—for example, the creation of the world by God—*means* creation *in time*, from which it of course logically follows that if the world had no beginning in time, then it cannot be the creation of God. This, however, is erroneous, for creation means essentially *dependence*, even in Christian theology. If one thing is the creation of another, then it depends for its existence on that other, and this is perfectly consistent with saying that both are eternal, that neither ever came into being, and hence, that neither was ever created at any point of time. Perhaps an analogy will help convey this point. Consider, then, a flame that is casting beams of light. Now there seems to be a clear sense in which the beams of light are dependent for their existence upon the flame, which is their source, while the flame, on the other hand, is not similarly dependent for its existence upon them. The beams of light arise from the flame, but the flame does not arise from them. In this sense, they are the creation of the flame; they derive their existence from it. And none of this has any reference to time; the relationship of dependence in such a case would not be altered in the slightest if we supposed that the flame, and with it the beams of light, had always existed, that neither had ever *come* into being.

Now if the world is the creation of God, its relationship to God should be thought of in this fashion; namely, that the world depends for its existence upon God, and could not exist independently of God. If God is eternal, as those who believe in God generally assume, then the world may (though it need not) be eternal too, without that altering in the least its dependence upon God for its existence, and hence without altering its being the creation of God. The supposition of God's eternality, on the other hand, does not by itself imply that the world is eternal too; for there is not the least reason why something of finite duration might not depend for its existence upon something of infinite duration—though the reverse is, of course, impossible.

If we think of God as "the creator of heaven and earth," and if we consider heaven and earth to include everything that exists except God, then we appear to have, in the foregoing considerations, fairly strong reasons for asserting that God, as so conceived, exists. Now of course most people have much more in mind than this when they think of God, for religions have ascribed to God ever so many attributes that are not at all implied by describing him merely as the creator of the world; but that is not relevant here. Most religious persons do, in any case, think of God as being at least the creator, as that being upon which everything ultimately depends, no matter what else they may say about him in addition. It is, in fact, the first item in the creeds of Christianity that God is the "creator of heaven and earth." And, it seems, there are good metaphysical reasons, as distinguished from the persuasions of faith, for thinking that such a creative being exists.

If, as seems clearly implied by the principle of sufficent reason, there must be a reason for the existence of heaven and earth—i.e., for the world—then that reason must be found either in the world itself, or outside it, in something that is literally supranatural, or outside heaven and earth. Now if we suppose that the world—i.e., the totality of all things except God—contains within itself the reason for its existence, we are supposing that it exists by its very nature, that is, that it is a necessary being. In that case there would, of course, be no reason for saying that it must depend upon God or anything else for its existence; for if it exists by its very nature, then it depends upon nothing but itself, much as the sun depends upon nothing but itself for its heat. This, however, is implausible, for we find nothing about the world or anything in it to suggest that it exists by its own nature, and we do find, on the contrary, ever so many things to suggest that it does not. For in the first place, anything which exists by its very nature must necessarily be eternal and indestructible. It would be a self-contradiction to say of anything that it exists by its own nature, or is a necessarily existing thing, and at the same time to say that it comes into being or passes away, or that it ever could come into being or pass away. Nothing about the world seems at all like this, for concerning anything in the world, we can perfectly easily think of it as being annihilated, or as never having existed in the first place, without there being the slightest hint of any absurdity in such a supposition. Some of the things in the universe are, to be sure, very old; the moon, for example, or the stars and the planets. It is even possible to imagine that they have always existed. Yet it seems quite impossible to suppose that they owe their existence to nothing but themselves, that they bestow existence upon themselves by their very natures, or that they are in themselves things of such nature that it would be impossible for them not to exist. Even if we suppose that something, such as the sun, for instance, has existed forever, and will never cease, still we cannot conclude just from this that it exists by its own nature. If, as is of course very doubtful, the sun has existed forever and will never cease, then it is possible that its heat and light have also existed forever and will never cease; but that would not show that the heat and light of the sun exist by their own natures. They are obviously contingent and depend on the sun for their existence, whether they are beginningless and everlasting or not.

There seems to be nothing in the world, then, concerning which it is at all plausible to suppose that it exists by its own nature, or contains within itself the reason for its existence. In fact, everything in the world appears to be quite plainly the opposite, namely, something that not only need not exist, but at some time or other, past or future or both, does not in fact exist. Everything in the world seems to have a finite duration, whether long or short. Most things, such as ourselves, exist only for a short while; they come into being, then soon cease. Other things, like the heavenly bodies, last longer, but they are still corruptible, and from all that we can gather about them, they too seem destined eventually to perish. We arrive at the conclusion, then, that while the world may contain some things which have always existed and are destined never to perish, it is nevertheless doubtful that it contains any such thing and, in any case, everything in the world is capable of perishing, and nothing in it, however long it may already have existed and however long it may yet remain, exists by its own nature, but depends instead upon something else.

While this might be true of everything in the world, is it necessarily true of the world itself? That is, if we grant, as we seem forced to, that nothing in the world exists by its own nature, that everything in the world is contingent and perishable, must we also say that the world itself, or the totality of all these perishable things, is also contingent and perishable? Logically, we are not forced to, for it is logically possible that the totality of all perishable things might itself be imperishable, and hence, that the world might exist by its own nature, even though it is comprised exclusively of things which are contingent. It is not logically necessary that a totality should share the defects of its members. For example, even though every man is mortal, it does not follow from this that the human race, or the totality of all men, is also mortal; for it is possible that there will always be human beings, even though there are no human beings which will always exist. Similarly, it is possible that the world is in itself a necessary thing, even though it is comprised entirely of things that are contingent.

This is logically possible, but it is not plausible. For we find nothing whatever about the world, any more than in its parts, to suggest that it exists by its own nature. Concerning anything in the world, we have not the slightest difficulty in supposing that it should perish, or even, that it should never have existed in the first place. We have almost as little difficulty in supposing this of the world itself. It might be somewhat hard to think of everything as utterly perishing and leaving no trace whatever of its ever having been, but there seems to be not the slightest difficulty in imagining that the world should never have existed in the first place. We can, for instance, perfectly easily suppose that nothing in the world had ever existed except, let us suppose, a single grain of sand, and we can thus suppose that this grain of sand has forever constituted the whole universe. Now if we consider just this grain of sand, it is quite impossible for us to suppose that it exists by its very nature, and could never have failed to exist. It clearly depends for its existence upon something other than itself, if it depends on anything at all. The same will be true if we consider the world to consist, not of one grain of sand, but of two, or of a million, or, as we in fact find, of a vast number of stars and planets and all their minuter parts.

It would seem, then, that the world, in case it happens to exist at all—and this is quite beyond doubt—is contingent and thus dependent upon something other than itself for its existence, if it depends upon anything at all. And it must depend upon something, for otherwise there could be no reason why it exists in the first place. Now that upon which the world depends must be something that either exists by its own nature or does not. If it does not exist by its own nature, then it, in turn, depends for its existence upon something else, and so on. Now then, we can say either of two things; namely, (1) that the world depends for its existence upon something else, which in turn depends on still another thing, this depending upon still another, *ad infinitum;* or (2) that the world derives its existence from something that exists by its own nature and which is accordingly eternal and imperishable, and is the creator of heaven and earth. The first of these alternatives, however, is impossible, for it does not render a sufficient reason why anything should exist in the first place. Instead of supplying a reason why any world should exist, it repeatedly begs off giving a reason. It explains what is dependent and perishable in terms of what is itself dependent and perishable, leaving us still without a reason why perishable things should exist at all, which is what we are seeking. Ultimately, then, it would seem that the world, or the totality of contingent or perishable things, in case it exists at all, must depend upon something that is necessary and imperishable, and which accordingly exists, not in dependence upon something else, but by its own nature.

What has been said thus far gives some intimation of what meaning should be attached to the concept of a self-caused being, a concept that is quite generally misunderstood, sometimes even by scholars. To say that something—God, for example—is self-caused, or is the cause of its own existence, does not mean that this being brings itself into existence, which is a perfectly absurd idea. Nothing can *bring* itself into existence. To say that something is self-caused (*causa sui*) means only that it exists, not contingently or in dependence upon something else, but by its own nature, which is only to say that it is a being which is such that it can neither come into being nor perish. Now whether such a being in fact exists or not, there is in any case no absurdity in the idea. We have found, in fact, that the principle of sufficient reason seems to point to the existence of such a being, as upon which the world, with everything in it, must ultimately depend for its existence.

A being that depends for its existence upon nothing but itself, and is in this sense self-caused, can equally be described as a necessary being; that is to say, a being that is not contingent, and hence not perishable. For in the case of anything which exists by its own nature, and is dependent upon nothing else, it is impossible that it should not exist, which is equivalent to saying that it is necessary. Many persons have professed to find the gravest difficulties in this concept, too, but that is partly because it has been confused with other notions. If it makes sense to speak of anything as an *impossible* being, or something which by its very nature does not exist, then it is hard to see why the idea of a necessary being, or something which in its very nature exists, should not be just as comprehensible. And of course, we have not the slightest difficulty in speaking of something, such as a square circle or a formless body, as an impossible being. And if it makes sense to speak of something as being perishable, contingent, and dependent upon something other than itself for its existence, as it surely does, then there seems to be no difficulty in thinking of something as imperishable and dependent upon nothing other than itself for its existence.

From these considerations we can see also what is properly meant by a first cause, an appellative that has often been applied to God by theologians, and which many persons have deemed an absurdity. It is a common criticism of this notion to say that there need not be any first cause, since the series of causes and effects which constitute the history of the universe might be infinite or beginningless and must, in fact, be infinite in case the universe itself had no beginning in time. This criticism, however, reflects a total misconception of what is meant by a first cause. *First* here does not mean first in time, and when God is spoken of as a first cause, he is not being described as a being which, at some time in the remote past, *started* everything. To describe God as a first cause is only to say that he is literally a *primary* rather than a secondary cause, an *ultimate* rather than a derived cause, or a being upon which all other things, heaven and earth, ultimately depend for their existence. It is, in short, only to say that God is the creator, in the sense of creation explained above. Now this, of course, is perfectly consistent with saying that the world is eternal or beginningless. As we have seen, one gives no reason for the existence of a world merely by giving it an age, even if it is supposed to have an infinite age. To use a helpful analogy, we can say that the sun is the first cause of daylight and, for that matter, of the moonlight of the night as well, which means only that daylight and moonlight ultimately depend upon the sun for their existence. The moon, on the other hand, is only a seondary or derivative cause of its light. This light would be no less dependent upon the sun if we affirmed that it had no beginning, for an ageless and beginningless light requires a source no less than an ephemeral one. If we supposed that the sun has always existed, and with it its light, then we would have to say that the sun has always been the first—i.e., the primary or ultimate—cause of its light. Such is precisely the manner in which God should be thought of, and is by theologians often thought of, as the first cause of heaven and earth.

The Cosmological Argument

PAUL EDWARDS

I

The so-called "cosmological proof" is one of the oldest and most popular arguments for the existence of God. It was forcibly criticized by Hume,[1] Kant,[2] and Mill,[3] but it would be inaccurate to consider the argument dead or even moribund. Catholic philosophers, with hardly any exception, appear to believe that it is as solid and conclusive as ever. Thus Father F. C. Copleston confidently championed it in his Third Programme debate with Bertrand Russell[4]; and in America, where Catholic writers are more sanguine, we are told by a Jesuit professor of physics that "the existence of an intelligent being as the First Cause of the universe can be established by *rational scientific inference*."[5]

I am absolutely convinced [the same writer continues] that any one who would give the same consideration to that proof (the cosmological argument), as outlined for example in William Brosnan's *God and Reason*, as he would give to a line of argumentation found in the *Physical Review* or the *Proceedings of the Royal Society* would be forced to admit that the cogency of this argument for the existence of God far outstrips that which is found in the reasoning which Chadwick uses to prove the existence of the neutron, which today is accepted as certain as any conclusion in the physical sciences.[6]

Mild theists like the late Professor Dawes Hicks[7] and Dr. [A. C.] Ewing,[8] who concede many of Hume's and Kant's criticisms, nevertheless contend that the argument possesses a certain core of truth. In popular discussions it also crops up again and again—for example, when believers address atheists with such questions as "You tell me where the universe came from!" Even philosophers who reject the cosmological proof sometimes embody certain of its confusions in the formulation of their own position. In the light of all this, it may be worth while to undertake a fresh examination of the argument with special attention to the fallacies that were not emphasized by the older critics.

II

The cosmological proof has taken a number of forms, the most important of which are known as the "causal argument" and "the argument from contingency," respectively. In some writers, in Samuel Clarke for example, they are combined, but it is best to keep them apart as far as possible. The causal argument is the second of the "five ways" of Aquinas and roughly proceeds as follows: we find that the things around us come into being as the result of the activity of other things. These causes are themselves the result of the activity of other things. But such a causal series cannot "go back to infinity." Hence there must be a first member, a member which is not itself caused by any preceding member—an uncaused or "first" cause.

Paul Edwards is professor of philosophy at City University of New York.

From *The Rationalist Annual for the Year 1959*, edited by Hector Hawton. Reprinted by permission of Paul Edwards.

It has frequently been pointed out that even if this argument were sound it would not establish the existence of *God.* It would not show that the first cause is all-powerful or all-good or that it is in any sense personal. Somebody believing in the eternity of atoms, or of matter generally, could quite consistently accept the conclusion. Defenders of the causal argument ususally concede this and insist that the argument is not in itself meant to prove the existence of God. Supplementary arguments are required to show that the first cause must have the attributes assigned to the deity. They claim, however, that the argument, if valid, would at least be an important step towards a complete proof of the existence of God.

Does the argument succeed in proving so much as a first cause? This will depend mainly on the soundness of the premise that an infinite series of causes is impossible. Aquinas supports this premise by maintaining that the opposite belief involves a plain absurdity. To suppose that there is an infinite series of causes logically implies that nothing exists now; but we know that plenty of things do exist now; and hence any theory which implies that nothing exists now must be wrong. Let us take some causal series and refer to its members by the letters of the alphabet:

$$A \rightarrow B \ldots W \rightarrow X \rightarrow Y \rightarrow Z$$

Z stands here for something presently existing, e.g. Margaret Truman. Y represents the cause or part of the cause of Z, say Harry Truman. X designates the cause or part of the cause of Y, say Harry Truman's father, etc. Now, Aquinas reasons, whenever we take away the cause, we also take away the effect: if Harry Truman had never lived, Margaret Truman would never have been born. If Harry Truman's father had never lived, Harry Truman and Margaret Truman would never have been born. If A had never existed, none of the subsequent members of the series would have come into existence. But it is precisely A that the believer in the infinite series is "taking away." For in maintaining that the series is infinite he is denying that it has a first member; he is denying that there is such a thing as a first cause; he is in other words denying the existence of A. Since without A, Z could not have existed, his position implies that Z does not exist now; and that is plainly false.

This argument fails to do justice to the supporter of the infinite series of causes. Aquinas has failed to distinguish between the two statements:

(1) A did not exist, and
(2) A is not uncaused.

To say that the series is infinite implies (2), but it does not imply (1). The following parallel may be helpful here: Suppose Captain Spaulding had said, "I am the greatest explorer who ever lived," and somebody replied, "No, you are not." This answer would be denying that the Captain possessed the exalted attribute he had claimed for himself, but it would not be denying his existence. It would not be "taking him away." Similarly, the believer in the infinite series is not "taking A away." He is taking away the privileged status of A; he is taking away its "first causiness." He does not deny the *existence* of A or of any particular member of the series. He denies that A or anything else *is the first member* of the series. Since he is not taking A away, he is not taking B away, and thus he is also not taking X, Y, or Z away. His view, then, does not commit him to the absurdity that nothing exists now, or more specifically, that Margaret Truman does not exist now. It may be noted in this connection that a believer in the infinite series is not necessarily denying the existence of supernatural beings. He is merely committed to denying that such a being, if it exists, is uncaused. He is committed to holding that whatever other impressive attributes a supernatural being might possess, the attribute of being a first cause is not among them.

The causal argument is open to several other objections. Thus, even if otherwise valid, the argument would not prove a *single* first cause. For there does not seem to be any good ground for supposing that the various causal series in the universe ultimately merge. Hence even if it is granted that no series of causes can be infinite the possibility of a plurality of first members has not been ruled out. Nor does the argument establish the *present* existence of the first cause. It does not prove this, since experience clearly shows that an effect may exist long after its cause has been destroyed.

III

Many defenders of the causal argument would contend that at least some of these criticisms rest on a misunderstanding. They would probably go further and contend that the argument was not quite fairly stated in the first place—or at any rate that if it was fair to some of its adherents it was not fair to others. They would in this connection distinguish between two types of causes—what they call "causes *in fieri*" and what they call "causes *in esse*." A cause *in fieri* is a factor which brought or helped to bring an effect into existence. A cause *in esse* is a factor which "sustains" or helps to sustain the effect "in being." The parents of a human being would be an example of a cause *in fieri*. If somebody puts a book in my hand and I keep holding it up, his putting it there would be the cause *in fieri*, and my holding it would be the cause *in esse* of the book's position. To quote Father [G. H.] Joyce:

> If a smith forges a horse-shoe, he is only a cause *in fieri* of the shape given to the iron. That shape persists after his action has ceased. So, too, a builder is a cause *in fieri* of the house which he builds. In both these cases the substances employed act as causes *in esse* as regards the continued existence of the effect produced. Iron, in virtue of its natural rigidity, retains in being the shape which it has once received; and, similarly, the materials employed in building retain in being the order and arrangement which constitute them into a house.[9]

Using this distinction, a defender of the argument now reasons in the following way. To say that there is an infinite series of causes *in fieri* does not lead to any absurd conclusions. But Aquinas is concerned only with causes *in esse* and an infinite series of *such* causes is impossible. In the words of the contemporary American Thomist, R. P. Phillips:

> Each member of the series of causes possesses being solely by virtue of the actual present operation of a superior cause. . . . Life is dependent, *inter alia*, on a certain atmospheric pressure, this again on the continual operation of physical forces, whose being and operation depends on the position of the earth in the solar system, which itself must endure relatively unchanged, a state of being which can only be continuously produced by a definite—if unknown—constitution of the material universe. This constitution, however, cannot be its own cause. That a thing should cause itself is impossible: for in order that it may cause it is necessary for it to exist, which it cannot do, on the hypothesis, until it has been caused. So it must *be* in order to cause itself. Thus, not being uncaused nor yet its own cause, it must be caused by another, which produces and preserves it. It is plain, then, that as no member of this series possesses being except in virtue of the actual present operation of a superior cause, if there be no first cause actually operating none of the dependent causes could operate either. We are thus irresistibly led to posit a first efficient cause which, while itself uncaused, shall impart causality to a whole series. . . .
>
> The series of causes which we are considering is not one which stretches back into the past; so that we are not demanding a beginning of the world at some definite moment reckoning back from the present, but an actual cause now operating, to account for the present being of things.[10]

Professor Phillips offers the following parallel to bring out his point:

> In a goods train each truck is moved and moves by the action of the one immediately in front of it. If then we suppose the train to be infinite, i.e. that there is no end to it, and so no engine which starts the motion, it is plain that no truck will move. To lengthen it out to infinity will not give it what no member of it possesses of itself, viz. the power of drawing the truck behind it. If then we see any truck in motion we know there must be an end to the series of trucks which gives causality to the whole.[11]

Father Joyce introduces an illustration from Aquinas to explain how the present existence of things may be compatible with an infinite series of causes *in fieri* but not with an infinite series of causes *in esse*.

> When a carpenter is at work, the series of efficient causes on which his work depends is necessarily limited. The final effect, e.g. the fastening of a nail is caused by a hammer: the hammer is moved by the arm: and the motion of his arm is determined by the motor-impulses communicated from the nerve centres of the brain. Unless the subordinate causes were limited in number, and were connected with a starting-point of motion, the hammer must remain inert; and the nail will never be driven in. If the series be supposed infinite, no work will ever take place. But if there is question of causes on

which the work is not essentially dependent, we cannot draw the same conclusion. We may suppose the carpenter to have broken an infinite number of hammers, and as often to have replaced the broken tool by a fresh one. There is nothing in such a supposition which excludes the driving home of the nail.[12]

The supporter of the infinite series of causes, Joyce also remarks, is

. . . asking us to believe that although each link in a suspended chain is prevented from falling simply because it is attached to the one above it, yet if only the chain be long enough, it will, taken as a whole, need no support, but will hang loose in the air suspended from nothing.[13]

This formualtion of the causal argument unquestionably circumvents one of the objections mentioned previously. If Y is the cause *in esse* of an effect, Z, then it must exist as long as Z exists. If the argument were valid in this form it would therefore prove the present and not merely the past existence of a first cause. In this form the argument is, however, less convincing in another respect. To maintain that all "natural" or "phenomenal" objects—things like tables and mountains and human beings—require a cause *in fieri* is not implausible, though even here Mill and others have argued that strictly speaking only *changes* require a causal explanation. It is far from plausible, on the other hand, to claim that all natural objects require a cause *in esse*. It may be granted that the air around us is a cause *in esse* of human life and further that certain gravitational forces are among the causes *in esse* of the air being where it is. But when we come to gravitational forces or, at any rate, to material particles like atoms or electrons it is difficult to see what cause *in esse* they require. To those not already convinced of the need for a supernatural First Cause some of the remarks by Professor Phillips in this connection appear merely dogmatic and question-begging. Most people would grant that such particles as atoms did not cause themselves, since, as Professor Phillips observes, they would in that event have had to exist before they began existing. It is not at all evident, however, that these particles cannot be uncaused. Professor Phillips and all other supporters of the causal argument immediately proceed to claim that there is something else which needs no cause *in esse*. They themselves admit thus, that there is nothing self-evident about the proposition that everything must have a cause *in esse*. Their entire procedure here lends substance to Schopenhauer's gibe that supporters of the cosmological argument treat the law of universal causation like "a hired cab which we dismiss when we have reached our destination."[14]

But waiving this and all similar objections, the restatement of the argument in terms of causes *in esse* in no way avoids the main difficulty which was previously mentioned. A believer in the infinite series would insist that his position was just as much misrepresented now as before. He is no more removing the member of the series which is supposed to be the first cause *in esse* than he was removing the member which had been declared to be the first cause *in fieri*. He is again merely denying a privileged status to it. He is not denying the reality of the cause *in esse* labelled "A." He is not even necessarily denying that it possesses supernatural attributes. He is again merely taking away its "first causiness."

The advocates of the causal argument in either form seem to confuse an infinite series with one which is long but finite. If a book, Z, is to remain in its position, say 100 miles up in the air, there must be another object, say another book, Y, underneath it to serve as its support. If Y is to remain where it is, it will need another support, X, beneath it. Suppose that this series of supports, one below the other, continues for a long time, but eventually, say after 100,000 members, comes to a first book which is not resting on any other book or indeed on any other support. In that event the whole collection would come crashing down. What we seem to need is a first member of the series, a first support (such as the earth) which does not need another member as *its* support, which in other words is "self-supporting."

This is evidently the sort of picture that supporters of the First Cause argument have before their minds when they rule out the possibility of an infinite series. But such a picture is not a fair representation of the theory of the infinite series. A *finite* series of books would indeed come crashing down, since the first or lowest member would not have a predecessor on which it could be supported. If the series, however, were infinite this would not be the case. In that event every member *would* have a predecessor to support itself on and there would be no crash. That is to say: a crash can be avoided either by a finite series with a first self-supporting member or by an infinite series. Similarly, the present existence of motion is equally compatible with the theory of a first unmoved mover and with the theory of an infinite series of moving objects; and the present existence of causal activity is compatible with the theory of a first cause *in esse* as much as with the theory of an infinite series of such causes.

The illustrations given by Joyce and Phillips are hardly to the point. It is true that a carpenter would not, *in a finite time-span,* succeed in driving in a nail if he had to carry out an infinite number of movements. For that matter, he would not accomplish this goal in a finite time if he broke an infinite number of hammers. However, to make the illustrations relevant we must suppose that he has infinite time at his disposal. In that case he would succeed in driving in the nail even if he required an infinite number of movements for this purpose. As for the goods train, it may be granted that the trucks do not move unless the train has an engine. But this illustration is totally irrelevant as it stands. A relevant illustration would be that of engines, each moved by the one in front of it. Such a train would move if it were infinite. For every member of this series there would be one in front capable of drawing it along. The advocate of the infinite series of causes does not, as the original illustration suggests, believe in a series whose members are not really causally connected with one another. In the series he believes in every member is genuinely the cause of the one that follows it.

IV

No staunch defender of the cosmological argument would give up at this stage. Even if there were an infinite series of causes *in fieri* or *in esse,* he would contend, this still would not do away with the need for an ultimate, a first cause. As Father Copleston put it in his debate with Bertrand Russell:

> Every object has a phenomenal cause, if you insist on the infinity of the series. But the series of phenomenal causes is an insufficient explanation of the series. Therefore, the series has not a phenomenal cause, but a transcendent cause. . . .[15]
>
> An infinite series of contingent beings will be, to my way of thinking, as unable to cause itself as one contingent being.[16]

The demand to find the cause of the series as a whole rests on the erroneous assumption that the series is something over and above the members of which it is composed. It is tempting to suppose this, at least by implication, because the word "series" is a noun like "dog" or "man." Like the expression "this dog" or "this man" the phrase "this series" is easily taken to designate an individual object. But reflection shows this to be an error. If we have explained the individual members there is nothing additional left to be explained. Supposing I see a group of five Eskimos standing on the corner of Sixth Avenue and 50th Street and I wish to explain why the group came to New York. Investigation reveals the following stories:

Eskimo No. 1 did not enjoy the extreme cold in the polar region and decided to move to a warmer climate.
No. 2 is the husband of Eskimo No. 1. He loves her dearly and did not wish to live without her.
No. 3 is the son of Eskimos 1 and 2. He is too small and too weak to oppose his parents.
No. 4 saw an advertisement in the *New York Times* for an Eskimo to appear on television.
No. 5 is a private detective engaged by the Pinkerton Agency to keep an eye on Eskimo No. 4.

Let us assume that we have now explained in the case of each of the five Eskimos why he or she is in New York. Somebody then asks: "All right, but what about the group as a whole; why is *it* in New York?" This would plainly be an absurd question. There is no group over and above the five members, and if we have explained why each of the five members is in New York we have *ipso facto* explained why the group is there. It is just as absurd to ask for the cause of the series as a whole as distinct from asking for the causes of individual members.

V

It is most unlikely that a determined defender of the cosmological line of reasoning would surrender even here. He would probably admit that the series is not a thing over and above its members and that it does not make sense to ask for the cause of the series if the cause of each member has already been found. He would insist, however, that when he asked for the explanation of the entire series, he was not asking for its *cause*. He was really saying that a series, finite or infinite, is not "intelligible" or "explained" if it consists of nothing but "contingent" members. To quote Father Copleston once more:

> What we call the world is intrinsically unintelligible apart from the existence of God. The infinity of the series of events, if such an infinity could be proved, would not be in the slightest degree relevant to the situation. If you add up chocolates, you get chocolates after all, and not a sheep. If you add up chocolates to infinity, you presumably get an infinite number of chocolates. So, if you add up contingent beings to infinity, you still get contingent beings, not a necessary being.[17]

This last quotation is really a summary of the "contingency argument," the other main form of the cosmological proof and the third of the five ways of Aquinas. It may be stated more fully in these words: All around us we perceive contingent beings. This includes all physical objects and also all human minds. In calling them "contingent" we mean that they might not have existed. We mean that the universe can be *conceived* without this or that physical object, without this or that human being, however certain their actual existence may be. These contingent beings we can trace back to other contingent beings—e.g. a human being to his parents. However, since these other beings are also contingent, they do not provide a real or full explanation. The contingent beings we originally wanted explained have not yet become intelligible, since the beings to which they have been traced back are no more necessary than they were. It is just as true of our parents, for example, as it is of ourselves, that they might not have existed. We can then properly explain the contingent beings around us only by tracing them back ultimately to some necessary being, to something which exists necessarily, which has "the reason for its existence within itself." The existence of contingent beings, in other words, implies the existence of a necessary being.

This form of the cosmological argument is even more beset with difficulties than the causal variety. In the first place, there is the objection, stated with great force by Kant, that it really commits the same error as the ontological argument in tacitly regarding existence as an attribute or characteristic. To say that there is a necessary being is to say that it would be a self-contradiction to deny its existence. This would mean that at least one existential statement is a necessary truth; and this in turn presupposes that in at least one case existence is contained in a concept. But only a characteristic can be contained in a concept and it has seemed plain to most philosophers since Kant that existence is not a characteristic, that it can hence never be contained in a concept, and that hence no existential statement can ever be a necessary truth. To talk about anything "existing necessarily" is in their view about as sensible as to talk about round squares, and they have concluded that the contingency-argument is quite absurd.

It would lead too far to discuss here the reasons for denying that existence is a characteristic. I will assume that this difficulty can somehow be surmounted and that the expression "necessary being," as it is intended by the champions of the contingency-argument, might conceivably apply to something. There remain other objections which are of great weight. I shall try to state these by first quoting again from the debate between Bertrand Russell and Father Copleston:

> RUSSELL: . . . It all turns on this question of sufficient reason, and I must say you haven't defined "sufficient reason" in a way that I can understand—what do you mean by sufficient reason? You don't mean cause?
>
> COPLESTON: Not necessarily. Cause is a kind of sufficient reason. Only contingent being can have a cause. God is his own sufficient reason; and he is not cause of himself. By sufficient reason in the full sense I mean an explanation adequate for the existence of some particular being.
>
> RUSSELL: But when is an explanation adequate? Suppose I am about to make a flame with a match.

You may say that the adequate explanation of that is that I rub it on the box.

COPLESTON: Well for practical purposes—but theoretically, that is only a partial explanation. An adequate explanation must ultimately be a total explanation, to which nothing further can be added.

RUSSELL: Then I can only say that you're looking for something which can't be got, and which one ought not to expect to get.

COPLESTON: To say that one has not found it is one thing; to say that one should not look for it seems to me rather dogmatic.

RUSSELL: Well, I don't know. I mean, the explanation of one thing is another thing which makes the other thing dependent on yet another, and you have to grasp this sorry scheme of things entire to do what you want, and that we can't do.[18]

Russell's main point here may be expanded in the following way. The contingency-argument rests on a misconception of what an explanation is and does, and similarly on what it is that makes phenomena "intelligible." Or else it involves an obscure and arbitrary redefinition of "explanation," "intelligible," and related terms. Normally, we are satisfied that we have explained a phenomenon if we have found its cause or if we have exhibited some other uniform or near-uniform connection between it and something else. Confining ourselves to the former case, which is probably the most common, we might say that a phenomenon, Z, has been explained if it has been traced back to a group of factors, a, b, c, d, etc., which are its cause. These factors are the full and real explanation of Z, quite regardless of whether they are pleasing or displeasing, admirable or contemptible, necessary or contingent. The explanation would not be adequate only if the factors listed are not really the cause of Z. If they are the cause of Z, the explanation would be adequate, even though each of the factors is merely a "contingent" being.

Let us suppose that we have been asked to explain why General Eisenhower won the elections of 1952. "He was an extremely popular general," we might answer, "while Stevenson was relatively little known; moreover there was a great deal of resentment over the scandals in the Truman Administration." If somebody complained that this was only a partial explanation we might mention additional antecedents, such as the widespread belief that the Democrats had allowed communist agents to infiltrate the State Department, that Eisenhower was a man with a winning smile, and that unlike Stevenson he had shown the good sense to say one thing on race relations in the North and quite another in the South. Theoretically, we might go further and list the motives of all American voters during the weeks or months preceding the elections. If we could do this we would have explained Eisenhower's victory. We would have made it intelligible. We would "understand" why he won and why Stevenson lost. Perhaps there is a sense in which we might make Eisenhower's victory even more intelligible if we went further back and discussed such matters as the origin of American views on Communism or of racial attitudes in the North and South. However, to explain the outcome of the election in any ordinary sense, loose or strict, it would not be necessary to go back to prehistoric days or to the amœba or to a first cause, if such a first cause exists. Nor would our explanation be considered in any way defective because each of the factors mentioned was a "contingent" and not a necessary being. The only thing that matters is whether the factors were really the cause of Eisenhower's election. If they were, then it has been explained although they are contingent beings. If they were not the cause of Eisenhower's victory, we would have failed to explain it even if each of the factors were a necessary being.

If it is granted that, in order to explain a phenomenon or to make it intelligible, we need not bring in a necessary being, then the contingency-argument breaks down. For a series, as was already pointed out, is not something over and above its members; and every contingent member of it could in that case be explained by reference to other contingent beings. But I should wish to go further than this and it is evident from Russell's remarks that he would do so also. Even if it were granted, both that the phrase "necessary being" is meaningful and that all explanations are defective unless the phenomena to be explained are traced back to a necessary being, the conclusion would still not have been established. The conclusion follows from this premise together with the additional premise that *there are* explanations of phenomena in the special sense just mentioned. It is this further premise which Russell (and many other philosophers) would question. They do not merely question, as Copleston implies, whether human beings can ever obtain explanations in this sense, but whether they *exist.* To assume without further ado that phenomena have explanations or an explanation in this sense is to beg the very point at issue. The use of the same word "explanation" in two crucially different ways lends the additional premise a plausibility it does not really possess. It may indeed be highly plausible to assert that phenomena have explanations, whether we have found them or not, in the ordinary sense in which this usually means that they have causes. It is then tempting to suppose, because of the use of the same word, that they also have explanations in a sense in which this implies dependence on a necessary being. But this is a gross *non sequitur.*

VI

It is necessary to add a few words about the proper way of formulating the position of those who reject the main premise of the cosmological argument, in either of the forms we have considered. It is sometimes maintained in this connection that in order to reach a "self-existing" entity it is not necessary to go beyond the universe: the universe itself (or "Nature") is "self-existing." And this in turn is sometimes expanded into the statement that while all individual things "within" the universe are caused, the universe itself is uncaused. Statements of this kind are found in Büchner, Bradlaugh, Haeckel, and other free-thinkers of the nineteenth and early twentieth century. Sometimes the assertion that the universe is "self-existing" is elaborated to mean that *it* is the "necessary being." Some eighteenth-century unbelievers, apparently accepting the view that there is a necessary being, asked why Nature or the material universe could not fill the bill as well or better than God.

"Why," asks one of the characters in Hume's *Dialogues,* "may not the material universe be the necessarily existent Being? . . . We dare not affirm that we know all the qualitites of matter; and for aught we can determine, it may contain some qualities, which, were they known, would make its non-existence appear as great a contradiction as that twice two is five."[19]

Similar remarks can be found in Holbach and several of the Encyclopedists.

The former of these formualtions immediately invites the question why the universe, alone of all "things," is exempted from the universal sway of causation. "The strong point of the cosmological argument," writes Dr. Ewing, "is that after all it does remain incredible that the physical universe should just have happened . . . It calls out for some further explanation of some kind."[20] The latter formulation is exposed to the criticism that there is nothing any more "necessary" about the existence of the universe or Nature as a whole than about any particular thing within the universe.

I hope some of the earlier discussions in this article have made it clear that in rejecting the cosmological argument one is not committed to either of these propositions. If I reject the view that there is a supernatural first cause, I am not thereby committed to the proposition that there is a *natural* first cause, and even less to the proposition that a mysterious "thing" called "the universe" qualifies for this title. I may hold that there is no "universe" over and above individual things of various sorts; and, accepting the causal principle, I may proceed to assert that all these things are caused by other things, and these other things by yet other things, and so on, *ad infinitum.* In this way no arbitrary exception is made to the principle of causation. Similarly, if I reject the assertion that God is a "necessary being," I am not committed to the view that the universe is such an entity. I may hold that it does not make sense to speak of anything as a "necessary being" and that even if there were such a thing as the universe it could not be properly considered a necessary being.

However, in saying that nothing is uncaused or that there is no necessary being, one is not committed to the view that everything, or for that matter anything, is merely a "brute fact." Dr. Ewing laments that "the usual modern philosophical views opposed to theism do not try to give any rational explanation of the world at all, but just take it as a brute fact not to be explained." They thus fail to "rationalize" the universe. Theism, he concedes, cannot completely rationalize things either since it does not show "how God can be his own cause or how it is that he does not need a cause."[21] Now, if one means by "brute fact" something for which there *exists* no explanation (as distinct from something for which no explanation is in our possession), then the theists have at least one brute fact on their hands, namely God. Those who adopt Büchner's formulation also have one brute fact on their hands, namely "the universe." Only the position I have been supporting dispenses with brute facts altogether. I don't know if this is any special virtue, but the defenders of the cosmological argument seem to think so.

NOTES

1. *Dialogues Concerning Natural Religion* (London, 1958), Part IX.
2. *The Critique of Pure Reason*, Transcendental Dialectic, Book II, Chapter III.
3. "Theism," *Three Essays on Religion*, Part I.
4. Reprinted in the British edition of Russell's *Why I Am Not a Christian*.
5. J. S. O'Connor, "A Scientific Approach to Religion," *The Scientific Monthly* (1940), p. 369; my italics.
6. *Ibid.*, pp. 369-70.
7. *The Philosophical Bases of Theism*, Lecture V.
8. *The Fundamental Questions of Philosophy*, Chapter XI.
9. *The Principles of Natural Theology*, p. 58.
10. *Modern Thomistic Philosophy*, Vol. II, pp. 284-85.
11. *Ibid.*, p. 278.
12. *Op. cit.*, pp. 67-68.
13. *Ibid.*, p. 82.
14. *The Fourfold Root of the Principle of Sufficient Reason*, pp. 42-43. My attention to this passage was drawn by Professor C. J. Ducasse. See his excellent discussion of the arguments for the existence of God in *A Philosophical Scrutiny of Religion*, Chapter 15.
15. *Why I Am Not a Christian*, pp. 152-53.
16. *Ibid.*, p. 151.
17. *Ibid.*
18. *Ibid.*, p. 150.
19. *Op. cit.*, Part IX.
20. *Op. cit.*, p. 225.
21. *Ibid.*

The Teleological Argument

DAVID HUME

I must own, Cleanthes, said Demea, that nothing can more surprise me than the light in which you have all along put this argument. By the whole tenor of your discourse, one would imagine that you were maintaining the Being of a God against the cavils of atheists and infidels, and were necessitated to become a champion for that fundamental principle of all religion. But this, I hope, is not by any means a question among us. No man, no man at least of common sense, I am persuaded, ever entertained a serious doubt with regard to a truth so certain and self-evident. The question is not concerning the *being* but the *nature* of God. This I affirm, from the infirmities of human understanding, to be altogether incomprehensible and unknown to us. The essence of that supreme Mind, his attributes, the manner of his existence, the very nature of his duration—these and every particular which regards so divine a Being are mysterious to men. Finite, weak, and blind creatures, we ought to humble ourselves in his august presence, and, conscious of our frailties, adore in silence his infinite perfections which eye hath not seen, ear hath not heard, neither hath it entered into the heart of man to conceive. They are covered in a deep cloud from human curiosity; it is profaneness to attempt penetrating through these sacred obscurities, and, next to the impiety of denying his existence, is the temerity of prying into his nature and essence, decrees and attributes.

But lest you should think that my *piety* has here got the better of my *philosophy*, I shall support my opinion, if it needs any support, by a very great authority. I might cite all the divines, almost from the foundation of Christianity, who have ever treated of this or any other theological subject; but I shall confine myself, at present, to one equally celebrated for piety and philosophy. It is Father Malebranche who, I remember, thus expresses himself.[1] "One ought not so much," says he, "to call God a spirit in order to express positively what he is, as in order to signify that he is not matter. He is a Being infinitely perfect—of this we cannot doubt. But in the same manner as we ought not to imagine, even supposing him corporeal, that he is clothed with a human body, as the anthropomorphites asserted, under colour that that figure was the most pefect of any, so neither ought we to imagine that the spirit of God has human ideas or bears any resemblance to our spirit, under colour that we know nothing more perfect than a human mind. We ought rather to believe that as he comprehends the perfections of matter without being material . . . he comprehends also the perfections of created spirits without being spirit, in the manner we conceive spirit: that his true name is *He that is,* or, in other words, Being without restriction, All Being, the Being infinite and universal."

After so great an authority, Demea, replied Philo, as that which you have produced, and a thousand more which you might produce, it

---

David Hume (1711-1776) was the most influential British empiricist.

This selection includes Parts II and V from Hume's *Dialogues on Natural Religion*.

would appear ridiculous in me to add my sentiment or express my approbation of your doctrine. But surely, where reasonable men treat these subjects, the question can never be concerning the *being* but only the *nature* of the Deity. The former truth, as you well observe, is unquestionable and self-evident. Nothing exists without a cause; and the original cause of this universe (whatever it be) we call God, and piously ascribe to him every species of perfection. Whoever scruples this fundamental truth deserves every punishment which can be inflicted among philosophers, to wit, the greatest ridicule, contempt, and disapprobation. But as all perfection is entirely relative, we ought never to imagine that we comprehend the attributes of this divine Being, or to suppose that his perfections have any analogy or likeness to the perfections of a human creature. Wisdom, thought, design, knowledge—these we justly ascribe to him because these words are honourable among men, and we have no other language or other conceptions by which we can express our adoration of him. But let us beware lest we think that our ideas anywise correspond to his perfections, or that his attributes have any resemblance to these qualities among men. He is infinitely superior to our limited view and comprehension, and is more the object of worship in the temple than of disputation in the schools.

In reality, Cleanthes, continued he, there is no need of having recourse to that affected scepticism so displeasing to you in order to come at this determination. Our ideas reach no farther than our experience. We have no experience of divine attributes and operations. I need not conclude my syllogism, you can draw the inference yourself. And it is a pleasure to me (and I hope to you, too) that just reasoning and sound piety here concur in the same conclusion, and both of them establish the adorably mysterious and incomprehensible nature of the Supreme Being.

Not to lose any time in circumlocutions, said Cleanthes, addressing himself to Demea, much less in replying to the pious declamations of Philo, I shall briefly explain how I conceive this matter. Look round the world, contemplate the whole and every part of it: you will find it to be nothing but one great machine, subdivided into an infinite number of lesser machines, which again admit of subdivisions to a degree beyond what human senses and faculties can trace and explain. All these various machines, and even their most minute parts, are adjusted to each other with an accuracy which ravishes into admiration all men who have ever contemplated them. The curious adapting of means to ends, throughout all nature, resembles exactly, though it much exceeds, the productions of human contrivance—of human design, thought, wisdom, and intelligence. Since therefore the effects resemble each other, we are led to infer, by all the rules of analogy, that the causes also resemble, and that the Author of nature is somewhat similar to the mind of man, though possessed of much larger faculties, proportioned to the grandeur of the work which he has executed. By this argument *a posteriori,* and by this argument alone, do we prove at once the existence of a Deity and his similarity to human mind and intelligence.

I shall be so free, Cleanthes, said Demea, as to tell you that from the beginning I could not approve of your conclusion concerning the similarity of the Deity to men, still less can I approve of the mediums by which you endeavour to establish it. What! No demonstration of the being of God! No abstract arguments! No proofs *a priori!* Are these which have hitherto been so much insisted on by philosophers all fallacy, all sophism? Can we reach no farther in this subject than experience and probability? I will not say that this is betraying the cause of a Deity; but surely, by this affected candour, you give advantages to atheists which they never could obtain by the mere dint of argument and reasoning.

What I chiefly scruple in this subject, said Philo, is not so much that all religious arguments are by Cleanthes reduced to experience, as that they appear not to be even the most certain and irrefragable of that inferior kind. That a stone will fall, that fire will burn, that the earth has solidity, we have observed a thousand and a thousand times; and when any new instance of this nature is presented, we draw without hesitation the accustomed inference. The exact similarity of the cases gives us a perfect assurance of a similar event and a stronger evidence is never desired nor sought after. But wherever you depart, in the least, from the similarity of the cases, you diminish proportionably the evidence, and may at last bring it to a very weak *analogy*, which is confessedly liable to error and uncertainty. After having experienced the circulation of the blood in human creatures, we make no doubt that it takes place in Titius and Maevius; but from its circulation in frogs and fishes it is only a presumption, though a strong one, from analogy that it takes place in men and other animals. The analogical reasoning is much weaker when we infer the circulation of the sap in vegetables from our experience that the blood circulates in animals; and those who hastily followed that imperfect analogy are found, by more accurate experiments, to have been mistaken.

If we see a house, Cleanthes, we conclude, with the greatest certainty, that it had an architect or builder because this is precisely that species of effect which we have experienced to proceed from that species of cause. But surely you will not affirm that the universe bears such a resemblance to a house that we can with the same certainty infer a similar cause, or that the analogy is here entire and perfect. The dissimilitude is so striking that the utmost you can here pretend to is a guess, a conjecture, a presumption concerning a similar cause; and how that pretension will be received in the world, I leave you to consider.

It would surely be very ill received, replied Cleanthes; and I should be deservedly blamed and detested did I allow that the proofs of a Deity amounted to no more than a guess or conjecture. But is the whole adjustment of means to ends in a house and in the universe so slight a resemblance? the economy of final causes? the order, proportion, and arrangement of every part? Steps of a stair are plainly contrived that human legs may use them in mounting; and this inference is certain and infallible. Human legs are also contrived for walking and mounting; and this inference, I allow, is not altogether so certain because of the dissimilarity which you remark; but does it, therefore, deserve the name only of presumption or conjecture?

Good God! cried Demea, interrupting him, where are we? Zealous defenders of religion allow that the proofs of a Deity fall short of perfect evidence! And you, Philo, on whose assistance I depended in proving the adorable mysteriousness of the Divine Nature, do you assent to all these extravagant opinions of Cleanthes? For what other name can I give them? or, why spare my censure when such principles are advanced, supported by such an authority, before so young a man as Pamphilus?

You seem not to apprehend, replied Philo, that I argue with Cleanthes in his own way, and, by showing him the dangerous consequences of his tenets, hope at last to reduce him to our opinion. But what sticks most with you, I observe, is the representation which Cleanthes has made of the argument *a posteriori;* and, finding that that argument is likely to escape your hold and vanish into air, you think it so disguised that you can scarcely believe it to be set in its true light. Now, however much I may dissent, in other respects, from the dangerous principle of Cleanthes, I must allow that he has fairly represented that argument, and I shall endeavour so to state the matter to you that you will entertain no further scruples with regard to it.

Were a man to abstract from everything which he knows or has seen, he would be altogether incapable, merely from his own ideas, to determine what kind of scene the universe must be, or to give the preference to one state or situation of things above another. For as nothing which he clearly conceives could be esteemed impossible or implying a contradiction, every chimera of his fancy would be upon an equal footing; nor could he assign any just reason why he adheres to one idea or system, and rejects the others which are equally possible.

Again, after he opens his eyes and contemplates the world as it really is, it would be impossible for him at first to assign the cause of any one event, much less of the whole of things, or of the universe. He might set his fancy a rambling, and she might bring him in an infinite variety of reports and representations. These would all be possible, but, being all equally possible, he would never of himself give a satisfactory account for his preferring one of them to the rest. Experience alone can point out to him the true cause of any phenomenon.

Now, according to this method of reasoning, Demea, it follows (and is, indeed, tacitly allowed by Cleanthes himself) that order, arrangement, or the adjustment of final causes, is not of itself any proof of design, but only so far as it has been experienced to proceed from that principle. For aught we can know *a priori,* matter may contain the source or spring of order originally within itself, as well as mind does; and there is no more difficulty in conceiving that the several elements, from an internal unknown cause, may fall into the most exquisite arrangement, than to conceive that their ideas, in the great universal mind, from a like internal unknown cause, fall into that arrangement. The equal possibility of both these suppositions is allowed. But, by experience, we find (according to Cleanthes) that there is a difference between them. Throw several pieces of steel together, without shape or form, they will never arrange themselves so as to compose a watch. Stone and mortar and wood, without an architect, never erect a house. But the ideas in a human mind, we see, by an unknown, inexplicable economy, arrange themselves so as to form the plan of a watch or house. Experience, therefore, proves that there is an original principle of order in mind, not in matter. From similar effects we infer similar causes. The adjustment of means to ends is alike in the universe, as in a machine of human contrivance. The causes, therefore, must be resembling.

I was from the beginning scandalized, I must own, with this resemblance which is asserted between the Deity and human creatures, and must conceive it to imply such a degradation of the Supreme Being as no sound theist could endure. With your assistance, therefore, Demea, I shall endeavour to defend what you justly call the adorable mysteriousness of the Divine Nature, and shall refute this reasoning of Cleanthes, provided he allows that I have made a fair representation of it.

When Cleanthes had assented, Philo, after a short pause, proceeded in the following manner.

That all inferences, Cleanthes, concerning fact are founded on experience, and that all experimental reasonings are founded on the supposition that similar causes prove similar effects, and similar effects similar causes, I shall not at present much dispute with you. But observe, I entreat you, with what extreme caution all just reasoners proceed in the transferring of experiments to similar cases. Unless the cases be exactly similar, they repose no perfect confidence in applying their past observation to any particular phenomenon. Every alteration of circumstances occasions a doubt concerning the event; and it requires new experiments to prove certainly that the new circumstances are of no moment or importance. A change in bulk, situation, arrangement, age, disposition of the air, or surrounding bodies—any of these particulars may be attended with the most unexpected consequences. And unless the objects be quite familiar to us, it is the highest temerity to expect with assurance, after any of these changes, an event similar to that which before fell under our observation. The slow and deliberate steps of philosophers here, if anywhere, are distinguished from the precipitate march of the vulgar, who, hurried on by the smallest similitude, are incapable of all discernment or consideration.

But can you think, Cleanthes, that your usual phlegm and philosophy have been preserved in so wide a step as you have taken when you compared to the universe houses, ships, furniture, machines, and, from their similarity in some circumstances, inferred a similarity in their causes? Thought, design, intelligence, such as we discover in men and other animals, is no more than one of the springs and principles of the universe, as well as heat or cold, attraction or repulsion, and a hundred others which fall under daily observation. It is an active cause by which some particular parts of nature, we find, produce alterations on other parts. But can a conclusion, with any propriety, be transferred from parts to the whole? Does not the great disproportion bar all comparison and inference? From observing the growth of a hair, can we learn anything concerning the generation of a man? Would the manner of a leaf's blowing, even though perfectly known, afford us any instruction concerning the vegetation of a tree?

But allowing that we were to take the *operations* of one part of nature upon another for the foundation of our judgment concerning the *origin* of the whole (which never can be admitted), yet why select so minute, so weak, so bounded a principle as the reason and design of animals is found to be upon this planet? What peculiar privilege has this little agitation of the brain which we call *thought*, that we must thus make it the model of the whole universe? Our partiality in our own favour does indeed present it on all occasions, but sound philosophy ought carefully to guard against so natural an illusion.

So far from admitting, continued Philo, that the operations of a part can afford us any just conclusion concerning the origin of the whole, I will not allow any one part to form a rule for another part if the latter be very remote from the former. Is there any reasonable ground to conclude that the inhabitants of other planets possess thought, intelligence, reason, or anything similar to these faculties in men? When nature has so extremely diversified her manner of operation in this small globe, can we imagine that she incessantly copies herself throughout so immense a universe? And if thought, as we may well suppose, be confined merely to this narrow corner and has even there so limited a sphere of action, with what propriety can we assign it for the original cause of all things? The narrow views of a peasant who makes his domestic economy the rule for the government of kingdoms is in comparison a pardonable sophism.

But were we ever so much assured that a thought and reason resembling the human were to be found throughout the whole universe, and were its activity elsewhere vastly greater and more commanding than it appears in this globe, yet I cannot see why the operations of a world constituted, arranged, adjusted, can with any propriety be extended to a world which is in its embryo state, and is advancing towards that constitution and arrangement. By observation we know somewhat of the economy, action, and nourishment of a finished animal, but we must transfer with great caution that observation to the growth of a fœtus in the womb, and still more to the formation of an animalcule in the loins of its male parent. Nature, we find, even from our limited experience, possesses an infinite number of springs and principles which incessantly discover themselves on every change of her position and situation. And what new and unknown principles would actuate her in so new and unknown a situation as that of the formation of a universe, we cannot, without the utmost temerity, pretend to determine.

A very small part of this great system, during a very short time, is very imperfectly discovered to us; and do we thence pronounce decisively concerning the origin of the whole?

Admirable conclusion! Stone, wood, brick, iron, brass, have not, at this time, in this minute globe of earth, an order or arrangement without human art and contrivance; therefore, the universe could not originally attain its order and arrangement without something similar to human art. But is a part of nature a rule for another part very wide of the former? Is it a rule for the whole? Is a very small part a rule for the universe? Is nature in one situation a certain rule for nature in another situation vastly different from the former?

And can you blame me, Cleanthes, if I here imitate the prudent reserve of Simonides, who, according to the noted story, being asked by Hiero, *What God was?* desired a day to think of it, and then two days more; and after that manner continually prolonged the term, without ever bringing in his definition or description? Could you even blame me if I had answered, at first, *that I did not know*, and was sensible that this subject lay vastly beyond the reach of my faculties? You might cry out sceptic and rallier, as much as you pleased; but, having found in so many other subjects much more familiar the imperfections and even contradictions of human reason, I never should expect any success from its feeble conjectures in a subject so sublime and so remote from the sphere of our observation. When two *species* of objects have always been observed to be conjoined together, I can *infer*, by custom, the existence of one wherever I *see* the existence of the other; and this I call an argument from experience. But how this argument can have place where the objects, as in the present case, are single, individual, without parallel or specific resemblance, may be difficult to explain. And will any man tell me with a serious countenance that an orderly universe must arise from some thought and art like the human because we have experience of it? To ascertain this reasoning it were requisite that we had experience of the origin of worlds; and it is not sufficient, surely, that we have seen ships and cities arise from human art and contrivance.

Philo was proceeding in this vehement manner, somewhat between jest and earnest, as it appeared to me, when he observed some signs of impatience in Cleanthes, and then immediately stopped short. What I had to suggest, said Cleanthes, is only that you would not abuse terms, or make use of popular expressions to subvert philosophical reasonings. You know that the vulgar often distinguish reason from experience, even where the question relates only to matter of fact and existence, though it is found, where that *reason* is properly analyzed, that it is nothing but a species of experience. To prove by experience the origin of the universe from mind is not more contrary to common speech than to prove the motion of the earth from the same principle. And a caviller might raise all the same objections to the Copernican system which you have urged against my reasonings. Have you other earths, might he say, which you have seen to move? Have . . .

Yes! cried Philo, interrupting him, we have other earths. Is not the moon another earth, which we see to turn round its centre? Is not Venus another earth, where we observe the same phenomenon? Are not the revolutions of the sun also a confirmation, from analogy, of the same theory? All the planets, are they not earths which revolve about the sun? Are not the satellites moons which move round Jupiter and Saturn, and along with these primary planets round the sun? These analogies and resemblances, with others which I have not mentioned, are the sole proofs of the Copernican system; and to you it belongs to consider whether you have any analogies of the same kind to support your theory.

In reality, Cleanthes, continued he, the modern system of astronomy is now so much received by all inquirers, and has become so essential a part even of our earliest education, that we are not commonly very scrupulous in examining the reasons upon which it is founded. It is now become a matter of mere curiosity to study the first writers on that subject who had the full force of prejudice to encounter, and were obliged to turn their arguments on every side in order to render them popular and convincing. But if we peruse Galileo's famous *Dialogues*[2] concerning the system of the world, we shall find that that great genius, one of the sublimest that ever existed, first bent all his endeavours to prove that there was no foundation for the distinction commonly made between elementary and celestial substances. The schools, proceeding from the illusions of sense, had carried this distinction very far; and had established the latter substances to be ingenerable, incorruptible, unalterable, impassible; and had assigned all the opposite qualities to the former. But Galileo, beginning with the moon, proved its similarity in every particular to the earth: its convex figure, its natural darkness when not illuminated, its density, its distinction into solid and liquid, the variations of its phases, the mutual illuminations of the earth and moon, their mutual eclipses, the inequalities of the lunar surface, etc. After many instances of this kind, with regard to all the planets, men plainly saw that these bodies became proper objects of experience, and that the similarity of their nature enabled us to extend the same arguments and phenomena from one to the other.

In this cautious proceeding of the astronomers you may read your own condemnation, Cleanthes, or rather may see that the subject in which you are engaged exceeds all human reason and inquiry. Can you pretend to show any such similarity between the fabric of a house and the generation of a universe? Have you ever seen nature in any such situation as resembles the first arrangement of the elements? Have worlds ever been formed under your eye, and have you had leisure to observe the whole progress of the phenomenon, from the first appearance of order to its final consummation? . . .

But to show you still more inconveniences, continued Philo, in your anthropomorphism, please to take a new survey of your principles. *Like effects prove like causes.* This is the experimental argument; and this, you say too, is the sole theological argument. Now it is certain that the liker the effects are which are seen and the liker the causes which are inferred, the stronger is the argument. Every departure on either side diminishes the probability and renders the experiment less conclusive. You cannot doubt of the principle; neither ought you to reject its consequences.

All the new discoveries in astronomy which prove the immense grandeur and maginificence of the works of nature are so many additional arguments for a Deity, according to the true system of theism; but, according to your hypothesis of experimental theism, they become so many objections, by removing the effect still farther from all resemblance to the effects of human art and contrivance. For if Lucretius, even following the old system of the world, could exclaim:

Quis regere immensi summam, quis habere profundi
Indu manu validas potis est moderanter habenas?
Quis pariter cœlos omnes convertere? et omnes
Ignibus ætheriis terras suffire feraces?
Omnibus inque locis esse omni tempore præsto?[3]

If Tully [Cicero] esteemed this reasoning so natural as to put it into the mouth of his Epicurean:

Quibus enim oculis animi intueri potuit vester Plato fabricam illam tanti operis, qua construi a Deo atque ædificari mundum facit? quæ molitio? quæ ferramenta? qui vectes? quæ machinæ? qui minstri tanti muneris fuerunt? quemadmodum autem obedire et parere voluntati architecti aer, ignis, aqua, terra potuerunt?[4]

If this argument, I say, had any force in former ages, how much greater must it have at present when the bounds of Nature are so infinitely enlarged and such a magnificent scene is opened to us? It is still more unreasonable to form our idea of so unlimited a cause from our experience of the narrow productions of human design and invention.

The discoveries by microscopes, as they open a new universe in miniature, are still objections, according to you, arguments, according to me. The further we push our researches of this kind, we are still led to infer the universal cause of all to be vastly different from mankind, or from any object of human experience and observation.

And what say you to the discoveries in anatomy, chemistry, botany?... These surely are no objections, replied Cleanthes; they only discover new instances of art and contrivance. It is still the image of mind reflected on us from innumerable objects. Add a mind *like the human,* said Philo. I know of no other, replied Cleanthes. And the liker, the better, insisted Philo. To be sure, said Cleanthes.

Now, Cleanthes, said Philo, with an air of alacrity and triumph, mark the consequences. *First,* by this method of reasoning you renounce all claim to infinity in any of the attributes of the Deity. For, as the cause ought only to be proportioned to the effect, and the effect, so far as it falls under our cognizance, is not infinite, what pretensions have we, upon your suppositions, to ascribe that attribute to the Divine Being? You will still insist that, by removing him so much from all similarity to human creatures, we give in to the most arbitrary hypothesis, and at the same time weaken all proofs of his existence.

Secondly, you have no reason, on your theory, for ascribing perfection to the Deity, even in his finite capacity, or for supposing him free from every error, mistake, or incoherence, in his undertakings. There are many inexplicable difficulties in the works of nature which, if we allow a perfect author to be proved *a priori,* are easily solved, and become only seeming difficulties from the narrow capacity of man, who cannot trace infinite relations. But according to your method of reasoning, these difficulties become all real, and, perhaps, will be insisted on as new instances of likeness to human art and contrivance. At least, you must acknowledge that it is impossible for us to tell, from our limited views, whether this system contains any great faults or deserves any considerable praise if compared to other possible and even real systems. Could a peasant, if the *Aeneid* were read to him, pronounce that poem to be absolutely faultless, or even assign to it its proper rank among the productions of human wit, he who had never seen any other production?

But were this world ever so perfect a production, it must still remain uncertain whether all the excellences of the work can justly be ascribed to the workman. If we survey a ship, what an exalted idea must we form of the ingenuity of the carpenter who framed so complicated, useful, and beautiful a machine? And what surprise must we feel when we find him a stupid mechanic who imitated others, and copied an art which, through a long succession of ages, after multiplied trials, mistakes, corrections, deliberations, and controversies, had been gradually improving? Many worlds might have been botched and bungled, throughout an eternity, ere this system was struck out; much labour lost, many fruitless trials made, and a slow but continued improvement carried on during infinite ages in the art of world-making. In such subjects, who can determine where the truth, nay, who can conjecture where the probability lies, amidst a great number of hypotheses which may be proposed, and a still greater which may be imagined?

And what shadow of an argument, continued Philo, can you produce from your hypothesis to prove the unity of the Deity? A great number of men join in building a house or ship, in rearing a city, in framing a commonwealth; why may not several deities combine in contriving and framing a world? This is only so much greater similarity to human affairs. By sharing the work among several, we may so much further limit the attributes of each, and get rid of that extensive power and knowledge which must be supposed in one deity, and which, according to you, can only serve to weaken the proof of his existence. And if such foolish, such vicious creatures as man can yet often unite in framing and executing one plan, how much more those deities or demons, whom we may suppose several degrees more perfect!

To multiply causes without necessity is indeed contrary to true philosophy, but this principle applies not to the present case. Were one deity antecedently proved by your theory who were possessed of every attribute requisite to the production of the universe, it would be needless, I own, (though not absurd) to suppose any other deity existent. But while it is still a question whether all these attributes are united in one subject or dispersed among several independent beings, by what phenomena in nature can we pretend to decide the controversy? Where we see a body raised in a scale, we are sure that there is in the opposite scale, however concealed from sight, some counterpoising weight equal to it; but it is still allowed to doubt whether that weight be an aggregate of several distinct bodies or one uniform united mass. And if the weight requisite very much exceeds anything which we have ever seen conjoined in any single body, the former supposition becomes still more probable and natural. An intelligent being of such vast power and capacity as is necessary to produce the universe, or, to speak in the language of ancient philosophy, so prodigious an animal exceeds all analogy and even comprehension.

But further, Cleanthes: Men are mortal, and renew their species by generation; and this is common to all living creatures. The two great sexes of male and female, says Milton, animate the world. Why must this circumstance, so universal, so essential, be excluded from those numerous and limited deities? Behold, then, the theogeny of ancient times brought back upon us.

And why not become a perfect anthropomorphite? Why not assert the deity or deities to be corporeal, and to have eyes, a nose, mouth, ears, etc.? Epicurus maintained that no man had ever seen reason but in a human figure; therefore, the gods must have a human figure. And this argument, which is deservedly so much ridiculed by Cicero, becomes, according to you, solid and philosophical.

In a word, Cleanthes, a man who follows your hypothesis is able, perhaps, to assert or conjecture that the universe sometime arose from something like design; but beyond that position he cannot ascertain one single circumstance and is left afterwards to fix every point of his theology by the utmost license of fancy and hypothesis. This world, for aught he knows, is very faulty and imperfect, compared to a superior standard, and was only the first rude essay of some infant deity who afterwards abandoned it, ashamed of his lame performance; it is the work only of some dependent, inferior deity, and is the object of derision to his superiors; it is the production of old age and dotage in some superannuated deity, and ever since his death has run on at adventures, from the first impulse and active force which it received from him. You justly give signs of horror, Demea, at these strange suppositions; but these, and a thousand more of the same kind, are Cleanthes' suppositions, not mine. From the moment the attributes of the Deity are supposed finite, all these have place. And I cannot, for my part, think that so wild and unsettled a system of theology is, in any respect, preferable to none at all.

These suppositions I absolutely disown, cried Cleanthes: they strike me, however, with no horror, especially when proposed in that rambling way in which they drop from you. On the contrary, they give me pleasure when I see that, by the utmost indulgence of your imagination, you never get rid of the hypothesis of design in the universe, but are obliged at every turn to have recourse to it. To this concession I adhere steadily; and this I regard as a sufficient foundation for religion.

NOTES

1. Recherche de la Vérité, liv. 3, cap. 9.

2. [*Dialogo dei due Massimi Sistemi del Mondo (1632.*]

3. [*De Rerum Natura*], lib. XI [II], 1094. [Who can rule the sum, who hold in his hand with controlling force the strong reins, of the immeasurable deep? Who can at once make all the different heavens to roll and warm with ethereal fires all the fruitful earths, or be present in all places at all times? (Translation by H. A. J. Munro, G. Bell & Sons, 1920.)]

4. *De Natura Deorum,* lib. I; [cap. VIII.] [For with what eyes could your Plato see the construction of so vast a work which, according to him, God was putting together and building? What materials, what tools, what bars, what machines, what servants were employed in such gigantic work? How could the air, fire, water, and earth pay obedience and submit to the will of the architect?]

The Argument from Evil

DAVID HUME

It is my opinion, I own, replied Demea, that each man feels, in a manner, the truth of religion within his own breast, and, from a consciousness of his imbecility and misery rather than from any reasoning, is led to seek protection from that Being on whom he and all nature is dependent. So anxious or so tedious are even the best scenes of life that futurity is still the object of all our hopes and fears. We incessantly look forward and endeavour, by prayers, adoration, and sacrifice, to appease those unknown powers whom we find, by experience, so able to afflict and oppress us. Wretched creatures that we are! What resource for us amidst the innumerable ills of life did not religion suggest some methods of atonement, and appease those terrors with which we are incessantly agitated and tormented?

I am indeed persuaded, said Philo, that the best and indeed the only method of bringing everyone to a due sense of religion is by just representations of the misery and wickedness of men. And for that purpose a talent of eloquence and strong imagery is more requisite than that of reasoning and argument. For is it necessary to prove what everyone feels within himself? It is only necessary to make us feel it, if possible, more intimately and sensibly.

The people, indeed, replied Demea, are sufficiently convinced of this great and melancholy truth. The miseries of life, the unhappiness of man, the general corruptions of our nature, the unsatisfactory enjoyment of pleasures, riches, honours—these phrases have become almost proverbial in all languages. And who can doubt of what all men declare from their own immediate feeling and experience?

In this point, said Philo, the learned are perfectly agreed with the vulgar; and in all letters, *sacred* and *profane,* the topic of human misery has been insisted on with the most pathetic eloquence that sorrow and melancholy could inspire. The poets, who speak from sentiment, without a system, and whose testimony has therefore the more authority, abound in images of this nature. From Homer down to Dr. Young, the whole inspired tribe have ever been sensible that no other representation of things would suit the feeling and observation of each individual.

As to authorities, replied Demea, you need not seek them. Look round this library of Cleanthes. I shall venture to affirm that, except authors of particular sciences, such as chemistry or botany, who have no occasion to treat of human life, there is scarce one of those innumerable writers from whom the sense of human misery has not, in some passage or other, extorted a complaint and confession of it. At least, the chance is entirely on that side; and no one author has ever, so far as I can recollect, been so extravagant as to deny it.

There you must excuse me, said Philo: Leibniz has denied it, and is perhaps the first[1] who ventured upon so bold and paradoxical an opinion; at least, the first who made it essential to his philosophical system.

And by being the first, replied Demea, might he not have been sensible of his error?

Taken from Parts X and XI of Hume's *Dialogues*.

For is this a subject in which philosophers can propose to make discoveries especially in so late an age? And can any man hope by a simple denial (for the subject scarcely admits of reasoning) to bear down the united testimony of mankind, founded on sense and consciousness?

And why should man, added he, pretend to an exemption from the lot of all other animals? The whole earth, believe me, Philo, is cursed and polluted. A perpetual war is kindled amongst all living creatures. Necessity, hunger, want stimulate the strong and courageous; fear, anxiety, terror agitate the weak and infirm. The first entrance into life gives anguish to the new-born infant and to its wretched parent; weakness, impotence, distress attend each stage of that life, and it is, at last, finished in agony and horror.

Observe, too, says Philo, the curious artifices of nature in order to embitter the life of every living being. The stronger prey upon the weaker and keep them in perpetual terror and anxiety. The weaker, too, in their turn, often prey upon the stronger, and vex and molest them without relaxation. Consider that innumerable race of insects, which either are bred on the body of each animal or, flying about, infix their stings in him. These insects have others still less than themselves which torment them. And thus on each hand, before and behind, above and below, every animal is surrounded with enemies which incessantly seek his misery and destruction.

Man alone, said Demea, seems to be, in part, an exception to this rule. For by combination in society he can easily master lions, tigers, and bears, whose greater strength and agility naturally enable them to prey upon him.

On the contrary, it is here chiefly, cried Philo, that the uniform and equal maxims of nature are most apparent. Man, it is true, can, by combination, surmount all his *real* enemies and become master of the whole animal creation; but does he not immediately raise up to himself *imaginary* enemies, the demons of his fancy, who haunt him with superstitious terrors and blast every enjoyment of life? His pleasure, as he imagines, becomes in their eyes a crime; his food and repose give them umbrage and offence; his very sleep and dreams furnish new materials to anxious fear; and even death, his refuge from every other ill, presents only the dread of endless and innumerable woes. Nor does the wolf molest more the timid flock than superstition does the anxious breast of wretched mortals.

Besides, consider, Demea: This very society by which we surmount those wild beasts, our natural enemies, what new enemies does it not raise to us? What woe and misery does it not occasion? Man is the greatest enemy of man. Oppression, injustice, contempt, contumely, violence, sedition, war, calumny, treachery, fraud—by these they mutually torment each other, and they would soon dissolve that society which they had formed were it not for the dread of still greater ills which must attend their separation.

But though these external insults, said Demea, from animals, from men, from all the elements, which assault us form a frightful catalogue of woes, they are nothing in comparison of those which arise within ourselves, from the distempered condition of our mind and body. How many lie under the lingering torment of diseases? Hear the pathetic enumeration of the great poet.

> Intestine stone and ulcer, colic-pangs,
> Demoniac frenzy, moping melancholy,
> And moon-struck madness, pining atrophy,
> Marasmus, and wide-wasting pestilence.
> Dire was the tossing, deep the groans: *Despair*
> Tended the sick, busiest from couch to couch.
> And over them triumphant *Death* his dart
> Shook: but delay'd to strike, though oft invok'd
> With vows, as their chief good and final hope.[2]

The disorders of the mind, continued Demea, though more secret, are not perhaps less dismal and vexatious. Remorse, shame, anguish, rage, disappointment, anxiety, fear, dejection, despair—who has ever passed through life without cruel inroads from these tormentors? How many have scarcely ever felt any better sensations? Labour and poverty, so abhorred by everyone, are the certain lot of the far greater number; and those few privileged persons who enjoy ease and opulence never reach contentment or true felicity. All the goods of life united would not make a very happy man, but all the ills united would make a wretch indeed; and any one of them almost (and who can be free from every one?), nay, often the absence of one good (and who can possess all?) is sufficient to render life ineligible.

Were a stranger to drop on a sudden into this world, I would show him, as a specimen of its ills, an hospital full of diseases, a prison crowded with malefactors and debtors, a field of battle strewed with carcases, a fleet foundering in the ocean, a nation languishing under tyranny, famine, or pestilence. To turn the gay side of life to him and give him a notion of its pleasures—whither should I conduct him? To a ball, to an opera, to court? He might justly think that I was only showing him a diversity of distress and sorrow.

There is no evading such striking instances, said Philo, but by apologies which still further aggravate the charge. Why have all men, I ask, in all ages, complained incessantly of the miseries of life? . . . They have no just reason, says one: these complaints proceed only from their discontented, repining, anxious disposition. . . . And can there possibly, I reply, be more certain foundation of misery than such a wretched temper? my antagonist, why do they remain in life? . . .

But if they were really as unhappy as they pretend, says my antagonist, why do they remain in life? . . .

> Not satisfied with life, afraid of death—

this is the secret chain, say I, that holds us. We are terrified, not bribed to the continuance of our existence.

It is only a false delicacy, he may insist, which a few refined spirits indulge, and which has spread these complaints among the whole race of mankind . . . And what is this delicacy, I ask, which you blame? Is it anything but a greater sensibility to all the pleasures and pains of life? And if the man of a delicate, refined temper, by being so much more alive than the rest of the world, is only so much more unhappy, what judgment must we form in general of human life?

Let men remain at rest, says our adversary, and they will be easy. They are willing artificers of their own misery. . . . No! reply I: an anxious languor follows their repose; disappointment, vexation, trouble, their activity and ambition.

I can observe something like what you mention in some others, replied Cleanthes, but I confess I feel little or nothing of it in myself, and hope that it is not so common as you represent it.

If you feel not human misery yourself, cried Demea, I congratulate you on so happy a singularity. Others, seemingly the most prosperous, have not been ashamed to vent their complaints in the most melancholy strains. Let us attend to the great, the fortunate emperor, Charles V, when, tired with human grandeur, he resigned all his extensive dominions into the hands of his son. In the last harangue which he made on that memorable occasion, he publicly avowed *that the greatest prosperities which he had ever enjoyed had been mixed with so many adversities that he might truly say he had never enjoyed any satisfaction or contentment.* But did the retired life in which he sought for shelter afford him any greater happiness? If we may credit his son's account, his repentance commenced the very day of his resignation.

Cicero's fortune, from small beginnings, rose to the greatest lustre and renown; yet what pathetic complaints of the ills of life do his familiar letters, as well as philosophical discourses, contain? And suitably to his own experience, he introduces Cato, the great, the fortunate Cato protesting in his old age that had he a new life in his offer he would reject the present.

Ask yourself, ask any of your acquaintance, whether they would live over again the last ten or twenty years of their life. No! but the next twenty, they say, will be better:

> And from the dregs of life, hope to receive
> What the first sprightly running could not give.[3]

Thus, at last, they find (such is the greatness of human misery, it reconciles even contradictions) that they complain at once of the shortness of life and of its vanity and sorrow.

And is it possible, Cleanthes, said Philo, that after all these reflections, and infinitely more which might be suggested, you can still persevere in your anthropomorphism, and assert the moral attributes of the Diety, his justice, benevolence, mercy, and rectitude, to be of the same nature with these virtues in human creatures? His power, we allow, is infinite; whatever he wills is executed; but neither man nor any other animal is happy; therefore, he does not will their happiness. His wisdom is infinite; he is never mistaken in choosing the means to any end; but the course of nature tends not to human or animal felicity; therefore, it is not established for that purpose. Through the whole compass of human knowledge there are no inferences more certain and infallible than these. In what respect, then, do his benevolence and mercy resemble the benevolence and mercy of men?

Epicurus' old questions are yet unanswered.

Is he willing to prevent evil, but not able? then is he impotent. Is he able, but not willing? then is he malevolent. Is he both able and willing? whence then is evil?

You ascribe, Cleanthes, (and I believe justly) a purpose and intention to nature. But what, I beseech you, is the object of that curious artifice and machinery which she has displayed in all animals—the preservation alone of individuals, and propagation of the species? It seems enough for her purpose, if such a rank be barely upheld in the universe, without any care or concern for the happiness of the members that compose it. No resource for this purpose: no machinery in order merely to give pleasure or ease; no fund of pure joy and contentment; no indulgence without some want or necessity accompanying it. At least, the few phenomena of this nature are overbalanced by opposite phenomena of still greater importance.

Our sense of music, harmony, and indeed beauty of all kinds, gives satisfaction, without being absolutely necessary to the preservation and propagation of the species. But what racking pains, on the other hand, arise from gouts, gravels, megrims, toothaches, rheumatisms, where the injury to the animal machinery is either small or incurable? Mirth, laughter, play, frolic seem gratuitous satisfactions which have no further tendency; spleen, melancholy, discontent, superstition are pains of the same nature. How then does the Divine benevolence display itself, in the sense of you anthropomorphites? None but we mystics, as you were pleased to call us, can account for this strange mixture of phenomena, by deriving it from attributes infinitely perfect but incomprehensible.

And have you, at last, said Cleanthes smiling, betrayed your intentions, Philo? Your long agreement with Demea did indeed a little surprise me, but I find you were all the while erecting a concealed battery against me. And I must confess that you have now fallen upon a subject worthy of your noble spirit of opposition and controversy. If you can make out the present point, and prove mankind to be unhappy or corrupted, there is an end at once of all religion. For to what purpose establish the natural attributes of the Deity, while the moral are still doubtful and uncertain?

You take umbrage very easily, replied Demea, at opinions the most innocent and the most generally received, even amongst the religious and devout themselves; and nothing can be more surprising than to find a topic like this—concerning the wickedness and misery of man—charged with no less than atheism and profaneness. Have not all pious divines and preachers who have indulged their rhetoric on so fertile a subject, have they not easily, I say, given a solution of any difficulties which may attend it? This world is but a point in comparison of the universe; this life but a moment in comparison of eternity. The present evil phenomena, therefore, are rectified in other regions, and in some future period of existence. And the eyes of men, being then opened to larger views of things, see the whole connection of general laws, and trace, with adoration, the benevolence and rectitude of the Deity through all the mazes and intricacies of his providence.

No! replied Cleanthes, no! These arbitrary suppositions can never be admitted, contrary to matter of fact, visible and uncontroverted. Whence can any cause be known but from its known effects? Whence can any hypothesis be proved but from the apparent phenomena? To establish one hypothesis upon another is building entirely in the air; and the utmost we ever attain by these conjectures and fictions is to ascertain the bare possibility of our opinion, but never can we, upon such terms, establish its reality.

The only method of supporting Divine benevolence—and it is what I willingly embrace—is to deny absolutely the misery and wickedness of man. Your representations are exaggerated; your melancholy views mostly fictitious; your inferences contrary to fact and experience. Health is more common than sickness; pleasure than pain; happiness than misery. And for one vexation which we meet with, we attain, upon computation, a hundred enjoyments.

Admitting your position, replied Philo, which yet is extremely doubtful, you must at the same time allow that, if pain be less frequent than pleasure, it is infinitely more violent and durable. One hour of it is often able to outweigh a day, a week, a month of our common insipid enjoyments; and how many days, weeks, and months are passed by several in the most acute torments? Pleasure, scarcely in one instance, is ever able to reach ecstasy and rapture; and in no one instance can it continue for any time at its highest pitch and altitude. The spirits evaporate, the nerves relax, the fabric is disordered, and the enjoyment quickly degenerates into fatigue and uneasiness. But pain often, good God, how often! rises to torture and agony; and the longer it continues, it becomes still more genuine agony and torture. Patience is exhausted, courage languishes, melancholy seizes us, and nothing terminates our misery but the removal of its cause or another event which is the sole cure of all evil, but which, from our natural folly, we regard with still greater horror and consternation.

But not to insist upon these topics, continued Philo, though most obvious, certain, and important, I must use the freedom to admonish you, Cleanthes, that you have put the controversy upon a most dangerous issue, and are unawares introducing a total scepticism into the most essential articles of natural and revealed theology. What! no method of fixing a just foundation for religion unless we allow the happiness of human life, and maintain a continued existence even in this world, with all our present pains, infirmities, vexations, and follies, to be eligible and desirable! But this is contrary to everyone's feeling and experience; it is contrary to an authority so established as nothing can subvert. No decisive proofs can ever be produced against this authority; nor is it possible for you to compute, estimate, and compare all the pains and all the pleasures in the lives of all men and of all animals; and thus, by your resting the whole system of religion on a point which, from its very nature, must for ever be uncertain, you tacitly confess that that system is equally uncertain.

But allowing you what never will be believed, at least, what you never possibly can prove, that animal or, at least, human happiness in this life exceeds its misery, you have yet done nothing; for this is not, by any means, what we expect from infinite power, infinite wisdom, and infinite goodness. Why is there any misery at all in the world? Not by chance, surely. From some cause then. Is it from the intention of the Deity? But he is perfectly benevolent. Is it contrary to his intention? But he is almighty. Nothing can shake the solidity of this reasoning, so short, so clear, so decisive, except we assert that these subjects exceed all human capacity, and that our common measures of truth and falsehood are not applicable to them—a topic which I have all along insisted on, but which you have, from the beginning, rejected with scorn and indignation.

But I will be contented to retire still from this intrenchment, for I deny that you can ever force me in it. I will allow that pain or misery in man is *compatible* with infinite power and goodness in the Deity, even in your sense of these attributes: what are you advanced by all these concessions? A mere possible compatibility is not sufficient. You must *prove* these pure, unmixt, and uncontrollable attributes from the present mixed and confused phenomena, and from these alone. A hopeful undertaking! Were the phenomena ever so pure and unmixed, yet, being finite, they would be insufficient for that purpose. How much more, where they are also so jarring and discordant!

Here, Cleanthes, I find myself at ease in my argument. Here I triumph. Formerly, when we argued concerning the natural attributes of intelligence and design, I needed all my sceptical and metaphysical subtilty to elude your grasp. In many views of the universe and of its parts, particularly the latter, the beauty and fitness of final causes strike us with such irresistible force that all objections appear (what I believe they really are) mere cavils and sophisms; nor can we then imagine how it was ever possible for us to repose any weight on them. But there is no view of human life or of the condition of mankind from which, without the greatest violence, we can infer the moral attributes or learn that infinite benevolence, conjoined with infinite power and infinite wisdom, which we must discover by the eyes of faith alone. It is your turn now to tug the labouring oar, and to support your philosophical subtilties against the dictates of plain reason and experience.

I scruple not to allow, said Cleanthes, that I have been apt to suspect the frequent repetition of the word *infinite,* which we meet with in all theological writers, to savour more of panegyric than of philosophy, and that any purposes of reasoning, and even of religion, would be better served were we to rest contented with more accurate and more moderate expressions. The terms *admirable, excellent, superlatively great, wise,* and *holy*—these sufficiently fill the imaginations of men, and anything beyond, besides that it leads into absurdities, has no influence on the affections or sentiments. Thus, in the present subject, if we abandon all human analogy, as seems your intention, Demea, I am afraid we abandon all religion and retain no conception of the great object of our adoration. If we preserve human analogy, we must forever find it impossible to reconcile any mixture of evil in the universe with infinite attributes; much less can we ever prove the latter from the former. But supposing the Author of nature to be finitely perfect, though far exceeding mankind, a satisfactory account may then be given of natural and moral evil, and every untoward phenomenon be explained and adjusted. A less evil may then be chosen in order to avoid a greater; inconveniences be submitted to in order to reach a desirable end; and, in a word, benevolence, regulated by wisdom and limited by necessity, may produce just such a world as the present. You, Philo, who are so prompt at starting views and reflections and analogies, I would gladly hear, at length, without interruption, your opinion of this new theory; and if it deserve our attention, we may afterwards, at more leisure, reduce it into form.

My sentiments, replied Philo, are not worth being made a mystery of; and, therefore, without any ceremony, I shall deliver what occurs to me with regard to the present subject. It must, I think, be allowed that, if a very limited intelligence whom we shall suppose utterly unacquainted with the universe were assured that it were the production of a very good, wise, and powerful Being, however finite, he would, from his conjectures, form *beforehand* a different notion of it from what we find it to be by experience; nor would he ever imagine, merely from these attributes of the cause of which he is informed, that the effect could be so full of vice and misery and disorder, as it appears in this life. Supposing now that this person were brought into the world, still assured that it was the workmanship of such a sublime and benevolent Being, he might, perhaps, be surprised at the disappointment, but would never retract his former belief if founded on any very solid argument, since such a limited intelligence must be sensible of his own blindness and ignorance, and must allow that there may be many solutions of those phenomena which will for ever escape his comprehension. But supposing, which is the real case with regard to man, that this creature is not antecedently convinced of a supreme intelligence, benevolent, and powerful, but is left to gather such a belief from the appearances of things—this entirely alters the case, nor will he ever find any reason for such a conclusion. He may be fully convinced of the narrow limits of his understanding, but this will not help him in forming an inference concerning the goodness of superior powers, since he must form that inference from what he knows, not from what he is ignorant of. The more you exaggerate his weakness and ignorance, the more diffident you render him, and give him the greater suspicion that such subjects are beyond the reach of his faculties. You are obliged, therefore, to reason with him merely from the known phenomena, and to drop every arbitrary supposition or conjecture.

Did I show you a house or palace where there was not one apartment convenient or agreeable, where the windows, doors, fires, passages, stairs, and the whole economy of the building were the source of noise, confusion, fatigue, darkness, and the extremes of heat and cold, you would certainly blame the contrivance, without any further examination. The architect would in vain display his subtilty, and prove to you that, if this door or that window were altered, greater ills would ensue. What he says may be strictly true: the alteration of one particular, while the other parts of the building remain, may only augment the inconveniences. But still you would assert in general that, if the architect had had skill and good intentions, he might have formed such a plan of the whole, and might have adjusted the parts in such a manner as would have remedied all or most of these inconveniences. His ignorance, or even your own ignorance of such a plan, will never convince you of the impossibility of it. If you find any inconveniences and deformities in the building, you will always, without entering into any detail, condemn the architect.

In short, I repeat the question: Is the world, considered in general and as it appears to us in this life, different from what a man or such a limited being would, *beforehand,* expect from a very powerful, wise, and benevolent Deity? It must be strange prejudice to assert the contrary. And from thence I conclude that, however consistent the world may be, allowing certain suppositions and conjectures with the idea of such a Deity, it can never afford us an inference concerning his existence. The consistency is not absolutely denied, only the inference. Conjectures, especially where infinity is excluded from the Divine attributes, may perhaps be sufficient to prove a consistency, but can never be foundations for any inference.

There seem to be *four* circumstances on which depend all or the greatest part of the ills that molest sensible creatures; and it is not impossible but all these circumstances may be necessary and unavoidable. We know so little beyond common life, or even of common life, that, with regard to the economy of a universe, there is no conjecture, however wild, which may not be just, nor any one, however plausible, which may not be erroneous. All that belongs to human understanding, in this deep ignorance and obscurity, is to be sceptical or at least cautious, and not to admit of any hypothesis whatever, much less of any which is supported by no appearance of probability. Now this I assert to be the case with regard to all the causes of evil and the circumstances on which it depends. None of them appear to human reason in the least degree necessary or unavoidable, nor can we suppose them such, without the utmost license of imagination.

The *first* circumstance which introduces evil is that contrivance or economy of the animal creation by which pains, as well as pleasures, are employed to excite all creatures to action, and make them vigilant in the great work of self-preservation. Now pleasure alone, in its various degrees, seems to human understanding sufficient for this purpose. All animals might be constantly in a state of enjoyment; but when urged by any of the necessities of nature, such as thirst, hunger, weariness, instead of pain, they might feel a diminution of pleasure by which they might be prompted to seek that object which is necessary to their subsistence. Men pursue pleasure as eagerly as they avoid pain; at least, they might have been so constituted. It seems, therefore, plainly possible to carry on the business of life without any pain. Why then is any animal ever rendered susceptible of such a sensation? If animals can be free from it an hour, they might enjoy a perpetual exemption from it, and it required as particular a contrivance of their organs to produce that feeling as to endow them with sight, hearing, or any of the senses. Shall we conjecture that such a contrivance was necessary, without any appearance of reason, and shall we build on that conjecture as on the most certain truth?

But a capacity of pain would not alone produce pain were it not for the *second* circumstance, viz., the conducting of the world by general laws; and this seems nowise necessary to a very perfect Being. It is true, if everything were conducted by particular volitions, the course of nature would be perpetually broken, and no man could employ his reason in the conduct of life. But might not other particular volitions remedy this inconvenience? In short, might not the Deity exterminate all ill, wherever it were to be found, and produce all good, without any preparation or long progress of causes and effects?

Besides, we must consider that, according to the present economy of the world, the course of nature, though supposed exactly regular, yet to us appears not so, and many events are uncertain, and many disappoint our expectations. Health and sickness, calm and tempest, with an infinite number of other accidents whose causes are unknown and variable, have a great influence both on the fortunes of particular persons and on the prosperity of public societies; and indeed all human life, in a manner, depends on such accidents. A Being, therefore, who knows the secret springs of the universe might easily, by particular volitions, turn all these accidents to the good of mankind and render the whole world, happy, without discovering himself in any operation. A fleet whose purposes were salutary to society might always meet with a fair wind. Good princes enjoy sound health and long life. Persons born to power and authority be framed with good tempers and virtuous dispositions. A few such events as these, regularly and wisely conducted, would change the face of the world, and yet would no more seem to disturb the course of nature or confound human conduct than the present economy of things where the causes are secret and variable and compounded. Some small touches given to Caligula's brain in his infancy might have converted him into a Trajan. One wave, a little higher than the rest, by burying Caesar and his fortune in the bottom of the ocean, might have restored liberty to a considerable part of mankind. There may, for aught we know, be good reasons why Providence interposes not in this manner, but they are unknown to us; and, though the mere supposition that such reasons exist may be sufficient to *save* the conclusion concerning the Divine attributes, yet surely it can never be sufficient to *establish* that conclusion.

If everything in the universe be conducted by general laws, and if animals be rendered susceptible of pain, it scarcely seems possible but some ill must arise in the various shocks of matter and the various concurrence and opposition of general laws; but this ill would be very rare were it not for the *third* circumstance which I proposed to mention, viz., the great frugality with which all powers and faculties are distributed to every particular being. So well adjusted are the organs and capacities of all animals, and so well fitted to their preservation, that, as far as history or tradition reaches, there appears not to be any single species which has yet been extinguished in the universe. Every animal has the requisite endowments, but these endowments are bestowed with so scrupulous an economy that any considerable diminution must entirely destroy the creature. Wherever one power is increased, there is a proportional abatement in the others. Animals which excel in swiftness are commonly defective in force. Those which possess both are either imperfect in some of their senses or are oppressed with the most craving wants. The human species, whose chief excellence is reason and sagacity, is of all others the most necessitous, and the most deficient in bodily advantages, without clothes, without arms, without food, without lodging, without any convenience of life, except what they owe to their own skill and industry. In short, nature seems to have formed an exact calculation of the necessities of her creatures, and, like a *rigid master,* has afforded them little more powers or endowments than what are strictly sufficient to supply those necessities. An *indulgent parent* would have bestowed a large stock in order to guard against accidents, and secure the happiness and welfare of the creature in the most unfortunate concurrence of circumstances. Every course of life would not have been so surrounded with precipices that the least departure from the true path, by mistake or necessity, must involve us in misery and ruin. Some reserve, some fund, would have been provided to ensure happiness, nor would the powers and the necessities have been adjusted with so rigid an economy. The Author of nature is inconceivably powerful; his force is supposed great, if not altogether inexhaustible, nor is there any reason, as far as we can judge, to make him observe this strict frugality in his dealings with his creatures. It would have been better, were his power extremely limited, to have created fewer animals, and to have endowed these with more faculties for their happiness and preservation. A builder is never esteemed prudent who undertakes a plan beyond what his stock will enable him to finish.

In order to cure most of the ills of human life, I require not that man should have the wings of the eagle, the swiftness of the stag, the force of the ox, the arms of the lion, the scales of the crocodile or rhinoceros; much less do I demand the sagacity of an angel or cherubim. I am contented to take an increase in one single power or faculty of his soul. Let him be endowed with a greater propensity to industry and labour, a more vigorous spring and activity of mind, a more constant bent to business and application. Let the whole species possess naturally an equal diligence with that which many individuals are able to attain by habit and reflection, and the most beneficial consequences, without any allay of ill, is the immediate and necessary result of this endowment. Almost all the moral as well as natural evils of human life arise from idleness; and were our species, by the original constitution of their frame, exempt from this vice or infirmity, the perfect cultivation of land, the improvement of arts and manufactures, the exact execution of every office and duty, immediately follow; and men at once may fully reach that state of society which is so imperfectly attained by the best regulated government. But as industry is a power, and the most valuable of any, nature seems determined, suitably to her usual maxims, to bestow it on men with a very sparing hand, and rather to punish him severely for his deficiency in it than to reward him for his attainments. She has so contrived his frame that nothing but the most violent necessity can oblige him to labour; and she employs all his other wants to overcome, at least in part, the want of diligence, and to endow him with some share of a faculty of which she has thought fit naturally to bereave him. Here our demands may be allowed very humble, and therefore the more reasonable. If we required the endowments of superior penetration and judgment, of a more delicate taste of beauty, of a nicer sensibility to benevolence and friendship, we might be told that we impiously pretend to break the order of nature, that we want to exalt ourselves into a higher rank of being, that the presents which we require, not being suitable to our state and condition, would only be pernicious to us. But it is hard, I dare to repeat it, it is hard that, being placed in a world so full of wants and necessities, where almost every being and element is either our foe or refuses its assistance . . . we should also have our own temper to struggle with, and should be deprived of that faculty which can alone fence against these multiplied evils.

The *fourth* circumstance whence arises the misery and ill of the universe is the inaccurate workmanship of all the springs and principles of the great machine of nature. It must be acknowledged that there are few parts of the universe which seem not to serve some purpose, and whose removal would not produce a visible defect and disorder in the whole. The parts hang all together, nor can one be touched without affecting the rest, in a greater or less degree. But at the same time, it must be observed that none of these parts or principles, however useful, are so accurately adjusted as to keep precisely within those bounds in which their utility consists; but they are, all of them, apt, on every occasion, to run into the one extreme or the other. One would imagine that this grand production had not received the last hand of the maker—so little finished is every part, and so coarse are the strokes with which it is executed. Thus the winds are requisite to convey the vapours along the surface of the globe, and to assist men in navigation; but how often, rising up to tempests and hurricanes, do they become pernicious? Rains are necessary to nourish all the plants and animals of the earth; but how often are they defective? how often excessive? Heat is requisite to all life and vegetation, but is not always found in the due proportion. On the mixture and secretion of the humours and juices of the body depend the health and prosperity of the animal; but the parts perform not regularly their proper function. What more useful than all the passions of the mind, ambition, vanity, love, anger? But how often do they break their bounds and cause the greatest convulsions in society? There is nothing so advantageous in the universe but what frequently becomes pernicious, by its excess or defect; nor has nature guarded, with the requisite accuracy, against all disorder or confusion. The irregularity is never perhaps so great as to destroy any species, but is often sufficient to involve the individuals in ruin and misery.

On the concurrence, then, of these *four* circumstances does all or the greatest part of natural evil depend. Were all living creatures incapable of pain, or were the world administered by particular volitions, evil never could have found access into the universe; and were animals endowed with a large stock of powers and faculties, beyond what strict necessity requires, or were the several springs and principles of the universe so accurately framed as to preserve always the just temperament and medium, there must have been very little ill in comparison of what we feel at present. What then shall we pronounce on this occasion? Shall we say that these circumstances are not necessary, and that they might easily have been altered in the contrivance of the universe? This decision seems too presumptuous for creatures so blind and ignorant. Let us be more modest in our conclusions. Let us allow that, if the goodness of the Deity (I mean a goodness like the human) could be established on any tolerable reasons *a priori,* these phenomena, however untoward, would not be sufficient to subvert that principle, but might easily, in some unknown manner, be reconcilable to it. But let us still assert that, as this goodness is not antecedently established but must be inferred from the phenomena, there can be no grounds for such an inference while there are so many ills in the universe, and while these ills might so easily have been remedied, as far as human understanding can be allowed to judge on such a subject. I am sceptic enough to allow that the bad appearances, notwithstanding all my reasonings, may be compatible with such attributes as you suppose, but surely they can never prove these attributes. Such a conclusion cannot result from scepticism, but must arise from the phenomena, and from our confidence in the reasonings which we deduce from these phenomena.

Look round this universe. What an immense profusion of beings, animated and organized, sensible and active! You admire this prodigious variety and fecundity. But inspect a little more narrowly these living existences, the only beings worth regarding. How hostile and destructive to each other! How insufficient all of them for their own happiness! How contemptible or odious to the spectator! The whole presents nothing but the idea of a blind nature, impregnated by a great vivifying principle, and pouring forth from her lap, without discernment or parental care, her maimed and abortive children!

Here the Manichaean system occurs as a proper hypothesis to solve the difficulty; and, no doubt, in some respects it is very specious and has more probability than the common hypothesis, by giving a plausible account of the strange mixture of good and ill which appears in life. But if we consider, on the other hand, the perfect uniformity and agreement of the parts of the universe, we shall not discover in it any marks of the combat of a malevolent with a benevolent being. There is indeed an opposition of pains and pleasures in the feelings of sensible creatures; but are not all the operations of nature carried on by an opposition of principles, of hot and cold, moist and dry, light and heavy? The true conclusion is that the original Source of all things is entirely indifferent to all these principles, and has no more regard to good above ill than to heat above cold, or to drought above moisture, or to light above heavy.

There may *four* hypotheses be framed concerning the first causes of the universe; that they are endowed with perfect goodness; that they have perfect malice; that they are opposite and have both goodness and malice; that they have neither goodness nor malice. Mixed phenomena can never prove the two former unmixed principles; and the uniformity and steadiness of general laws seem to oppose the third. The fourth, therefore, seems by far the most probable.

What I have said concerning natural evil will apply to moral with little or no variation; and we have no more reason to infer that the rectitude of the Supreme Being resembles human rectitude than that his benevolence resembles the human. Nay, it will be thought that we have still greater cause to exclude from him moral sentiments, such as we feel them, since moral evil, in the opinion of many, is much more predominant above moral good than natural evil above natural good.

But even though this should not be allowed, and though the virtue which is in mankind should be acknowledged much superior to the vice, yet, so long as there is any vice at all in the universe, it will very much puzzle you anthropomorphites how to account for it. You must assign a cause for it, without having recourse to the first cause. But as every effect must have a cause, and that cause another, you must either carry on the progression *in infinitum* or rest on that original principle, who is the ultimate cause of all things. . . .

Hold! hold! cried Demea: Whither does your imagination hurry you? I joined in alliance with you in order to prove the incomprehensible nature of the Divine Being, and refute the principles of Cleanthes, who would measure everything by human rule and standard. But I now find you running into all the topics of the greatest libertines and infidels, and betraying that holy cause which you seemingly espoused. Are you secretly, then, a more dangerous enemy than Cleanthes himself?

And are you so late in perceiving it? replied Cleanthes. Believe me, Demea, your friend Philo, from the beginning, has been amusing himself at both our expense; and it must be confessed that the injudicious reasoning of our vulgar theology has given him but too just a handle of ridicule. The total infirmity of human reason, the absolute incomprehensibility of the Divine Nature, the great and universal misery, and still greater wickedness of men—these are strange topics, surely, to be so fondly cherished by orthodox divines and doctors. In ages of stupidity and ignorance, indeed, these principles may safely be espoused; and perhaps no views of things are more proper to promote superstition than such as encourage the blind amazement, the diffidence, and melancholy of mankind. But at present . . .

Blame not so much, interposed Philo, the ignorance of these reverend gentlemen. They know how to change their style with the times. Formerly, it was a most popular theological topic to maintain that human life was vanity and misery, and to exaggerate all the ills and pains which are incident to men. But of late years, divines, we find, begin to retract this position and maintain, though still with some hesitation, that there are more goods than evils, more pleasures than pains, even in this life. When religion stood entirely upon temper and education, it was thought proper to encourage melancholy, as, indeed, mankind never have recourse to superior powers so readily as in that disposition. But as men have now learned to form principles and to draw consequences, it is necessary to change the batteries, and to make use of such arguments as will endure at least some scrutiny and examination. This variation is the same (and from the same causes) with that which I formerly remarked with regard to scepticism.

Thus Philo continued to the last his spirit of opposition, and his censure of established opinions. But I could observe that Demea did not at all relish the latter part of the discourse; and he took occasion soon after, on some pretence or other, to leave the company.

NOTES

1. That sentiment had been maintained by Dr. King and some few others before Leibniz, though by none of so great fame as that German Philosopher.

2. [Milton: *Paradise Lost,* Bk. XI.]

3. [John Dryden, *Aureng-Zebe,* Act IV, sc. I.]

God, Evil, and the Metaphysics of Freedom

ALVIN PLANTINGA

Perhaps the most impressive objection to theistic belief is to be found in what is called "The Problem of Evil." Many philosophers[1] have held that the existence of evil constitutes at least an embarrassment for those who accept belief in God. And most contemporary philosophers who hold that evil constitutes a difficulty for theistic belief claim to detect *logical inconsistency* in beliefs a theist typically accepts. So, for example, according to H.J. McCloskey,

> Evil is a problem for the theist in that a *contradiction* is involved in the fact of evil, on the one hand, and the belief in the omnipotence and perfection of God on the other.[2]

J.L. Mackie urges the same charge:

> I think, however, that a more telling criticism can be made by way of the traditional problem of evil. Here it can be shown, not that religious beliefs lack rational support, but that they are positively irrational, that the several parts of the essential theological doctrine are *inconsistent* with one another.[3]

And Henry David Aiken substantially repeats this allegation.[4] Now the alleged contradiction arises, of course, when we consider the fact that evil exists together with the belief that God exists and is omniscient, omnipotent, and wholly good or morally perfect. But obviously these propositions are not *formally* inconsistent: the resources of logic alone do not enable us to deduce an explicit contradiction from their conjunction. Presumably, then, the atheologian never meant to hold that there was a formal contradiction here; he meant instead that the conjunction of these two propositions is necessarily false, false in every possible world. So what he must do to show that he is right is produce a proposition that is at least plausibly thought to be necessary and whose conjunction with our original two formally yields a contradiction.

I have argued elsewhere[5] that it is extremely difficult to find any such proposition. I have also argued[6] that the *Free Will Defense* can be used to show that in fact these propositions are not inconsistent. In what follows I wish to take another look at the issues involved in the Free Will Defense—this time from the vantage point of some recent ideas about possible worlds.

I THE FREE WILL DEFENSE

The Free Will Defense is an effort to show that

(1) God is omnipotent, omniscient, and wholly good

is not consistent with

(2) There is evil in the world.

Alvin Plantinga is professor of philosophy at Calvin College in Grand Rapids, Michigan.

This is an original article published with the permission of the author.

That is, the Free Will Defender aims to show that there is a possible world in which (1) and (2) are both true. Now, one way to show that a proposition P is consistent with a proposition Q is to produce a third proposition whose conjunction with P is consistent and entails Q. This third proposition, of course, need not be known to be true; it need not be so much as plausible. All that is required of it is that it be consistent with P, and in conjunction with the latter entail Q. What the Free Will Defender must do, therefore, is find such a proposition.

But first, some preliminary definitions and distinctions. What does the Free Will Defender mean when he says that people are or may be *free*? If a man is free with respect to a given action, then he is free to perform that action and free to refrain; causal laws and antecedent conditions determine neither that he will perform the action, nor that he will not. It is within his power, at the time in question, to perform the action, and within his power to refrain. Further, let's say that an action is *morally significant,* for a given person at a given time, if it would be wrong for him to perform the action but right to refrain, or *vice versa*. Keeping a promise, for example, would typically be morally significant, as would refusing induction into the army; having Cheerios for breakfast (instead of Wheaties) would not. And let us say that a person *goes wrong with respect to a morally significant action* if it is wrong for him to perform it and he does, or wrong for him not to and he does not. Still further, suppose we say that a person is *significantly free,* on a given occasion if he is then free with respect to an action that is morally significant for him. And finally, we must distinguish between *moral* evil and *natural* evil. The former is evil that results from some human being's going wrong with respect to an action that is morally significant for him; any other evil is natural evil.[7] Suffering due to human cruelty—Hiltler's treatment of the Jews, for example—would be an example of the former; suffering resulting from an earthquake or tidal wave, an example of the latter. An analogous distinction is made between moral and natural good.

Given these definitions and distinctions, we can make a preliminary statement of the Free Will Defense as follows. A world containing creatures who are sometimes significantly free (and freely perform more good than evil actions) is more valuable, all else being equal, than a world containing no free creatures at all. Now, God can create free creatures, but he can't *cause* or *determine* them to do only what is right. For if he does so, then they aren't significantly free after all; they do not do what is right *freely*. To create creatures capable of *moral good,* therefore, he must create creatures capable of *moral evil*; and he can't leave these creatures *free* to perform evil and at the same time prevent them from doing so. God did in fact create significantly free creatures; but as it turned out, sadly enough, some of them went wrong in the exercise of their freedom; this is the source of moral evil. The fact that these free creatures sometimes go wrong, however, counts neither against God's omnipotence nor against his goodness; for he could have forestalled the occurrence of moral evil only by excising the possibility of moral good.

I said earlier that the Free Will Defender tries to find a proposition that is consistent with

(1) God is omniscient, omnipotent, and wholly good

and together with (1) entails that there is evil. According to the Free Will Defense, we must find this proposition somewhere in the above story. The heart of the Free Will Defense is the claim that it is *possible* that God could not have created a universe containing moral good (or as much moral good as this one contains) without creating one containing moral evil.

II AN OBJECTION

A formidable objection goes like this. Surely it is logically possible that there be a world containing significantly free creatures who always do what is right. There is certainly no contradiction or inconsistency in this idea. If so, however, there are possible worlds containing moral good but no moral evil. Now the theist says that God is omnipotent—which means, roughly, that there are no nonlogical limits to his power. Accordingly, he could have created just any possible world he chose, including those containing moral good but no moral evil. If it is possible that there be a world containing significantly free creatures who never do what is wrong, then it follows that an omnipotent God could have created such a world. If so, however, the Free Will Defense must be mistaken in its insistence upon the possibility that God, though omnipotent, could not have created a world containing moral good without permitting moral evil. As Mackie puts it,

> If God has made men such that in their free choices they sometimes prefer what is good and sometimes what is evil, why could he not have made men such that they always freely choose the good? If there is no logical impossibility in a man's freely choosing good on one, or on several occasions, there cannot be logical impossibility in his freely choosing the good on every occasion. God was not, then, faced with a choice between making innocent automata and making beings who, in acting freely, would sometimes go wrong; there was open to him the obviously better possibility of making beings who would act freely but always go right. Clearly his failure to avail himself of this possibility is inconsistent with his being both omnipotent and wholly good.[8]

Was it within the power of an omnipotent God to create just any logically possible world? This is the important question for the Free Will Defense, and a subtle question it is. Leibniz, as you recall, insisted that *this* world, the actual world, must be the best of all possible worlds. His reasoning is as follows. Before God created anything at all, he was confronted with an enormous range of choices; he could create or bring into acutality any of the myriads of different possible worlds. Being perfectly good, he must have chosen the best of all possible worlds; and hence *this* world, the one he did create, must be (despite appearances) the best possible. Now Mackie, of course, agrees with Leibniz that God, if omnipotent, could have created just any possible world he pleased and would have created the best world he could. But while Leibniz draws the conclusion that the actual world must be the best possible, Mackie concludes instead that there is no omnipotent, wholly good God. For, he says, it is obvious enough that the actual world could be improved upon.

The Free Will Defender disagrees with both. In the first place, he might say, what is the reason for supposing that *there is* such a thing as the best of all possible worlds? But what is really characteristic and central to the Free Will Defense is the claim that God, though omnipotent, could not have actualized just any possible world he pleased; and this is the claim we must investigate.

III GOD AND POSSIBLE WORLDS

What, first of all, is a possible world? A possible world is a *way things could have been*: a possible state of affairs. Some states of affairs obtain or are actual: *the sun's being 93,000,000 miles from the earth*, for example. Other states of affairs do not obtain, but *could have: there being just seven planets* would be an example. Still others—those that are impossible—do not obtain and could not have: for example, *Henry Kissinger's having grandparents who never had children*. So a possible world is a possible state of affairs. But not every possible state of affairs is a possible world; to claim this title, a state of affairs must be maximal. *The sun's being 93,000,000 miles from the earth* is a possible state of affairs, as is, perhaps, *Paul C. Zwier's being a good tennis player;* but neither of these is fully determinate. Let us say that a state of affairs S *precludes* a state of affairs S' if it is not possible that both S and S' obtain; S *includes* S', on the other hand, if it is not possible that S obtain and S' *not obtain*. A state of affairs S is maximal if for any state of affairs S', S either includes or precludes S'; and a possible world is just a possible state of affairs that is maximal.[9] Obviously there is exactly one possible world that is actual; the others are merely possible. For ease of reference, let us name the actual world α; α alone, of all 'the possible worlds, has the distinction of being actual. We should also note that objects *have properties* in possible worlds. To say that an object X has a property P in a possible world W is to say that if W had been actual, X would have had P. The same object, clearly enough, has different properties in different possible worlds. In the actual world, Raquel Welch has many impressive assets; in some other possible world she is 50 pounds overweight and mousey.

Thus enlightened, let us return to our question. Was it within the power of an omnipotent God to create or actualize just any world he pleased?

Perhaps we can best procede by way of an example. Curley Smith, the mayor of Boston, is opposed to the proposed Freeway route. His objection is relatively trivial; the route would require destruction of the Old North Church along with some other antiquated and structurally unsound buildings. Lewis L. Smedes, the director of highways, asks him whether he'd drop his opposition for $1,000,000. "Of course," he replies. "Would you do it for $2?" asks Smedes. "What do you take me for?" comes the indignant reply. "We've already established that," smirks Smedes; "all that remains is to nail down your price." Smedes then offers him a bribe of $35,000; unwilling to break with the fine old traditions of Bay State politics, Curley accepts. Whereupon Smedes spends a sleepless night wondering whether he could have had Curley for $20,000.

Now what is it, exactly, that Smedes is wondering about? Whether, of course, Curley would have accepted a bribe of $20,000. Whether, that is, Curley would have accepted such a bribe *in a certain set of circumstances*. Call this set C*. C* includes Smedes having offered Curley a bribe of $20,000 rather than the $35,000 he did in fact propose. For the rest, these circumstances are as much as possible like those that did in fact obtain. In fact C* contains every circumstance that can obtain and is relevant to the question whether Curley would have taken a bribe of $20,000. So, for example, C* includes Curley's being free with respect to the action of taking the bribe; it also includes his notorious acquisitive tendencies along with the respect for tradition we've already noted.[10] And now the question is: given this set of circumstances, what would Curley have done? Would he have accepted the bribe, or would he have refused it? To put it another way, we are asking which of the following conditionals is true:

(3) If the circumstances in C* had obtained, Curley would have accepted the bribe

or

(4) If the circumstances in C* had obtained, Curley would have rejected the bribe.

IV LEIBNIZ' LAPSE

Was it within God's power, supposing him omnipotent, to actualize or create just any possible world? No. For either (3) or (4) is true. Suppose it is (3) that is true, and consider any possible world *W* that includes both C* and *Curley's not taking the bribe*. We know that there are such worlds, since C* does not include the state of affairs consisting in Curley's refusing the bribe; but not even an omnipotent God could have actualized it. For to do so he would have been obliged to create Curley and bring it about that the circumstances in C* obtain. But (3) is true; hence under these conditions Curley would have taken the bribe. But then the world thus actualized would not have been *W*; for there Curley is free to take the bribe but does not do so. So if God had actualized C* (thus causing Curley to be free with respect to the action in question), Curley would have taken the bribe, thereby precluding the actuality of *W*. If, on the other hand, God had *caused* Curley to refrain from taking the bribe, or *brought it about* that he didn't take it, then Curley would not have been *free* with respect to the action in question, so that once more it is not *W* that would have been actual. If (3) is true, therefore, then this world *W* is one that God could not have actualized, even though he is omnipotent and it is possible.[11]

Of course if it is (4) that is true, we get a similar result; then too there are possible worlds that God can't actualize. These would be worlds in which C* holds and in which Curley *does* take the bribe. But either (3) or (4) is true; so either way there are possible worlds that God could not have created. If we consider a world in which C* obtains and in which Curley freely rejects the bribe, we see that whether it was within God's power to actualize it depends in part upon what free choices Curley would have made in a certain situation. Accordingly, there are many possible worlds such that it is partly up to Curley whether or not God can actualize them. It is of course up to God whether or not to create Curley, and also up to God whether or not to make him free with respect to the action of taking the bribe at *t*. But if he creates him, and creates him free with respect to this action, then whether or not he takes it is up to Curley—not God.

Now we can return to the Free Will Defense and the problem of evil. The Free Will Defender, you recall, insists on the *possibility* that it is not within God's power to create a world containing moral good without creating one containing moral evil. His atheological opponent—Mackie, for example—agrees with Leibniz in insisting that *if* (as the theist holds) God is omnipotent, then it *follows* that he could have created just any possible world he pleased. We now see that this contention—call it "Leibniz' Lapse"—is a mistake. The atheologian is right in holding that there are many possible worlds containing moral good but no moral evil; his mistake lies in endorsing Leibniz' Lapse. So one of his central contentions—that God, if omnipotent, could have actualized just any world he pleased—is false.

V TRANSWORLD DEPRAVITY

Now suppose we recapitulate the logic of the situation. The Free Will Defender claims that the following is possible:

(5) God is omnipotent and it was not within his power to create a world containing moral good but no moral evil.

By way of retort the atheologian insists that there are possible worlds containing moral good but no moral evil. He adds that an omnipotent being could have actualized just any possible world he chose. So if God is omnipotent, it follows that he could have actualized a world containing moral good but no moral evil; hence (5) is not possible. What we have seen so far is that his second premiss—Leibniz' Lapse—is false.

Of course this does not settle the issue in the Free Will Defender's favor. Leibniz' Lapse (appropriately enough for a lapse) is false; but this doesn't show that (5) is possible. To show this latter we must show that it is possible that among the worlds God could not have actualized are all the worlds containing moral good but no moral evil. How can we approach this question?

Let's return to Curley and his venality. It could be that the latter is unbounded; Curley's bribability may be utter and absolute. We could put this possibility more exactly as follows. Taken any positive integer *n*. If (1) at *t* Smedes had offered Curley *n* dollars by way of a bribe, and (2) Curley had been free with respect to the action of taking the bribe, and (3) conditions had otherwise been as much as possible like those that did in fact obtain, then Curley would have accepted the bribe. Obviously Curley is less than incorruptible. But even this may not plumb the full depths of his lack of incorruptibility. For it is possible that Curley suffers from what I shall call *transworld depravity*. That is, the following is a possibility. Consider W^*, any of the worlds in which he is significantly free and never does what is wrong. In W^* Curley is significantly free, so in W^* there are some actions that are morally significant for him and with respect to which he is free. But at least one of these actions—call it *A*—has the following peculiar property. There is an appropriate set C^* of conditions that obtain in W^* and are such that

(6) If Curley were free with respect to *A* and the conditions in C^* obtained, he would go wrong with respect to A.

This means, of course, that God could not have actualized W^*. For to do so, he would have had to bring it about that Curley is free with respect to *A*, and that the conditions in C^* obtain. But then, as (6) assures us, Curley would have gone wrong with respect to *A*. And, since in W^* he always does what is right, the world thus actualized would not have been W^*. On the other hand, if God *causes* Curley to go right with respect to *A*, or *brings it about* that he does so, then Curley isn't free with respect to *A*; and once more it isn't W^* that is actual. Accordingly God could not have actualized W^*. But W^* was just any of the worlds in which Curley is significantly free but always does only what is right. It therefore follows that it was not within God's power to actualize a world in which Curley produces moral good but no moral evil. Every world God can actualize is such that if Curley is significantly free in it, he takes at least one wrong action.

I say all this is *possibly* true; if in fact it *is*

true, then Curley suffers from transworld depravity. (I leave as homework the problems of comparing transworld depravity with what the Calvinists call 'total depravity'.) By way of explicit definition:

(7) A person *P suffers from transworld depravity* if and only if for every world *W* such that *P* is significantly free in *W* and *P* does only what is right in *W*, there is an action *A* and an appropriate set of conditions C^* such that
   (1) *A* is morally significant for *P* in *W*
   (2) *P* is free with respect to A in W
   (3) the conditions in C^* obtain in *W*

and
   (4) If *P* were significantly free with respect to *A* and the conditions in C^* obtained, *P* would go wrong with respect to *A*.

(In thinking about this definition, remember that (4) is to be true in fact, in the actual world—not in that world W.)

What is important about the idea of transworld depravity is that if a person suffers from it, then it wasn't within God's power to actualize any world in which that person is significantly free but does no wrong—that is, a world in which he produces moral good but no moral evil. But clearly it is possible that *everybody* suffers from transworld depravity. If this possibility were actual, then of course God could not have created any of the possible worlds that contain the persons who do in fact exist and also contain moral good but no moral evil. For to do so he'd have had to create persons who were significantly free (otherwise there would be no moral good) but suffered from transworld depravity. Such persons go wrong with respect to at least one action in any world in which they exist; so the price for creating a world in which they produce moral good is creating one in which they also produce moral evil.

Now we might think this settles the question in favor of the Free Will Defender. But in fact it doesn't. For suppose all the people that exist in α, the actual world, suffer from transworld depravity; it doesn't follow that God could not have created a world containing moral good without creating one containing moral evil. God could have created *other people*. Instead of creating us, he could have created a world containing people all right, but not containing any of us. And perhaps if he'd done that, he could have created a world containing moral good but no moral evil.

Perhaps. But then again, perhaps not. Suppose we look into the matter a little further. Let *W* be a world distinct from α that contains a significantly free person who does not exist in α. Let us suppose that this person does only what is right. There is no reason to doubt that there *are* such worlds; but what reason do we have for supposing that God could have actualized any of them? How do we know that he can? To investigate this question, we must take a brief look at the idea of an *essence* or *individual concept*. Think again of Socrates and the fact that he exists in many different possible worlds. In some of these he has properties quite different from those he has in α, the actual world. But some of his properties are ones he has in every world in which he exists; call them his *essential* properties. Among these essential properties would be some that are *trivially* essential—such properties as *being unmarried if a bachelor, being either six feet tall or else not six feet tall, being self-identical*, and the like. Another and more interesting kind of essential property can be explained as follows. Socrates has the property of being snub-nosed. This property, presumably, is not essential to him; he could have had some other kind of nose. So there are possible worlds in which he is not snub-nosed. Let W^* be any such world. If W^* had been actual, Socrates would not have been snub-nosed; that is to say, Socrates has the *property of being non-snub-nosed in* W^*. For to say that an object *x* has a property of this sort—the property of having *P* in W, where *P* is a property and *W* is a possible world—is to say simply that *x would have had P if W had been actual*. Properties of this sort are *world-indexed* properties. Socrates has the world-indexed property of *being non-snub-nosed in* W^*. He has this property in α, the actual world. In W^*, however, he has the property of *being snub-nosed in* α. If W^* had been actual, Socrates would not have been snub-nosed; still, it would have been true that if α had been actual, Socrates would have been snub-nosed.

It is evident, I take it, that if indeed Socrates *is* snub-nosed in α, the actual world, then in all those worlds where Socrates exists it is true that Socrates is snub-nosed in α. So he has the property of *being snub-nosed in* α in every world in which he exists. This property, therefore, is essential to him; there is no world in which he exists and lacks it. Indeed, it is easy to see, I think, that every world-indexed property he has will be essential to him; and every world-indexed property he *lacks* will be such that its complement is essential to him.

Now suppose we define Socrates' *essence* as the set of properties essential to him. His essence is a set of properties, each of which is essential to him; and this set contains all his world-indexed properties, together with some others. It is evident that no *other* person has all of the properties in this set. Another person might have *some* of the same world-indexed properties as Socrates: he might be *snub-nosed in* α, for example. But he couldn't have *all* of Socrates' world-indexed properties, for then he would just *be* Socrates. So there is no person who shares Socrates' essence with him. But we can say something even stronger: there *couldn't* be any such person. For such a person would just be Socrates, and hence not *another* person. The essence of Socrates, therefore, is a set of properties each of which he has essentially. Furthermore, there neither is nor could be another person (a person distinct from Socrates) who has all of the properties in this set. And finally, Socrates' essence contains a *complete* set of world-indexed properties—that is, if P is world-indexed, then either P is a member of Socrates' essence or else its complement $\overline{P}$ is.[12]

Returning to Curley, we recall that he suffers from transworld depravity. This fact implies something interesting about Curleyhood, Curley's essence. Take those worlds W such that *is significantly free in W and never does what is wrong in W* is contained in Curley's essence. Each of these worlds has an important property, if Curley suffers from transworld depravity; each is such that God could not have actualized it. We can see this as follows. Suppose W is some world such that Curley's essence contains the property *is significantly free but never does what is wrong in W*. That is, W is a world in which Curley is significantly free but always does what is right. But of course Curley suffers from transworld depravity. This means that there is an appropriate set C^* of conditions and an action A such that

(a) the conditions in C^* obtain in W,

(b) Curley is significantly free with respect to A in W,

and

(c) if Curley were free with respect to A and the conditions in C^* obtained, then Curley would go wrong with respect to A.

So, (as we have already seen) God cannot actualize W. For to do so, he would have had to bring it about that the conditions in C^* obtain, and that Curley is free with respect to A. But then (since (c) is true) Curley would have gone wrong with respect to A. Since in W^* he always does what is right, W^* would not have been actual. So if Curley suffers from transworld depravity, then Curleyhood, Curley's essence, has this property: God could not have created any world W such that Curleyhood contains the properties *is significantly free in W* and *always does what is right in W*.

We can use this connection between Curley's transworld depravity and his essence as the basis for a definition of transworld depravity as applied to essences rather than persons. We should note first that if E is a person's essence, then he is the instantiation of E; he is the thing that has (or instantiates) every property in E. To instantiate an essence, God creates a person who has that essence; and in creating a person he instantiates an essence. Now we can say that

(8) An essence E *suffers from transworld depravity* if and only if for every world W such that E contains the properties *is significantly free in W* and *always does what is right in W*, there is an action A and an appropriate set C^* of conditions such that

(1) E contains the property *is significantly free with respect to A in W*

(2) the conditions in C^* obtain in W

and

(3) E were instantiated and its instantiation were free with respect to A and the conditions in C^* obtained, then E's instantiation would go wrong with respect to A.

By now it is evident, I take it, that if an essence E suffers from transworld depravity, then it was not within God's power to actualize a possible world *W* such that *E* contains the properties *is significantly free in W* and *always does what is right in W*. Hence it was not within God's power to create a world in which E's instantiation is significantly free but always does what is right.

Now the interesting fact here is this: it is possible that every essence suffers from transworld depravity. But this possibility has some interesting consequences. For God can create a world containing moral good only by creating significantly free persons. And since every person is the instantiation of an essence, he can create significantly free persons only by instantiating some essences. But if every essence suffers from transworld depravity, then no matter which essences God instantiated, the resulting persons, if free with respect to morally significant actions, would always perform at least some wrong actions. If every essence suffers from transworld depravity, then it was beyond the power of God to create a world containing moral good but no moral evil. He might have been able to create worlds in which moral evil is very considerably outweighed by moral good; but it was not within the power of omnipotence to create worlds containing moral good but no moral evil. Under these conditions God could have created a world containing no moral evil only by creating one without significantly free persons. But it is possible that every essence suffers from transworld depravity; so it's possible that God could not have created a world containing moral good but no moral evil.

VI THE FREE WILL DEFENSE TRIUMPHANT

Put formally, you remember, the Free Will Defender's project was to show that

(1) God is omniscient, omnipotent and wholly good

is consistent with

(2) There is evil.

What we have just seen is that

(9) It was not within God's power to create a world containing moral good but no moral evil

is possible and consistent with God's omnipotence and omniscience. But then it is clearly consistent with (1). So we can use it to show that (1) is consistent with (2). For consider

(9) God couldn't create a world containing moral good without creating one containing moral evil

and

(10) God created a world containing moral good.

The conjunction of (1) with (9) and (10) is evidently consistent; it is possibly true. But (1), (9) and (10) together entail

(2) There is evil.

Accordingly, (1) is consistent with (2); the Free Will Defense is successful.

VII GOD'S EXISTENCE AND THE *AMOUNT* OF MORAL EVIL

The world, after all, contains a *great deal* of moral evil; and what we've seen so far is only that God's existence is compatible with *some* evil. Perhaps the atheologian could regroup, and argue that at any rate God's existence is not consistent with the vast amount and variety of evil the universe actually contains. Of course there doesn't seem to be any way to measure moral evil—that is, we don't have units like volts or pounds or kilowatts so that we could say "this situation contains exactly 35 turps of moral evil." Still, we can compare situations in terms of evil; we can see that some contain more moral evil than others. And perhaps the atheologian could maintain that it is at any rate obvious that God, if omnipotent, could have created a world containing a better mixture of moral good and evil than α —one, let's say, that contained as much moral good but less moral evil.

But is this really obvious? I don't think so. Possibly this was *not* within God's power, which is all the Free Will Defender needs. We can see this as follows. Of course there are many possible worlds containing as much moral good as α but less moral evil. Let W^* be any such world. If W^* had been actual, there would have been as much moral good (past, present, and future) as in fact there was, is, and will be; and there would have been less moral evil in all. Now in W^* a certain set S of essences is instantiated (that is, there is a set S of essences such that if W^* had been actual, then each member of S would have been instantiated). So to actualize W^*, God would have had to create persons who were the instantiations of these essences. The following, however, is possible. There is an action A, an appropriate set of conditions C^* and a member E of S such that

(a) E contains the properties *is significantly free with respect to A in W* and *goes right with respect to A in W**;

(b) the conditions in C^* obtain in W^*

and

(c) if E were instantiated and its instantiation were free with respect to A and the conditions in C^* obtained, E's instantiation would go wrong with respect to A.

If this possibility is actual, then God could not have actualized W^*. For to do so, he would have had to instantiate E, bring it about that E's instantiation was free with respect to A, and cause the conditions in C^* to obtain. But then the instantiation of E would have gone wrong with respect to A, so that the world thus actualized would not have been W^*; in W^* E's instantiation goes *right* with respect to A.

More generally, it's possible that every world containing as much moral good as the actual world, but less moral evil, resembles W^* in that God could not have actualized it. For it is possible that

(11) For every world W containing as much moral good as α but less moral evil, there is at least one essence E, an action A and a set C^* of conditions such that

(a) E contains the properties *is significantly free with respect to A in W* and *goes right with respect to A in W*

(b) The conditions in C^* obtain in W^*, and

(c) if E were instantiated and E's instantiation were free with respect to A and the conditions in C^* obtained, E's instantiation would go wrong with respect to A.

(11) is possible; if it is also true, then it wasn't within the power of God to create a world containing as much moral good as α contains but less moral evil. So it's possible that this was not within God's power; but if so, then (1) is compatible with the proposition that there is as much moral evil as α does in fact contain. And, of course, what the Free Will Defender claims is not that (11) is *true*; he claims only that it is compatible with the existence of a wholly good, omnipotent, and omniscient God.

The upshot, I believe, is that the existence of God is not inconsistent with the existence of evil. Of course suffering and misfortune may nonetheless constitute a *problem* for the theist; but the problem is not that presented by holding beliefs that are logically incompatible. The theist may find a *religious* problem in evil; in the presence of his own suffering or that of someone near to him, he may find it difficult to maintain what he takes to be the proper attitude towards God. Faced with great personal suffering or misfortune, he may be tempted to rebel against God, to shake his fist in God's face, or even to give up belief in God altogether. But this is a problem of a different dimension. Such a problem calls for pastoral rather than philosophical counsel.

NOTES

1. Epicurus, for example, as well as David Hume, some of the French Encyclopedists, F. H. Bradley, J. McTaggert, J. S. Mill, and many others.

2. "God and Evil," *Philosophical Quarterly* 10 (1960), 97.

3. "Evil and Omnipotence," *Mind* 64 (1955), 200.

4. "God and Evil," *Ethics* 48 (1957), 79.

5. *God and Other Minds*, Chap. 5

6. *Ibid.*, Chap. 6

7. This distinction is not very precise (how,

exactly, are we to construe 'results from'?); but perhaps it will serve our present purposes.

8. *Op. cit.*

9. For more on possible worlds, see my book *The Nature of Necessity* (Oxford: 1974) Chapter IV.

10. Of course C* includes neither Curley's taking the bribe nor his rejecting it.

11. For a fuller development of this argument, see *The Nature of Necessity*, pp. 169-184.

12. For more about essences and essential properties, see *The Nature of Necessity*, chapters IV and V.

Theology and Falsification

ANTONY FLEW, R. M. HARE,
AND BASIL MITCHELL

ANTONY FLEW

Let us begin with a parable. It is a parable developed from a tale told by John Wisdom in his haunting and revelatory article 'Gods'.[1] Once upon a time two explorers came upon a clearing in the jungle. In the clearing were growing many flowers and many weeds. One explorer says, 'Some gardener must tend this plot'. The other disagrees, 'There is no gardener'. So they pitch their tents and set a watch. No gardener is ever seen. 'But perhaps he is an invisible gardener'. So they set up a barbed-wire fence. They electrify it. They patrol with bloodhounds. (For they remember how H. G. Wells's *The Invisible Man* could be both smelt and touched though he could not be seen.) But no shrieks ever suggest that some intruder has received a shock. No movements of the wire ever betray an invisible climber. The bloodhounds never give cry. Yet still the Believer is not convinced. 'But there is a gardener, invisible, intangible, insensible to electric shocks, a gardener who has no scent and makes no sound, a gardener who comes secretly to look after the garden which he loves'. At last the Sceptic despairs, 'But what remains of your original assertion? Just how does what you call an invisible, intangible, eternally elusive gardener differ from an imaginary gardener or even from no gardener at all?'

In this parable we can see how what starts as an assertion, that something exists or that there is some analogy between certain complexes of phenomena, may be reduced step by step to an altogether different status, to an expression perhaps of 'a picture preference'.[2] The Sceptic says there is no gardener. The Believer says there is a gardener (but invisible, etc.). One man talks about sexual behaviour. Another man prefers to talk of Aphrodite (but knows that there is not really a superhuman person additional to, and somehow responsible for, all sexual phenomena).[3] The process of qualification may be checked at any point before the original assertion is completely withdrawn and something of that first assertion will remain (Tautology). Mr. Wells's invisible man could not, admittedly, be seen, but in all other respects he was a man like the rest of us. But though the process of qualification may be, and of course usually is, checked in time, it is not always judiciously so halted. Someone may dissipate his assertion completely without noticing that he has done so. A fine brash hypothesis may thus be killed by inches, the death by a thousand qualifications.

And in this, it seems to me, lies the peculiar danger, the endemic evil, of theological utterance. Take such utterances as 'God has a

---

Antony Flew is professor of philosophy at the University of Reading.

Reprinted with permission of Macmillan Publishing Co., Inc. from *New Essays in Philosophical Theology* edited by Antony Flew and Alasdair MacIntyre. Published in the United States by Macmillan Publishing Co., Inc., 1955.

plan', 'God created the world', 'God loves us as a father loves his children'. They look at first sight very much like assertions, vast cosmological assertions. Of course, this is no sure sign that they either are, or are intended to be, assertions. But let us confine ourselves to the cases where those who utter such sentences intend them to express assertions. (Merely remarking parenthetically that those who intend or interpret such utterances as crypto-commands, expressions of wishes, disguised ejaculations, concealed ethics, or as anything else but assertions, are unlikely to succeed in making them either properly orthodox or practically effective.)

Now to assert that such and such is the case is necessarily equivalent to denying that such and such is not the case.[4] Suppose then that we are in doubt as to what someone who gives vent to an utterance is asserting, or suppose that, more radically, we are sceptical as to whether he is really asserting anything at all, one way of trying to understand (or perhaps it will be to expose) his utterance is to attempt to find what he would regard as counting against, or as being incompatible with, its truth. For if the utterance is indeed an assertion, it will necessarily be equivalent to a denial of the negation of that assertion. And anything which would count against the assertion, or which would induce the speaker to withdraw it and to admit that it had been mistaken, must be part of (or the whole of) the meaning of the negation of that assertion. And to know the meaning of the negation of an assertion, is as near as makes no matter, to know the meaning of that assertion.[5] And if there is nothing which a putative assertion denies then there is nothing which it asserts either: and so it is not really an assertion. When the Sceptic in the parable asked the Believer, 'Just how does what you call an invisible, intangible, eternally elusive gardener differ from an imaginary gardener or even from no gardener at all?' he was suggesting that the Believer's earlier statement had been so eroded by qualification that it was no longer an assertion at all.

Now it often seems to people who are not religious as if there was no conceivable event or series of events the occurrence of which would be admitted by sophisticated religious people to be a sufficient reason for conceding 'There wasn't a God after all' or 'God does not really love us then'. Someone tells us that God loves us as a father loves his children. We are reassured. But then we see a child dying of inoperable cancer of the throat. His earthly father is driven frantic in his efforts to help, but his Heavenly Father reveals no obvious sign of concern. Some qualification is made—God's love is 'not a merely human love' or it is 'an inscrutable love', perhaps—and we realize that such sufferings are quite compatible with the truth of the assertion that 'God loves us as a father (but, of course, . . .)'. We are reassured again. But then perhaps we ask: what is this assurance of God's (appropriately qualified) love worth, what is this apparent guarantee really a guarantee against? Just what would have to happen not merely (morally and wrongly) to tempt but also (logically and rightly) to entitle us to say 'God does not love us' or even 'God does not exist'? I therefore put to the succeeding symposiasts the simple central questions, 'What would have to occur or to have occurred to constitute for you a disproof of the love of, or of the existence of, God?'

R. M. HARE

I wish to make it clear that I shall not try to defend Christianity in particular, but religion in general—not because I do not belive in Christianity, but because you cannot understand what Christianity is, until you have understood what religion is.

I must begin by confessing that, on the ground marked out by Flew, he seems to me to be completely victorious. I therefore shift my ground by relating another parable. A certain lunatic is convinced that all dons want to murder him. His friends introduce him to all the mildest and most respectable dons that they can find, and after each of them has retired, they say, 'You see, he doesn't really want to murder you; he spoke to you in a most cordial manner; surely you are convinced now?' But the lunatic replies, 'Yes, but that was only his diabolical cunning; he's really

---

R. M. Hare is professor of Moral Philosophy at Corpus Christi College, Oxford.

plotting against me the whole time, like the rest of them; I know it I tell you'. However many kindly dons are produced, the reaction is still the same.

Now we say that such a person is deluded. But what is he deluded about? About the truth or falsity of an assertion? Let us apply Flew's test to him. There is no behaviour of dons that can be enacted which he will accept as counting against his theory; and therefore his theory, on this test, asserts nothing. But it does not follow that there is no difference between what he thinks about dons and what most of us think about them—otherwise we should not call him a lunatic and ourselves sane, and dons would have no reason to feel uneasy about his presence in Oxford.

Let us call that in which we differ from this lunatic, our respective *bliks*. He has an insane *blik* about dons; we have a sane one. It is important to realize that we have a sane one, not no *blik* at all; for there must be two sides to any argument—if he has a wrong *blik*, then those who are right about dons must have a right one. Flew has shown that a *blik* does not consist in an assertion or system of them; but nevertheless it is very important to have the right *blik*.

Let us try to imagine what it would be like to have different *bliks* about other things than dons. When I am driving my car, it sometimes occurs to me to wonder whether my movements of the steering-wheel will always continue to be followed by corresponding alterations in the direction of the car. I have never had a steering failure, though I have had skids, which must be similar. Moreover, I know enough about how the steering of my car is made, to know the sort of thing that would have to go wrong for the steering to fail—steel joints would have to part, or steel rods break, or something—but how do I know that this won't happen? The truth is, I don't know; I just have a *blik* about steel and its properties, so that normally I trust the steering of my car; but I find it not at all difficult to imagine what it would be like to lose this *blik* and acquire the opposite one. People would say I was silly about steel; but there would be no mistaking the reality of the difference between our respective *bliks*—for example, I should never go in a motor-car. Yet I should hesitate to say that the difference between us was the difference between contradictory assertions. No amount of safe arrivals or bench-tests will remove my *blik* and restore the normal one; for my *blik* is compatible with any finite number of such tests.

It was Hume who taught us that our whole commerce with the world depends upon our *blik* about the world; and that differences between *bliks* about the world cannot be settled by observation of what happens in the world. That was why, having performed the interesting experiment of doubting the ordinary man's *blik* about the world, and showing that no proof could be given to make us adopt one *blik* rather than another, he turned to backgammon to take his mind off the problem. It seems, indeed, to be impossible even to formulate as an assertion the normal *blik* about the world which makes me put my confidence in the future reliability of steel joints, in the continued ability of the road to support my car, and not gape beneath it revealing nothing below; in the general non-homicidal tendencies of dons; in my own continued well-being (in some sense of that word that I may not now fully understand) if I continue to do what is right according to my lights; in the general likelihood of people like Hitler coming to a bad end. But perhaps a formulation less inadequate than most is to be found in the Psalms: 'The earth is weak and all the inhabiters thereof: I bear up the pillars of it'.

The mistake of the position which Flew selects for attack is to regard this kind of talk as some sort of *explanation*, as scientists are accustomed to use the word. As such, it would obviously be ludicrous. We no longer believe in God as an Atlas—*nous n'avons pas besoin de cette hypothèse*. But it is nevertheless true to say that, as Hume saw, without a *blik* there can be no explanation; for it is by our *bliks* that we decide what is and what is not an explanation. Suppose we believed that everything that happened, happened by pure chance. This would not of course be an assertion; for it is compatible with anything happening or not happening, and so, incidentally, is its contradictory. But if we had this belief, we should not be able to explain or predict or plan anything. Thus, although we should not be *asserting* anything different from those of a more normal belief, there would be a great difference between us; and this is the sort of difference that there is between those who really believe in God and those who really disbelieve in him.

The word 'really' is important, and may excite suspicion. I put it in, because when people have had a good Christian upbringing, as have most of those who now profess not to believe in any sort of religion, it is very hard to discover what they really believe. The reason why they find it so easy to think that they are not religious, is that they have never got into the frame of mind of one who suffers from the doubts to which religion is the answer. Not for them the terrors of the primitive jungle. Having abandoned some of the more picturesque fringes of religion, they think that they have abandoned the whole thing—whereas in fact they still have got, and could not live without, a religion of a comfortably substantial, albeit highly sophisticated, kind, which differs from that of many 'religious people' in little more than this, that 'religious people' like to sing Psalms about theirs—a very natural and proper thing to do. But nevertheless there may be a big difference lying behind—the difference between two people who, though side by side, are walking in different directions. I do not know in what direction Flew is walking; perhaps he does not know either. But we have had some examples recently of various ways in which one can walk away from Christianity, and there are any number of possibilities. After all, man has not changed biologically since primitive times; it is his religion that has changed, and it can easily change again. And if you do not think that such changes make a difference, get acquainted with some Sikhs and some Mussulmans of the same Punjabi stock; you will find them quite different sorts of people.

There is an important difference between Flew's parable and my own which we have not yet noticed. The explorers do not *mind* about their garden; they discuss it with interest, but not with concern. But my lunatic, poor fellow, minds about dons; and I mind about the steering of my car; it often has people in it that I care for. It is because I mind very much about what goes on in the garden in which I find myself, that I am unable to share the explorers' detachment.

BASIL MITCHELL

Flew's article is searching and perceptive, but there is, I think, something odd about his conduct of the theologian's case. The theologian surely would not deny that the fact of pain counts against the assertion that God loves men. This very incompatibility generates the most intractable of theological problems—the problem of evil. So the theologian *does* recognize the fact of pain as counting against Christian doctrine. But it is true that he will not allow it—or anything—to count decisively against it; for he is committed by his faith to trust in God. His attitude is not that of the detached observer, but of the believer.

Perhaps this can be brought out by yet another parable. In time of war in an occupied country, a member of the resistance meets one night a stranger who deeply impresses him. They spend that night together in conversation. The Stranger tells the partisan that he himself is on the side of the resistance—indeed that he is in command of it, and urges the partisan to have faith in him no matter what happens. The partisan is utterly convinced at that meeting of the Stranger's sincerity and constancy and undertakes to trust him.

They never meet in conditions of intimacy again. But sometimes the Stranger is seen helping members of the resistance, and the partisan is grateful and says to his friends, 'He is on our side'.

Sometimes he is seen in the uniform of the police handing over patriots to the occupying power. On these occasions his friends murmur against him: but the partisan still says, 'He is on our side'. He still believes that, in spite of appearances, the Stranger did not deceive him. Sometimes he asks the Stranger for help and receives it. He is then thankful. Sometimes he asks and does not receive it. Then he says, 'The Stranger knows best'. Sometimes his friends, in exasperation, say 'Well, what *would* he have to do for you to admit that you were wrong and that he is not on our side?' But the partisan refuses to answer. He will not consent to put the

---

Basil Mitchell is a professor in Oriel College at Oxford University.

Stranger to the test. And sometimes his friends complain, 'Well, if *that's* what you mean by his being on our side, the sooner he goes over to the other side the better'.

The partisan of the parable does not allow anything to count decisively against the proposition 'The Stranger is on our side'. This is because he has committed himself to trust the Stranger. But he of course recognizes that the Stranger's ambiguous behaviour *does* count against what he believes about him. It is precisely this situation which constitutes the trial of his faith.

When the partisan asks for help and doesn't get it, what can he do? He can *(a)* conclude that the stranger is not on our side or; *(b)* maintain that he is on our side, but that he has reasons for withholding help.

The first he will refuse to do. How long can he uphold the second position without its becoming just silly?

I don't think one can say in advance. It will depend on the nature of the impression created by the Stranger in the first place. It will depend, too, on the manner in which he takes the Stranger's behaviour. If he blandly dismisses it as of no consequence, as having no bearing upon his belief, it will be assumed that he is thoughtless or insane. And it quite obviously won't do for him to say easily, 'Oh, when used of the Stranger the phrase "is on our side" *means* ambiguous behaviour of this sort'. In that case he would be like the religious man who says blandly of a terrible disaster 'It is God's will'. No, he will only be regarded as sane and reasonable in his belief, if he experiences in himself the full force of the conflict.

It is here that my parable differs from Hare's. The partisan admits that many things may and do count against his belief: whereas Hare's lunatic who has a *blik* about dons doesn't admit that anything counts against his *blik*. Nothing *can* count against *bliks*. Also the partisan has a reason for having in the first instance committed himself, viz. the character of the Stranger; whereas the lunatic has no reason for his *blik* about dons—because, of course, you can't have reasons for *bliks*.

This means that I agree with Flew that theological utterances must be assertions. The partisan is making an assertion when he says, 'The Stranger is on our side'.

Do I want to say that the partisan's belief about the Stranger is, in any sense, an explanation? I think I do. It explains and makes sense of the Stranger's behaviour: it helps to explain also the resistance movement in the context of which he appears. In each case it differs from the interpretation which the others put upon the same facts.

'God loves men' resembles the 'Stranger is on our side' (and many other significant statements, e.g. historical ones) in not being conclusively falsifiable. They can both be treated in at least three different ways: (1) As provisional hypotheses to be discarded if experience tells against them; (2) As significant articles of faith; (3) As vacuous formulae (expressing, perhaps, a desire for reassurance) to which experience makes no difference and which make no difference to life.

The Christian, once he has committed himself, is precluded by his faith from taking up the first attitude: 'Thou shalt not tempt the Lord thy God'. He is in constant danger, as Flew has observed, of slipping into the third. But he need not; and, if he does, it is a failure in faith as well as in logic.

ANTONY FLEW

It has been a good discussion: and I am glad to have helped to provoke it. But now—at least in *University*—it must come to an end: and the Editors of *University* have asked me to make some concluding remarks. Since it is impossible to deal with all the issues raised or to comment separately upon each contribution, I will concentrate on Mitchell and Hare, as representative of two very different kinds of response to the challenge made in 'Theology and Falsification'.

The challenge, it will be remembered, ran like this. Some theological utterances seem to, and are intended to, provide explanations or express assertions. Now an assertion, to be an assertion at all, must claim that things stand thus and thus; *and not otherwise*. Similarly an explanation, to be an explanation at all, must explain why this particular thing occurs; *and not something else*. Those last clauses are crucial. And yet sophisticated religious people—or so it seemed to me—are apt to overlook this, and tend to refuse to allow, not merely that anything actually does occur, but that anything conceivably could occur, which would count against their theological assertions and explanations. But in so far as they do this their supposed explanations are actually bogus, and their seeming assertions are really vacuous.

Mitchell's response to this challenge is admirably direct, straightforward, and understanding. He agrees that 'theological utterances must be assertions'. He agrees that if they are to be assertions, there must be something that would count against their truth. He agrees, too, that believers are in constant danger of transforming their would-be assertions into 'vacuous formulae'. But he takes me to task for an oddity in my 'conduct of the theologian's case. The theologian surely would not deny that the fact of pain counts against the assertion that God loves men. This very incompatibility generates the most intractable of theological problems, the problem of evil'. I think he is right. I should have made a distinction between two very different ways of dealing with what looks like evidence against the love of God: the way I stressed was the expedient of qualifying the original assertion; the way the theologian usually takes, at first, is to admit that it looks bad but to insist that there is—there must be—some explanation which will show that, in spite of appearances, there really is a God who loves us. His difficulty, it seems to me, is that he has given God attributes which rule out all possible saving explanations. In Mitchell's parable of the Stranger it is easy for the believer to find plausible excuses for ambiguous behaviour: for the Stranger is a man. But suppose the Stranger is God. We cannot say that he would like to help but cannot: God is omnipotent. We cannot say that he would help if he only knew: God is omniscient. We cannot say that he is not responsible for the wickedness of others: God creates those others. Indeed an omnipotent, omniscient God must be an accessory before (and during) the fact to every human misdeed; as well as being responsible for every non-moral defect in the universe. So, though I entirely concede that Mitchell was absolutely right to insist against me that the theologian's first move is to look for an *explanation*, I still think that in the end, if relentlessly pursued, he will have to resort to the avoiding action of *qualification*. And there lies the danger of that death by a thousand qualifications, which would, I agree, constitute 'a failure in faith as well as in logic'.

Hare's approach is fresh and bold. He confesses that 'on the ground marked out by Flew, he seems to me to be completely victorious'. He therefore introduces the concept of *blik*. But while I think that there is room for some such concept in philosophy, and that philosophers should be grateful to Hare for his invention, I nevertheless want to insist that any attempt to analyse Christian religious utterances as expressions or affirmations of a *blik* rather than as (at least would-be) assertions about the cosmos is fundamentally misguided. *First*, because thus interpreted they would be entirely unorthodox. If Hare's religion really is a *blik*, involving no cosmological assertions about the nature and activities of a supposed personal creator, then surely he is not a Christian at all? *Second*, because thus interpreted, they could scarcely do the job they do. If they were not even intended as assertions then many religious activities would become fraudulent, or merely silly. If 'You ought *because* it is God's will' asserts no more than 'You ought', then the person who prefers the former phraseology is not really giving a reason, but a fraudulent substitute for one, a dialectical dud cheque. If 'My soul must be immortal *because* God loves his children, etc.' asserts no more than 'My soul must be immortal', then the man who reassures himself with theological arguments for immortality is being as silly as the man who tries to clear his overdraft by writing his bank a cheque on the same account. (Of course neither of these utterances would be distinctively Christian: but this discussion never pretended to be so confined.) Religious utterances may indeed express false or even bogus assertions: but I simply do not believe that they are not both intended and interpreted to be or at any rate to presuppose assertions, at least in the context of religious practice; whatever shifts may be demanded, in another context, by the exigencies of theological apologetic.

One final suggestion. The philosophers of

religion might well draw upon George Orwell's last appalling nightmare *1984* for the concept of *doublethink*. '*Doublethink* means the power of holding two contradictory beliefs simultaneously, and accepting both of them. The party intellectual knows that he is playing tricks with reality, but by the exercise of *doublethink* he also satisfies himself that reality is not violated' (*1984*, p. 220). Perhaps religious intellectuals too are sometimes driven to doublethink in order to retain their faith in a loving God in face of the reality of a heartless and indifferent world. But of this more another time, perhaps.

NOTES

1. *P.A.S.*, 1944-5, reprinted as Ch. X of *Logic and Language*, Vol. I (Blackwell, 1951), and in his *Philosophy and Psychoanalysis* (Blackwell, 1953).

2. Cf. J. Wisdom, 'Other Minds', *Mind*, 1940; reprinted in his *Other Minds* (Blackwell, 1952).

3. Cf. Lucretius, *De Rerum Natura*, II, 655-60,

Hic siquis mare Neptunum Cereremque vocare
Constituet fruges et Bacchi nomine abuti
Mavolat quam laticis proprium proferre vocamen
Concedamus ut hic terrarum dictitet orbem
Esse deum matrem dum vera re tamen ipse
Religione animum turpi contingere parcat.

4. For those who prefer symbolism: $p \equiv \sim\sim p$.

5. For by simply negating $\sim p$ we get p: $\sim\sim p \equiv p$.

A Free Man's Worship

BERTRAND RUSSELL

To Dr. Faustus in his study Mephistopheles told the history of the Creation, saying:

"The endless praises of the choirs of angels had begun to grow wearisome; for, after all, did he not deserve their praise? Had he not given them endless joy? Would it not be more amusing to obtain undeserved praise, to be worshipped by beings whom he tortured? He smiled inwardly, and resolved that the great drama should be performed.

"For countless ages the hot nebula whirled aimlessly through space. At length it began to take shape, the central mass threw off planets, the planets cooled, boiling seas and burning mountains heaved and tossed, from black masses of cloud hot sheets of rain deluged the barely solid crust. And now the first germ of life grew in the depths of the ocean, and developed rapidly in the fructifying warmth into vast forest trees, huge ferns springing from the damp mould, sea monsters breeding, fighting, devouring, and passing away. And from the monsters, as the play unfolded itself, Man was born, with the power of thought, the knowledge of good and evil, and the cruel thirst for worship. And Man saw that all is passing in this mad, monstrous world, that all is struggling to snatch, at any cost, a few brief moments of life before Death's inexorable decree. And Man said: 'There is a hidden purpose, could we but fathom it, and the purpose is good; for we must reverence something, and in the visible world there is nothing worthy of reverence.' And Man stood aside from the struggle, resolving that God intended harmony to come out of chaos by human efforts. And when he followed the instincts which God had transmitted to him from his ancestry of beasts of prey, he called it Sin, and asked God to forgive him. But he doubted whether he could be justly forgiven, until he invented a divine Plan by which God's wrath was to have been appeased. And seeing the present was bad, he made it yet worse, that thereby the future might be better. And he gave God thanks for the strength that enabled him to forgo even the joys that were possible. And God smiled; and when he saw that Man had become perfect in renunciation and worship, he sent another sun through the sky, which crashed into Man's sun; and all returned again to nebula.

" 'Yes,' he murmured, 'it was a good play; I will have it performed again.' "

Such, in outline, but even more purposeless, more void of meaning, is the world which Science presents for our belief. Amid such a world, if anywhere, our ideals henceforward must find a home. That Man is the product of causes which had no prevision of the end they were achieving; that his origin, his growth, his hopes and fears, his loves and his beliefs, are but the outcome of accidental collocations of atoms; that no fire, no heroism, no intensity of thought and feeling, can preserve an individual life beyond the grave; that all the labours of the ages, all the

---

Bertrand Russell (1872-1970) was one of the most influential philosophers in the twentieth-century Anglo-American tradition.

devotion, all the inspiration, all the noonday brightness of human genius, are destined to extinction in the vast death of the solar system, and that the whole temple of Man's achievement must inevitably be buried beneath the débris of a universe in ruins—all these things, if not quite beyond dispute, are yet so nearly certain, that no philosophy which rejects them can hope to stand. Only within the scaffolding of these truths, only on the firm foundation of unyielding despair, can the soul's habitation henceforth be safely built.

How, in such an alien and inhuman world, can so powerless a creature as Man preserve his aspirations untarnished? A strange mystery it is that Nature, omnipotent but blind, in the revolutions of her secular hurryings through the abysses of space, has brought forth at last a child, subject still to her power, but gifted with sight, with knowledge of good and evil, with the capacity of judging all the works of his unthinking Mother. In spite of Death, the mark and seal of the parental control, Man is yet free, during his brief years, to examine, to criticise, to know, and in imagination to create. To him alone, in the world with which he is acquainted, this freedom belongs; and in this lies his superiority to the resistless forces that control his outward life.

The savage, like ourselves, feels the oppression of his impotence before the powers of Nature; but having in himself nothing that he respects more than Power, he is willing to prostrate himself before his gods, without inquiring whether they are worthy of his worship. Pathetic and very terrible is the long history of cruelty and torture, of degradation and human sacrifice, endured in the hope of placating the jealous gods: surely, the trembling believer thinks, when what is most precious has been freely given, their lust for blood must be appeased, and more will not be required. The religion of Moloch—as such creeds may be generically called—is in essence the cringing submission of the slave, who dare not, even in his heart, allow the thought that his master deserves no adulation. Since the independence of ideals is not yet acknowledged, Power may be freely worshipped, and receive an unlimited respect, despite its wanton infliction of pain.

But gradually, as morality grows bolder, the claim of the ideal world begins to be felt; and worship, if it is not to cease, must be given to gods of another kind than those created by the savage. Some, though they feel the demands of the ideal, will still consciously reject them, still urging that naked Power is worthy of worship. Such is the attitude inculcated in God's answer to Job out of the whirlwind: the divine power and knowledge are paraded, but of the divine goodness there is no hint. Such also is the attitude of those who, in our own day, base their morality upon the struggle for survival, maintaining that the survivors are necessarily the fittest. But others, not content with an answer so repugnant to the moral sense, will adopt the position which we have become accustomed to regard as specially religious, maintaining that, in some hidden manner, the world of fact is really harmonious with the world of ideals. Thus Man creates God, all-powerful and all-good, the mystic unity of what is and what should be.

But the world of fact, after all, is not good; and, in submitting our judgment to it, there is an element of slavishness from which our thoughts must be purged. For in all things it is well to exalt the dignity of Man, by freeing him as far as possible from the tyranny of non-human Power. When we have realised that Power is largely bad, that man, with his knowledge of good and evil, is but a helpless atom in a world which has no such knowledge, the choice is again presented to us: Shall we worship Force, or shall we worship Goodness? Shall our God exist and be evil, or shall he be recognised as the creation of our own conscience?

The answer to this question is very momentous, and affects profoundly our whole morality. The worship of Force, to which Carlyle and Nietzsche and the creed of Militarism have accustomed us, is the result of failure to maintain our own ideals against a hostile universe: it is itself a prostrate submission to evil, a sacrifice of our best to Moloch. If strength indeed is to be respected, let us respect rather the strength of those who refuse that false "recognition of facts" which fails to recognise that facts are often bad. Let us admit that, in the world we know, there are many things that would be better otherwise, and that the ideals to which we do and must adhere are not realised in the realm of matter. Let us preserve our respect for truth, for beauty, for the ideal of perfection which life does not permit us to attain, though none of these things meet with the approval of the unconscious universe. If Power is bad, as it seems to be, let us reject it from our hearts. In this lies Man's true freedom: in determination to worship only the God created by our own love of the good, to respect only the heaven which inspires the insight of our best moments. In action, in desire, we must submit perpetually to the tyranny of outside forces; but in thought, in aspiration, we are free, free from our fellowmen, free from the petty planet on which our bodies impotently crawl, free even, while we live, from the tyranny of death. Let us learn, then, that energy of faith which enables us to live constantly in the vision of the good; and let us descend, in action, into the world of fact, with that vision always before us.

When first the opposition of fact and ideal grows fully visible, a spirit of fiery revolt, of fierce hatred of the gods, seems necessary to the assertion of freedom. To defy with Promethean constancy a hostile universe, to keep its evil always in view, always actively hated, to refuse no pain that the malice of Power can invent, appears to be the duty of all who will not bow before the inevitable. But indignation is still a bondage, for it compels our thoughts to be occupied with an evil world; and in the fierceness of desire from which rebellion springs there is a kind of self-assertion which it is necessary for the wise to overcome. Indignation is a submission of our thoughts, but not of our desires; the Stoic freedom in which wisdom consists is found in the submission of our desires, but not of our thoughts. From the submission of our desires springs the virtue of resignation; from the freedom of our thoughts springs the whole world of art and philosophy, and the vision of beauty by which, at last, we half reconquer the reluctant world. But the vision of beauty is possible only to unfettered contemplation, to thoughts not weighted by the load of eager wishes; and thus Freedom comes only to those who no longer ask of life that it shall yield them any of those personal goods that are subject to the mutations of Time.

Although the necessity of renunciation is evidence of the existence of evil, yet Christianity, in preaching it, has shown a wisdom exceeding that of the Promethean philosophy of rebellion. It must be admitted that, of the things we desire, some, though they prove impossible, are yet real goods; others, however, as ardently longed for, do not form part of a fully purified ideal. The belief that what must be renounced is bad, though sometimes false, is far less often false than untamed passion supposes; and the creed of religion, by providing a reason for proving that it is never false, has been the means of purifying our hopes by the discovery of many austere truths.

But there is in resignation a further good element: even real goods, when they are unattainable, ought not to be fretfully desired. To every man comes, sooner or later, the great renunciation. For the young, there is nothing unattainable; a good thing desired with the whole force of a passionate will, and yet impossible, is to them not credible. Yet, by death, by illness, by poverty, or by the voice of duty, we must learn, each one of us, that the world was not made for us, and that, however beautiful may be the things we crave, Fate may nevertheless forbid them. It is the part of courage, when misfortune comes, to bear without repining the ruin of our hopes, to turn away our thoughts from vain regrets. This degree of submission to Power is not only just and right: it is the very gate of wisdom.

But passive renunciation is not the whole of wisdom; for not by renunciation alone can we build a temple for the worship of our own ideals. Haunting foreshadowings of the temple appear in the realm of imagination, in music, in architecture, in the untroubled kingdom of reason, and in the golden sunset magic of lyrics, where beauty shines and glows, remote from the touch of sorrow, remote from the fear of change, remote from the failures and disenchantments of the world of fact. In the contemplation of these things the vision of heaven will shape itself in our hearts, giving at once a touchstone to judge the world about us, and an inspiration by which to fashion to our needs whatever is not incapable of serving as a stone in the sacred temple.

Except for those rare spirits that are born without sin, there is a cavern of darkness to be traversed before that temple can be entered. The gate of the cavern is despair, and its floor is paved with the gravestones of abandoned hopes. There Self must die; there the eagerness, the greed of untamed desire must be slain, for only so can the soul be freed from the empire of Fate. But out of the cavern the Gate of Renunciation leads again to the daylight of wisdom, by whose radiance a new insight, a new joy, a new tenderness, shine forth to gladden the pilgrim's heart.

When, without the bitterness of impotent rebellion, we have learnt both to resign ourselves to the outward rule of Fate and to recognise that the non-human world is unworthy of our worship, it becomes possible at last so to transform and refashion the unconscious universe, so to transmute it in the crucible of imagination, that a new image of shining gold replaces the old idol of clay. In all the multiform facts of the world—in the visual shapes of trees and mountains and clouds, in the events of the life of man, even in the very omnipotence of Death—the insight of creative idealism can find the reflection of a beauty which its own thoughts first made. In this way mind asserts its subtle mastery over the thoughtless forces of Nature. The more evil the material with which it deals, the more thwarting to untrained desire, the greater is its achievement in inducing the reluctant rock to yield up its hidden treasures, the prouder its victory in compelling the opposing forces to swell the pageant of its triumph. Of all the arts, Tragedy is the proudest, the most triumphant; for it builds its shining citadel in the very centre of the enemy's country, on the very summit of his highest mountain; from its impregnable watchtowers, his camps and arsenals, his columns and forts, are all revealed; within its walls the free life continues, while the legions of Death and Pain and Despair, and all the servile captains of tyrant Fate, afford the burghers of that dauntless city new spectacles of beauty. Happy those sacred ramparts, thrice happy the dwellers on that all-seeing eminence. Honour to those brave warriors who, through countless ages of warfare, have preserved for us the priceless heritage of liberty, and have kept undefiled by sacrilegious invaders the home of the unsubdued.

But the beauty of Tragedy does but make visible a quality which, in more or less obvious shapes, is present always and everywhere in life. In the spectacle of Death, in the endurance of intolerable pain, and in the irrevocableness of a vanished past, there is a sacredness, an overpowering awe, a feeling of the vastness, the depth, the inexhaustible mystery of existence, in which, as by some strange marriage of pain, the sufferer is bound to the world by bonds of sorrow. In these moments of insight, we lose all eagerness of temporary desire, all struggling and striving for petty ends, all care for the little trivial things that, to a superficial view, make up the common life of day by day; we see, surrounding the narrow raft illumined by the flickering light of human comradeship, the dark ocean on whose rolling waves we toss for a brief hour; from the great night without, a chill blast breaks in upon our refuge; all the loneliness of humanity amid hostile forces is concentrated upon the individual soul, which must struggle alone, with what of courage it can command, against the whole weight of a universe that cares nothing for its hopes and fears. Victory, in this struggle with the powers of darkness, is the true baptism into the glorious company of heroes, the true initiation into the overmastering beauty of human existence. From that awful encounter of the soul with the outer world, renunciation, wisdom, and charity are born; and with their birth a new life begins. To take into the inmost shrine of the soul the irresistible forces whose puppets we seem to be—Death and change, the irrevocableness of the past, and the powerlessness of man before the blind hurry of the universe from vanity to vanity—to feel these things and know them is to conquer them.

This is the reason why the Past has such magical power. The beauty of its motionless and silent pictures is like the enchanted purity of late autumn, when the leaves, though one breath would make them fall, still glow against the sky in golden glory. The Past does not change or strive; like Duncan, after life's fitful fever it sleeps well; what was eager and grasping, what was petty and transitory, has faded away, the things that were beautiful and eternal shine out of it like stars in the night. Its beauty, to a soul not worthy of it, is unendurable; but to a soul which has conquered Fate it is the key of religion.

The life of Man, viewed outwardly, is but a small thing in comparison with the forces of Nature. The slave is doomed to worship Time and Fate and Death, because they are greater than anything he finds in himself, and because all his thoughts are of things which they devour. But, great as they are, to think of them greatly, to feel their passionless splendour, is greater still. And such thought makes us free men; we no longer bow before the inevitable in Oriental subjection, but we absorb it, and make it a part of ourselves. To abandon the struggle for private happiness, to expel all eagerness of temporary desire, to burn with passion for eternal things—this is emancipation, and this is the free man's worship. And this liberation is effected by a contemplation of Fate; for Fate itself is subdued by the mind which leaves nothing to be purged by the purifying fire of Time.

United with his fellow-men by the strongest of all ties, the tie of a common doom, the free man finds that a new vision is with him always, shedding over every daily task the light of love. The life of Man is a long march through the night, surrounded by invisible foes, tortured by weariness and pain, towards a goal that few can hope to reach, and where none may tarry long. One by one, as they march, our comrades vanish from our sight, seized by the silent orders of omnipotent Death. Very brief is the time in which we can help them, in which their happiness or misery is decided. Be it ours to shed sunshine on their path, to lighten their sorrows by the balm of sympathy, to give them the pure joy of a nevertiring affection, to strengthen failing courage, to instil faith in hours of despair. Let us not weigh in grudging scales their merits and demerits, but let us think only of their need—of the sorrows, the difficulties, perhaps the blindnesses, that make the misery of their lives; let us remember that they are fellow-sufferers in the same darkness, actors in the same tragedy with ourselves. And so, when their day is over, when their good and their evil have become eternal by the immortality of the past, be it ours to feel that, where they suffered, where they failed, no deed of ours was the cause; but wherever a spark of the divine fire kindled in their hearts, we were ready with encouragement, with sympathy, with brave words in which high courage glowed.

Brief and powerless is Man's life; on him and all his race the slow, sure doom falls pitiless and dark. Blind to good and evil, reckless of destruction, omnipotent matter rolls on its relentless way; for Man, condemned to-day to lose his dearest, to-morrow himself to pass through the gate of darkness, it remains only to cherish, ere yet the blow falls, the lofty thoughts that ennoble his little day; disdaining the coward terrors of the slave of Fate, to worship at the shrine that his own hands have built; undismayed by the empire of chance, to preserve a mind free from the wanton tyranny that rules his outward life; proudly defiant of the irresistible forces that tolerate, for a moment, his knowledge and his condemnation, to sustain alone, a weary but unyielding Atlas, the world that his own ideals have fashioned despite the trampling march of unconscious power.

The Absolute Paradox: A Metaphysical Crotchet

SØREN KIERKEGAARD

In spite of the fact that Socrates studied with all diligence to acquire a knowledge of human nature and to understand himself, and in spite of the fame accorded him through the centuries as one who beyond all other men had an insight into the human heart, he has himself admitted that the reason for his shrinking from reflection upon the nature of such beings as Pegasus and the Gorgons was that he, the life-long student of human nature, had not yet been able to make up his mind whether he was a stranger monster than Typhon, or a creature of a gentler and simpler sort, partaking of something divine (*Phaedrus*, 229 E). This seems to be a paradox. However, one should not think slightingly of the paradoxical; for the paradox is the source of the thinker's passion, and the thinker without a paradox is like a lover without feeling: a paltry mediocrity. But the highest pitch of every passion is always to will its own downfall; and so it is also the supreme passion of the Reason to seek a collision, though this collision must in one way or another prove its undoing. The supreme paradox of all thought is the attempt to discover something that thought cannot think. This passion is at bottom present in all thinking, even in the thinking of the individual, in so far as in thinking he participates in something transcending himself. But habit dulls our sensibilities, and prevents us from perceiving it. So for example the scientists tell us that our walking is a constant falling. But a sedate and proper gentleman who walks to his office in the morning and back again at noon, probably thinks this to be an exaggeration, for his progress is clearly a case of mediation; how should it occur to him that he is constantly falling when he religiously follows his nose!

But in order to make a beginning, let us now assume a daring proposition; let us assume that we know what man is.[1] Here we have that criterion of the Truth, which in the whole course of Greek philosophy was either *sought*, or *doubted*, or *postulated*, or *made fruitful*. Is it not remarkable that the Greeks should have borne us this testimony? And is it not an epitome, as it were, of the significance of Greek culture, an epigram of its own writing, with which it is also better served than with the frequently voluminous disquisitions sometimes devoted to it? Thus the proposition is well worth positing . . . while anyone who attempts to explain Socrates differently may well beware lest he fall into the snare of the earlier or later Greek scepticism. For unless

Kierkegaard (1813-1855) was a Danish philosopher, influential in the development of Existentialist philosophy.

"The Absolute Paradox: A Metaphysical Crotchet," by Søren Kierkegaard, *Philosophical Fragments or A Fragment of Philosophy*, 2nd ed. originally translated and introduced by David Swenson. New Introduction and Commentary by Niels Thulstrup. Transl. Rev. and Commentary Transl. by Howard V. Hong (copyright © 1936, 1962 by Princeton University Press), pp. 46-60. Reprinted by permission of Princeton University Press.

we hold fast to the Socratic doctrine of Recollection, and to his principle that every individual man is Man, Sextus Empiricus stands ready to make the transition involved in "teaching" not only difficult but impossible; and Protagoras will begin where Sextus Empiricus leaves off, maintaining that man is the measure of all things, in the sense that the individual man is the measure for others, but by no means in the Socratic sense that each man is his own measure, neither more nor less.

So then we know what man is, and this wisdom, which I shall be the last to hold in light esteem, may progressively become richer and more significant, and with it also the Truth. But now the Reason stands still, just as Socrates did; for the paradoxical passion of the Reason is aroused and seeks a collision; without rightly understanding itself, it is bent upon its own downfall. This is like what happens in connection with the paradox of love. Man lives undisturbed a self-centered life, until there awakens within him the paradox of self-love, in the form of love for another, the object of his longing. (Self-love lies as the ground of all love or is the ground in which all love perishes; therefore if we conceive a religion of love, this religion need make but one assumption, as epigrammatic as true, and take its actuality for granted, namely, the condition that man loves himself, in order to command him to love his neighbor as himself.) The lover is so completely transformed by the paradox of love that he scarcely recognizes himself; so say the poets, who are the spokesmen of love, and so say also the lovers themselves, since they permit the poets merely to take the words from their lips, but not the passion from their hearts. In like manner the paradoxical passion of the Reason, while as yet a mere presentiment, retroactively affects man and his self-knowledge, so that he who thought to know himself is no longer certain whether he is a more strangely composite animal than Typhon, or if perchance his nature contains a gentler and diviner part. (*σκοπῶ οὐ ταῦτα, ἀλλὰ ἐμαυτόν, εἴτε τι θηρίον ὢν τυγκάνω πολυπλοκώτερον καὶ μᾶλλον ἐπιτεθυμμένον εἴτε ἡμερώτερόν τε καὶ ἁπλούστερον ζῶον, θείας τινος καὶ ἀτύφου μοίρας φύσει μετέχον*. *Phaedrus*, 230 A).

But what is this unknown something with which the Reason collides when inspired by its paradoxical passion, with the result of unsettling even man's knowledge of himself? It is the Unknown. It is not a human being, in so far as we know what man is; nor is it any other known thing. So let us call this unknown something: *the God*. It is nothing more than a name we assign to it. The idea of demonstrating that this unknown something (the God) exists, could scarcely suggest itself to the Reason. For if the God does not exist it would of course be impossible to prove it; and if he does exist it would be folly to attempt it. For at the very outset, in beginning my proof, I would have presupposed it, not as doubtful but as certain (a presupposition is never doubtful, for the very reason that it is a presupposition), since otherwise I would not begin, readily understanding that the whole would be impossible if he did not exist. But if when I speak of proving the God's existence I mean that I propose to prove that the Unknown, which exists, is the God, then I express myself unfortunately. For in that case I do not prove anything, least of all an existence, but merely develop the content of a conception. Generally speaking, it is a difficult matter to prove that anything exists; and what is still worse for the intrepid souls who undertake the venture, the difficulty is such that fame scarcely awaits those who concern themselves with it. The entire demonstration always turns into something very different and becomes an additional development of the consequences that flow from my having assumed that the object in question exists. Thus I always reason from existence, not toward existence, whether I move in the sphere of palpable sensible fact or in the realm of thought. I do not for example prove that a stone exists, but that some existing thing is a stone. The procedure in a court of justice does not prove that a criminal exists, but that the accused, whose existence is given, is a criminal. Whether we call existence an *accessorium* or the eternal *prius*, it is never subject to demonstration. Let us take ample time for consideration. We have no such reason for haste as have those who from concern for themselves or for the God or for some other thing, must make haste to get existence demonstrated. Under such circumstances there may indeed be need for haste, especially if the prover sincerely seeks to appreciate the danger that he himself, or the thing in question, may be non-existent unless the proof is finished and does not surreptitiously entertain the thought that it exists whether he succeeds in proving it or not.

If it were proposed to prove Napoleon's existence from Napoleon's deeds, would it not be a most curious proceeding? His existence does indeed explain his deeds, but the deeds do not prove *his* existence, unless I have already understood the word "his" so as thereby to have assumed his existence. But Napoleon is only an individual, and in so far there exists no absolute relationship between him and his deeds; some other person might have performed the same deeds. Perhaps this is the reason why I cannot pass from the deeds to existence. If I call these deeds the deeds of Napoleon the proof becomes superfluous, since I have already named him; if I ignore this, I can never prove from the deeds that they are Napoleon's, but only in a purely ideal manner that such deeds are the deeds of a great general, and so forth. But between the God and his works there is an absolute relationship; God is not a name but a concept. Is this perhaps the reason that his *essentia involvit existentiam*?[2] The works of God are such that only the God can perform them. Just so, but where then are the works of the God? The works from which I would deduce his existence are not directly and immediately given. The wisdom in nature, the goodness, the wisdom in the governance of the world—are all these manifest, perhaps, upon the very face of things? Are we not here confronted with the most terrible temptations to doubt, and is it not impossible finally to dispose of all these doubts? But from such an order of things I will surely not attempt to prove God's existence; and even if I began I would never finish, and would in addition have to live constantly in suspense, lest something so terrible should suddenly happen that my bit of proof would be demolished. From what works then do I propose to derive the proof? From the works as apprehended through an ideal interpretation, i.e., such as they do not immediately reveal themselves. But in that case it is not from the works that I make the proof; I merely develop the ideality I have presupposed, and because of my confidence in *this* I make so bold as to defy all objections, even those that have not yet been made. In beginning my proof I presuppose the ideal interpretation, and also that I will be successful in carrying it through; but what else is this but to presuppose that the God exists, so that I really begin by virtue of confidence in him?

And how does the God's existence emerge from the proof? Does it follow straightway, without any breach of continuity? Or have we not here an analogy to the behaviour of the little Cartesian dolls? As soon as I let go of the doll it stands on its head. As soon as I let it go—I must therefore let it go. So also with the proof. As long as I keep my hold on the proof, i.e., continue to demonstrate, the existence does not come out, if for no other reason than that I am engaged in proving it; but when I let the proof go, the existence is there. But this act of letting go is surely also something; it is indeed a contribution of mine. Must not this also be taken into the account, this little moment, brief as it may be—it need not be long, for it is a *leap*. However brief this moment, if only an instantaneous now, this "now" must be included in the reckoning. If anyone wishes to have it ignored, I will use it to tell a little anecdote, in order to show that it nevertheless does exist. Chrysippus was experimenting with a sorites to see if he could not bring about a break in its quality, either progressively or retrogressively. But Carneades could not get it in his head when the new quality actually emerged. Then Chrysippus told him to try making a little pause in the reckoning, and so—so it would be easier to understand. Carneades replied: With the greatest pleasure, please do not hesitate on my account; you may not only pause, but even lie down to sleep, and it will help you just as little; for when you awake we will begin again where you left off. Just so; it boots as little to try to get rid of something by sleeping as to try to come into the possession of something in the same manner.

Whoever therefore attempts to demonstrate the existence of God (except in the sense of clarifying the concept, and without the *reservatio finalis* noted above, that the existence emerges from the demonstration by a leap) proves in lieu thereof something else, something which at times perhaps does not need a proof, and in any case needs none better; for the fool says in his heart that there is no God, but whoever says in his heart or to men: Wait just a little and I will prove it—what a rare man of wisdom is he![3] If in the moment of beginning his proof it is not absolutely undetermined whether the God exists or not, he does not prove it; and if it is thus undetermined in the beginning he will never come to begin, partly from fear of failure, since the God perhaps does not exist, and partly because he has nothing with which to begin.—A project of this kind would scarcely have been undertaken by the ancients. Socrates at least, who is credited with having put forth the physico-teleological proof for God's existence, did not go about it in any such manner. He always presupposes the God's existence, and under this presupposition seeks to interpenetrate nature with the idea of purpose. Had he been asked why he pursued this method, he would doubtless have explained that he lacked the courage to venture out upon so perilous a voyage of discovery without having made sure of the God's existence behind him. At the word of the God he casts his net as if to catch the idea of purpose; for nature herself finds many means of frightening the inquirer, and distracts him by many a digression.

The paradoxical passion of the Reason thus comes repeatedly into collision with this Unknown, which does indeed exist, but is unknown, and in so far does not exist. The Reason cannot advance beyond this point, and yet it cannot refrain in its paradoxicalness from arriving at this limit and occupying itself therewith. It will not serve to dismiss its relation to it simply by asserting that the Unknown does not exist, since this itself involves a relationship. But what then is the Unknown, since the designation of it as the God merely signifies for us that it is unknown? To say that it is the Unknown because it cannot be known, and even if it were capable of being known, it could not be expressed, does not satisfy the demands of passion, though it correctly interprets the Unknown as a limit; but a limit is precisely a torment for passion, though it also serves as an incitement. And yet the Reason can come no further, whether it risks an issue *via negationis* or *via eminentia*.

What then is the Unknown? It is the limit to which the Reason repeatedly comes, and in so far, substituting a static form of conception for the dynamic, it is the different, the absolutely different. But because it is absolutely different, there is no mark by which it could be distinguished. When qualified as absolutely different it seems on the verge of disclosure, but this is not the case; for the Reason cannot even conceive an absolute unlikeness. The Reason cannot negate itself absolutely, but uses itself for the purpose, and thus conceives only such an unlikeness within itself as it can conceive by means of itself; it cannot absolutely transcend itself, and hence conceives only such a superiority over itself as it can conceive by means of itself. Unless the Unknown (the God) remains a mere limiting conception, the single idea of difference will be thrown into a state of confusion, and become many ideas of many differences. The Unknown is then in a condition of dispersion (διασπορά), and the Reason may choose at pleasure from what is at hand and the imagination may suggest (the monstrous, the ludicrous, etc.).

But it is impossible to hold fast to a difference of this nature. Every time this is done it is essentially an arbitrary act, and deepest down in the heart of piety lurks the mad caprice which knows that it has itself produced the God. If no specific determination of difference can be held fast, because there is no distinguishing mark, like and unlike finally become identified with one another, thus sharing the fate of all such dialectical opposites. The unlikeness clings to the Reason and confounds it, so that the Reason no longer knows itself and quite consistently confuses itself with the unlikeness. On this point paganism has been sufficiently prolific in fantastic inventions. As for the last named supposition, the self-irony of the Reason, I shall attempt to delineate it merely by a stroke or two, without raising any question of its being historical. There exists an individual whose appearance is precisely like that of other men; he grows up to manhood like others, he marries, he has an occupation by which he earns his livelihood, and he makes provision for the future as befits a man. For though it may be beautiful to live like the birds of the air, it is not lawful, and may lead to the sorriest of consequences: either starvation if one has enough persistence, or dependence on the bounty of others. This man is also the God. How do I know? I cannot know it, for in order to know it I would have to know the God, and the nature of the difference between the God and man; and this I cannot know, because the Reason has reduced it to likeness with that from which it was unlike. Thus the God becomes the most terrible of deceivers, because the Reason has deceived itself. The Reason has brought the God as near as possible, and yet he is as far away as ever.

Now perhaps someone will say: "You are certainly a crotcheteer, as I know very well. But you surely do not believe that I would pay any attention to such a crotchet, so strange or so ridiculous that it has doubtless never occurred to anyone, and above all so absurd that I must exclude from my consciousness everything that I have in it in order to hit upon it."—And so indeed you must. But do you think yourself warranted in retaining all the presuppositions you have in your consciousness, while pretending to think about your consciousness without presuppositions? Will you deny the consistency of our exposition: that the Reason, in attempting to determine the Unknown as the unlike, at last goes astray, and confounds the unlike with the like? From this there would seem to follow the further consequence, that if man is to receive any true knowledge about the Unknown (the God) he must be made to know that it is unlike him, absolutely unlike him. This knowledge the Reason cannot possibly obtain of itself; we have already seen that this would be a self-contradiction. It will therefore have to obtain this knowledge from the God. But even if it obtains such knowledge it cannot understand it, and thus is quite unable to possess such knowledge. For how should the Reason be able to understand what is absolutely different from itself? If this is not immediately evident, it will become clearer in the light of the consequences; for if the God is absolutely unlike man, then man is absolutely unlike the God; but how could the Reason be expected to understand this? Here we seem to be confronted with a paradox. Merely to obtain the knowledge that the God is unlike him, man needs the help of the God; and now he learns that the God is absolutely different from himself. But if the God and man are absolutely different, this cannot be accounted for on the basis of what man derives from the God, for in so far they are akin. Their unlikeness must therefore be explained by what man derives from himself, or by what he has brought upon his own head. But what can this unlikeness be? Aye, what can it be but sin; since the unlikeness, the absolute unlikeness, is something that man has brought upon himself. We have expressed this in the preceding by saying that man was in Error, and had brought this upon his head by his own guilt; and we came to the conclusion, partly in jest and yet also in earnest, that it was too much to expect of man that he should find this out for himself. Now we have again arrived at the same conclusion. The connoisseur in self-knowledge was perplexed over himself to the point of bewilderment when he came to grapple in thought with the unlike; he scarcely knew any longer whether he was a stranger monster than Typhon, or if his nature partook of something divine. What then did he lack? The consciousness of sin, which he indeed could no more teach to another than another could teach it to him, but only the God—if the God consents to become a Teacher. But this was his purpose, as we have imagined it. In order to be man's Teacher, the God proposed to make himself like the individual man, so that he might understand him fully. Thus our paradox is rendered still more appalling, or the same paradox has the double aspect which proclaims it as the Absolute Paradox; negatively by revealing the absolute unlikeness of sin, positively by proposing to do away with the absolute unlikeness in absolute likeness.

But can such a paradox be conceived? Let us not be over-hasty in replying; and since we strive merely to find the answer to a question, and not as those who run a race, it may be well to remember that success is to the accurate rather than to the swift. The Reason will doubtless find it impossible to conceive it, could not of itself have discovered it, and when it hears it announced will not be able to understand it, sensing merely that its downfall is threatened. In so far the Reason will have much to urge against it; and yet we have on the other hand seen that the Reason, in its paradoxical passion, precisely desires its own downfall. But this is what the Paradox also desires, and thus they are at bottom linked in understanding; but this understanding is present only in the moment of passion. Consider the analogy presented by love, though it is not a perfect one. Self-love lies as the ground of love; but the paradoxical passion of self-love when at its highest pitch wills precisely its own downfall. This is also what love desires, so that these two are linked in mutual understanding in the passion of the moment, and this passion is love. Why should not the lover find this conceivable? But he who in self-love shrinks from the touch of love can neither understand it nor summon the courage to venture it, since it means his downfall. Such is then the passion of love; self-love is indeed submerged but not annihilated; it is taken captive and become love's *spolia opima*, but may again come to life, and this is love's temptation. So also with the Paradox in its relation to the Reason, only that the passion in this case has another name; or rather, we must seek to find a name for it.

NOTES

1. It may seem ridiculous to give this proposition a doubtful form by "assuming" it, for in this theocentric age such matters are of course known to all. Aye, if it were only so well with us! Democritus also knew what man is, for he defines man as follows: "Man is what we all know," and then goes on to say: "for we all know what a dog, a horse, a plant is, and so forth; but none of these is a man." We do not aspire to the malice of Sextus Empiricus, nor have we his wit; for he concludes as we know, from the above definition, and quite correctly, that man is a dog; for man is what we all know, and we all know what a dog is, *ergo*—but let us not be so malicious. Nevertheless, has this question been so thoroughly cleared up in our own time that no one need feel a little uneasy about himself when he is reminded of poor Socrates and his predicament?

2. So Spinoza, who probes the depths of the God-idea in order to bring being out of it by way of thought, but not, it should be noted, as if being were an accidental characteristic, but rather as if it constituted an essential determination of content. Here lies Spinoza's profundity, but let us examine his reasoning. In *principia philosophiae Cartesianae, pars I, propositio VII, lemma I,* he says: "*quo res sua natura perfectior est, eo majorem existentiam et magis necessariam involvit; et contra, quo magis necessariam existentiam res sua natura involvit, eo perfectior.*" The more perfect therefore a thing is, the more being it has; the more being it has, the more perfect it is. This is however a tautology, which becomes still more evident in a note, *nota II: "quod hic non loquimur de pulchritudine et aliis perfectionibus, quas homines ex superstitione et ignorantia perfectiones vocare voluerunt. Sed per perfectionem intelligo tantum realitatem sive esse.*" He explains *perfectio* by *realitas, esse*; so that the more perfect a thing is, the more it is; but its perfection consists in having more *esse* in itself; that is to say, the more a thing is, the more it is. So much for the tautology, but now further. What is lacking here is a distinction between factual being and ideal being. The terminology which permits us to speak of more or less of being, and consequently of degrees of reality or being, is in itself lacking in clearness, and becomes still more confusing when the above distinction is neglected—in other words, when Spinoza does indeed speak profoundly but fails first to consider the difficulty. In the case of factual being it is meaningless to speak of more or less of being. A fly, when it is, has as much being as the God; with respect to factual being the stupid remark I here set down has as much being as Spinoza's profundity, for factual being is subject to the dialectic of Hamlet: to be or not to be. Factual being is wholly indifferent to any and all variations in essence, and everything that exists participates without petty jealousy in being, and participates in the same degree. Ideally, to be sure, the case is quite different. *But the moment I speak of being in the ideal sense I no longer speak of being, but of essence.* Highest ideality has this necessity and therefore it is. But this its being is identical with its essence; such being does not involve it dialectically in the determinations of factual being, since it is; nor can it be said to have more or less of being in relation to other things. In the old days this used to be expressed, if somewhat imperfectly, by saying that if God is possible, he is *eo ipso* necessary (Leibniz). Spinoza's principle is thus quite correct and his tautology in order; but it is also certain that he

altogether evades the difficulty. For the difficulty is to lay hold of God's factual being and to introduce God's ideal essence dialectically into the sphere of factual being.

3. What an excellent subject for a comedy of the higher lunacy!

FURTHER READINGS

Baillie, John. *The Interpretation of Religion*. Nashville: Abingdon Press, 1928.

Braithwaite, R. B. *An Empiricist's View of Religious Belief*. Cambridge: Cambridge University Press, 1955.

Cahn, Steven. *Philosophy of Religion*. New York: Harper & Row, 1970.

Cohen, Jack. *The Case for Religious Naturalism*. New York: Reconstructionist Press, 1958.

Flew, A. G. N. and MacIntyre, Alasdair. *New Essays in Philosophical Theology*. New York: Macmillan, 1955.

Hick, John. *The Philosophy of Religion*. Englewood Cliffs, N.J.: Prentice-Hall, 1963.

James, William. *The Varieties of Religious Experience*. London: Longmans & Green, 1902.

Matson, Wallace. *The Existence of God*. Ithaca, N.Y.: Cornell University Press, 1965.

Pascal, Blaise. *Pensées*. Edited by H. F. Stewart. London: Routledge & Kegan Paul, 1950.

Plantinga, Alvin. *God, Freedom, and Evil*. New York: Harper & Row, 1974.

PART TWO

Knowledge

Introduction

C. F. DELANEY

Most of the things we believe we believe because "someone told us," either in the conventional sense of "telling" or by means of books or other media. Historical facts are an obvious case in point, but even our ordinary beliefs about the world we live in are most often the products, if not of social conditioning, at least of very indirect evidence. The great majority of our beliefs bear on states of affairs we have never witnessed and depend on evidence we are in no position to appreciate. A little reflection gives rise to the specific question—are beliefs so based on "heresay" reasonable?—which in turn leads to the more general issue of the conditions of reasonable belief. Philosophers have taken very seriously these and related questions, on the assumption that we have a responsibility to be reasonable not only in action but also in the sphere of belief.

The various conceptions of reasonable belief (and the various strategies for effecting it) which philosophers have fixed upon have differed widely. Socrates had a modest proposal. He suggested that we should replace our prejudices by beliefs which at least are capable of surviving a certain dialectical scrutiny. Strict proof may be unattainable, but we should at least be capable of giving *reasons* for our belief, reasons which are able to stand up under cross-examination. Aristotle and the medievals were harder to satisfy and fixed on the notion of *demonstration* as the key to reasonable belief. The paradigm case of a reasonable belief was a belief for which one had a conclusive argument. It remained for Descartes, however, to bring this line of thinking to its natural culmination. He was even harder to satisfy and saw in the notion of *demonstrative system* the only hope for generating truly reasonable beliefs. Reasons, simply speaking, were seen to be less than conclusive, and even demonstration left the status of the premises dangling. Nothing short of a conclusive argument from premises which themselves were beyond question was deemed satisfactory. With Descartes the philosopher's ideal of securely founded beliefs received its definitive statement.

The adoption of this general picture of the conditions of reasonable belief, however, falls considerably short of deciding the details of the case. What exactly are these foundational beliefs whose surety grounds our whole edifice of knowledge? What would be instances of these claims which are beyond all doubt?

Descartes fixed upon a foundational belief that could not be doubted without self-contradiction and then associated with it a set of abstract principles which he thought shared the same features. So, from the indubitable truth of his own existence, together with self-evident principles such as that of causality, he endeavored to demonstrate a whole range of truths about God, mathematics, and the physical universe. The model was clearly geometry, and beliefs were seen to be ultimately reasonable to the degree that they were either axioms or theorems in the system.

Driven by the same motives, some empirical-minded philosophers fixed upon the "deliverances of sense" as the objects of their foundational beliefs and attempted to build upon them a similar edifice of knowledge. That which was immediately given in sense experience was seen to be indubitable, and other beliefs were truly credible to the degree that they were translatable into these. Russell's attempt to build up our system of "knowings-about" on a foundation of "knowledge-by-acquaintance" is a case in point. Hence, while radically different in most other regards, both the rationalist and the empiricist traditions shared this foundational picture of knowledge which can be called the "Cartesian ideal."

However, it is one thing to have an ideal and another to realize it successfully in practice. Almost as soon as the ink was dry on Descartes' impressive system of knowledge, the objections started rolling in. And, as is common in the case of reactions, the pendulum swung to the other extreme. In reaction to Descartes' quest of absolute knowledge and to the empiricist's more modest quest for empirically grounded knowledge, the specter of skepticism again loomed on the horizon. Maybe we can't have good reasons for our beliefs after all. Maybe everything is really a matter of subjective opinion.

David Hume was the principal spokesman for this recall from reason (or at least from what he saw as the excesses thereof). Neither the reason of the rationalists nor the sense faculties of the empiricists is really a bona fide source of knowledge. When the operations of reason and the information supplied by the senses are subjected to careful scrutiny, it becomes obvious that they not only fall short of the Cartesian ideal but fall short even of more modest construals of reasonable belief. Theoretical skepticism is the only defensible stand, with 'nature saving us' from the practical consequences of our cognitive inability.

Hume's considerations were directed against both formulations of the foundationalist program. On the one hand he attempted to show that abstract reason was ultimately self-destructive. While on first consideration reason seems to generate instances of knowledge which are beyond doubt, these are shown necessarily to degenerate into probabilities and even these probabilities, by further reasoning, continually to diminish until they all converge on zero. Hence, on reflection, abstract reason is seen really to give us no knowledge at all of anything.

The information provided by the senses proves to be no more reliable, at least insofar as it pretends to give us knowledge of physical objects in the world. Physical objects such as the table in this room are the kinds of things which are supposed to exist distinct from the perceiver and to continue to exist when they are no longer being perceived. Here is the rub. If these properties of distinct and continued existence are essential to physical objects, surely only if we can know that objects have them can we be said to know physical objects. But neither the senses themselves nor the senses supplemented by reason can reveal these properties to us. Hence, experience gives us no knowledge at all of the physical world around us. Hume thus concludes that neither reason nor sense experience can give rise to real knowledge and that habit alone saves us from the dire practical consequences of complete skepticism.

So, as the battle lines were drawn up in modern philosophy, the alternatives seemed to be *foundationalism* or *skepticism*. Either our knowledge system was an edifice built on a firm foundation or real knowledge was not to be had at all. Since there were profound difficulties with each alternative, it is not at all surprising that a third option emerged, an option which would present itself as a mean between the two extremes.

Thomas Reid emerged as the defender of "common sense." From his perspective, Humean skepticism was the natural result of the Cartesian construal of the problem of knowledge. The foundationalist and the skeptical positions each contained features which naturally impelled the inquirer to the other. Accordingly, the dictated course of action seemed to be to reexamine the way in which the whole problem was set and thus to reexamine the criteria of success which so quickly led to failure. Reid did this and suggested that the difficulty lay in the austere conception of knowledge (characterized by incorrigibility) with which Descartes was operating, a conception which was easy prey for Hume's arguments. In its stead he proposed the more modest conception of an edifice of knowledge grounded on the beliefs of *common sense*. From this perspective he attempted to answer the skeptical arguments of Hume.

But common sense is a slippery notion: it can as often mask prejudices as attest to real objective certainties. The very notion of common sense was one concerning which one had to be extremely cautious. It was in this spirit that C. S. Peirce proposed his "critical common-sensism." It may well be that the touchstones of our conceptions of the world are our common-sense beliefs, but even these are revisable within limits. Our individual common-sense beliefs are the beginnings but not the end of the process of critical inquiry. Moreover, rather than view the problem of knowledge in the abstract (i.e., as atemporal and asocial) he situated it within the dynamic social setting of an ongoing inquiry whose goal is the fixation of belief, and thus transformed the question into one bearing on the appropriate method for the fixing of beliefs. In the concrete, what are the conditions of reasonable belief? Is there a way of going about the determination of our beliefs which is ultimately reasonable in that it will lead to the truth in the long run? Peirce's answer was "yes," and the basis of his "yes" was a conception of *method* which took our ordinary perceptual beliefs as foundational but which was self-corrective through and through. It was not that the individual beliefs were deemed beyond doubt, but that the method of inquiry in which they functioned in a privileged way was deemed ultimately reliable.

Whatever one may think of the specific suggestions made by Reid and Peirce (and there are, of course, important differences between them), the overarching question is whether or not there is a genuine mean between the Cartesian ideal of knowledge and Humean skepticism, and if there is not, whether some form of foundationalism or skepticism should be embraced.

Meditations on First Philosophy

RENÉ DESCARTES

MEDITATION I

Of the things which may be brought within the sphere of the doubtful.

It is now some years since I detected how many were the false beliefs that I had from my earliest youth admitted as true, and how doubtful was everything I had since constructed on this basis; and from that time I was convinced that I must once for all seriously undertake to rid myself of all the opinions which I had formerly accepted, and commence to build anew from the foundation, if I wanted to establish any firm and permanent structure in the sciences. But as this enterprise appeared to be a very great one, I waited until I had attained an age so mature that I could not hope that at any later date I should be better fitted to execute my design. This reason caused me to delay so long that I should feel that I was doing wrong were I to occupy in deliberation the time that yet remains to me for action. To-day, then, since very opportunely for the plan I have in view I have delivered my mind from every care [and am happily agitated by no passions] and since I have procured for myself an assured leisure in a peaceable retirement, I shall at last seriously and freely address myself to the general upheaval of all my former opinions.

Now for this object it is not necessary that I should show that all of these are false—I shall perhaps never arrive at this end. But inasmuch as reason already persuades me that I ought no less carefully to withhold my assent from matters which are not entirely certain and indubitable than from those which appear to me manifestly to be false, if I am able to find in each one some reason to doubt, this will suffice to justify my rejecting the whole. And for that end it will not be requisite that I should examine each in particular, which would be an endless undertaking; for owing to the fact that the destruction of the foundations of necessity brings with it the downfall of the rest of the edifice, I shall only in the first place attack those principles upon which all my former opinions rested.

All that up to the present time I have accepted as most true and certain I have learned either from the senses or through the senses; but it is sometimes proved to me that these senses are deceptive, and it is wiser not to trust entirely to any thing by which we have once been deceived.

But it may be that although the senses sometimes deceive us concerning things which are hardly perceptible, or very far away, there are yet many others to be met with as to which we cannot reasonably have any doubt, although we recognise them by their means. For example, there is the fact that I am here, seated by the fire, attired in a dressing gown, having this paper in my hands and

René Descartes (1596-1650) was probably the leading representative of the "rationalist" tradition in philosophy.

From *The Philosophical Works of Descartes*, translated by E. S. Haldane and G. R. T. Ross (Cambridge: Cambridge University Press, 1911). Reprinted by permission of Cambridge University Press.

other similar matters. And how could I deny that these hands and this body are mine, were it not perhaps that I compare myself to certain persons, devoid of sense, whose cerebella are so troubled and clouded by the violent vapours of black bile, that they constantly assure us that they think they are kings when they are really quite poor, or that they are clothed in purple when they are really without covering, or who imagine that they have an earthenware head or are nothing but pumpkins or are made of glass. But they are mad, and I should not be any the less insane were I to follow examples so extravagant.

At the same time I must remember that I am a man, and that consequently I am in the habit of sleeping, and in my dreams representing to myself the same things or sometimes even less probable things, than do those who are insane in their waking moments. How often has it happened to me that in the night I dreamt that I found myself in this particular place, that I was dressed and seated near the fire, whilst in reality I was lying undressed in bed! At this moment it does indeed seem to me that it is with eyes awake that I am looking at this paper; that this head which I move is not asleep, that it is deliberately and of set purpose that I extend my hand and perceive it; what happens in sleep does not appear so clear nor so distinct as does all this. But in thinking over this I remind myself that on many occasions I have in sleep been deceived by similar illusions, and in dwelling carefully on this reflection I see so manifestly that there are no certain indications by which we may clearly distinguish wakefulness from sleep that I am lost in astonishment. And my astonishment is such that it is almost capable of persuading me that I now dream.

Now let us assume that we are asleep and that all these particulars, e.g. that we open our eyes, shake our head, extend our hands, and so on, are but false delusions; and let us reflect that possibly neither our hands nor our whole body are such as they appear to us to be. At the same time we must at least confess that the things which are represented to us in sleep are like painted representations which can only have been formed as the counterparts of something real and true, and that in this way those general things at least, i.e. eyes, a head, hands, and a whole body, are not imaginary things, but things really existent. For, as a matter of fact, painters, even when they study with the greatest skill to represent sirens and satyrs by forms the most strange and extraordinary, cannot give them natures which are entirely new, but merely make a certain medley of the members of different animals; or if their imagination is extravagant enough to invent something so novel that nothing similar has ever before been seen, and that then their work represents a thing purely fictitious and absolutely false, it is certain all the same that the colours of which this is composed are necessarily real. And for the same reason, although these general things, to wit, [a body], eyes, a head, hands, and such like, may be imaginary, we are bound at the same time to confess that there are at least some other objects yet more simple and more universal, which are real and true; and of these just in the same way as with certain real colours, all these images of things which dwell in our thoughts, whether true and real or false and fantastic, are formed.

To such a class of things pertains corporeal nature in general, and its extension, the figure of extended things, their quantity or magnitude and number, as also the place in which they are, the time which measures their duration, and so on.

That is possibly why our reasoning is not unjust when we conclude from this that Physics, Astronomy, Medicine and all other sciences which have as their end the consideration of composite things, are very dubious and uncertain; but that Arithmetic, Geometry and other sciences of that kind which only treat of things that are very simple and very general, without taking great trouble to ascertain whether they are actually existent or not, contain some measure of certainty and an element of the indubitable. For whether I am awake or asleep, two and three together always form five, and the square can never have more than four sides, and it does not seem possible that truths so clear and apparent can be suspected of any falsity [or uncertainty].

Nevertheless I have long had fixed in my mind the belief that an all-powerful God existed by whom I have been created such as I am. But how do I know that He has not brought it to pass that there is no earth, no heaven, no extended body, no magnitude, no place, and that nevertheless [I possess the perceptions of all these things and that] they seem to me to exist just exactly as I now see them? And, besides, as I sometimes imagine that others deceive themselves in the things which they think they know best, how do I know that I am not deceived every time that I add two and three, or count the sides of a square, or judge of things yet simpler, if anything simpler can be imagined? But possibly God has not desired that I should be thus deceived, for He is said to be supremely good. If, however, it is contrary to His goodness to have made me such that I constantly deceive myself, it would also appear to be contrary to His goodness to permit me to be sometimes deceived, and nevertheless I cannot doubt that He does permit this.

There may indeed be those who would prefer to deny the existence of a God so powerful, rather than believe that all other things are uncertain. But let us not oppose them for the present, and grant that all that is here said of a God is a fable; nevertheless in whatever way they suppose that I have arrived at the state of being that I have reached—whether they attribute it to fate or to accident, or make out that it is by a continual succession of antecedents, or by some other method—since to err and deceive oneself is a defect, it is clear that the greater will be the probability of my being so imperfect as to deceive myself ever, as is the Author to whom they assign my origin the less powerful. To these reasons I have certainly nothing to reply, but at the end I feel constrained to confess that there is nothing in all that I formerly believed to be true, of which I cannot in some measure doubt, and that not merely through want of thought or through levity, but for reasons which are very powerful and maturely considered; so that henceforth I ought not the less carefully to refrain from giving credence to these opinions than to that which is manifestly false, if I desire to arrive at any certainty [in the sciences].

But it is not sufficient to have made these remarks, we must also be careful to keep them in mind. For these ancient and commonly held opinions still revert frequently to my mind, long and familiar custom having given them the right to occupy my mind against my inclination and rendered them almost masters of my belief; nor will I ever lose the habit of deferring to them or of placing my confidence in them, so long as I consider them as they really are, i.e. opinions in some measure doubtful, as I have just shown, and at the same time highly probable, so that there is much more reason to believe in than to deny them. That is why I consider that I shall not be acting amiss, if, taking of set purpose a contrary belief, I allow myself to be deceived, and for a certain time pretend that all these opinions are entirely false and imaginary, until at last, having thus balanced my former prejudices with my latter [so that they cannot divert my opinions more to one side than to the other], my judgment will no longer be dominated by bad usage or turned away from the right knowledge of the truth. For I am assured that there can be neither peril nor error in this course, and that I cannot at present yield too much to distrust, since I am not considering the question of action, but only of knowledge.

I shall then suppose, not that God who is supremely good and the fountain of truth, but some evil genius not less powerful than deceitful, has employed his whole energies in deceiving me; I shall consider that the heavens, the earth, colours, figures, sound, and all other external things are nought but the illusions and dreams of which this genius has availed himself in order to lay traps for my credulity; I shall consider myself as having no hands, no eyes, no flesh, no blood, nor any senses, yet falsely believing myself to possess all these things; I shall remain obstinately attached to this idea, and if by this means it is not in my power to arrive at the knowledge of any truth, I may at least do what is in my power [i.e. suspend my judgment], and with firm purpose avoid giving credence to any false thing, or being imposed upon by this arch deceiver, however powerful and deceptive he may be. But this task is a laborious one, and insensibly a certain lassitude leads me into the course of my ordinary life. And just as a captive who in sleep enjoys an imaginary liberty, when he begins to suspect that his liberty is but a dream, fears to awaken, and conspires with these agreeable illusions that the deception may be prolonged, so insensibly of my own accord I fall back into my former opinions, and I dread awakening from this slumber, lest the laborious wakefulness which would follow the tranquillity of this repose should have to be spent not in daylight, but in the excessive darkness of the difficulties which have just been discussed.

MEDITATION II

Of the Nature of the Human Mind; and that it is more easily known than the Body.

The Meditation of yesterday filled my mind with so many doubts that it is no longer in my power to forget them. And yet I do not see in what manner I can resolve them; and, just as if I had all of a sudden fallen into very deep water, I am so disconcerted that I can neither make certain of setting my feet on the bottom, nor can I swim and so support myself on the surface. I shall nevertheless make an effort and follow anew the same path as that on which I yesterday entered, i.e. I shall proceed by setting aside all that in which the least doubt could be supposed to exist, just as if I had discovered that it was absolutely false; and I shall ever follow in this road until I have met with something which is certain, or at least, if I can do nothing else, until I have learned for certain that there is nothing in the world that is certain. Archimedes, in order that he might draw the terrestrial globe out of its place, and transport it elsewhere, demanded only that one point should be fixed and immoveable; in the same way I shall have the right to conceive high hopes if I am happy enough to discover one thing only which is certain and indubitable.

I suppose, then, that all the things that I see are false; I persuade myself that nothing has ever existed of all that my fallacious memory represents to me. I consider that I possess no senses; I imagine that body, figure, extension, movement and place are but the fictions of my mind. What, then, can be esteemed as true? Perhaps nothing at all, unless that there is nothing in the world that is certain.

But how can I know there is not something different from those things that I have just considered, of which one cannot have the slightest doubt? Is there not some God, or some other being by whatever name we call it, who puts these reflections into my mind? That is not necessary, for is it not possible that I am capable of producing them myself? I myself, am I not at least something? But I have already denied that I had senses and body. Yet I hesitate, for what follows from that? Am I so dependent on body and senses that I cannot exist without these? But I was persuaded that there was nothing in all the world, that there was no heaven, no earth, that there were no minds, nor any bodies: was I not then likewise persuaded that I did not exist? Not at all; of a surety I myself did exist since I persuaded myself of something [or merely because I thought of something]. But there is some deceiver or other, very powerful and very cunning, who ever employs his ingenuity in deceiving me. Then without doubt I exist also if he deceives me, and let him deceive me as much as he will, he can never cause me to be nothing so long as I think that I am something. So that after having reflected well and carefully examined all things, we must come to the definite conclusion that this proposition: I am, I exist, is necessarily true each time that I pronounce it, or that I mentally conceive it.

But I do not yet know clearly enough what I am, I who am certain that I am; and hence I must be careful to see that I do not imprudently take some other object in place of myself, and thus that I do not go astray in respect of this knowledge that I hold to be the most certain and most evident of all that I have formerly learned. That is why I shall now consider anew what I believed myself to be before I embarked upon these last reflections; and of my former opinions I shall withdraw all that might even in a small degree be invalidated by the reasons which I have just brought forward, in order that there may be nothing at all left beyond what is absolutely certain and indubitable.

What then did I formerly believe myself to be? Undoubtedly I believed myself to be a man. But what is a man? Shall I say a reasonable animal? Certainly not; for then I should have to inquire what an animal is, and what is reasonable; and thus from a single question I should insensibly fall into an infinitude of others more difficult; and I should not wish to waste the little time and leisure remaining to me in trying to unravel subtleties like these. But I shall rather stop here to consider the thoughts which of themselves spring up in my mind, and which were not inspired by anything beyond my own nature alone when I applied myself to the consideration of my being. In the first place, then, I considered myself as having a face, hands, arms, and all that system of members composed of bones and flesh as seen in a corpse which I designated by the name of body. In addition to this I considered that I was nourished, that I walked, that I felt, and that I thought, and I referred all these actions to the soul: but I did not stop to consider what the soul was, or if I did stop, I imagined that it was something extremely rare and subtle like a wind, a flame, or an ether, which was spread throughout my grosser parts. As to body I had no manner of doubt about its nature, but thought I had a very clear knowledge of it; and if I had desired to explain it according to the notions that I had then formed of it, I should have described it thus: By the body I understand all that which can be defined by a certain figure: something which can be confined in a certain place, and which can fill a given space in such a way that every other body will be excluded from it; which can be perceived either by touch, or by sight, or by hearing, or by taste, or by smell: which can be moved in many ways not, in truth, by itself, but by something which is foreign to it, by which it is touched [and from which it receives impressions]: for to have the power of self-movement, as also of feeling or of thinking, I did not consider to appertain to the nature of body: on the contrary, I was rather astonished to find that faculties similar to them existed in some bodies.

But what am I, now that I suppose that there is a certain genius which is extremely powerful, and, if I may say so, malicious, who employs all his powers in deceiving me? Can I affirm that I possess the least of all those things which I have just said pertain to the nature of body? I pause to consider, I revolve all these things in my mind, and I find none of which I can say that it pertains to me. It would be tedious to stop to enumerate them. Let us pass to the attributes of soul and see if there is any one which is in me? What of nutrition or walking [the first mentioned]? But if it is so that I have no body it is also true that I can neither walk nor take nourishment. Another attribute is sensation. But one cannot feel without body, and besides I have thought I perceived many things during sleep that I recognised in my waking moments as not having been experienced at all. What of thinking? I find here that thought is an attribute that belongs to me; it alone cannot be separated from me. I am, I exist, that is certain. But how often? Just when I think; for it might possibly be the case if I ceased entirely to think, that I should likewise cease altogether to exist. I do not now admit anything which is not necessarily true: to speak accurately I am not more than a thing which thinks, that is to say a mind or a soul, or an understanding, or a reason, which are terms whose significance was formerly unknown to me. I am, however, a real thing and really exist; but what thing? I have answered: a thing which thinks.

And what more? I shall exercise my imagination [in order to see if I am not something more]. I am not a collection of members which we call the human body: I am not a subtle air distributed through these members, I am not a wind, a fire, a vapour, a breath, nor anything at all which I can imagine or conceive; because I have assumed that all these were nothing. Without changing that supposition I find that I only leave myself certain of the fact that I am somewhat. But perhaps it is true that these same things which I supposed were non-existent because they are unknown to me, are really not different from the self which I know. I am not sure about this, I shall not dispute about it now; I can only give judgment on things that are known to me. I know that I exist, and I inquire what I am, I whom I know to exist. But it is very certain that the knowledge of my existence taken in its precise significance does not depend on things whose existence is not yet known to me; consequently it does not depend on those which I can feign in imagination. And indeed the very term *feign* in imagination[1] proves to me my error, for I really do this if I image myself a something, since to imagine is nothing else than to contemplate the figure or image of a corporeal thing. But I already know for certain that I am, and that it may be that all these images, and, speaking generally, all things that relate to the nature of body are nothing but dreams [and chimeras]. For this reason I see clearly that I have as little reason to say, 'I shall stimulate my imagination in order to know more distinctly what I am,' than if I were to say, 'I am now awake, and I perceive somewhat that is real and true: but because I do not yet perceive it distinctly enough, I shall go to sleep of express purpose, so that my dreams may represent the perception with greatest truth and evidence.' And, thus, I know for certain that nothing of all that I can understand by means of my imagination belongs to this knowledge which I have of myself, and that it is necessary to recall the mind from this mode of thought with the utmost diligence in order that it may be able to know its own nature with perfect distinctness.

But what then am I? A thing which thinks. What is a thing which thinks? It is a thing which doubts, understands, [conceives], affirms, denies, wills, refuses, which also imagines and feels.

Certainly it is no small matter if all these things pertain to my nature. But why should they not so pertain? Am I not that being who now doubts nearly everything, who nevertheless understands certain things, who affirms that one only is true, who denies all the others, who desires to know more, is averse from being deceived, who imagines many things, sometimes indeed despite his will, and who perceives many likewise, as by the intervention of the bodily organs? Is there nothing in all this which is as true as it is certain that I exist, even though I should always sleep and though he who has given me being employed all his ingenuity in deceiving me? Is there likewise any one of these attributes which can be distinguished from my thought, or which might be said to be separated from myself? For it is so evident of itself that it is I who doubts, who understands, and who desires, that there is no reason here to add anything to explain it. And I have certainly the power of imagining likewise; for although it may happen (as I formerly supposed) that none of the things which I imagine are true, nevertheless this power of imagining does not cease to be really in use, and it forms part of my thought. Finally, I am the same who feels, that is to say, who perceives certain things, as by the organs of sense, since in truth I see light, I hear noise, I feel heat. But it will be said that these phenomena are false and that I am dreaming. Let it be so; still it is at least quite certain that it seems to me that I see light, that I hear noise and that I feel heat. That cannot be false; properly speaking it is what is in me called feeling[2]; and used in this precise sense that is no other thing than thinking.

From this time I begin to know what I am with a little more clearness and distinction than before; but nevertheless it still seems to me, and I cannot prevent myself from thinking, that corporeal things, whose images are framed by thought, which are tested by the senses, are much more distinctly known than that obscure part of me which does not come under the imagination. Although really it is very strange to say that I know and understand more distinctly these things whose existence seems to me dubious, which are unknown to me, and which do not belong to me, than others of the truth of which I am convinced, which are known to me and which pertain to my real nature, in a word, than myself. But I see clearly how the case stands: my mind loves to wander, and cannot yet suffer itself to be retained within the just limits of truth. Very good, let us once more give it the freest rein, so that, when afterwards we seize the proper occasion for pulling up, it may the more easily be regulated and controlled.

Let us begin by considering the commonest matters, those which we believe to be the most distinctly comprehended, to wit, the bodies which we touch and see; not indeed bodies in general, for these general ideas are usually a little more confused, but let us consider one body in particular. Let us take, for example, this piece of wax: it has been taken quite freshly from the hive, and it has not yet lost the sweetness of the honey which it contains; it still retains somewhat of the odour of the flowers from which it has been culled; its colour, its figure, its size are apparent; it is hard, cold, easily handled, and if you strike it with the finger, it will emit a sound. Finally all the things which are requisite to cause us distinctly to recognise a body, are met with in it. But notice that while I speak and approach the fire what remained of the taste is exhaled, the smell evaporates, the colour alters, the figure is destroyed, the size increases, it becomes liquid, it heats, scarcely can one handle it, and when one strikes it, no sound is emitted. Does the same wax remain after this change? We must confess that it remains; none would judge otherwise. What then did I know so distinctly in this piece of wax? It could certainly be nothing of all that the senses brought to my notice, since all these things which fall under taste, smell, sight, touch, and hearing, are found to be changed, and yet the same wax remains.

Perhaps it was what I now think, viz. that this wax was not that sweetness of honey, nor that agreeable scent of flowers, nor that particular whiteness, nor that figure, nor that sound, but simply a body which a little while before appeared to me as perceptible under these forms, and which is now perceptible under others. But what, precisely, is it that I imagine when I form such conceptions? Let us attentively consider this, and, abstracting from all that does not belong to the wax, let us see what remains. Certainly nothing remains excepting a certain extended thing which is flexible and movable. But what is the meaning of flexible and movable? Is it not that I imagine that this piece of wax being round is capable of becoming square and of passing from a square to a triangular figure? No, certainly it is not that, since I imagine it admits of an infinitude of similar changes, and I nevertheless do not know how to compass the infinitude by my imagination, and consequently this conception which I have of the wax is not brought about by the faculty of imagination. What now is this extension? Is it not also unknown? For it becomes greater when the wax is melted, greater when it is boiled, and greater still when the heat increases; and I should not conceive [clearly] according to truth what wax is, if I did not think that even this piece that we are considering is capable of receiving more variations in extension than I have ever imagined. We must then grant that I could not even understand through the imagination what this piece of wax is, and that it is my mind[3] alone which perceives it. I say this piece of wax in particular, for as to wax in general it is yet clearer. But what is this piece of wax which cannot be understood excepting by the [understanding or] mind? It is certainly the same that I see, touch, imagine, and finally it is the same which I have always believed it to be from the beginning. But what must particularly be observed is that its perception is neither an act of vision, nor of touch, nor of imagination, and has never been such although it may have appeared formerly to be so, but only an intuition[4] of the mind, which may be imperfect and confused as it was formerly, or clear and distinct as it is at present, according as my attention is more or less directed to the elements which are found in it, and of which it is composed.

Yet in the meantime I am greatly astonished when I consider [the great feebleness of mind] and its proneness to fall [insensibly] into error; for although without giving expression to my thoughts I consider all this in my own mind, words often impede me and I am almost deceived by the terms of ordinary language. For we say that we see the same wax, if it is present, and not that we simply judge that it is the same from its having the same colour and figure. From this I should conclude that I knew the wax by means of vision and not simply by the intuition of the mind; unless by chance I remember that, when looking from a window and saying I see men who pass in the street, I really do not see them, but infer that what I see is men, just as I say that I see wax. And yet what do I see from the window but hats and coats which may cover automatic machines? Yet I judge these to be men. And similarly solely by the faculty of judgment which rests in my mind, I comprehend that which I believed I saw with my eyes.

A man who makes it his aim to raise his knowledge above the common should be ashamed to derive the occasion for doubting from the forms of speech invented by the vulgar; I prefer to pass on and consider whether I had a more evident and perfect conception of what the wax was when I first perceived it, and when I believed I knew it by means of the external senses or at least by the common sense[5] as it is called, that is to say by the imaginative faculty, or whether my present conception is clearer now that I have most carefully examined what it is, and in what way it can be known. It would certainly be absurd to doubt as to this. For what was there in this first perception which was distinct?

What was there which might not as well have been perceived by any of the animals? But when I distinguish the wax from its external forms, and when, just as if I had taken from it its vestments, I consider it quite naked, it is certain that although some error may still be found in my judgment, I can nevertheless not perceive it thus without a human mind.

But finally what shall I say of this mind, that is, of myself, for up to this point I do not admit in myself anything but mind? What then, I who seem to perceive this piece of wax so distinctly, do I not know myself, not only with much more truth and certainty, but also with much more distinctness and clearness? For if I judge that the wax is or exists from the fact that I see it, it certainly follows much more clearly that I am or that I exist myself from the fact that I see it. For it may be that what I see is not really wax, it may also be that I do not possess eyes with which to see anything; but it cannot be that when I see, or (for I no longer take account of the distinction) when I think I see, that I myself who think am nought. So if I judge that the wax exists from the fact that I touch it, the same thing will follow, to wit, that I am; and if I judge that my imagination, or some other cause, whatever it is, persuades me that the wax exists, I shall still conclude the same. And what I have here remarked of wax may be applied to all other things which are external to me [and which are met with outside of me]. And further, if the [notion or] perception of wax has seemed to me clearer and more distinct, not only after the sight or the touch, but also after many other causes have rendered it quite manifest to me, with how much more [evidence] and distinctness must it be said that I now know myself, since all the reasons which contribute to the knowledge of wax, or any other body whatever, are yet better proofs of the nature of my mind! And there are so many other things in the mind itself which may contribute to the elucidation of its nature, that those which depend on body such as these just mentioned, hardly merit being taken into account.

But finally here I am, having insensibly reverted to the point I desired, for, since it is now manifest to me that even bodies are not properly speaking known by the senses or by the faculty of imagination, but by the understanding only, and since they are not known from the fact that they are seen or touched, but only because they are understood, I see clearly that there is nothing which is easier for me to know than my mind. But because it is difficult to rid oneself so promptly of an opinion to which one was accustomed for so long, it will be well that I should halt a little at this point, so that by the length of my meditation I may more deeply imprint on my memory this new knowledge.

MEDITATION III

Of God: that He exists.

I shall now close my eyes, I shall stop my ears, I shall call away all my senses, I shall efface even from my thoughts all the images of corporeal things, or at least (for that is hardly possible) I shall esteem them as vain and false; and thus holding converse only with myself and considering my own nature, I shall try little by little to reach a better knowledge of and a more familiar acquaintanceship with myself. I am a thing that thinks, that is to say, that doubts, affirms, denies, that knows a few things, that is ignorant of many [that loves, that hates], that wills, that desires, that also imagines and perceives; for as I remarked before, although the things which I perceive and imagine are perhaps nothing at all apart from me and in themselves, I am nevertheless assured that these modes of thought that I call perceptions and imaginations, inasmuch only as they are modes of thought, certainly reside [and are met with] in me.

And in the little that I have just said, I think I have summed up all that I really know, or at least all that hitherto I was aware that I knew. In order to try to extend my knowledge further, I shall now look around more carefully and see whether I cannot still discover in myself some other things which I have not hitherto perceived. I am certain that I am a thing which thinks; but do I not then likewise know what is requisite to render me certain of a truth? Certainly in this first knowledge there is nothing that assures me of its truth, excepting the clear and distinct perception of that which I state, which would not indeed suffice to assure me that what I say is true, if it could ever happen that a thing which I conceived so clearly and distinctly could be false; and accordingly it seems to me that already I can establish as a general rule that all things which I perceive[6] very clearly and very distinctly are true.

At the same time I have before received and admitted many things to be very certain and manifest, which yet I afterwards recognised as being dubious. What then were these things? They were the earth, sky, stars and all other objects which I apprehended by means of the senses. But what did I clearly [and distinctly] perceive in them? Nothing more than that the ideas or thoughts of these things were presented to my mind. And not even now do I deny that these ideas are met with in me. But there was yet another thing which I affirmed, and which, owing to the habit which I had formed of believing it, I thought I perceived very clearly, although in truth I did not perceive it at all, to wit, that there were objects outside of me from which these ideas proceeded, and to which they were entirely similar. And it was in this that I erred, or, if perchance my judgment was correct, this was not due to any knowledge arising from my perception.

But when I took anything very simple and easy in the sphere of arithmetic or geometry into consideration, e.g. that two and three together made five, and other things of the sort, were not these present to my mind so clearly as to enable me to affirm that they were true? Certainly if I judged that since such matters could be doubted, this would not have been so for any other reason than that it came into my mind that perhaps a God might have endowed me with such a nature that I may have been deceived even concerning things which seemed to me most manifest. But every time that this preconceived opinion of the sovereign power of a God presents itself to my thought, I am constrained to confess that it is easy to Him, if He wishes it, to cause me to err, even in matters in which I believe myself to have the best evidence. And, on the other hand, always when I direct my attention to things which I believe myself to perceive very clearly, I am so persuaded of their truth that I let myself break out into words such as these: Let who will deceive me, He can never cause me to be nothing while I think that I am, or some day cause it to be true to say that I have never been, it being true now to say that I am, or that two and three make more or less than five, or any such thing in which I see a manifest contradiction. And, certainly, since I have no reason to believe that there is a God who is a deceiver, and as I have not yet satisfied myself that there is a God at all, the reason for doubt which depends on this opinion alone is very slight, and so to speak metaphysical. But in order to be able altogether to remove it, I must inquire whether there is a God as soon as the occasion presents itself; and if I find that there is a God, I must also inquire whether He may be a deceiver; for without a knowledge of these two truths I do not see that I can ever be certain of anything.

And in order that I may have an opportunity of inquiring into this in an orderly way [without interrupting the order of meditation which I have proposed to myself, and which is little by little to pass from the notions which I find first of all in my mind to those which I shall later on discover in it] it is requisite that I should here divide my thoughts into certain kinds, and that I should consider in which of these kinds there is, properly speaking, truth or error to be found. Of my thoughts some are, so to speak, images of the things, and to these alone is the title 'idea' properly applied; examples are my thought of a man or of a chimera, of heaven, of an angel, or [even] of God. But other thoughts possess other forms as well. For example in willing, fearing, approving, denying, though I always perceive something as the subject of the action of my mind[7], yet by this action I always add something else to the idea[8] which I have of that thing; and of the thoughts of this kind some are called volitions or affections, and others judgments.

Now as to what concerns ideas, if we consider them only in themselves and do not relate them to anything else beyond themselves, they cannot properly speaking be false; for whether I imagine a goat or a chimera, it is not less true that I imagine the one than the other.We must not fear likewise that falsity can enter into will and into affections, for although I may desire evil things, or even things that never existed, it is not the less true that I desire them. Thus there remains no more than the judgments which we make, in which I must take the greatest care not to deceive myself. But the principal error and the commonest which we may meet with in them, consists in my judging that the ideas which are in me are similar or conformable to the things which are outside me; for without doubt if I considered the ideas only as certain modes of my thoughts, without trying to relate them to anything beyond, they could scarcely give me material for error.

But among these ideas, some appear to me to be innate, some adventitious, and others to be formed [or invented] by myself; for, as I have the power of understanding what is called a thing, or a truth, or a thought, it appears to me that I hold this power from no other source than my own nature. But if I now hear some sound, if I see the sun, or feel heat, I have hitherto judged that these sensations proceeded from certain things that exist outside of me; and finally it appears to me that sirens, hippogryphs, and the like, are formed out of my own mind. But again I may possibly persuade myself that all these ideas are of the nature of those which I term adventitious, or else that they are all innate, or all fictitious: for I have not yet clearly discovered their true origin.

And my principal task in this place is to consider, in respect to those ideas which appear to me to proceed from certain objects that are outside me, what are the reasons which cause me to think them similar to these objects. It seems indeed in the first place that I am taught this lesson by nature; and, secondly, I experience in myself that these ideas do not depend on my will nor therefore on myself—for they often present themselves to my mind in spite of my will. Just now, for instance, whether I will or whether I do not will, I feel heat, and thus I persuade myself that this feeling, or at least this idea of heat, is produced in me by something which is different from me, i.e. by the heat of the fire near which I sit. And nothing seems to me more obvious than to judge that this object imprints its likeness rather than anything else upon me.

Now I must discover whether these proofs are sufficiently strong and convincing. When I say that I am so instructed by nature, I merely mean a certain spontaneous inclination which impels me to believe in this connection, and not a natural light which makes me recognise that it is true. But these two things are very different; for I cannot doubt that which the natural light causes me to believe to be true, as, for example, it has shown me that I am from the fact that I doubt, or other facts of the same kind. And I possess no other faculty whereby to distinguish truth from falsehood, which can teach me that what this light shows me to be true is not really true, and no other faculty that is equally trustworthy. But as far as [apparently] natural impulses are concerned, I have frequently remarked, when I had to make active choice between virtue and vice, that they often enough led me to the part that was worse; and this is why I do not see any reason for following them in what regards truth and error.

And as to the other reason, which is that these ideas must proceed from objects outside me, since they do not depend on my will, I do not find it any the more convincing. For just as these impulses of which I have spoken are found in me, nothwithstanding that they do not always concur with my will, so perhaps there is in me some faculty fitted to produce these ideas without the assistance of any external things, even though it is not yet known by me; just as, apparently, they have hitherto always been found in me during sleep without the aid of any external objects.

And finally, though they did proceed from objects different from myself, it is not a necessary consequence that they should resemble these. On the contrary, I have noticed that in many cases there was a great difference between the object and its idea. I find, for example two completely diverse ideas of the sun in my mind; the one derives its origin from the senses, and should be placed in the category of adventitious ideas; according to this idea the sun seems to be extremely small; but the other is derived from astronomical reasonings, i.e. is elicited from certain notions that are innate in me, or else it is formed by me in some other manner; in accordance with it the sun appears to be several times greater than the earth. These two ideas cannot, indeed, both resemble the same sun, and reason makes me believe that the one which seems to have originated directly from the sun itself, is the one which is most dissimilar to it.

All this causes me to believe that until the present time it has not been by a judgment that was certain [or premeditated], but only by a sort of blind impulse that I believed that things existed outside of, and different from me, which, by the organs of my senses, or by some other method whatever it might be, conveyed these ideas or images to me [and imprinted on me their similitudes].

But there is yet another method of inquiring whether any of the objects of which I have ideas within me exist outside of me. If ideas are only taken as certain modes of thought, I recognise amongst them no difference or inequality, and all appear to proceed from me in the same manner; but when we consider them as images, one representing one thing and the other another, it is clear that they are very different one from the other. There is no doubt that those which represent to me substances are something more, and contain so to speak more objective reality within them [that is to say, by representation participate in a higher degree of being or perfection] than those that simply represent modes or accidents; and that idea again by which I understand a supreme God, eternal, infinite, [immutable], omniscient, omnipotent, and Creator of all things which are outside of Himself, has certainly more objective reality in itself than those ideas by which finite substances are represented.

Now it is manifest by the natural light that there must at least be as much reality in the efficient and total cause as in its effect. For, pray, whence can the effect derive its reality, if not from its cause? And in what way can this cause communicate this reality to it, unless it possessed it in itself? And from this it follows, not only that something cannot proceed from nothing, but likewise that what is more perfect—that is to say, which has more reality within itself—cannot proceed from the less perfect. And this is not only evidently true of those effects which possess actual or formal reality, but also of the ideas in which we consider merely what is termed objective reality. To take an example, the stone which has not yet existed not only cannot now commence to be unless it has been produced by something which possesses within itself, either formally or eminently, all that enters into the composition of the stone [i.e. it must possess the same things or other more excellent things than those which exist in the stone] and heat can only be produced in a subject in which it did not previously exist by a cause that is of an order [degree or kind] at least as perfect as heat, and so in all other cases. But further, the idea of heat, or of a stone, cannot exist in me unless it has been placed within me by some cause which possesses within it at least as much reality as that which I conceive to exist in the heat or the stone. For although this cause does not transmit anything of its actual or formal reality to my idea, we must not for that reason imagine that it is necessarily a less real cause; we must remember that [since every idea is a work of the mind] its nature is such that it demands of itself no other formal reality than that which it borrows from my thought, of which it is only a mode [i.e. a manner or way of thinking]. But in order that an idea should contain some one certain objective reality rather than another, it must without doubt derive it from some cause in which there is at least as much formal reality as this idea contains of objective reality. For if we imagine that something is found in an idea which is not found in the cause, it must then have been derived from nought; but however imperfect may be this mode of being by which a thing is objectively [or by representation] in the understanding by its idea, we cannot certainly say that this mode of being is nothing, nor, consequently, that the idea derives its origin from nothing.

Nor must I imagine that, since the reality that I consider in these ideas is only objective, it is not essential that this reality should be formally in the causes of my ideas, but that it is sufficient that it should be found objectively. For just as this mode of objective existence pertains to ideas by their proper nature, so does the mode of formal existence pertain to the causes of those ideas (this is at least true of the first and principal) by the nature peculiar to them. And although it may be the case that one idea gives birth to another idea, that cannot continue to be so indefinitely; for in the end we must reach an idea whose cause shall be so to speak an archetype, in which the whole reality [or perfection] which is so to speak objectively [or by representation] in these ideas is contained formally [and really]. Thus the light of nature causes me to know clearly that the ideas in me are like [pictures or] images which can, in truth, easily fall short of the perfection of the objects from which they have been derived, but which can never contain anything greater or more perfect.

And the longer and the more carefully that I investigate these matters, the more clearly and distinctly do I recognise their truth. But what am I to conclude from it all in the end? It is this, that if the objective reality of any one of my ideas is of such a nature as clearly to make me recognise that it is not in me either formally or eminently, and that consequently I cannot myself be the cause of it, it follows of necessity that I am not alone in the world, but that there is another being which exists, or which is the cause of this idea. On the other hand, had no such an idea existed in me, I should have had no sufficient argument to convince me of the existence of any being beyond myself; for I have made very careful investigation everywhere and up to the present time have been able to find no other ground.

But of my ideas, beyond that which represents me to myself, as to which there can here be no difficulty, there is another which represents a God, and there are others representing corporeal and inanimate things, others angels, others animals, and others again which represent to me men similar to myself.

As regards the ideas which represent to me other men or animals, or angels, I can however easily conceive that they might be formed by an admixture of the other ideas which I have of myself, of corporeal things, and of God, even although there were apart from me neither men nor animals, nor angels, in all the world.

And in regard to the ideas of corporeal objects, I do not recognise in them anything so great or so excellent that they might not have possibly proceeded from myself; for if I consider them more closely, and examine them individually, as I yesterday examined the idea of wax, I find that there is very little in them which I perceive clearly and distinctly. Magnitude or extension in length, breadth, or depth, I do so perceive; also figure which results from a termination of this extension, the situation which bodies of different figure preserve in relation to one another, and movement or change of situation; to which we may also add substance, duration and number. As to other things such as light, colours, sounds, scents, tastes, heat, cold and the other tactile qualities, they are thought by me with so much obscurity and confusion that I do not even know if they are true or false, i.e. whether the ideas which I form of these qualities are actually the ideas of real objects or not [or whether they only represent chimeras which cannot exist in fact]. For although I have before remarked that it is only in judgments that falsity, properly speaking, or formal falsity, can be met with, a certain material falsity may nevertheless be found in ideas, i.e. when these ideas represent what is nothing as though it were something. For example, the ideas which I have of cold and heat are so far from clear and distinct that by their means I cannot tell whether cold is merely a privation of heat, or heat a privation of cold, or whether both are real qualities, or are not such. And inasmuch as [since ideas resemble images] there cannot be any ideas which do not appear to represent some things, if it is correct to say that cold is merely a privation of heat, the idea which represents it to me as something real and positive will not be improperly termed false, and the same holds good of other similar ideas.

To these it is certainly not necessary that I should attribute any author other than myself. For if they are false, i.e if they represent things which do not exist, the light of nature shows me that they issue from nought, that is to say, that they are only in me in so far as something is lacking to the perfection of my nature. But if they are true, nevertheless because they exhibit so little reality to me that I cannot even clearly distinguish the thing represented from non-being, I do not see any reason why they should not be produced by myself.

As to the clear and distinct idea which I have of corporeal things, some of them seem as though I might have derived them from the idea which I possess of myself, as those which I have of substance, duration, number, and such like. For [even] when I think that a stone is a substance, or at least a thing capable of existing of itself, and that I am a substance also, although I conceive that I am a thing that thinks and not one that is extended, and that the stone on the other hand is an extended thing which does not think, and that thus there is a notable difference between the two conceptions—they seem, nevertheless to agree in this, that both represent substances. In the same way, when I perceive that I now exist and further recollect that I have in former times existed, and when I remember that I have various thoughts of which I can recognise the number, I acquire ideas of duration and number which I can afterwards transfer to any object that I please. But as to all the other qualities of which the ideas of corporeal things are composed, to wit, extension, figure, situation and motion, it is true that they are not formally in me, since I am only a thing that thinks; but because they are merely certain modes of substance [and so to speak the vestments under which corporeal substance appears to us] and because I myself am also a substance, it would seem that they might be contained in me eminently.

Hence there remains only the idea of God, concerning which we must consider whether it is something which cannot have proceeded from me myself. By the name God I understand a substance that is infinite [eternal, immutable], independent, all-knowing, all-powerful, and by which I myself and everything else, if anything else does exist, have been created. Now all these characteristics are such that the more diligently I attend to them, the less do they appear capable of proceeding from me alone; hence, from what has been already said, we must conclude that God necessarily exists.

For although the idea of substance is within me owing to the fact that I am substance, nevertheless I should not have the idea of an infinite substance—since I am finite—if it had not proceeded from some substance which was veritably infinite.

Nor should I imagine that I do not perceive the infinite by a true idea, but only by the negation of the finite, just as I perceive repose and darkness by the negation of movement and of light; for, on the contrary, I see that there is manifestly more reality in infinite substance than in finite, and therefore that in some way I have in me the notion of the infinite earlier than the finite—to wit, the notion of God before that of myself. For how would it be possible that I should know that I doubt and desire, that is to say, that something is lacking to me, and that I am not quite perfect, unless I had within me some idea of a Being more perfect than myself, in comparison with which I should recognise the deficiencies of my nature?

And we cannot say that this idea of God is perhaps materially false and that consequently I can derive it from nought [i.e. that possibly it exists in me because I am imperfect], as I have just said is the case with ideas of heat, cold and other such things; for, on the contrary, as this idea is very clear and distinct and contains within it more objective reality than any other, there can be none which is of itself more true, nor any in which there can be less suspicion of falsehood. The idea, I say, of this Being who is absolutely perfect and infinite, is entirely true; for although, perhaps, we can imagine that such a Being does not exist, we cannot nevertheless imagine that His idea represents nothing real to me, as I have said of the idea of cold. This idea is also very clear and distinct; since all that I conceive clearly and distinctly of the real and the true, and of what conveys some perfection, is in its entirety contained in this idea. And this does not cease to be true although I do not comprehend the infinite, or though in God there is an infinitude of things which I cannot comprehend, nor possibly even reach in any way by thought; for it is of the nature of the infinite that my nature, which is finite and limited, should not comprehend it; and it is sufficient that I should understand this, and that I should judge that all things which I clearly perceive and in which I know that there is some perfection, and possibly likewise an infinitude of properties of which I am ignorant, are in God formally or eminently, so that the idea which I have of Him may become the most true, most clear, and most distinct of all the ideas that are in my mind.

But possibly I am something more than I suppose myself to be, and perhaps all those perfections which I attribute to God are in some way potentially in me, although they do not yet disclose themselves, or issue in action. As a matter of fact I am already sensible that my knowledge increases [and perfects itself] little by little, and I see nothing which can prevent it from increasing more and more into infinitude; nor do I see, after it has thus been increased [or perfected], anything to prevent my being able to acquire by its means all the other perfections of the Divine nature; nor finally why the power I have of acquiring these perfections, if it really exists in me, shall not suffice to produce the ideas of them.

At the same time I recognise that this cannot be. For, in the first place, although it were true that every day my knowledge acquired new degrees of perfection, and that there were in my nature many things potentially which are not yet there actually, nevertheless these excellences do not pertain to [or make the smallest approach to] the idea which I have of God in whom there is nothing merely potential [but in whom all is present really and actually]; for it is an infallible token of imperfection in my knowledge that it increases little by little. And further, although my knowledge grows more and more, nevertheless I do not for that reason believe that it can ever be actually infinite, since it can never reach a point so high that it will be unable to attain to any greater increase. But I understand God to be actually infinite, so that He can add nothing to His supreme perfection. And finally I perceive that the objective being of an idea cannot be produced by a being that exists potentially only, which properly speaking is nothing, but only by a being which is formal or actual.

To speak the truth, I see nothing in all that I have just said which by the light of nature is not manifest to anyone who desires to think attentively on the subject; but when I slightly relax my attention, my mind, finding its vision somewhat obscured and so to speak blinded by the images of sensible objects, I do not easily recollect the reason why the idea that I possess of a being more perfect than I, must necessarily have been placed in me by a being which is really more perfect; and this is why I wish here to go on to inquire whether I, who have this idea, can exist if no such being exists.

And I ask, from whom do I then derive my existence? Perhaps from myself or from my parents, or from some other source less perfect than God; for we can imagine nothing more perfect than God, or even as perfect as He is.

But [were I independent of every other and] were I myself the author of my being, I should doubt nothing and I should desire nothing, and finally no perfection would be lacking to me; for I should have bestowed on myself every perfection of which I possessed any idea and should thus be God. And it must not be imagined that those things that are lacking to me are perhaps more difficult of attainment than those which I already possess; for, on the contrary, it is quite evident that it was a matter of much greater difficulty to bring to pass that I, that is to say, a thing or a substance that thinks, should emerge out of nothing, than it would be to attain to the knowledge of many things of which I am ignorant, and which are only the accidents of this thinking substance. But it is clear that if I had of myself possessed this greater perfection of which I have just spoken [that is to say, if I had been the author of my own existence], I should not at least have denied myself the things which are the more easy to acquire [to wit, many branches of knowledge of which my nature is destitute]; nor should I have deprived myself of any of the things contained in the idea which I form of God, because there are none of them which seem to me specially difficult to acquire: and if there were any that were more difficult to acquire, they would certainly appear to me to be such (supposing I myself were the origin of the other things which I possess) since I should discover in them that my powers were limited.

But though I assume that perhaps I have always existed just as I am at present, neither can I escape the force of this reasoning, and imagine that the conclusion to be drawn from this is, that I need not seek for any author of my existence. For all the course of my life may be divided into an infinite number of parts, none of which is in any way dependent on the other; and thus from the fact that I was in existence a short time ago it does not follow that I must be in existence now, unless some cause at this instant, so to speak, produces me anew, that is to say, conserves me. It is as a matter of fact perfectly clear and evident to all those who consider with attention the nature of time, that, in order to be conserved in each moment in which it endures, a substance has need of the same power and action as would be necessary to produce and create it anew, supposing it did not yet exist, so that the light of nature shows us clearly that the distinction between creation and conservation is solely a distinction of the reason.

All that I thus require here is that I should interrogate myself, if I wish to know whether I possess a power which is capable of bringing it to pass that I who now am shall still be in the future; for since I am nothing but a thinking thing, or at least since thus far it is only this portion of myself which is precisely in question at present, if such a power did reside in me, I should certainly be conscious of it. But I am conscious of nothing of the kind, and by this I know clearly that I depend on some being different from myself.

Possibly, however, this being on which I depend is not that which I call God, and I am created either by my parents or by some other cause less perfect than God. This cannot be, because, as I have just said, it is perfectly evident that there must be at least as much reality in the cause as in the effect; and thus since I am a thinking thing, and possess an idea of God within me, whatever in the end be the cause assigned to my existence, it must be allowed that it is likewise a thinking thing and that it possesses in itself the idea of all the perfections which I attribute to God. We may again inquire whether this cause derives its origin from itself or from some other thing. For if from itself, it follows by the reasons before brought forward, that this cause must itself be God; for since it possesses the virtue of self-existence, it must also without doubt have the power of actually possessing all the perfections of which it has the idea, that is, all those which I conceive as existing in God. But if it derives its existence from some other cause than itself, we shall again ask, for the same reason, whether this second cause exists by itself or through another, until from one step to another, we finally arrive at an ultimate cause, which will be God.

And it is perfectly manifest that in this there can be no regression into infinity, since what is in question is not so much the cause which formerly created me, as that which conserves me at the present time.

Nor can we suppose that several causes may have concurred in my production, and that from one I have received the idea of one of the perfections which I attribute to God, and from another the idea of some other, so that all these perfections indeed exist somewhere in the universe, but not as complete in one unity which is God. On the contrary, the unity, the simplicity or the inseparability of all things which are in God is one of the principal perfections which I conceive to be in Him. And certainly the idea of this unity of all Divine perfections cannot have been placed in me by any cause from which I have not likewise received the ideas of all the other perfections; for this cause could not make me able to comprehend them as joined together in an inseparable unity without having at the same time caused me in some measure to know what they are [and in some way to recognise each one of them].

Finally, so far as my parents [from whom it appears I have sprung] are concerned, although all that I have ever been able to believe of them were true, that does not make it follow that it is they who conserve me, nor are they even the authors of my being in any sense, in so far as I am a thinking being; since what they did was merely to implant certain dispositions in that matter in which the self—i.e. the mind, which alone I at present identify with myself—is by me deemed to exist. And thus there can be no difficulty in their regard, but we must of necessity conclude from the fact alone that I exist, or that the idea of a Being supremely perfect—that is of God—is in me, that the proof of God's existence is grounded on the highest evidence.

It only remains to me to examine into the manner in which I have acquired this idea from God; for I have not received it through the senses, and it is never presented to me unexpectedly, as is usual with the ideas of sensible things when these things present themselves, or seem to present themselves, to the external organs of my senses; nor is it likewise a fiction of my mind, for it is not in my power to take from or to add anything to it; and consequently the only alternative is that it is innate in me, just as the idea of myself is innate in me.

And one certainly ought not to find it strange that God, in creating me, placed this idea within me to be like the mark of the workman imprinted on his work; and it is likewise not essential that the mark shall be something different from the work itself. For from the sole fact that God created me it is most probable that in some way he has placed his image and similitude upon me, and that I perceive this similitude (in which the idea of

God is contained) by means of the same faculty by which I perceive myself—that is to say, when I reflect on myself I not only know that I am something [imperfect], incomplete and dependent on another, which incessantly aspires after something which is better and greater than myself, but I also know that He on whom I depend possesses in Himself all the great things towards which I aspire [and the ideas of which I find within myself], and that not indefinitely or potentially alone, but really, actually and infinitely; and that thus He is God. And the whole strength of the argument which I have here made use of to prove the existence of God consists in this, that I recognise that it is not possible that my nature should be what it is, and indeed that I should have in myself the idea of a God, if God did not veritably exist—a God, I say, whose idea is in me, i.e. who possesses all those supreme perfections of which our mind may indeed have some idea but without understanding them all, who is liable to no errors or defect [and who has none of all those marks which denote imperfection]. From this it is manifest that He cannot be a deceiver, since the light of nature teaches us that fraud and deception necessarily proceed from some defect.

But before I examine this matter with more care, and pass on to the consideration of other truths which may be derived from it, it seems to me right to pause for a while in order to contemplate God Himself, to ponder at leisure His marvellous attributes, to consider, and admire, and adore, the beauty of this light so resplendent, at least as far as the strength of my mind, which is in some measure dazzled by the sight, will allow me to do so. For just as faith teaches us that the supreme felicity of the other life consists only in this contemplation of the Divine Majesty, so we continue to learn by experience that a similar meditation, though incomparably less perfect, causes us to enjoy the greatest satisfaction of which we are capable in this life.

MEDITATION IV

Of the True and the False.

I have been well accustomed these past days to detach my mind from my senses, and I have accurately observed that there are very few things that one knows with certainty respecting corporeal objects, that there are many more which are known to us respecting the human mind, and yet more still regarding God Himself; so that I shall now without any difficulty abstract my thoughts from the consideration of [sensible or] imaginable objects, and carry them to those which, being withdrawn from all contact with matter, are purely intelligible. And certainly the idea which I possess of the human mind inasmuch as it is a thinking thing, and not extended in length, width and depth, nor participating in anything pertaining to body, is incomparably more distinct than is the idea of any corporeal thing. And when I consider that I doubt, that is to say, that I am an incomplete and dependent being, the idea of a being that is complete and independent, that is of God, presents itself to my mind with so much distinctness and clearness—and from the fact alone that this idea is found in me, or that I who possess this idea exist, I conclude so certainly that God exists, and that my existence depends entirely on Him in every moment of my life—that I do not think that the human mind is capable of knowing anything with more evidence and certitude. And it seems to me that I now have before me a road which will lead us from the contemplation of the true God (in whom all the treasures of science and wisdom are contained) to the knowledge of the other objects of the universe.

For, first of all, I recognise it to be impossible that He should ever deceive me; for in all fraud and deception some imperfection is to be found, and although it may appear that the power of deception is a mark of subtilty or power, yet the desire to deceive without doubt testifies to malice or feebleness, and accordingly cannot be found in God.

In the next place I experienced in myself a certain capacity for judging which I have doubtless received from God, like all the other things that I possess; and as He could not desire to deceive me, it is clear that He has not given me a faculty that will lead me to err if I use it aright.

And no doubt respecting this matter could remain, if it were not that the consequence would seem to follow that I can thus never be deceived; for if I hold all that I possess from God, and if He has not placed in me the capacity for error, it seems as though I could never fall into error. And it is true that when I think only of God [and direct my mind wholly to Him][9], I discover [in myself] no cause of error, or falsity; yet directly afterwards, when recurring to myself, experience shows me that I am nevertheless subject to an infinitude of errors, as to which, when we come to investigate them more closely, I notice that not only is there a real and positive idea of God or of a Being of supreme perfection present to my mind, but also, so to speak, a certain negative idea of nothing, that is, of that which is infinitely removed from any kind of perfection; and that I am in a sense something intermediate between God and nought, i.e. placed in such a manner between the supreme Being and nonbeing, that there is in truth nothing in me that can lead to error in so far as a sovereign Being has formed me; but that, as I in some degree participate likewise in nought or in non-being, i.e. in so far as I am not myself the supreme Being, and as I find myself subject to an infinitude of imperfections, I ought not to be astonished if I should fall into error. Thus do I recognise that error, in so far as it is such, is not a real thing depending on God, but simply a defect; and therefore, in order to fall into it, that I have no need to possess a special faculty given me by God for this very purpose, but that I fall into error from the fact that the power given me by God for the purpose of distinguishing truth from error is not infinite. . . .

MEDITATION VI

Of the Existence of Material Things, and of the real distinction between the Soul and Body of Man.

Nothing further now remains but to inquire whether material things exist. And certainly I at least know that these may exist in so far as they are considered as the objects of pure mathematics, since in this aspect I perceive them clearly and distinctly. For there is no doubt that God possesses the power to produce everything that I am capable of perceiving with distinctness, and I have never deemed that anything was impossible for Him, unless I found a contradiction in attempting to conceive it clearly. Further, the faculty of imagination which I possess, and of which, experience tells me, I make use when I apply myself to the consideration of material things, is capable of persuading me of their existence; for when I attentively consider what imagination is, I find that it is nothing but a certain application of the faculty of knowledge to the body which is immediately present to it, and which therefore exists.

And to render this quite clear, I remark in the first place the difference that exists between the imagination and pure intellection [or conception].[10] For example, when I imagine a triangle, I do not conceive it only as a figure comprehended by three lines, but I also apprehend[11] these three lines as present by the power and inward vision of my mind[12], and this is what I call imagining. But if I desire to think of a chiliagon, I certainly conceive truly that it is a figure composed of a thousand sides, just as easily as I conceive of a triangle that it is a figure of three sides only; but I cannot in any way imagine the thousand sides of a chiliagon [as I do the three sides of a triangle], nor do I, so to speak, regard them as present [with the eyes of my mind]. And although in accordance with the habit I have formed of always employing the aid of my imagination when I think of corporeal things, it may happen that in imagining a chiliagon I confusedly represent to myself some figure, yet it is very evident that this figure is not a chiliagon, since it in no way differs from that which I represent to myself when I think of a myriagon or any other many-sided figure; nor does it serve my purpose in discovering the properties which go to form the distinction between a chiliagon and other polygons. But if the question turns upon a pentagon, it is quite true that I can conceive its figure as well as that of a chiliagon without the help of my imagination; but I can also imagine it by applying the attention of my mind to each of its five sides, and at the same time to the space which they enclose. And thus I clearly recognise that I have need of a particular effort of mind in order to effect the act of imagination, such as I do not require in order to understand, and this particular effort of mind clearly manifests the difference which exists between imagination and pure intellection[13].

I remark besides that this power of imagination which is in one, inasmuch as it differs from the power of understanding, is in no wise a necessary element in my nature, or in [my essence, that is to say, in] the essence of my mind; for although I did not possess it I should doubtless ever remain the same as I now am, from which it appears that we might conclude that it depends on something which differs from me. And I easily conceive that if some body exists with which my mind is conjoined and united in such a way that it can apply itself to consider it when it pleases, it may be that by this means it can imagine corporeal objects; so that this mode of thinking differs from pure intellection only inasmuch as mind in its intellectual activity in some manner turns on itself, and considers some of the ideas which it possesses in itself; while in imagining it turns towards the body, and there beholds in it something conformable to the idea which it has either conceived of itself or perceived by the senses. I easily understand, I say, that the imagination could be thus constituted if it is true that body exists; and because I can discover no other convenient mode of explaining it, I conjecture with probability that body does exist; but this is only with probability, and although I examine all things with care, I nevertheless do not find that from this distinct idea of corporeal nature, which I have in my imagination, I can derive any argument from which there will necessarily be deduced the existence of body.

But I am in the habit of imagining many other things besides this corporeal nature which is the object of pure mathematics, to wit, the colours, sounds, scents, pain, and other such things, although less distinctly. And inasmuch as I perceive these things much better through the senses, by the medium of which, and by the memory, they seem to have reached my imagination, I believe that, in order to examine them more conveniently, it is right that I should at the same time investigate the nature of sense perception, and that I should see if from the ideas which I apprehend by this mode of thought, which I call feeling, I cannot derive some certain proof of the existence of corporeal objects.

And first of all I shall recall to my memory those matters which I hitherto held to be true, as having perceived them through the senses, and the foundations on which my belief has rested; in the next place I shall examine the reasons which have since obliged me to place them in doubt; in the last place I shall consider which of them I must now believe.

First of all, then, I perceived that I had a head, hands, feet, and all other members of which this body—which I considered as a part, or possibly even as the whole, of myself—is composed. Further I was sensible that this body was placed amidst many others, from which it was capable of being affected in many different ways, beneficial and hurtful, and I remarked that a certain feeling of pleasure accompanied those that were beneficial, and pain those which were harmful. And in addition to this pleasure and pain, I also experienced hunger, thirst, and other similar appetites, as also certain corporeal inclinations towards joy, sadness, anger, and other similar passions. And outside myself, in addition to extension, figure, and motions of bodies, I remarked in them hardness, heat, and all other tactile qualities, and, further, light and colour, and scents and sounds, the variety of which gave me the means of distinguishing the sky, the earth, the sea, and generally all the other bodies, one from the other. And certainly, considering the ideas of all these qualities which presented themselves to my mind, and which alone I perceived properly or immediately, it was not without reason that I believed myself to perceive objects quite different from my thought, to wit, bodies from which those ideas proceeded; for I found by experience that these ideas presented themselves to me without my consent being requisite, so that I could not perceive any object, however desirous I might be, unless it were present to the organs of sense; and it was not in my power not to perceive it, when it was present. And because the ideas which I received through the senses were much more lively, more clear, and even, in their own way, more distinct than any of those which I could of myself frame in meditation, or than those I found impressed on my memory, it appeared as though they could not have proceeded from my mind, so that they must necessarily have been produced in me by some other things. And having no knowledge of those objects excepting the knowledge which the ideas themselves gave me, nothing was more likely to occur to my mind than that the objects were similar to the ideas which were caused. And because I likewise remembered that I had formerly made use of my senses rather than my reason, and recognised that the ideas which I formed of myself were not so distinct as those which I perceived through the senses, and that they were most frequently even composed of portions of these last, I persuaded myself easily that I had no idea in my mind which had not formerly come to me through the senses. Nor was it without some reason that I believed that this body (which by a certain special right I call my own) belonged to me more properly and more strictly than any other; for in fact I could never be separated from it as from other bodies; I experienced in it and on account of it all my appetites and affections, and finally I was touched by the feeling of pain and the titillation of pleasure in its parts, and not in the parts of other bodies which were separated from it. But when I inquired, why, from some, I know not what, painful sensation, there follows sadness of mind, and from the pleasurable sensation there arises joy, or why this mysterious pinching of the stomach which I call hunger causes me to desire to eat, and dryness of throat causes a desire to drink, and so on, I could give no reason excepting that nature taught me so; for there is certainly no affinity (that I at least can understand) between the craving of the stomach and the desire to eat, any more than between the perception of whatever causes pain and the thought of sadness which arises from this perception. And in the same way it appeared to me that I had learned from nature all the other judgments which I formed regarding the objects of my senses, since I remarked that these judgments were formed in me before I had the leisure to weigh and consider any reasons which might oblige me to make them.

But afterwards many experiences little by little destroyed all the faith which I had rested in my senses; for I from time to time observed that those towers which from afar appeared to me to be round, more closely observed seemed square, and that colossal statues raised on the summit of these towers, appeared as quite tiny statues when viewed from the bottom; and so in an infinitude of other cases I found error in judgments founded on the external senses. And not only in those founded on the external senses, but even in those founded on the internal as well; for is there anything more intimate or more internal than pain? And yet I have learned from some persons whose arms or legs have been cut off, that they sometimes seemed to feel pain in the part which had been amputated, which made me think that I could not be quite certain that it was a certain member which pained me, even although I felt pain in it. And to those grounds of doubt I have lately added two others, which are very general; the first is that I never have believed myself to feel anything in waking moments which I cannot also sometimes believe myself to feel when I sleep, and as I do not think that these things which I seem to feel in sleep, proceed from objects outside of me, I do not see any reason why I should have this belief regarding objects which I seem to perceive while awake. The other was that being still ignorant, or rather supposing myself to be ignorant, of the author of my being, I saw nothing to prevent me from having been so constituted by nature that I might be deceived even in matters which seemed to me to be most certain. And as to the grounds on which I was formerly persuaded of the truth of sensible objects, I had not much trouble in replying to them. For since nature seemed to cause me to lean towards many things from which reason repelled me, I did not believe that I should trust much to the teachings of nature. And although the ideas which I receive by the senses do not depend on my will, I did not think that one should for that reason conclude that they proceeded from things different from myself, since possibly some faculty might be discovered in me—though hitherto unknown to me—which produced them.

But now that I begin to know myself better, and to discover more clearly the author of my being, I do not in truth think that I should rashly admit all the matters which the senses seem to teach us, but, on the other hand, I do not think that I should doubt them all universally.

And first of all, because I know that all things which I apprehend clearly and distinctly can be created by God as I apprehend them, it suffices that I am able to apprehend one thing apart from another clearly and distinctly in order to be certain that the one is different from the other, since they may be made to exist in separation at least by the omnipotence of God; and it does not signify by what power this separation is made in order to compel me to judge them to be different: and, therefore, just because I know certainly that I exist, and that meanwhile I do not remark that any other thing necessarily pertains to my nature or essence, excepting that I am a thinking thing, I rightly conclude that my essence consists solely in the fact that I am a thinking thing [or a substance whose whole essence or nature is to think]. And although possibly (or rather certainly, as I shall say in a moment) I possess a body with which I am very intimately conjoined, yet because, on the one side, I have a clear and distinct idea of myself inasmuch as I am only a thinking and unextended thing, and as, on the other, I possess a distinct idea of body, inasmuch as it is only an extended and unthinking thing, it is certain that this I [that is to say, my soul by which I am what I am], is entirely and absolutely distinct from my body, and can exist without it.

I further find in myself faculties employing modes of thinking peculiar to themselves, to wit, the faculties of imagination and feeling, without which I can easily conceive myself clearly and distinctly as a complete being; while, on the other hand, they cannot be so conceived apart from me, that is without an intelligent substance in which they reside, for [in the notion we have of these faculties, or, to use the language of the Schools] in their formal concept, some kind of intellection is comprised, from which I infer that they are distinct from me as its modes are from a thing. I observe also in me some other faculties such as that of change of position, the assumption of different figures and such like, which cannot be conceived, any more than can the preceding, apart from some substance to which they are attached, and consequently cannot exist without it; but it is very clear that these faculties, if it be true that they exist, must be attached to some corporeal or extended substance, and not to an intelligent substance, since in the clear and distinct conception of these there is some sort of extension found to be present, but no intellection at all. There is certainly further in me a certain passive faculty of perception, that is, of receiving and recognising the ideas of sensible things, but this would be useless to me [and I could in no way avail myself of it], if there were not either in me or in some other thing another active faculty capable of forming and producing these ideas. But this active faculty cannot exist in me [inasmuch as I am a thing that thinks] seeing that it does not presuppose thought, and also that those ideas are often produced in me without my contributing in any way to the same, and often even against my will; it is thus necessarily the case that the faculty resides in some substance different from me in which all the reality which is objectively in the ideas that are produced by this faculty is formally or eminently contained, as I remarked before. And this substance is either a body, that is, a corporeal nature in which there is contained formally [and really] all that which is objectively [and by representation] in those ideas, or it is God Himself, or some other creature more noble than body in which that same is contained eminently. But, since God is no deceiver, it is very manifest that He does not communicate to me these ideas immediately and by Himself, nor yet by the intervention of some creature in which their reality is not formally, but only eminently, contained. For since He has given me no faculty to recognise that this is the case, but, on the other hand, a very great inclination to believe [that they are sent to me or] that they are conveyed to me by corporeal objects, I do not see how He could be defended from the accusation of deceit if these ideas were produced by causes other than corporeal objects. Hence we must allow that corporeal things exist. However, they are perhaps not exactly what we perceive by the senses, since this comprehension by the senses is in many instances very obscure and confused; but we must at least admit that all things which I conceive in them clearly and distinctly, that is to say, all things which, speaking generally, are comprehended in the object of pure mathematics, are truly to be recognised as external objects. . . .

NOTES

1. Or 'form an image' (effingo).
2. Sentire.
3. entendement F., mens L.
4. inspectio.
5. sensus communis.
6. Percipio, F. nous concevons.
7. The French version is followed here as being more explicit. In it 'action de mon esprit' replaces 'mea cogitatio.'
8. In the Latin version 'similitudinem.'
9. Not in the French version.
10. 'Conception,' French version. 'intellectionem,' Latin version.
11. intueor.
12. acie mentis.
13. intellectionem.

Knowledge by Acquaintance and Knowledge by Description

BERTRAND RUSSELL

In the preceding chapter we saw that there are two sorts of knowledge: knowledge of things, and knowledge of truths. In this chapter we shall be concerned exclusively with knowledge of things, of which in turn we shall have to distinguish two kinds. Knowledge of things, when it is of the kind we call knowledge by *acquaintance*, is essentially simpler than any knowledge of truths, and logically independent of knowledge of truths, though it would be rash to assume that human beings ever, in fact, have acquaintance with things without at the same time knowing some truth about them. Knowledge of things by *description*, on the contrary, always involves, as we shall find in the course of the present chapter, some knowledge of truths as its source and ground. But first of all we must make clear what we mean by 'acquaintance' and what we mean by 'description'.

We shall say that we have *acquaintance* with anything of which we are directly aware, without the intermediary of any process of inference or any knowledge of truths. Thus in the presence of my table I am acquainted with the sense-data that make up the appearance of my table—its colour, shape, hardness, smoothness, etc.; all these are things of which I am immediately conscious when I am seeing and touching my table. The particular shade of colour that I am seeing may have many things said about it—I may say that it is brown, that it is rather dark, and so on. But such statements, though they make me know truths *about* the colour, do not make me know the colour itself any better than I did before: so far as concerns knowledge of the colour itself, as opposed to knowledge of truths about it, I know the colour perfectly and completely when I see it, and no further knowledge of it itself is even theoretically possible. Thus the sense-data which make up the appearance of my table are things with which I have acquaintance, things immediately known to me just as they are.

My knowledge of the table as a physical object, on the contrary, is not direct knowledge. Such as it is, it is obtained through acquaintance with the sense-data that make up the appearance of the table. We have seen that it is possible, without absurdity, to doubt whether there is a table at all, whereas it is not possible to doubt the sense-data. My knowledge of the table is of the kind which we shall call 'knowledge by description'. The table is 'the physical object which causes such-and-such sense-data'. This *describes* the table by means of the sense-data. In order to know anything at all about the table, we must know truths connecting it with things with which we have acquaintance: we must know

---

Bertrand Russell (1872-1970) held philosophical appointments in England and in America and is generally regarded as one of the most influential philosophers of the twentieth century.

Reprinted from Bertrand Russell, *The Problems of Philosophy* by permission of the Oxford University Press, Oxford.

that 'such-and-such sense-data are caused by a physical object'. There is no state of mind in which we are directly aware of the table; all our knowledge of the table is really knowledge of *truths*, and the actual thing which is the table is not, strictly speaking, known to us at all. We know a description, and we know that there is just one object to which this description applies, though the object itself is not directly known to us. In such a case, we say that our knowledge of the object is knowledge by description.

All our knowledge, both knowledge of things and knowledge of truths, rests upon acquaintance as its foundation. It is therefore important to consider what kinds of things there are with which we have acquaintance.

Sense-data, as we have already seen, are among the things with which we are acquainted; in fact, they supply the most obvious and striking example of knowledge by acquaintance. But if they were the sole example, our knowledge would be very much more restricted than it is. We should only know what is now present to our senses: we could not know anything about the past—not even that there was a past—nor could we know any truths about our sense-data, for all knowledge of truths, as we shall show, demands acquaintance with things which are of an essentially different character from sense-data, the things which are sometimes called 'abstract ideas', but which we shall call 'universals'. We have therefore to consider acquaintance with other things besides sense-data if we are to obtain any tolerably adequate analysis of our knowledge.

The first extension beyond sense-data to be considered is acquaintance by *memory*. It is obvious that we often remember what we have seen or heard or had otherwise present to our senses, and that in such cases we are still immediately aware of what we remember, in spite of the fact that it appears as past and not as present. This immediate knowledge by memory is the source of all our knowledge concerning the past: without it, there could be no knowledge of the past by inference, since we should never know that there was anything past to be inferred.

The next extension to be considered is acquaintance by *introspection*. We are not only aware of things, but we are often aware of being aware of them. When I see the sun, I am often aware of my seeing the sun; thus 'my seeing the sun' is an object with which I have acquaintance. When I desire food, I may be aware of my desire for food; thus 'my desiring food' is an object with which I am acquainted. Similarly we may be aware of our feeling pleasure or pain, and generally of the events which happen in our minds. This kind of acquaintance, which may be called self-consciousness, is the source of all our knowledge of mental things. It is obvious that it is only what goes on in our own minds that can be thus known immediately. What goes on in the minds of others is known to us through our perception of their bodies, that is, through the sense-data in us which are associated with their bodies. But for our acquaintance with the contents of our own minds, we should be unable to imagine the minds of others, and therefore we could never arrive at the knowledge that they have minds. It seems natural to suppose that self-consciousness is one of the things that distinguish men from animals: animals, we may suppose, though they have acquaintance with sense-data, never become aware of this acquaintance. I do not mean that they *doubt* whether they exist, but that they have never become conscious of the fact that they have sensations and feelings, nor therefore of the fact that they, the subjects of their sensations and feelings, exist.

We have spoken of acquaintance with the contents of our minds as *self*-consciousness, but it is not, of course, consciousness of our *self*: it is consciousness of particular thoughts and feelings. The question whether we are also acquainted with our bare selves, as opposed to particular thoughts and feelings, is a very difficult one, upon which it would be rash to speak positively. When we try to look into ourselves we always seem to come upon some particular thought or feeling, and not upon the 'I' which has the thought or feeling. Nevertheless there are some reasons for thinking that we are acquainted with the 'I', though the acquaintance is hard to disentangle from other things. To make clear what sort of reason there is, let us consider for a moment what our acquaintance with particular thoughts really involves.

When I am acquainted with 'my seeing the sun', it seems plain that I am acquainted with two different things in relation to each other. On the one hand there is the sense-datum which represents the sun to me, on the other hand there is that which sees this sense-datum. All acquaintance, such as my acquaintance with the sense-datum which represents the sun, seems obviously a relation between the person acquainted and the object with which the person is acquainted. When a case of acquaintance is one with which I can be acquainted (as I am acquainted with my acquaintance with the sense-datum representing the sun), it is plain that the person acquainted is myself. Thus, when I am acquainted with my seeing the sun, the whole fact with which I am acquainted is 'Self-acquainted-with-sense-datum'.

Further, we know the truth 'I am acquainted with this sense-datum'. It is hard to see how we could know this truth, or even understand what is meant by it, unless we were acquainted with something which we call 'I'. It does not seem necessary to suppose that we are acquainted with a more or less permanent person, the same to-day as yesterday, but it does seem as though we must be acquainted with that thing, whatever its nature, which sees the sun and has acquaintance with sense-data. Thus, in some sense it would seem we must be acquainted with our Selves as opposed to our particular experiences. But the question is difficult, and complicated arguments can be adduced on either side. Hence, although acquaintance with ourselves seems *probably* to occur, it is not wise to assert that it undoubtedly does occur.

We may therefore sum up as follow what has been said concerning acquaintance with things that exist. We have acquaintance in sensation with the data of the outer senses, and in introspection with the data of what may be called the inner sense—thoughts, feelings, desires, etc.; we have acquaintance in memory with things which have been data either of the outer senses or of the inner sense. Further, it is probable, though not certain, that we have acquaintance with Self, as that which is aware of things or has desires towards things.

In addition to our acquaintance with particular existing things, we also have acquaintance with what we shall call *universals*, that is to say, general ideas, such as *whiteness*, *diversity*, *brotherhood*, and so on. Every complete sentence must contain at least one word which stands for a universal, since all verbs have a meaning which is universal. We shall return to universals later on, in Chapter IX; for the present, it is only necessary to guard against the supposition that whatever we can be acquainted with must be something particular and existent. Awareness of universals is called *conceiving*, and a universal of which we are aware is called a *concept*.

It will be seen that among the objects with which we are acquainted are not included physical objects (as opposed to sense-data), nor other people's minds. These things are known to us by what I call 'knowledge by description', which we must now consider.

By a 'description' I mean any phrase of the form a 'so-and-so' or the 'so-and-so'. A phrase of the form a 'so-and-so' I shall call an 'ambiguous' description; a phrase of the form 'the so-and-so' (in the singular) I shall call a 'definite' description. Thus 'a man' is an ambiguous description, and 'the man with the iron mask' is a definite description. There are various problems connected with ambiguous descriptions, but I pass them by, since they do not directly concern the matter we are discussing, which is the nature of our knowledge concerning objects in cases where we know that there is an object answering to a definite description, though we are not *acquainted* with any such object. This is a matter which is concerned exclusively with *definite* descriptions. I shall therefore, in the sequel, speak simply of 'descriptions' when I mean 'definite descriptions'. Thus a description will mean any phrase of the form 'the so-and-so' in the singular.

We shall say that an object is 'known by description' when we know that it is the 'so-and-so', i.e. when we know that there is one object, and no more, having a certain property; and it will generally be implied that we do not have knowledge of the same object by acquaintance. We know that the man with the iron mask existed, and many propositions are known about him; but we do not know who he was. We know that the candidate who gets the most votes will be elected, and in this case we are very likely also acquainted (in the only sense in which one can be acquainted with some one else) with the man who is, in fact, the candidate who will get most votes; but we do not know which of the candidates he is, i.e. we do not know any proposition of the form 'A is the candidate who will get most votes' where A is one of the candidates by name. We shall say that we have 'merely descriptive knowledge' of the so-and-so when, although we know that the so-and-so exists, and although we may possibly be acquainted with the object which is, in fact, the so-and-so, yet we do not know any proposition '*a* is the so-and-so', where *a* is something with which we are acquainted.

When we say the 'so-and-so exists', we mean that there is just one object which is the so-and-so. The proposition '*a* is the so-and-so' means that *a* has the property so-and-so, and nothing else has. 'Mr. A. is the Unionist candidate for this constituency' means 'Mr. A. is a Unionist candidate for this constituency, and no one else is'. 'The Unionist candidate for this constituency exists' means 'some one is a Unionist candidate for this constituency, and no one else is'. Thus, when we are acquainted with an object which is the so-and-so, we know that the so-and-so exists; but we may know that the so-and-so exists when we are not acquainted with any object which we know to be the so-and-so, and even when we are acquainted with any object which, in fact, is the so-and-so.

Common words, even proper names, are usually really descriptions. That is to say, the thought in the mind of a person using a proper name correctly can generally only be expressed explicitly if we replace the proper name by a description. Moreover, the description required to express the thought will vary for different people, or for the same person at different times. The only thing constant (so long as the name is rightly used) is the object to which the name applies. But so long as this remains constant, the particular description involved usually makes no difference to the truth or falsehood of the proposition in which the name appears.

Let us take some illustrations. Suppose some statement made about Bismarck. Assuming that there is such a thing as direct acquaintance with oneself, Bismarck himself might have used his name directly to designate the particular person with whom he was acquainted. In this case, if he made a judgement about himself, he himself might be a constituent of the judgement. Here the proper name has the direct use which it always wishes to have, as simply standing for a certain object, and not for a description of the object. But if a person who knew Bismarck made a judgement about him, the case is different. What this person was acquainted with were certain sense-data which he connected (rightly, we will suppose) with Bismarck's body. His body, as a physical object, and still more his mind, were only known as the body and the mind connected with these sense-data. That is, they were known by description. It is, of course, very much a matter of chance which characteristics of a man's appearance will come into a friend's mind when he thinks of him; thus the description actually in the friend's mind is accidental. The essential point is that he knows that the various descriptions all apply to the same entity, in spite of not being acquainted with the entity in question.

When we, who did not know Bismarck, make a judgement about him, the description in our minds will probably be some more or less vague mass of historical knowledge—far more, in most cases, than is required to identify him. But, for the sake of illustration, let us assume that we think of him as 'the first Chancellor of the German Empire'. Here all the words are abstract except 'German'. The word 'German' will, again, have different meanings for different people. To some it will recall travels in Germany, to some the look of Germany on the map, and so on. But if we are to obtain a description which we know to be applicable, we shall be compelled, at some point, to bring in a reference to a particular with which we are acquainted. Such reference is involved in any mention of past, present, and future (as opposed to definite dates), or of here and there, or of what others have told us. Thus it would seem that, in some way or other, a description known to be applicable to a particular must involve some reference to a particular with which we are acquainted, if our knowledge about the thing described is not to be merely what follows *logically* from the description. For example, 'the most longlived of men' is a description involving only universals, which must apply to some man, but we can make no judgements concerning this man which involve knowledge about him beyond what the description gives. If, however, we say, 'The first Chancellor of the German Empire was an astute diplomatist', we can only be assured of the truth of our judgement in virtue of something with which we are acquainted—usually a testimony heard or read. Apart from the information we convey to others, apart from the fact about the actual Bismarck, which gives importance to our judgement, the thought we really have contains the one or more particulars involved, and otherwise consists wholly of concepts.

All names of places—London, England, Europe, the Earth, the Solar System—similarly involve, when used, descriptions which start from some one or more particulars with which we are acquainted. I suspect that even the Universe, as considered by metaphysics, involves such a connexion with particulars. In logic, on the contrary, where we are concerned not merely with what does exist, but with whatever might or could exist or be, no reference to actual particulars is involved.

It would seem that, when we make a statement about something only known by description, we often *intend* to make our statement, not in the form involving the description, but about the actual thing described. That is to say, when we say anything about Bismarck, we should like, if we could, to make the judgement which Bismarck alone can make, namely, the judgement of which he himself is a constituent. In this we are necessarily defeated, since the actual Bismarck is unknown to us. But we know that there is an object B, called Bismarck, and that B was an astute diplomatist. We can thus *describe* the proposition we should like to affirm, namely, 'B was an astute diplomatist', where B is the object which was Bismarck. If we are describing Bismarck as 'the first Chancellor of the German Empire', the proposition we should like to affirm may be described as 'the proposition asserting, concerning the actual object which was the first Chancellor of the German Empire, that this object was an astute diplomatist'. What enables us to communicate in spite of the varying descriptions we employ is that we know there is a true proposition concerning the actual Bismarck, and that however we may vary the description (so long as the description is correct) the proposition described is still the same. This proposition, which is described and is known to be true, is what interests us; but we are not acquainted with the proposition itself, and do not know *it*, though we know it is true.

It will be seen that there are various stages in the removal from acquaintance with particulars: there is Bismarck to people who knew him; Bismarck to those who only know of him through history; the man with the iron mask; the longest-lived of men. These are progressively further removed from acquaintance with particulars; the first comes as near to acquaintance as is possible in regard to another person; in the second, we shall still be said to know 'who Bismarck was'; in the third, we do not know who was the man with the iron mask, though we can know many propositions about him which are not logically deducible from the fact that he wore an iron mask; in the fourth, finally, we know nothing beyond what is logically deducible from the definition of the man. There is a similar hierarchy in the region of universals. Many universals, like many particulars, are only known to us by description. But here, as in the case of particulars, knowledge concerning what is known by description is ultimately reducible to knowledge concerning what is known by acquaintance.

The fundamental principle in the analysis of propositions containing descriptions is this: *Every proposition which we can understand must be composed wholly of constituents with which we are acquainted.*

We shall not at this stage attempt to answer all the objections which may be urged against this fundamental principle. For the present, we shall merely point out that, in some way or other, it must be possible to meet these objections, for it is scarcely conceivable that we can make a judgement or entertain a supposition without knowing what it is that we are judging or supposing about. We must attach *some* meaning to the words we use, if we are to speak significantly and not utter mere noise; and the meaning we attach to our words must be something with which we are acquainted. Thus when, for example, we make a statement about Julius Caesar, it is plain that Julius Caesar himself is not before our minds, since we are not acquainted with him. We have in mind some *description* of Julius Caesar: 'the man who was assassinated on the Ides of March', 'the founder of the Roman Empire', or, perhaps, merely 'the man whose name was *Julius Caesar*'. (In this last description, *Julius Caesar* is a noise or shape with which we are acquainted.) Thus our statement does not mean quite what it seems to mean, but means something involving, instead of Julius Caesar, some description of him which is composed wholly of particulars and universals with which we are acquainted.

The chief importance of knowledge by description is that it enables us to pass beyond the limits of our private experience. In spite of the fact that we can only know truths which are wholly composed of terms which we have experienced in acquaintance, we can yet have knowledge by description of things which we have never experienced. In view of the very narrow range of our immediate experience, this result is vital, and until it is understood, much of our knowledge must remain mysterious and therefore doubtful.

Of the Sceptical and Other Systems of Philosophy

DAVID HUME

I

OF SCEPTICISM WITH REGARD TO REASON

In all demonstrative sciences the rules are certain and infallible; but when we apply them, our fallible and uncertain faculties are very apt to depart from them, and fall into error. We must, therefore, in every reasoning form a new judgment, as a check or controul on our first judgment or belief; and must enlarge our view to comprehend a kind of history of all the instances, wherein our understanding has deceiv'd us, compar'd with those, wherein its testimony was just and true. Our reason must be consider'd as a kind of cause, of which truth is the natural effect; but such-a-one as by the irruption of other causes, and by the inconstancy of our mental powers, may frequently be prevented. By this means all knowledge degenerates into probability; and this probability is greater or less, according to our experience of the veracity or deceitfulness of our understanding, and according to the simplicity of intricacy of the question.

There is no Algebraist nor Mathematician so expert in his science, as to place entire confidence in any truth immediately upon his discovery of it, or regard it as any thing, but a mere probability. Every time he runs over his proofs, his confidence encreases; but still more by the approbation of his friends; and is rais'd to its utmost perfection by the universal assent and applauses of the learned world. Now 'tis evident, that this gradual encrease of assurance is nothing but the addition of new probabilities, and is deriv'd from the constant union of causes and effects, according to past experience and observation.

In accompts of any length or importance, Merchants seldom trust to the infallible certainty of numbers for their security; but by the artificial structure of the accompts, produce a probability beyond what is deriv'd from the skill and experience of the accomptant. For that is plainly of itself some degree of probability; tho' uncertain and variable, according to the degrees of his experience and length of the accompt. Now as none will maintain, that our assurance in a long numeration exceeds probability, I may safely affirm, that there scarce is any proposition concerning numbers, of which we can have a fuller security. For 'tis easily possible, by gradually diminishing the numbers, to reduce the longest series of addition to the most simple question, which can be form'd, to an addition of two single numbers; and upon this supposition we shall find it impracticable to shew the precise limits of knowledge and of probability, or discover that particular number, at which the one ends and the other begins. But knowledge and probability are of such contrary and disagreeing natures, that they cannot well run

---

David Hume (1711-1776) is probably the principal representative of the "British empiricist" tradition in philosophy.

From Hume's *A Treatise of Human Nature* (1739).

insensibly into each other, and that because they will not divide, but must be either entirely present, or entirely absent. Besides, if any single addition were certain, every one wou'd be so, and consequently the whole or total sum; unless the whole can be different from all its parts. I had almost said, that this was certain; but I reflect, that it must reduce *itself*, as well as every other reasoning, and from knowledge degenerate into probability.

Since therefore all knowledge resolves itself into probability, and becomes at last of the same nature with that evidence, which we employ in common life, we must now examine this latter species of reasoning, and see on what foundation it stands.

In every judgment, which we can form concerning probability, as well as concerning knowledge, we ought always to correct the first judgment, deriv'd from the nature of the object, by another judgment, deriv'd from the nature of the understanding. 'Tis certain a man of solid sense and long experience ought to have, and usually has, a greater assurance in his opinions, than one that is foolish and ignorant, and that our sentiments have different degrees of authority, even with ourselves, in proportion to the degrees of our reason and experience. In the man of the best sense and longest experience, this authority is never entire; since even such-a-one must be conscious of many errors in the past, and must still dread the like for the future. Here then arises a new species of probability to correct and regulate the first, and fix its just standard and proportion. As demonstration is subject to the controul of probability, so is probability liable to a new correction by a reflex act of the mind, wherein the nature of our understanding, and our reasoning from the first probability become our objects.

Having thus found in every probability, beside the original uncertainty inherent in the subject, a new uncertainty deriv'd from the weakness of that faculty, which judges, and having adjusted these two together, we are oblig'd by our reason to add a new doubt deriv'd from the possibility of error in the estimation we make of the truth and fidelity of our faculties. This is a doubt, which immediately occurs to us, and of which, if we wou'd closely pursue our reason, we cannot avoid giving a decision. But this decision, tho' it shou'd be favourable to our preceeding judgment, being founded only on probability, must weaken still further our first evidence, and must itself be weaken'd by a fourth doubt of the same kind, and so on *in infinitum*; till at last there remain nothing of the original probability, however great we may suppose it to have been, and however small the diminution by every new uncertainty. No finite object can subsist under a decrease repeated *in infinitum*; and even the vastest quantity, which can enter into human imagination, must in this manner be reduc'd to nothing. Let our first belief be never so strong, it must infallibly perish by passing thro' so many new examinations, of which each diminishes somewhat of its force and vigour. When I reflect on the natural fallibility of my judgment, I have less confidence in my opinions, than when I only consider the objects concerning which I reason; and when I proceed still farther, to turn the scrutiny against every successive estimation I make of my faculties, all the rules of logic require a continual diminution, and at last a total extinction of belief and evidence.

Shou'd it here be ask'd me, whether I sincerely assent to this argument, which I seem to take such pains to inculcate, and whether I be really one of those sceptics, who hold that all is uncertain, and that our judgment is not in *any* thing possest of *any* measures of truth and falshood; I shou'd reply, that this question is entirely superfluous, and that neither I, nor any other person was ever sincerely and constantly of that opinion. Nature, by an absolute and uncontroulable necessity has determin'd us to judge as well as to breathe and feel; nor can we any more forbear viewing certain objects in a stronger and fuller light, upon account of their customary connexion with a present impression, than we can hinder ourselves from thinking as long as we are awake, or seeing the surrounding bodies, when we turn our eyes towards them in broad sunshine. Whoever has taken the pains to refute the cavils of this *total* scepticism, has really disputed without an antagonist, and endeavour'd by arguments to establish a faculty, which nature has antecedently implanted in the mind, and render'd unavoidable.

My intention then in displaying so carefully the arguments of that fantastic sect, is only to make the reader sensible of the truth of my hypothesis, *that all our reasonings concerning causes and effects are deriv'd from nothing but custom; and that belief is more properly an act of the sensitive, than of the cogitative part of our natures*. I have here prov'd, that the very same principles, which make us form a decision upon any subject, and correct that decision by the consideration of our genius and capacity, and of the situation of our mind, when we examin'd that subject; I say, I have prov'd, that these same principles, when carry'd farther, and apply'd to every new reflex judgment, must, by continually diminishing the original evidence, at last reduce it to nothing, and utterly subvert all belief and opinion. If belief, therefore, were a simple act of the thought, without any peculiar manner of conception, or the addition of a force and vivacity, it must infallibly destroy itself, and in every case terminate in a total suspense of judgment. But as experience will sufficiently convince any one, who thinks it worth while to try, that tho' he can find no error in the foregoing arguments, yet he still continues to believe, and think, and reason as usual, he may safely conclude, that his reasoning and belief is some sensation or peculiar manner of conception, which 'tis impossible for mere ideas and reflections to destroy.

But here, perhaps, it may be demanded, how it happens, even upon my hypothesis, that these arguments above-explain'd produce not a total suspense of judgment, and after what manner the mind ever retains a degree of assurance in any subject? For as these new probabilities, which by their repetition perpetually diminish the original evidence, are founded on the very same principles, whether of thought or sensation, as the primary judgment, it may seem unavoidable, that in either case they must equally subvert it, and by the opposition, either of contrary thoughts or sensations, reduce the mind to a total uncertainty. I suppose, there is some question propos'd to me, and that after revolving over the impressions of my memory and senses, and carrying my thoughts from them to such objects, as are commonly conjoin'd with them, I feel a stronger and more forcible conception on the one side, than on the other. This strong conception forms my first decision. I suppose, that afterwards I examine my judgment itself, and observing from experience, that 'tis sometimes just and sometimes erroneous, I consider it as regulated by contrary principles or causes, of which some lead to truth, and some to error; and in ballancing these contrary causes, I diminish by a new probability the assurance of my first decision. This new probability is liable to the same diminution as the foregoing, and so on, *in infinitum*. 'Tis therefore demanded, *how it happens, that even after all we retain a degree of belief, which is sufficient for our prupose, either in philosophy or common life*.

I answer, that after the first and second decision; as the action of the mind becomes forc'd and unnatural, and the ideas faint and obscure; tho' the principles of judgment, and the ballancing of opposite causes be the same as at the very beginning; yet their influence on the imagination, and the vigour they add to, or diminish from the thought, is by no means equal. Where the mind reaches not its objects with easiness and facility, the same principles have not the same effect as in a more natural conception of the ideas; nor does the imagination feel a sensation, which holds any proportion with that which arises from its common judgments and opinions. The attention is on the stretch: The posture of the mind is uneasy; and the spirits being diverted from their natural course, are not govern'd in their movements by the same laws, at least not to the same degree, as when they flow in their usual channel.

If we desire similar instances, 'twill not be very difficult to find them. The present subject of metaphysics will supply us abundantly. The same argument, which wou'd have been esteem'd convincing in a reasoning concerning history or politics, has little or no influence in these abstruser subjects, even tho' it be perfectly comprehended; and that because there is requir'd a study and an effort of thought, in order to its being comprehended: And this effort of thought disturbs the operation of our sentiments, on which the belief depends. The case is the same in other subjects. The straining of the imagination always hinders the regular flowing of the passions and sentiments. A tragic poet, that wou'd represent his heroes as very ingenious and witty in their misfortunes, wou'd never touch the passions. As the emotions of the soul prevent any subtile reasoning and reflection, so these latter actions of the mind are equally prejudicial to the former. The mind, as well as the body, seems to be endow'd with a certain precise degree of force and activity, which it never employs in one action, but at the expence of all the rest. This is more evidently true, where the actions are of quite different natures; since in that case the force of the mind is not only diverted, but even the disposition chang'd, so as to render us incapable of a sudden transition from one action to the other, and still more of performing both at once. No wonder, then, the conviction, which arises from a subtile reasoning, diminishes in proportion to the efforts, which the imagination makes to enter into the reasoning, and to conceive it in all its parts. Belief, being a lively conception, can never be entire, where it is not founded on something natural and easy.

This I take to be the true state of the question, and cannot approve of that expeditious way, which some take with the sceptics, to reject at once all their arguments without enquiry or examination. If the sceptical reasonings be strong, say they, 'tis a proof, that reason may have some force and authority: if weak, they can never be sufficient to invalidate all the conclusions of our understanding. This argument is not just; because of the sceptical reasonings, were it possible for them to exist, and were they not destroy'd by their subtility, wou'd be successively both strong and weak, according to the successive dispositions of the mind. Reason first appears in possession of the throne, prescribing laws, and imposing maxims, with an absolute sway and authority. Her enemy, therefore, is oblig'd to take shelter under her protection, and by making use of rational arguments to prove the fallaciousness and imbecility of reason, produces, in a manner, a patent under her hand and seal. This patent has at first an authority, proportion'd to the present and immediate authority of reason, from which it is deriv'd. But as it is suppos'd to be contradictory to reason, it gradually diminishes the force of that governing power, and its own at the same time; till at last they both vanish away into nothing, by a regular and just diminution. The sceptical and dogmatical reasons are of the same kind, tho' contrary in their operation and tendency; so that where the latter is strong, it has an enemy of equal force in the former to encounter; and as their forces were at first equal, they still continue so, as long as either of them subsists; nor does one of them lose any force in the contest, without taking as much from its antagonist. 'Tis happy, therefore, that nature breaks the force of all sceptical arguments in time, and keeps them from having any considerable influence on the understanding. Were we to trust entirely to their self-destruction, that can never take place, 'till they have first subverted all conviction, and have totally destroy'd human reason.

II

OF SCEPTICISM WITH REGARD TO THE SENSES

Thus the sceptic still continues to reason and believe, even tho' he asserts, that he cannot defend his reason by reason; and by the same rule he must assent to the principle concerning the existence of body, tho' he cannot pretend by any arguments of philosophy to maintain its veracity. Nature has not left this to his choice, and has doubtless esteem'd it an affair of too great importance to be trusted to our uncertain reasonings and speculations. We may well ask, *What causes induce us to believe in the existence of body?* but 'tis in vain to ask, *Whether there be body or not?* That is a point, which we must take for granted in all our reasonings.

The subject, then, of our present enquiry is concerning the *causes* which induce us to belive in the existence of body: And my reasonings on this head I shall begin with a distinction, which at first sight may seem superfluous, but which will contribute very much to the perfect understanding of what follows. We ought to examine apart those two questions, which are commonly confounded together, *viz*. Why we attribute a CONTINU'D existence to objects, even when they are not present to the senses; and why we suppose them to have an existence DISTINCT from the mind and perception. Under this last head I comprehend their situation as well as relations, their *external* position as well as the *independence* of their existence and operation. These two questions concerning the continu'd and distinct existence of body are intimately connected together. For if the objects of our senses continue to exist, even when they are not perceiv'd, their existence is of course independent of and distinct from the perception; and *vice versa*, if their existence be independent of the perception and distinct from it, they must continue to exist, even tho' they be not perceiv'd. But tho' the decision of the one question decides the other; yet that we may the more easily discover the principles of human nature, from whence the decision arises, we shall carry along with us this distinction, and shall consider, whether it be the *senses*, *reason*, or the *imagination*, that produces the opinion of a *continu'd* or of a *distinct* existence. These are the only questions, that are intelligible on the present subject. For as to the notion of external existence, when taken for something specifically different from our perceptions, we have already shewn its absurdity.

To begin with the SENSES, 'tis evident these faculties are incapable of giving rise to the notion of the *continu'd* existence of their objects, after they no longer appear to the senses. For that is a contradiction in terms, and supposes that the senses continue to operate, even after they have ceas'd all manner of operation. These faculties, therefore, if they have any influence in the present case, must produce the opinion of a distinct, not of a continu'd existence; and in order to that, must present their impressions either as images and representations, or as these very distinct and external existences.

That our senses offer not their impressions as the images of something *distinct*, or *independent*, and *external*, is evident; because they convey to us nothing but a single perception, and never give us the least intimation of any thing beyond. A single perception can never produce the idea of a double existence, but by some inference either of the reason or imagination. When the mind looks farther than what immediately appears to it, its conclusions can never be put to the account of the senses; and it certainly looks farther, when from a single perception it infers a double existence, and supposes the relations of resemblance and causation betwixt them.

If our senses, therefore, suggest any idea of distinct existences, they must convey the impressions as those very existences, by a kind of fallacy and illusion. Upon this head we may observe, that all sensations are felt by the mind, such as they really are, and that when we doubt, whether they present themselves as distinct objects, or as mere impressions, the difficulty is not concerning their nature, but concerning their relations and situation. Now if the senses presented our impressions as external to, and independent of ourselves, both the objects and ourselves must be obvious to our senses, otherwise they cou'd not be compar'd by these faculties. The difficulty, then, is how far we are *ourselves* the objects of our senses.

'Tis certain there is no question in philosophy more abstruse than that concerning identity, and the nature of the uniting principle, which constitutes a person. So far from being able by our senses merely to determine this question, we must have recourse to the most profound metaphysics to give a satisfactory answer to it; and in common life 'tis evident these ideas of self and person are never very fix'd nor determinate. 'Tis absurd, therefore, to imagine the senses can ever distinguish betwixt ourselves and external objects.

Add to this, that every impression, external and internal, passions, affections, sensations, pains and pleasures, are originally on the same footing; and that whatever other differences we may observe among them, they appear all of them, in their true colours, as impressions or perceptions. And indeed, if we consider the matter aright, 'tis scarce possible it shou'd be otherwise, nor is it conceivable that our senses shou'd be more capable of deceiving us in the situation and relations, than in the nature of our impressions. For since all actions and sensations of the mind are known to us by consciousness, they must necessarily appear in every particular what they are, and be what they appear. Every thing that enters the mind, being in *reality* as the perception, 'tis impossible any thing shou'd to *feeling* appear different. This were to suppose, that even where we are most intimately conscious, we might be mistaken.

But not to lose time in examining, whether 'tis possible for our senses to deceive us, and represent our perceptions as distinct from ourselves, that is as *external* to and *independent* of us; let us consider whether they really do so, and whether this error proceeds from an immediate sensation, or from some other causes.

To begin with the question concerning *external* existence, it may perhaps be said, that setting aside the metaphysical question of the identity of a thinking substance, our own body evidently belongs to us; and as several impressions appear exterior to the body, we suppose them also exterior to ourselves. The paper, on which I write at present, is beyond my hand. The table is beyond the paper. The walls of the chamber beyond the table. And in casting my eye towards the window, I perceive a great extent of fields and buildings beyond my chamber. From all this it may be infer'd, that no other faculty is requir'd, beside the senses, to convince us of the external existence of body. But to prevent this inference, we need only weigh the three following considerations. *First*, That, properly speaking, 'tis not our body we perceive, when we regard our limbs and members, but certain impressions, which enter by the senses; so that the ascribing a real and corporeal existence to these impressions, or to their objects, is an act of the mind as difficult to explain, as that which we examine at present. *Secondly*, Sounds, and tastes, and smells, tho' commonly regarded by the mind as continu'd independent qualities, appear not to have any existence in extension, and consequently cannot appear to the senses as situated externally to the body. The reason, why we ascribe a place to them, shall be consider'd afterwards. *Thirdly*, Even our sight informs us not of distance or outness (so to speak) immediately and without a certain reasoning and experience, as is acknowledg'd by the most rational philosophers.

As to the *independency* of our perceptions on ourselves, this can never be an object of the senses; but any opinion we form concerning it, must be deriv'd from experience and observation: And we shall see afterwards, that our conclusions from experience are far from being favourable to the doctrine of the independency of our perceptions. Meanwhile we may observe that when we talk of real distinct existences, we have commonly more in our eye their independency than external situation in place, and think an object has a sufficient reality, when its Being is uninterrupted, and independent of the incessant revolutions, which we are conscious of in ourselves.

Thus to resume what I have said concerning the senses; they give us no notion of continu'd existence, because they cannot operate beyond the extent, in which they really operate. They as little produce the opinion of a distinct existence, because they neither can offer it to the mind as represented, nor as original. To offer it as represented, they must present both an object and an image. To make it appear as original, they must convey a falshood; and this falshood must lie in the relations and situation: In order to which they must be able to compare the object with ourselves; and even in that case they do not, nor is it possible they shou'd, deceive us. We may, therefore, conclude with certainty, that the opinion of a continu'd and of a distinct existence never arises from the senses.

To confirm this we may observe, that there are three different kinds of impressions convey'd by the senses. The first are those of the figure, bulk, motion and solidity of bodies. The second those of colours, tastes, smells, sounds, heat and cold. The third are the pains and pleasures, that arise from the application of objects to our bodies, as by the cutting of our flesh with steel, and such like. Both philosophers and the vulgar suppose the first of these to have a distinct continu'd existence. The vulgar only regard the second as on the same footing. Both philosophers and the vulgar, again, esteem the third to be merely perceptions; and consequently interrupted and dependent beings.

Now 'tis evident, that, whatever may be our philosophical opinion, colours, sounds, heat and cold, as far as appears to the senses, exist after the same manner with motion and solidity, and that the difference we make betwixt them in this respect, arises not from the mere perception. So strong is the prejudice for the distinct continu'd existence of the former qualities, that when the contrary opinion is advanc'd by modern philosophers, people imagine they can almost refute it from their feeling and experience, and that their very senses contradict this philosophy. 'Tis also evident, that colours, sounds, &c. are originally on the same footing with the pain that arises from steel, and pleasure that proceeds from a fire; and that the difference betwixt them is founded neither on perception nor reason, but on the imagination. For as they are confest to be, both of them, nothing but perceptions arising from the particular configurations and motions of the parts of body, wherein possibly can their difference consist? Upon the whole, then, we may conclude, that as far as the senses are judges, all perceptions are the same in the manner of their existence.

We may also observe in this instance of sounds and colours, that we can attribute a distinct continu'd existence to objects without ever consulting REASON, or weighing our opinions by any philosophical principles. And indeed, whatever convincing arguments philosophers may fancy they can produce to establish the belief of objects independent of the mind, 'tis obvious these arguments are known but to very few, and that 'tis not by them, that children, peasants, and the greatest part of mankind are induc'd to attribute objects to some impressions, and deny them to others. Accordingly we find, that all the conclusions, which the vulgar form on this head, are directly contrary to those, which are confirm'd by philosophy. For philosophy informs us, that every thing, which appears to the mind, is nothing but a perception, and is interrupted, and dependent on the mind; whereas the vulgar confound perceptions and objects, and attribute a distinct continu'd existence to the very things they feel or see. This sentiment, then, as it is entirely unreasonable, must proceed from some other faculty than the understanding. To which we may add, that as long as we take our perceptions and objects to be the same, we can never infer the existence of the one from that of the other, nor form any argument from the relation of cause and effect; which is the only one that can assure us of matter of fact. Even after we distinguish our perceptions from our objects, 'twill appear presently, that we are still incapable of reasoning from the existence of one to that of the other: So that upon the whole our reason neither does, nor is it possible it ever shou'd, upon any supposition, give us an assurance of the continu'd and distinct existence of body. That opinion must be entirely owing to the IMAGINATION: which must now be the subject of our enquiry.

Since all impressions are internal and perishing existences, and appear as such, the notion of their distinct and continu'd existence must arise from a concurrence of some of their qualities with the qualities of the imagination; and since this notion does not extend to all of them, it must arise from certain qualities peculiar to some impressions. 'Twill therefore be easy for us to discover these qualities by a comparison of the impressions, to which we attribute a distinct and continu'd existence, with those, which we regard as internal and perishing.

We may observe, then, that 'tis neither upon account of the involuntariness of certain impressions, as is commonly suppos'd, nor of their superior force and violence, that we attribute to them a reality, and continu'd existence, which we refuse to others, that are voluntary or feeble. For 'tis evident our pains and pleasures, our passions and affections, which we never suppose to have any existence beyond our perception, operate with greater violence, and are equally involuntary, as the impressions of figure and extension, colour and sound, which we suppose to be permanent beings. The heat of a fire, when moderate, is suppos'd to exist in the fire; but the pain, which it causes upon a near approach, is not taken to have any being except in the perception.

These vulgar opinions, then, being rejected, we must search for some other hypothesis, by which we may discover those peculiar qualities in our impressions, which makes us attribute to them a distinct and continu'd existence.

After a little examination, we shall find, that all those objects, to which we attribute a continu'd existence, have a peculiar *constancy*, which distinguishes them from the impressions, whose existence depends upon our perception. Those mountains, and houses, and trees, which lie at present under my eye, have always appear'd to me in the same order; and when I lose sight of them by shutting my eyes or turning my head, I soon after find them return upon me without the least alteration. My bed and table, my books and papers, present themselves in the same uniform manner, and change not upon account of any interruption in my seeing or perceiving them. This is the case with all the impressions, whose objects are suppos'd to have an external existence; and is the case with no other impressions, whether gentle or violent, voluntary or involuntary.

This constancy, however, is not so perfect as not to admit of very considerable exceptions. Bodies often change their position and qualities, and after a little absence or interruption may become hardly knowable. But here 'tis observable, that even in these changes they preserve a *coherence*, and have a regular dependence on each other; which is the foundation of a kind of reasoning from causation, and produces the opinion of their continu'd existence. When I return to my chamber after an hour's absence, I find not my fire in the same situation, in which I left it: But then I am accustom'd in other instances to see a like alteration produc'd in a like time, whether I am present or absent, near or remote. This coherence, therefore, in their changes in one of the characteristics of external objects, as well as their constancy.

Having found that the opinion of the continu'd existence of body depends on the COHERENCE and CONSTANCY of certain impressions, I now proceed to examine after what manner these qualities give rise to so extraordinary an opinion. To begin with the coherence; we may observe, that tho' those internal impressions, which we regard as fleeting and perishing, have also a certain coherence or regularity in their appearances, yet 'tis of somewhat a different nature, from that which we discover in bodies. Our passions are found by experience to have a mutual connexion with and dependance on each other; but on no occasion is it necessary to suppose, that they have existed and operated, when they were not perceiv'd, in order to preserve the same dependance and connexion, of which we have had experience. The case is not the same with relation to external objects. Those require a continu'd existence, or otherwise lose, in a great measure, the regularity of their operation. I am here seated in my chamber with my face to the fire; and all the objects, that strike my senses, are contain'd in a few yards around me. My memory, indeed, informs me of the existence of many objects; but then this information extends not beyond their past existence, nor do either my senses or memory give any testimony to the continuance of their being. When therefore I am thus seated, and revolve over these thoughts, I hear on a sudden a noise as of a door turning upon its hinges; and a little after see a porter, who advances towards me. This gives occasion to many new reflexions and reasonings. First, I never have observ'd, that this noise cou'd proceed from anything but the motion of a door; and therefore conclude, that the present phænomenon is a contradiction to all past experience, unless the door, which I remember on t'other side the chamber, be still in being. Again, I have always found, that a human body was possest of a quality, which I call gravity, and which hinders it from mounting in the air, as this porter must have done to arrive at my chamber, unless the stairs I remember be not annihilated by my absence. But this is not all. I receive a letter, which upon opening it I perceive by the hand-writing and subscription to have come from a friend, who says he is two hundred leagues distant. 'Tis evident I can never account for this phænomenon, conformable to my experience in other instances, without spreading out in my mind the whole sea and continent between us, and supposing the effects and continu'd existence of posts and ferries, according to my memory and observation. To consider these phænomena of the porter and letter in a certain light, they are contradictions to common experience, and may be regarded as objections to those maxims, which we form concerning the connexions of causes and effects. I am accustom'd to hear such a sound, and see such an object in motion at the same time. I have not receiv'd in this particular instance both these perceptions. These observations are contrary, unless I suppose that the door still remains, and that it was open'd without my perceiving it: And this supposition, which was at first entirely arbitrary and hypothetical, acquires a force and evidence by its being the only one, upon which I can reconcile these contradictions. There is scarce a moment of my life, wherein there is not a similar instance presented to me, and I have not occasion to suppose the continu'd existence of objects, in order to connect their past and present appearances, and give them such an union with each other, as I have found by experience to be suitable to their particular natures and circumstances. Here then I am naturally led to regard the world, as something real and durable, and as preserving its existence, even when it is no longer present to my perception.

But tho' this conclusion from the coherence of appearances may seem to be of the same nature with our reasonings concerning causes and effects; as being deriv'd from custom, and regulated by past experience; we shall find upon examination, that they are at the bottom considerably different from each other, and that this inference arises from the understanding, and from custom in an indirect and oblique manner. For 'twill readily be allow'd, that since nothing is ever really present to the mind, besides its own perceptions, 'tis not only impossible, that any habit shou'd ever be acquir'd otherwise than by the regular succession of these perceptions, but also that any habit shou'd ever exceed that degree of regularity. Any degree, therefore, of regularity in our perceptions, can never be a foundation for us to infer a greater degree of regularity in some objects, which are not perceiv'd; since this supposes a contradiction, *viz.* a habit acquir'd by what was never present to the mind. But 'tis evident, that whenever we infer the continu'd existence of the objects of sense from their coherence, and the frequency of their union, 'tis in order to bestow on the objects a greater regularity than what is observ'd in our mere perceptions. We remark a connexion betwixt two kinds of objects in their past appearance to the senses, but are not able to observe this connexion to be perfectly constant, since the turning about of our head, or the shutting of our eyes is able to break it. What then do we suppose in this case, but that these objects still continue their usual connexion, notwithstanding their apparent interruption, and that the irregular appearances are join'd by something, of which we are insensible? But as all reasoning concerning matters of fact arises only from custom, and custom can only be the effect of repeated perceptions, the extending of custom and reasoning beyond the perceptions can never be the direct and natural effect of the constant repetition and connexion, but must arise from the co-operation of some other principles.

I have already observ'd, in examining the foundation of mathematics, that the imagination, when set into any train of thinking, is apt to continue, even when its object fails it, and like a galley put in motion by the oars, carries on its course without any new impulse. This I have assign'd for the reason, why, after considering several loose standards of equality, and correcting them by each other, we proceed to imagine so correct and exact a standard of that relation, as is not liable to the least error or variation. The same principle makes us easily entertain this opinion of the continu'd existence of body. Objects have a certain coherence even as they appear to our senses; but this coherence is much greater and more uniform, if we suppose the objects to have a continu'd existence; and as the mind is once in the train of observing an uniformity among objects, it naturally continues, till it renders the uniformity as compleat as possible. The simple supposition of their continu'd existence suffices for this purpose, and gives us a notion of a much greater regularity among objects, than what they have when we look no farther than our senses.

But whatever force we may ascribe to this principle, I am afraid 'tis too weak to support alone so vast an edifice, as is that of the continu'd existence of all external bodies; and that we must join the *constancy* of their appearance to the *coherence*, in order to give a satisfactory account of that opinion. As the explication of this will lead me into a considerable compass of very profound reasoning; I think it proper, in order to avoid confusion, to give a short sketch or abridgment of my system, and afterwards draw out all its parts in their full compass. This inference from the constancy of our perceptions, like the precedent from their coherence, gives rise to the opinion of the *continu'd* existence of body, which is prior to that of its *distinct* existence, and produces that latter principle.

When we have been accustom'd to observe a constancy in certain impressions, and have found, that the perception of the sun or ocean, for instance, returns upon us after an absence or annihilation with like parts and in a like order, as at its first appearance, we are not apt to regard these interrupted perceptions as different, (which they really are) but on the contrary consider them as individually the same, upon account of their resemblance. But as this interruption of their existence is contrary to their perfect identity, and makes us regard the first impression as annihilated, and the second as newly created, we find ourselves somewhat at a loss, and are involv'd in a kind of contradiction. In order to free ourselves from this difficulty, we disguise, as much as possible, the interruption, or rather remove it entirely, by supposing that these interrupted perceptions are connected by a real existence, of which we are insensible. This supposition, or idea of continu'd existence, acquires a force and vivacity from the memory of these broken impressions, and from that propensity, which they give us, to suppose them the same; and according to the precedent reasoning, the very essence of belief consists in the force and vivacity of the conception. . . .

But tho' we are led after this manner, by the natural propensity of the imagination, to ascribe a continu'd existence to those sensible objects or perceptions, which we find to resemble each other in their interrupted appearance; yet a very little reflection and philosophy is sufficient to make us perceive the fallacy of that opinion. I have already observ'd, that there is an intimate connexion betwixt those two principles, of a *continu'd* and of a *distinct* or *independent* existence, and that we no sooner establish the one than the other follows, as a necessary consequence. 'Tis the opinion of a continu'd existence, which first takes place, and without much study or reflection draws the other along with it, wherever the mind follows its first and most natural tendency. But when we compare experiments, and reason a little upon them, we quickly perceive, that the doctrine of the independent existence of our sensible perceptions is contrary to the plainest experience. This leads us backward upon our footsteps to perceive our error in attributing a continu'd existence to our perceptions, and is the origin of many very curious opinions, which we shall here endeavour to account for.

'Twill first be proper to observe a few of those experiments, which convince us, that our perceptions are not possest of any independent existence. When we press one eye with a finger, we immediately perceive all the objects to become double, and one half of them to be remov'd from their common and natural position. But as we do not attribute a continu'd existence to both these perceptions, and as they are both of the same nature, we clearly perceive, that all our perceptions are dependent on our organs, and the disposition of our nerves and animal spirits. This opinion is confirm'd by the seeming encrease and diminution of objects, according to their distance; by the apparent alterations in their figure; by the changes in their colour and other qualities from our sickness and distempers; and by an infinite number of other experiments of the same kind; from all which we learn, that our sensible perceptions are not possest of any distinct or independent existence.

The natural consequence of this reasoning shou'd be, that our perceptions have no more a continu'd than an independent existence; and indeed philosophers have so far run into this opinion, that they change their system, and distinguish, (as we shall do for the future) betwixt perceptions and objects, of which the former are suppos'd to be interrupted, and perishing, and different at every different return; the latter to be uninterrupted, and to preserve a continu'd existence and identity. But however philosophical this new system may be esteem'd, I assert that 'tis only a palliative remedy, and that it contains all the difficulties of the vulgar system, with some others, that are peculiar to itself. There are no principles either of the understanding or fancy, which lead us directly to embrace this opinion of the double existence of perceptions and objects, nor can we arrive at it but by passing thro' the common hypothesis of the identity and continuance of our interrupted perceptions. Were we not first perswaded, that our perceptions are our only objects, and continue to exist even when they no longer make their appearance to the senses, we sou'd never be led to think, that our perceptions and objects are different, and that our objects alone preserve a continu'd existence. 'The latter hypothesis has no primary recommendation either to reason or the imagination, but acquires all its influence on the imagination from the former.' This proposition contains two parts, which we shall endeavour to prove as distinctly and clearly, as such abstruse subjects will permit.

As to the first part of the proposition, *that this philosophical hypothesis has no primary recommendation, either to reason or the imagination*, we may soon satisfy ourselves with regard to *reason* by the following reflections. The only existences, of which we are certain, are perceptions, which being immediately present to us by consciousness, command our strongest assent, and are the first foundation of all our conclusions. The only conclusion we can draw from the existence of one thing to that of another, is by means of the relation of cause and effect, which shews, that there is a connexion betwixt them, and that the existence of one is dependent on that of the other. The idea of this relation is deriv'd from past experience, by which we find, that two beings are constantly conjoin'd together, and are always present at once to the mind. But as no beings are ever present to the mind but perceptions; it follows that we may observe a conjunction or a relation of cause and effect between different perceptions, but can never observe it between perceptions and objects. 'Tis impossible, therefore, that from the existence or any of the qualities of the former, we can ever form any conclusion concerning the existence of the latter, or ever satisfy our reason in this particular.

'Tis no less certain, that this philosophical system has no primary recommendation to the *imagination*, and that that faculty wou'd never, of itself, and by its original tendency, have fallen upon such a principle. I confess it will be somewhat difficult to prove this to the full satisfaction of the reader; because it implies a negative, which in many cases will not admit of any positive proof. If any one wou'd take the pains to examine this question, and wou'd invent a system, to account for the direct origin of this opinion from the imagination, we shou'd be able, by the examination of that system, to pronounce a certain judgment in the present subject. Let it be taken for granted, that our perceptions are broken, and interrupted, and however like, are still different from each other; and let any one upon this supposition shew why the fancy, directly and immediately, proceeds to the belief of another existence, resembling these perceptions in their nature, but yet continu'd, and uninterrupted, and identical; and after he has done this to my satisfaction, I promise to renounce my present opinion. Mean while I cannot forbear concluding, from the very abstractedness and difficulty of the first supposition, that 'tis an improper subject for the fancy to work upon. Whoever wou'd explain the origin of the *common* opinion concerning the continu'd and distinct existence of body, must take the mind in its *common* situation, and must proceed upon the supposition, that our perceptions are our only objects, and continue to exist even when they are not perceiv'd. Tho' this opinion be false, 'tis the most natural of any, and has alone any primary recommendation to the fancy.

As to the second part of the proposition, *that the philosophical system acquires all its influence on the imagination from the vulgar one*; we may observe, that this is a natural and unavoidable consequence of the foregoing conclusion, *that it has no primary recommendation to reason or the imagination*. For as the philosophical system is found by experience to take hold of many minds, and in particular of all those, who reflect ever so little on this subject, it must derive all its authority from the vulgar system; since it has no original authority of its own. The manner, in which these two systems, tho' directly contrary, are connected together, may be explain'd, as follows.

The imagination naturally runs on in this train of thinking. Our perceptions are our only objects: Resembling perceptions are the same, however broken or uninterrupted in their appearance: This appearing interruption is contrary to the identity: The interruption consequently extends not beyond the appearance, and the perception or object really continues to exist, even when absent from us: Our sensible perceptions have, therefore, a continu'd and uninterrupted existence. But as a little reflection destroys this conclusion, that our perceptions have a continu'd existence, by shewing that they have a dependent one, 'twou'd naturally be expected, that we must altogether reject the opinion, that there is such a thing in nature as a continu'd existence, which is preserv'd even when it no longer appears to the senses. The case, however, is otherwise. Philosophers are so far from rejecting the opinion of a continu'd existence upon rejecting that of the independence and continuance of our sensible perceptions, that tho' all sects agree in the latter sentiment, the former, which is, in a manner, its necessary consequence, has been peculiar to a few extravagant sceptics; who after all maintain'd that opinion in words only, and were never able to bring themselves sincerely to believe it.

There is a great difference betwixt such opinions as we form after a calm and profound reflection, and such as we embrace by a kind of instinct or natural impulse, on account of their suitableness and conformity to the mind. If these opinions become contrary, 'tis not difficult to foresee which of them will have the advantage. As long as our attention is bent upon the subject, the philosophical and study'd principle may prevail; but the moment we relax our thoughts, nature will display herself, and draw us back to our former opinion. Nay she has sometimes such an influence, that she can stop our progress, even in the midst of our most profound reflections, and keep us from running on with all the consequences of any philosophical opinion. Thus tho' we clearly perceive the dependence and interruption of our perceptions, we stop short in our carreer, and never upon that account reject the notion of an independent and continu'd existence. That opinion has taken such deep root in the imagination, that 'tis impossible ever to eradicate it, nor will any strain'd metaphysical conviction of the dependence of our perceptions be sufficient for that purpose.

But tho' our natural and obvious principles here prevail above our study'd reflections, 'tis certain there must be some struggle and opposition in the case; at least so long as these reflections retain any force or vivacity. In order to set ourselves at ease in this particular, we contrive a new hypothesis, which seems to comprehend both these principles of reason and imagination. This hypothesis is the philosophical one of the double existence of perceptions and objects; which pleases our reason, in allowing, that our dependent perceptions are interrupted and different; and at the same time is agreeable to the imagination, in attributing a continu'd existence to something else, which we call *objects*. This philosophical system, therefore, is the monstrous offspring of two principles, which are contrary to each other, which are both at once embrac'd by the mind, and which are unable mutually to destroy each other. The imagination tells us, that our resembling perceptions have a continu'd and uninterrupted existence, and are not annihilated by their absence. Reflection tells us, that even our resembling perceptions are interrupted in their existence, and different from each other. The contradiction betwixt these opinions we elude by a new fiction, which is conformable to the hypotheses both of reflection and fancy, by ascribing these contrary qualities to different existences; the *interruption* to perceptions, and the *continuance* to objects. Nature is obstinate, and will not quit the field, however strongly attack'd by reason; and at the same time reason is so clear in the point, that there is no possibility of disguising her. Not being able to reconcile these two enemies, we endeavour to set ourselves at ease as much as possible, by successively granting to each whatever it demands, and by feigning a double existence, where each may find something, that has all the conditions it desires. Were we fully convinc'd, that our resembling perceptions are continu'd, and identical, and independent, we shou'd never run into this opinion of a double existence; since we shou'd find satisfaction in our first supposition, and wou'd not look beyond. Again, were we fully convinc'd, that our perceptions are dependent, and interrupted, and different, we shou'd be as little inclin'd to embrace the opinion of a double existence; since in that case we shou'd clearly perceive the error of our first supposition of a continu'd existence, and wou'd never regard it any farther. 'Tis therefore from the intermediate situation of the mind, that this opinion arises, and from such an adherence to these two contrary principles, as makes us seek some pretext to justify our receiving both; which happily at last is found in the system of a double existence.

Another advantage of this philosophical system is its similarity to the vulgar one; by which means we can humour our reason for a moment, when it becomes troublesome and sollicitous; and yet upon its least negligence or inattention, can easily return to our vulgar and natural notions. Accordingly we find, that philosophers neglect not this advantage; but immediately upon leaving their closets, mingle with the rest of mankind in those exploded opinions, that our perceptions are our only objects, and continue identically and uninterruptedly the same in all their interrupted appearances.

There are other particulars of this system, wherein we may remark its dependence on the fancy, in a very conspicuous manner. Of these, I shall observe the two following. *First,* We suppose external objects to resemble internal perceptions. I have already shewn, that the relation of cause and effect can never afford us any just conclusion from the existence or qualities of our perceptions to the existence of external continu'd objects: And I shall farther add, that even tho' they cou'd afford such a conclusion, we shou'd never have any reason to infer, that our objects resemble our perceptions. That opinion, therefore, is deriv'd from nothing but the quality of the fancy above-explain'd, *that it borrows all its ideas from some precedent perception.* We never can conceive any thing but perceptions, and therefore must make every thing resemble them.

Secondly, As we suppose our objects in general to resemble our perceptions, so we take it for granted, that every particular object resembles that perception, which it causes. The relation of cause and effect determines us to join the other of resemblance; and the ideas of these existences being already united together in the fancy by the former relation, we naturally add the latter to compleat the union. We have a strong propensity to compleat every union by joining new relations to those which we have before observ'd betwixt any ideas, as we shall have occasion to observe presently.

Having thus given an account of all the systems both popular and philosophical, with regard to external existences, I cannot forbear giving vent to a certain sentiment, which arises upon reviewing those systems. I begun this subject with premising, that we ought to have an implicit faith in our senses, and that this wou'd be the conclusion, I shou'd draw from the whole of my reasoning. But to be ingenuous, I feel myself *at present* of a quite contrary sentiment, and am more inclin'd to repose no faith at all in my senses, or rather imagination, than to place in it such an implicit confidence. I cannot conceive how such trivial qualities of the fancy, conducted by such false suppositons, can ever lead to any solid and rational system. They are the coherence and constancy of our perceptions, which produce the opinion of their continu'd existence; tho' these qualities of perceptions have no perceivable connexion with such an existence. The constancy of our perceptions has the most considerable effect, and yet is attended with the greatest difficulties. 'Tis a gross illusion to suppose, that our resembling perceptions are numerically the same; and 'tis this illusion, which leads us into the opinion, that these perceptions are uninterrupted, and are still existent, even when they are not present to the senses. This is the case with our popular system. And as to our philosophical one, 'tis liable to the same difficulties; and is over-and-above loaded with this absurdity, that it at once denies and establishes the vulgar supposition. Philosophers deny our resembling perceptions to be identically the same, and uninterrupted; and yet have so great a propensity to believe them such, that they arbitrarily invent a new set of perceptions, to which they attribute these qualities. I say, a new set of perceptions: For we may well suppose in general, but 'tis impossible for us distinctly to conceive, objects to be in their nature any thing but exactly the same with perceptions. What then can we look for from this confusion of groundless and extraordinary opinions but error and falshood? And how can we justify to ourselves any belief we repose in them?

This sceptical doubt, both with respect to reason and the senses, is a malady, which can never be radically cur'd, but must return upon us every moment, however we may chace it away, and sometimes may seem entirely free from it. 'Tis impossible upon any system to defend either our understanding or senses; and we but expose them farther when we endeavour to justify them in that manner. As the sceptical doubt arises naturally from a profound and intense reflection on those subjects, it always encreases, the farther we carry our reflections, whether in opposition or conformity to it. Carelessness and in-attention alone can afford us any remedy. For this reason I rely entirely upon them; and take it for granted, whatever may be the reader's opinion at this present moment, that an hour hence he will be persuaded there is both an external and internal world; and going upon that supposition, I intend to examine some general systems both ancient and modern, which have been propos'd of both, before I proceed to a more particular enquiry concerning our impressions. This will not, perhaps, in the end be found foreign to our present purpose.

Skeptical Doubts Concerning the Operations of the Understanding

DAVID HUME

I

All the objects of human reason or inquiry may naturally be divided into two kinds, to wit, "Relations of Ideas," and "Matters of Fact." Of the first kind are the sciences of Geometry, Algebra, and Arithmetic, and, in short, every affirmation which is either intuitively or demonstratively certain. *That the square of the hypotenuse is equal to the square of the two sides* is a proposition which expresses a relation between these figures. *That three times five is equal to the half of thirty* expresses a relation between these numbers. Propositions of this kind are discoverable by the mere operation of thought, without dependence on what is anywhere existent in the universe. Though there never were a circle or triangle in nature, the truths demonstrated by Euclid would forever retain their certainty and evidence.

Matters of fact, which are the second objects of human reason, are not ascertained in the same manner, nor is our evidence of their truth, however great, of a like nature with the foregoing. The contrary of every matter of fact is still possible, because it can never imply a contradiction and is conceived by the mind with the same facility and distinctness as if ever so conformable to reality. *That the sun will not rise tomorrow* is no less intelligible a proposition and implies no more contradiction than the affirmation *that it will rise*. We should in vain, therefore, attempt to demonstrate its falsehood. Were it demonstratively false, it would imply a contradiction and could never be distinctly conceived by the mind.

It may, therefore, be a subject worthy of curiosity to inquire what is the nature of that evidence which assures us of any real existence and matter of fact beyond the present testimony of our senses or the records of our memory. This part of philosophy, it is observable, had been little cultivated either by the ancients or moderns; and, therefore, our doubts and errors in the prosecution of so important an inquiry may be the more excusable while we march through such difficult paths without any guide or direction. They may even prove useful by exciting curiosity and destroying that implicit faith and security which is the bane of all reasoning and free inquiry. The discovery of defects in the common philosophy, if any such there be, will not, I presume, be a discouragement, but rather an incitement, as is usual, to attempt something more full and satisfactory than has yet been proposed to the public.

All reasonings concerning matter of fact seem to be founded on the relation of *cause* and *effect*. By means of that relation alone we can go beyond the evidence of our memory and senses. If you were to ask a man why he believes any matter of fact which is absent, for instance, that his friend is in the country or in France, he would give you a reason, and

From Hume's *An Enquiry Concerning Human Understanding* (1748).

this reason would be some other fact: as a letter received from him or the knowledge of his former resolutions and promises. A man finding a watch or any other machine in a desert island would conclude that there had once been men in that island. All our reasonings concerning fact are of the same nature. And here it is constantly supposed that there is a connection between the present fact and that which is inferred from it. Were there nothing to bind them together, the inference would be entirely precarious. The hearing of an articulate voice and rational discourse in the dark assures us of the presence of some person. Why? Because these are the effects of the human make and fabric, and closely connected with it. If we anatomize all the other reasonings of this nature, we shall find that they are founded on the relation of cause and effect, and that this relation is either near or remote, direct or collateral. Heat and light are collateral effects of fire, and the one effect may justly be inferred from the other.

If we would satisfy ourselves, therefore, concerning the nature of that evidence which assures us of matters of fact, we must inquire how we arrive at the knowledge of cause and effect.

I shall venture to affirm, as a general proposition which admits of no exception, that the knowledge of this relation is not, in any instance, attained by reasonings *a priori,* but arises entirely from experience, when we find that any particular objects are constantly conjoined with each other. Let an object be presented to a man of ever so strong natural reason and abilities—if that object be entirely new to him, he will not be able, by the most accurate examination of its sensible qualities, to discover any of its causes or effects. Adam, though his rational faculties be supposed, at the very first, entirely perfect, could not have inferred from the fluidity and transparency of water that it would suffocate him, or from the light and warmth of fire that it would consume him. No object ever discovers, by the qualities which appear to the senses, either the causes which produced it or the effects which will arise from it; nor can our reason, unassisted by experience, ever draw any inference concerning real existence and matter of fact.

This proposition, *that causes and effects are discoverable, not by reason, but by experience,* will readily be admitted with regard to such objects as we remember to have once been altogether unknown to us, since we must be conscious of the utter inability which we then lay under of foretelling what would arise from them. Present two smooth pieces of marble to a man who has no tincture of natural philosophy; he will never discover that they will adhere together in such a manner as to require great force to separate them in a direct line, while they make so small a resistance to a lateral pressure. Such events as bear little analogy to the common course of nature are also readily confessed to be known only by experience, nor does any man imagine that the explosion of gunpowder or the attraction of a loadstone could ever be discovered by arguments *a priori*. In like manner, when an effect is supposed to depend upon an intricate machinery or secret structure of parts, we make no difficulty in attributing all our knowledge of it to experience. Who will assert that he can give the ultimate reason why milk or bread is proper nourishment for a man, not for a lion or tiger?

But the same truth may not appear at first sight to have the same evidence with regard to events which have become familiar to us from our first appearance in the world, which bear a close analogy to the whole course of nature, and which are supposed to depend on the simple qualities of objects without any secret structure of parts. We are apt to imagine that we could discover these effects by the mere operation of our reason without experience. We fancy that, were we brought on a sudden into this world, we could at first have inferred that one billiard ball would communicate motion to another upon impulse, and that we needed not to have waited for the event in order to pronounce with certainty concerning it. Such is the influence of custom that where it is strongest it not only covers our natural ignorance but even conceals itself, and seems not to take place, merely because it is found in the highest degree.

But to convince us that all the laws of nature and all the operations of bodies without exception are known only by experience, the following reflections may perhaps suffice. Were any object presented to us, and were we required to pronounce concerning the effect which will result from it without consulting past observation, after what manner, I beseech you, must the mind proceed in this operation? It must invent or imagine some event which it ascribes to the object as its effect; and it is plain that this invention must be entirely arbitrary. The mind can never possibly find the effect in the supposed cause by the most accurate scrutiny and examination. For the effect is totally different from the cause, and consequently can never be discovered in it. Motion in the second billiard ball is a quite distinct event from motion in the first, nor is there anything in the one to suggest the smallest hint of the other. A stone or piece of metal raised into the air and left without any support immediately falls. But to consider the matter *a priori,* is there anything we discover in this situation which can beget the idea of a downward rather than an upward or any other motion in the stone or metal?

And as the first imagination or invention of a particular effect in all natural operations is arbitrary where we consult not experience, so must we also esteem the supposed tie or connection between the cause and effect which binds them together and renders it impossible that any other effect could result from the operation of that cause. When I see, for instance, a billiard ball moving in a straight line toward another, even suppose motion in the second ball should by accident be suggested to me as the result of their contact or impulse, may I not conceive that a hundred different events might as well follow from that cause? May not both these balls remain at absolute rest? May not the first ball return in a straight line or leap off from the second in any line or direction? All these suppositions are consistent and conceivable. Why, then, should we give the preference to one which is no more consistent or conceivable than the rest? All our reasonings *a priori* will never be able to show us any foundation for this preference.

In a word, then, every effect is a distinct event from its cause. It could not, therefore, be discovered in the cause, and the first invention or conception of it, *a priori,* must be entirely arbitrary. And even after it is suggested, the conjunction of it with the cause must appear equally arbitrary, since there are always many other effects which, to reason, must seem fully as consistent and natural. In vain, therefore, should we pretend to determine any single event or infer any cause or effect without the assistance of observation and experience.

Hence we may discover the reason why no philosopher who is rational and modest has ever pretended to assign the ultimate cause of any natural operation, or to show distinctly the action of that power which produces any single effect in the universe. It is confessed that the utmost effort of human reason is to reduce the principles productive of natural phenomena to a greater simplicity, and to resolve the many particular effects into a few general causes, by means of reasonings from analogy, experience, and observation. But as to the causes of these general causes, we should in vain attempt their discovery, nor shall we ever be able to satisfy ourselves by any particular explication of them. These ultimate springs and principles are totally shut up from human curiosity and inquiry. Elasticity, gravity, cohesion of parts, communication of motion by impulse—these are probably the ultimate causes and principles which we shall ever discover in nature; and we may esteem ourselves sufficiently happy if, by accurate inquiry and reasoning, we can trace up the particular phenomena to, or near to, these general principles. The most perfect philosophy of the natural kind only staves off our ignorance a little longer, as perhaps the most perfect philosophy of the moral or metaphysical kind serves only to discover larger portions of it. Thus the observation of human blindness and weakness is the result of all philosophy, and meets us, at every turn, in spite of our endeavors to elude or avoid it.

Nor is geometry, when taken into the assistance of natural philosophy, ever able to remedy this defect or lead us into the knowledge of ultimate causes by all that accuracy of reasoning for which it is so justly celebrated. Every part of mixed mathematics proceeds upon the supposition that certain laws are established by nature in her operations, and abstract reasonings are employed either to assist experience in the discovery of these laws or to determine their influence in particular instances where it depends upon any precise degree of distance and quantity. Thus it is a law of motion, discovered by experience, that the moment or force of any body in motion is in the compound ratio or proportion of its solid contents and its velocity, and, consequently, that a small force may remove the greatest obstacle or raise the greatest weight if by any contrivance or machinery we can increase the velocity of that force so as to make it an overmatch for its antagonist. Geometry assists us in the application of this law by giving us the just dimensions of all the parts and figures which can enter into any species of machine, but still the discovery of the law itself is owing merely to experience; and all the abstract reasonings in the world could never lead us one step toward the knowledge of it. When we reason *a priori* and consider merely any object or cause as it appears to the mind, independent of all observation, it never could suggest to us the notion of any distinct object, such as its effect, much less show us the inseparable and inviolable connection between them. A man must be very sagacious who could discover by reasoning that crystal is the effect of heat, and ice of cold, without being previously acquainted with the operation of these qualities.

II

But we have not yet attained any tolerable satisfaction with regard to the question first proposed. Each solution still gives rise to a new question as difficult as the foregoing and leads us on to further inquiries. When it is asked, *What is the nature of all our reasonings concerning matter of fact?* the proper answer seems to be, That they are founded on the relation of cause and effect. When again it is asked, *What is the foundation of all our reasonings and conclusions concerning that relation?* it may be replied in one word, *experience*. But if we still carry on our sifting humor and ask, *What is the foundation of all conclusions from experience?* this implies a new question which may be of more difficult solution and explication. Philosophers that give themselves airs of superior wisdom and sufficiency have a hard task when they encounter persons of inquisitive dispositions, who push them from every corner to which they retreat, and who are sure at last to bring them to some dangerous dilemma. The best expedient to prevent this confusion is to be modest in our pretensions and even to discover the difficulty ourselves before it is objected to us. By this means we may make a kind of merit of our very ignorance.

I shall content myself in this section with an easy task and shall pretend only to give a negative answer to the question here proposed. I say, then, that even after we have experience of the operations of cause and effect, our conclusions from that experience are *not* founded on reasoning or any process of the understanding. This answer we must endeavor both to explain and to defend.

It must certainly be allowed that nature has kept us at a great distance from all her secrets and has afforded us only the knowledge of a few superficial qualities of objects, while she conceals from us those powers and principles on which the influence of these objects entirely depends. Our senses inform us of the color, weight, and consistency of bread, but neither sense nor reason can ever inform us of those qualities which fit it for the nourishment and support of the human body. Sight or feeling conveys an idea of the actual motion of bodies, but as to that wonderful force or power which would carry on a moving body forever in a continued change of place, and which bodies never lose but by communicating it to others, of this we cannot form the most distant conception. But notwithstanding this ignorance of natural powers[1] and principles, we always presume when we see like sensible qualities that they have like secret powers, and expect that effects similar to those which we have experienced will follow from them. If a body of like color and consistency with that bread which we have formerly eaten be presented to us, we make no scruple of repeating the experiment and foresee with certainty like nourishment and support. Now this is a process of the mind or thought of which I would willingly know the foundation. It is allowed on all hands that there is no known connection between the sensible qualities and the secret powers, and, consequently, that the mind is not led to form such a conclusion concerning their constant and regular conjunction by anything which it knows of their nature. As to past *experience*, it can be allowed to give *direct* and *certain* information of those precise objects only, and that precise period of time which fell under its cognizance: But why this experience should be extended to future times and to other objects which, for aught we know, may be only in appearance similar, this is the main question on which I would insist. The bread which I formerly ate nourished me; that is, a body of such sensible qualities was, at that time, endued with such secret powers. But does it follow that other bread must also nourish me at another time, and that like sensible qualities must always be attended with like secret powers? The consequence seems nowise necessary. At least, it must be acknowledged that there is here a consequence drawn by the mind that there is a certain step taken, a process of thought, and an inference which wants to be explained. These two propositions are far from being the same: *I have found that such an object has always been attended with such an effect,* and *I foresee that other objects which are in appearance similar will be attended with similar effects.* I shall allow, if you please, that the one proposition may justly be inferred from the other: I know, in fact, that it always is inferred. But if you insist that the inference is made by a chain of reasoning, I desire you to produce that reasoning. The connection between these propositions is not intuitive. There is required a medium which may enable the mind to draw such an inference, if indeed it be drawn by reasoning and argument. What that medium is I must confess passes my comprehension; and it is incumbent on those to produce it who assert that it really exists and is the original of all our conclusions concerning matter of fact.

This negative argument must certainly, in process of time, become altogether convincing if many penetrating and able philosophers shall turn their inquiries this way, and no one be ever able to discover any connecting proposition or intermediate step which supports the understanding in this conclusion. But as the question is yet new, every reader may not trust so far to his own penetration as to conclude, because an argument escapes his inquiry, that therefore it does not really exist. For this reason it may be requisite to venture upon a more difficult task, and, enumerating all the branches of human knowledge, endeavor to show that none of them can afford such an argument.

All reasonings may be divided into two kinds, namely, demonstrative reasoning, or that concerning relations of ideas, and moral[2] reasoning, or that concerning matter of fact and existence. That there are no demonstrative arguments in the case seems evident, since it implies no contradiction that the course of nature may change and that an object, seemingly like those which we have experienced, may be attended with different or contrary effects. May I not clearly and distinctly conceive that a body, falling from the clouds and which in all other respects resembles snow, has yet the taste of salt or feeling of fire? Is there any more intelligible proposition than to affirm that all the trees will flourish in December and January, and will decay in May and June? Now, whatever is intelligible and can be distinctly conceived implies no contradiction and can never be proved false by any demonstrative argument or abstract reasoning *a priori*.

If we be, therefore, engaged by arguments to put trust in past experience and make it the standard of our future judgment, these arguments must be probable only, or such as regard matter of fact and real existence, according to the division above mentioned. But that there is no argument of this kind must appear if our explication of that species of reasoning be admitted as solid and satisfactory. We have said that all arguments concerning existence are founded on the relation of cause and effect, that our knowledge of that relation is derived entirely from experience, and that all our experimental conclusions proceed upon the supposition that the future will be conformable to the past. To endeavor, therefore, the proof of this last supposition by probable arguments, or arguments regarding existence, must be evidently going in a circle and taking that for granted which is the very point in question.

In reality, all arguments from experience are founded on the similarity which we discover among natural objects, and by which we are induced to expect effects similar to those which we have found to follow from such objects. And though none but a fool or madman will ever pretend to dispute the authority of experience or to reject that great guide of human life, it may surely be allowed a philosopher to have so much curiosity at least as to examine the principle of human nature which gives this mighty authority to experience and makes us draw advantage from that similarity which nature has placed among different objects. From causes which appear similar, we expect similar effects. This is the sum of all our experimental conclusions. Now it seems evident that, if this conclusion were formed by reason, it would be as perfect at first, and upon one instance, as after ever so long a course of experience; but the case is far otherwise. Nothing so like as eggs, yet no one, on account of this appearing similarity, expects the same taste and relish in all of them. It is only after a long course of uniform experiments in any kind that we attain a firm reliance and security with regard to a particular event. Now, where is that process of reasoning which, from one instance, draws a conclusion so different from that which it infers from a hundred instances that are nowise different from that single one? This question I propose as much for the sake of information as with an intention of raising difficulties. I cannot find, I cannot imagine any such reasoning. But I keep my mind still open to instruction if anyone will vouchsafe to bestow it on me.

Should it be said that, from a number of uniform experiments, we *infer* a connection between the sensible qualities and the secret powers, this, I must confess, seems the same difficulty, couched in different terms. The question still occurs, On what process of argument is this *inference* founded? Where is the medium, the interposing ideas which join propositions so very wide of each other? It is confessed that the color, consistency, and other sensible qualities of bread appear not of themselves to have any connection with the secret powers of nourishment and support; for otherwise we could infer these secret powers from the first appearance of these sensible qualities without the aid of experience, contrary to the sentiment of all philosophers, and contrary to plain matter of fact. Here, then, is our natural state of ignorance with regard to the powers and influence of all objects. How is this remedied by experience? It only shows us a number of uniform effects resulting from certain objects, and teaches us that those particular objects, at that particular time, were endowed with such powers and forces. When a new object endowed with similar sensible qualities is produced, we expect similar powers and forces, and look for a like effect. From a body of like color and consistency with bread, we expect like nourishment and support. But this surely is a step or progress of the mind which wants to be explained. When a man says, *I have found, in all past instances, such sensible qualities, conjoined with such secret powers,* and when he says, *similar sensible qualities will always be conjoined with similar secret powers,* he is not guilty of a tautology, nor are these propositions in any respect the same. You say that the one proposition is an inference from the other; but you must confess that the inference is not intuitive, neither is it demonstrative. Of what nature is it then? To say it is experimental is begging the question. For all inferences from experience suppose, as their foundation, that the future will resemble the past and that similar powers will be conjoined with similar sensible qualities. If there be any suspicion that the course of nature may change, and that the past may be no rule for the future, all experience becomes useless and can give rise to no inference or conclusion. It is impossible, therefore, that any arguments from experience can prove this resemblance of the past to the future, since all these arguments are founded on the supposition of that resemblance. Let the course of things be allowed hitherto ever so regular, that alone, without some new argument or inference, proves not that for the future it will continue so. In vain do you pretend to have learned the nature of bodies from your past experience. Their secret nature, and consequently all their effects and influence, may change without any change in their sensible qualities. This happens sometimes, and with regard to some objects. Why may it not happen always, and with regard to all objects? What logic, what process of argument secures you against this supposition? My practice, you say, refutes my doubts. But you mistake the purport of my question. As an agent, I am quite satisfied in the point; but as a philosopher who has some share of curiosity, I will not say skepticism, I want to learn the foundation of this inference. No reading, no inquiry has yet been able to remove my difficulty or give me satisfaction in a matter of such importance. Can I do better than propose the difficulty to the public, even though, perhaps, I have small hopes of obtaining a solution? We shall at least, by this means, be sensible of our ignorance, if we do not augment our knowledge.

I must confess that a man is guilty of unpardonable arrogance who concludes, because an argument has escaped his own investigation, that therefore it does not really exist. I must also confess that, though all the learned, for several ages, should have employed themselves in fruitless search upon any subject, it may still, perhaps, be rash to conclude positively that the subject must therefore pass all human comprehension. Even though we examine all the sources of our knowledge and conclude them unfit for such a subject, there may still remain a suspicion that the enumeration is not complete or the examination not accurate. But with regard to the present subject, there are some considerations which seem to remove all this accusation of arrogance or suspicion of mistake.

It is certain that the most ignorant and stupid peasants, nay infants, nay even brute beasts, improve by experience and learn the qualities of natural objects by observing the effects which result from them. When a child has felt the sensation of pain from touching the flame of a candle, he will be careful not to put his hand near any candle, but will expect a similar effect from a cause which is similar in its sensible qualities and appearance. If you assert, therefore, that the understanding of the child is led into this conclusion by any process of argument or ratiocination, I may justly require you to produce that argument, nor have you any pretense to refuse so equitable a demand. You cannot say that the argument is abstruse and may possibly escape your inquiry, since you confess that it is obvious to the capacity of a mere infant. If you hesitate, therefore, a moment or if, after reflection, you produce an intricate or profound argument, you, in a manner, give up the question and confess that it is not reasoning which engages us to suppose the past resembling the future, and to expect similar effects from causes which are to appearance similar. This is the proposition which I intended to enforce in the present section. If I be right, I pretend not to have made any mighty discovery. And if I be wrong, I must acknowledge myself to be indeed a very backward scholar, since I cannot now discover an argument which, it seems, was perfectly familiar to me long before I was out of my cradle.

NOTES

1. The word "power" is here used in a loose and popular sense. The more accurate explication of it would give additional evidence to this argument. See Section VII. [This note was added in Edition L.]

2. [Editions K and L: "moral or probable."]

Of Mr. Hume's Skepticism with Regard to Reason

THOMAS REID

In the Treatise of Human Nature, book 1. part 4. sect. 1. the author undertakes to prove two points: 1st, that all that is called human knowledge, meaning demonstrative knowledge, is only probablity; and 2dly, that this probability, when duly examined, vanishes by degrees, and leaves at last no evidence at all: so that in the issue, there is no ground to believe any one proposition rather than its contrary, and "all those are certainly fools who reason or believe any thing."

According to this account, reason, that boasted prerogative of man, and the light of his mind, is an *ignis fatuus*, which misleads the wandering traveller, and leaves him at last in absolute darkness.

How unhappy is the condition of man, born under a necessity of believing contradictions, and of trusting to a guide who confesses herself to be a false one!

It is some comfort, that this doctrine can never be seriously adopted by any man in his senses. And after this author had shown that "all the rules of logic require a total extinction of all belief and evidence," he himself, and all men that are not insane, must have believed many things, and yielded assent to the evidence which he had extinguished.

This indeed he is so candid as to acknowledge. "He finds himself absolutely and necessarily determined to live and talk and act like other people in the common affairs of life. And since reason is incapable of dispelling these clouds, most fortunately it happens, that nature herself suffices to that purpose, and cures him of this philosophical melancholy and delirium." See sect. 7.

This was surely a very kind and friendly interposition of nature; for the effects of this philosophical delirium, if carried into life, must have been very melancholy.

But what pity is it, that nature, whatever is meant by that personage, so kind in curing this delirium, should be so cruel as to cause it. Doth the same fountain send forth sweet waters and bitter? Is it not more probable, that if the cure was the work of nature, the disease came from another hand, and was the work of the philosopher?

To pretend to prove by reasoning that there is no force in reason, does indeed look like a philosophical delirium. It is like a man's pretending to see clearly, that he himself and all other men are blind.

A common symptom of delirium is, to think that all other men are fools or mad. This appears to have been the case of our author, who concluded, "That all those are certainly fools who reason or believe any thing."

Whatever was the cause of this delirium, it must be granted, that if it was real and not feigned, it was not to be cured by reasoning: for what can be more absurd than to attempt to convince a man by reasoning who disowns the authority of reason. It was therefore very for-

---

Thomas Reid (1710-1796) was the originator of the Scottish philosophy of common sense.

From Reid's *Essays on the Intellectual Powers of Man* (1785).

tunate that nature found other means of curing it.

It may, however, not be improper to inquire, whether, as the author thinks, it was produced by a just application of the rules of logic, or, as others may be apt to think, by the misapplication and abuse of them.

First, Because we are fallible, the author infers that all knowledge degenerates into probability.

That man, and probably every created being, is fallible; and that a fallible being cannot have that perfect comprehension and assurance of truth which an infallible being has, I think ought to be granted. It becomes a fallible being to be modest, open to new light, and sensible, that by some false bias, or by rash judging, he may be misled. If this be called a degree of skepticism, I cannot help approving of it, being persuaded, that the man who makes the best use he can of the faculties which God has given him, without thinking them more perfect than they really are, may have all the belief that is necessary in the conduct of life, and all that is necessary to his acceptance with his Maker.

It is granted then, that human judgments ought always to be formed with an humble sense of our fallibility in judging.

This is all that can be inferred by the rules of logic from our being fallible. And if this be all that is meant by our knowledge degenerating into probability, I know no person of a different opinion.

But it may be observed, that the author here uses the word *probability* in a sense for which I know no authority but his own. Philosophers understand probability as opposed to demonstration; the vulgar as opposed to certainty; but this author understands it as opposed to infallibility, which no man claims.

One who believes himself to be fallible, may still hold it to be certain that two and two make four, and that two contradictory propositions cannot both be true. He may believe some things to be probable only, and other things to be demonstrable, without making any pretence to infallibility.

If we use words in their proper meaning, it is impossible that demonstration should degenerate into probability from the imperfection of our faculties. Our judgment cannot change the nature of the things about which we judge. What is really demonstration, will still be so, whatever judgment we form concerning it. It may likewise be observed, that when we mistake that for demonstration, which really is not, the consequence of this mistake is, not that demonstration degenerates into probability, but that what we took to be demonstration is no proof at all; for one false step in a demonstration destroys the whole, but cannot turn it into another kind of proof.

Upon the whole, then, this first conclusion of our author, that the fallibility of human judgment turns all knowledge into probability, if understood literally, is absurd; but if it be only a figure of speech, and means no more, but that, in all our judgments, we ought to be sensible of our fallibility, and ought to hold our opinions with that modesty that becomes fallible creatures, which I take to be what the author meant, this, I think, nobody denies, nor was it necessary to enter into a laborious proof of it.

One is never in greater danger of transgressing against the rules of logic, than in attempting to prove what needs no proof. Of this we have an instance in this very case: for the author begins his proof, that all human judgments are fallible, with affirming that some are infallible.

"In all demonstrative sciences," says he, "the rules are certain and infallible; but when we apply them, our fallible and uncertain faculties are very apt to depart from them, and fall into error."

He had forgot, surely, that the rules of demonstrative sciences are discovered by our fallible and uncertain faculties, and have no authority but that of human judgment. If they be infallible, some human judgments are infallible; and there are many in various branches of human knowledge which have as good a claim to infallibility as the rules of the demonstrative sciences.

We have reason here to find fault with our author for not being skeptical enough, as well as for a mistake in reasoning, when he claims infallibility to certain decisions of the human faculties, in order to prove that all their decisions are fallible.

The *second* point which he attempts to prove, is, that this probability, when duly examined, suffers a continual diminution, and at last a total extinction.

The obvious consequence of this is, that no fallible being can have good reason to believe any thing at all; but let us hear the proof.

"In every judgment, we ought to correct the first judgment derived from the nature of the object, by another judgment derived from the nature of the understanding. Besides the original uncertainty inherent in the subject, there arises another, derived from the weakness of the faculty which judges. Having adjusted these two uncertainties together, we are obliged, by our reason, to add a new uncertainty, derived from the possibility of error in the estimation we make of the truth and fidelity of our faculties. This is a doubt, of which, if we would closely pursue our reasoning, we cannot avoid giving a decision. But this decision, though it should be favourable to our preceding judgment, being founded only on probability, must weaken still further our first evidence. The third uncertainty must in like manner be criticised by a fourth, and so on without end.

"Now, as every one of these uncertainties takes away a part of the original evidence, it must at last be reduced to nothing. Let our first belief be ever so strong, it must infallibly perish, by passing through so many examinations, each of which carries off somewhat of its force and vigour. No finite object can subsist under a decrease repeated *in infinitum*.

"When I reflect on the natural fallibility of my judgment, I have less confidence in my opinions, than when I only consider the objects concerning which I reason. And when I proceed still further, to turn the scrutiny against every successive estimation I make of my faculties, all the rules of logic require a continual diminution, and at last a total extinction of belief and evidence."

This is the author's Achillean argument against the evidence of reason, from which he concludes, that a man who would govern his belief by reason, must believe nothing at all, and that belief is an act not of the cogitative, but of the sensitive part of our nature.

If there be any such thing as motion, said an ancient skeptic, the swift-footed Achilles could never overtake an old man in a journey. For, suppose the old man to set out a thousand paces before Achilles, and that while Achilles has travelled the thousand paces, the old man has gone five hundred; when Achilles has gone the five hundred, the old man has gone two hundred and fifty; and when Achilles has gone the two hundred and fifty, the old man is still one hundred and twenty-five before him. Repeat these estimations *in infinitum*, and you will still find the old man foremost; therefore Achilles can never overtake him; therefore there can be no such thing as motion.

The reasoning of the modern skeptic against reason is equally ingenious, and equally convincing. Indeed, they have a great similarity.

If we trace the journey of Achilles two thousand paces, we shall find the very point where the old man is overtaken: but this short journey, by dividing it into an infinite number of stages, with corresponding estimations, is made to appear infinite. In like manner, our author, subjecting every judgment to an infinite number of successive probable estimations, reduces the evidence to nothing.

To return then to the argument of the modern skeptic. I examine the proof of a theorem of Euclid. It appears to me to be strict demonstration. But I may have overlooked some fallacy; therefore I examine it again and again, but can find no flaw in it. I find all that have examined it agree with me. I have now that evidence of the truth of the proposition, which I and all men call demonstration, and that belief of it, which we call certainty.

Here my skeptical friend interposes, and assures me, that the rules of logic reduce this demonstration to no evidence at all. I am willing to hear what step in it he thinks fallacious, and why. He makes no objection to any part of the demonstration, but pleads my fallibility in judging. I have made the proper allowance for this already, by being open to conviction. But, says he, there are two uncertainties, the first inherent in the subject, which I have already shown to have only probable evidence; the second arising from the weakness of the faculty that judges. I answer, It is the weakness of the faculty only that reduces this demonstration to what you call probability. You must not therefore make it a second uncertainty; for it is the same with the first. To take credit twice in an account for the same article is not agreeable to the rules of logic. Hitherto therefore there is but one uncertainty; to wit, my fallibility in judging.

But, says my friend, you are obliged by reason to add a new uncertainty, derived from the possibility of error in the estimation you make of the truth and fidelity of your faculties. I answer,

This estimation is ambiguously expressed; it may either mean an estimation of my liableness to err by the misapplication and abuse of my faculties; or it may mean an estimation of my liableness to err, by conceiving my faculties to be true and faithful while they may be false and fallacious in themselves, even when applied in the best manner. I shall consider this estimation in each of these senses.

If the first be the estimation meant, it is true that reason directs us, as fallible creatures, to carry along with us, in all our judgments, a sense of our fallibility. It is true also, that we are in greater danger of erring in some cases, and less in others; and that this danger of erring may, according to the circumstances of the case, admit of an estimation, which we ought likewise to carry along with us in every judgment we form.

When a demonstration is short and plain; when the point to be proved does not touch our interest or our passions; when the faculty of judging in such cases, has acquired strength by much exercise, there is less danger of erring; when the contrary circumstances take place, there is more.

In the present case, every circumstance is favourable to the judgment I have formed. There cannot be less danger of erring in any case, excepting perhaps when I judge of a self-evident axiom.

The skeptic further urges, that this decision, though favourable to my first judgment, being founded only on probability, must still weaken the evidence of that judgment.

Here I cannot help being of a quite contrary opinion, nor can I imagine how an ingenious author could impose upon himself so grossly, for surely he did not intend to impose upon his reader.

After repeated examination of a proposition of Euclid, I judge it to be strictly demonstrated; this is my first judgment. But as I am liable to err from various causes, I consider how far I may have been misled by any of these causes in this judgment. My decision upon this second point is favourable to my first judgment, and therefore, as I apprehend, must strengthen it. To say, that this decision, because it is only probable, must weaken the first evidence, seems to me contrary to all rules of logic, and to common sense.

The first judgment may be compared to the testimony of a credible witness; the second, after a scrutiny into the character of the witness, wipes off every objection that can be made to it, and therefore surely must confirm and not weaken his testimony.

But let us suppose, that, in another case, I examine my first judgment upon some point, and find, that it was attended with unfavourable circumstances. What, in reason, and according to the rules of logic, ought to be the effect of this discovery?

The effect surely will be, and ought to be, to make me less confident in my first judgment, until I examine the point anew in more favourable circumstances. If it be a matter of importance, I return to weigh the evidence of my first judgment. If it was precipitate before, it must now be deliberate in every point. If at first I was in passion, I must now be cool. If I had an interest in the decision, I must place the interest on the other side.

It is evident, that this review of the subject may confirm my first judgment, notwithstanding the suspicious circumstances that attended it. Though the judge was biassed or corrupted, it does not follow, that the sentence was unjust. The rectitude of the decision does not depend upon the character of the judge, but upon the nature of the case. From that only, it must be determined whether the decision be just. The circumstances that rendered it suspicious are mere presumptions, which have no force against direct evidence.

Thus, I have considered the effect of this estimation of our liableness to err in our first judgment, and have allowed to it all the effect that reason and the rules of logic permit. In the case I first supposed, and in every case where we can discover no cause of error, it affords a presumption in favour of the first judgment. In other cases, it may afford a presumption against it. But the rules of logic require, that we should not judge by presumptions, where we have direct evidence. The effect of an unfavourable presumption should only be, to make us examine the evidence with the greater care.

The skeptic urges, in the last place, that this estimation must be subjected to another estimation, that to another, and so on *in infinitum;* and as every new estimation takes away from the evidence of the first judgment, it must at last be totally annihilated.

I answer, *first,* It has been shown above, that the first estimation, supposing it unfavourable, can only afford a presumption against the first judgment; the second, upon the same supposition, will be only the presumption of a presumption; and the third, the presumption that there is a presumption of a presumption. This infinite series of presumption resembles an infinite series of quantities decreasing in geometrical proportion, which amounts only to a finite sum. The infinite series of stages of Achilles's journey after the old man, amounts only to two thousand paces; nor can this infinite series of presumptions outweigh one solid argument in favour of the first judgment, supposing them all to be unfavourable to it.

2dly, I have shown, that the estimation of our first judgment may strengthen it; and the same thing may be said of all the subsequent estimations. It would, therefore, be as reasonable to conclude, that the first judgment will be brought to infallible certainty when this series of estimations is wholly in its favour, as that its evidence will be brought to nothing by such a series supposed to be wholly unfavourable to it. But, in reality, one serious and cool re-examination of the evidence by which our first judgment is supported, has, and in reason ought to have, more force to strengthen or weaken it, than an infinite series of such estimations as our author requires.

3dly, I know no reason nor rule in logic, that requires that such a series of estimations should follow every particular judgment.

A wise man who has practised reasoning knows that he is fallible, and carries this conviction along with him in every judgment he forms. He knows likewise, that he is more liable to err in some cases than in others. He has a scale in his mind, by which he estimates his liableness to err, and by this he regulates the degree of his assent in his first judgment upon any point.

The author's reasoning supposes, that a man, when he forms his first judgment, conceives himself to be infallible; that by a second and subsequent judgment, he discovers that he is not infallible; and that by a third judgment, subsequent to the second, he estimates his liableness to err in such a case as the present.

If the man proceed in this order, I grant, that his second judgment will, with good reason, bring down the first from supposed infallibility to fallibility; and that his third judgment will, in some degree, either strengthen or weaken the first, as it is corrected by the second.

But every man of understanding proceeds in a contrary order. When about to judge in any particular point, he knows already that he is not infallible. He knows what are the cases in which he is most or least liable to err. The conviction of these things is always present to his mind, and influences the degree of his assent in his first judgment, as far as to him appears reasonable.

If he should afterward find reason to suspect his first judgment, and desires to have all the satisfaction his faculties can give, reason will direct him not to form such a series of estimations upon estimations, as this author requires, but to examine the evidence of his first judgment carefully and cooly; and this review may very reasonably, according to its result, either strengthen or weaken, or totally overturn his first judgment.

This infinite series of estimations, therefore, is not the method that reason directs in order to form our judgment in any case. It is introduced without necessity, without any use but to puzzle the understanding, and to make us think, that to judge, even in the simplest and plainest cases, is a matter of insurmountable difficulty and endless labour; just as the ancient skeptic, to make a journey of two thousand paces appear endless, divided it into an infinite number of stages.

But we observed, that the estimation which our author requires may admit of another meaning, which indeed is more agreeable to the expression, but inconsistent with what he advanced before.

By the possibility of error in the estimation of the truth and fidelity of our faculties, may be meant, that we may err by esteeming our faculties true and faithful, while they may be false and fallacious, even when used according to the rules of reason and logic.

If this be meant, I answer, 1st, that the truth and fidelity of our faculty of judging is, and must be taken for granted in every judgment and in every estimation.

If the skeptic can seriously doubt of the truth and fidelity of his faculty of judging when properly used, and suspend his judgment upon that point till he finds proof, his skepticism admits of no cure by reasoning, and he must even continue in it until he have new faculties given him, which shall have authority to sit in judgment upon the old. Nor is there any need of an endless succession of doubts upon this subject, for the first puts an end to all judgment and reasoning, and to the possibility of conviction by that means. The skeptic has here got possession of a strong hold which is impregnable to reasoning, and we must leave him in possession of it, till nature, by other means, makes him give it up.

2dly, I observe, that this ground of skepticism, from the supposed infidelity of our faculties, contradicts what the author before advanced in this very argument; to wit, that "the rules of the demonstrative sciences are certain and infallible, and that truth is the natural effect of reason, and that error arises from the irruption of other causes."

But perhaps he made these concessions unwarily. He is therefore at liberty to retract them, and to rest his skepticism upon this sole foundation, that no reasoning can prove the truth and fidelity of our faculties. Here he stands upon firm ground: for it is evident, that every argument offered to prove the truth and fidelity of our faculties, takes for granted the thing in question, and is therefore that kind of sophism which logicians call *petitio principi*.

All we would ask of this kind of skeptic is, that he would be uniform and consistent, and that his practice in life do not belie his profession of skepticism with regard to the fidelity of his faculties: for the want of faith, as well as faith itself, is best shown by works. If a skeptic avoid the fire as much as those who believe it dangerous to go into it, we can hardly avoid thinking his skepticism to be feigned, and not real.

Our author indeed was aware, that neither his skepticism, nor that of any other person, was able to endure this trial, and therefore enters a caveat against it. "Neither I," says he, "nor any other person, was ever sincerely and constantly of that opinion. Nature, by an absolute and uncontrollable necessity, has determined us to judge, as well as to breathe and feel. My intention, therefore," says he, "in displaying so carefully the arguments of that fantastic sect, is only to make the reader sensible of the truth of my hypothesis, that all our reasonings concerning causes and effects, are derived from nothing but custom, and that belief is more properly an act of the sensitive than of the cogitative part of our nature."

We have before considered the first part of this hypothesis, Whether our reasoning about causes be derived only from custom?

The other part of the author's hypothesis here mentioned is darkly expressed, though the expression seems to be studied, as it is put in italics. It cannot surely mean that belief is not an act of thinking. It is not, therefore, the power of thinking that he calls the cogitative part of our nature. Neither can it be the power of judging, for all belief implies judgment; and to believe a proposition means the same thing as to judge it to be true. It seems, therefore, to be the power of reasoning that he calls the cogitative part of our nature.

If this be the meaning, I agree to it in part. The belief of first principles is not an act of the reasoning power: for all reasoning must be grounded upon them. We judge them to be true, and believe them without reasoning. But why this power of judging of first principles should be called the sensitive part of our nature, I do not understand.

As our belief of first principles is an act of pure judgment without reasoning; so our belief of the conclusions drawn by reasoning from first principles, may, I think, be called an act of the reasoning faculty.

Upon the whole, I see only two conclusions that can be fairly drawn from this profound and intricate reasoning against reason. The first is, that we are fallible in all our judgments and in all our reasonings. The second, that the truth and fidelity of our faculties can never be proved by reasoning; and therefore our belief of it cannot be founded on reasoning. If the last be what the author calls his hypothesis, I subscribe to it, and think it not an hypothesis, but a manifest truth; though I conceive it to be very improperly expressed, by saying, that belief is more properly an act of the sensitive than of the cognitative part of our nature.

The Fixation of Belief

C. S. PEIRCE

1. SCIENCE AND LOGIC

358. Few persons care to study logic, because everybody conceives himself to be proficient enough in the art of reasoning already. But I observe that this satisfaction is limited to one's own ratiocination, and does not extend to that of other men.

359. We come to the full possession of our power of drawing inferences, the last of all our faculties; for it is not so much a natural gift as a long and difficult art. The history of its practice would make a grand subject for a book. The medieval schoolman, following the Romans, made logic the earliest of a boy's studies after grammar, as being very easy. So it was as they understood it. Its fundamental principle, according to them, was, that all knowledge rests either on authority or reason; but that whatever is deduced by reason depends ultimately on a premiss derived from authority. Accordingly, as soon as a boy was perfect in the syllogistic procedure, his intellectual kit of tools was held to be complete.

360. To Roger Bacon, that remarkable mind who in the middle of the thirteenth century was almost a scientific man, the schoolmen's conception of reasoning appeared only an obstacle to truth. He saw that experience alone teaches anything—a proposition which to us seems easy to understand, because a distinct conception of experience has been handed down to us from former generations; which to him likewise seemed perfectly clear, because its difficulties had not yet unfolded themselves. Of all kinds of experience, the best, he thought, was interior illumination, which teaches many things about Nature which the external senses could never discover, such as the transubstantiation of bread.

361. Four centuries later, the more celebrated Bacon, in the first book of his *Novum Organum,* gave his clear account of experience as something which must be open to verification and reëxamination. But, superior as Lord Bacon's conception is to earlier notions, a modern reader who is not in awe of his grandiloquence is chiefly struck by the inadequacy of his view of scientific procedure. That we have only to make some crude experiments, to draw up briefs of the results in certain blank forms, to go through these by rule, checking off everything disproved and setting down the alternatives, and that thus in a few years physical science would be finished up—what an idea! "He wrote on science like a Lord Chancellor,"[1] indeed, as Harvey, a genuine man of science said.

362. The early scientists, Copernicus, Tycho Brahe, Kepler, Galileo, Harvey, and Gilbert, had methods more like those of their modern brethren. Kepler undertook to draw a curve through the places of Mars,[2] and to state the times occupied by the planet in describing

---

C.S. Peirce (1839-1914) was the father of the pragmatic tradition and the most significant philosopher yet produced in America.

Reprinted by permission of the publishers from *Collected Papers of Charles Sanders Peirce,* Volume V, Charles Hartshorne and Paul Weiss, eds., Cambridge, Massachusetts: The Belknap Press of Harvard University Press, © 1934, 1962 by the President and Fellows of Harvard College.

the different parts of that curve; but perhaps his greatest service to science was in impressing on men's minds that this was the thing to be done if they wished to improve astronomy; that they were not to content themselves with inquiring whether one system of epicycles was better than another but that they were to sit down to the figures and find out what the curve, in truth, was. He accomplished this by his incomparable energy and courage, blundering along in the most inconceivable way (to us), from one irrational hypothesis to another, until, after trying twenty-two of these, he fell, by the mere exhaustion of his invention, upon the orbit which a mind well furnished with the weapons of modern logic would have tried almost at the outset.[3]

363. In the same way, every work of science great enough to be well remembered for a few generations affords some exemplification of the defective state of the art of reasoning of the time when it was written; and each chief step in science has been a lesson in logic. It was so when Lavoisier and his contemporaries took up the study of Chemistry. The old chemist's maxim had been, "Lege, lege, lege, labora, ora, et relege." Lavoisier's method was not to read and pray, but to dream that some long and complicated chemical process would have a certain effect, to put it into practice with dull patience, after its inevitable failure, to dream that with some modification it would have another result, and to end by publishing the last dream as a fact: his way was to carry his mind into his laboratory, and literally to make of his alembics and cucurbits instruments of thought, giving a new conception of reasoning as something which was to be done with one's eyes open, in manipulating real things instead of words and fancies.

364. The Darwinian controversy is, in large part, a question of logic. Mr. Darwin proposed to apply the statistical method to biology.[4] The same thing has been done in a widely different branch of science, the theory of gases. Though unable to say what the movements of any particular molecule of gas would be on a certain hypothesis regarding the constitution of this class of bodies, Clausius and Maxwell were yet able, eight years before the publication of Darwin's immortal work, by the application of the doctrine of probabilities, to predict that in the long run such and such a proportion of the molecules would, under given circumstances, acquire such and such velocities; that there would take place, every second, such and such a relative number of collisions, etc.; and from these propositions were able to deduce certain properties of gases, especially in regard to their heat-relations. In like manner, Darwin, while unable to say what the operation of variation and natural selection in any individual case will be, demonstrates that in the long run they will, or would, adapt animals to their circumstances. Whether or not existing animal forms are due to such action, or what position the theory ought to take, forms the subject of a discussion in which questions of fact and questions of logic are curiously interlaced.

2. GUIDING PRINCIPLES

365. The object of reasoning is to find out, from the consideration of what we already know, something else which we do not know. Consequently, reasoning is good if it be such as to[5] give a true conclusion from true premisses, and not otherwise. Thus, the question of validity is purely one of fact and not of thinking. A being the facts stated in the premisses and B being that concluded, the question is, whether these facts are really so related that if A were B would generally be. If so, the inference is valid; if not, not. It is not in the least the question whether, when the premisses are accepted by the mind, we feel an impulse to accept the conclusion also. It is true that we do generally reason correctly by nature. But that is an accident; the true conclusion would remain true if we had no impulse to accept it; and the false one would remain false, though we could not resist the tendency to believe in it.

366. We are, doubtless, in the main logical animals, but we are not perfectly so. Most of us, for example, are naturally more sanguine and hopeful than logic would justify. We seem to be so constituted that in the absence of any facts to go upon we are happy and self-satisfied; so that the effect of experience is continually to contract our hopes and aspirations. Yet a lifetime of the application of this

corrective does not usually eradicate our sanguine disposition. Where hope is unchecked by any experience, it is likely that our optimism is extravagant. Logicality in regard to practical matters (if this be understood, not in the old sense, but as consisting in a wise union of security with fruitfulness of reasoning) is the most useful quality an animal can possess, and might, therefore, result from the action of natural selection; but outside of these it is probably of more advantage to the animal to have his mind filled with pleasing and encouraging visions, independently of their truth; and thus, upon unpractical subjects, natural selection might occasion a fallacious tendency of thought.[6]

367. That which determines us, from given premisses, to draw one inference rather than another, is some habit of mind, whether it be constitutional or acquired. The habit is good or otherwise, according as it produces true conclusions from true premisses or not; and an inference is regarded as valid or not, without reference to the truth or falsity of its conclusion specially, but according as the habit which determines it is such as to produce true conclusions in general or not. The particular habit of mind which governs this or that inference may be formulated in a proposition whose truth depends on the validity of the inferences which the habit determines; and such a formula is called a *guiding principle* of inference. Suppose, for example, that we observe that a rotating disk of copper quickly comes to rest when placed between the poles of a magnet, and we infer that this will happen with every disk of copper. The guiding principle is, that what is true of one piece of copper is true of another. Such a guiding principle with regard to copper would be much safer than with regard to many other substances—brass, for example.

368. A book might be written to signalize all the most important of these guiding principles of reasoning. It would probably be, we must confess, of no service to a person whose thought is directed wholly to practical subjects, and whose activity moves along thoroughly-beaten paths. The problems that present themselves to such a mind are matters of routine which he has learned once for all to handle in learning his business. But let a man venture into an unfamiliar field, or where his results are not continually checked by experience, and all history shows that the most masculine intellect will ofttimes lose his orientation and waste his efforts in directions which bring him no nearer to his goal, or even carry him entirely astray. He is like a ship in the open sea, with no one on board who understands the rules of navigation. And in such a case some general study of the guiding principles of reasoning would be sure to be found useful.

369. The subject could hardly be treated, however, without being first limited; since almost any fact may serve as a guiding principle. But it so happens that there exists a division among facts, such that in one class are all those which are absolutely essential as guiding principles, while in the others are all which have any other interest as objects of research. This division is between those which are necessarily taken for granted in asking why a certain conclusion is thought to follow from certain premisses, and those which are not implied in such a question. A moment's thought will show that a variety of facts are already assumed when the logical question is first asked. It is implied, for instance, that there are such states of mind as doubt and belief—that a passage from one to the other is possible, the object of thought remaining the same, and that this transition is subject to some rules by which all minds are alike bound. As these are facts which we must already know before we can have any clear conception of reasoning at all, it cannot be supposed to be any longer of much interest to inquire into their truth or falsity. On the other hand, it is easy to believe that those rules of reasoning which are deduced from the very idea of the process are the ones which are the most essential; and, indeed, that so long as it conforms to these it will, at least, not lead to false conclusions from true premisses. In point of fact, the importance of what may be deduced from the assumptions involved in the logical question turns out to be greater than might be supposed, and this for reasons which it is difficult to exhibit at the outset. The only one which I shall here mention is, that conceptions which are really products of logical reflection, without being readily seen to be so, mingle with our ordinary thoughts, and are frequently the causes of great confusion. This

is the case, for example, with the conception of quality. A quality, as such, is never an object of observation. We can see that a thing is blue or green, but the quality of being blue and the quality of being green are not things which we see; they are products of logical reflections. The truth is, that common-sense, or thought as it first emerges above the level of the narrowly practical, is deeply imbued with that bad logical quality to which the epithet *metaphysical* is commonly applied; and nothing can clear it up but a severe course of logic.

3. DOUBT AND BELIEF

370. We generally know when we wish to ask a question and when we wish to pronounce a judgment, for there is a dissimilarity between the sensation of doubting and that of believing.

371. But this is not all which distinguishes doubt from belief. There is a practical difference. Our beliefs guide our desires and shape our actions. The Assassins, or followers of the Old Man of the Mountain, used to rush into death at his least command, because they believed that obedience to him would insure everlasting felicity. Had they doubted this, they would not have acted as they did. So it is with every belief, according to its degree. The feeling of believing is a more or less sure indication of there being established in our nature some habit which will determine our actions.[7] Doubt never has such an effect.

372. Nor must we overlook a third point of difference. Doubt is an uneasy and dissatisfied state from which we struggle to free ourselves and pass into the state of belief;[8] while the latter is a calm and satisfactory state which we do not wish to avoid, or to change to a belief in anything else.[9] On the contrary, we cling tenaciously, not merely to believing, but to believing just what we do believe.

373. Thus, both doubt and belief have positive effects upon us, though very different ones. Belief does not make us act at once, but puts us into such a condition that we shall behave in some certain way, when the occasion arises. Doubt has not the least such active effect, but stimulates us to inquiry until it is destroyed. This reminds us of the irritation of a nerve and the reflex action produced thereby; while for the analogue of belief, in the nervous system, we must look to what are called nervous associations—for example, to that habit of the nerves in consequence of which the smell of a peach will make the mouth water.[10]

4. THE END OF INQUIRY

374. The irritation of doubt causes a struggle to attain a state of belief. I shall term this struggle *Inquiry*, though it must be admitted that this is sometimes not a very apt designation.

375. The irritation of doubt is the only immediate motive for the struggle to attain belief. It is certainly best for us that our beliefs should be such as may truly guide our actions so as to satisfy our desires; and this reflection will make us reject every belief which does not seem to have been so formed as to insure this result. But it will only do so by creating a doubt in the place of that belief.[11] With the doubt, therefore, the struggle begins, and with the cessation of doubt it ends. Hence, the sole object of inquiry is the settlement of opinion. We may fancy that this is not enough for us, and that we seek, not merely an opinion, but a true opinion. But put this fancy to the test, and it proves groundless; for as soon as a firm belief is reached we are entirely satisfied, whether the belief be true or false. And it is clear that nothing out of the sphere of our knowledge can be our object, for nothing which does not affect the mind can be the motive for mental effort. The most that can be maintained is, that we seek for a belief that we shall *think* to be true. But we think each one of our beliefs to be true, and, indeed, it is mere tautology to say so.[12]

That the settlement of opinion is the sole end of inquiry is a very important proposition. It sweeps away, at once, various vague and erroneous conceptions of proof. A few of these may be noticed here.

376. 1. Some philosophers have imagined that to start an inquiry it was only necessary to utter a question whether orally or by setting it down on paper, and have even recommended us to begin our studies with questioning everything! But the mere putting of a proposi-

tion into the interrogative form does not stimulate the mind to any struggle after belief. There must be a real and living doubt, and without this all discussion is idle.[13]

2. It is a very common idea that a demonstration must rest on some ultimate and absolutely indubitable propositions. These, according to one school, are first principles of a general nature; according to another, are first sensations. But, in point of fact, an inquiry, to have that completely satisfactory result called demonstration, has only to start with propositions perfectly free from all actual doubt. If the premisses are not in fact doubted at all, they cannot be more satisfactory than they are.[14]

3. Some people seem to love to argue a point after all the world is fully convinced of it. But no further advance can be made. When doubt ceases, mental action on the subject comes to an end; and, if it did go on, it would be without a purpose.[15]

5. METHODS OF FIXING BELIEF

377. If the settlement of opinion is the sole object of inquiry, and if belief is of the nature of a habit, why should we not attain the desired end, by taking as answer to a question any we may fancy, and constantly reiterating it to ourselves, dwelling on all which may conduce to that belief, and learning to turn with contempt and hatred from anything that might disturb it? This simple and direct method is really pursued by many men. I remember once being entreated not to read a certain newspaper lest it might change my opinion upon free-trade. "Lest I might be entrapped by its fallacies and misstatements," was the form of expression. "You are not," my friend said, "a special student of political economy. You might, therefore, easily be deceived by fallacious arguments upon the subject. You might, then, if you read this paper, be led to believe in protection. But you admit that free-trade is the true doctrine; and you do not wish to believe what is not true." I have often known this system to be deliberately adopted. Still oftener, the instinctive dislike of an undecided state of mind, exaggerated into a vague dread of doubt, makes men cling spasmodically to the views they already take. The man feels that, if he only holds to his belief without wavering, it will be entirely satisfactory. Nor can it be denied that a steady and immovable faith yields great peace of mind. It may, indeed, give rise to inconveniences, as if a man should resolutely continue to believe that fire would not burn him, or that he would be eternally damned if he received his *ingesta* otherwise than through a stomach-pump. But then the man who adopts this method will not allow that its inconveniences are greater than its advantages. He will say, "I hold steadfastly to the truth, and the truth is always wholesome." And in many cases it may very well be that the pleasure he derives from his calm faith overbalances any inconveniences resulting from its deceptive character. Thus, if it be true that death is annihilation, then the man who believes that he will certainly go straight to heaven when he dies, provided he have fulfilled certain simple observances in this life, has a cheap pleasure which will not be followed by the least disappointment.[16] A similar consideration seems to have weight with many persons in religious topics, for we frequently hear it said, "Oh, I could not believe so-and-so, because I should be wretched if I did." When an ostrich buries its head in the sand as danger approaches, it very likely takes the happiest course. It hides the danger, and then calmly says there is no danger, and, if it feels perfectly sure there is none, why should it raise its head to see? A man may go through life, systematically keeping out of view all that might cause a change in his opinions, and if he only succeeds—basing his method, as he does, on two fundamental psychological laws—I do not see what can be said against his doing so. It would be an egotistical impertinence to object that his procedure is irrational, for that only amounts to saying that his method of settling belief is not ours. He does not propose to himself to be rational, and, indeed, will often talk with scorn of man's weak and illusive reason. So let him think as he pleases.

378. But this method of fixing belief, which may be called the method of tenacity, "will be unable to hold its ground in practice." The social impulse is against it. The man who adopts it will find that other men think differently from him, and it will be apt

to occur to him, in some saner moment, that their opinions are quite as good as his own, and this will shake his confidence in his belief. This conception, that another man's thought or sentiment may be equivalent to one's own, is a distinctly new step, and a highly important one. It arises from an impulse too strong in man to be suppressed, without danger of destroying the human species. Unless we make ourselves hermits, we shall necessarily influence each other's opinions; so that the problem becomes how to fix belief, not in the individual merely, but in the community.

379. Let the will of the state act, then, instead of that of the individual. Let an institution be created which shall have for its object to keep correct doctrines before the attention of the people, to reiterate them perpetually, and to teach them to the young; having at the same time power to prevent contrary doctrines from being taught, advocated, or expressed. Let all possible causes of a change of mind be removed from men's apprehensions. Let them be kept ignorant, lest they should learn of some reason to think otherwise than they do. Let their passions be enlisted, so that they may regard private and unusual opinions with hatred and horror. Then, let all men who reject the established belief be terrified into silence. Let the people turn out and tar-and-feather such men, or let inquisitions be made into the manner of thinking of suspected persons, and when they are found guilty of forbidden beliefs, let them be subjected to some signal punishment. When complete agreement could not otherwise be reached, a general massacre of all who have not thought in a certain way has proved a very effective means of settling opinion in a country. If the power to do this be wanting, let a list of opinions be drawn up, to which no man of the least independence of thought can assent, and let the faithful be required to accept all these propositions, in order to segregate them as radically as possible from the influence of the rest of the world.

This method has, from the earliest times, been one of the chief means of upholding correct theological and political doctrines, and of preserving their universal or catholic character. In Rome, especially, it has been practised from the days of Numa Pompilius to those of Pius Nonus. This is the most perfect example in history; but wherever there is a priesthood—and no religion has been without one—this method has been more or less made use of. Wherever there is an aristocracy, or a guild, or any association of a class of men whose interests depend, or are supposed to depend, on certain propositions, there will be inevitably found some traces of this natural product of social feeling. Cruelties always accompany this system; and when it is consistently carried out, they become atrocities of the most horrible kind in the eyes of any rational man. Nor should this occasion surprise, for the officer of a society does not feel justified in surrendering the interests of that society for the sake of mercy, as he might his own private interests. It is natural, therefore, that sympathy and fellowship should thus produce a most ruthless power.

380. In judging this method of fixing belief, which may be called the method of authority, we must, in the first place, allow its immeasurable mental and moral superiority to the method of tenacity. Its success is proportionately greater; and, in fact, it has over and over again worked the most majestic results. The mere structures of stone which it has caused to be put together—in Siam, for example, in Egypt, and in Europe—have many of them a sublimity hardly more than rivaled by the greatest works of Nature. And, except the geological epochs, there are no periods of time so vast as those which are measured by some of these organized faiths.[17] If we scrutinize the matter closely, we shall find that there has not been one of their creeds which has remained always the same; yet the change is so slow as to be imperceptible during one person's life, so that individual belief remains sensibly fixed. For the mass of mankind, then, there is perhaps no better method than this. If it is their highest impulse to be intellectual slaves, then slaves they ought to remain.

381. But no institution can undertake to regulate opinions upon every subject. Only the most important ones can be attended to, and on the rest men's minds must be left to the action of natural causes. This imperfection will be no source of weakness so long as men are in such a state of culture that one opinion does not influence another—that is, so long as

they cannot put two and two together. But in the most priest-ridden states some individuals will be found who are raised above that condition. These men possess a wider sort of social feeling; they see that men in other countries and in other ages have held to very different doctrines from those which they themselves have been brought up to believe; and they cannot help seeing that it is the mere accident of their having been taught as they have, and of their having been surrounded with the manners and associations they have, that has caused them to believe as they do and not far differently. Nor can their candour resist the reflection that there is no reason to rate their own views at a higher value than those of other nations and other centuries; thus giving rise to doubts in their minds.

382. They will further perceive that such doubts as these must exist in their minds with reference to every belief which seems to be determined by the caprice either of themselves or of those who originated the popular opinions. The willful adherence to a belief, and the arbitrary forcing of it upon others, must, therefore, both be given up. A different new method of settling opinions must be adopted, that shall not only produce an impulse to believe, but shall also decide what proposition it is which is to be believed. Let the action of natural preferences be unimpeded, then, and under their influence let men, conversing together and regarding matters in different lights, gradually develop beliefs in harmony with natural causes. This method resembles that by which conceptions of art have been brought to maturity. The most perfect example of it is to be found in the history of metaphysical philosophy. Systems of this sort have not usually rested upon any observed facts, at least not in any great degree. They have been chiefly adopted because their fundamental propositions seemed "agreeable to reason." This is an apt expression; it does not mean that which agrees with experience, but that which we find ourselves inclined to believe. Plato, for example, finds it agreeable to reason that the distances of the celestial spheres from one another should be proportional to the different lengths of strings which produce harmonious chords. Many philosophers have been led to their main conclusions by considerations like this;[18] but this is the lowest and least developed form which the method takes, for it is clear that another man might find Kepler's theory, that the celestial spheres are proportional to the inscribed and circumscribed spheres of the different regular solids, more agreeable to *his* reason. But the shock of opinions will soon lead men to rest on preferences of a far more universal nature. Take, for example, the doctrine that man only acts selfishly—that is, from the consideration that acting in one way will afford him more pleasure than acting in another. This rests on no fact in the world, but it has had a wide acceptance as being the only reasonable theory.[19]

383. This method is far more intellectual and respectable from the point of view of reason than either of the others which we have noticed. Indeed, as long as no better method can be applied, it ought to be followed, since it is then the expression of instinct which must be the ultimate cause of belief in all cases. But its failure has been the most manifest. It makes of inquiry something similar to the development of taste; but taste, unfortunately, is always more or less a matter of fashion, and accordingly metaphysicians have never come to any fixed agreement, but the pendulum has swung backward and forward between a more material and a more spiritual philosophy, from the earliest times to the latest. And so from this, which has been called the *a priori* method, we are driven, in Lord Bacon's phrase, to a true induction. We have examined into this *a priori* method as something which promised to deliver our opinions from their accidental and capricious element. But development, while it is a process which eliminates the effect of some casual circumstances, only magnifies that of others. This method, therefore, does not differ in a very essential way from that of authority. The government may not have lifted its finger to influence my convictions; I may have been left outwardly quite free to choose, we will say, between monogamy and polygamy, and, appealing to my conscience only, I may have concluded that the latter practice is in itself licentious. But when I come to see that the chief obstacle to the spread of Christianity among a people of as high culture as the Hindoos has been a conviction of the immorality of our way of treating

women, I cannot help seeing that, though governments do not interfere, sentiments in their development will be very greatly determined by accidental causes. Now, there are some people, among whom I must suppose that my reader is to be found, who, when they see that any belief of theirs is determined by any circumstance extraneous to the facts, will from that moment not merely admit in words that that belief is doubtful, but will experience a real doubt of it, so that it ceases in some degree at least to be a belief.

384. To satisfy our doubts, therefore, it is necessary that a method should be found by which our beliefs may be determined by nothing human, but by some external permanency—by something upon which our thinking has no effect.[20] Some mystics imagine that they have such a method in a private inspiration from on high. But that is only a form of the method of tenacity, in which the conception of truth as something public is not yet developed. Our external permanency would not be external, in our sense, if it was restricted in its influence to one individual. It must be something which affects, or might affect, every man. And, though these affections are necessarily as various as are individual conditions, yet the method must be such that the ultimate conclusion of every man shall be the same.[21] Such is the method of science. Its fundamental hypothesis, restated in more familiar language, is this: There are Real things, whose characters are entirely independent of our opinions about them; those Reals affect our senses according to regular laws, and, though our sensations are as different as are our relations to the objects, yet, by taking advantage of the laws of perception, we can ascertain by reasoning how things really and truly are; and any man, if he have sufficient experience and he reason enough about it, will be led to the one True conclusion. The new conception here involved is that of Reality. It may be asked how I know that there are any Reals. If this hypothesis is the sole support of my method of inquiry, my method of inquiry must not be used to support my hypothesis. The reply is this: 1. If investigation cannot be regarded as proving that there are Real things, it at least does not lead to a contrary conclusion; but the method and the conception on which it is based remain ever in harmony. No doubts of the method, therefore, necessarily arise from its practice, as is the case with all the others. 2. The feeling which gives rise to any method of fixing belief is a dissatisfaction at two repugnant propositions. But here already is a vague concession that there is some *one* thing which a proposition should represent. Nobody, therefore, can really doubt that there are Reals, for, if he did, doubt would not be a source of dissatisfaction. The hypothesis, therefore, is one which every mind admits. So that the social impulse does not cause men to doubt it. 3. Everybody uses the scientific method about a great many things, and only ceases to use it when he does not know how to apply it. 4. Experience of the method has not led us to doubt it, but, on the contrary, scientific investigation has had the most wonderful triumphs in the way of settling opinion. These afford the explanation of my not doubting the method or the hypothesis which it supposes; and not having any doubt, nor believing that anybody else whom I could influence has, it would be the merest babble for me to say more about it. If there be anybody with a living doubt upon the subject, let him consider it.[22]

385. To describe the method of scientific investigation is the object of this series of papers. At present I have only room to notice some points of contrast between it and other methods of fixing belief.

This is the only one of the four methods which presents any distinction of a right and a wrong way. If I adopt the method of tenacity, and shut myself out from all influences, whatever I think necessary to doing this, is necessary according to that method. So with the method of authority: the state may try to put down heresy by means which, from a scientific point of view, seem very ill — calculated to accomplish its purposes; but the only test *on that method* is what the state thinks; so that it cannot pursue the method wrongly. So with the *a priori* method. The very essence of it is to think as one is inclined to think. All metaphysicians will be sure to do that, however they may be inclined to judge each other to be perversely wrong. The Hegelian system recognizes every natural tendency of thought as logical, although it be certain to be abolished by counter-tendencies. Hegel thinks there is a regular system in the succession of these tendencies, in consequence of which, after drifting one way and the other for a long time, opinion will at last go right. And it is true that metaphysicians do get the right ideas at last; Hegel's system of Nature represents tolerably the science of his day; and one may be sure that whatever scientific investigation shall have put out of doubt will presently receive *a priori* demonstration on the part of the metaphysicians. But with the scientific method the case is different. I may start with known and observed facts to proceed to the unknown; and yet the rules which I follow in doing so may not be such as investigation would approve. The test of whether I am truly following the method is not an immediate appeal to my feelings and purposes, but, on the contrary, itself involves the applicaiton of the method. Hence it is that bad reasoning as well as good reasoning is possible; and this fact is the foundation of the practical side of logic.

386. It is not to be supposed that the first three methods of settling opinion present no advantage whatever over the scientific method. On the contrary, each has some peculiar convenience of its own. The *a priori* method is distinguished for its comfortable conclusions. It is the nature of the process to adopt whatever belief we are inclined to, and there are certain flatteries to the vanity of man which we all believe by nature, until we are awakened from our pleasing dream by rough facts. The method of authority will always govern the mass of mankind; and those who wield the various forms of organized force in the state will never be convinced that dangerous reasoning ought not to be suppressed in some way. If liberty of speech is to be untrammeled from the grosser forms of constraint, then uniformity of opinion will be secured by a moral terrorism to which the respectability of society will give its thorough approval. Following the method of authority is the path of peace. Certain non-conformities are permitted; certain others (considered unsafe) are forbidden. These are different in different countries and in different ages; but, wherever you are, let it be known that you seriously hold a tabooed belief, and you may be perfectly sure of being treated with a cruelty less brutal but more refined than hunting you like a wolf. Thus, the greatest intellectual benefactors of mankind have never dared, and dare not now, to utter the whole of their thought; and thus a shade of *prima facie* doubt is cast upon every proposition which is considered essential to the security of society. Singularly enough, the persecution does not all come from without; but a man torments himself and is oftentimes most distressed at finding himself believing propositons which he has been brought up to regard with aversion. The peaceful and sympathetic man will, therefore, find it hard to resist the temptation to submit his opinions to authority. But most of all I admire the method of tenacity for its strength, simplicity, and directness. Men who pursue it are distinguished for their decision of character, which becomes very easy with such a mental rule. They do not waste time in trying to make up their minds what they want, but, fastening like lightning upon whatever alternative comes first, they hold to it to the end, whatever happens, without an instant's irresolution. This is one of the splendid qualities which generally accompany brilliant, unlasting success. It is impossible not to envy the man who can dismiss reason, although we know how it must turn out at last.

387. Such are the advantages which the other methods of settling opinion have over scientific investigation. A man should consider well of them; and then he should consider that, after all, he wishes his opinions to coincide with the fact, and that there is no reason why the results of those three first methods should do so. To bring about this effect is the prerogative of the method of science. Upon such considerations he has to make his choice—a choice which is far more than the adoption of any intellectual opinion, which is one of the ruling decisions of his life, to which, when once made, he is bound to adhere. The force of habit will sometimes cause a man to hold on to old beliefs, after he is in a condition to see that they have no sound basis. But reflection upon the state of the case will overcome these habits, and he ought to allow reflection its full weight. People sometimes shrink from doing this, having an idea that beliefs are wholesome which they cannot help feeling rest on nothing. But let such persons suppose an analogous though differ-

ent case from their own. Let them ask themselves what they would say to a reformed Mussulman who should hesitate to give up his old notions in regard to the relations of the sexes; or to a reformed Catholic who should still shrink from reading the Bible. Would they not say that these persons ought to consider the matter fully, and clearly understand the new doctrine, and then ought to embrace it, in its entirety? But, above all, let it be considered that what is more wholesome than any particular belief is integrity of belief, and that to avoid looking into the support of any belief from a fear that it may turn out rotten is quite as immoral as it is disadvantageous. The person who confesses that there is such a thing as truth, which is distinguished from falsehood simply by this, that if acted on it should, on full consideration, carry us to the point we aim at and not astray, and then, though convinced of this, dares not know the truth and seeks to avoid it, is in a sorry state of mind indeed.

[23]Yes, the other methods do have their merits: a clear logical conscience does cost something—just as any virtue, just as all that we cherish, costs us dear. But we should not desire it to be otherwise. The genius of a man's logical method should be loved and reverenced as his bride, whom he has chosen from all the world. He need not contemn the others; on the contrary, he may honor them deeply, and in doing so he only honors her the more. But she is the one that he has chosen, and he knows that he was right in making that choice. And having made it, he will work and fight for her, and will not complain that there are blows to take, hoping that there may be as many and as hard to give, and will strive to be the worthy knight and champion of her from the blaze of whose splendors he draws his inspiration and his courage.

NOTES

1. Cf. J. Aubrey's *Brief Lives* (Oxford ed. 1898), I, 299.

2. Not quite so, but as nearly so as can be told in a few words.

3. I am ashamed at being obliged to confess that this volume contains a very false and foolish remark about Kepler. When I wrote it, I had never studied the original book as I have since. It is now my deliberate opinion that it is the most marvellous piece of inductive reasoning I have been able to find.—1893.

4. What he did, a most instructive illustration of the logic of science, will be described in another chapter; and we now know what was authoritatively denied when I first suggested it, that he took a hint from Malthus' book on Population.—1903

5. I.e., be dominated by such a habit as generally to give.—1903.

6. Let us not, however, be cocksure that natural selection is the only factor of evolution; and until this momentous proposition has been much better proved than as yet it has been, let it not blind us to the force [of] very sound reasoning.—1903.

7. Let us recall the nature of a sign and ask ourselves how we can know that a feeling of any sort is a sign that we have a habit implanted within us.

We can understand one habit by likening it to another habit. But to understand what any habit is, there must be some habit of which we are directly conscious in its generality. That is to say, we must have a certain generality in our direct consciousness. Bishop Berkeley and a great many clear thinkers laugh at the idea of our being able to imagine a triangle that is neither equilateral, isosceles, nor scalene. They seem to think the object of imagination must be precisely determinate in every respect. But it seems certain that something general we must imagine. I do not intend, in this book, to go into questions of psychology. It is not necessary for us to know in detail how our thinking is done, but only how it can be done. Still, I may as well say, at once, that I think our direct consciousness covers a duration of time, although only an infinitely brief duration. At any rate, I can see no way of escaping the proposition that to attach any general significance to a sign and to know that we do attach a general significance to it, we must have a direct imagination of something not in all respects determinate.—1893..

8. In this, it is like any other stimulus. It is true that just as men may, for the sake of the pleasures of the table, like to be hungry and take means to make themselves so, although hunger always involves a desire to fill the stomach, so for the sake of the pleasures of inquiry, men may like to seek out

doubts. Yet, for all that, doubt essentially involves a struggle to escape it.—1893.

9. I am not speaking of secondary effects occasionally produced by the interference of other impulses.

10. Doubt, however, is not usually hesitancy about what is to be done then and there. It is anticipated hesitancy about what I shall do hereafter, or a feigned hesitancy about a fictitious state of things. It is the power of making believe we hesitate, together with the pregnant fact that the decision upon the merely make-believe dilemma goes toward forming a bona fide habit that will be operative in a real emergency. It is these two things in conjunction that constitute us intellectual beings.

Every answer to a question that has any meaning is a decision as to how we would act under imagined circumstances, or how the world would be expected to react upon our senses. Thus, suppose I am told that if two straight lines in one plane are cut by a third making the sum of the internal angles on one side less than two right angles, then those lines if sufficiently produced will meet on the side on which the said sum is less than two right angles. This means to me that if I had two lines drawn on a plane and wished to find where they would meet, I could draw a third line cutting them and ascertaining on which side the sum of the two interval angles was less than two right angles, and should lengthen the lines on that side. In like manner, all doubt is a state of hesitancy about an imagined state of things.—1893.

11. Unless, indeed, it leads us to modify our desires.—1903.

12. For truth is neither more nor less than that character of a proposition which consists in this, that belief in the proposition would, with sufficient experience and reflection, lead us to such conduct as would tend to satisfy the desires we should then have. To say that truth means more than this is to say that it has no meaning at all.—1903.

13. So long as we cannot put our fingers on our erroneous opinions, they remain our opinions, still. It will be wholesome enough for us to make a general review of the causes of our beliefs; and the result will be that most of them have been taken upon trust and have been held since we were too young to discriminate the credible from the incredible. Such reflections may awaken real doubts about some of our positions. But in cases where no real doubt exists in our minds inquiry will be an idle farce, a mere whitewashing commission which were better let alone. This fault in philosophy was very widespread in those ages in which Disputations were the principal exercises in the universities; that is, from their rise in the thirteenth century down to the middle of the eighteenth, and even to this day in some Catholic institutions. But since those disputations went out of vogue, this philosophic disease is less virulent.—1893.

14. We have to acknowledge that doubts about them may spring up later; but we can find no propositions which are not subject to this contingency. We ought to construct our theories so as to provide for such discoveries; first, by making them rest on as great a variety of different considerations as possible, and second, by leaving room for the modifications which cannot be foreseen but which are pretty sure to prove needful. Some systems are much more open to this criticism than others. All those which repose heavily upon an "inconceivability of the opposite" have proved particularly fragile and short-lived. Those, however, which rest upon positive evidences and which avoid insisting upon the absolute precision of their dogmas are hard to destroy.—1893.

15. Except that of self-criticism. Insert here a section upon self-control and the analogy between Moral and Rational self-control.—1903.

16. Although it certainly may be that it will cause a line of conduct leading to pains that deeper reflection would have avoided.—1903.

17. Unify them in the sense of Alexander Pope's *Universal Prayer,* and who is the individual whose conceit shall stand up and place his dictum against theirs? These faiths lay claim to divine authorship; and it is true that men have no more *invented* them, than the birds have invented their songs. It is a relapse toward the method of tenacity that segregates them and blinds the ecclesiastic to the value of anything but hatred. Every distinctive creed was as a historical fact invented to harm somebody. Still, the upshot has, on the whole, been success unparalleled. If slavery of opinion is natural and wholesome for men, then slaves they ought to remain.

Every such system was first established by some individual legislator or prophet; and once established it grew of itself. But within this principle of growth lurk germs of decay. The power of individualism becomes extinct; the organization alone has life. Now, in the course of ages old questions pass out of mind: new questions become urgent. The sea advances or recedes; some horde which has always lived by conquest happens to make a conquest of consequence to the world at large. In one way or another, commerce is diverted from its ancient roads. Such change brings novel experiences and new ideas. Men begin to rebel at doings of the authorities to which in former times they would have submitted. Questions never before raised come up for decision; yet an individual legislator would no longer be listened to. Never has the instinct of rulers failed to see that the summoning of a council of the people was a measure fraught with peril to authority. Yet however they strive to avoid it, they in effect invoke public opinion, which is a momentous appeal to a new method of settling opinion. Disturbances occur; knots of men discuss the state of affairs; and a suspicion is kindled, which runs about like a train of gun powder, that the Dicta men have been reverencing, originated in caprice, in the pertinacity of some busybody, in the schemes of an ambitious man, or in other influences which are seen to edify a deliberative assembly. Men now begin to demand that, as the power which maintains the belief has become no longer capricious but public and methodical, so the propositions to be believed shall be determined in a public and methodical manner.—1893.

18. Let us see in what manner a few of the greatest philosophers have undertaken to settle opinion, and what their success has been. Descartes, who would have a man begin by doubting everything, remarks that there is one thing he will find himself unable to doubt, and that is, that he does doubt; and when he reflects that he doubts, he can no longer doubt that he exists. Then, because he is all the while doubting whether there are any such things as shape and motion, Descartes thinks he must be persuaded that shape and motion do not belong to his nature, or anything else but consciousness. This is taking it for granted that nothing in his nature lies hidden beneath the surface. Next, Descartes asks the doubter to remark that he has the idea of a Being, in the highest degree intelligent, powerful, and perfect. Now a Being would not have these qualities unless he existed necessarily and eternally. By existing necessarily he means existing by virture of the existence of the idea. Consequently, all doubt as to the existence of this Being must cease. This plainly supposes that belief is to be fixed by what men find in their minds. He is reasoning like this: I find it written in the volume of my mind that there is something X, which is such a sort of thing that the moment it is written down it exists. Plainly, he is aiming at a kind of truth which saying so can make to be so. He gives two further proofs of God's existence. Descartes makes God easier to know than anything else; for whatever we think He is, He is. He fails to remark that this is precisely the definition of a *figment*. In particular, God cannot be a deceiver; whence it follows, that whatever we quite clearly and distinctly think to be true about any subject, must *be* true. Accordingly, if people will thoroughly discuss a subject, and quite clearly and distinctly make up their minds what they think about it, the desired settlement of the question will be reached. I may remark that the world has pretty thoroughly deliberated upon that theory and has quite distinctly come to the conclusion that it is utter nonsense; whence that judgment is indisputably right.

Many critics have told me that I misrepresent the *a priori* philosophers, when I represent them as adopting whatever opinion there seems to be a natural inclination to adopt. But nobody can say the above does not accurately define the position of Descartes, and upon what does he repose except natural ways of thinking? Perhaps I shall be told however, that since Kant, that vice has been cured. Kant's great boast is that he critically examines into our natural inclinations toward certain opinions. An opinion that something is *universally* true clearly goes further than experience can warrant. An opinion that something is *necessarily* true (that is, not merely is true in the existing state of things, but would be true in every state of things) equally goes further than experience will warrant. Those remarks had been made by Leibniz and admitted by Hume; and Kant reiterates them. Though they are propositions of a nominalistic cast, they can hardly be denied. I may add that whatever is held to be precisely true goes further than experience can possibly warrant. Accepting those criteria of the origin of ideas, Kant proceeds to reason as follows: Geometrical propositions are held to be universally true. Hence, they are not given by experience. Consequently, it must be owing to an inward necessity of man's nature that he sees everything in space. Ergo, the sum of the angles of a triangle will be equal to two right angles for all the objects of our vision. Just that, and nothing more, is Kant's line of thought. But the dry-rot of reason in the seminaries has gone to the point where such stuff is held to be admirable argumentation. I might go through the *Critic of the Pure Reason,* section by section, and show that the thought throughout is precisely of this character. He everywhere shows that ordinary objects, such as trees and goldpieces, involve elements not contained in the first presentations of sense. But we cannot persuade ourselves to give up the reality of trees and goldpieces. There is a general inward insistence upon them, and that is the warrant for swallowing the entire bolus of general belief about them. This is merely accepting without question a belief as soon as it is shown to please a great many people very much. When he comes to the ideas of God, Freedom, and Immortality, he hesitates; because people who think only of bread and butter, pleasure and power, are indifferent to those ideas. He subjects these ideas to a different kind of examination, and finally admits them upon grounds which appear to the seminarists more or less suspicious, but which in the eyes of laboratorists are infinitely stronger than the grounds upon which he has accepted space, time, and causality. Those last grounds amount to nothing but this, that what there is a very decided and general inclination to believe must be true. Had Kant merely said, I shall adopt for the present the belief that the three angles of a triangle are equal to two right angles because nobody but brother Lambert and some Italian has ever called it in question, his attitude would be well enough. But on the contrary, he and those who today represent his school distinctly maintain the proposition is *proved*, and the Lambertists *refuted*, by what comes merely to general disinclination to think with them.

As for Hegel, who led Germany for a generation, he recognizes clearly what he is about. He simply launches his boat into the current of thought and allows himself to be carried wherever the current leads. He himself calls his method *dialectic*, meaning that a frank discussion of the difficulties to which any opinion spontaneously gives rise will lead to modification after modification until a tenable position is attained. This is a distinct profession of faith in the method of inclinations.

Other philosophers appeal to "the test of inconceivability of the opposite," to "Presuppositions" (by which they mean *Voraussetzungen*, properly translated, *postulates*), and other devices; but all these are but so many systems of rummaging the garret of the skull to find an enduring opinion about the Universe.

When we pass from the perusal of works upholding the method of authority to those of the philosophers, we not only find ourselves in a vastly higher intellectual atmosphere, but also in a clearer, freer, brighter, and more refreshing moral atmosphere. All this, however, is beside the one significant question of whether the method succeeds in fixing men's opinions. The projects of these authors are most persuasive. One dare swear they should succeed. But in point of fact, up to date they decidedly do not; and the outlook in this direction is most discouraging. The difficulty is that the opinions which today seem most unshakable are found tomorrow to be out of fashion. They are really far more changeable than they appear to a hasty reader to be; since the phrases made to dress out defunct opinions are worn at second hand by their successors.

We still talk of "cause and effect" although, in the mechanical world, the opinion that phrase was meant to express has been shelved long ago. We now know that the acceleration of a particle at any instant depends upon its position relative to other particles at that same instant; while the old idea was that the past affects the future, while the future does not affect the past. So the "law of demand and supply" has utterly different meanings with different economists.—1893.

19. An acceptance whose real support has been the opinion that pleasure is the only ultimate good. But this opinion, or even the opinion that pleasure *per se* is any good at all, is only tenable so long as he who holds it remains without any distinct idea of what he means by "good."—1903.

20. But which, on the other hand, unceasingly tends to influence thought; or in other words, by something Real.—1903.

21. Or would be the same if inquiry were sufficiently persisted in.—1903.

22. Changes of opinion are brought about by events beyond human control. All mankind were so firmly of opinion that heavy bodies must fall faster than light ones, that any other view was scouted as absurd, eccentric, and probably insincere. Yet as soon as some of the absurd and eccentric men could succeed in inducing some of the adherents of common sense to look at their experiments—no easy task—it became apparent that nature would not follow human opinion, however unanimous. So there was nothing for it but human opinion must move to nature's position. That was a lesson in humility. A few men, the small band of laboratory men, began to see that they had to abandon the pride of an opinion assumed absolutely final in any respect, and to use all their endeavors to yield as unresistingly as possible to the overwhelming tide of experience, which must master them at last, and to listen to what nature seems to be telling us. The trial of this method of experience in natural science for these three centuries—though bitterly detested by the majority of men—encourages us to hope that we are approaching nearer and nearer to an opinion which is not destined to be broken down—though we cannot expect ever quite to reach that ideal goal.—1893.

23. Delete the remainder.—marginal note, 1893, 1903.

FURTHER READINGS

Ayer, A. J. *The Problem of Knowledge*. New York: Penguin Books, 1956.

Chisholm, R. M. *Theory of Knowledge*. Englewood Cliffs, N. J.: Prentice-Hall, 1956.

Chisholm, R. M., and Swartz, R. J. *Empirical Knowledge: Readings from Contemporary Sources*. Englewood Cliffs, N. J.: Prentice-Hall, 1973.

Danto, A. *Analytical Philosophy of Knowledge*. Cambridge: University Press, 1968.

Hamlyn, D. W. *The Theory of Knowledge*. Garden City, N. Y.: Doubleday, 1970.

Lehrer, K. *Knowledge*. Oxford: Clarendon Press, 1974.

Polanyi, M. *Personal Knowledge: Towards a Post-Critical Philosophy*. Chicago: University of Chicago Press, 1958.

Pollock, J. *Knowledge and Justification*. Princeton: Princeton University Press, 1974.

Unger, P. *Ignorance: A Case for Skepticism*. Oxford: Clarendon Press, 1975.

Will, F. *Induction and Justification*. Ithaca, N. Y.: Cornell University Press, 1974.

PART THREE

Human Freedom

Introduction

GARY GUTTING

A view of ourselves as free agents, as the controlling sources of at least many of our actions, pervades our lives. Our language bristles with distinctions between what we do "on purpose" and what we do "by accident," between what we "couldn't help doing" and what we did because we "wanted to," between "freely choosing" and "being compelled." The same view pervades our social institutions, from the freely given "I do" which constitutes a marriage to a jury's deliberation as to whether the defendant purposely pulled the trigger. And underlying this linguistic and social commitment to freedom is a continuing and, it seems, irrefutable personal experience of ourselves as free agents. I decide to buy a green rather than a yellow coat, to give a compliment rather than withhold it, to apply to law school rather than medical school; and in each case it is overwhelmingly obvious to me that I could have made the opposite choice. As Descartes said, ". . . it is so evident that we are possessed of a free will . . . that this may be counted as one of the first and most ordinary notions that are found innately in us."

Beyond these overwhelming indications of the sheer fact of freedom, there is another fact which, all on its own, would seem sufficient to establish the reality of our freedom. This is the fact of moral responsibility. Each of us is convinced that there are certain things that it would be morally wrong to do (or leave undone). I am certain, for example, that it is wrong for me to torture small children for my own amusement. (This point remains true quite independently of the question of whether any moral obligations are absolute in the sense of applying to all individuals. At a minimum, I know there are moral obligations applying to me.) Now it seems clear that the claim that I am morally obligated to do an action A cannot be rightly made unless I am free either to do or not do A. It is simply false to say that I ought to do something if I either can't do it or can't help doing it. Consider, for example, the absurdity of saying that it is morally wrong for me to blink when bright lights are shined in my eyes or that I have a moral obligation to run a mile in two minutes. If, then, we are not free, there is no moral right or wrong, no moral responsibility. But there is moral responsiblity (at least for the individual). Therefore, we are free.

The view of ourselves as free which pervades human life seems especially obvious in the literature which mirrors, analyzes, and comments on that life. The Jews' desire to leave Egypt, Achilles' refusal to fight, Hamlet's indecision (to cite a few classic examples) are typical of the myriad ways in which literature presents and scrutinizes the fact of our freedom. As Sartre puts it, ". . . the work of art, from whichever side you approach it, is an act of confidence in the freedom of men." But this appeal to art turns out to be a two-edged sword and reveals that freedom is not the unproblematic given that our discussion so far has suggested it is. For we also find in our literature themes of fate, providence, and psychological or social inevitability that appear incompatible with the idea of human freedom. The Jews fleeing Egypt are presented as instruments of the divine plan of redemption, Achilles as a tool of the Fates, and Hamlet (perhaps) as the victim of his unconscious drives. Very frequently, the vision of the literary artist sees freedom not as an irrefutable reality but as an illusion due to our ignorance of the cosmic, social, or psychological causes that in fact determine our actions.

We might of course ignore the tendency of literature to exclude freedom on the grounds that art distorts reality for aesthetic effect. Individual actions are more interesting when viewed as part of some deeper plot, and there is aesthetic satisfaction in seeing events as inevitable; but here truth is sacrificed to art. But whatever our view on this question, the idea that our freedom is an illusion, a deception based on our ignorance of the external forces that in fact rule our actions, is by no means limited to artistic portrayals of human life. The idea also haunts religion and science, one or the other of which most people think yields the essential truth about reality. The idea is particularly strong in Judaeo-Christian religion and modern (post-17th-century) science.

In spite of a whole range of notorious conflicts, Judaeo-Christian religion and modern science are built on a shared fundamental presupposition: the rejection of any ultimate role for *chance* in the cosmic scheme of things. (I will ignore the question of the role of chance in quantum mechanics.) For both, every least detail of the universe is under complete control—in the one case of a pervasive divine providence, in the other of an implacable system of natural laws. Everything, from the fall of a sparrow to the fall of an empire, from the path of a planet in the heavens to the path of a wind-blown leaf takes place in accord with the will of God or Newton's laws of motion. (And for those who accept both religion and science, the scientific order of things can be viewed as an expression of the divine order.) Philosophical formulations of this shared fundamental presuppostion eliminate the concept of chance in favor of the concept of *causality*. The Greeks had talked about causes of various sorts and had sought them in their science and philosophy. But chance—the presence of brute, inexplicable, uncaused facts—was always maintained as a correlate of causality. But for the philosophers of Judaeo-Christian religion and of modern science, nothing happens without a cause, every event can be understood as the product of something outside it. Such a view may be acceptable—even exciting or edifying—when applied to inanimate nature and animals; but when applied to ourselves it seems disconcertingly at odds with what seemed to be the overwhelming fact of our freedom.

There is, accordingly, a problem of freedom in the following sense: It seems, on the one hand, that we are free, the independent sources of our actions; but on the other hand, it seems that everything, including our apparently free actions, is caused, produced by occurrences external to it. But surely our actions cannot be both free and caused. Initially, at least, the problem of freedom presents itself as the question: Are our actions (at least some of them) free or are they all caused? The view that at least some of our actions are uncaused and hence free is called *libertarianism*. The view that all our actions are caused (determined by external facts) is called *determinism*.

The debate between the libertarian and the determinist takes two different forms, depending on whether the case for determinism is made on a religious or on a scientific basis. The religious determinist (at least in the Judaeo-Chritian tradition) can argue that freedom is incompatible with both the omniscience and the omnipotence of God. The argument from God's omniscience is particularly striking: Since God knows everything, he knows what all my future decisions and actions will be; for example, he knows whether I will decide to vote for the Democrat in the next presidential election. But what God knows is true. Hence, if God knows that I will vote for the Democrat, then it is true right now that I will vote for the Democrat. But then it seems that how I will vote is already determined; nothing I do between now and the next election (including the apparently free choices I make) can alter the fact, known even now to God, that I will vote for the Democrat. Hence, it seems I am determined to vote for the Democrat; so my vote is not a free action. An exactly similar argument will show that any other action is likewise determined. Hence, nothing I do is free. (The same sort of argument can be developed even if we do not assume the existence of God simply on the basis of the idea that, if I am going to vote for the Democrat, then *right now* the statement, "I will vote for the Democrat," is true.)

This argument for determinism has been discussed by theologians and philosophers with incredible thoroughness and subtlety. However, it seems to me (and to many others) that the argument fails for a very simple reason. Granted that there is an exact correlation between God's knowledge of what I will do and what I will in fact do; this does not show, as the argument assumes, that the former determines the latter. That is, God's knowing that I will vote Democratic does not cause me to vote Democratic any more than my knowledge that the leaves will fall next autumn causes the leaves to fall. Quite the contrary, God's knowledge is determined by what I will do; that is, the reason he knows that I will vote Democratic is because that is in fact how I will freely decide to vote. Knowing X entails that X is true; but it does not cause X to be true.

But the religious determinist can also argue from God's omnipotence. Here the argument is simply that there is an incompatibility between human freedom and the fact that God, as omnipotent creator of all things, is the ultimate source of everything a creature is and does, including all allegedly free actions. Here the religious libertarian seems faced with the difficult alternative of either denying that God is the omnipotent creator of everything in the universe or else explaining how God's omnipotent creative power is compatible with the existence of uncaused (free) actions. However, the libertarian can respond with what seems to be a decisive in-principle argument: The religious viewpoint, he can urge, is (at least in part) a *moral* viewpoint. It presents us with an ideal way of life and says that we ought to adopt it. When, for example, Christ says, "Come follow me," he is extending an invitation which we are free to accept or reject. The essential character of religious belief as a decision for or commitment to a way of life is wholly lost if freedom is denied. This is not to say that there are not great (even in fact insuperable) difficulties in our understanding *how* our freedom and God's omnipotence can be reconciled. But, the libertarian can argue, the moral sigificance of religion requires that the reconciliation be in principle possible. (The same sort of argument could, of course, be applied to the question of reconciling God's omniscience and human freedom.)

The scientific determinist argues that freedom is incompatible with the universal scope of scientific laws. In particular, he claims that there are scientific laws determining all human actions. There are two lines of argument supporting this claim, one direct, one indirect. The direct line is to point to laws governing human actions that have been formulated by psychology and the social sciences. But this line of argument suffers from the *de facto* paucity and inexactness of laws in psychology and the social sciences, features signalled by the behavioral scientist's general inability to predict the behavior of *individuals*. The indirect line of argument points to the laws (of the physical sciences) governing the behavior of material bodies in general and claims that these apply to human beings because a human being is just a particular kind of material body. This approach avoids the weakness of the direct argument, since it appeals to the predictively powerful system of laws developed by the physical sciences. But it must further show that these laws govern the actions of human beings. Typically, this is done by claiming that a human being is just a material body, perhaps more complex than other bodies but of essentially the same nature. How can we establish this materialist claim? Although it is obvious that, as human beings, we have a material dimension, there are also obvious differences between us and the general run of material bodies; for example, we think abstractly, act for long-term goals, and have highly developed linguistic abilities. These differences do not prove that we are not just material bodies, but they do show that the materialist claim is not obvious and needs proof. However, it seems that the only conclusive proof of the materialist claim would be to exhibit in fact the complete adequacy of the laws of the physical sciences for describing and predicting human behavior. For a human being is just another material body if and only if the laws that govern its behavior are the same as those that govern material bodies in general. At this point, however, the scientific determinist's argument has become circular: To establish the applicability of the laws of the physical sciences to human actions, the determinist has argued that human beings are just material bodies; but now to establish this latter claim he must show the applicability of the laws of the physical sciences to human actions.

The above discussion does not, of course, refute scientific determinism. But is does suggest that the case for determinism will have to be based on the actual formulation of scientific laws (governing human behavior) that have not yet been formulated. Whether or not they will or can be formulated is an open question.

At this point the libertarian might well claim that the question is not open, on the grounds—invoked also at a crucial point in the discussion of religious determinism—that determinism conflicts with the undeniable reality of moral obligation. Since we know we have moral obligations and also know that being free is a necessary condition for being morally obligated, we can be sure that there are no scientific laws inconsistent with our freedom.

So far, then, the defense of determinism has come up short before the fact of moral obligation. The determinist might, of course, simply grit his teeth and deny the reality of moral obligation, claiming that it, like freedom itself, is an illusion. But such a move is as unwarranted as it is unpalatable. Lacking theological or scientific *proof* that all our actions are caused, why should we deny something so obvious as moral obligation?

But the determinist has a more subtle and more promising approach available. Why, he can ask, should we assume (as we have so far) that the freedom required for moral responsibility cannot exist if all our actions are causally determined? Perhaps an action can be free (at least from a moral point of view) even if it is caused. This suggestion may seem bizarre, but on reflection it becomes more attractive. Notice for example that when we praise someone for avoiding a moral temptation (e.g., for not betraying friends to the secret police), we often heighten the praise by saying that the person was *incapable* of such an action, a person whom we are certain would never do such a thing. (By contrast, it may be very faint praise indeed to say, "You didn't betray your friends, but I was very afraid you might.") In such a case, the fact than an action is causally determined (e.g., by a person's character or personality) seems to make it all the more morally admirable. Consider also the following argument: To say an action has no cause at all is equivalent to saying that its occurrence is an accident in the most genuine sense of that term—something that "just happened," with no source at all. But we are surely not responsible for what is an accident in this sense; so if our actions are uncaused, we are not morally responsible for them.

These sorts of considerations suggest that, from a moral point of view, an action is free not by *being uncaused* but by *having a particular type of cause*. Roughly, we might say, an action is free when it is caused by *internal* factors such as my decisions, intentions, character, etc., rather than by *external* factors such as physical constraints, drugs, hypnosis, etc. To cite a classic example: I am not free to leave a room if all the exits are locked and I have no key, or if I am chained to a wall, or if I am unconscious. But if there are no such external compulsions, if it is in my power to leave, then I am free, even if my action is causally determined by internal factors such as my choices, habits, or character traits. Consequently, it seems we can distinguish free human actions as a subclass of causally determined actions; namely, as those which are not externally compelled. This view of freedom is one form of what is called *compatibilism,* so called since it urges that freedom and causal determination are compatible with one another. Compatibilism, if correct, provides a way of being a determinist without taking the unacceptably hard line of denying moral responsibility. (Hence compatibilism is sometimes called "soft," as oppposed to "hard" determinism.) In fact, a compatibilist need not actually be a determinist. He may only claim that *if* determinism is true, its truth poses no threat to human freedom. However, most philosophers who defend a form of compatibilism do accept determinism, or at least think that it is probably true.

Although compatibilism is an attractive approach, the particular version of it we have formulated above is very hard to defend. For the success of this version depends on our ability to distinguish actions caused by internal factors from those caused by external factors. We must be able to distinguish actions which *I* cause (via my character, intentions, choices) from those which are caused by factors outside of me. But it seems that this distinction cannot be maintained. If, as determinism asserts, *everything* is causally determined, then all the internal factors that cause my actions are themselves caused. Some of these factors may be caused by other internal factors; e.g., my choice of a particular job may be caused by my general desire to earn as much money as possible, and this desire may itself be caused by the presence of avarice in my character. But eventually this chain of internal causes will lead to a cause that is external to me. (E.g., my avarice may be due to genetic factors or unconscious desires.) Consequently, it seems that, for determinism, all my actions are ultimately determined by external factors (factors beyond my control); and so the compatibilist cannot draw the distinction he needs between internal and external determination.

But, as we noted, the position formulated above is just one form of compatibilism, a form based on a definition of a free action as one which is caused by internal factors. Let us next consider another version of compatibilism, one based on a very different approach. This version begins by noting that there is an important difference between *what a person does* and *what happens to a person*. Being born, tripping on the steps, accidentally finding a $100 bill are things that happen to me; they are *events*. Running away from home, buying a car, jumping off a building are things that I *do;* they are *actions*. Given this distinction of events and actions, the following two points can be made: (1) Only actions, not events, can be free; (2) Only events, not actions, are caused. Point (1) is obvious, since only what I do, as opposed to what happens to me, can in any sense be under my control. The line of thought behind (2) is as follows: If someone asks, "Why did that *happen* to you?" (e.g., "Why did you fall down the stairs?"), I can answer only by citing a cause of the event in question (e.g., "I slipped on a Barbie doll"). But if someone asks, "Why did you *do* that?" (e.g., "Why did you throw yourself down the stairs?"), I can answer only by citing a *reason*—e.g., a purpose or goal—for my action (e.g., "I was trying to avoid the tear gas"). To cite a cause rather than a reason (e.g., to say, "I was pushed") is to deny that I performed an action. Accordingly, it seems that while events are properly regarded as explained by causes, actions are properly explained by reasons. This is a conceptual, not a factual, point: It is not that actions might have causes but don't happen to; rather, they are not the sorts of things that could have causes (just as ideas are not the sort of things that could have color).

(1) and (2) effect a sharp conceptual division between occurrences which are *actions* (what we do for *reasons*) and occurrences which are *events* (what is produced by *causes*). Further, it is only actions which can be properly characterized as free, while only events can be properly characterized as caused. But of course the same occurrence may be both an event and an action; that is, there may be one way of describing an occurrence which presents it as something that happens as the result of causes and another which presents it as something done by an agent for reasons. Thus, the pulling of a gun's trigger could be described (e.g., by a physiologist) as an event which is the result of a complex set of events happening within a human body, beginning with certain electro-chemical changes in the brain and ending with the pushing of a finger against the trigger with a certain force. But the same occurrence could be also described (e.g., by a prosecuting attorney) as an attempt to foment revolution by assassinating a political leader. Under the first description, the occurrence is a causally determined event; under the second, is an action, possibly free. Since the two descriptions are equally valid and do not contradict one another, there is no incompatibility in saying that the same occurrence is both caused and free. It is caused as an event and free as an action.

Of course not everything describable as an action is free. A psychopathic killer, for example, performs actions. He has his purposes and takes steps to achieve them; so he is acting for reasons in contrast, for example, to someone suffering an epileptic seizure. But we do not regard the psychopath as free. Why not? The most plausible suggestion is that, although he is acting for reasons, there is no way of rationally persuading him to act otherwise than he does. A pacifist might sensibly try to persuade a mentally normal soldier that killing is wrong and that he should refuse to engage in battle. But if the soldier were a psychopathic killer, such persuasive attempts would be completely futile. This suggests that we can characterize actions as free just in case the agent could have been (in principle if not in fact) rationally persuaded to act otherwise than he did.

The above definition of freedom—and the general approach to compatibilism it embodies—is not without difficulties. For example, might not behavioral or depth psychology someday reveal the process of rational persuasion to be itself but a subtle type of causal determination (e.g., a complex way of stimulating a behavioral response, a covert appeal to unconscious motivations)? If so, even given the distinction of action and event, it would seem impossible to designate a subclass of actions as free. An adequate response to this objection would require a detailed examination of the nature of rational persuasion, showing that it is necessarily an action and not an event. Further, and more fundamentally, the distinction of actions and events needs a much fuller elucidation and defense than I have given it here. So this second version of compatibilism needs much more development before it is fully convincing. However, of all the aproaches to the problem of freedom we have discussed, it seems to be by far the most promising.

In the following selections, Ledger Wood defends hard determinism and C. A. Campbell defends libertarianism. W. T. Stace develops the first version of compatibilism discussed above, and John Hospers raises some problems for this view. In the discussion on determinism, P. F. Strawson suggests an action-theory approach to compatibilism.

The Free Will Controversy

LEDGER WOOD

Few philosophical controversies have been waged with greater acrimony than the controversy between the libertarians and the determinists; the vigour with which both sides of the question have been espoused is due not only to the metaphysical importance of the issue—which is indeed considerable—but more especially to its moral and religious implications. No other philosophical issues, with the exception of those pertaining to God and the immortality of the soul, are of greater ethical and theological moment. So thoroughly has the question been debated that further consideration of it may seem futile. Has not the evidence been so completely canvassed on both sides of the controversy that further discussion will be a fruitless reiteration of long familiar arguments? The free will problem is considered by many contemporary thinkers an admittedly unsolved but completely outmoded problem to which they respond with impatience or complete indifference. This attitude toward the problem is quite indefensible since the question of the freedom of the will is one of those perennially significant philosophical issues which takes on new meaning in every age and is particularly significant in the context of contemporary science and philosophy. Recent psychology, in large measure through the influence of Freud, has achieved a more penetrating analysis of human motivation by bringing to the fore certain hitherto obscure factors which are operative in volition. The psychology of the subconscious by filling in apparent gaps in the psychological causation of volition has furthered the case for determinism. Furthermore, behaviouristic psychology by subjecting all human behaviour, including so-called volitional acts, to a mechanistic formula bears directly on the free will issue and like the Freudian psychology seems to strengthen the deterministic position. Recent developments in the physical sciences are not without their significance for the free-will issue; the principle of indeterminacy in quantum mechanics has been eagerly seized upon by the libertarians in the belief that it affords a physical foundation for their position. Finally, in philosophy proper the progress of philosophical analysis and of the philosophical theory of meaning renders possible a more exact statement of the free will issue and permits a more just appraisal of the traditional arguments on both sides of the free will controversy than has hitherto been possible. The concepts of determinacy, indeterminacy, compulsion, choice, etc., are elucidated by analysis in accordance with the theory of meaning of recent positivism and radical empiricism. It is for these reasons that a contemporary re-examination of the free will issue is not only legitimate but most imperative.

The question of the freedom of the will, reduced to its barest essentials, is simply this: *Are all human acts of will causally produced by antecedent conditions or are at least some volitional actions exempt from causal determination?* The determinist insists that all actions, even the most carefully planned and

---

Ledger Wood was a professor at Princeton University.

Reprinted with permission from *Philosophy*, vol. 16 (1941), pp. 386-389.

deliberate, can be causally explained and that if we knew enough about a man's hereditary traits and the environmental influences which have moulded his character, we could predict just how he would behave under any specified set of circumstances. The free-willist or libertarian, on the other hand, asserts that there are at least some human actions of the volitional type in which the individual by the exercise of his will-power, acts independently of conditioning factors—that he, so to speak, "lifts himself up by his boot-straps."

The freedom of caprice (the traditional *liberum arbitrium*) when precisely defined means that some, and perhaps all, volitional acts are causally indeterminate, that is to say, are not conjoined in any uniform way with antecedent conditions. The uniform antecedents of free acts are, on this view, undiscoverable for the simple reason that they do not exist. Free acts are the products of pure chance and, therefore, remain unexplained because they are inherently inexplicable; they are, in the strict sense of the word, miracles—a miracle being defined as any occurrence which cannot be brought within the compass of natural law. The freedom of chance, conceived in this extreme fashion, would, if it existed, utterly disrupt social intercourse, for, no one could possibly anticipate when another, or even himself, might act freely, or in other words, miraculously. Perhaps the closest approximation to a capricious free will is to be found in a lunatic—but even his acts are not genuinely free, since a psychiatrist can, at least ideally, explain and even predict them. The maniac's actions, however strange they may seem when judged by the sane man's standards of normal behaviour, are psychologically explicable; they conform to certain uniform patterns of abnormal psychology, which, in turn, are assimilable to the laws of general psychology. The free willist—however much he may seek to disguise the fact—introduces an element of indeterminacy into human behaviour; he admits an effect, namely, the volitional action, without a sufficient and adequate natural cause. The free will of man, according to the extreme defenders of the free will doctrine, swoops down from above and injects into the volitional situation an arbitrary, capricious, and incalculable factor.

I propose to give a brief résumé of the free will controversy, examining first the arguments for the freedom of the will and then stating the case for determinism. Although the position taken throughout the present paper is avowedly deterministic, the attempt will be made to state with fairness the case for and against both of the rival positions and on the basis of these arguments, to give a just appraisal of the two positions. The strength of the deterministic position will be found to lie not only in the positive evidence which may be adduced to support it, but also in its easy ability to meet the arguments advanced by the free-willists.

ARGUMENTS FOR THE FREEDOM OF THE WILL

The arguments of the free-willist are for the most part humanistic and non-scientific in character and may be conveniently considered under the following heads:

(1) the introspective or psychological argument,
(2) the moral and religious arguments,
(3) the argument from physical indeterminacy.

(1) *The Introspective or Psychological Argument*

Most advocates of the free will doctrine believe that the mind is directly aware of its freedom in the very act of making a decision, and thus that freedom is an immediate datum of our introspective awareness. "I feel myself free, *therefore,* I am free," runs the simplest and perhaps the most compelling of the arguments for freedom. In the elaboration of his argument, the free-willist offers a detailed description of what in his opinion, is introspectively observable whenever the self makes a free choice. Suppose I find myself forced to choose between conflicting and incompatible lines of action. At such a time, I stand, so to speak, at the moral cross-roads, I deliberate, and finally by some mysterious and inexplicable power of mind, I decide to go one way rather than the other. Deliberative decision, if this description is correct, is analysable into these three constituents: *(a)* the envisaging of two or more incompatible courses of action, *(b)* the review of considerations favourable and unfavourable to each of the conflicting possibilities of action, and *(c)* the choice among the alternative possibilities.

Deliberative, or so-called "moral" decisions, are fairly numerous in the lives of all of us and are made on the most trivial occasions, as well as on matters of grave import. The university undergraduate's resolution of the conflict between his desire to see the latest cinema at the local playhouse and his felt obligation to devote the evening to his studies, trivial and inconsequential as it may seem, is the *type* of all moral decisions and differs in no essential respect from such a momentous decision as his choice of a life career. Each of these decisions to the extent that it is truly deliberative involves *(a)* the imaginative contemplation of alternative actions, *(b)* the weighing of considerations *for* and *against* the several alternatives involving, perhaps, an appeal to ideals and values approved by the moral agent, and finally *(c)* the choice between the several possibilities of action. At the moment of making the actual decision, the mind experiences a *feeling* of self-assertion and of independence of determining influences both external and internal. The libertarian rests his case for free will on the authenticity of this subjective feeling of freedom.

The phenomenon of decision after deliberation is an indubitable *fact* which determinist and free-willist alike must acknowledge, but the real issue is whether this fact warrants the *construction* which the free-willist puts upon it. The determinist, replying to the introspective argument, urges that the *feeling* of freedom is nothing but a sense of relief following upon earlier tension and indecision. After conflict and uncertainty, the pent-up energies of the mind—or rather of the underlying neural processes—are released and this process is accompanied by an inner sense of power. Thus the feeling of freedom or of voluntary control over one's actions is a mere subjective illusion which cannot be considered evidence for psychological indeterminacy.

Besides the direct appeal to the sense of freedom, there is a psychological argument which *infers* freedom from the mind's ability to resolve an equilibrium of opposing motives. The allegedly "prerogative" or "critical" instance of free will, is that in which the will makes a choice between two or more actions which are equally attractive, or equally objectionable. If, after a careful weighing of all the considerations *for* and *against* each of the alternative actions, the mind finds the rival claimants exactly equal, a decision is possible, argues the libertarian, only by a free act of will. We weigh the motives against one another, find the scale balanced, and then, in the words of William James, . . . "we feel, in deciding as if we ourselves by our wilful act inclined the beam."[1] This argument from the equilibrium of motives is indeed plausible, but the determinist has a ready reply. *If* the motives really had been exactly equal and opposite, then the mind would have remained indefinitely in a state of suspended judgment and consequent inaction or would, in Hamlet fashion, have oscillated between the two incompatibles, never able to yield to one or to the other. The analogy of the balanced scale would lead one to expect the will under these circumstances to do just this. Indeed, there are undoubtedly some pathological minds which are in a perpetual tug-of-war between conflicting tendencies of action and whose wills, as a consequence, are completely paralysed. But in normal minds the "motives" on the one side or the other become momentarily stronger because of some new external factor injected into the situation or because of the inner reorganization of forces and then action immediately ensues. Often the decision is determined by accidental and contingent circumstances—a literal flip of the coin—or perhaps one allows one's action to be decided by a chance idea or impulse, that is to say, by a "mental flip of the coin." In any case the fact that a decision is actually made testifies to the eventual inequality of the opposing forces. Under no circumstances is it necessary to resort to a mysterious, inner force of will to "incline the beam" one way rather than the other.

Still another introspective fact cited by the libertarian in support of his doctrine is that the moral agent is in retrospect convinced that he might, *if he had chosen,* have followed a course of action different from that which he actually pursued. The belief that there are genuine alternatives of action and that the choice between them is indeterminate is usually stronger in prospect and in retrospect than at the time of actual decision. The alternatives exist in prospect as imaginatively envisaged possibilities of action and in retrospect as the memory of the state of affairs before the agent had, so to speak, "made up his mind." Especially in retrospect does the agent recall his earlier decision with remorse and repentance, dwelling sorrowfully upon rejected possibilities of action which now loom up as opportunities missed. How frequently one hears the lament: "I regret that decision; I should, and I could, have acted otherwise." Now the contemplation of supposed alternatives of action along with the sentiment of regret produces the illusion of indeterminate choice between alternatives, but a careful analysis of the import of the retrospective judgment, "I could have acted otherwise than I did," will, I believe, disclose it to be an empirically meaningless statement. If I decided in favour of this alternative, rather than that, it can only mean that the circumstances being what they were, and I in the frame of mind I was at the time, no other eventuation was really possible. My statement that I could have acted differently expresses only my memory of an earlier state of suspense, indecision, and uncertainty, intensified by my present remorse and the firm determination that if, in the future, I am faced with a similar choice, I shall profit by my earlier mistake. There is, however, in the deliberate situation no evidence of genuine alternatives of action, or the indeterminacy of my choice between them.

(2) *The Moral and Religious Arguments*

The moral argument assumes a variety of forms, but they all agree in their attempt to infer volitional freedom of the moral agent from some feature of the moral situation. The most characteristic feature of moral action is that it seems to be directed toward the realization of an ideal or the fulfilment of an obligation. But, argues the free-willest, it is of the very nature of an ideal or an obligation that it shall be *freely* embraced; the acceptance or rejection of a moral ideal and the acknowledgement of an obligation as binding can only be accounted for on the assumption of the agent's free choice. The very existence of moral ideals, norms, or standards which, though *coercive* or not *compulsive*, testifies to the freedom of the agent who acknowledges them. Thus did Kant in his famous formula: "I ought, therefore I can" directly infer the agent's freedom from his recognition of moral obligation.

The moral argument is so loose in its logic that unable to put one's finger on its fallacy one is tempted to resort to the logicians' "catch-all," and call it a *non sequitur*. A moral agent's adoption of a moral ideal or recognition of a moral obligation simply does *not* imply that he possesses a free will in the sense of psychological indeterminacy. An adequate critique of the moral argument would require a detailed psychological account of the genesis of moral ideals and duties without recourse to freedom of the libertarian sort and I am convinced that such an account is forthcoming. The emergence of ideals in the mind of an individual moral agent along with the feeling that such ideals are coercive is largely non-volitional and even when it rises to the volitional level and represents a choice between competing ideals, there is even then no reason for abandoning psychological determinism. The moral argument for freedom is found, on close examination, to be the psychological argument in disguise and like it, is introspectively false; there is no indication of volitional freedom either in the original adoption of moral standards nor in subsequent moral decisions in accordance with those standards once they have been embraced.

The moral argument for freedom has sometimes been stated from the point of view not the moral agent but of the moral critic who passes judgment on the action of another or even upon his own actions. A judgment of praise or blame, of approval or condemnation, so the argument runs, imputes freedom to the agent whose action is judged. When I praise your unselfish and benevolent acts, I imply that you could, if you had chosen, have been cruel and selfish instead. Condemnation of another's conduct seems even more surely to suggest that he acted willingly, or rather "wilfully." Otherwise, would it not be in order to pity rather than condemn the wrong-doer? Should we not say with condescension, "Poor misguided fool, he can't help what he does, he is simply that kind of man"? Instead, we reprove his action and by so doing implicitly acknowledge that he is a free moral agent. A novel variant of this argument is contained in William James's essay "The Dilemma of Determinism." The determinist, so James argues, finds himself in a curious logical predicament whenever he utters a judgment of regret. If I, a determinist, pass an adverse judgment on my own or another's actions, I thereby acknowledge that they ought not to have been, that others ought to have been performed in their place. But how can I meaningfully make such a statement if these particular actions, and no others, were possible?[2] "What sense can there be in condemning ourselves for taking the wrong way, unless the right way was open to us as well?"[3] James advanced the moral argument, not as an absolute *proof* of freedom (he admits that it is not intellectually coercive), but rather as a belief to be *freely* embraced. As a pragmatically effective, moral fiction, freedom has much to be said in its favour: the belief in freedom no doubt fosters moral earnestness, whereas the belief in determinism may, at least in certain persons, induce moral lassitude. Most defenders of the free-will doctrine do not, however, share James's cautious restraint: they advance the moral argument as a conclusive proof of an indeterminate free-will. The fallacy again can only be described as a *non sequitur*. Moral appraisal has nothing to do with the freedom of the will; the mere fact that *I* approve certain of *your* actions because I consider them good and condemn others as wrong may give some indication of *my* moral make-up, but it proves nothing whatsoever regarding the freedom of *your* will. Your moral acts, even though completely determined, may be judged in accordance with prevailing standards to be laudable or reprehensible. I praise your good conduct and condemn your bad conduct even though both are inexorably determined and—the determinist would add—I too am determined to judge them as I do. Hence the freedom of a moral agent cannot possibly be inferred from the judgments of approbation and disapprobation passed upon him by a moral critic.

The determinist finds no difficulty in assimilating to his deterministic scheme the facts of moral approval and disapproval. Moral valuation is not the detached and disinterested judgment of a moral critic, but is an instrumentality for the social propagation of norms of conduct. Morality is essentially a social phenomenon; society has gradually evolved its patterns of social behaviour which it imposes upon its individual members by means of various sanctions including the favourable or adverse judgments which members of society pass upon one another. Judgments of moral valuation rest upon the socially constituted norms of action and are the media through which these norms are communicated from individual to individual. I reprove your unsocial or antisocial behaviour in the belief that my adverse judgment may influence you to desist therefrom. When I pass a moral judgment on another, far from implying his free will, I tacitly assume that my judgment of him, in so far as he takes cognizance of it, operates as a determining influence on his conduct. Thus moral criticism when interpreted naturalistically harmonizes with the theory of moral determinism.

Another moral argument, closely paralleling the argument from obligation, stresses the concept of moral responsibility. The free-willist considers freedom a *sine qua non* of responsibility; his argument runs: "Without freedom, there can be no responsibility, but there *must* be responsibility, hence man is free." There are *two* ways of attacking this argument: (1) we may pertinently ask: "But *why* must there be responsibility?", or, (2) we may challenge the underlying assumption of the argument, namely, that freedom is an indispensable condition of responsibility. The first criticism is a rejection of the minor and usually tacit premise of the free-willist's argument, the conviction, namely, that there must be responsibility. The conviction prevalent among moralists that responsibility, obligation, etc., because they are morally significant must actually exist, would seem to be the outcome of a curiously perverse ontological argument. Whatever is morally useful and significant must actually exist. But why must it? What assurance have we that reality is constituted so as to satisfy the insistent demands of our moral nature? Even if responsibility could be shown to be an indispensable adjunct of genuine morality, this would not suffice to guarantee its factuality. There is only one way of establishing the fact of responsibility, and that is by exhibiting actual instances of morally responsible actions. The concept of moral responsibility no doubt admits of precise empirical definition and exemplification; there is a real distinction between responsible and irresponsible actions. But when responsibility is analysed in this empirical and positivistic fashion, it will be found in no wise to imply volitional freedom. A careful analysis of responsible actions will show them to be if anything no more indeterminate than non-responsible and irresponsible actions. And this brings us to the second criticism of the argument from responsibility: *viz.*, the failure to establish the alleged implication of the concept of freedom by the concept of responsibility. The concepts of freedom and responsibility are by no means indissolubly connected; on the contrary, the freedom of indeterminacy, far from guaranteeing responsibility, would, if it existed, actually be prejudicial to it. If freedom is the complete divorce of the will from antecedent conditions, including my moral character, I cannot then be held accountable for my actions. A will which descends upon me like "a bolt from the blue" is not *my* will and it is manifestly unfair to take me to task for its caprices.

Closely allied with—perhaps in the last analysis indistinguishable from—the moral argument is the *religious* argument for free will. The free will dogma is deeply rooted in the Hebraic-Christian theology. The essential connection between freedom and responsibility to God is the real theme of the Book of *Genesis:* Man's freedom is necessary to insure what William James has aptly referred to as man's "forensic responsibility before God."[4] Were man not free, he could not be held accountable for his action, but he *must* be held accountable, therefore, man is free. The Hebraic doctrine of the freedom of the will arises from a paternalistic conception of the relation between God and man. On this view, moral principles are the commandments of God to which man yields as does the child to parental authority. But, just as a recalcitrant child may defy his father, so man may, at his own peril, rebel against the divine moral code. The principles of morality are authoritative in that they emanate from God, but they are not compulsive since man may or may not choose to conform to them. The paternalism of the Hebraic conception of God is embodied in the myth of creation. God created Adam and endowed him with a will, free to choose between good and evil. Adam yielded to temptation and his original sin has been transmitted to all his descendants. The story of the fall of man is a highly symbolic expression of the theological doctrine that man is accountable for his actions only on the assumption that they are free. Incidentally, the ascription of a free will to man, absolves God from any responsibility for the sins of mankind and thus affords an easy solution to one of the most perplexing of theological problems, the problem of evil.

The religious argument may be dismissed quite summarily by rejecting outright the conception of God as a task-master who maintains discipline over humanity by conferring upon it a freedom which shall insure its responsibility and justify its punishment. If the Hebraic conception of an austere and vengeful God be renounced, the religious argument for freedom loses all force; it then reduces to the simple moral argument from responsibility to freedom, the fallacies of which have already been exposed. The determinist by his rejection of this particular conception of divinity is not necessarily committed to atheism. Determinism and theology in certain of its forms are entirely compatible; thus the theological doctrine of predestination, though of course very different in its emphasis from physical and psychological determinism of the naturalistic sort, is by no means inconsistent with the latter. There is then no strictly theological argument proof for freedom and theological considerations can at best serve to reinforce the moral argument for freedom.

(3) The Argument from Physical Indeterminacy

Free-willists have recently derived not a little encouragement from the advent of the principle of physical indeterminacy which even if it does not suffice to demonstrate freedom of the will, at least seems to remove a serious obstacle to its acceptance. If there is a real indeterminacy at the subatomic level of quantum mechanics, this affords at least the *possibility* of the physiological and ultimately of the psychological indeterminacy which constitutes the freedom of the will. Recent quantum theory seems on the surface to afford a physical basis for a volitional indeterminacy much as the swerve of the atoms invoked by the ancient Epicureans seemed to justify their free-will doctrine. But the contemporary argument is defective and in very much the same respects as its historic prototype.

Against the modern version of the indeterminacy argument, it may be urged in the first place that the physical theory of indeterminacy merely expresses an observational difficulty encountered in the attempt to determine both the position and the velocity of an electron and that consequently it posits a methodological and not the physical or ontological indeterminacy which is requisite for the purposes of the free will doctrine. But secondly, even supposing that the indeterminacy principle is physical and not merely methodological, it has not been shown that this subatomic indeterminacy manifests itself in the behaviour of ordinary mass-objects and in particular that it is exemplified in just those neural processes which are supposedly the basis of the act of free will. The psychophysical correlation of a neural indeterminacy with its psychological counterpart, could be effected only by the introspective observation of the volitional indeterminacy along with the underlying physical indeterminacy, and thus the evidence of introspection is an essential link in the argument from physical indeterminacy. The physical theory of indeterminacy is at the present time far from demonstrating the existence of or giving a complete picture of the *modus operandi* of a free will and thus the freedom of indeterminacy remains, even on the background of physical indeterminacy, a more speculative possibility.

THE CASE FOR DETERMINISM

Whereas the evidence for the free will doctrine is largely humanistic and moralistic, the case for determinism is an appeal to scientific evidence; the determinist finds that the sciences of *physiology, psychology,* and *sociology* afford evidence that human behaviour is no exception to the causal uniformity of nature.

(1) *Physiological Evidence*

The more we know about the physiological and neural processes which go on inside the human organism, even when it reacts to the most complicated of stimuli, the more evident it becomes that there is no break in the continuous chain of causation. Physiology gives us a reasonably clear picture of the mechanism of human behaviour. The behaviourists, the most recent recruits to the cause of determinism, have with infinite patience applied the objective method of the physiologists to human conduct; they have described in the minutest detail the mechanism of reflexes and the manner of their conditioning. There seems to remain no missing link in the causal chain from stimulus to ultimate response—even when that response is long "delayed." Delayed responses are mediated by very complex neural processes which on their subjective side are called conflict, indecision, and deliberation, but they are no exception to the behaviouristic formula.

(2) *Psychological Evidence*

While the deterministic thesis receives its most obvious support from physiology and behaviouristic psychology, introspective psychology makes its contribution also. An unbiased introspective examination of volition supports the theory of psychological determinism. The more carefully I scrutinize my decisions, the more clearly do I discern the motives which determine them. If one's powers of introspection were sufficiently developed, one could presumably after any decision discover the exact psychological influences which rendered that particular decision inevitable. Doubtless for a complete explanation of certain decisions it is necessary in addition to the conscious antecedents of the volitional act to recover the more recondite sub-conscious and unconscious influences; the extensive researches of the Freudians into the submerged factors in human motivation provide the explanation of otherwise inexplicable mental acts and therefore tend to supply the missing links in the chain of psychic causation. Indeed, the existence of consciously inexplicable conscious events was one of the most compelling reasons for the original positing of an unconscious or subconscious mind. It remains true, however, that a fairly complete account of the psychological causation of volitional decisions is possible even without recourse to an unconscious mind.

Perhaps the best classical statement of the case for psychological determinism was given by David Hume. Hume, whose introspective subtlety has rarely been surpassed, commits himself unequivocally to psychological determinism in his assertion that "There is a great uniformity among the actions of men. . . . *The same motives always produce the same actions*."[5] Every historian, as Hume points out, appeals to this principle in judging the accuracy of historical documents; he asks himself whether the reported actions conform to what is known of human nature. And we might add, the same criterion is appealed to even in the evaluation of works of fiction. The novelist or the playwright gives a portrayal of his characters; he places them in definite situations, and then describes how they act. If his account of their behaviour under these precisely defined circumstances violates any of the recognized laws of human motivation, his literary and dramatic artistry is to that extent defective. Thus the principle of psychological determinism serves as a recognized canon on historical, literary, and dramatic criticism, and while this does not "prove" the correctness of psychological determinism, it does afford confirmation of it from an unsuspected quarter.

(3) *Sociological Evidence*

The social sciences yield abundant evidence for a deterministic view of human behaviour. The fact that the conduct of large aggregates of individuals is expressible in terms of statistical law, although it is by no means a conclusive proof of individual determinism, certainly points in that direction. I may not be able to predict how you as an individual will behave in any specified circumstances, but I can formulate a statistical law applicable to a large group of individuals of which you are a member. It is difficult to reconcile the possibility of the laws of groups or mass action with individual free will.

The conclusion reached as a result of the survey of the arguments on both sides of the free will controversy is that the strength of the deterministic position lies not only in the overwhelming array of psychological, physiological, and sociological evidence for the uniformity of human behaviour, but also in its ability to meet the psychological, moral, and religious "proofs" of free will. Accordingly, we seem fully justified in concluding that a capricious free will, that is to say, a will capable of acting independently of antecedent conditions, psychological or physiological, is a philosophical absurdity.

NOTES

1. *The Principles of Psychology*, vol. ii, p. 534.
2. William James, *The Will to Believe and Other Essays in Popular Philosophy*, p. 163.
3. *Ibid.*, p. 175.
4. *The Principles of Psychology*, vol. ii, p. 349.
5. *Enquiry Concerning Human Understanding*, section viii.

In Defense of Free Will

C. A. CAMPBELL

Mighty issues turn, and turn directly, on the solution of the free will problem. It is in no way surprising that for centuries past it has exercised a fascination for thinkers both within and without the ranks of the professional philosophers that is probably not paralleled in the case of any of the other great problems of metaphysics.

There are, however, other considerations also which have governed my choice of subject. More particularly, I have been influenced by a conviction that the present state of philosophical opinion on free will is, for certain definitely assignable reasons, profoundly unsatisfactory. In my judgment, a thoroughly perverse attitude to the whole problem has been created by the almost universal acquiescence in the view that free will in what is often called the 'vulgar' sense is too obviously nonsensical a notion to deserve serious discussion. Free will in a more 'refined' sense—which is apt to mean free will purged of all elements that may cause embarrassment to a Deterministic psychology or a Deterministic metaphysics—is, it is understood, a conception which may be defended by the philosopher without loss of caste. But in its 'vulgar' sense, as maintained, for example, by the plain man, who clings to a belief in genuinely open possibilities, it is (we are told) a wild and even obnoxious delusion, long ago discredited for sober thinkers.

Now, as it happens, I myself firmly believe that free will, in something extremely like the 'vulgar' sense, is a fact. And I am anxious to-day to do what I can, within the limits of a single lecture, to justify that belief. I propose therefore to develop a statement of the Libertarian's position which will try to make clear why he finds himself obliged to hold what he does hold, and to follow this up with a critical examination of the grounds most in vogue among philosophers for impugning this position. Considerations of time will, I fear, compel a somewhat close economy in my treatment of objections. But I shall hope to say enough to instigate a doubt in some minds concerning the validity of certain very fashionable objections whose authority is often taken to be virtually final. And if no other good purpose is served, it will at least be of advantage if I can offer, in my positive statement, a target for the missiles of the critics more truly representative of Libertarianism than the targets at which they sometimes direct their fire—targets, I may add, upon which even the clumsiest of marksmen could hardly fail to register bull's-eyes.

Let us begin by noting that the problem of free will gets its urgency for the ordinary educated man by reason of its close connection with the conception of moral responsibility. When we regard a man as morally responsible for an act, we regard him as a legitimate object of moral praise or blame in respect of it. But it seems plain that a man cannot be a legitimate object of moral praise or blame for

---

C. A. Campbell is professor emeritus at the University of Glasgow.

Reprinted from Campbell's *In Defence of Free Will*, by permission of the publisher. New Jersey: Humanities Press, Inc.

an act unless in willing the act he is in some important sense a 'free' agent. Evidently free will in some sense, therefore, is a precondition of moral responsibility. Without doubt it is the realization that any threat to freedom is thus a threat to moral responsibility—with all that that implies—combined with the knowledge that there are a variety of considerations, philosophic, scientific, and theological, tending to place freedom in jeopardy, that gives to the problem of free will its perennial and universal appeal. And it is therefore in close connection with the question of the conditions of moral responsibility that any discussion of the problem must proceed, if it is not to be academic in the worst sense of the term.

We raise the question at once, therefore, what are the conditions, in respect of freedom, which must attach to an act in order to make it a morally responsible act? It seems to me that the fundamental conditions are two. I shall state them with all possible brevity, for we have a long road to travel.

The first condition is the universally recognised one that the act must be *self*-caused, *self*-determined. But it is important to accept this condition in its full rigour. The agent must be not merely *a* cause but the *sole* cause of that for which he is deemed morally responsible. If entities other than the self have also a causal influence upon an act, then that act is not one for which we can say without qualification that the *self* is morally responsible. If in respect of it we hold the self responsible at all, it can only be for some feature of the act—assuming the possibility of disengaging such a feature—of which the self *is* the sole cause. I do not see how this conclusion can be evaded. But it has awkward implications which have led not a few people to abandon the notion of individual moral responsibility altogether.

This first condition, however, is quite clearly not sufficient. It is possible to conceive an act of which the agent is the sole cause, but which is at the same time an act *necessitated* by the agent's nature. Some philosophers have contended, for example, that the act of Divine creation is an act which issues necessarily from the Divine nature. In the case of such an act, where the agent could not do otherwise than he did, we must all agree, I think, that it would be inept to say that he *ought* to have done otherwise and is thus morally blameworthy, or *ought not* to have done otherwise and is thus morally praiseworthy. It is perfectly true that we do sometimes hold a person morally responsible for an act, even when we believe that he, being what he now is, virtually could not do otherwise. But underlying that judgment is always the assumption that the person has *come* to be what he now is in virtue of past acts of will in which he *was* confronted by real alternatives, by genuinely open possibilities: and, strictly speaking, it is in respect of these *past* acts of his that we praise or blame the agent *now*. For ultimate analysis, the agent's power of alternative action would seem to be an inexpugnable condition of his liability to moral praise or blame, i.e. of his moral responsibility.

We may lay down, therefore, that an act is a 'free' act in the sense required for moral responsibility only if the agent (*a*) is the sole cause of the act; and (*b*) could exert his causality in alternative ways. And it may be pointed out in passing that the acceptance of condition (*b*) implies the recognition of the inadequacy for moral freedom of mere 'self-determination'. The doctrine called 'Self-determinism'* is often contrasted by its advocates with mere Determinism on the one hand and Indeterminism on the other, and pronounced to be the one true gospel. I must insist, however, that if 'Self-determinism' rejects condition (*b*), it cannot claim to be a doctrine of free will in the sense required to vindicate moral responsibility. The doctrine which demands, and asserts, the fulfilment of both conditions is the doctrine we call 'Libertarianism'. And it would in my opinion minister greatly to clarity if it were more widely recognized that for any doctrine which is not a species of Libertarianism to pose as a doctrine of 'free will' is mere masquerade.

And now, the conditions of free will being defined in these general terms, we have to ask whether human beings are in fact capable of performing free acts; and if so, where precisely such acts are to be found. In order to prepare the way for an answer, it is desirable, I think, that we should get clear at once about

*'Self-determinism' is another term for 'compatibilism' (editor's note).

the significance of a certain very familiar, but none the less formidable, criticism of free will which the Self-determinist as well as the Libertarian has to meet. This is the criticism which bases itself upon the facts of heredity on the one hand and of environment on the other. I may briefly summarize the criticism as follows.

Every historic self has an hereditary nature consisting of a group of inborn propensities, in range more or less common to the race, but specific to the individual in their respective strengths. With this equipment the self just *happens* to be born. Strictly speaking, it antedates the existence of the self proper, i.e. the existence of the self-conscious subject, and it is itself the effect of a series of causes leading back to indefinitely remote antiquity. It follows, therefore, that any of the self's choices that manifests the influence of his hereditary nature is not a choice of which *he*, the actual historic self, is the sole cause. The choice is determined, at least in part, by factors external to the self. The same thing holds good of 'environment'. Every self is born and bred in a particular physical and social environment, not of his own choosing, which plays upon him in innumerable ways, encouraging this propensity, discouraging that, and so on. Clearly any of the self's choices that manifests the influence of environmental factors is likewise a choice which is determined, at least in part, by factors external to the self. But if we thus grant, as seems inevitable, that heredity and environment are external influences, where shall we find a choice in the whole history of a self that is not subject to external influence? Surely we must admit that every particular act of choice bears the marks of the agent's hereditary nature and environmental nurture; in which case a free act, in the sense of an act determined solely by the self, must be dismissed as a mere chimaera.

To this line of criticism the Self-determinist—T. H. Green is a typical example—has a stock reply. He urges that these factors, heredity and environment, are not, in so far as their operation in willing (and therefore in conduct proper) is concerned, 'external' to the self at all. For the act of willing, when we analyse it, reveals itself to be in its nature such that no end can be willed save in so far as it is conceived by the self as a good for the self. A 'native propensity' cannot function *as such* in willing. It can function only in so far as the self conceives its object as a good for the self. It follows that the self in willing is essentially *self*-determining; not moved from the outside, but moved always by its own conception of its own good. Inherited nature and environmental circumstance do play their part; but not as factors external to the self. They can function only in so far as their suggestions are, as it were, incorporated by the self in its conception of its own good. Consequently—so we are told—the threat to self-determination from the side of inheritance and environment disappears on an adequate analysis of the act of willing.

I am afraid, however, that this argument, though it contains important truth, cannot bear the heavy weight that is here imposed upon it. Let us grant that inheritance and environment can operate in willing only in the medium of the self's conception of its own good. But then let us ask, how is the self's conception of its own good constituted? Self-consciousness is required, of course: but mere self-conscious reflection *in vacuo* will not furnish the self with any conception of a personal good whatsoever. Obviously to answer the question in regard to any agent we are obliged to make reference to certain sheer external facts; viz., to the quality and strength of that person's inherited propensities, and to the nature of the influences that are brought to bear upon him from the side of environment. It seems certain, then, that the self's conception of its own good is influenced directly by its particular inheritance and environment. But to admit this surely involves the admission that external determination enters into choices. It may be true that the self's choices are always determined by its conception of its own good. But if what it conceives to be its own good is always dependent, at least partly, upon inheritance and environment, as external facts, then it is idle to deny that the self's choices are externally influenced likewise.

Indeed I cannot but regard the attempt to save self-determination by denying the externality of the influence of heredity and environment as a quite desperate expedient. It is significant that nobody really believes it in practice. The externality of these influences is taken for granted in our reflective practical judgments upon persons. On those occasions when we are in real earnest about giving a critical and considered estimate of a man's moral calibre—as, e.g., in any serious biographical study—we impose upon ourselves as a matter of course the duty of enquiring with scrupulous care into his hereditary propensities and environmental circumstances, with a view to discovering how far his conduct is influenced by these factors. And having traced these influences, we certainly do not regard the result as having no bearing on the question of the man's moral responsibility for his conduct. On the contrary, the very purpose of the enquiry is to enable us, by due appreciation of the *external* influences that affect his conduct, to gain as accurate a view as possible of that which can justly be attributed to the man's own *self*-determination. The allowances that we all of us do in practice make for hereditary and environmental influences in passing judgment on our fellows would be meaningless if we did not suppose these influences to be in a real sense 'external' to the self.

Now the recognition of this externality is, of course, just as serious a matter for the Libertarian as for the Self-determinist. For the Libertarian, as we saw, accepts condition (*a*) no less whole-heartedly than the Self-determinist does: i.e. that an act is free only if it is determined by the self and nothing but the self. But though we have not been *directly* advancing our course by these recent considerations, we have been doing so indirectly, by narrowing and sharpening the issue. We know now that condition (*a*) is not fulfilled by any act in respect of which inheritance or environment exerts a causal influence. For that type of influence has been shown to be in a real sense external to the self. The free act of which we are in search has therefore got to be one into which influences of this kind do not enter at all.

Moreover, one encouraging portent has emerged in the course of our brief discussion. For we noticed that our reflective practical judgments on persons, while fully recognizing the externality of the influence of heredity and environment, do nevertheless presuppose throughout that there *is something* in conduct which is genuinely self-determined; something which the agent contributes solely on his own initiative, unaffected by external influences; something for which, accordingly, he may justly be held morally responsible. That conviction may, of course, be a false one. But the fact of its widespread existence can hardly be without significance for our problem.

Let us proceed, then, by following up this clue. Let us ask, why do human beings so obstinately persist in believing that there is an indissoluble core of purely *self*-originated activity which even heredity and environment are powerless to affect? There can be little doubt, I think, of the answer in general terms. They do so, at bottom, because they feel certain of the existence of such activity from their immediate practical experience of themselves. Nor can there be in the end much doubt, I think, in what function of the self that activity is to be located. There seems to me to be one, and only one, function of the self with respect to which the agent can even pretend to have an assurance of that absolute self-origination which is here at issue. But to render precise the nature of that function is obviously of quite paramount importance: and we can do so, I think, only by way of a somewhat thorough analysis—which I now propose to attempt—of the experiential situation in which it occurs, viz., the situation of 'moral temptation'.

It is characteristic of that situation that in it I am aware of an end A which I believe to be morally right, and also of an end B, incompatible with A, towards which, in virtue of that system of conative dispositions which constitutes my 'character' as so far formed, I entertain a strong desire. There may be, and perhaps must be, desiring elements in my nature which are directed to A also. But what gives to the situation its specific character as one of moral temptation is that the urge of our desiring nature towards the right end, A, is felt to be *relatively* weak. We are sure that if our desiring nature is permitted to issue directly in action, it is end B that we shall choose. That is what is meant by saying, as William James does, that end B is 'in the line of least resistance' relatively to our conative dispositions. The expression is, of course, a metaphorical one, but it serves to describe, graphically enough, a situation of which we all have frequent experience, viz., where we recognize a specific end as that towards which the 'set' of our desiring nature most strongly inclines us, and which we shall indubitably choose if no inhibiting factor intervenes.

But inhibiting factors, we should most of us say, *may* intervene: and that in two totally different ways which it is vital to distinguish clearly. The inhibiting factor may be of the nature of another desire (or aversion), which operates by changing the balance of the desiring situation. Though at one stage I desire B, which I believe to be wrong, more strongly than I desire A, which I believe to be right, it may happen that before action is taken I become aware of certain hitherto undiscerned consequences of A which I strongly desire, and the result may be that now not *B* but *A* presents itself to me as the end in the line of least resistance. Moral temptation is here overcome by the simple process of ceasing to be a moral temptation.

That is one way, and probably by far the commoner way, in which an inhibiting factor intervenes. But it is certainly not regarded by the self who is confronted by moral temptation as the *only* way. In such situations we all believe, rightly or wrongly, that even although B *continues* to be in the line of least resistance, even although, in other words, the situation remains one with the characteristic marks of moral temptation, we *can* nevertheless align ourselves with A. We can do so, we believe, because we have the power to introduce a new energy, to make what we call an 'effort of will', whereby we are able to act contrary to the felt balance of mere desire, and to achieve the higher end despite the fact that it continues to be in the line of greater resistance relatively to our desiring nature. The self in practice believes that it has this power; and believes, moreover, that the decision rests solely with its self, here and now, whether this power be exerted or not.

Now the objective validity or otherwise of this belief is not at the moment in question. I am here merely pointing to its existence as a psychological fact. No amount of introspective analysis, so far as I can see, even tends to disprove that we do as a matter of fact believe, in situations of moral temptation, that it rests with our self absolutely to decide whether we exert the effort of will which will enable us to rise to duty, or whether we shall allow our desiring nature to take its course.

I have now to point out, further, how this act of moral decision, at least in the significance which it has for the agent himself, fulfils in full the two conditions which we found it necessary to lay down at the beginning for the kind of 'free' act which moral responsibility presupposes.

For obviously it is, in the first place, an act which the agent believes he could perform in alternative ways. He believes that it is genuinely open to him to put forth effort—in varying degrees, if the situation admits of that—or withhold it altogether. And when he *has* decided—in whatever way—he remains convinced that these alternative courses were really open to him.

It is perhaps a little less obvious, but, I think, equally certain, that the agent believes the second condition to be fulfilled likewise, i.e. that the act of decision is determined *solely* by his self. It appears less obvious, because we all realize that formed character has a great deal to do with the choices that we make; and formed character is, without a doubt, partly dependent on the external factors of heredity and environment. But it is crucial here that we should not misunderstand the precise nature of the influence which formed character brings to bear upon the choices that constitute conduct. No one denies that it determines, at least largely, what things we desire, and again how greatly we desire them. It may thus fairly be said to determine the felt balance of desires in the situation of moral temptation. But all that that amounts to is that formed character prescribes the nature of the situation *within* which the act of moral decision takes place. It does not in the least follow that it has any influence whatsoever in determining the act of decision itself—the decision as to whether we shall exert effort or take the easy course of following the bent of our desiring nature: take, that is to say, the course which, in virtue of the determining influence of our character as so far formed, we feel to be in the line of least resistance.

When one appreciates this, one is perhaps better prepared to recognize the fact that the agent himself in the situation of moral temptation does not, and indeed could not, regard his formed character as having any influence whatever upon his act of decision as such. For the very nature of that decision, as it presents itself to him, is as to whether he will or will not permit his formed character to dictate his action. In other words, the agent distinguishes sharply between the self which makes the decision, and the self which, as formed character, determines not the decision but the situation within which the decision takes place. Rightly or wrongly, the agent believes that through his act of decision he can oppose and transcend his own formed character in the interest of duty. We are therefore obliged to say, I think, that the agent *cannot* regard his formed character as in any sense a determinant of the act of decision as such. The act is felt to be a genuinely creative act, originated by the self *ad hoc*, and by the self alone.

Here then, if my analysis is correct, in the function of moral decision in situations of moral temptation, we have an act of the self which at least *appears to the agent* to satisfy both of the conditions of freedom which we laid down at the beginning. The vital question now is, is this 'appearance' true or false? Is the act of decision really what it appears to the agent to be, determined solely by the self, and capable of alternative forms of expression? If it is, then we have here a free act which serves as an adequate basis for moral responsibility. We shall be entitled to regard the agent as morally praiseworthy or morally blameworthy according as he decides to put forth effort or to let his desiring nature have its way. We shall be entitled, in short, to judge the agent as he most certainly judges himself in the situation of moral temptation. If, on the other hand, there is good reason to believe that the agent is the victim of illusion in supposing his act of decision to bear this character, then in my opinion the whole conception of moral responsibility must be jettisoned altogether. For it seems to me certain that there is no other function of the self that even looks as though it satisfied the required conditions of the free act.

Now in considering the claim to truth of this belief of our practical consciousness, we should begin by noting that the onus of proof rests upon the critic who rejects this belief. Until cogent evidence to the contrary is adduced, we are entitled to put our trust in a belief which is so deeply embedded in our experience as practical beings as to be, I venture to say, ineradicable from it. Anyone who doubts whether it is ineradicable may be invited to think himself imaginatively into a situation of moral temptation as we have above described it, and then to ask himself whether in that situation he finds it possible to *disbelieve* that his act of decision has the characteristics in question. I have no misgivings about the answer. It is possible to disbelieve only when we are thinking abstractly about the situation; not when we are living through it, either actually or in imagination. This fact certainly establishes a strong prima facie presumption in favour of the Libertarian position. Nevertheless I agree that we shall have to weigh carefully several criticisms of high authority before we can feel justified in asserting free will as an ultimate and unqualified truth.

Fortunately for our purpose, however, there are some lines of criticism which, although extremely influential in the recent past, may at the present time be legitimately ignored. We are not to-day confronted, for example, by any widely accepted system of metaphysic with implications directly hostile to free will. Only a decade or two ago one could hardly hope to gain a sympathetic hearing for a view which assigned an ultimate initiative to finite selves, unless one were prepared first to show reason for rejecting the dominant metaphysical doctrine that all things in the universe are the expression of a single Mind or Spirit. But the challenge so lately offered by monistic Idealism has in the present age little more significance than the challenge once offered by monistic Materialism.

Much the same thing holds good of the challenge from the side of physical science. Libertarianism is certainly inconsistent with a rigidly determinist theory of the physical world. It is idle to pretend that there can be open possibilities for psychical decision, while at the same time holding that the physical events in which such decisions manifest themselves are determined in accordance with irrevocable law. But whereas until a few years ago the weight of scientific authority was thrown overwhelmingly on the side of a universal determinism of physical phenomena, the situation has, as everybody knows, profoundly altered during the present century more especially since the advent of Planck's Quantum Theory and Heisenberg's Principle of Uncertainty. Very few scientists to-day would seek to impugn free will on the ground of any supposed implications of the aims or achievements of physical science. I am not myself, I should perhaps add in passing, disposed to rest any part of the case against a universal physical determinism upon these recent dramatic developments of physical science. In my view there never were in the established results of physical science cogent reasons for believing that the apparently universal determinism of inorganic processes holds good also of the processes of the human body. The only inference I here wish to draw from the trend of present-day science is that it removes from any *contemporary* urgency the problem of meeting one particular type of objection to free will. And it is with the contemporary situation that I am in this paper anxious to deal.

I may turn at once, therefore, to lines of argument which do still enjoy a wide currency among anti-Libertarians. And I shall begin with one which, though it is a simple matter to show its irrelevance to the Libertarian doctrine as I have stated it, is so extremely popular that it cannot safely be ignored.

The charge made is that the Libertarian view is incompatible with the *predictability* of human conduct. For we do make rough predictions of people's conduct, on the basis of what we know of their character, every day of our lives, and there can be no doubt that the practice, within certain limits, is amply justified by results. Indeed if it were not so, social life would be reduced to sheer chaos. The close relationship between character and conduct which prediction postulates really seems to be about as certain as anything can be. But the Libertarian view, it is urged, by ascribing to the self a mysterious power of decision uncontrolled by character, and capable of issuing in acts inconsistent with character, denies that continuity between character and conduct upon which prediction depends. If Libertarianism is true, prediction is impossible. But prediction *is* possible, therefore Libertarianism is untrue.

My answer is that the Libertarian view is perfectly compatible with prediction within certain limits, and that there is no empirical evidence at all that prediction is in fact possible beyond these limits. The following considerations will, I think, make the point abundantly clear.

(1) There is no question, on our view, of a free will that can will just anything at all. The range of possible choices is limited by the agent's character in every case; for nothing can be an object of possible choice which is not suggested by either the agent's desires or his moral ideals, and these depend on 'character' for us just as much as for our opponents. We have, indeed explicitly recognized at an earlier stage that character determines the situation within which the act of moral decision takes place, although not the act of moral decision itself. This consideration obviously furnishes a broad basis for at least approximate predictions.

(2) There is *one* experiential situation, and *one only*, on our view, in which there is any possibility of the act of will not being in accordance with character; viz. the situation in which the course which formed character prescribes is a course in conflict with the agent's moral ideal: in other words, the situation of moral temptation. Now this is a situation of comparative rarity. Yet with respect to all other situations in life we are in full agreement with those who hold that conduct is the response of the agent's formed character to the given situation. Why should it not be so? There could be no reason, on our view any more than on another, for the agent even to consider deviating from the course which his formed character prescribes and he most strongly desires, *unless* that course is believed by him to be incompatible with what is right.

(3) Even within that one situation which is relevant to free will, our view can still recognize a certain basis for prediction. In that situation our character as so far formed prescribes a course opposed to duty, and an effort of will is required if we are to deviate from that course. But of course we are all aware that a greater effort of will is required in proportion to the degree in which we have to transcend our formed character in order to will the right. Such action is, as we say, 'harder'. But if action is 'harder' in proportion as it involves deviation from formed character, it seems reasonable to suppose that, on the whole, action will be of rarer

occurrence in that same proportion: though perhaps we may not say that at any level of deviation it becomes flatly impossible. It follows that even with respect to situations of moral temptation we may usefully employ our knowledge of the agent's character as a clue to prediction. It will be a clue of limited, but of by no means negligible, value. It will warrant us in predicting, e.g., of a person who has become enslaved to alcohol, that he is unlikely, even if fully aware of the moral evil of such slavery, to be successful immediately and completely in throwing off its shackles. Predictions of this kind we all make often enough in practice. And there seems no reason at all why a Libertarian doctrine should wish to question their validity.

Now when these three considerations are borne in mind, it becomes quite clear that the doctrine we are defending is compatible with a very substantial measure of predictability indeed. And I submit that there is not a jot of empirical evidence that any larger measure than this obtains in fact.

Let us pass on then to consider a much more interesting and, I think, more plausible criticism. It is constantly objected against the Libertarian doctrine that it is fundamentally *unintelligible*. Libertarianism holds that the act of moral decision is the *self's* act, and yet insists at the same time that it is not influenced by any of those determinate features in the self's nature which go to constitute its 'character'. But, it is asked, do not these two propositions contradict one another? Surely a *self*-determination which is determination by something other than the self's *character* is a contradiction in terms? What meaning is there in the conception of a 'self' in abstraction from its 'character'? If you really wish to maintain, it is urged, that the act of decision is not determined by the self's character, you ought to admit frankly that it is not determined by the *self* at all. But in that case, of course, you will not be advocating a freedom which lends any kind of support to moral responsibility; indeed very much the reverse.

Now this criticism, and all of its kind, seem to me to be the product of a simple, but extraordinarily pervasive, error: the error of confining one's self to the categories of the external observer in dealing with the actions of human agents. Let me explain.

It is perfectly true that the standpoint of the external observer, which we are obliged to adopt in dealing with physical processes, does not furnish us with even a glimmering of a notion of what can be meant by an entity which acts causally and yet not through any of the determinate features of its character. So far as we confine ourselves to external observation, I agree that this notion must seem to us pure nonsense. But then we are *not* obliged to confine ourselves to external observation in dealing with the human agent. Here, though here alone, we have the inestimable advantage of being able to apprehend operations from the *inside*, from the standpoint of *living experience*. But if we do adopt this internal standpoint—surely a proper standpoint, and one which we should be only too glad to adopt if we could in the case of other entities—the situation is entirely changed. We find that we not merely can, but constantly do, attach meaning to a causation which is the self's causation but is yet not exercised by the self's character. We have seen as much already in our analysis of the situation of moral temptation. When confronted by such a situation, we saw, we are certain that it lies with our *self* to decide whether we shall let our character as so far formed dictate our action or whether we shall by effort oppose its dictates and rise to duty. We are certain, in other words, that the act is *not* determined by our *character*, while we remain equally certain that the act *is* determined by our *self*.

Or look, for a further illustration (since the point we have to make here is of the very first importance for the whole free will controversy), to the experience of effortful willing itself, where the act of decision has found expression in the will to rise to duty. In such an experience we are certain that it is our self which makes the effort. But we are equally certain that the effort does not flow from that system of conative dispositions which we call our formed character; for the very function that the effort has for us is to enable us to act against the 'line of least resistance', i.e. to act in a way *contrary* to that to which our formed character inclines us.

I conclude, therefore, that those who find the Libertarian doctrine of the self's causality in moral decision inherently unintelligible find it so simply because they restrict themselves, quite arbitrarily, to an inadequate standpoint: a standpoint from which, indeed, a genuinely creative activity, if it existed, never *could* be apprehended.

It will be understood, of course, that it is no part of my purpose to deny that the act of moral decision is in *one* sense 'unintelligible'. If by the 'intelligibility' of an act we mean that it is capable, at least in principle, of being inferred as a consequence of a given ground, then naturally my view is that the act in question is '*un*intelligible'. But that, presumably, is not the meaning of 'intelligibility' in the critic's mind when he says that the Libertarian holds an 'unintelligible' doctrine. If it were all he meant, he would merely be pointing out that Libertarianism is not compatible with Determinism! And that tautologous pronouncement would hardly deserve the title of 'criticism'. Yet, strangely enough, not all of the critics seem to be quite clear on this matter. The Libertarian often has the experience of being challenged by the critic to tell him *why*, on his view, the agent now decides to put forth moral effort and now decides not to, with the obviously intended implication that if the Libertarian cannot say 'why' he should give up his theory. Such critics apparently fail to see that if the Libertarian *could* say why he would already have given up his theory! Obviously to demand 'intelligibility' in this sense is simply to prejudge the whole issue in favour of Determinism. The sense in which the critic is entitled to demand intelligibility of our doctrine is simply this; he may demand that the kind of action which our doctrine imputes to human selves should not be, for ultimate analysis, meaningless. And in that sense, as I have already argued, our doctrine is perfectly intelligible.

Let us suppose, then, that the Determinist, confronted by the plain evidence of our practical self-consciousness, now recognizes his obligation to give up the position that the Libertarian doctrine is without qualification 'meaningless', and concedes that from the standpoint of our practical self-consciousness at any rate it is 'meaningful'. And let us ask what will be his next move. So far as I can see, his most likely move now will be to attack the value of that 'internal' standpoint, contrasting it unfavourably, in respect of its claim to truth, with the rational, objective, standpoint of 'pure philosophy'. 'I admit,' he may tell us, 'that there is begotten in the self, in the practical experience you refer to, a belief in a self-causality which is yet not a causality exercised through the self's character. But surely this must weigh but lightly in the balance against the proposition, which appeals to our reason with axiomatic certainty, that an act cannot be caused by a self if it has no ground in the determinate nature of that self. If the choice lies between either disbelieving that rational proposition, or dismissing the evidence of practical self-consciousness as illusion, it is the latter alternative which in my opinion any sane philosophy is bound to adopt.'

But a very little reflection suffices to show that this position is in reality no improvement at all on that from which the critic has just fallen back. For it is evident that the proposition alleged to be axiomatic is axiomatic, at most, only to a reason which knows nothing of acts or events save as they present themselves to an external observer. It obviously is *not* axiomatic to a reason whose field of apprehension is broadened to include the data furnished by the direct experience of acting. In short, the proposition is axiomatic, at most, only to reason functioning *abstractly*; which most certainly cannot be identified with reason functioning *philosophically*.

What is required of the critic, of course, if he is to make good his case, is a reasoned justification of his cavalier attitude towards the testimony of practical self-consciousness. That is the primary desideratum. And the lack of it in the bulk of Determinist literature is in my opinion something of a scandal. Without it, the criticism we have just been examining is sheer dogmatism. It is, indeed, dogmatism of a peculiarly perverse kind. For the situation is, in effect, as follows. From our practical self-consciousness we gain a notion of a genuinely creative act—which might be defined as an act which nothing determines save the agent's doing of it. Of such a character is the act of moral decision as we experience it. But the critic says 'No! This sort of thing cannot be. A person cannot without affront to reason be conceived to be the author of an act which bears, *ex hypothesi*, no intelligible relation to his character. A mere intuition of practical self-consciousness is the solitary prop of this fantastic notion, and surely that is quite incapable of bearing the weight that you would thrust upon it.' Now observe the perversity! The critic says, excluding the evidence of practical self-consciousness, the notion makes nonsense. In other words, excluding the only evidence there ever *could* be for such a notion, the notion makes nonsense! For, of course, if there should be such a thing as creative activity, there is absolutely no other way save an intuition of practical self-consciousness in which we could become aware of it. Only from the inside, from the standpoint of the agent's living experience, can 'activity' possibly be apprehended. So that what the critic is really doing is to condemn a notion as nonsensical on the ground that the only evidence for it is the only evidence there ever could be for it.

Up to the present I have deemed it advisable, in order better to cover the ground, to deal with typical rather than with individual criticisms of the Libertarian position. I wish, however, to depart from that precedent in one instance before I conclude. I am anxious to come to somewhat closer grips with the criticism which Professor C. D. Broad makes in an inaugural lecture published under the title 'Determinism, Indeterminism, and Libertarianism': a work which, short as it is, seems to me to offer incomparably the best elucidation of the problem of freedom that we have. Mr Broad's criticism does not, as I shall try to show, raise any really new point of principle. But its author's pre-eminence in contemporary philosophy, combined with the recency of this pronouncement, makes it desirable to give a rather particular attention to his views.

The business of elucidation—with which by far the greater part of his lecture is concerned—is in my opinion executed almost to perfection. I acquiesce with especial pleasure in the position Mr Broad adopts on three important aspects of the problem. (1) He takes as his starting-point the conditions implied in moral obligability; the only starting-point, as I believe, which will ensure that the freedom to be discussed will be the freedom which constitutes the real problem. (2) He is entirely clear that the freedom implied in moral obligability is a freedom in which there are genuinely open possibilities before the self: a freedom in which, to use Mr Broad's terminology, our volition is not merely 'conditionally' but 'categorically' substitutable: i.e. a freedom in which the agent 'could have done otherwise than he did' even though the whole set of conditions environing his decision remained constant. And (3) his analysis culminates in the frank recognition of what he calls the 'effortful factor' in willing as the crux of the whole problem. It is by reference to this that the Libertarian position has got to be defined. What the Libertarian wants to say, he tells us, is that where an effort of will is put forth to reinforce my desire for a course A, 'it is logically consistent with all the nomic, occurrent, dispositional, and background facts that no effort should have been made, or that it should have been directed towards reinforcing the desire for B instead of the desire for A, or that it should have been put forth more or less strongly than it actually was in favour of the desire for A'; and that, nevertheless, the putting forth of the effort was no mere *accident*, but was 'in a unique and peculiar way' determined *'by the agent or self'*.

Now up to this point, p. 43 of a book of less than fifty pages, I am, with only a few relatively unimportant reservations, in almost verbal agreement with what Mr Broad says. Yet I doubt whether even those who, unlike myself, are in sympathy also with Mr Broad's ultimate verdict will escape disappointment from the remaining few pages. The problem of free will has at this juncture been no more than stated. But for Mr Broad, apparently, the mere statement is virtually tantamount to a Determinist solution. In one single paragraph he now proceeds to offer his reasons for rejecting the Libertarian position as certainly false. Let me quote from it the passage on which this summary dismissal turns. 'The putting forth of an effort', he says, 'of a certain intensity, in a certain direction, at a certain moment, for a certain duration, is quite clearly an event or process, however unique and peculiar it may be in other respects. It is therefore subject to any conditions which self-evidently apply to every event, as such.

Now it is surely quite evident that, if the beginning of a certain process at a certain time is determined at all, its total cause *must* contain as an essential factor another event or process which *enters into* the moment from which the determined event or process *issues*. I see no prima facie objection to there being events that are not completely determined. But, in so far as an event *is* determined, an essential factor in its total cause must be other events' (p. 44).

I wish to suggest, with all respect, that we have here merely another manifestation of the cardinal fallacy of anti-Libertarian criticism, the fallacy of bringing to the interpretation of human action categories derived solely from the standpoint of the external observer.

For consider. 'It is surely quite evident', says Mr Broad, 'that if the beginning of a certain process at a certain time is determined at all, its total cause *must* contain as an essential factor another event or process which *enters into* the moment from which the determined event or process *issues*.' On this contention his whole argument rests. On this, and this alone, depends his conclusion that the act of moral decision is preconditioned, and therefore not, as Libertarianism holds, creative. But *is* this contention evident? It may seem evident with respect to those events to which we stand in the relation solely of external observer. But that is not the only relation in which we can stand to events. If the decision to put forth or forbear from putting forth effort in the situation of moral temptation is an event—and I agree that from one point of view it may rightly be called so—it is an event which we can know from within. And, as known from within, it is the *reverse* of evident that its total cause must contain another event which enters into the moment from which the determined event issues. On the contrary, from the internal standpoint of the agent himself, it is evident that while the event which is the moral decision is determined, in that the self is recognized as its author, there is no *other* event concerned in the matter at all. What determines my 'deed', in the act of moral decision, is felt to be nothing but my doing of it. And this 'doing' is of course not some other event antecedent to the deed itself. It is just the deed (or decision) as *act*, which is the other side of the deed (or decision) as *event*. It seems to me perfectly clear, therefore, that the proposition which Mr Broad says is 'quite evident' must in fact appear to be a false proposition to any moral agent engaged in the actual function of moral decision.

It will be seen, then, that my objection to Mr Broad's criticism is identical in principle with the general objection which I urged earlier. Mr Broad is not entitled to say that certain conditions of the occurrence of an event as such are 'self-evidently' necessary, if that 'self-evidence' is achieved only by ignoring the testimony of our practical self-consciousness. This holds good, it seems to me, irrespective of any question as to the ultimate value of that testimony. The point is that if that testimony is relevant to the problem at all—and if it is not, I should very much like to know *why* it is not—then it *cannot* be 'self-evident' that the conditions Mr Broad alleges are necessary conditions. It may possibly be the case, though I do not believe it to be so, that Mr Broad's ultimate verdict is the correct one: that Libertarianism is a false theory, and the notion of 'categorical obligability' in consequence a delusive notion. But it is not the case that, in Mr Broad's words, 'Libertarianism is self-evidently impossible'. Mr Broad has helped enormously towards the solution of the free will problem by his masterly statement of the issues involved. But, if I am right, much laborious analysis and deliberation upon *pros* and *cons* (which to Mr Broad, for the reasons we have seen, appears as a work of mere supererogation) must ensue before we can possibly be in a position to say that the problem is 'solved' one way or the other.

And here, to my regret, my own too brief discussion must terminate. There is much more that I should have liked to say: much more, in my opinion, that badly requires to be said. I should have liked, perhaps above all, to have been able to give more space to an analysis of the experience we call 'effort of will', and to have attempted to expose the fallacies which seem to me to underlie all attempts to explain away that experience by resolving it into something other than itself. That, however, is a matter with which I have partially dealt on a previous occasion, and to which I propose to return under conditions more appropriate to the full-length treatment which can alone be of much service on a difficult psychological theme of this kind. Meantime I can only hope that the little I have been able to say may do something towards regaining for free will in the 'vulgar' sense a place in serious philosophical discussion: that it may do something—to use language of an appropriate vulgarity—towards putting Libertarianism 'on the map' once more. It is not, in my opinion, 'on the map' at all at present. It cannot be, when critics are so often content to make slogans and shibboleths do the work of analysis and argument; when a few satirical references to the 'mysterious fiat' of a 'pure ego' are regarded in so many quarters as a sufficient rejoinder to the Libertarian's claims. Prejudicial phrases like these have certainly a good deal of power. They are evocative of an acutely hostile emotional atmosphere. But, unless accompanied by the most careful analysis, they seem to me to stand for bad habits rather than for good reasons. And it would be no disservice to philosophy if they were extruded from the literature of the free will problem altogether.

A Defense of Compatibilism

W. T. STACE

. . .if there is no free will there can be no morality. Morality is concerned with what men ought and ought not to do. But if a man has no freedom to choose what he will do, if whatever he does is done under compulsion, then it does not make sense to tell him that he ought not to have done what he did and that he ought to do something different. All moral precepts would in such case be meaningless. Also if he acts always under compulsion, how can he be held morally responsible for his actions? How can he, for example, be punished for what he could not help doing?

It is to be observed that those learned professors of philosophy or psychology who deny the existence of free will do so only in their professional moments and in their studies and lecture rooms. For when it comes to doing anything practical, even of the most trivial kind, they invariably behave as if they and others were free. They inquire from you at dinner whether you will choose this dish or that dish. They will ask a child why he told a lie, and will punish him for not having chosen the way of truthfulness. All of which is inconsistent with a disbelief in free will. This should cause us to suspect that the problem is not a real one; and this, I believe, is the case. The dispute is merely verbal, and is due to nothing but a confusion about the meanings of words. It is what is now fashionably called a semantic problem.

How does a verbal dispute arise? Let us consider a case which, although it is absurd in the sense that no one would ever make the mistake which is involved in it, yet illustrates the principle which we shall have to use in the solution of the problem. Suppose that someone believed that the word "man" means a certain sort of five-legged animal; in short that "five-legged animal" is the correct *definition* of man. He might then look around the world, and rightly observing that there are no five-legged animals in it, he might proceed to deny the existence of men. This preposterous conclusion would have been reached because he was using an incorrect definition of "man." All you would have to do to show him his mistake would be to give him the correct definition; or at least to show him that his definition was wrong. Both the problem and its solution would, of course, be entirely verbal. The problem of free will, and its solution, I shall maintain, is verbal in exactly the same way. The problem has been created by the fact that learned men, especially philosophers, have assumed an incorrect definition of free will, and then finding that there is nothing in the world which answers to their definition, have denied its existence. As far as logic is concerned, their conclusion is just as absurd as that of the man who denies the existence of men. The only difference is that the mistake in the latter case is obvious and crude, while the mistake which the deniers of free will have made is rather subtle and difficult to detect.

The late Professor Stace was for many years professor of philosophy at Princeton.

From *Religion and the Modern Mind* by W. T. Stace. Copyright 1952 by W. T. Stace. Reprinted by permission of J. B. Lippincott Company. This chapter appears under the title "The Problem of Morals."

Throughout the modern period, until quite recently, it was assumed, both by the philosophers who denied free will and by those who defended it, that *determinism is inconsistent with free will*. If a man's actions were wholly determined by chains of causes stretching back into the remote past, so that they could be predicted beforehand by a mind which knew all the causes, it was assumed that they could not in that case be free. This implies that a certain definition of actions done from free will was assumed, namely that they are actions *not* wholly determined by causes or predictable beforehand. Let us shorten this by saying that free will was defined as meaning indeterminism. This is the incorrect definition which has led to the denial of free will. As soon as we see what the true definition is we shall find that the question whether the world is deterministic, as Newtonian science implied, or in a measure indeterministic, as current physics teaches, is wholly irrelevant to the problem.

Of course there is a sense in which one can define a word arbitrarily in any way one pleases. But a definition may nevertheless be called correct or incorrect. It is correct if it accords with a *common usage* of the word defined. It is incorrect if it does not. And if you give an incorrect definition, absurd and untrue results are likely to follow. For instance, there is nothing to prevent you from arbitrarily defining a man as a five-legged animal, but this is incorrect in the sense that it does not accord with the ordinary meaning of the word. Also it has the absurd result of leading to a denial of the existence of men. This shows that *common usage is the criterion for deciding whether a definition is correct or not*. And this is the principle which I shall apply to free will. I shall show that indeterminism is not what is meant by the phrase "free will" *as it is commonly used*. And I shall attempt to discover the correct definition by inquiring how the phrase is used in ordinary conversation.

Here are a few samples of how the phrase might be used in ordinary conversation. It will be noticed that they include cases in which the question whether a man acted with free will is asked in order to determine whether he was morally and legally responsible for his acts.

JONES: I once went without food for a week.
SMITH: Did you do that of your own free will?
JONES: No. I did it because I was lost in a desert and could find no food.

But suppose that the man who had fasted was Mahatma Gandhi. The conversation might then have gone:

GANDHI: I once fasted for a week.
SMITH: Did you do that of your own free will?
GANDHI: Yes. I did it because I wanted to compel the British Government to give India its independence.

Take another case. Suppose that I had stolen some bread, but that I was as truthful as George Washington. Then, if I were charged with the crime in court, some exchange of the following sort might take place:

JUDGE: Did you steal the bread of your own free will?
STACE: Yes. I stole it because I was hungry.

Or in different circumstances the conversation might run:

JUDGE: Did you steal of your own free will?
STACE: No. I stole because my employer threatened to beat me if I did not.

At a recent murder trial in Trenton some of the accused had signed confessions, but afterwards asserted that they had done so under police duress. The following exchange might have occurred:

JUDGE: Did you sign this confession of your own free will?
PRISONER: No. I signed it because the police beat me up.

Now suppose that a philosopher had been a member of the jury. We could imagine this conversation taking place in the jury room.

FOREMAN OF THE JURY: The prisoner says he signed the confession because he was beaten, and not of his own free will.
PHILOSOPHER: This is quite irrelevant to the case. There is no such thing as free will.
FOREMAN: Do you mean to say that it makes no difference whether he signed because his conscience made him want to tell the truth or because he was beaten?
PHILOSOPHER: None at all. Whether he was caused to sign by a beating or by some desire of his own—the desire to tell the truth, for example—in either case his signing was causally determined, and therefore in neither case

> did he act of his own free will. Since there is no such thing as free will, the question whether he signed of his own free will ought not to be discussed by us.

The foreman and the rest of the jury would rightly conclude that the philosopher must be making some mistake. What sort of a mistake could it be? There is only one possible answer. The philosopher must be using the phrase "free will" in some peculiar way of his own which is not the way in which men usually use it when they wish to determine a question of moral responsibility. That is, he must be using an incorrect definition of it as implying action not determined by causes.

Suppose a man left his office at noon, and were questioned about it. Then we might hear this:

JONES: Did you leave your office of your own free will?
SMITH: No. I was forcibly removed by the police.

We have now collected a number of cases of actions which, in the ordinary usage of the English language, would be called cases in which people have acted of their own free will. We should also say in all these cases that they *chose* to act as they did. We should also say that they could have acted otherwise, if they had chosen. For instance, Mahatma Gandhi was not compelled to fast; he chose to do so. He could have eaten if he had wanted to. When Smith went out to get his lunch, he chose to do so. He could have stayed and done some more work, if he had wanted to. We have also collected a number of cases of the opposite kind. They are cases in which men were not able to exercise their free will. They had no choice. They were compelled to do as they did. The man in the desert did not fast of his own free will. He had no choice in the matter. He was compelled to fast because there was nothing for him to eat. And so with the other cases. It ought to be quite easy, by an inspection of these cases, to tell what we ordinarily mean when we say that a man did or did not exercise free will. We ought therefore to be able to extract from them the proper definition of the term. Let us put the cases in a table:

Free Acts

Gandhi fasting because he wanted to free India.
Stealing bread because one is hungry.
Signing a confession because one wanted to tell the truth.
Leaving the office because one wanted one's lunch.

Unfree Acts

The man fasting in the desert because there was no food.
Stealing because one's employer threatened to beat one.
Signing because the police beat one.
Leaving because forcibly removed.

It is obvious that to find the correct definition of free acts we must discover what characteristic is common to all the acts on the first list, and is, at the same time, absent from all the acts on the second list. This characteristic which all free acts have, and which no unfree acts have, will be the defining characteristic of free will.

Is being uncaused, or not being determined by causes, the characteristic of which we are in search? It cannot be, because although it is true that all the acts on the second list have causes, such as the beating by the police or the absence of food in the desert, so also do the acts on the first list. Mr. Gandhi's fasting was caused by his desire to free India, the man leaving his office by his hunger, and so on. Moreover there is no reason to doubt that these causes of the free acts were in turn caused by prior conditions, and that these were again the results of causes, and so on back indefinitely into the past. Any physiologist can tell us the causes of hunger. What caused Mr. Gandhi's tremendously powerful desire to free India is no doubt more difficult to discover. But it must have had causes. Some of them may have lain in peculiarities of his glands or brain, others in his past experiences, others in his heredity, others in his education. Defenders of free will have usually tended to deny such facts. But to do so is plainly a case of special pleading, which is unsupported by any scrap of evidence. The only reasonable view is that all human actions, both those which are freely done and those which are not, are either wholly determined by causes, or at least as much determined as other events in nature. It may be true, as the physicists tell us, that nature is not as deterministic as was once thought. But whatever degree of determinism prevails in the world, human actions appear to be as much determined as anything else. And if this is so, it cannot be the case that what distinguishes actions freely chosen from those which are not free is that the latter are determined by causes while the former are not. Therefore, being uncaused or being undetermined by causes, must be an incorrect definition of free will.

What, then, is the difference between acts which are freely done and those which are not? What is the characteristic which is present to all the acts on the first list and absent from all those on the second list? Is it not obvious that, although both sets of actions have causes, the causes of those on the first list are *of a different kind* from the causes of those on the second list? The free acts are all caused by desires, or motives, or by some sort of internal psychological states of the agent's mind. The unfree acts, on the other hand, are all caused by physical forces or physical conditions, outside the agent. Police arrest means physical force exerted from the outside; the absence of food in the desert is a physical condition of the outside world. We may therefore frame the following rough definitions. *Acts freely done are those whose immediate causes are psychological states in the agent. Acts not freely done are those whose immediate causes are states of affairs external to the agent.*

It is plain that if we define free will in this way, then free will certainly exists, and the philosopher's denial of its existence is seen to be what it is—nonsense. For it is obvious that all those actions of men which we should ordinarily attribute to the exercise of their free will, or of which we should say that they freely chose to do them, are in fact actions which have been caused by their own desires, wishes, thoughts, emotions, impulses, or other psychological states.

In applying our definition we shall find that it usually works well, but that there are some puzzling cases which it does not seem exactly to fit. These puzzles can always be solved by paying careful attention to the ways in which words are used, and remembering that they are not always used consistently. I have space for only one example. Suppose that a thug threatens to shoot you unless you give him your wallet, and suppose that you do so. Do you, in giving him your wallet, do so of your own free will or not? If we apply our definition, we find that you acted freely, since the immediate cause of the action was not an actual outside force but the fear of death, which is a psychological cause. Most people, however, would say that you did not act of your own free will but under compulsion. Does this show that our definition is wrong? I do not think so. Aristotle, who gave a solution of the problem of free will substantially the same as ours (though he did not use the term "free will") admitted that there are what he called "mixed" or borderline cases in which it is difficult to know whether we ought to call the acts free or compelled. In the case under discussion, though no actual force was used, the gun at your forehead so nearly approximated to actual force that we tend to say the case was one of compulsion. It is a borderline case.

Here is what may seem like another kind of puzzle. According to our view an action may be free though it could have been predicted beforehand with certainty. But suppose you told a lie, and it was certain beforehand that you would tell it. How could one then say, "You could have told the truth"? The answer is that it is perfectly true that you could have told the truth *if* you had wanted to. In fact you would have done so, for in that case the causes producing your action, namely your desires, would have been different, and would therefore have produced different effects. It is a delusion that predictability and free will are incompatible. This agrees with common sense. For if, knowing your character, I predict that you will act honorably, no one would say when you do act honorably, that this shows you did not do so of your own free will.

Since free will is a condition of moral responsibility, we must be sure that our theory of free will gives a sufficient basis for it. To be held morally responsible for one's actions means that one may be justly punished or rewarded, blamed or praised, for them. But it is not just to punish a man for what he cannot help doing. How can it be just to punish him for an action which it was certain beforehand that he would do? We have not attempted to decide whether, as a matter of fact, all events, including human actions, are completely determined. For that question is irrelevant to the problem of free will. But if we assume for the purposes of argument that complete determinism is true, but that we are nevertheless free, it may then be asked whether such a deterministic free will is compatible with moral responsibility. For it may seem unjust to punish a man for an action which it could have been predicted with certainty beforehand that he would do.

But that determinism is incompatible with moral responsibility is as much a delusion as that it is incompatible with free will. You do not excuse a man for doing a wrong act because, knowing his character, you felt certain beforehand that he would do it. Nor do you deprive a man of a reward or prize because, knowing his goodness or his capabilities, you felt certain beforehand that he would win it.

Volumes have been written on the justification of punishment. But so far as it affects the question of free will, the essential principles involved are quite simple. The punishment of a man for doing a wrong act is justified, either on the ground that it will correct his own character, or that it will deter other people from doing similar acts. The instrument of punishment has been in the past, and no doubt still is, often unwisely used; so that it may often have done more harm than good. But that is not relevant to our present problem. Punishment, if and when it is justified, is justified only on one or both of the grounds just mentioned. The question then is how, if we assume determinism, punishment can correct character or deter people from evil actions.

Suppose that your child develops a habit of telling lies. You give him a mild beating. Why? Because you believe that his personality is such that the usual motives for telling the truth do not cause him to do so. You therefore supply the missing cause, or motive, in the shape of pain and the fear of future pain if he repeats his untruthful behavior. And you hope that a few treatments of this kind will condition him to the habit of truth-telling, so that he will come to tell the truth without the infliction of pain. You assume that his actions are determined by causes, but that the usual causes of truth-telling do not in him produce their usual effects. You therefore supply him with an artificially injected motive, pain and fear, which you think will in the future cause him to speak truthfully.

The principle is exactly the same where you hope, by punishing one man, to deter others from wrong actions. You believe that the fear of punishment will cause those who might otherwise do evil to do well.

We act on the same principle with nonhuman, and even with inanimate, things, if they do not behave in the way we think they ought to behave. The rose bushes in the garden produce only small and poor blooms, whereas we want large and rich ones. We supply a cause which will produce large blooms, namely fertilizer. Our automobile does not go properly. We supply a cause which will make it go better, namely oil in the works. The punishment for the man, the fertilizer for the plant, and the oil for the car, are all justified by the same principle and in the same way. The only difference is that different kinds of things require different kinds of causes to make them do what they should. Pain may be the appropriate remedy to apply, in certain cases, to human beings, and oil to the machine. It is, of course, of no use to inject motor oil into the boy or to beat the machine.

Thus we see that moral responsibility is not only consistent with determinism, but requires it. The assumption on which punishment is based is that human behavior is causally determined. If pain could not be a cause of truth-telling there would be no justification at all for punishing lies. If human actions and volitions were uncaused, it would be useless either to punish or reward, or indeed to do anything else to correct people's bad behavior. For nothing that you could do would in any way influence them. Thus moral responsibility would entirely disappear. If there were no determinism of human beings at all, their actions would be completely unpredictable and capricious, and therefore irresponsible. And this is in itself a strong argument against the common view of philosophers that free will means being undetermined by causes.

Freedom and Psychoanalysis

JOHN HOSPERS

Perhaps the most obvious conception of freedom is this: an act is free if and only if it is a voluntary act. A response that occurs spontaneously, not as a result of your willing it, such as a reflex action, is not a free act. I do not know that this view is ever held in its pure form, but it is the basis for other ones. As it stands, of course, it is ambiguous: does "voluntary" entail "premeditated?" are acts we perform semi-automatically through habit to be called free acts? To what extent is a conscious decision to act required for the act to be classified as voluntary? What of sudden outbursts of feeling? They are hardly premeditated or decided upon, yet they may have their origin in the presence or absence of habit-patterns due to self-discipline which may have been consciously decided upon. Clearly the view needs to be refined.

Now, however we may come to define "voluntary," it is perfectly possible to maintain that all voluntary acts are free acts and vice versa; after all, it is a matter of what meaning we are giving to the word "free" and we can give it this meaning if we choose. But it soon becomes apparent that this is not the meaning which most of us *want* to give it: for there *are* classes of action which we want to refrain from calling "free" even though they are voluntary (not that we have this denial in mind when we use the word "free"—still, it is significant that we do not use the word in some situations in which the act in question is nevertheless voluntary).

When a man tells a state secret under torture, he does choose voluntarily between telling and enduring more torture; and when he submits to a bandit's command at the point of a gun, he voluntarily chooses to submit rather than to be shot. And still such actions would not generally be called free; it is clear that they are performed under compulsion. Voluntary acts performed under compulsion would not be called free; and the cruder view is to this extent amended.

For some persons, this is as far as we need to go. Schlick, for example, says that the free will issue is the scandal of philosophy and nothing but so much wasted ink and paper, because the whole controversy is nothing but an inexcusable confusion between compulsion and universal causality.[1] The free act is the uncompelled act, says Schlick, and controversies about causality and determinism have nothing to do with the case. When one asks whether an act done of necessity is free, the question is ambiguous: if "of necessity" means "by compulsion," then the answer is no; if, on the other hand, "of necessity" is a way of referring to "causal uniformity" in nature—the sense in which we may misleadingly speak of the laws of nature as "necessary" simply because there are no exceptions to them—then the answer is clearly yes; every act is an instance of some causal law (uniformity) or other, but this has nothing to do with its being free in the sense of uncompelled.

John Hospers is professor of philosophy at the University of Southern California.

From the article "Meaning and Free Will" by John Hospers, *Philosophy and Phenomenological Research*, vol. 10, no. 3 (March 1950), pp. 313-330. Reprinted by permission of the publisher.

For Schlick, this is the end of the matter. Any attempt to discuss the matter further simply betrays a failure to perceive the clarifying distinctions that Schlick has made.

> Freedom means the opposite of compulsion; a man is *free* if he does not act under *compulsion*, and he is compelled or unfree when he is hindered from without in the realization of his natural desires. Hence he is unfree when he is locked up, or chained, or when someone forces him at the point of a gun to do what otherwise he would not do. This is quite clear, and everyone will admit that the everyday or legal notion of the lack of freedom is thus correctly interpreted, and that a man will be considered quite free . . . if no such external compulsion is exerted upon him.[2]

This all seems clear enough. And yet if we ask whether it ends the matter, whether it states what we "really mean" by "free," many of us will feel qualms. We remember statements about human beings being pawns of their environment, victims of conditions beyond their control, the result of causal influences stemming from parents, etc., and we think, "Still, are we really free?" We do not want to say that the uniformity of nature itself binds us or renders us unfree; yet is there not something in what generations of wise men have said about man being fettered? Is there not something too facile, too sleight-of-hand, in Schlick's cutting of the Gordian knot?

It will be noticed that we have slipped from talking about acts as being free into talking about human beings as free. Both locutions are employed, I would say about 50-50. Sometimes an attempt is made to legislate definitely between the two: Stebbing, for instance, says that one must never call acts free, but only the doers of the acts.[3]

Let us pause over this for a moment. If it is we and not our acts that are to be called free, the most obvious reflection to make is that we are free to do some things and not free to do other things; we are free to lift our hands but not free to lift the moon. We cannot simply call ourselves free or unfree *in toto*; we must say at best that we are free in respect of certain actions only. G. E. Moore states the criterion as follows: we are free to do an act if we can do it *if* we want to; that which we can do if we want to is what we are free to do.[4] Some things certain people are free to do while others are not; most of us are free to move our legs, but paralytics are not; some of us are free to concentrate on philosophical reading matter for three hours at a stretch while others are not. In general, we could relate the two approaches by saying that a *person* is free *in respect of* a given action if he can do it if he wants to, and in this case his *act* is free.

Moore himself, however, has reservations that Schlick has not. He adds that there *is* a sense of "free" which fulfills the criterion he has just set forth; but that there may be *another* sense in which man cannot be said to be free in all the situations in which he could rightly be said to be so in the first sense.

And surely it is not necessary for me to multiply examples of the sort of thing we mean. In practice most of us would not call free many persons who behave voluntarily and even with calculation aforethought, and under no compulsion either of any obvious sort. A metropolitan newspaper headlines an article with the words "Boy Killer Is Doomed Long before He Is Born,"[5] and then goes on to describe how a twelve-year-old boy has just been sentenced to thirty years in Sing Sing for the murder of a girl; his family background includes records of drunkenness, divorce, social maladjustment, epilepsy, and paresis. He early displays a tendency to sadistic activity to hide an underlying masochism and "prove that he's a man"; being coddled by his mother only worsens this tendency, until, spurned by a girl in his attempt on her, he kills her—not simply in a fit of anger, but calculatingly, deliberately. Is he free in respect of his criminal act, or for that matter in most of the acts of his life? Surely to ask this question is to answer it in the negative. Perhaps I have taken an extreme case; but it is only to show the superficiality of the Schlick analysis the more clearly. Though not everyone has criminotic tendencies, everyone has been moulded by influences which in large measure at least determine his present behavior; he is literally the product of these influences, stemming from periods prior to his "years of discretion," giving him a host of character traits that he cannot change now even if he would. So obviously does what a man is depend upon how a man comes to be, that it is small wonder that philosophers and sages have considered man far indeed from being the master of his fate. It is not as if man's will were standing high and serene above the flux of events that have moulded him; it is itself caught up in this flux, itself carried along on the current. An act is free when it is determined by the man's character, say moralists; but when there was nothing the man could do to shape his character, and even the degree of will power available to him in shaping his habits and disciplining himself to overcome the influence of his early environment is a factor over which he has no control, what are we to say of this kind of "freedom?" Is it not rather like the freedom of the machine to stamp labels on cans when it has been devised for just that purpose? Some machines can do so more efficiently than others, but only because they have been better constructed.

It is not my purpose here to establish this thesis in general, but only in one specific respect which has received comparatively little attention, namely, the field referred to by psychiatrists as that of unconscious motivation. In what follows I shall restrict my attention to it because it illustrates as clearly as anything the points I wish to make.

Let me try to summarize very briefly the psychoanalytic doctrine on this point.[6] The conscious life of the human being, including the conscious decisions and volitions, is merely a mouthpiece for the unconscious—not directly for the enactment of unconscious drives but of the compromise between unconscious drives and unconscious reproaches. There is a Big Three behind the scenes which the automaton called the conscious personality carries out: the id, an "eternal gimme," presents its wish and demands its immediate satisfaction; the super-ego says no to the wish immediately upon presentation, and the unconscious ego, the mediator between the two, tries to keep peace by means of compromise.[7]

To go into examples of the functioning of these three "bosses" would be endless; psychoanalytic case books supply hundreds of them. The important point for us to see in the present context is that it is the unconscious that determines what the conscious impulse and the conscious action shall be. Hamlet, for example, had a strong Oedipus wish, which was violently counteracted by super-ego reproaches; these early wishes were vividly revived in an unusual adult situation in which his uncle usurped the coveted position from Hamlet's father and won his mother besides. This situation evoked strong strictures on the part of Hamlet's super-ego, and it was this that was responsible for his notorious delay in killing his uncle. A dozen times Hamlet could have killed Claudius easily; but every time Hamlet "decided" not to: a free choice, moralists would say—but no, listen to the super-ego: "What you feel such hatred toward your uncle for, what you are plotting to kill him for, is precisely the crime which you yourself desire to commit: to kill your father and replace him in the affections of your mother. Your fate and your uncle's are bound up together." This paralyzes Hamlet into inaction. Consciously all he knows is that he is unable to act; this conscious inability he rationalizes, giving a different excuse each time.[8]

We have always been conscious of the fact that we are not masters of our fate in every respect—that there are many things which we cannot do, that nature is more powerful than we are, that we cannot disobey laws without danger of reprisals, etc. Lately we have become more conscious, too, though novelists and dramatists have always been fairly conscious of it, that we are not free with respect to the emotions that we feel—whom we love or hate, what types we admire, and the like. More lately still we have been reminded that there are unconscious motivations for our basic attractions and repulsions, our compulsive actions or inabilities to act. But what is not welcome news is that our very acts of volition, and the entire train of deliberations leading up to them, are but facades for the expression of unconscious wishes, or rather, unconscious compromises and defenses.

A man is faced by a choice: shall he kill another person or not? Moralists would say, here is a free choice—the result of deliberation, an act consciously entered into. And yet, though the agent himself does not know it, and has no awareness of the forces that are at work within him, his choice is already determined for him: his conscious will is only an instrument, a slave, in the hands of a deep unconscious motivation which determines his action. If he has a great deal of what the analyst calls "free-floating guilt," he will not; but if the guilt is such as to demand immediate absorption in the form of self-damaging behavior, this accumulated guilt will have to be discharged in some criminal action. The man himself does not know what the inner clockwork is; he is like the hands on the clock, thinking they move freely over the face of the clock.

A woman has married and divorced several husbands. Now she is faced with a choice for the next marriage: shall she marry Mr. A, or Mr. B, or nobody at all? She may take considerable time to "decide" this question, and her decision may appear as a final triumph of her free will. Let us assume that A is a normal, well-adjusted, kind, and generous man, while B is a leech, an impostor, one who will become entangled constantly in quarrels with her. If she belongs to a certain classifiable psychological type, she will inevitably choose B, and she will do so even if her previous husbands have resembled B, so that one would think that she "had learned from experience." Consciously, she will of course "give the matter due consideration," etc., etc. To the psychoanalyst all this is irrelevant chaff in the wind—only a camouflage for the inner workings about which she knows nothing consciously. If she is of a certain kind of masochistic strain, as exhibited in her previous set of symptoms, she *must* choose B: her super-ego, always out to maximize the torment in the situation, seeing what dazzling possibilities for self-damaging behavior are promised by the choice of B, compels her to make the choice she does, and even to conceal the real basis of the choice behind an elaborate facade of rationalizations.

A man is addicted to gambling. In the service of his addiction he loses all his money, spends what belongs to his wife, even sells his property and neglects his children. For a time perhaps he stops; then, inevitably, he takes it up again, although he himself may think he chose to. The man does not know that he is a victim rather than an agent; or, if he sometimes senses that he is in the throes of something-he-knows-not-what, he will have no inkling of its character and will soon relapse into the illusion that he (his conscious self) is freely deciding the course of his own actions. What he does not know, of course, is that he is still taking out on his mother the original lesion to his infantile narcissism, getting back at her for her fancied refusal of his infantile wishes—and this by rejecting everything identified with her, namely education, discipline, logic, common sense, training. At the roulette wheel, almost alone among adult activities, chance—the opposite of all these things—rules supreme; and his addiction represents his continued and emphatic reiteration of his rejection of Mother and all she represents to his unconscious.

This pseudo-aggression of his is of course masochistic in its effects. In the long run he always loses; he can never quit while he is winning. And far from playing in order to win, rather one can say that his losing is a *sine qua non* of his psychic equilibrium (as it was for example with Dostoyevsky): guilt demands punishment, and in the ego's "deal" with the super-ego the super-ego has granted satisfaction of infantile wishes in return for the self-damaging conditions obtaining. Winning would upset the neurotic equilibrium.[9]

A man has wash-compulsion. He must be constantly washing his hands—he uses up perhaps 400 towels a day. Asked why he does this, he says "I need to, my hands are dirty"; and if it is pointed out to him that they are not really dirty, he says "They feel dirty anyway, I feel better when I wash them." So once again he washes them. He "freely decides" every time; he feels that he must wash them, he deliberates for a moment perhaps; but always ends by washing them. What he does not see, of course, is the invisible wires inside him pulling him inevitably to do the thing he does: the infantile id-wish concerns preoccupation with dirt, the super-ego charges him with this, and the terrified ego must respond, "No, I don't like dirt, see how clean I like to be, look how I wash my hands!"

Let us see what further "free acts" the same patient engages in (this is an actual case history): he is taken to a concentration camp, and given the worst of treatment by the Nazi guards. In the camp he no longer chooses to be clean, does not even try to be—on the contrary, his choice is now to wallow in filth as much as he can. All he is aware of now is a disinclination to be clean, and every time he must choose he chooses not to be. Behind the scenes, however, another drama is being enacted: the super-ego, perceiving that enough torment is being administered from the outside, can afford to cease pressing its charges in this quarter—the outside world is doing the torturing now, so the super-ego is relieved of the responsibility. Thus the ego is relieved of the agony of constantly making terrified replies in the form of washing to prove that the super-ego is wrong. The defense no longer being needed, the person slides back into what is his natural predilection anyway, for filth. This becomes too much even for the Nazi guards: they take hold of him one day, saying "We'll teach you how to be clean!" drag him into the snow, and pour bucket after bucket of icy water over him until he freezes to death. Such is the end-result of an original id-wish, caught in the machinations of a destroying super-ego.

Let us take, finally, a less colorful, more everyday example. A student at a university, possessing wealth, charm, and all that is usually considered essential to popularity, begins to develop the following personality-pattern: although well taught in the graces of social conversation, he always makes a *faux pas* somewhere, and always in the worst possible situation; to his friends he makes cutting remarks which hurt deeply—and always apparently aimed in such a way as to hurt the most: a remark that would not hurt A but would hurt B he invariably makes to B rather than to A, and so on. None of this is conscious. Ordinarily he is considerate of people, but he contrives always (unconsciously) to impose on just those friends who would resent it most, and at just the times when he should know that he should not impose: at 3 o'clock in the morning, without forewarning, he phones a friend in a near-by city demanding to stay at his apartment for the weekend; naturally the friend is offended, but the person himself is not aware that he has provoked the grievance ("common sense" suffers a temporary eclipse when the neurotic pattern sets in, and one's intelligence, far from being of help in such a situation, is used in the interest of the neurosis), and when the friend is cool to him the next time they meet, he wonders why and feels unjustly treated. Aggressive behavior on his part invites resentment and aggression in turn, but all that he consciously sees is other's behavior toward him—and he considers himself the innocent victim of an unjustified "persecution."

Each of these choices is, from the moralist's point of view, free: he chose to phone his friend at 3 a.m.; he chose to make the cutting remark that he did, etc. What he does not know is that an ineradicable masochistic pattern has set in. His unconscious is far more shrewd and clever than is his conscious intellect; it sees with uncanny accuracy just what kind of behavior will damage him most, and unerringly forces him into that behavior. Consciously, the student "doesn't know why he did it"—he gives different "reasons" at different times, but they are all, once again, rationalizations cloaking the unconscious mechanism which propels him willy-nilly into actions that his "common sense" eschews.

The more of this sort of thing you see, the more you can see what the psychoanalyst means when he talks about "the illusion of free will." And the more of a psychiatrist you become, the more you are overcome with a sense of what an illusion this precious free will really is. In some kinds of cases most of us can see it already: it takes no psychiatrist to look at the epileptic and sigh with sadness at the thought that soon this person before you will be as one possessed, not the same thoughtful intelligent person you knew. But people are not aware of this in other contexts, for example when they express surprise at how a person whom they have been so good to could treat them so badly. Let us suppose that you help a person financially or morally or in some other way, so that he is in your debt; suppose further that he is one of the many neurotics who unconsciously identify kindness with weakness and aggression with strength, then he will unconsciously take your kindness to him as weakness and use it as the occasion for enacting some aggression against you. He can't help it, he may regret it himself later; still, he will be driven to do it. If we gain a little knowledge of psychiatry, we can look at him with pity, that a person otherwise so worthy should be so unreliable—but we will exercise realism too and be aware that there are some types of people that you cannot be good to; in "free" acts of their conscious volition, they will use your own goodness against you.

Sometimes the persons themselves will become dimly aware that "something behind the scenes" is determining their behavior. The divorcee will sometimes view herself with detachment, as if she were some machine (and indeed the psychoanalyst does call her a "repeating-machine"): "I know I'm caught in a net, that I'll fall in love with this guy and marry him and the whole ridiculous merry-go-round will start all over again."

We talk about free will, and we say, yes, the person is free to do so-and-so if he can do so *if* he wants to—and we forget that his wanting to is itself caught up in the stream of determinism, that unconscious forces drive him into the wanting or not wanting to do the thing in question. The idea of the puppet whose motions are manipulated from behind by invisible wires, or better still, by springs inside, is no mere figure of speech. The analogy is a telling one at almost every point.

And the pity of it is that it all started so early, before we knew what was happening. The personality-structure is inelastic after the age of five, and comparatively so in most cases after the age of three. Whether one acquires a neurosis or not is determined by that age—and just as involuntarily as if it had been a curse of God. If, for example, a masochistic pattern was set up, under pressure of hyper-narcissism combined with real or fancied infantile deprivation, then the masochistic snowball was on its course downhill long before we or anybody else knew what was happening, and long before anyone could do anything about it. To speak of human beings as "puppets" in such a context is no mere metaphor, but a stark rendering of a literal fact: only the psychiatrist knows what puppets people really are; and it is no wonder that the protestations of philosophers that "the act which is the result of a volition, a deliberation, a conscious decision, is free" leave these persons, to speak mildly, somewhat cold.

But, one may object, all the states thus far described have been abnormal, neurotic ones. The well-adjusted (normal) person at least is free.

Leaving aside the question of now clearly and on what grounds one can distinguish the neurotic from the normal, let me use an illustration of a proclivity that everyone would call normal, namely, the decision of a man to support his wife and possibly a family, and consider briefly its genesis.[10]

Every baby comes into the world with a full-fledged case of megalomania—interested only in himself, naively assuming that he is the center of the universe and that others are present only to fulfill his wishes, and furious when his own wants are not satisfied immediately no matter for what reason. Gratitude, even for all the time and worry and care expended on him by the mother, is an emotion entirely foreign to the infant, and as he grows older it is inculcated in him only with the greatest difficulty; his natural tendency is to assume that everything that happens to him is due to himself, except for denials and frustrations, which are due to the "cruel, denying" outer world, in particular the mother; and that he owes nothing to anyone, is dependent on no one. This omnipotence-complex, or illusion of nondependence, has been called the "autarchic fiction." Such a conception of the world is actually fostered in the child by the conduct of adults, who automatically attempt to fulfill the infant's every wish concerning nourishment, sleep, and attention. The child misconceives causality and sees in these wish-fulfillments not the results of maternal kindness and love, but simply the result of his own omnipotence.

This fiction of omnipotence is gradually destroyed by experience, and its destruction is probably the deepest disappointment of the early years of life. First of all, the infant discovers that he is the victim of organic urges and necessities: hunger, defecation, urination. More important, he discovers that the maternal breast, which he has not previously distinguished from his own body (he has not needed to, since it was available when he wanted it), is not a part of himself after all, but of another creature upon whom he is dependent. He is forced to recognize this, e.g., when he wants nourishment and it is at the moment not present; even a small delay is most damaging to the "autarchic fiction." Most painful of all is the experience of weaning, probably the greatest tragedy in every baby's life, when his dependence is most cruelly emphasized; it is a frustrating experience because what he wants is no longer there at all; and if he has been able to some extent to preserve the illusion of non-dependence heretofore, he is not able to do so now—it is plain that the source of his nourishment is not dependent on him, but he on it. The shattering of the autarchic fiction is a great disillusionment to every child, a tremendous blow to his ego which he will, in one way or another, spend the rest of his life trying to repair. How does he do this?

First of all, his reaction to frustration is anger and fury; and he responds by kicking, biting, etc., the only ways he knows. But he is motorically helpless, and these measures are ineffective, and only serve to emphasize his dependence the more. Moreover, against such responses of the child the parental reaction is one of prohibition, generally accompanied by physical force of some kind. Gradually the child soon learns that this form of rebellion is profitless, and brings him more harm than good. He wants to respond to frustration with violent aggression, and at the same time learns that he will be punished for such aggression, and that in any case the latter is ineffectual. What face-saving solution does he find? Since he must "face facts," since he must in any case "conform" if he is to have any peace at all, he tries to make it seem as if he himself is the source of the commands and prohibitions: the *external* prohibitive force is *internalized*—and here we have the origin of conscience. By making the prohibitive agency seem to come from within himself, the child can "save face"—as if saying, "The prohibition comes from within me, not from outside, so I'm not subservient to external rule, I'm only obeying rules I've set up myself," thus to some extent saving the autarchic fiction, and at the same time avoiding unpleasant consequences directed against himself by complying with parental commands.

Moreover, the boy[11] has unconsciously never forgiven the mother for his dependence on her in early life, for nourishment and all other things. It has upset his illusion of non-dependence. These feelings have been repressed and are not remembered; but they are acted out in later life in many ways—e.g., in the constant deprecation man has for woman's duties such as cooking and housework of all sorts ("All she does is stay home and get together a few meals, and she calls that work"), and especially in the man's identification with the mother in his sex experiences with women. By identifying with someone one cancels out in effect the person with whom he identifies—replacing that person, unconsciously denying his existence, and the man, identifying with his early mother, playing the active role in "giving" to his wife as his mother has "given" to him, is in effect the denial of his mother's existence, a fact which is narcissistically embarrassing to his ego because it is chiefly responsible for shattering his autarchic fiction. In supporting his wife, he can unconsciously deny that his mother gave to him, and that he was dependent on her giving. Why is it that the husband plays the provider, and wants his wife to be dependent on no one else, although twenty years before he was nothing but a parasitic baby? This is a face-saving device on his part; he can act out the reasoning "See, I'm not the parasitic baby, on the contrary I'm the provider, the giver." His playing the provider is a constant face-saving device, to deny his early dependence which is so embarrassing to his ego. It is no wonder that men generally dislike to be reminded of their babyhood, when they were dependent on woman.

Thus we have here a perfectly normal adult reaction which is unconsciously motivated. The man "chooses" to support a family—and his choice is as unconsciously motivated as anything could be. (I have described here only the "normal" state of affairs, uncomplicated by the well-nigh infinite number of variations that occur in actual practice.)

Now, what of the notion of responsibility? What happens to it on our analysis?

Let us begin with an example, not a fictitious one. A woman and her two-year-old baby are riding on a train to Montreal in mid-winter. The child is ill. The woman wants badly to get to her destination. She is, unknown to herself, the victim of a neurotic conflict whose nature is irrelevant here except for the fact that it forces her to behave aggressively toward the child, partly to spite her husband whom she despises and who loves the child, but chiefly to ward off super-ego charges of masochistic attachment. Consciously she loves the child, and when she says this she says it sincerely, but she must behave aggressively toward it nevertheless, just as many children love their mothers but are nasty to them most of the time in neurotic pseudo-aggression. The child becomes more ill as the train approaches Montreal; the heating system of the train is not working, and the conductor advises the woman to get off the train at the next town and get the child to a hospital at once. The woman says no, she must get to Montreal. Shortly afterward, the child's condition worsens, and the mother does all she can to keep it alive, without, however, leaving the train, for she declares that it is absolutely necessary that she reach her destination. But before she gets there the child is dead. After that, of course, the mother grieves, blames herself, weeps hysterically, and joins the church to gain surcease from the guilt that constantly overwhelms her when she thinks of how her aggressive behavior has killed her child.

Was she responsible for her deed? In ordinary life, after making a mistake, we say, "Chalk it up to experience." Here we say, "Chalk it up to the neurosis." No, she is not responsible. She could not help it if her neurosis forced her to act this way—she didn't even know what was going on behind the scenes, she merely acted out the part assigned to her. This is far more true than is generally realized: criminal actions in general are not actions for which their agents are responsible; the agents are passive, not active—they are victims of a neurotic conflict. Their very hyper-activity is unconsciously determined.

To say this is, of course, not to say that we should not punish criminals. Clearly, for our own protection, we must remove them from our midst so that they can no longer molest and endanger organized society. And, of course, if we use the word "responsible" in such a way that justly to hold someone responsible for a deed is by definition identical with being justified in punishing him, then we can and do hold people responsible. But this is like the sense of "free" in which free acts are voluntary ones. It does not go deep enough. In a deeper sense we cannot hold the person responsible: we may hold his neurosis responsible, but he is not responsible for the neurosis, particularly since the age at which its onset was inevitable was an age before he could even speak.

The neurosis is responsible—but isn't the neurosis a part of *him*? We have been speaking all the time as if the person and his unconscious were two separate beings; but isn't he one personality, including conscious and unconscious departments together?

I do not wish to deny this. But it hardly helps us here; for what people want when they talk about freedom, and what they hold to when they champion it, is the idea that the *conscious* will is the master of their destiny. "I am the master of my fate, I am the captain of my soul"—and they surely mean their conscious selves, the self that they can recognize and search and introspect. Between an unconscious that willy-nilly determines your actions, and an external force which pushes you, there is little if anything to choose. The unconscious is just *as if* it were an outside force; and indeed, psychiatrists will assert that the inner Hitler can torment you far more than any external Hitler can. Thus the kind of freedom that people want, the only kind they will settle for, is precisely the kind that psychiatry says that they cannot have.

Heretofore it was pretty generally thought that, while we could not rightly blame a person for the color of his eyes or the morality of his parents, or even for what he did at the age of three, or to a large extent what impulses he had and whom he fell in love with, one *could* do so for other of his adult activities, particularly the acts he performed voluntarily and with premeditation. Later this attitude was shaken. Many voluntary acts came to be recognized, at least in some circles, as compelled by the unconscious. Some philosophers recognized this too—Ayer[12] talks about the kleptomaniac being unfree, and about a person being unfree when another person exerts a habitual ascendancy over his personality. But this is as far as he goes. The usual examples, such as the kleptomaniac and the schizophrenic, apparently satisfy most philosophers, and with these exceptions removed, the rest of mankind is permitted to wander in the vast and alluring fields of freedom and responsibility. So far, the inroads upon freedom left the vast majority of humanity untouched; they began to hit home when psychiatrists began to realize, though philosophers did not, that the domination of the conscious by the unconscious extended, not merely to a few exceptional individuals, but to all human beings, that the "big three behind the scenes" are not respecters of persons, and dominate us all, even including that *sanctum sanctorum* of freedom, our conscious will. To be sure, the domination in the case of "normal" individuals is somewhat more benevolent than the tyranny and despotism exercised in neurotic cases, and therefore the former have evoked less comment; but the principle remains in all cases the same: the unconscious is the master of every fate and the captain of every soul.

We speak of a machine turning out good products most of the time but every once in a while it turns out a "lemon." We do not, of course, hold the product responsible for this, but the machine, and via the machine, its maker. Is it silly to extend to inanimate objects the idea of responsibility? Of course. But is it any less silly to employ the notion in speaking of human creatures? Are not the two kinds of cases analogous in countless important ways? Occasionally a child turns out badly too, even when his environment and training are the same as that of his brothers and sisters who turn out "all right." He is the "bad penny." His acts of rebellion against parental discipline in adult life (such as the case of the gambler, already cited) are traceable to early experiences of real or fancied denial of infantile wishes. Sometimes the denial has been real, though many denials are absolutely necessary if the child is to grow up to observe the common decencies of civilized life; sometimes, if the child has an unusual quantity of narcissism, every event that occurs is interpreted by him as a denial of his wishes, and nothing a parent could do, even granting every humanly possible wish, would help. In any event, the later neurosis can be attributed to this. Can the person himself be held responsible? Hardly. If he engages in activities which are a menace to society, he must be put into prison, of course, but responsibility is another matter. The time when the events occurred which rendered his neurotic behavior inevitable was a time long before he was capable of thought and decision. As an adult, he is a victim of a world he never made—only this world is inside him.

What about the children who turn out "all right"? All we can say is that "it's just lucky for them" that what happened to their unfortunate brother didn't happen to them; *through no virtue of their own* they are not doomed to the life of unconscious guilt, expiation, conscious depression, terrified ego-gestures for the appeasement of a tyrannical super-ego that he is. The machine turned them out with a minimum of damage. But if the brother cannot be blamed for his evils, neither can they be praised for their good. It will take society a long time to come round to this attitude. We do not blame people for the color of their eyes, but we have not attained the same attitude toward their socially significant activities.

We all agree that machines turn out "lemons", we all agree that nature turns out misfits in the realm of biology—the blind, the crippled, the diseased; but we hesitate to include the realm of the personality, for here, it seems, is the last retreat of our dignity as human beings. Our ego can endure anything but this; this island at least must remain above the encroaching flood. But may not precisely the same analysis be made here also? Nature turns out psychological "lemons" too, in fa greater quantities than any other kind; and indeed all of us are "lemons" in some respect or other, the difference being one of degree. Some of us are lucky enough not to have a gambling-neurosis or criminotic tendencies or masochistic mother-attachment or overdimensional repetition-compulsion to make our lives miserable, but most of our actions, those usually considered the most important, are unconsciously dominated just the same. And, if a neurosis may be likened to a curse of God, let those of us, the elect, who are enabled to enjoy a measure of life's happiness without the hell-fire of neurotic guilt, take this, not as our own achievement, but simply for what it is—a gift of God.

Let us, however, quit metaphysics and put the situation schematically in the form of a deductive argument.

1. An occurrence over which we had no control is something we cannot be held responsible for.

2. Events E, occurring during our babyhood, were events over which we had no control.

3. Therefore events E were events which we cannot be held responsible for.

4. But if there is something we cannot be

held responsible for, neither can we be held responsible for something that inevitably results from it.

5. Events E have as inevitable consequence Neurosis N, which in turn has as inevitable consequence Behavior B.

6. Since N is the inevitable consequence of E and B is the inevitable consequence of N, B is the inevitable consequence of E.

7. Hence, not being responsible for E, we cannot be responsible for B.

In Samuel Butler's Utopian satire *Erewhon* there occurs the following passage, in which a judge is passing sentence on a prisoner:

> It is all very well for you to say that you came of unhealthy parents, and had a severe accident in your childhood which permanently undermined your constitution; excuses such as these are the ordinary refuge of the criminal; but they cannot for one moment be listened to by the ear of justice. I am not here to enter upon curious metaphysical questions as to the origin of this or that—questions to which there would be no end were their introduction once tolerated, and which would result in throwing the only guilt on the tissues of the primordial cell, or on the elementary gases. There is no question of how you came to be wicked, but only this—namely, are you wicked or not? This has been decided in the affirmative, neither can I hesitate for a single moment to say that it has been decided justly. You are a bad and dangerous person, and stand branded in the eyes of your fellow countrymen with one of the most heinous known offenses.[13]

As moralists read this passage, they may perhaps nod with approval. But the joke is on them. The sting comes when we realize what the crime is for which the prisoner is being sentenced: namely, consumption. The defendant is reminded that during the previous year he was sentenced for aggravated bronchitis, and is warned that he should profit from experience in the future. Butler is employing here his familiar method of presenting some human tendency (in this case, holding people responsible for what isn't their fault) to a ridiculous extreme and thereby reducing it to absurdity. How soon will mankind appreciate the keen edge of Butler's bitter irony? How long will they continue to read such a passage, but fail to smile, or yet to wince?

. . .The psychoanalytic examples we have adduced have (if one was not acquainted with them before) added, so to speak, a new dimension to the term "free." In our ordinary use of this word we probably had nothing in mind as concrete as the sort of thing brought to light in our examples; but now that we have, we hesitate to label many actions as free which previously we had so labeled without hesitation. And we would, I think, call people "free" in far fewer respects than we would have previously.

Can human beings, in the light of psychiatric knowledge, be called "free" in any respect at all? We must remember that every term that can be significantly used must have a significant opposite. If the opposite cannot significantly be asserted, neither can its original. If the term "unfree" can be significantly used, so can the term "free." Even though there may be no actual denotation of a term naming an opposite, one must know what it would be like—what it would mean to speak of it; even though there are no white crows, it must be significant, as indeed it is, to speak of them. Now is the case of freedom like that of the white crows that don't exist but can be significantly spoken of, or like the black crows that do exist and can be significantly spoken of as well?

Unless "freedom" is taken to mean the same as "lack of cause" and a principle of universal causality is taken for granted, I think the latter must be the case.

If we asked the psychoanalysts for their opinion on this, they would doubtless reply somewhat as follows. They would say that they were not accustomed to using the term "free" at all, but that if they had to suggest a criterion for distinguishing the free from the unfree, they would say that a person's freedom occurs in inverse proportion to his neuroticism; the more he is compelled in his behavior by a *malevolent* unconscious, the less free he is. We speak of degrees of freedom—and the psychologically normal and well-adjusted individual is comparatively the freest, even though most of his behavior is determined by his unconscious.

But suppose it is the determination of his behavior by his unconscious, no matter what kind, that we balk at? We may then say that a man is free only to the extent that his behavior is *not* unconsciously motivated at all. If this be our criterion, most of our behavior could not be called free: everything, including both impulses and volitions, having to do with our basic attitudes toward life, the general tenor of our tastes, whether we become philosophers or artists or business men, our whole affective life including our preferences for blondes or brunettes, active or passive, older or younger, has its inevitable basis in the unconscious. Only those comparatively vanilla-flavored aspects of life—such as our behavior toward people who don't really matter to us—are exempted from this rule.

These, I think, are the two principal criteria for distinguishing freedom from the lack of it which we might set up on the basis of psychoanalytic knowledge. Conceivably we might set up others. In every case, of course, it remains trivially true that "it all depends on how we choose to use the word." The facts are what they are, regardless of how we choose to label them. But if we choose to label facts in a way which is out of accordance with people's deep-seated and traditional methods of labeling them, as we would be doing if we labeled "free" human actions which we know as much about as we now do through modern psychiatry, then we shall only be manipulating words to mislead our fellow creatures.

NOTES

1. Moritz Schlick, *The Problems of Ethics*, Chapter VII.

2. *Ibid.*, p. 150.

3. L. Susan Stebbing, *Philosophy and the Physicists*, p. 242.

4. G. E. Moore, *Ethics*, p. 205.

5. *New York Times Post*, Tuesday, May 18, 1948, p.4.

6. I am aware that the theory presented below is not accepted by all practicing psychoanalysts. Many non-Freudians would disagree with the conclusions presented below. But I do not believe that this fact affects my argument, as long as the concept of unconscious motivation is accepted. I am aware, too, that much of the language employed in the following descriptions is animistic and metaphorical; but as long as I am presenting a view I would prefer to "go the whole hog" and present it in its strongest possible light. The theory can in any case be made clearest by the use of such language, just as atomic theory can often be made clearest to students with the use of models.

7. This view is very clearly developed in Edmund Bergler, *Divorce Won't Help*, especially Chapter I.

8. See *The Basic Writings of Sigmund Freud*, Modern Library Edition, p. 310. (In *The Interpretaton of Dreams*.) Cf. also the essay by Ernest Jones, "A Psycho-analytical Study of Hamlet."

9. See Edmund Bergler's article on the pathological gambler in *Diseases of the Nervous System* (1943). Also "Suppositions about the Mechanism of Criminosis," *Journal of Criminal Psychopathology* (1944) and "Clinical Contributions to the Psychogenesis of Alcohol Addiction," *Quarterly Journal of Studies on Alcohol*, 5:434 (1944).

10. Edmund Bergler, *The Battle of the Conscience*, Chapter I.

11. The girl's development after this point is somewhat different. Society demands more aggressiveness of the adult male, hence there are more super-ego strictures on tendencies toward passivity in the male; accordingly his defenses must be stronger.

12. A. J. Ayer, "Freedom and Necessity," *Polemic* (September-October 1946), pp. 40-43.

13. Samuel Butler, *Erewhon* (Modern Library edition), p. 107.

Determinism

DISCUSSION: G. J. WARNOCK, J. F. THOMSON, P. F. STRAWSON

GEOFFREY J. WARNOCK: 'Determinism' has meant so many different things to different people that perhaps it will be better to avoid asking straight out what it is. We should only find ourselves with a long list of not very clear theses. A list of that sort would be an interesting place to start a discussion from, but compiling the list and explaining the items would leave us no time for discussion of it. So I suggest we ask instead: How do people become determinists? What motives or reasons draw them in this direction?

J. F. THOMSON: Isn't it often that determinism of some kind seems to be enjoined by a scientific way of looking at human beings? Suppose you are an experimental psychologist. Then you may very well say: 'For my purposes, a human being is just something with an input and an output. And I am interested in discovering what correlations hold between input and output. Now the output at a given moment doesn't depend simply on the input then or immediately preceding. This is a fact of everyday observation. So I suppose that it depends on, at most, the input then and the state of the organism; the latter depending on, at most, past inputs, past outputs, and perhaps innate factors. But this means that the organism's output—what you call the man's behaviour, how he responds to a situation—is completely determined by (*a*) what happens to him and (*b*) how he is.'

P. F. STRAWSON: And this picture completely leaves out and ignores choice.

J. F. T.: It leaves it out. It doesn't deny it.

P. F. S.: But you, quite naturally, made your experimentalist say: 'For my purposes.' This is surely important. If he had said: 'A human being is just something with an input and an output', that would have been a statement, a thesis, but it would almost certainly turn out to be either blatantly false or quite trivially true, because true by definition. But your experimentalist, I think, isn't asserting a thesis or not one about his subject-matter. He is saying that it is convenient to start off with a certain kind of model. He wants, for his own professional purposes, to regard human beings and their behaviour in a certain light. He certainly needn't say that this is the only way of regarding them; and obviously it isn't.

J. F. T.: Yes, I think that is quite right. What I described could be called an engineer's way of looking at human beings.

G. J. W.: But now doesn't this mean that the kind of 'determinism' you hinted at isn't a philosophical thesis either?

J. F. T.: Well, I agree that if it is one, then it's very difficult to see just what thesis it is or what would count as a refutation of it. Our imaginary psychologist says that what the organism does at any given moment is uniquely

---

This selection is a discussion among three prominent contemporary British philosophers. It was originally broadcast by the BBC.

From *Freedom and the Will*, edited by David Pears (New York: St. Martin's Press, 1963). Reprinted by permission of the editor and Macmillan, London, and Basingstoke.

determined by the situation it is in—or, perhaps, by how it 'sees' that situation, and also by the state of the organism. It seems that 'determined' here has something like its mathematical meaning, as when we say that the volume of a sphere is uniquely determined by its radius. The volume is a function of the radius—a function of just one variable. So we should ask, just what are the variables on which the behaviour is held to depend? Since these aren't in fact specified, there isn't really a determinate thesis to discuss. It isn't enough to say that how a man behaves depends on something; you have to be able to say on what it depends.

G. J. W.: And if the psychologist were actually to list some measurable quantities and then say that behaviour is some function of these and these alone, what he says might well be wrong—I mean untrue in a quite straightforward way.

P. F. S.: Exactly. Whereas if he doesn't, if what the relevant variables are is left completely open, they might be anything—for example, they might for all that has been said, include variables connected somehow with acts of choice.

J. F. T.: So it now seems that this kind of determinism is either not a thesis at all, or is a thesis so vague and ill-defined as not to be really discussable. Perhaps we should say that it is the form of a thesis.

P. F. S.: Yes, but all the same you were right in implying that it must have seemed much more than this to many people. And we shan't have answered Warnock's original questions until we have seen why.

G. J. W.: Yes, there is still the question why some form of determinism is so often taken for granted.

J. F. T.: Well, I suppose that we are inclined to extrapolate from particular examples of success in explaining and predicting human behaviour.

G. J. W.: How do you mean? I might explain your behaviour to a friend in a quite satisfactory way simply by telling him what your own acknowledged reasons were for acting in the way you did. Or again, I might succeed in telling him correctly what your future course of action was going to be, simply by quoting your own statement of your intentions. These would be, wouldn't they, 'particular examples of success in explanation and prediction of human behaviour'. But it's hard to see how any amount of 'extrapolation' from such examples as these could lead one to determinism.

P. F. S.: Would you really say that you were 'predicting' Thomson's behaviour when you merely reproduced his own statement of his intentions?

G. J. W.: I don't see why not. I shouldn't merely be passing his statement on. I should be committing myself to the belief that he would actually do what he said he would do. In any case, even if the word 'prediction' isn't quite right for this kind of case, the word 'explanation' seems perfectly satisfactory for the other kind.

J. F. T.: But it wasn't either of these kinds of case that I had in mind. It seems, on the face of it, that there are two quite different and contrasting ways in which human actions can be explained; and similarly two quite different and contrasting ways in which we can come to hold beliefs about what men's future courses of action are going to be. One of these ways in each case essentially involves going by a man's acknowledged reasons or disclosed intentions. Insincerity and unforeseen obstacles apart, these are simply accepted as explanations of what was done or as statements of what will be done. The other way of coming to hold such beliefs is sharply contrasted with this. Acknowledged reasons and declared intentions either play no part at all, or play quite a different part. They are not accepted as the answers to our questions. At the most, they are treated as additional bits of the evidence in the light of which we frame our own answers. It was explanations of this kind which I had in mind when I said what I did say about extrapolation from successes.

P. F. S.: If I understand you, you're suggesting two things: first, that the thesis of determinism is simply that the whole field of human action could be covered by explanation and predictions of your second kind; and, second, that particular examples of success in this kind of explanation and prediction incline us, or some of us, to think that the thesis may be true.

J. F. T.: Well, for the moment, yes.

G. J. W.: I'm afraid I'm not altogether clear. Is the suggestion that, if the second kind of explanation or prediction is available, the first somehow lapses or doesn't count, or embodies an illusion? Are the two kinds of explanation opposed? If you can explain an action of mine in the second way, does this mean that my giving my reason for it is no explanation at all? If you can predict an action of mine in the second way, does this mean that I am under an illusion in thinking that I decided to do it for certain reasons, that I was carrying out such-and-such an intention in doing it?

J. F. T.: Well, it certainly seems that sometimes these consequences follow. We dismiss some reasons as rationalizations. But I don't think that the determinist—my determinist—has to claim that these consequences necessarily, or even usually, follow. Won't his point simply be that, on the hypothesis in question, we should be able adequately to explain and predict human actions without, as it were, taking anything on trust from the agent?

G. J. W.: If this is all his point is, it doesn't seem to me to be enough to make him a determinist. When I rely on a man's announced intentions, I don't have to be taking anything on trust from him. I may simply know that he is not a man to misrepresent his intentions, or to change his mind unless his knowledge of the circumstances changes. Quite apart from announced intentions, I might very well be able to explain a man's actions and to predict, within rough limits, what he will do in important situations, without taking anything on trust from him, simply because I know him very well. Knowing him, I know what sort of reasons weigh with him, what sort of decisions he may be expected to make. This doesn't mean that the reasons don't really weigh with him, that he doesn't really make the decisions. And since it doesn't, I see nothing determinist at all in this possibility.

P. F. S.: But I don't think this possibility can be quite what Thomson had in mind, though I agree it seems to be covered by the concessive form of words he adopted. When you spoke of knowing a man well, you were thinking, and indeed you spoke, of knowing what sort of reasons weighed with him, what sort of decisions he might be expected to make. This is what we mean, or part of what we mean, by knowing a man's character. But suppose we had a different and deeper kind of knowledge. Suppose we were able to give a complete explanation, in terms of factors that didn't themselves include a man's reasons or decisions, of the fact that the reasons that weighed with a man did weigh with him. Then, in a sense, we could still admit that a man's action was explained by the reasons he gave for it; that these were his reasons. And this was the point of Thomson's concessions. But the fact that those reasons weighed with him would, by this hypothesis, be completely explained by factors of a quite different kind. And if an explanation of this second kind were available, the availability of the explanation of the first kind might seem to be a matter of smaller significance than it currently does. For we should have, as it were, two stages of explanation. There would be the question: 'Why did he act as he did?' answered by mentioning, among other things, the reasons that weighed with him. Then there would be the question: 'Why did those reasons weigh with him?' answered by mentioning only factors which were not reasons for him at all. If now we put the first question again—'Why did he act as he did?'—we might well feel that we could give a complete answer to it simply by mentioning the factors referred to in the answer to the second question, together with a description of the stimuli the man was exposed to. The sense of the word 'Why?' will have changed, of course, just because, in the answer to it, we no longer mention the man's reasons. This is not to say that he didn't have those reasons. Only now it will not seem so important that he had them.

G. J. W.: That sounds more like determinism to me. But it also sounds enormously hypothetical. Is there any reason at all to suppose that one kind of explanation could be undermined in this way by the other?

P. F. S.: Well, if you mean 'Could one kind of explanation ever be undermined by the other?' the answer surely is 'Yes'. Suppose that someone is, habitually, painfully shrinking and hesitant about entering a room full of strangers. We ask why. Well, his reason, the reason he gives, is just that to go into a room full of strangers frightens him; the situation just strikes him as frightening. But of course we want to know why he is frightened. Now the answer to this question, let's assume, is some fact about his early upbringing—some fact of which he may be completely unaware, so that it would not figure in the explanation given by him. Now, surely in this case, the fact about his early upbringing would quite naturally and properly be taken as the explanation of his odd behaviour; the explanation he gives, that he finds the situation frightening, would be regarded as having, by comparison, no explanatory force.

J. F. T.: Yes, but I suppose the question Warnock had in mind was not whether this displacing of one type of explanation by the other ever occurs, but whether there is the slightest reason to suppose that it might occur universally, in absolutely every case.

G. J. W.: Yes, that was what seemed to me enormously doubtful. And I think I can explain why. You said earlier, you remember, that probably what inclines some people to accept a general determinist thesis is a simple propensity to generalize from examples of success in explaining and predicting human behaviour. But now, if we see what kind of explanation and prediction the determinist needs, doesn't there seem to be an objection in principle to generalizing from the examples of success? You see, the sort of behaviour Strawson mentioned in his example—excessive hesitancy about entering a crowded room—is abnormal behaviour; and this is just why the example suited his book. The reason the man gives—that the situation frightens him—is quite easily undermined as the explanation of his behaviour just because normal people are not frightened in this situation; so of course we have to look for a further explanation of his abnormality. Now I strongly suspect that our successes—successes of the kind that the determinist needs—are all achieved in this field of abnormal behaviour—typically psychotic and neurotic behaviour, and some kinds of criminal and generally anti-social behaviour. But if so, to generalize on the basis of these successes would be to propound the obviously absurd thesis that all human behaviour is abnormal.

J. F. T.: Neat, but unconvincing.

G. J. W.: Well, what's wrong with it?

J. F. T.: Well, what worries me about it is really, I think, a general point about explanation. It's broadly true, isn't it, for fairly obvious reasons, that what we tend to have an interest in explaining is abnormality, deviation from the normally expected course of events. When things go as we expect them to, we don't raise any questions—it's when something odd happens that we look round for an explanation. But of course that doesn't mean that the normal course of events can't be explained. When aeroplanes crash, we want to know why, we look for an explanation; when they don't crash no questions are asked. But of course there is a reason why aeroplanes usually stay up in the air and come down safely—that they do this depends, furthermore, on factors of exactly the same kind as those we invoke to explain why they sometimes crash. So the thesis you nearly presented as obviously ridiculous could be put in a quite sensible way—not as the thesis that all human behaviour is abnormal, but as the thesis that all human behavior could in principle be explained in the same way as some kinds of abnormal behaviour can in fact be explained already. And that makes perfectly good sense.

P. F. S.: But wait a moment. In making this general point about explanation, I think you're ignoring the special difficulty about human behaviour (as I think Warnock did too). People, unlike aeroplanes, often have reason for what they do, and often can say what their reasons are. Well, wasn't the significant feature of the example I produced, not just that this man's neurotic behaviour was abnormal (as Warnock said), but that the reason he gave for it was plainly inadequate? He is frightened, as he tells us—but by something which just isn't really frightening. It's not just that normal people aren't frightened of going into rooms full of people, but that there is no reason to be frightened. And that is why the reason he gives 'It frightens me' is regarded as having no, or insufficient, explanatory force, and is accordingly displaced by explaining how he came to be afflicted with baseless fright in this situation.

G. J. W.: All right, but I don't retract my point; I amend it. The position seems to be that the reasons people give for what they do are sometimes undermined by explanations of the other kind—which explain, in fact, why they are such as to be influenced by the reasons they give—but this second kind of explanation displaces or undermines the first kind in those cases in which (and precisely because) the reasons these people give are not good or adequate reasons for behaving as they do. But if so, to erect a general determinist thesis by generalizing on the basis of these cases still looks absurd: because it seems to imply the obvious falsehood that the reasons people give for what they do are never good reasons, and never have explanatory force.

J. F. T.: But no, surely this isn't what the determinist is committed to saying. (I think I can now amend the point I made before.) It's admitted, or anyway it seems to be, that sometimes, when the reasons people give for what they do are very bad or inadequate reasons, we can further explain how they came to be influenced by such reasons—and in doing this we shall normally mention factors of a quite different kind from any they do give or could give, as their reasons; for instance, facts about their early upbringing, or perhaps about their physiological make-up. Now surely the determinist is not committed to saying that the reasons people give for what they do are never good reasons; but only that whether the reasons they give are good or bad, there will always be a further explanation of the fact that those reasons weighed with them. And is there anything patently absurd in that suggestion?

P. F. S.: No, I don't think it's patently absurd. But isn't it in some danger of turning out to be rather trivial? As the thesis stands, it contains too many blank cheques, so to speak, for one to be sure what it amounts to. We have to ask, surely, what kind of 'further explanation' is envisaged here. For example, if someone has, and avows, a perfectly good reason for something that he does, it is, I suppose, some sort of further explanation of his behaviour to say that he is quite an intelligent person, whose upbringing and background and present circumstances are perfectly normal and satisfactory, so that he is, in short, a rational man—the sort of man who tends to adopt good reasons as his reasons for doing things. But then two questions arise: first, it seems to me highly doubtful whether a 'further explanation' of this kind lends any support to any thesis that could aptly be called determinism—the points that add up to his being a rational man may explain his behaviour, but why should we say that they determine it? And, secondly, surely a 'further explanation' to the general effect that someone is a rational man has no tendency to undermine the explanation he himself gives of his own behaviour. Just the contrary, in fact; if the reasons he gives are good reasons, the fact that he is a rational man strengthens the view that the good reasons he gives do really explain his behaviour. So—either the 'further explanations' which the determinist claims could always be given do not (always) undermine explanations of the kind the agent himself gives in giving his reasons, or the determinist must have in mind some special sort of further explanation, something different from the kind of thing I mentioned just now.

J. F. T.: Well, he won't, I think, have in mind the kind of 'further explanation' you've just mentioned. If 'being rational' comes in, it will come in because he is someone who sets himself certain ideals, prides himself on—or even makes a thing of—rationality, and then this latter fact—supposing it to be one—will be put down to parental influence or something like that. But before we ask what kind of further explanation the determinist does envisage as being available in all cases, I think we ought to retrace our steps a little and ask what we mean by one kind of reason undermining another. I think you, Warnock, had in mind that the existence of the 'outside' kind of explanation (call it a B-explanation) would typically undermine the agent's own explanation (call this an A-explanation) in cases where the reasons given by the agent were not good ones. Hence you said that determinism as a general thesis seemed to imply 'the obvious falsehood that the reasons people give for what they do are never good reasons'. But surely there is quite a different way in which the existence of a B-explanation might undermine or discredit an A-explanation; it might tend to show that the reasons given by the agent, whether adequate or inadequate, weren't really his reasons, or weren't all of them.

P. F. S.: I think what you're now calling attention to isn't, or isn't only, an obscurity in the notion of undermining; it's a general difficulty about A-explanations. If we ask someone why he did something, he may reply by 'giving his reasons'—or by 'giving the reasons'. In the former case, what is in question is, roughly, whether what he did was a reasonable thing to do; he will aim to show that it was, and to do this by telling us of good reasons for doing it. And his standpoint here is that of an agent who is, or wants to be thought, reasonable and responsible. But in the second case, he is not concerned with the reasonableness of the action, but only with explaining it.

G. J. W.: Is this distinction as clear as you suggest? Take 'I hit her because she was becoming hysterical'. That she was hysterical is here put forward as showing that an action was reasonable and justified. But it also explains it in a quite straightforward way.

P. F. S.: But I think all that matters for our purposes is that we can distinguish two ways in which such a statement might be attacked. It might be attacked, first by denying that she was becoming hysterical, or by denying that this is the right way of handling someone who is becoming hysterical. Or, quite differently, it might be met with the suggestion that it doesn't correctly or doesn't completely state the agent's motive. For example, it might be suggested that although she was becoming hysterical and although this was the best way of handling the situation, the man in question hit her partly because he wanted to or because it gave him pleasure.

J. F. T.: Exactly. And the reason I wanted to draw this distinction is that it enables us to see that determinism needn't have the absurd consequence that Warnock mentioned, that no reasons are really good reasons. The consequence that would presumably remain—that many and perhaps all of the assessments we make of our own motives, and our statements about how we came to do the things we did, are at best incomplete and partial—this consequence doesn't seem absurd, at least to me.

P. F. S.: But I still don't see just how every such statement could turn out to be 'incomplete'. And this brings us back to the question I asked: what sort of further explanations does the determinist envisage being available in every case?

G. J. W.: Your question is a pressing one, I think. It's now generally recognized that behind, or besides, acknowledged reasons there sometimes lie unacknowledged reasons—generally of a less reputable kind—of which the agent may not be wholly conscious or of which he may be wholly unconscious. But, first, it would seem difficult to generalize this thesis without trouble; and, second, and more important, it is hard to see that it offers even limited support to determinism. When a man is brought to acknowledge an unacknowledged reason as his, he certainly sees his action in a different light; but not as an action for which he can disclaim responsibility.

J. F. T.: Perhaps the would-be determinist might look altogether elsewhere for his further explanations. What about this? All human action is ultimately a matter of physical movement, of movement of parts of the body, including, of course, the organs of speech. All such movements may be completely explained as the consequences of events within the body, of the kind studied in physiology and neurophysiology. And all these events may themselves be completely explained, in terms of physical laws, as the result of physical stimuli acting upon a body of a certain physical constitution. Is this deterministic enough for you?

G. J. W.: You would agree that you describe at best a programme rather than an achievement?

J. F. T.: Certainly. But not an absurd one.

P. F. S.: I think you must agree too, that it's a different sort of programme from the one you initially mentioned. Initially you spoke of finding explanations of why certain reasons weighed with a man, in the light of which we might be inclined to think of his action as wholly explained by factors which were not reasons for him. The reasons were to be first explained, then by-passed. But the new programme doesn't even mention reasons. It just envisages physical explanations of physical movements.

J. F. T.: Yes. I said, I think, that the would-be determinist might look altogether elsewhere for his further explanations.

P. F. S.: I think the new programme is rather a lot to take on at this stage. But my first reactions are these. First, and concessively, it seems to me pure folly for any philosopher to declare, about any scientific aim that can intelligibly be stated, that that aim is in principle unattainable for philosophical reasons. But I think that what you said wasn't simply the statement of an intelligible scientific programme. It began with the purely philosophical remark that all human action is ultimately a matter of movement of parts of the body. It is this which makes me suspicious. I agree that we might, for some purposes, describe a particular bit of human behaviour in terms of 'moving parts'. But I don't agree that such descriptions would be adequate to the concept of human action. So long as we are the sort of creatures we are, the possible availability of descriptions of particular bits of human behaviour in these terms wouldn't dispense us from the need to see and interpret human actions in terms of a quite different set of concepts. The first sort of descriptions might indeed all find a place in, or under, physical explanatory laws of the kind you envisage. But the second and indispensable sort could find no such place. They belong to a different kind of vocabulary and call for a place in a wholly different dimension of explanation.

J. F. T.: But this sounds like a mere evasion. Wouldn't they just be the same events under different names? If I completely explain an event under one name, calling it a different name doesn't mean that I haven't completely explained it.

G. J. W.: Isn't Strawson's point precisely that it wouldn't be simply a matter of different names for, or descriptions of, the same event? The two names, as you call them, belong to wholly different systems of classification. Unless those systems of classification exhibited a kind of correlation which we can be quite sure they won't exhibit, then however much neuro-physiology advances, no interesting thesis of determinism can be based on that advance. There may be as complete a system as you like of physical laws of movements of bodily parts; but there will still be no physical laws of human action.

J. F. T.: But I'm afraid this still sounds to me like a mere evasion. You seem to me to be saying that the thesis that all movements of bodily parts might be brought under a system of physical laws is, in a sense, not interesting, for the reason that the system (if we can call it such) within which we employ the concepts of human action is, and would remain, a quite different system. Well, that can scarcely be denied. But aren't you also assuming that these systems are not just different, but also independent?

P. F. S.: How do you mean?

J. F. T.: Well, you seem to me to be suggesting that we now have a way of talking about, and a way of seeing, human behaviour (bringing in such ideas as those of reasons, intentions, choices, decisions and responsibility)—and that it would just make no difference to this whether or not it were also possible to explain all bodily movements completely in physical terms.

P. F. S.: Well, what difference would it make?

J. F. T.: I'm sure you'd really agree, anyway, that it isn't just obvious that it wouldn't make any. What about this, for instance (though I'm talking pretty vaguely here)—mightn't one say that our current way of thinking and talking about human action tacitly makes a claim (which, by most people, is tacitly conceded) to being indispensable to the explanation of what goes on in the world, so far at least as human beings are concerned in what goes on? That is, isn't it perhaps taken for granted that where human beings are involved, what goes on can neither be predicted, nor explained, without employing the notions of reasoning, choosing, deciding and the rest. But your thesis denies this, at any rate; and that's quite enough to make it far from uninteresting.

P. F. S.: I really must disagree with you about this. You speak of 'what goes on, where human beings are concerned'. But what does go on? Certainly, bodily parts move. Equally certainly, people do things. The blanket expression, 'what goes on', conceals the fact that there are no effective correlations between the two vocabularies for talking about what goes on, the vocabulary of human action and the vocabulary of physical science. If, for example, every case of someone's telling a lie were an instance of one physically specifiable class of sets of physical movements (and vice versa), and every case of someone's jilting his girl friend were an instance of another such class (and vice versa), then the reign of law in the field of physical movements would mean that lying and jilting could be deterministically explained. There would, as far as lying and jilting were concerned, be physical laws of human action as well as physical laws of physical movement. But there is no question of any such correlations ever being established. And it's no good saying that every description of a type of human action must in fact be correlated with some disjunction or other of descriptions in purely physical terms. This would be a pointless piece of logic, which could never be the basis of a scientific theory of human action, and could never yield deterministic explanations of human action.

J. F. T.: Well, I think I must disagree with you in turn. First, if we assume, as it were, unlimited success in physical explanation of physical movements, then it's by no means clear to me that people in general would find your point about absence of correlations an adequate defence against determinism. To many this defence will seem rather like surrender. And, second, why are you so sure that 'effective correlations', as you call them, can't be established? This sounds like a piece of dogmatism, on a matter which should be left to scientific investigation.

P. F. S.: On the first point—I can't help it if people are confused. And on the second—I don't think it is a matter for scientific investigation, but for philosophical argument.

G. J. W.: I'm afraid it's too late to pursue this disagreement any further. I think perhaps we ought to try to summarize what's emerged so far. We've referred to more than one type of thesis as deterministic, or possibly deterministic, and I think we ought to end by listing and distinguishing them. The thesis we've just been discussing might be labelled 'physical determinism'. This was the thesis that human behaviour, at least in so far as it consists in movements of bodily parts, might be brought under a system of purely physical laws. This was agreed to be a programme, not an achievement. But there seems to be room for disagreement as to whether even the fulfilment of the programme would establish what might be called a physical determinism of human action. Perhaps, for this, some other conditions would need to be fulfilled. And there seems to be room for disagreement about whether they could be fulfilled.

J. F. T.: What we were discussing earlier, of course, was something quite different from this—it could be called psychological determinism.

G. J. W.: Yes—but it's important to notice that we actually considered two possibilities, both broadly 'psychological' I suppose, but different. The first was the thesis that explanations of human behaviour in terms of the agent's own reasons could always be supplemented by explanations, in quite different terms, of the fact that those reasons weighed with him; and what we chiefly discussed here was whether, and, if so, in what sense, this kind of supplementary explanation could properly be regarded as undermining, by-passing, or somehow displacing the other kind. Then Thomson mentioned the rather different thesis that the reasons an agent gives for his action might be held to be always incomplete—that he always has further, unacknowledged, perhaps unconscious reasons (or motives). What I said about this, you remember, and I still think rightly, is that, although no doubt it is a somehow worrying thesis, it is very doubtful whether it should be called a species of determinism; and also very doubtful whether it could plausibly, or even reasonably, be put forward as true of all human behaviour.

P. F. S.: But that last remark, of course, applies to any kind of determinism which is really a thesis, and not just a programme. Perhaps the clearest point of all is that no such thesis worth taking seriously is known to be true.

J. F. T.: Or false.

FURTHER READINGS

Augustine. *On Free Choice of the Will*. Indianapolis: Bobbs-Merrill, 1964.

Campbell, C. A. "Is 'Freewill' a Pseudo-Problem?" *Mind* 60 (1951), 446-465.

D'Holbach, P. *System of Nature*, chaps. 11 and 12. Boston, 1853.

James, W. "The Dilemma of Determinism." In *The Will to Believe and Other Essays* London: Longmans, 1931.

MacIntyre, A. "Determinism." *Mind* 66 (1957), 28-41.

Mill, J. S. *System of Logic*, Book VI, chap. 2. 1843.

Ree, P. "Determinism and the Illusion of Moral Responsibility." In *A Modern Introduction to Philosophy*, edited by A. Pap and P. Edwards. 3rd ed. New York: The Free Press, 1973.

Sartre, J.-P. *Being and Nothingness*, pp. 433-484. New York; Philosophical Library, 1956.

Schlick, M. "When Is a Man Responsible?" In *Problems of Ethics*, pp. 143-156. New York: Prentice-Hall, 1939.

Taylor, R. *Metaphysics*, chap. 4. Englewood Cliffs, N. J.: Prentice-Hall, 1963.

PART FOUR

Personal Survival

Introduction

C. F. DELANEY

Most of us most of the time have very mundane conceptions of personal survival, i.e., as an indefinitely long continuation of some presently enjoyable state of affairs. As philosophers, however, we are not interested in these flights of imagination but rather in those conceptions of survival that have been maintained on reflection. Even here there is much unclarity, and the specific notions of *personal immortality* and *personal resurrection* are but two of many concepts people entertain when they reflect on death and the hereafter. Accordingly, our first task will be to clarify these concepts by distinguishing them both from each other and from other kindred notions. This clarification will set the boundaries for a discussion of the intelligibility of these notions which itself is a necessary preliminary to any discussion of the truth or falsity of the corresponding assertion.

What exactly is involved in the notions of personal immortality and personal resurrection? The adjective "personal" is common to both and is meant to single out that which is believed to survive, whereas the nouns "immortality" and "resurrection" designate different modes of survival one believes to be true of the person. Both features of these complex notions should be clarified by contrasting each with the alternative it excludes.

Let us concentrate first on "personal" and indicate what kindred notions are meant to be excluded by this adjective. First, there is the belief that I will live on in my children or in my work, or, more generally, in the memory of mankind. This is not an uncommon notion and in fact was dominant in Roman times. Now this belief is meant to be excluded by the adjective "personal" because it is not a belief in personal survival at all but a rather straightforward prediction that others will survive and remember me. Secondly, there is the Aristotelian notion that my "mind," in a sense of that term which would make it distinct from my personal history and memory thereof, is transcendent and will survive. To the degree that I am not my mind and that my mind is but a part of me, this belief in its survival is no more interesting than the conviction that my arm will be preserved for posterity inasmuch as neither involves the survival of the person. This leaves the Platonic-Christian notion of the persistence of the integral person which would involve at least the persistence of experiences continuous (or connected) with past experiences and accompanied by the memory thereof.

We must now shift to the notions of resurrection and immortality to distinguish them not only from each other but from other conceptions bearing on the transcendence and/or survival of the person. These are the modes of survival various traditions have seen fit to ascribe to persons.

First, there is the distinctively religious belief in *resurrection*. This is the belief that although the person ceases to exist at the death of the body, at some later time he will be reconstituted and enjoy life everlasting. Since on this account the person does die (although he rises again), this is quite different from the belief in personal immortality. Secondly, there is the generic belief in disembodied life. This is the belief that I am not identical with my body so that right here and now I enjoy a kind of existence which is trans-bodily, and, accordingly, the existence of my person need not and will not cease with the corruption of my body. Usually the term "soul" is used in this context, but it is important to note that fundamentally I must *be* my soul if the continued existence of my soul is to be *my* continued existence.

This notion of disembodied life admits of at least three varieties, i.e., eternality, immortality, and mere survival. The *eternality* of the person is a matter of the existent involved having neither beginning nor end so that it involves the notion of my preexistence as well survival of my bodily state. *Immortality* is a matter of the existent involved being such that once posited it is without end. Mere *survival* is a matter of the existent involved being such that it need not cease with the corruption of the body but will continue on for some finite period.

There are two other notions which are conceptually more complicated than the above, namely, the notion of reincarnation and the Thomistic notion of disembodied life plus reembodiment. Both seem logically committed to the prior notion of disembodied life, with reincarnation adding the feature of successive embodiments and the Thomistic view adding the feature of eventual reembodiment. Hence, if they are not to collapse back into the resurrection notion (some remnant of me persists and I will be reconstituted around it), both cases presuppose the notion of the person as fundamentally not identical with his body such that he can either perdure through successive embodiments or wait out his eventual completeness. Accordingly, we will focus our attention on the two simple notions of resurrection and immortality.

Hopefully, the discussion to this point has enabled us to get clear about these two notions. By way of summary, *the belief in personal resurrection is the belief that although I will cease to exist at the death of my body, I will be reconstituted and enjoy life everlasting; the belief in personal immortality is the belief that my existence as a person transcends my embodiment such that the eventual corruption of my body need not and will not involve the cessation of my existence and I will persist everlastingly*. It still remains to be seen whether or not these beliefs are intelligible and whether or not they are true.

Many philosophers have found these beliefs not merely unwarranted or false but radically meaningless. The belief in personal resurrection is at least initially puzzling because of the complexities that would be involved in bodily reconstitution. Given the decomposition and dispersal of the bodily person at death, what exactly is involved in his bodily reconstitution. From a material point of view a person's makeup changes over time; which elements would figure in his resurrection? Moreover, nature's cyclic character being what it is, the very same elements could be parts of many different people. Of which resurrected person would they be the elements? The standard response to these and similar objections invokes the notion of the "glorified body" as opposed to the ordinary one, but with this move the doctrine of bodily resurrection loses the conceptual simplicity that originally recommended it.

The belief in personal immortality is open to more serious charges. As we have seen, this belief involves the notion of a disembodied person whose experiences are continuous with those it underwent in its embodied state. But does it even make sense to speak of instances of disembodied life as undergoing experiences? Does it make any sense to think of instances of disembodied life as seeing, feeling, remembering, or even thinking or choosing? To the degree that our concept of an experience involves the body as a necessary condition, this feature of the belief in personal immortality will be seen to be incoherent.

Peter Geach among others has argued that our concepts of seeing, feeling, etc., are used only in association with a whole host of other concepts bearing on the physical characteristics of what is seen and the behavior of those who see such that when enough of these connecting threads are broken (as they would have to be in the case of disembodied life) these concepts collapse. Even our concepts of thinking and choosing are so bound up with sensation, imagination, and emotion that it is not at all clear what it would mean for them to be ascribed in situations where the latter ones are clearly inapplicable. And if we propose to ascribe only thinking-in-a-special-sense and choosing-in-a-special-sense to instances of disembodied life, these modes of experiencing would have to be so radically different from the ordinary ones as to render suspect not only the identification of the disembodied experiencer with the embodied one but even his similarity to him. If Geach is right, then, all our specific concepts falling under the generic notion "having an experience" are so bound up with our bodily existence that it would make no sense to think of an instance of disembodied life as having an experience. But this latter notion is a necessary ingredient in our concept of personal immortality.

But even granted that we can render intelligible the notions of "the resurrected body" or of "disembodied life undergoing experiences" one fundamental objection to both views remains. Both beliefs involve the notion of personal *identity* through death, and to the degree that *bodily continuity* is seen to be a necessary condition of personal identity, obviously it will be a manifest contradiction to talk of the same person persisting independently of his body or even reappearing following a time gap.

One of the most forceful arguments for the thesis that bodily continuity is a necessary condition for personal identity is the reduplication argument put forward by Bernard Williams. The argument presupposes that personal identity requires numerical identity and not mere qualitative similarity and then attempts to show that only bodily continuity can provide a basis for the former in this case. He asks us to imagine the following case. A certain friend of ours undergoes a personality change through the night and in the morning has a character exactly like that of some person known to have existed in the past. Or, he could undergo plastic surgery so as to look exactly like some person known to have existed in the past. He then proceeds to make sincere memory claims which exactly fit the life of that previous person. Is this sufficient for us to identify our contemporary as he is now with that previous person? Williams maintains that it obviously is not sufficient. For another of our friends might simultaneously undergo an exactly similar change, and if the conditions were sufficient to say that our first friend really was the previous person obviously they would be sufficient to say that our second friend also was. But if both our friends really are identical with the same previous person, they have to be identical with each other—which is clearly absurd. And we can't avoid the absurdity by abandoning simply one of the identifications of our contemporaries with the previous person because there is nothing to choose between them. Hence, we are constrained to abandon both identifications.

The point of the argument is to show that in situations where bodily continuity is excluded from the case and we are dealing only with physical similarity or with character traits and experiences such as memories, there is always the possibility of duplication. And where that is a possibility we are necessarily dealing with a one-many relation and consequently the concept of identity (which is a one-one relation) can't get a toehold. Bringing this back to the issue of survival construed either as resurrection or as immortality, the only conditions under which we would be entitled to say that a successor existent is really a continuation of the previously embodied person (i.e., is numerically identical with it as opposed to being merely similar to it) are conditions which by definition cannot obtain. Bodily continuity is a necessary condition for identity, the 'continuity' feature telling against resurrection and the 'bodily' feature telling against immortality.

These objections to intelligibility, of course, are not without rejoinders. The incoherence which emerges with regard to the notion of immortality is the result of the conjunction of a purely nonphysical conception of the person with physicalist notions of numerical identity and the ascription of mental states. Hence, there are two avenues of escape. One could hold on to this stark conception of the person and attempt to defend nonphysicalist accounts of identity and the ascription of mental states, or, on the other hand, one could hold fast on the issues of identity and mental states and attempt to develop a more complex account of the integral person such that it is not completely nonphysical (as Geach himself does). The incoherence which arises with regard to the notion of resurrection could be avoided by developing a formal as opposed to a material conception of 'body' and by elaborating on the concept of a time-gap individual. On the assumption that these maneuvers can be carried out with some success, the question still remains as to the truth or falsity (plausibility or implausibility) of the belief in personal immortality.

Inasmuch as it is generally felt that there are no philosophical arguments for resurrection but only religious ones, I will focus simply on the belief in immortality. (Although if one had independent reasons for believing in resurrection, he might see the second and third arguments as having some bearing on that belief.) Arguments for the truth or plausibility of immortality can be categorized as either metaphysical, moral, or empirical. The classical metaphysical arguments are for the most part attempts to show that there is some human activity (usually 'thinking') that proceeds without any essential dependence on the body so that it is reasonable to believe that the subject of this activity can survive the corruption of the body. This kind of argument may or may not bear on personal immortality as we have defined it depending on whether the proper subject of this activity is seen to be the integral person or merely some feature thereof. It is this which determines whether it is truly the person (Aquinas, Descartes) or merely some remnant thereof (Aristotle) which is seen to be capable of survival.

Of moral arguments for personal immortality that of Immanual Kant is the best known. His analysis of moral experience leads him to see our perfection as consisting in bringing our wills into perfect conformity with the moral law. So, although the finite will cannot simply be perfect it is nevertheless obligated to become perfect, and the only way in which this can be done is by its making endless progress toward the condition of perfect adequation with the moral law as an ideal limit. But this endless progress toward perfection presumes the everlasting existence of the moral agent. Hence, personal immortality is seen to be a necessary condition of plenary obedience to the moral law. Again, this argument may or may not bear on personal immortality as we have defined it depending on whether it is the integral person or merely some feature thereof such as his will which is the true moral agent.

This brings us finally to the realm of the empirical. Two quite different kinds of appeal to experience have been made in support of the belief in personal immortality. On the one hand, reference has always been made to entities such as ghosts as well as to other less striking parapsychological phenomena which seem to be manifestations of beyond. What better evidence of survival could we have than the actual showing up of one of the survivors? For most people, however, the data invoked in these arguments appear to be far more suspect than the conclusions they are brought in to support. On the other hand, a quite different sort of appeal to experience is made by those who claim to find in their own present experience certain features which indicate that the person right here and now lives a deeper life than that of the bodily organism, one that, given the features isolated, it is reasonable to believe will survive the death of the latter. Even granted the conflation of evidence and aspiration in most cases, the history of the human spirit is replete with moving testimonies to this deeper life.

Phaedo

PLATO

And now, O my judges, I desire to prove to you that the real philosopher has reason to be of good cheer when he is about to die, and that after death he may hope to obtain the greatest good in the other world. And how this may be, Simmias and Cebes, I will endeavour to explain. For I deem that the true votary of philosophy is likely to be misunderstood by other men; they do not perceive that he is always pursuing death and dying; and if this be so, and he has had the desire of death all his life long, why when his time comes should he repine at that which he had been always pursuing and desiring?

Simmias said laughingly: Though not in a laughing humour, you have made me laugh, Socrates; for I cannot help thinking that the many when they hear your words will say how truly you have described philosophers, and our people at home will likewise say that the life which philosophers desire is in reality death, and that they have found them out to be deserving of the death which they desire.

And they are right, Simmias, in thinking so, with the exception of the words "they have found them out"; for they have not found out either what is the nature of that death which the true philosopher deserves, or how he deserves or desires death. But enough of them:—let us discuss the matter among ourselves. Do we believe that there is such a thing as death?

To be sure, replied Simmias.

Is it not the separation of soul and body? And to be dead is the completion of this; when the soul exists in herself, and is released from the body and the body is released from the soul, what is this but death?

Just so, he replied.

There is another question, which will probably throw light on our present enquiry if you and I can agree about it:—Ought the philosopher to care about the pleasures—if they are to be called pleasures—of eating and drinking?

Certainly not, answered Simmias.

And what about the pleasures of love—should he care for them?

By no means.

And will he think much of the other ways of indulging the body, for example, the acquisition of costly raiment, or sandals, or other adornments of the body? Instead of caring about them, does he not rather despise anything more than nature needs? What do you say?

I should say that the true philosopher would despise them.

Would you not say that he is entirely concerned with the soul and not with the body? He would like, as far as he can, to get away from the body and to turn to the soul.

Quite true.

In matters of this sort philosophers, above all other men, may be observed in every sort of way to dissever the soul from the communion of the body.

Very true.

Plato (429-347 BC) through his many dialogues was one of the principal influences on the intellectual development of the Western world.

This selection is an excerpt from *Phaedo* in *The Dialogues of Plato*, trans. by Benjamin Jowett. (Macmillan, 1892).

Whereas, Simmias, the rest of the world are of opinion that to him who has no sense of pleasure and no part in bodily pleasure, life is not worth having; and that he who is indifferent about them is as good as dead.

That is also true.

What again shall we say of the actual acquirement of knowledge?—is the body, if invited to share in the enquiry, a hinderer or a helper? I mean to say, have sight and hearing any truth in them? Are they not, as the poets are always telling us, inaccurate witnesses? and yet, if even they are inaccurate and indistinct, what is to be said of the other senses?—for you will allow that they are the best of them?

Certainly, he replied.

Then when does the soul attain truth?—for in attempting to consider anything in company with the body she is obviously deceived.

True.

Then must not true existence be revealed to her in thought, if at all?

Yes.

And thought is best when the mind is gathered into herself and none of these things trouble her—neither sounds nor sights nor pain nor any pleasure,—when she takes leave of the body, and has as little as possible to do with it, when she has no bodily sense or desire, but is aspiring after true being?

Certainly.

And in this the philosopher dishonours the body; his soul runs away from his body and desires to be alone and by herself?

That is true.

Well, but there is another thing, Simmias: Is there or is there not an absolute justice?

Assuredly, there is.

And an absolute beauty and absolute good?

Of course.

But did you ever behold any of them with your eyes?

Certainly not.

Or did you ever reach them with any other bodily sense?—and I speak not of these alone, but of absolute greatness, and health, and strength, and of the essence or true nature of everything. Has the reality of them ever been perceived by you through the bodily organs? or rather, is not the nearest approach to the knowledge of their several natures made by him who so orders his intellectual vision as to have the most exact conception of the essence of each thing which he considers?

Certainly.

And he attains to the purest knowledge of them who goes to each with the mind alone, not introducing or intruding in the act of thought sight or any other sense together with reason, but with the very light of the mind in her own clearness searches into the very truth of each; he who has got rid, as far as he can, of eyes and ears and, so to speak, of the whole body, these being in his opinion distracting elements which when they infect the soul hinder her from acquiring truth and knowledge—who, if not he, is likely to attain to the knowledge of true being?

What you say has a wonderful truth in it, Socrates, replied Simmias.

And when real philosophers consider all these things, will they not be led to make a reflection which they will express in words something like the following? "Have we not found," they will say, "a path of thought which seems to bring us and our argument to the conclusion, that while we are in the body, and while the soul is infected with the evils of the body, our desire will not be satisfied, and our desire is of the truth? For the body is a source of endless trouble to us by reason of the mere requirement of food; and is liable also to diseases which overtake and impede us in the search after true being: it fills us full of loves, and lusts, and fears, and fancies of all kinds, and endless foolery, and, in fact, as men say, takes away from us the power of thinking at all. Whence come wars, and fightings, and factions? whence but from the body and the lusts of the body? Wars are occasioned by the love of money, and money has to be acquired for the sake and service of the body; and by reason of all these impediments we have no time to give to philosophy; and, last and worst of all, even if we are at leisure and betake ourselves to some speculation, the body is always breaking in upon us, causing turmoil and confusion in our enquiries, and so amazing us that we are prevented from seeing the truth. It has been proved to us by experience that if we would have pure knowledge of anything we must be quit of the body—the soul in herself must behold things in themselves: and then we shall attain the wisdom which we desire, and of which we say that we are lovers; not while we live, but after death; for if while in company with the body, the soul cannot have pure knowledge, one of two things follows—either knowledge is not to be attained at all, or, if at all, after death. For then, and not till then, the soul will be parted from the body and exist in herself alone. In this present life, I reckon that we make the nearest approach to knowledge when we have the least possible intercourse or communion with the body, and are not surfeited with the bodily nature, but keep ourselves pure until the hour when God himself is pleased to release us. And thus having got rid of the foolishness of the body we shall be pure and hold converse with the pure, and know of ourselves the clear light everywhere, which is no other than the light of truth." For the impure are not permitted to approach the pure. These are the sort of words, Simmias, which the true lovers of knowledge cannot help saying to one another, and thinking. You would agree; would you not?

Undoubtedly, Socrates.

But, O my friend, if this be true, there is great reason to hope that, going whither I go, when I have come to the end of my journey, I shall attain that which has been the pursuit of my life. And therefore I go on my way rejoicing, and not I only, but every other man who believes that his mind has been made ready and that he is in a manner purified.

Certainly, replied Simmias.

And what is purification but the separation of the soul from the body, as I was saying before; the habit of the soul gathering and collecting herself into herself from all sides out of the body; the dwelling in her own place alone, as in another life, so also in this, as far as she can;—the release of the soul from the chains of the body?

Very true, he said.

And this separation and release of the soul from the body is termed death?

To be sure, he said.

And the true philosophers, and they only, are ever seeking to release the soul. Is not the separation and release of the soul from the body their especial study?

That is true.

And, as I was saying at first, there would be a ridiculous contradiction in men studying to live as nearly as they can in a state of death, and yet repining when it comes upon them.

Clearly.

And the true philosophers, Simmias, are always occupied in the practice of dying, wherefore also to them least of all men is death terrible. Look at the matter thus:—if they have been in every way the enemies of the body, and are wanting to be alone with the soul, when this desire of theirs is granted, how inconsistent would they be if they trembled and repined, instead of rejoicing at their departure to that place where, when they arrive, they hope to gain that which in life they desired—and this was wisdom—and at the same time to be rid of the company of their enemy. Many a man has been willing to go to the world below animated by the hope of seeing there an earthly love, or wife, or son, and conversing with them. And will he who is a true lover of wisdom, and is strongly persuaded in like manner that only in the world below he can worthily enjoy her, still repine at death? Will he not depart with joy? Surely he will, O my friend, if he be a true philosopher. For he will have a firm conviction that there, and there only, he can find wisdom in her purity. And if this be true, he would be very absurd, as I was saying, if he were afraid of death.

He would indeed, replied Simmias.

And when you see a man who is repining at the approach of death, is not his reluctance a sufficient proof that he is not a lover of wisdom, but a lover of the body, and probably at the same time a lover of either money or power, or both?

Quite so, he replied. . . .

Cebes answered: I agree, Socrates, in the greater part of what you say. But in what concerns the soul, men are apt to be incredulous; they fear that when she has left the body her place may be nowhere, and that on the very day of death she may perish and come to an end—immediately on her release from the body, issuing forth dispersed like smoke or air and in her flight vanishing away into nothingness. If she could only be collected into herself after she has obtained release from the evils of which you were speaking, there would be good reason to hope, Socrates, that what you say is true. But surely it requires a great deal of argument and many proofs to show that when the man is dead his soul yet exists, and has any force or intelligence.

True, Cebes, said Socrates; and shall I suggest that we converse a little of the probabilities of these things?

I am sure, said Cebes, that I should greatly like to know your opinion about them.

I reckon, said Socrates, that no one who heard me now, not even if he were one of my old enemies, the comic poets, could accuse me of idle talking about matters in which I have no concern:—If you please, then, we will proceed with the enquiry.

Suppose we consider the question whether the souls of men after death are or are not in the world below. There comes into my mind an ancient doctrine which affirms that they go from hence into the other world, and returning hither, are born again from the dead. Now, if it be true that the living come from the dead, then our souls must exist in the other world, for if not, how could they have been born again? And this would be conclusive, if there were any real evidence that the living are only born from the dead; but if this is not so, then other arguments will have to be adduced.

Very true, replied Cebes.

Then let us consider the whole question, not in relation to man only, but in relation to animals generally, and to plants, and to everything of which there is generation, and the proof will be easier. Are not all things which have opposites generated out of their opposites? I mean such things as good and evil, just and unjust—and there are innumerable other opposites which are generated out of opposites. And I want to show that in all opposites there is of necessity a similar alternation; I mean to say, for example, that anything which becomes greater must become greater after being less.

True.

And that which becomes less must have been once greater and then have become less.

Yes.

And the weaker is generated from the stronger, and the swifter from the slower.

Very true.

And the worse is from the better, and the more just is from the more unjust.

Of course.

And is this true of all opposites? and are we convinced that all of them are generated out of opposites?

Yes.

And in this universal opposition of all things, are there not also two intermediate processes which are ever going on, from one to the other opposite, and back again; where there is a greater and a less there is also an intermediate process of increase and diminution, and that which grows is said to wax, and that which decays to wane?

Yes, he said.

And there are many other processes, such as division and composition, cooling and heating, which equally involve a passage into and out of one another. And this necessarily holds of all opposites, even though not always expressed in words—they are really generated out of one another, and there is a passing or process from one to the other of them?

Very true, he replied.

Well, and is there not an opposite of life, as sleep is the opposite of waking?

True, he said.

And what is it?

Death, he answered.

And these, if they are opposites, are generated the one from the other, and have their two intermediate processes also?

Of course.

Now, said Socrates, I will analyze one of the two pairs of opposites which I have mentioned to you, and also its intermediate processes, and you shall analyze the other to me. One of them I term sleep, the other waking. The state of sleep is opposed to the state of waking, and out of sleeping waking is generated, and out of waking, sleeping; and the process of generation is in the one case falling asleep, and in the other waking up. Do you agree?

I entirely agree.

Then suppose that you analyze life and death to me in the same manner. Is not death opposed to life?

Yes.

And they are generated one from the other?

Yes.

What is generated from the living?

The dead.

And what from the dead?

I can only say in answer—the living.

Then the living, whether things or persons, Cebes, are generated from the dead?

That is clear, he replied.

Then the inference is that our souls exist in the world below?

That is true.

And one of the two processes or generations is visible—for surely the act of dying is visible?

Surely, he said.

What then is to be the result? Shall we exclude the opposite process? and shall we suppose nature to walk on one leg only? Must we not rather assign to death some corresponding process of generation?

Certainly, he replied.

And what is that process?

Return to life.

And return to life, if there be such a thing, is the birth of the dead into the world of the living?

Quite true.

Then here is a new way by which we arrive at the conclusion that the living come from the dead, just as the dead come from the living; and this, if true, affords a most certain proof that the souls of the dead exist in some place out of which they come again.

Yes, Socrates, he said; the conclusion seems to flow necessarily out of our previous admissions.

And that these admissions were not unfair, Cebes, he said, may be shown, I think, as follows: If generation were in a straight line only, and there were no compensation or circle in nature, no turn or return of elements into their opposites, then you know that all things would at last have the same form and pass into the same state, and there would be no more generation of them.

What do you mean? he said.

A simple thing enough, which I will illustrate by the case of sleep, he replied. You know that if there were no alternation of sleeping and waking, the tale of the sleeping Endymion would in the end have no meaning, because all other things would be asleep too, and he would not be distinguishable from the rest. Or if there were composition only, and no division of substances, then the chaos of Anaxagoras would come again. And in like manner, my dear Cebes, if all things which partook of life were to die, and after they were dead remained in the form of death, and did not come to life again, all would at last die, and nothing would be alive—what other result could there be? For if the living spring from any other things, and they too die, must not all things at last be swallowed up in death?

There is no escape, Socrates, said Cebes; and to me your argument seems to be absolutely true.

Yes, he said, Cebes, it is and must be so, in my opinion; and we have not been deluded in making these admissions; but I am confident that there truly is such a thing as living again, and that the living spring from the dead, and that the souls of the dead are in existence and that the good souls have a better portion than the evil.

Cebes added: Your favourite doctrine, Socrates, that knowledge is simply recollection, if true, also necessarily implies a previous time in which we have learned that which we now recollect. But this would be impossible unless our soul had been in some place before existing in the form of man; here then is another proof of the soul's immortality.

But tell me, Cebes, said Simmias, interposing, what arguments are urged in favour of this doctrine of recollection. I am not very sure at the moment that I remember them.

One excellent proof, said Cebes, is afforded by questions. If you put a question to a person in a right way, he will give a true answer of himself, but how could he do this unless there were knowledge and right reason already in him? And this is most clearly shown when he is taken to a diagram or to anything of that sort.

But if, said Socrates, you are still incredulous, Simmias, I would ask you whether you may not agree with me when you look at the matter in another way;—I mean, if you are still incredulous as to whether knowledge is recollection?

Incredulous I am not, said Simmias; but I want to have this doctrine of recollection brought to my own recollection, and, from what Cebes has said, I am beginning to recollect and be convinced: but I should still like to hear what you were going to say.

This is what I would say, he replied:—We should agree, if I am not mistaken, that what a man recollects he must have known at some previous time.

Very true.

And what is the nature of this knowledge or recollection? I mean to ask, Whether a person who, having seen or heard or in any way perceived anything, knows not only that, but has a conception of something else which is the subject, not of the same but of some other kind of knowledge, may not be fairly said to recollect that of which he has the conception?

What do you mean?

I mean what I may illustrate by the following instance:—The knowledge of a lyre is not the same as the knowledge of a man?

True.

And yet what is the feeling of lovers when they recognize a lyre, or a garment, or anything else which the beloved has been in the habit of using? Do not they, from knowing the lyre, form in the mind's eye an image of the youth to whom the lyre belongs? And this is recollection. In like manner any one who sees Simmias may remember Cebes; and there are endless examples of the same thing.

Endless, indeed, replied Simmias.

And recollection is most commonly a process of recovering that which has been already forgotten through time and inattention.

Very true, he said.

Well; and may you not also from seeing the picture of a horse or a lyre remember a man? and from the picture of Simmias, you may be led to remember Cebes?

True.

Or you may also be led to the recollection of Simmias himself?

Quite so.

And in all these cases, the recollection may be derived from things either like or unlike?

It may be.

And when the recollection is derived from like things, then another consideration is sure to arise, which is—whether the likeness in any degree falls short or not of that which is recollected?

Very true, he said.

And shall we proceed a step further, and affirm that there is such a thing as equality, not of one piece of wood or stone with another, but that, over and above this, there is absolute equality? Shall we say so?

Say so, yes, replied Simmias, and swear to it, with all the confidence in life.

And do we know the nature of this absolute essence?

To be sure, he said.

And whence did we obtain our knowledge? Did we not see equalities of material things, such as pieces of wood and stones, and gather from them the idea of an equality which is different from them? For you will acknowledge that there is a difference. Or look at the matter in another way:—Do not the same pieces of wood or stone appear at one time equal, and at another time unequal?

That is certain.

But are real equals ever unequal? or is the idea of equality the same as of inequality?

Impossible, Socrates.

Then these (so-called) equals are not the same with the idea of equality?

I should say, clearly not, Socrates.

And yet from these equals, although differing from the idea of equality, you conceived and attained that idea?

Very true, he said.

Which might be like, or might be unlike them?

Yes.

But that makes no difference: whenever from seeing one thing you conceived another, whether like or unlike, there must surely have been an act of recollection?

Very true.

But what would you say of equal portions of wood and stone, or other material equals? and what is the impression produced by them? Are they equals in the same sense in which absolute equality is equal? or do they fall short of this perfect equality in a measure?

Yes, he said, in a very great measure too.

And must we not allow, that when I or any one, looking at any object, observes that the thing which he sees aims at being some other thing, but falls short of, and cannot be, that other thing, but is inferior, he who makes this observation must have had a previous knowledge of that to which the other, although similar, was inferior?

Certainly.

And has not this been our own case in the matter of equals and of absolute equality?

Precisely.

Then we must have known equality previously to the time when we first saw the material equals, and reflected that all these apparent equals strive to attain absolute equality, but fall short of it?

Very true.

And we recognize also that this absolute equality has only been known, and can only be known, through the medium of sight or touch, or of some other of the senses, which are all alike in this respect?

Yes, Socrates, as far as the argument is concerned, one of them is the same as the other.

From the senses then is derived the knowledge that all sensible things aim at an absolute equality of which they fall short?

Yes.

Then before we began to see or hear or perceive in any way, we must have had a knowledge of absolute equality, or we could not have referred to that standard the equals which are derived from the senses?—for to that they all aspire, and of that they fall short.

No other inference can be drawn from the previous statements.

And did we not see and hear and have the use of our other senses as soon as we were born?

Certainly.

Then we must have acquired the knowledge of equality at some previous time?

Yes.

That is to say, before we were born, I suppose?

True.

And if we acquired this knowledge before we were born, and were born having the use of it, then we also knew before we were born and at the instant of birth not only the equal or the greater or the less, but all other ideas; for we are not speaking only of equality, but of beauty, goodness, justice, holiness, and of all which we stamp with the name of essence in the dialectical process, both when we ask and when we answer questions. Of all this we may certainly affirm that we acquired the knowledge before birth?

We may.

But if, after having acquired, we have not forgotten what in each case we acquired, then we must always have come into life having knowledge, and shall always continue to know as long as life lasts—for knowing is the acquiring and retaining knowledge and not forgetting. Is not forgetting, Simmias, just the losing of knowledge?

Quite true, Socrates.

But if the knowledge which we acquired before birth was lost by us at birth, and if afterwards by the use of the senses we recovered what we previously knew, will not the process which we call learning be a recovering of the knowledge which is natural to us, and may not this be rightly termed recollection?

Very true.

So much is clear—that when we perceive something, either by the help of sight, or hearing, or some other sense, from that perception we are able to obtain a notion of some other thing like or unlike which is associated with it but has been forgotten. Whence, as I was saying, one of two alternatives follows:—either we had this knowledge at birth, and continued to know through life; or, after birth, those who are said to learn only remember, and learning is simply recollection.

Yes, that is quite true, Socrates.

And which alternative, Simmias, do you prefer? Had we the knowledge at our birth, or did we recollect the things which we knew previously to our birth?

I cannot decide at the moment.

At any rate you can decide whether he who has knowledge will or will not be able to render an account of his knowledge? What do you say?

Certainly, he will.

But do you think that every man is able to give an account of these very matters about which we are speaking?

Would that they could, Socrates, but I rather fear that to-morrow, at this time, there will no longer be any one alive who is able to give an account of them such as ought to be given.

Then you are not of opinion, Simmias, that all men know these things?

Certainly not.

They are in process of recollecting that which they learned before?

Certainly.

But when did our souls acquire this knowledge?—not since we were born as men?

Certainly not.

And therefore, previously?

Yes.

Then, Simmias, our souls must also have existed without bodies before they were in the form of man, and must have had intelligence.

Unless indeed you suppose, Socrates, that these notions are given us at the very moment of birth; for this is the only time which remains.

Yes, my friend, but if so, when do we lose them? for they are not in us when we are born—that is admitted. Do we lose them at the moment of receiving them, or, if not, at what other time?

No, Socrates, I perceive that I was unconsciously talking nonsense.

Then may we not say, Simmias, that if, as we are always repeating, there is an absolute beauty, and goodness, and an absolute essence of all things; and if to this, which is now discovered to have existed in our former state, we refer all our sensations, and with this compare them, finding these ideas to be preexistent and our inborn possession—then our souls must have had a prior existence, but, if not, there would be no force in the argument? There is the same proof that these ideas must have existed before we were born, as that our souls existed before we were born; and if not the ideas, then not the souls.

Yes, Socrates; I am convinced that there is precisely the same necessity for the one as for the other; and the argument retreats successfully to the position that the existence of the soul before birth cannot be separated from the existence of the essence of which you speak. For there is nothing which to my mind is so patent as that beauty, goodness, and the other notions of which you were just now speaking, have a most real and absolute existence; and I am satisfied with the proof.

Well, but is Cebes equally satisfied? for I must convince him too.

I think, said Simmias, that Cebes is satisfied: although he is the most incredulous of mortals, yet I believe that he is sufficiently convinced of the existence of the soul before birth. But that after death the soul will continue to exist is not yet proven even to my own satisfaction. I cannot get rid of the feeling of the many to which Cebes was referring—the feeling that when the man dies the soul will be dispersed, and that this may be the extinction of her. For admitting that she may have been born elsewhere, and framed out of other elements, and was in existence before entering the human body, why after having entered in and gone out again may she not herself be destroyed and come to an end?

Very true, Simmias, said Cebes; about half of what was required has been proven; to wit, that our souls existed before we were born:—that the soul will exist after death as well as before birth is the other half of which the proof is still wanting, and has to be supplied; when that is given the demonstration will be complete.

But that proof, Simmias and Cebes, has been already given, said Socrates, if you put the two arguments together—I mean this and the former one, in which we admitted that everything living is born of the dead. For if the soul exists before birth, and in coming to life and being born can be born only from death and dying, must she not after death continue to exist, since she has to be born again?—Surely the proof which you desire has been already furnished. Still I suspect that you and Simmias would be glad to probe the argument further. Like children, you are haunted with a fear that when the soul leaves the body, the wind may really blow her away and scatter her; especially if a man should happen to die in a great storm and not when the sky is calm.

Cebes answered with a smile: Then, Socrates, you must argue us out of our fears—and yet, strictly speaking, they are not our fears, but there is a child within us to whom death is a sort of hobgoblin: him too we must persuade not to be afraid when he is alone in the dark.

Socrates said: Let the voice of the charmer be applied daily until you have charmed away the fear.

And where shall we find a good charmer of our fears, Socrates, when you are gone?

Hellas, he replied, is a large place, Cebes, and has many good men, and there are barbarous races not a few: seek for him among them all, far and wide, sparing neither pains nor money; for there is no better way of spending your money. And you must seek among yourselves too; for you will not find others better able to make the search.

The search, replied Cebes, shall certainly be made. And now, if you please, let us return to the point of the argument at which we digressed.

By all means, replied Socrates; what else should I please?

Very good.

Must we not, said Socrates, ask ourselves what that is which, as we imagine, is liable to be scattered, and about which we fear? and what again is that about which we have no fear? And then we may proceed further to enquire whether that which suffers dispersion is or is not of the nature of soul—our hopes and fears as to our own souls will turn upon the answers to these questions.

Very true, he said.

Now the compound or composite may be supposed to be naturally capable, as of being compounded, so also of being dissolved; but that which is uncompounded, and that only, must be, if anything is, indissoluble.

Yes; I should imagine so, said Cebes.

And the uncompounded may be assumed to be the same and unchanging, whereas the compound is always changing and never the same.

I agree, he said.

Then now let us return to the previous discussion. Is that idea or essence, which in the dialectical process we define as essence or true existence—whether essence of equality, beauty, or anything else—are these essences, I say, liable at times to some degree of change? or are they each of them always what they are, having the same simple self-existent and unchanging forms, not admitting of variation at all, or in any way, or at any time?

They must be always the same, Socrates, replied Cebes.

And what would you say of the many beautiful—whether men or horses or garments or any other things which are named by the same names and may be called equal or beautiful,—are they all unchanging and the same always, or quite the reverse? May they not rather be described as almost always changing and hardly ever the same, either with themselves or with one another?

The latter, replied Cebes; they are always in a state of change.

And these you can touch and see and perceive with the senses, but the unchanging things you can only perceive with the mind—they are invisible and are not seen?

That is very true, he said.

Well, then, added Socrates, let us suppose that there are two sorts of existences—one seen, the other unseen.

Let us suppose them.

The seen is the changing, and the unseen is the unchanging?

That may be also supposed.

And, further, is not one part of us body, another part soul?

To be sure.

And to which class is the body more alike and akin?

Clearly to the seen—no one can doubt that.

And is the soul seen or not seen?

Not by man, Socrates.

And what we mean by "seen" and "not seen" is that which is or is not visible to the eye of man?

Yes, to the eye of man.

And is the soul seen or not seen?

Not seen.

Unseen then?

Yes.

Then the soul is more like to the unseen, and the body to the seen?

That follows necessarily, Socrates.

And were we not saying long ago that the soul when using the body as an instrument of perception, that is to say, when using the sense of sight or hearing or some other sense (for the meaning of perceiving through the body is perceiving through the senses)—were we not saying that the soul too is then dragged by the body into the region of the changeable, and wanders and is confused; the world spins round her, and she is like a drunkard, when she touches change?

Very true.

But when returning into herself she reflects, then she passes into the other world, the region of purity, and eternity, and immortality, and unchangeableness, which are her kindred, and with them she ever lives, when she is by herself and is not let or hindered; then she ceases from her erring ways, and being in communion with the unchanging is unchanging. And this state of the soul is called wisdom?

That is well and truly said, Socrates, he replied.

And to which class is the soul more nearly alike and akin, as far as may be inferred from this argument, as well as from the preceding one?

I think, Socrates, that, in the opinion of every one who follows the argument, the soul will be infinitely more like the unchangeable—even the most stupid person will not deny that.

And the body is more like the changing?

Yes.

Yet once more consider the matter in another light: When the soul and the body are united, then nature orders the soul to rule and govern, and the body to obey and serve. Now, which of these two functions is akin to the divine? and which to the mortal? Does not the divine appear to you to be that which naturally orders and rules, and the mortal to be that which is subject and servant?

True.

And which does the soul resemble?

The soul resembles the divine, and the body the mortal—there can be no doubt of that, Socrates.

Then reflect, Cebes: of all which has been said is not this the conclusion?—that the soul is in the very likeness of the divine, and immortal, and intellectual, and uniform, and indissoluble, and unchangeable; and that the body is in the very likeness of the human, and mortal, and unintellectual, and multiform, and dissoluble, and changeable. Can this, my dear Cebes, be denied?

It cannot.

But if it be true, then is not the body liable to speedy dissolution? and is not the soul almost or altogether indissoluble?

Certainly.

And do you further observe, that after a man is dead, the body, or visible part of him, which is lying in the visible world, and is called a corpse, and would naturally be dissolved and decomposed and dissipated, is not dissolved or decomposed at once, but may remain for some time, nay, even for a long time, if the constitution be sound at the time of death, and the season of the year favourable? For the body when shrunk and embalmed, as the manner is in Egypt, may remain almost entire through infinite ages; and even in decay, there are still some portions, such as the bones and ligaments, which are practically indestructible:—Do you agree?

Yes.

And is it likely that the soul, which is invisible, in passing to the place of the true Hades, which like her is invisible, and pure, and noble, and on her way to the good and wise God, whither, if God will, my soul is also soon to go,—that the soul, I repeat, if this be her nature and origin, will be blown away and destroyed immediately on quitting the body, as the many say? That can never be, my dear Simmias and Cebes. . . .

When Socrates had done speaking, for a considerable time there was silence; he himself appeared to be meditating, as most of us were, on what had been said; only Cebes and Simmias spoke a few words to one another. And Socrates observing them asked what they thought of the argument, and whether there was anything wanting? For, said he, there are many points still open to suspicion and attack, if any one were disposed to sift the matter thoroughly. Should you be considering some other matter I say no more, but if you are still in doubt do not hesitate to say exactly what you think, and let us have anything better which you can suggest; and if you think that I can be of any use, allow me to help you.

Simmias said: I must confess, Socrates, that doubts did arise in our minds, and each of us was urging and inciting the other to put the question which we wanted to have answered but which neither of us liked to ask, fearing that our importunity might be troublesome at such a time.

Socrates replied with a smile: O Simmias, what are you saying? I am not very likely to persuade other men that I do not regard my present situation as a misfortune, if I cannot even persuade you that I am no worse off now than at any other time in my life. Will you not allow that I have as much of the spirit of prophecy in me as the swans? For they, when they perceive that they must die, having sung all their life long, do then sing more lustily than ever, rejoicing in the thought that they are about to go away to the god whose ministers they are. But men, because they are themselves afraid of death, slanderously affirm of the swans that they sing a lament at the last, not considering that no bird sings when cold, or hungry, or in pain, not even the nightingale, nor the swallow, nor yet the hoopoe; which are said indeed to tune a lay of sorrow, although I do not believe this to be true of them any more than of the swans. But because they are sacred to Apollo, they have the gift of prophecy, and anticipate the good things of another world; wherefore they sing and rejoice in that day more than ever they did before. And I, too, believing myself to be the consecrated servant of the same God, and the fellow-servant of the swans, and thinking that I have received from my master gifts of prophecy which are not inferior to theirs, would not go out of life less merrily than the swans. Never mind then, if this be your only objection, but speak and ask anything which you like, while the eleven magistrates of Athens allow.

Very good, Socrates, said Simmias; then I will tell you my difficulty, and Cebes will tell you his. I feel myself (and I dare say that you have the same feeling) how hard or rather impossible is the attainment of any certainty about questions such as these in the present life. And yet I should deem him a coward who did not prove what is said about them to the uttermost, or whose heart failed him before he had examined them on every side. For he should persevere until he has achieved one of two things: either he should discover, or be taught the truth about them; or, if this be impossible, I would have him take the best and most irrefragable of human theories, and let this be the raft upon which he sails through life—not without risk, as I admit, if he cannot find some word of God which will more surely and safely carry him. And now, as you bid me, I will venture to question you, and then I shall not have to reproach myself hereafter with not having said at the time what I think. For when I consider the matter, either alone or with Cebes, the argument does certainly appear to me, Socrates, to be not sufficient.

Socrates answered: I dare say, my friend, that you may be right, but I should like to know in what respect the argument is insufficient.

In this respect, replied Simmias:—Suppose a person to use the same argument about harmony and the lyre—might he not say that harmony is a thing invisible, incorporeal, perfect, divine, existing in the lyre which is harmonized, but that the lyre and the strings are matter and material, composite, earthy, and akin to mortality? And when some one breaks the lyre, or cuts and rends the strings, then he who takes this view would argue as you do, and on the same analogy, that the harmony survives and has not perished—you cannot imagine, he would say, that the lyre without the strings and the broken strings themselves which are mortal remain, and yet that the harmony, which is of heavenly and immortal nature and kindred, has perished—perished before the mortal. The harmony must still be somewhere, and the wood and strings will decay before anything can happen to that. The thought, Socrates, must have occurred to your own mind that such is our conception of the soul; and that when the body is in a manner strung and held together by the elements of hot and cold, wet and dry, then the soul is the harmony or due proportionate admixture of them. But if so, whenever the strings of the body are unduly loosened or overstrained through disease or other injury, then the soul, though most divine, like other harmonies of music or of works of art, of course perishes at once; although the material remains of the body may last for a considerable time, until they are either decayed or burnt. And if any one maintains that the soul, being the harmony of the elements of the body, is first to perish in that which is called death, how shall we answer him?

Socrates looked fixedly at us as his manner was, and said with a smile: Simmias has reason on his side; and why does not some one of you who is better able than myself answer him? for there is force in his attack upon me. But perhaps, before we answer him, we had better also hear what Cebes has to say that we may gain time for reflection, and when they have both spoken, we may either assent to them, if there is truth in what they say, or if not, we will maintain our position. Please to tell me then, Cebes, he said, what was the difficulty which troubled you?

Cebes said: I will tell you. My feeling is that the argument is where it was, and open to the same objections which were urged before; for I am ready to admit that the existence of the soul before entering into the bodily form has been very ingeniously, and, if I may say so, quite sufficiently proven; but the existence of the soul after death is still, in my judgment, unproven. Now, my objection is not the same as that of Simmias; for I am not disposed to deny that the soul is stronger and more lasting than the body, being of opinion that in all such respects the soul very far excels the body. Well, then, says the argument to me, why do you remain unconvinced?—When you see that the weaker continues in existence after the man is dead, will you not admit that the more lasting must also survive during the same period of time? Now, I will ask you to consider whether the objection, which, like Simmias, I will express in a figure, is of any weight. The analogy which I will adduce is that of an old weaver, who dies, and after his death somebody says:—He is not dead, he must be alive;—see, there is the coat which he himself wove and wore, and which remains whole and undecayed. And then he proceeds to ask of some one who is incredulous, whether a man lasts longer, or the coat which is in use and wear; and when he is answered that a man lasts far longer, thinks that he has thus certainly demonstrated the survival of the man, who is the more lasting, because the less lasting remains. But that, Simmias, as I would beg you to remark, is a mistake; any one can see that he who talks thus is talking nonsense. For the truth is, that the weaver aforesaid, having woven and worn many such coats, outlived several of them; and was outlived by the last; but a man is not therefore proved to be slighter and weaker than a coat. Now the relation of the body to the soul may be expressed in a similar figure; and any one may very fairly say in like manner that the soul is lasting, and the body weak and short-lived in comparison. He may argue in like manner that every soul wears out many bodies, especially if a man live many years. While he is alive the body deliquesces and decays, and the soul always weaves another garment and repairs the waste. But of course, whenever the soul perishes, she must have on her last garment, and this will survive her; and then at length, when the soul is dead, the body will show its native weakness, and quickly decompose and pass away. I would therefore rather not rely on the argument from superior strength to prove the continued existence of the soul after death. For granting even more than you affirm to be possible, and acknowledging not only that the soul existed before birth, but also that the souls of some exist, and will continue to exist after death, and will be born and die again and again, and that there is a natural strength in the soul which will hold out and be born many times—nevertheless, we may be still inclined to think that she will weary in the labours of successive births, and may at last succumb in one of her deaths and utterly perish; and this death and dissolution of the body which brings destruction to the soul may be unknown to any of us, for no one of us can have had any experience of it: and if so, then I maintain that he who is confident about death has but a foolish confidence, unless he is able to prove that the soul is altogether immortal and imperishable. But if he cannot prove the soul's immortality, he who is about to die will always have reason to fear that when the body is disunited, the soul also may utterly perish.

All of us, as we afterwards remarked to one another, had an unpleasant feeling at hearing what they said. When we had been so firmly convinced before, now to have our faith shaken seemed to introduce a confusion and uncertainty, not only into the previous argument, but into any future one; either we were incapable of forming a judgment, or there were no grounds of belief. . . .

And now let us proceed, he said. And first of all let me be sure that I have in my mind what you were saying; Simmias, if I remember rightly, has fears and misgivings whether the soul, although a fairer and diviner thing than the body, being as she is in the form of harmony, may not perish first. On the other hand, Cebes appeared to grant that the soul was more lasting than the body, but he said that no one could know whether the soul, after having worn out many bodies, might not perish herself and leave her last body behind her; and that this is death, which is the destruction not of the body but of the soul, for in the body the work of destruction is ever going on. Are not these, Simmias and Cebes, the points which we have to consider?

They both agreed to this statement of them.

He proceeded: And did you deny the force of the whole preceding argument, or of a part only?

Of a part only, they replied.

And what did you think, he said, of that part of the argument in which we said that knowledge was recollection, and hence inferred that the soul must have previously existed somewhere else before she was enclosed in the body?

Cebes said that he had been wonderfully impressed by that part of the argument, and that his conviction remained absolutely unshaken. Simmias agreed, and added that he himself could hardly imagine the possibility of his ever thinking differently.

But, rejoined Socrates, you will have to think differently, my Theban friend, if you still maintain that harmony is a compound, and that the soul is a harmony which is made out of strings set in the frame of the body; for you will surely never allow yourself to say that a harmony is prior to the elements which compose it.

Never, Socrates.

But do you not see that this is what you imply when you say that the soul existed before she took the form and body of man, and was made up of elements which as yet had no existence? For harmony is not like the soul, as you suppose; but first the lyre, and the strings, and the sounds exist in a state of discord, and then harmony is made last of all, and perishes first. And how can such a notion of the soul as this agree with the other?

Not at all, replied Simmias.

And yet, he said, there surely ought to be harmony in a discourse of which harmony is the theme?

There ought, replied Simmias.

But there is no harmony, he said, in the two propositions that knowledge is recollection, and that the soul is a harmony. Which of them will you retain?

I think, he replied, that I have a much stronger faith, Socrates, in the first of the two, which has been fully demonstrated to me, than in the latter, which has not been demonstrated at all, but rests only on probable and plausible grounds; and is therefore believed by the many. I know too well that these arguments from probabilities are impostors, and unless great caution is observed in the use of them, they are apt to be deceptive—in geometry, and in other things too. But the doctrine of knowledge and recollection has been proven to me on trustworthy grounds: and the proof was that the soul must have existed before she came into the body, because to her belongs the essence of which the very name implies existence. Having, as I am convinced, rightly accepted this conclusion, and on sufficient grounds, I must, as I suppose, cease to argue or allow others to argue that the soul is a harmony.

Let me put the matter, Simmias, he said, in another point of view: Do you imagine that a harmony or any other composition can be in a state other than that of the elements, out of which it is compounded?

Certainly not.

Or do or suffer anything other than they do or suffer?

He agreed.

Then a harmony does not, properly speaking, lead the parts or elements which make up the harmony, but only follows them.

He assented.

For harmony cannot possibly have any motion, or sound, or other quality which is opposed to its parts.

That would be impossible, he replied.

And does not the nature of every harmony depend upon the manner in which the elements are harmonized?

I do not understand you, he said.

I mean to say that a harmony admits of degrees, and is more of a harmony, and more completely a harmony, when more truly and fully harmonized, to any extent which is possible; and less of a harmony, and less completely a harmony, when less truly and fully harmonized.

True.

But does the soul admit of degrees? or is one soul in the very least degree more or less, or more or less completely, a soul than another?

Not in the least.

Yet surely of two souls, one is said to have intelligence and virtue, and to be good, and the other to have folly and vice, and to be an evil soul: and this is said truly?

Yes, truly.

But what will those who maintain the soul to be a harmony say of this presence of virtue and vice in the soul?—will they say that here is another harmony, and another discord, and that the virtuous soul is harmonized, and herself being a harmony has another harmony within her, and that the vicious soul is inharmonical and has no harmony within her?

I cannot tell, replied Simmias; but I suppose that something of the sort would be asserted by those who say that the soul is a harmony.

And we have already admitted that no soul is more a soul than another; which is equivalent to admitting that harmony is not more or less harmony, or more or less completely a harmony?

Quite true.

And that which is not more or less a harmony is not more or less harmonized?

True.

And that which is not more or less harmonized cannot have more or less of harmony, but only an equal harmony?

Yes, an equal harmony.

Then one soul not being more nor less absolutely a soul than another, is not more or less harmonized?

Exactly.

And therefore has neither more or less of discord, nor yet of harmony?

She has not.

And having neither more nor less of harmony or of discord, one soul has no more vice or virtue than another, if vice be discord and virtue harmony?

Not at all more.

Or speaking more correctly, Simmias, the soul, if she is a harmony, will never have any vice; because a harmony, being absolutely a harmony, has no part in the inharmonical.

No.

And therefore a soul which is absolutely a soul has no vice?

How can she have, if the previous argument holds?

Then, if all souls are equally by their nature souls, all souls of all living creatures will be equally good?

I agree with you, Socrates, he said.

And can all this be true, think you? he said; for these are the consequences which seem to follow from the assumption that the soul is a harmony?

It cannot be true.

Once more, he said, what ruler is there of the elements of human nature other than the soul, and especially the wise soul? Do you know of any?

Indeed, I do not.

And is the soul in agreement with the affections of the body? or is she at variance with them? For example, when the body is hot and thirsty, does not the soul incline us against drinking? and when the body is hungry, against eating? And this is only one instance out of ten thousand of the opposition of the soul to the things of the body.

Very true.

But we have already acknowledged that the soul, being a harmony, can never utter a note at variance with the tensions and relaxations and vibrations and other affections of the strings out of which she is composed; she can only follow, she cannot lead them?

It must be so, he replied.

And yet do we not now discover the soul to be doing the exact opposite—leading the elements of which she is believed to be composed; almost always opposing and coercing them in all sorts of ways throughout life, sometimes more violently with the pains of medicine and gymnastic; then again more gently; now threatening, now admonishing the desires, passions, fears, as if talking to a thing which is not herself, as Homer in the Odyssey represents Odysseus doing in the words—

He beat his breast, and thus reproached his heart:
Endure, my heart; far worse hast thou endured!

Do you think that Homer wrote this under the idea that the soul is a harmony capable of being led by the affections of the body, and not rather of a nature which should lead and master them—herself a far diviner thing than any harmony?

Yes, Socrates, I quite think so.

Then, my friend, we can never be right in saying that the soul is a harmony, for we should contradict the divine Homer, and contradict ourselves.

True, he said.

Thus much, said Socrates, of Harmonia, your Theban goddess, who has graciously yielded to us; but what shall I say, Cebes, to her husband Cadmus, and how shall I make peace with him?

I think that you will discover a way of propitiating him, said Cebes; I am sure that you have put the argument with Harmonia in a manner that I could never have expected. For when Simmias was mentioning his difficulty, I quite imagined that no answer could be given to him, and therefore I was surprised at finding that his argument could not sustain the first onset of yours, and not impossibly the other, whom you call Cadmus, may share a similar fate.

Nay, my good friend, said Socrates, let us not boast, lest some evil eye should put to flight the word which I am about to speak. That, however, may be left in the hands of those above; while I draw near in Homeric fashion, and try the mettle of your words. Here lies the point:—You want to have it proven to you that the soul is imperishable and immortal, and the philosopher who is confident in death appears to you to have but a vain and foolish confidence, if he believes that he will fare better in the world below than one who has led another sort of life, unless he can prove this: and you say that the demonstration of the strength and divinity of the soul, and of her existence prior to our becoming men, does not necessarily imply her immortality. Admitting the sôul to be longlived, and to have known and done much in a former state, still she is not on that account immortal; and her entrance into the human form may be a sort of disease which is the beginning of dissolution, and may at last, after the toils of life are over, end in that which is called death. And whether the soul enters into the body once only or many times, does not, as you say, make any difference in the fears of individuals. For any man, who is not devoid of sense, must fear, if he has no knowledge and can give no account of the soul's immortality. This, or something like this, I suspect to be your notion, Cebes; and I designedly recur to it in order that nothing may escape us, and that you may, if you wish, add or subtract anything.

But, said Cebes, as far as I see at present, I have nothing to add or subtract: I mean what you say that I mean.

Socrates paused awhile, and seemed to be absorbed in reflection. At length he said: You are raising a tremendous question, Cebes, involving the whole nature of generation and corruption, about which, if you like, I will give you my own experience; and if anything which I say is likely to avail towards the solution of your difficulty you may make use of it.

I should very much like, said Cebes, to hear what you have to say.

Then I will tell you, said Socrates. When I was young, Cebes, I had a prodigious desire to know that department of philosophy which is called the investigation of nature; to know the causes of things, and why a thing is and is created or destroyed appeared to me to be a lofty profession; and I was always agitating myself with the consideration of questions such as these:—Is the growth of animals the result of some decay which the hot and cold principle contracts, as some have said? Is the blood the element with which we think, or the air, or the fire? or perhaps nothing of the kind—but the brain may be the originating power of the perceptions of hearing and sight and smell, and memory and opinion may come from them, and science may be based on memory and opinion when they have attained fixity. And then I went on to examine the corruption of them, and then to the things of heaven and earth, and at last I concluded myself to be utterly and absolutely incapable of these enquiries, as I will satisfactorily prove to you. For I was fascinated by them to such a degree that my eyes grew blind to things which I had seemed to myself, and also to others, to know quite well; I forgot what I had before thought self-evident truths; for example, such a fact as that the growth of man is the result of eating and drinking; for when by the digestion of food flesh is added to flesh and bone to bone, and whenever there is an aggregation of congenial elements, the lesser bulk becomes larger and the small man great. Was not that a reasonable notion?

Yes, said Cebes, I think so.

Well; but let me tell you something more. There was a time when I thought that I understood the meaning of greater and less pretty well; and when I saw a great man standing by a little one, I fancied that one was taller than the other by a head; or one horse would appear to be greater than another horse: and still more clearly did I seem to perceive that ten is two more than eight, and that two cubits are more than one, because two is the double of one.

And what is now your notion of such matters? said Cebes.

I should be far enough from imagining, he replied, that I knew the cause of any of them, by heaven I should; for I cannot satisfy myself that, when one is added to one, the one to which the addition is made becomes two, or that the two units added together make two by reason of the addition. I cannot understand how, when separated from the other, each of them was one and not two, and now, when they are brought together, the mere juxtaposition or meeting of them should be the cause of their becoming two: neither can I understand how the division of one is the way to make two; for then a different cause would produce the same effect,—as in the former instance the addition and juxtaposition of one to one was the cause of two, in this the separation and subtraction of one from the other would be the cause. Nor am I any longer satisfied that I understand the reason why one or anything else is either generated or destroyed or is at all, but I have in my mind some confused notion of a new method, and can never admit the other.

Then I heard some one reading, as he said, from a book of Anaxagoras, that mind was the disposer and cause of all, and I was delighted at this notion, which appeared quite admirable, and I said to myself: If mind is the disposer, mind will dispose all for the best, and put each particular in the best place; and I argued that if any one desired to find out the cause of the generation or destruction or existence of anything, he must find out what state of being or doing or suffering was best for that thing, and therefore a man had only to consider the best for himself and others, and then he would also know the worse, since the same science comprehended both. And I rejoiced to think that I had found in Anaxagoras a teacher of the causes of existence such as I desired, and I imagined that he would tell me first whether the earth is flat or round; and whichever was true, he would proceed to explain the cause and the necessity of this being so, and then he would teach me the nature of the best and show that this was best; and if he said that the earth was in the centre, he would further explain that this position was the best, and I should be satisfied with the explanation given, and not want any other sort of cause. And I thought that I would then go on and ask him about the sun and moon and stars, and that he would explain to me their comparative swiftness, and their returnings and various states, active and passive, and how all of them were for the best. For I could not imagine that when he spoke of mind as the disposer of them, he would give any other account of their being as they are, except that this was best; and I thought that when he had explained to me in detail the cause of each and the cause of all, he would go on to explain to me what was best for each and what was good for all. These hopes I would not have sold for a large sum of money, and I seized the books and read them as fast as I could in my eagerness to know the better and the worse.

What expectations I had formed, and how grievously was I disappointed! As I proceeded, I found my philosopher altogether forsaking mind or any other principle of order, but having recourse to air, and ether, and water, and other eccentricities. I might compare him to a person who began by maintaining generally that mind is the cause of the actions of Socrates, but who, when he endeavoured to explain the causes of my several actions in detail, went on to show that I sit here because my body is made up of bone and muscles; and the bones, as he would say, are hard and have joints which divide them, and the muscles are elastic, and they cover the bones, which have also a covering or environment of flesh and skin which contains them; and as the bones are lifted at their joints by the contraction or relaxation of the muscles, I am able to bend my limbs, and this is why I am sitting here in a curved posture—that is what he would say; and he would have a similar explanation of my talking to you, which he would attribute to sound, and air, and hearing, and he would assign ten thousand other causes of the same sort, forgetting to mention the true cause, which is, that the Athenians have thought fit to condemn me, and accordingly I have thought it better and more right to remain here and undergo my sentence; for I am inclined to think that these muscles and bones of mine would have gone off long ago to Megara or Boeotia—by the dog they would, if they had been moved only by their own idea of what was best, and if I had not chosen the better and nobler part, instead of playing truant and running away, of enduring any punishment which the State inflicts. There is surely a strange confusion of causes and conditions in all this. It may be said, indeed, that without bones and muscles and the other parts of the body I cannot execute my purposes. But to say that I do as I do because of them, and that this is the way in which mind acts, and not from the choice of the best, is a very careless and idle mode of speaking. I wonder that they cannot distinguish the cause from the condition, which the many, feeling about in the dark, are always mistaking and misnaming. And thus one man makes a vortex all round and steadies the earth by the heaven; another gives the air as a support to the earth, which is a sort of broad trough. Any power which in arranging them as they are arranges them for the best never enters into their minds; and instead of finding any superior strength in it, they rather expect to discover another Atlas of the world who is stronger and more everlasting and more containing than the good;—of the obligatory and containing power of the good they think nothing; and yet this is the principle which I would fain learn if any one would teach me. But as I have failed either to discover myself, or to learn of any one else, the nature of the best, I will exhibit to you, if you like, what I have found to be the second best mode of enquiring into the cause.

I should very much like to hear, he replied.

Socrates proceeded:—I thought that as I had failed in the contemplation of true existence, I ought to be careful that I did not lose the eye of my soul; as people may injure their bodily eye by observing and gazing on the sun during an eclipse, unless they take the precaution of only looking at the image reflected in the water, or in some similar medium. So in my own case, I was afraid that my soul might be blinded altogether if I looked at things with my eyes or tried to apprehend them by the help of the senses. And I thought that I had better have recourse to the world of mind and seek there the truth of existence. I dare say that the simile is not perfect—for I am very far from admitting that he who contemplates existences through the medium of thought, sees them only "through a glass darkly," any more than he who considers them in action and operation. However, this was the method which I adopted: I first assumed some principle which I judged to be the strongest, and then I affirmed as true whatever seemed to agree with this, whether relating to the cause or to anything else; and that which disagreed I regarded as untrue. But I should like to explain my meaning more clearly, as I do not think that you as yet understand me.

No indeed, replied Cebes, not very well.

There is nothing new, he said, in what I am about to tell you; but only what I have been always and everywhere repeating in the previous discussion and on other occasions: I want to show you the nature of that cause which has occupied my thoughts. I shall have to go back to those familiar words which are in the mouth of every one, and first of all assume that there is an absolute beauty and goodness and greatness, and the like; grant me this, and I hope to be able to show you the nature of the cause, and to prove the immortality of the soul.

Cebes said: You may proceed at once with the proof, for I grant you this.

Well, he said, then I should like to know whether you agree with me in the next step; for I cannot help thinking, if there be anything beautiful other than absolute beauty, should there be such, that it can be beautiful only in so far as it partakes of absolute beauty—and I should say the same of everything. Do you agree in this notion of the cause?

Yes, he said, I agree.

He proceeded: I know nothing and can understand nothing of any other of those wise causes which are alleged; and if a person says to me that the bloom of colour, or form, or any such thing is a source of beauty, I leave all that, which is only confusing to me, and simply and singly, and perhaps foolishly, hold and am assured in my own mind that nothing makes a thing beautiful but the presence and participation of beauty in whatever way or manner obtained; for as to the manner I am uncertain, but I stoutly contend that by beauty all beautiful things become beautiful. This appears to me to be the safest answer which I can give, either to myself or to another, and to this I cling, in the persuasion that this principle will never be overthrown, and that to myself or to any who asks the question, I may safely reply, That by beauty beautiful things become beautiful. Do you not agree with me?

I do.

And that by greatness only great things become great and greater greater, and by smallness the less become less?

True.

Then if a person were to remark that A is taller by a head than B, and B less by a head than A, you would refuse to admit his statement, and would stoutly contend that what you mean is only that the greater is greater by, and by reason of, greatness, and the less is less only by, and by reason of, smallness; and thus you would avoid the danger of saying that the greater is greater and the less less by the measure of the head, which is the same in both, and would also avoid the monstrous absurdity of supposing that the greater man is greater by reason of the head, which is small. You would be afraid to draw such an inference, would you not?

Indeed, I should, said Cebes, laughing.

In like manner you would be afraid to say that ten exceeded eight by, and by reason of, two; but would say by, and by reason of, number; or you would say that two cubits exceed one cubit not by a half, but by magnitude?—for there is the same liability to error in all these cases.

Very true, he said.

Again, would you not be cautious of affirming that the addition of one to one, or the division of one, is the cause of two? And you would loudly asseverate that you know of no way in which anything comes into existence except by participation in its own proper essence, and consequently, as far as you know, the only cause of two is the participation in duality—this is the way to make two, and the participation in one is the way to make one. You would say: I will let alone puzzles of division and addition—wiser heads than mine may answer them; inexperienced as I am, and ready to start, as the proverb says, at my own shadow, I cannot afford to give up the sure ground of a principle. And if any one assails you there, you would not mind him, or answer him, until you had seen whether the consequences which follow agree with one another or not, and when you are further required to give an explanation of this principle, you would go on to assume a higher principle, and a higher, until you found a resting-place in the best of the higher; but you would not confuse the principle and the consequences in your reasoning, like the Eristics—at least if you wanted to discover real existence. Not that this confusion signifies to them, who never care or think about the matter at all, for they have the wit to be well pleased with themselves however great may be the turmoil of their ideas. But you, if you are a philosopher, will certainly do as I say.

What you say is most true, said Simmias and Cebes, both speaking at once.

Ech. Yes, Phaedo; and I do not wonder at their assenting. Any one who has the least sense will acknowledge the wonderful clearness of Socrates' reasoning.

Phaed. Certainly, Echecrates; and such was the feeling of the whole company at the time.

Ech. Yes, and equally of ourselves, who were not of the company, and are now listening to your recital. But what followed?

Phaed. After all this had been admitted, and they had agreed that ideas exist, and that other things participate in them and derive their names from them, Socrates, if I remember rightly, said:—

This is your way of speaking; and yet when you say that Simmias is greater than Socrates and less than Phaedo, do you not predicate of Simmias both greatness and smallness?

Yes, I do.

But still you allow that Simmias does not really exceed Socrates, as the words may seem to imply, because he is Simmias, but by reason of the size which he has; just as Simmias does not exceed Socrates because he is Simmias, any more than because Socrates is Socrates, but because he has smallness when compared with the greatness of Simmias?

True.

And if Phaedo exceeds him in size, this is not because Phaedo is Phaedo, but because Phaedo has greatness relatively to Simmias, who is comparatively smaller?

That is true.

And therefore Simmias is said to be great, and is also said to be small, because he is in a mean between them, exceeding the smallness of the one by his greatness, and allowing the greatness of the other to exceed his smallness. He added, laughing, I am speaking like a book, but I believe that what I am saying is true.

Simmias assented.

I speak as I do because I want you to agree with me in thinking, not only that absolute greatness will never be great and also small, but that greatness in us or in the concrete will never admit the small or admit of being exceeded: instead of this, one of two things will happen, either the greater will fly or retire before the opposite, which is the less, or at the approach of the less has already ceased to exist; but will not, if allowing or admitting of smallness, be changed by that; even as I, having received and admitted smallness when compared with Simmias, remain just as I was, and am the same small person. And as the idea of greatness cannot condescend ever to be or become small, in like manner the smallness in us cannot be or become great; nor can any other opposite which remains the same ever be or become its own opposite, but either passes away or perishes in the change.

That, replied Cebes, is quite my notion.

Hereupon one of the company, though I do not exactly remember which of them, said: In heaven's name, is not this the direct contrary of what was admitted before—that out of the greater came the less and out of the less the greater, and that opposites were simply generated from opposites; but now this principle seems to be utterly denied.

Socrates inclined his head to the speaker and listened. I like your courage, he said, in reminding us of this. But you do not observe that there is a difference in the two cases. For then we were speaking of opposites in the concrete, and now of the essential opposite which, as is affirmed, neither in us nor in nature can ever be at variance with itself: then, my friend, we were speaking of things in which opposites are inherent and which are called after them, but now about the opposites which are inherent in them and which give their name to them; and these essential opposites will never, as we maintain, admit of generation into or out of one another. At the same time, turning to Cebes, he said: Are you at all disconcerted, Cebes, at our friend's objection?

No, I do not feel so, said Cebes; and yet I cannot deny that I am often disturbed by objections.

Then we are agreed after all, said Socrates, that the opposite will never in any case be opposed to itself?

To that we are quite agreed, he replied.

Yet once more let me ask you to consider the question from another point of view, and see whether you agree with me:—There is a thing which you term heat, and another thing which you term cold?

Certainly.

But are they the same as fire and snow?

Most assuredly not.

Heat is a thing different from fire, and cold is not the same with snow?

Yes.

And yet you will surely admit, that when snow, as was before said, is under the influence of heat, they will not remain snow and heat; but at the advance of the heat, the snow will either retire or perish?

Very true, he replied.

And the fire too at the advance of the cold will either retire or perish; and when the fire is under the influence of the cold, they will not remain as before, fire and cold.

That is true, he said.

And in some cases the name of the idea is not only attached to the idea in an eternal connection, but anything else which, not being the idea, exists only in the form of the idea, may also lay claim to it. I will try to make this clearer by an example:—The odd number is always called by the name of odd?

Very true.

But is this the only thing which is called odd? Are there not other things which have their own name, and yet are called odd, because, although not the same as oddness, they are never without oddness?—that is what I mean to ask—whether numbers, such as the number three, are not of the class of odd. And there are many other examples: would you not say, for example, that three may be called by its proper name, and also be called odd, which is not the same with three? and this may be said not only of three but also of five, and of every alternate number—each of them without being oddness is odd; and in the same way two and four, and the other series of alternate numbers, has every number even, without being evenness. Do you agree?

Of course.

Then now mark the point at which I am aiming:—not only do essential opposites exclude one another, but also concrete things, which, although not in themselves opposed, contain opposites; these, I say, likewise reject the idea which is opposed to that which is contained in them, and when it approaches them they either perish or withdraw. For example: Will not the number three endure annihilation or anything sooner than be converted into an even number, while remaining three?

Very true, said Cebes.

And yet, he said, the number two is certainly not opposed to the number three?

It is not.

Then not only do opposite ideas repel the advance of one another, but also there are other natures which repel the approach of opposites.

Very true, he said.

Suppose, he said, that we endeavour, if possible, to determine what these are.

By all means.

Are they not, Cebes, such as compel the things of which they have possession, not only to take their own form, but also the form of some opposite?

What do you mean?

I mean, as I was just now saying, and as I am sure that you know, that those things which are possessed by the number three must not only be three in number, but must also be odd.

Quite true.

And on this oddness, of which the number three has the impress, the opposite idea will never intrude?

No.

And this impress was given by the odd principle?

Yes.

And to the odd is opposed the even?

True.

Then the idea of the even number will never arrive at three?

No.

Then three has no part in the even?

None.

Then the triad or number three is uneven?

Very true.

To return then to my distinction of natures which are not opposed, and yet do not admit opposites—as, in the instance given, three, although not opposed to the even, does not any the more admit of the even, but always brings the opposite into play on the other side; or as two does not receive the odd, or fire the cold—from these examples (and there are many more of them) perhaps you may be able to arrive at the general conclusion, that not only opposites will not receive opposites, but also that nothing which brings the opposite will admit the opposite of that which it brings, in that to which it is brought. And here let me recapitulate—for there is no harm in repetition. The number five will not admit the nature of the even, any more than ten, which is the double of five, will admit the nature of the odd. The double has another opposite, and is not strictly opposed to the odd, but nevertheless rejects the odd altogether. Nor again will parts in the ratio 3:2, nor any fraction in which there is a half, nor again in which there is a third, admit the notion of the whole, although they are not opposed to the whole: You will agree?

Yes, he said, I entirely agree and go along with you in that.

And now, he said, let us being again; and do not you answer my questions in the words in which I ask it: let me have not the old safe answer of which I spoke at first, but another equally safe, of which the truth will be inferred by you from what has been just said. I mean that if any one asks you "what that is, of which the inherence makes the body hot," you will reply not heat (this is what I call the safe and stupid answer), but fire, a far superior answer, which we are now in a condition to give. Or if any one asks you "why a body is diseased," you will not say from disease, but from fever; and instead of saying that oddness is the cause of odd numbers, you will say that the monad is the cause of them: and so of things in general, as I dare say that you will understand sufficiently without my adducing any further examples.

Yes, he said, I quite understand you.

Tell me, then, what is that of which the inherence will render the body alive?

The soul, he replied.

And is this always the case?

Yes, he said, of course.

Then whatever the soul possesses, to that she comes bearing life?

Yes, certainly.

And is there any opposite to life?

There is, he said.

And what is that?

Death.

Then the soul, as has been acknowledged, will never receive the opposite of what she brings.

Impossible, replied Cebes.

And now, he said, what did we just now call that principle which repels the even?

The odd.

And that principle which repels the musical or the just?

The unmusical, he said, and the unjust.

And what do we call that principle which does not admit of death?

The immortal, he said.

And does the soul admit of death?

No.

Then the soul is immortal?

Yes, he said.

And may we say that this has been proven?

Yes, abundantly proven, Socrates, he replied.

Supposing that the odd were imperishable, must not three be imperishable?

Of course.

And if that which is cold were imperishable, when the warm principle came attacking the snow, must not the snow have retired whole and unmelted—for it could never have perished, nor could it have remained and admitted the heat?

True, he said.

Again, if the uncooling or warm principle were imperishable, the fire when assailed by cold would not have perished or have been extinguished, but would have gone away unaffected?

Certainly, he said.

And the same may be said of the immortal: if the immortal is also imperishable, the soul when attacked by death cannot perish; for the preceding argument shows that the soul will not admit of death, or ever be dead, any more than three or the odd number will admit of the even, or fire, or the heat in the fire, of the cold. Yet a person may say: "But although the odd will not become even at the approach of the even, why may not the odd perish and the even take the place of the odd?" Now to him who makes this objection, we cannot answer that the odd principle is imperishable; for this has not been acknowledged, but if this had been acknowledged, there would have been no difficulty in contending that at the approach of the even the odd principle and the number three took their departure; and the same argument would have held good of fire and heat and any other thing.

Very true.

And the same may be said of the immortal: if the immortal is also imperishable, then the soul will be imperishable as well as immortal; but if not, some other proof of her imperishableness will have to be given.

No other proof is needed, he said; for if the immortal, being eternal, is liable to perish, then nothing is imperishable.

Yes, replied Socrates, and yet all men will agree that God, and the essential form of life, and the immortal in general, will never perish.

Yes, all men, he said—that is true; and what is more, gods, if I am not mistaken, as well as men.

Seeing then that the immortal is indestructible, must not the soul, if she is immortal, be also imperishable?

Most certainly.

Then when death attacks a man, the mortal portion of him may be supposed to die, but the immortal retires at the approach of death and is preserved safe and sound?

True.

Then, Cebes, beyond question, the soul is immortal and imperishable, and our souls will truly exist in another world!

I am convinced, Socrates, said Cebes, and have nothing more to object; but if my friend Simmias, or any one else, has any further objection to make, he had better speak out, and not keep silence, since I do not know to what other season he can defer the discussion, if there is anything which he wants to say or to have said.

But I have nothing more to say, replied Simmias; nor can I see any reason for doubt after what has been said. But I still feel and cannot help feeling uncertain in my own mind, when I think of the greatness of the subject and the feebleness of man.

Yes, Simmias, replied Socrates, that is well said: and I may add that first principles, even if they appear certain, should be carefully considered; and when they are satisfactorily ascertained, then, with a sort of hesitating confidence in human reason, you may, I think, follow the course of the argument; and if that be plain and clear, there will be no need for any further enquiry.

Very true. . . .

. . . Wherefore, I say, let a man be of good cheer about his soul, who having cast away the pleasures and ornaments of the body as alien to him and working harm rather than good, has sought after the pleasures of knowledge; and has arrayed the soul, not in some foreign attire, but in her own proper jewels, temperance, and justice, and courage, and nobility, and truth—in these adorned she is ready to go on her journey to the world below, when her hour comes. You, Simmias and Cebes, and all other men, will depart at some time or other. Me already, as a tragic poet would say, the voice of fate calls. Soon I must drink the poison; and I think that I had better repair to the bath first, in order that the women may not have the trouble of washing my body after I am dead.

When he had done speaking, Crito said: And have you any commands for us, Socrates—anything to say about your children, or any other matter in which we can serve you?

Nothing particular, Crito, he replied: only, as I have always told you, take care of yourselves; that is a service which you may be ever rendering to me and mine and to all of us, whether you promise to do so or not. But if you have no thought for yourselves, and care not to walk according to the rule which I have prescribed for you, not now for the first time, however much you may profess or promise at the moment, it will be of no avail.

We will do our best, said Crito: And in what way shall we bury you?

In any way that you like; but you must get hold of me, and take care that I do not run away from you. Then he turned to us, and added with a smile:—I cannot make Crito believe that I am the same Socrates who have been talking and conducting the argument; he fancies that I am the other Socrates whom he will soon see, a dead body—and he asks, How shall he bury me? And though I have spoken many words in the endeavour to show that when I have drunk the poison I shall leave you and go to the joys of the blessed,—these words of mine, with which I was comforting you and myself, have had, as I perceive, no effect upon Crito. And therefore I want you to be surety for me to him now, as at the trial he was surety to the judges for me: but let the promise be of another sort; for he was surety for me to the judges that I would remain, and you must be my surety to him that I shall not remain, but go away and depart; and then he will suffer less at my death, and not be grieved when he sees my body being burned or buried. I would not have him sorrow at my hard lot, or say at the burial, Thus we lay out Socrates, or, Thus we follow him to the grave or bury him; for false words are not only evil in themselves, but they inflict the soul with evil. Be of good cheer then, my dear Crito, and say that you are burying my body only, and do with that whatever is usual, and what you think best.

When he had spoken these words, he arose and went into a chamber to bathe; Crito followed him and told us to wait. So we remained behind, talking and thinking of the subject of discourse, and also of the greatness of our sorrow; he was like a father of whom we were being bereaved, and we were about to pass the rest of our lives as orphans. When he had taken the bath his children were brought to him (he had two young sons and an elder one); and the women of his family also came, and he talked to them and gave them a few directions in the presence of Crito; then he dismissed them and returned to us.

Now the hour of sunset was near, for a good deal of time had passed while he was within. When he came out, he sat down with us again after his bath, but not much was said. Soon the jailer, who was the servant of the Eleven, entered and stood by him, saying:—To you, Socrates, whom I know to be the noblest and gentlest and best of all who ever came to this place, I will not impute the angry feeling of other men, who rage and swear at me, when, in obedience to the authorities, I bid them drink the poison—indeed, I am sure that you will not be angry with me; for others, as you are aware, and not I, are to blame. And so fare you well, and try to bear lightly what must needs be—you know my errand. Then bursting into tears he turned away and went out.

Socrates looked at him and said: I return your good wishes, and will do as you bid. Then turning to us, he said, How charming the man is: since I have been in prison he has always been coming to see me, and at times he would talk to me, and was as good to me as could be, and now see how generously he sorrows on my account. We must do as he says, Crito; and therefore let the cup be brought, if the poison is prepared: if not, let the attendant prepare some.

Yet, said Crito, the sun is still upon the hill-tops, and I know that many a one has taken the draught late, and after the announcement has been made to him, he has eaten and drunk, and enjoyed the society of his beloved: do not hurry—there is time enough.

Socrates said: Yes, Crito, and they of whom you speak are right in so acting, for they think that they will be gainers by the delay; but I am right in not following their example, for I do not think that I should gain anything by drinking the poison a little later; I should only be ridiculous in my own eyes for sparing and saving a life which is already forfeit. Please then to do as I say, and not to refuse me.

Crito made a sign to the servant, who was standing by; and he went out, and having been absent for some time, returned with the jailer carrying the cup of poison. Socrates said: You, my good friend, who are experienced in these matters, shall give me directions how I am to proceed. The man answered: You have only to walk about until your legs are heavy, and then to lie down, and the poison will act. At the same time he handed the cup to Socrates, who in the easiest and gentlest manner, without the least fear or change of colour or feature, looking at the man with all his eyes. Echecrates, as his manner was, took the cup and said: What do you say about making a libation out of this cup to any god? May I, or not? The man answered: We only prepare, Socrates, just so much as we deem enough. I understand, he said: but I may and must ask the gods to prosper my journey from this to the other world—even so—and so be it according to my prayer. Then raising the cup to his lips, quite readily and cheerfully he drank off the poison. And hitherto most of us had been able to control our sorrow; but now when we saw him drinking, and saw too that he had finished the draught, we could no longer forbear, and in spite of myself my own tears were flowing fast; so that I covered my face and wept, not for him, but at the thought of my own calamity in having to part from such a friend. Nor was I the first; for Crito, when he found himself unable to restrain his tears, had got up, and I followed; and at that moment, Appollodorus, who had been weeping all the time, broke out in a loud and passionate cry which made cowards of us all. Socrates alone retained his calmness: What is this strange outcry? he said. I sent away the women mainly in order that they might not misbehave in this way, for I have been told that a man should die in peace. Be quiet then, and have patience. When we heard his words we were ashamed, and refrained our tears; and he walked about until, as he said, his legs began to fail, and then he lay on his back, according to directions, and the man who gave him the poison now and then looked at his feet and legs; and after a while he pressed his foot hard, and asked him if he could feel; and he said, No; and then his leg, and so upwards and upwards, and showed us that he was cold and stiff. And he felt them himself, and said: When the poison reaches the heart, that will be the end. He was beginning to grow cold about the groin, when he uncovered his face, for he had covered himself up, and said—they were his last words—he said: Crito, I owe a cock to Asclepius; will you remember to pay the debt? The debt shall be paid, said Crito; is there anything else? There was no answer to this question; but in a minute or two a movement was heard, and the attendants uncovered him; his eyes were set, and Crito closed his eyes and mouth.

Such was the end, Echecrates, of our friend; concerning whom I may truly say, that of all men of his time whom I have known, he was the wisest and justest and best.

On the Immortality of the Soul

DAVID HUME

By the mere light of reason it seems difficult to prove the immortality of the soul; the arguments for it are commonly derived either from metaphysical topics, or moral, or physical. But in reality it is the gospel, and the gospel alone, that has brought *life and immortality to light*.

I

Metaphysical topics suppose that the soul is immaterial, and that it is impossible for thought to belong to a material substance. But just metaphysics teach us, that the notion of substance is wholly confused and imperfect; and that we have no other idea of any substance, than as an aggregate of particular qualities inhering in an unknown something. Matter, therefore, and spirit, are at bottom equally unknown; and we cannot determine what qualities inhere in the one or in the other. They likewise teach us, that nothing can be decided *à priori* concerning any cause or effect; and that experience, being the only source of our judgments of this nature, we cannot know from any other principle, whether matter, by its structure or arrangement, may not be the cause of thought. Abstract reasonings cannot decide any question of fact or existence. But admitting a spiritual substance to be dispersed throughout the universe, like the ethereal fire of the Stoics, and to be the only inherent subject of thought, we have reason to conclude from *analogy*, that nature uses it after the manner she does the other substance, *matter*. She employs it as a kind of paste or clay; modifies it into a variety of forms and existences; dissolves after a time each modification, and from its substance erects a new form. As the same material substance may successively compose the bodies of all animals, the same spiritual substance may compose their minds: their consciousness or that system of thought which they formed during life, may be continually dissolved by death, and nothing interests them in the new modification. The most positive assertors of the mortality of the soul never denied the immortality of its substance; and that an immaterial substance, as well as a material, may lose its memory or consciousness, appears in part from experience, if the soul be immaterial. Reasoning from the common course of nature, and without supposing any new interposition of the Supreme Cause, which ought always to be excluded from philosophy, *what is incorruptible must also be ingenerable*. The soul therefore, if immortal, existed before our birth; and if the former existence noways concerned us, neither will the latter. Animals undoubtedly feel, think, love, hate, will, and even reason, though in a more imperfect manner than men: are their souls also immaterial and immortal?

II

Let us now consider the moral arguments,

David Hume (1711-1776) is probably the principal representative of the "British Empiricist" tradition in philosophy. This is a posthumously published essay from his *Two Essays on Suicide and Immortality* (1777).

chiefly those derived from the justice of God, which is supposed to be further interested in the future punishment of the vicious and reward of the virtuous. But these arguments are grounded on the supposition that God has attributes beyond what he has exerted in this universe, with which alone we are acquainted. Whence do we infer the existence of these attributes? It is very safe for us to affirm, that whatever we know the Deity to have actually done is best; but it is very dangerous to affirm that he must always do what to us seems best. In how many instances would this reasoning fail us with regard to the present world? But if any purpose of nature be clear, we may affirm, that the whole scope and intention of man's creation, so far as we can judge by natural reason, is limited to the present life. With how weak a concern from the original inherent structure of the mind and passions, does he ever look further? What comparison either for steadiness or efficacy, betwixt so floating an idea and the most doubtful persuasion of any matter of fact that occurs in common life? There arise indeed in some minds some unaccountable terrors with regard to futurity; but these would quickly vanish were they not artificially fostered by precept and education. And those who foster them, what is their motive? Only to gain a livelihood, and to acquire power and riches in this world. Their very zeal and industry, therefore, are an argument against them.

What cruelty, what iniquity, what injustice in nature, to confine all our concern, as well as all our knowledge, to the present life, if there be another scene still waiting us of infinitely greater consequence? Ought this barbarous deceit to be ascribed to a beneficent and wise Being? Observe with what exact proportion the task to be performed, and the performing powers, are adjusted throughout all nature. If the reason of man gives him great superiority above other animals, his necessities are proportionably multiplied upon him: his whole time, his whole capacity, activity, courage, and passion, find sufficient employment in fencing against the miseries of his present condition; and frequently, nay, almost always, are too slender for the business assigned them. A pair of shoes, perhaps, was never yet wrought to the highest degree of perfection which that commodity is capable of attaining; yet it is necessary, at least very useful, that there should be some politicians and moralists, even some geometers, poets, and philosophers among mankind. The powers of men are no more superior to their wants, considered merely in this life, than those of foxes and hares are, compared to *their* wants and to their period of existence. The inference from parity of reason is therefore obvious.

On the theory of the soul's mortality, the inferiority of women's capacity is easily accounted for. Their domestic life requires no higher faculties either of mind or body. This circumstance vanishes and becomes absolutely insignificant on the religious theory: the one sex has an equal task to perform as the other; their powers of reason and resolution ought also to have been equal, and both of them infinitely greater than at present. As every effect implies a cause, and that another, till we reach the first cause of all, which is the Deity; every thing that happens is ordained by him, and nothing can be the object of his punishment or vengeance. By what rule are punishments and rewards distributed? What is the Divine standard of merit and demerit? Shall we suppose that human sentiments have place in the Deity? How bold that hypothesis! We have no conception of any other sentiments. According to human sentiments, sense, courage, good-manners, industry, prudence, genius, etc. are essential parts of personal merits. Shall we therefore erect an elysium for poets and heroes like that of ancient mythology? Why confine all rewards to one species of virtue? Punishment, without any proper end or purpose, is inconsistent with *our* ideas of goodness and justice; and no end can be served by it after the whole scene is closed. Punishment, according to *our* conception, should bear some proportion to the offence. Why then eternal punishment for the temporary offences of so frail a creature as man? Can any one approve of Alexander's rage, who intended to exterminate a whole nation because they had seized his favorite horse Bucephalus?[1]

Heaven and hell suppose two distinct species of men, the good and the bad; but the greatest part of mankind float betwixt vice and virtue. Were one to go round the world with an intention of giving a good supper to the righteous and a sound drubbing to the wicked, he would frequently be embarrassed in his choice, and would find the merits and demerits of most men and women scarcely amount to the value of either. To suppose measures of approbation and blame different from the human confounds every thing. Whence do we learn that there is such a thing as moral distinctions, but from our own sentiments? What man who has not met with personal provocation (or what good-natured man who has) could inflict on crimes, from the sense of blame alone, even the common, legal, frivolous punishments? And does any thing steel the breast of judges and juries against the sentiments of humanity but reflection on necessity and public interest? By the Roman law, those who had been guilty of parricide, and confessed their crime, were put into a sack along with an ape, a dog, and a serpent, and thrown into the river. Death alone was the punishment of those who denied their guilt, however fully proved. A criminal was tried before Augustus, and condemned after a full conviction; but the humane emperor, when he put the last interrogatory, gave it such a turn as to lead the wretch into a denial of his guilt. "You surely (said the prince) did not kill your father?"[2] This lenity suits our natural ideas of *right* even towards the greatest of all criminals, and even though it prevents so inconsiderable a sufferance. Nay, even the most bigoted priest would naturally without reflection approve of it, provided the crime was not heresy or infidelity; for as these crimes hurt himself in his *temporal* interest and advantages, perhaps he may not be altogether so indulgent to them. The chief source of moral ideas is the reflection on the interests of human society. Ought these interests, so short, so frivolous, to be guarded by punishments eternal and infinite? The damnation of one man is an infinitely greater evil in the universe than the subversion of a thousand millions of kingdoms. Nature has rendered human infancy peculiarly frail and mortal, as it were on purpose to refute the notion of a probationary state; the half of mankind die before they are rational creatures.

III

The physical arguments from the analogy of nature are strong for the mortality of the soul; and are really the only philosophical arguments which ought to be admitted with regard to this question, or indeed any question of fact. Where any two objects are so closely connected that all alterations which we have ever seen in the one are attended with proportionable alterations in the other; we ought to conclude, by all rules of analogy, that, when there are still greater alterations produced in the former, and it is totally dissolved, there follows a total dissolution of the latter. Sleep, a very small effect on the body, is attended with a temporary extinction, at least a great confusion in the soul. The weakness of the body and that of the mind in infancy are exactly proportioned; their vigor in manhood, their sympathetic disorder in sickness, their common gradual decay in old age. The step further seems unavoidable; their common dissolution in death. The last symptoms which the mind discovers, are disorder, weakness, insensibility, and stupidity; the forerunners of its annihilation. The further progress of the same causes increasing, the same effects totally extinguish it. Judging by the usual analogy of nature, no form can continue when transferred to a condition of life very different from the original one in which it was placed. Trees perish in the water, fishes in the air, animals in the earth. Even so small a difference as that of climate is often fatal. What reason then to imagine, that an immense alteration, such as is made on the soul by the dissolution of its body, and all its organs of thought and sensation, can be effected without the dissolution of the whole? Every thing is in common betwixt soul and body. The organs of the one are all of them the organs of the other; the existence, therefore, of the one must be dependent on the other. The souls of animals are allowed to be mortal; and these bear so near a resemblance to the souls of men, that the analogy from one to the other forms a very strong argument. Their bodies are not more resembling, yet no one rejects the argument drawn from comparative anatomy. The Metempsychosis is therefore the only system of this kind that philosophy can hearken to.

Nothing in this world is perpetual; every thing, however, seemingly firm, is in continual flux and change: the world itself gives symptoms of frailty and dissolution. How contrary to analogy, therefore, to imagine that one single form, seeming the frailest of any, and subject to the greatest disorders, is immortal and indissoluble? What theory is that! how lightly, not to say how rashly, entertained! How to dispose of the infinite number of posthumous existences ought also to embarrass the religious theory. Every planet in every solar system, we are at liberty to imagine peopled with intelligent mortal beings, at least we can fix on no other supposition. For these then a new universe must every generation be created beyond the bounds of the present universe, or one must have been created at first so prodigiously wide as to admit of this continual influx of beings. Ought such bold suppositions to be received by any philosophy, and that merely on the pretext of a bare possibility? When it is asked, whether Agamemnon, Thersites, Hannibal, Varro, and every stupid clown that ever existed in Italy, Scythia, Bactria, or Guinea, are now alive; can any man think, that a scrutiny of nature will furnish arguments strong enough to answer so strange a question in the affirmative? The want of argument without revelation sufficiently establishes the negative. *Quanto facilius*, says Pliny,[3] *certiusque sibi quemque credere, ac specimen securitatis antigene tali sumere experimento.* Our insensibility before the composition of the body seems to natural reason a proof of a like state after dissolution. Were our horrors of annihilation an original passion, not the effect of our general love of happiness, it would rather prove the mortality of the soul: for as nature does nothing in vain, she would never give us a horror against an impossible event. She may give us a horror against an unavoidable event, provided our endeavors, as in the present case, may often remove it to some distance. Death is in the end unavoidable; yet the human species could not be preserved had not nature inspired us with an aversion towards it. All doctrines are to be suspected which are favored by our passions; and the hopes and fears which gave rise to this doctrine are very obvious.

It is an infinite advantage in every controversy to defend the negative. If the question be out of the common experienced course of nature, this circumstance is almost if not altogether decisive. By what arguments or analogies can we prove any state of existence, which no one ever saw, and which no way resembles any that ever was seen? Who will repose such trust in any pretended philosophy as to admit upon its testimony the reality of so marvellous a scene? Some new species of logic is requisite for that purpose, and some new faculties of the mind, that they may enable us to comprehend that logic.

Nothing could set in a fuller light the infinite obligations which mankind have to Divine revelation, since we find that no other medium could ascertain this great and important truth.

NOTES

1. Quintus Curtius [*History of Alexander*, VI. 5]

2. Suetonius, *The Deified Augustus*, II. 3.

3. ["But how much easier and safer for each to trust in himself, and for us to derive our idea of future tranquillity from our experience of it before birth!" Pliny, *Natural History* VII. 55, tr. H. Rackham (Cambridge, Mass.: "Loeb Classical Library," 1947).]

Immortality

PETER GEACH

Everybody knows that men die, and though most of us have read the advertisement 'Millions now living will never die', it is commonly believed that every man born will some day die; yet historically many men have believed that there is a life after death, and indeed that this after-life will never end. That is: there has been a common belief both in *survival* of bodily death and in *immortality*. Now a philosopher might interest himself specially in immortality, as opposed to survival; conceding survival for the sake of argument, he might raise and examine conceptual difficulties about *endless* survival. But the question of immortality cannot even arise unless men do survive bodily death; and, as we shall see, there are formidable difficulties even about survival. It is these difficulties I shall be discussing, not the special ones about endless survival.

There are various views as to the character of the afterlife. One view is that man has a subtle, ordinarily invisible, body which survives the death of the ordinary gross body. This view has a long history, and seems to be quite popular in England at the moment. So far as I can see, the view is open to no philosophical objection, but likewise wholly devoid of philosophical interest; the mind-body problem must after all be just the same for an ethereal body as for a gross one. There could clearly be no philosophical reasons for belief in such subtle bodies, but only empirical ones; such reasons are in fact alleged, and we are urged to study the evidence.

Philosophy can at this point say something: about what sort of evidence would be required. The existence of subtle bodies is a matter within the purview of physical science; evidence for it should satisfy such criteria of existence as physicists use, and should refer not only to what people say they have seen, heard, and felt, but also to effects produced by subtle bodies on physicists' apparatus. The believer in 'subtle bodies' must, I think, accept the physicists's criteria of existence; there would surely be a conceptual muddle in speaking of 'bodies' but saying they might be incapable of affecting any physical apparatus. For what distinguishes real physical objects from hallucinations, even collective hallucinations, is that physical objects act on one another, and do so in just the same way whether they are being observed or not; this is the point, I think, at which a phenomenalist account of physical objects breaks down. If, therefore, 'subtle bodies' produce no physical effects, they are not bodies at all.

How is it, then, that 'subtle bodies' have never forced themselves upon the attention of physicists, as X-rays did, by spontaneous interference with physical apparatus? There are supposed to be a lot of 'subtle bodies' around, and physicists have a lot of delicate apparatus; yet physicists not engaged in psychical research are never bothered by the interference of 'subtle bodies'. In the circumstances I think it wholly irrational to believe in 'subtle

Peter Geach is professor of logic at the University of Leeds, England.

Reprinted by permission of Schocken Books Inc. from *God and the Soul* by Peter Geach.

bodies'. Moreover, when I who am no physicist am invited to study the evidence for 'subtle bodies', I find that very fact suspicious. The discoverers of X-rays and electrons did not appeal to the lay public, but to physicists, to study the evidence; and so long as physicists (at least in general) refuse to take 'subtle bodies' seriously, a study of evidence for them by a layman like myself would be a waste of time.

When *philosophers* talk of life after death, what they mostly have in mind is a doctrine that may be called Platonic—it is found in its essentials in the *Phaedo*. It may be briefly stated thus: 'Each man's make-up includes a wholly immaterial thing, his mind and soul. It is the mind that sees and hears and feels and thinks and chooses—in a word, is conscious. The mind is the person; the body is extrinsic to the person, like a suit of clothes. Though body and mind affect one another, the mind's existence is quite independent of the body's; and there is thus no reason why the mind should not go on being conscious indefinitely after the death of the body, and even if it never again has with any body that sort of connexion which it now has.

This Platonic doctrine has a strong appeal, and there are plausible arguments in its favour. It appears a clearly intelligible supposition that I should go on after death having the same sorts of experience as I now have, even if I then have no body at all. For although these experiences are connected with processes in the body—sight, for example, with processes in the eyes, optic nerves, and brain—nevertheless there is no necessity of thought about the connexion—it is easy to conceive of someone who has no eyes having the experience called sight. He would be having the same experience as I who have eyes do, and I know what sort of experience that is because I have the experience.

Let us now examine these arguments. When a word can be used to stand for a private experience, like the words 'seeing' or 'pain', it is certainly tempting to suppose that the giving these words a meaning is itself a private experience—indeed that they get their meaning just from the experiences they stand for. But this is really nonsense: if a sentence I hear or utter contains the word 'pain', do I help myself to grasp its sense by giving myself a pain? Might not this be, on the contrary, rather distracting? As Wittgenstein said, to think you get the concept of pain by having a pain is like thinking you get the concept of a minus quantity by running up an overdraft. Our concepts of seeing, hearing, pain, anger, etc., apply in the first instance to human beings; we willingly extend them (say) to cats, dogs, and horses, but we rightly feel uncomfortable about extending them to very alien creatures and speaking of a slug's hearing or an angry ant. Do we know at all what it would be to apply such concepts to an immaterial being? I think not.

One may indeed be tempted to evade difficulties by saying: 'An immaterial spirit is angry or in pain if it feels *the same way* as I do when I am angry or in pain'. But, as Wittgenstein remarked, this is just like saying: Of course I know what it is for the time on the Sun to be five o'clock: it's five o'clock on the Sun at the very moment when it's five o'clock here!'—which plainly gets us no forrader. If there is a difficulty in passing from 'I am in pain' or 'Smith is in pain' to an 'immaterial spirit is in pain', there is equally a difficulty in passing from 'Smith feels the same way as I do' to an 'immaterial spirit feels the same way as I do'.

In fact, the question is, whether a private experience does suffice, as is here supposed, to give a meaning to a psychological verb like 'to see'. I am not trying to throw doubt on there being private experiences; of course men have thoughts they do not utter and pains they do not show; of course I may see something without any behaviour to show I see it; nor do I mean to emasculate these propositions with neo-behaviourist dialectics. But it is not a question of whether seeing is (sometimes) a private experience, but whether one can attach meaning to the verb 'to see' by a private uncheckable performance; and this is what I maintain one cannot do to any word at all.

One way to show that a word's being given a meaning cannot be a private uncheckable performance is the following: We can take a man's word for it that a linguistic expression has given him some private experience—e.g. has revived a painful memory, evoked a visual image, or given him a thrill in the pit of the stomach. But we cannot take his word for it that he attached a sense to the expression, even if we accept his *bona fides;* for later events may convince us that in fact he attached no sense to the expression. Attaching sense to an expression is thus not to be identified with any private experience that accompanies the expression; and I have argued this, not by attacking the idea of private experiences, but by contrasting the attaching of sense to an expression with some typical private experiences that may be connected with the expression.

We give words a sense—whether they are psychological words like 'seeing' and 'pain', or other words—by getting into a way of using them; and though a man can invent for himself a way of using a word, it must be a way that other people *could* follow—otherwise we are back to the idea of conferring meaning by a private uncheckable performance. Well, how do we eventually use such words as 'see', 'hear', 'feel', when we have got into the way of using them? We do not exercise these concepts only so as to pick our cases of seeing and the rest in our separate worlds of sense-experience; on the contrary, these concepts are used in association with a host of other concepts relating, e.g., to the physical characteristics of what is seen and the behaviour of those who do see. In saying this I am not putting forward a theory, but just reminding you of very familiar features in the everyday use of the verb 'to see' and related expressions; our ordinary talk about seeing would cease to be intelligible if there were cut out of it such expressions as 'I can't see, it's too far off', 'I caught his eye', 'Don't look round', etc. Do not let the bogy of behaviourism scare you off observing these features; I am not asking you to believe that 'to see' is itself a word for a kind of behaviour. But the concept of seeing can be maintained only because it has threads of connexion with these other non-psychological concepts; break enough threads, and the concept of seeing collapses.

We can now see the sort of difficulties that arise if we try to apply concepts like *seeing* and *feeling* to disembodied spirits. Let me give an acutal case of a psychological concept's collapsing when its connexions were broken. Certain hysterics claimed to have a magnetic sense; it was discovered, however, that their claim to be having magnetic sensations did not go with the actual presence of a magnet in their environment, but only with their belief that a magnet was present. Psychologists did not now take the line: We may take the patients' word for it that they have peculiar sensations—only the term 'magnetic sensations' has proved inappropriate, as having been based on a wrong causal hypothesis. On the contrary, patients' reports of magnetic sensations were thenceforward written off as being among the odd things that hysterical patients sometimes say. Now far fewer of the ordinary connexions of a sensation-concept were broken here than would be broken if we tried to apply a sensation-concept like seeing to a disembodied spirit.

If we conclude that the ascription of sensations and feelings to a disembodied spirit does not make sense, it does not obviously follow, as you might think, that we must deny the possibility of disembodied spirits altogether. Aquinas for example was convinced that there are disembodied spirits but ones that cannot see or hear or feel pain or fear or anger; he allowed them no mental operations except those of thought and will. Damned spirits would suffer from frustration of their evil will, but not from aches and pains or foul odours or the like. It would take me too far to discuss whether his reasons for thinking this were good; I want to show what follows from this view. In our human life thinking and choosing are intricately bound up with a play of sensations and mental images and emotions; if after a lifetime of thinking and choosing in this human way there is left only a disembodied mind whose thought is wholly nonsensuous and whose rational choices are unaccompanied by any human feelings—can we still say there remains the same person? Surely not: such a soul is not the person who died but a mere remnant of him. And this is just what Aquinas says (in his commentary on I Corinthians 15): *anima mea no est ego,* my soul is not I; and if only souls are saved, *I* am not saved, nor is any man. If some time after Peter Geach's death there is again a man identifiable as Peter Geach, then Peter Geach again, or still, lives: otherwise not.

Though a surviving mental remnant of a person, preserving some sort of physical continuity with the man you knew, would not be Peter Geach, this does not show that such a measure of survival is not possible; but its possibility does raise serious difficulties, even if such dehumanized thinking and willing is really conceivable at all. For *whose* thinking would this be? Could we tell whether *one* or *many* disembodied spirits thought the thoughts in question? We touch here on the old problem: what constitutes there being two disembodied minds (at the same time, that is)? Well, what constitutes there being two pennies? It may happen that one penny is bent and corroded while another is in mint condition; but such differences cannot be what make the two pennies to be two—the two pennies could not have these varied fortunes if they were not already distinct. In the same way, differences of memories or of aims could not constitute the difference between two disembodied minds, but could only supervene upon a difference already existing. What does constitute the difference between two disembodied human minds? If we could find no ground of differentiation, then not only would that which survived be a mere remnant of a person—there would not even be a surviving individuality.

Could we say that souls are different because in the first instance they were souls of different bodies, and then remain different on that account when they are no longer embodied? I do not think this solution would do at all if differentiation by reference to different bodies were merely retrospective. It might be otherwise if we held, with Aquinas, that the relation to a body was not merely retrospective—that each disembodied human soul permanently retained a capacity for reunion to such a body as would reconstitute a man identifiable with the man who died. This might satisfactorily account for the individuation of disembodied human souls; they would differ by being fitted for reunion to different bodies, but it would entail that the possibility of disembodied human souls stood or fell with the *possibility* of a dead man's living again *as a man*.

Some Scholastics held that just as two pennies or two cats differ by being different bits of matter, so human souls differ by containing different 'spiritual matter'. Aquinas regarded this idea as self-contradictory; it is at any rate much too obscure to count as establishing a possibility of distinct disembodied souls. Now this recourse to 'spiritual matter' might well strike us merely as the filling of a conceptual lacuna with a nonsensical piece of jargon. But it is not only Scholastic philosophers who assimilate mental processes to physical ones, only thinking of mental processes as taking place in an *immaterial* medium; and many people think it easy to conceive of distinct disembodied souls because they are illegitimately ascribing to souls a sort of differentiation—say, by existing *side by side*—that can be significantly ascribed only to bodies. The same goes for people who talk about souls as being 'fused' or 'merged' in a Great Soul; they are imagining some such change in the world of souls as occurs to a drop of water falling into a pool or to a small lump of wax that is rubbed into a big one. Now if only people *talked* about 'spiritual matter', instead of just thinking in terms of it unawares, their muddle could be more easily detected and treated.

To sum up what I have said so far: The possibility of life after death for Peter Geach appears to stand or fall with the possibility of there being once again a man identifiable as Peter Geach. The existence of a disembodied soul would not be a survival of the person Peter Geach; and even in such a truncated form, individual existence seems to require at least a persistent possibility of the soul's again entering into the make-up of a man who is identifiably Peter Geach.

This suggests a form of belief in survival that seems to have become quite popular of late in the West—at any rate as a half-belief—namely, the belief in reincarnation. Could it in fact have a clear sense to say that a baby born in Oxford this year is Hitler living again?

How could it be shown that the Oxford baby was Hitler? Presumably by memories and similarities of character. I maintain that no amount of such evidence would make it reasonable to identify the baby as Hitler. Similarities of character are of themselves obviously insufficient. As regards memories: If on growing up the Oxford baby reveals knowledge of what we should ordinarily say only Hitler can have known, does this establish a presumption that the child is Hitler? Not at all. In normal circumstances we know when to say 'only he can have known that'; when queer things start happening, we have no right to stick to our ordinary assumptions as to what can be known. And suppose that for some time the child 'is' Hitler by our criteria, and later on 'is' Goering? or might not several children simultaneously satisfy the criteria for 'being' Hitler?

These are not merely captious theoretical objections. Spirit-mediums, we are told, will in trance convincingly enact the part of various people: sometimes of fictitious characters, like Martians, or Red Indians ignorant of Red Indian languages, or the departed 'spirits' of Johnny Walker and John Jamieson; there are even stories of mediums' giving convincing 'messages' from people who were alive and normally conscious at the time of the 'message'. Now a medium giving messages from the dead is not said to be the dead man, but rather to be controlled by his spirit. What then can show whether the Oxford child 'is' Hitler or is merely 'controlled' by Hitler's spirit? For all these reasons the appearance that there might be good evidence for reincarnation dissolves on a closer view.

Nor do I see, for that matter, how the mental phenomena of mediumship could ever make it reasonable to believe that a human soul survived and communicated. For someone to carry on in a dramatic way quite out of his normal character is a common hysterical symptom; so if a medium does this in a trance, it is no evidence of anything except an abnormal condition of the medium's own mind. As for the medium's telling us things that 'only the dead can have known', I repeat that in these queer cases we have no right to stick to our ordinary assumptions about what can be known. Moreover, as I said, there are cases, as well-authenticated as any, in which the medium convincingly enacted the part of X and told things that 'Only X could have known' when X was in fact alive and normally conscious, so that his soul was certainly not trying to communicate by way of the medium! Even if we accept all the queer stories of spirit-messages, the result is only to open up a vast field of queer possibilities—not in the least to force us to say that mediums were possessed by such-and-such souls. This was argued by Bradley long ago in his essay 'The Evidences of Spiritualism', and he has never been answered.

How could a living man be rightly identifiable with a man who previously died? Let us first consider our normal criteria of personal identity. When we say an old man is the same person as the baby born seventy years before, we believe that the old man has material continuity with the baby. Of course this is not a criterion in the sense of being what we judge identity by; for the old man will not have been watched for seventy years continuously, even by rota! But something we regarded as disproving the material continuity (e.g. absence of a birthmark, different fingerprints) would disprove personal identity. Further, we believe that material continuity establishes a one-one relation: one baby grows up into one old man, and one old man has grown out of one baby. (Otherwise there would have to be at some stage a drastic change, a fusion or fission, which we should regard as destroying personal identity.) Moreover, the baby-body never coexists with the aged body, but develops into it.

Now it seems to me that we cannot rightly identify a man living 'again' with a man who died unless *material* conditions of identity are fulfilled. There must be some one-one relation of material continuity between the old body and the new. I am not saying that the new body need be even in part materially *identical* with the old; this, unlike material continuity, is not required for personal identity, for the old man need not have kept even a grain of matter from the baby of seventy years ago.

We must here notice an important fallacy. I was indicating just now that I favour Aquinas's doctrine that two coexisting souls differ by being related to two different bodies and that two coexisting human bodies, like two pennies or two cats, differ by being different bits of matter. Well, if it is difference of matter that makes two bodies different, it may seem to follow that a body can maintain its identity only if at least some identifiable matter remains in it all the time; otherwise it is no more the same body than the wine in a cask that is continuously emptied and refilled is the same wine. But just this is the fallacy: it does not follow, if difference in a certain respect at a certain time suffices to show non-identity, that sameness in that respect over a period of time is necessary to identity. Thus, Sir John Cutler's famous pair of stockings were the same pair all the time, although they started as silk and by much mending ended as worsted; people have found it hard to see this, because if at a given time there is a silk pair and also a worsted pair then there are two pairs. Again, it is clear that the same man may be in Birmingham at noon and in Oxford at 7 p.m., even though a man in Birmingham and a man in Oxford at a given time must be two different men. Once formulated, the fallacy is obvious, but it might be deceptive if not formulated.

'Why worry even about material continuity? Would not mental continuity be both necessary and sufficient?' Necessary, but not sufficient. Imagine a new 'Tichborne' trial. The claimant knows all the things he ought to know, and talks convincingly to the long-lost heir's friends. But medical evidence about scars and old fractures and so on indicates that he cannot be the man; moreover, the long-lost heir's corpse is decisively identified at an exhumation. Such a case would bewilder us, particularly if the claimant's *bona fides* were manifest. (He might, for example, voluntarily take a lie-detecting test.) But we should certainly not allow the evidence of mental connexions with the long-lost heir to settle the matter in the claimant's favour: the claimant cannot be the long-lost heir, whose body we know lies buried in Australia, and if he honestly thinks he is then we must try to cure him of a delusion.

'But if I went on being conscious, why should I worry which body I have?' To use the repeated 'I' prejudges the issue; a fairer way of putting the point would be: If there is going to be a consciousness that includes ostensible memories of my life, why should I worry about which body this consciousness goes with? When we put it that way, it is quite easy to imagine circumstances in which one would worry—particularly if the ostensible memories of my life were to be produced by processes that can produce entirely spurious memories.

If, however, memory is not enough for personal identity; if a man's living again does involve some bodily as well as mental continuity with the man who lived formerly; then we might fairly call his new bodily life a resurrection. So the upshot of our whole argument is that unless a man comes to life again by resurrection, he does not live again after death. At best some mental remnant of him would survive death; and I should hold that the possibility even of such survival involves at least a permanent *capacity* for renewed human life; if reincarnation is excluded, this means: a capacity for resurrection. It may be hard to believe in the resurrection of the body: but Aquinas argued in his commentary on I Corinthians 15, which I have already cited, that it is much harder to believe in an immortal but permanently disembodied human soul; for that would mean believing that a soul, whose very identity depends on the capacity for reunion with one human body rather than another, will continue to exist for ever with this capacity unrealized.

Speaking of the resurrection, St. Paul used the simile of a seed that is planted and grows into an ear of corn, to show the relation between the corpse and the body that rises again from the dead. This simile fits in well enough with our discussion. In this life, the bodily aspect of personal identity requires a one-one relationship and material continuity; one baby body grows into one old man's body by a continuous process. Now similarly there is a one-one relationship between the buried seed and the ear that grows out of it; one seed grows into one ear, one ear comes from one seed; and the ear of corn is materially continuous with the seed but need not have any material identity with it.

There is of course no philosophical reason to expect that from a human corpse there will arise at some future date a new human body, continuous in some way with the corpse; and in some particular cases there appear strong empirical objections. But apart from the *possibility* of resurrection, it seems to me a mere illusion to have any hope for life after death. I am of the mind of Judas Maccabeus: if there is no resurrection, it is superfluous and vain to pray for the dead.

The traditional faith of Christianity, inherited from Judaism, is that at the end of this age Messiah will come and men rise from their graves to die no more. That faith is not going to be shaken by inquiries about bodies burned to ashes or eaten by beasts; those who might well suffer just such death in martyrdom were those who were most confident of a glorious reward in the resurrection. One who shares that hope will hardly wish to take out an occultistic or philosophical insurance policy, to guarantee some sort of survival as an annuity, in case God's promise of resurrection should fail.

Empirical Arguments for Human Survival

C. D. BROAD

I must begin by saying exactly what I do and what I do not propose to discuss in this Chapter. I do not propose to discuss in any detail the special alleged facts (such as the Cross-correspondences in automatic writings) on which empirical arguments for human survival have been based. This is an extremely technical question which must be left to experts and would be out of place in a philosophical book. I do presuppose that the careful work of the Society for Psychical Research has elicited a mass of facts which may fairly be called "supernormal", in the sense that they cannot, if genuine, be explained on the usual assumptions of science and common-sense about the nature and powers of the human mind. And I do assume that a great many of the facts that come up to the extremely high standard of evidence required by the Society are "genuine", in the sense that they have been correctly reported and that they are not simply due to fraud or self-deception. I assume this on the basis of a fairly careful study of the literature; of a knowledge of the kind of persons who have controlled the policy of the Society and taken part in its investigations; and of some investigations of my own. I have, in fact, exactly the same kind of grounds for assuming the existence of genuinely supernormal phenomena as I have for assuming the existence of certain rare physical phenomena which are difficult to reproduce to order, and of certain rare diseases which competent doctors have described. I accept them on a mixed basis of authority and personal experience; and my authority is of the same kind and carries the same weight as the authority on which I accept the rarer and obscurer kinds of physical and medical phenomena as genuine. I do not think it is necessary to argue this point, because I have always found that those who deny it have not carefully read the relevant literature, have conducted very few careful investigations for themselves, and are ignorant of the intellectual calibre and the scrupulous accuracy of such men as Sidgwick, Gurney, and Podmore (to mention only the names of those who are no longer with us). Whenever we are told that "Science *proves* so-and-so to be impossible" we must remember that this is merely a rhetorical form of "Professor X and most of his colleagues *assert* so-and-so to be impossible". Those of us who have the privilege of meeting Professor X and his colleagues daily, and know from experience what kind of assertions they are capable of making when they leave their own subject, will, I am afraid, remain completely unmoved.

I take human survival then to be one hypothesis among others to account for certain reasonably well-established supernormal phenomena. The argument will be of the usual inverse-inductive type. Now, in such arguments we always have to consider the following points. (i) The antecedent probabilities of the various alternative hypotheses. And (ii) the completeness with which the var-

---

C. D. Broad (1887-1971) was professor of moral philosophy at Trinity College, Cambridge.

From C. D. Broad, *Mind and Its Place in Nature* (London: Routledge & Kegan Paul, 1925). Reprinted by permission of Routledge & Kegan Paul Ltd.

ious alternative hypotheses explain the special facts under consideration. If the antecedent probability of h_1 be very much less than that of h_2, then, even though h_1 explains the special facts better than h_2, it may be more prudent to try to make some modification of h_2 rather than to put much faith in h_1. I shall, therefore, begin by considering the antecedent probability of the hypothesis of human survival.

THE ANTECEDENT PROBABILITY OF HUMAN SURVIVAL

When we are considering the antecedent probability of a hypothesis put forward to explain certain special facts there are two points to be considered. (i) There is what may be called its "intrinsic probability". This depends on the structure of the proposition itself, and very little can be said about it here. (ii) There is the probability which the proposition has with respect to all known facts *other than* the special set of facts which it is put forward to explain. If p and q be two logically independent propositions, the proposition pq is intrinsically less probable than the proposition p. This is an instance of the first point. If a bishop falls down in the street it is antecedently more probable that this is due to a piece of orange-peel than to direct diabolic agency. For, although both hypotheses explain the observed fact equally well, the former fits in much better with the other facts which we know about the world than the latter does. This is an example of the latter point. I find myself quite unable to say much of importance about the intrinsic probabilities of human survival and its rival hypotheses. But there are a few logical points which are perhaps worth making. (I) Among alternative hypotheses to human survival which have been suggested we may mention (*a*) a very extended telepathy among living men, and (*b*) the action of non-human spirits who personate certain dead men. The second of these would seem to have the least intrinsic probability of the three hypotheses. For we have to postulate minds, for whose existence we have no other evidence, and to ascribe telepathic powers to them. The first hypothesis postulates no minds for whose existence we have not already independent evidence; but it has to ascribe to them telepathic powers of such great extent that we have little or no independent evidence for their existence. The hypothesis of human survival perhaps makes the minimum assumption of the three; since it merely postulates the continuance of something which we know independently to have existed, and it ascribes to this only such telepathic powers as we have reason to believe exist in embodied minds. (2) There is one very great logical difficulty which is inherent in the subject. We have not the least reason to believe that the hypotheses that have been put forward are exhaustive or even approximately so. Hence we have no ground for ascribing any very high antecedent probability to any one of them. We believe ourselves to know enough of the general structure of the material world to enable us to rule out all but a few hypotheses about the causation of a physical phenomenon. In such an unfamiliar region as we enter in doing Psychical Research we have not this advantage.

There is just one other remark that I will make before leaving this part of the subject. It is well known that many Roman Catholics and High Anglicans, not content with ascribing the phenomena to non-human spirits, ascribe them to "devils". Now I suppose that a "devil" means a non-human spirit who is morally much worse than the worst man. There appears to me to be absolutely nothing in the phenomena to warrant this hypothesis. (*a*) There is a certain amount of indecency in some automatic scripts. So there is in the writings of Petronius and in the conversation of many undergraduates; whilst Mr Gibbon informs us that "a learned prelate, now deceased, was fond of quoting . . . in conversation" a passage from Procopius about the Empress Theodora which the historian prudently "veils in the obscurity of a learned language". (*b*) Most spiritualistic communications which are not merely trivial consist of elevated, but to my mind "twaddling", ethico-religious "uplift". If they be the communications of devils it must be admitted that most devils who communicate are decorous to the verge of dulness; and that the aphorism "Heaven for the climate, but Hell for the company" stands in need of considerable modification. (*c*) It may be admitted that to personate a dead man and raise false hopes in his friends and relations would not be the mark of a very high morality. It would be a somewhat heartless practical joke. But it is not necessary to be a devil in order to play heartless practical jokes; such things have been done before now by quite kindly but somewhat thoughtless undergraduates. (*d*) It may be admitted that a certain number of weak-minded people go mentally and morally to the bad through excessive indulgence in spiritualistic séances. The same may be said of excessive indulgence in alcohol or religion. And a devil who chooses this particular method of leading men to damnation when there are so many more profitable alternatives open to him must be extremely incompetent as his own business. (*e*) There is a certain amount of "roughness" and horse-play at some séances for physical phenomena; there is a great deal more after a bump-supper or at many political meetings. In fact, if we can judge of Hell from those denizens of it whom we meet, on this theory, at spiritualistic séances, we must suppose that it is very much like what I believe is called a "Pleasant Sunday Afternoon" at a Nonconformist chapel, enlivened by occasional bump-suppers. Its nearest earthly analogy would probably be a Welsh University; and I should suppose that those who pass directly from the one institution to the other must often fail to notice the transition. To sum up, from a fairly extensive reading of spiritualistic literature, and from a certain amount of personal experience of séances, I should say that the average "spirit" is morally no worse than the average Fellow of Trinity, though there is a very marked difference in the intelligence of the two.

The motives which make the "devil-theory" so popular in ecclesiastical circles are tolerably obvious. In the first place, there is the perfectly legitimate desire to frighten one's congregation away from dabbling in practices which are very unlikely to do good to any of them and very likely to do positive harm to many of them. The second motive is probably just as strong, but is generally unrecognised or unadmitted. This is the objection which the members, and especially the officials, of all close corporations have to non-members who claim to perform the same functions. The objection of the orthodox churchman, and particularly the orthodox clergyman, to the spiritualistic medium is the same kind of objection which doctors feel towards "bone-setters" and trade-unionists feel towards blacklegs. It is necessary to disguise this to oneself and to others; and for this purpose the "devil-theory" is very handy, just as doctors find it highly convenient to remind us of the deaths of patients under quacks and to forget that patients sometimes die under doctors.

I propose now to consider whether there are any facts other than the special phenomena dealt with by Psychical Research which make the hypothesis of human survival antecedently probable. Although, as I have said, I do not think that such special propositions as the survival of man fall within the range of proof or disproof by metaphysical arguments, I can see of course that the antecedent probability of human survival will be greatly affected by one's general metaphysical position. If materialism or epiphenomenalism were strict metaphysical truth, survival, though perhaps still abstractly possible, would be in the last degree unlikely. If mentalism, in one of its forms, were strictly true, survival would not indeed necessarily follow. Lotze and Mr Bradley were mentalists; but they held quite consistently that their systems did not necessitate human survival and that it is on the whole improbable. Still, mentalism is decidedly more favourable to human survival than is the view of the world which is taken by common-sense, or by non-philosophical scientists, or by dualistic philosophers. Idealism (which I distinguish from mentalism, though most idealists have in fact been mentalists) is still more favourable to survival. For I take it that the essence of idealism is to hold that what we regard as the "higher" characteristics, such as life and consciousness, are fundamental categories which apply to Reality as such and are not just special and probably transitory features of certain specially complicated and probably unstable parts of Reality. It is possible to be an Idealist and yet to regard human survival as false or highly improbable. This position was taken by Professor Bosanquet. But it must be admitted that idealism would favour the antecedent probability of survival.

It might seem then that, in order to determine the antecedent probability of survival, it would be necessary to make up one's mind between various rival systems of metaphysics. I am certainly not prepared to do this. But I think I have a fairly good excuse. On my view no general metaphysical system can be proved deductively by reasoning from *a priori* premises. Idealism and materialism are just attempts to synthesise all the known facts; and their respective probabilities can be decided only by their respective success in doing this. There is then, in my view, no possibility of *first* deciding between alternative metaphysical systems on general grounds and *then* taking the system which we have accepted as a fixed datum from which to estimate the antecedent probability of survival. The question whether we probably do or probably do not survive the death of our bodies is just the kind of question that has to be answered *before* we can decide (say) between idealism and materialism or epiphenomenalism. What we must do then is to discuss the antecedent probability of survival on data which are common to all men, including the upholders of rival systems of metaphysics. And this means that we must consider the arguments for or against human survival which may be drawn from the constitution of the world as it presents itself to enlightened common-sense; for this is the common basis from which all the rival systems start. If we do this we may consistently use our result as one means of deciding tentatively between the various rival systems.

Now, on the face of it, the most striking feature of the world as we know it in daily life is, for our purpose, that it does not present the faintest trace of evidence for survival. Continued action is a criterion of the continued existence of any substance; and this is conspicuously lacking after death. The body ceases to give the characteristic responses, and very soon it decays and loses even its characteristic shape and appearance. Hence the only evidence that we ever had for the existence of a man's mind has ceased abruptly; and, apart from the alleged facts investigated by Psychical Research, it has ceased for ever so far as our experience goes. We do indeed often believe in the continued existence of substances in spite of long periods during which neither we nor anyone else are aware of them by any of their usual signs. *E.g.*, we believe that silver continues to exist though it be dissolved in nitric acid and kept for years as silver-nitrate. But in such cases we have reason to believe that at any moment we could restore a substance having the properties of the silver which we dissolved, and connected with it by identity of mass and continuity of spatial positions. Every such factor making for belief in the continued existence of dead men is lacking in our ordinary experience; and thus such a belief seems to have nothing whatever in its favour, and to be from a logical point of view a bare unmotivated possibility.

Yet of course, as a matter of history, this has seldom seriously militated against the belief in survival. Such a belief has been all but universal. Now, on the one hand, the mere universality of a belief is no proof of its truth. On the other hand, the fact that a belief has been widely held by ignorant and primitive men is no proof of its falsehood. Confronted then by a strong belief which seems to have arisen and persisted in spite of complete lack of evidence in its favour, we must consider what factors may have caused the belief, and whether any of them are *reasons* as well as *causes*.

A primitive man would certainly not accept the statement that there is no evidence in ordinary experience for survival. He would claim to know of dozens of cases of men seen and heard after death; and he might even think that he had met with such cases in his own experience. Now, without prejudice to the genuineness of abnormal phenomena in general or to the possibility that they occasionally happen among savages, we may be quite certain that in most cases the primitive man is mistaken in thinking that there is any need to assume the continued existence of the dead to explain the phenomena which he would regard as evidence for survival. We may divide such phenomena into two classes. The first consists of those which are capable of a perfectly normal explanation; the second of those which would now be dealt with by Psychical Research. There is no reason to suppose that the latter will be more numerous or striking among savages than among civilised men. The first group provides no evidence at all for survival, since the facts have simply been misinterpreted. The second, supposing it to exist, contains no evidence *antecedent* to Psychical Research; since, by hypothesis, it consists of precisely those phenomena which would now be treated by that science. Hence the primitive man had simply more *causes*, but no better *reasons*, for a belief in survival than we have; but a belief irrationally caused in him may have been handed on to us.

No doubt experiences of fainting and sleeping helped the belief in survival. In these conditions the mind gives no external manifestations of its existence, and the body in many ways resembles a corpse. Yet consciousness returns; and, if we remember our dreams, we remember that it was not really absent when our bodies were giving no external signs of its existence. What more natural then than to suppose that at these times the mind leaves the body for a while and follows its own adventures, and that at death it leaves the body for good? But the differences between sleep and death make it impossible to accept this undoubted cause of a belief in survival as a valid reason in its favour. If, after dissolving a bit of silver several times in nitric acid and getting it back again, we one day dissolved it in something else and found that no efforts of ours could restore anything with the properties of silver, the inference would be obvious. It was reasonable to think that the silver survived the nitric acid treatment, because it could be restored; it would not be reasonable to conclude from this that it also survived the treatment after which nothing like it can be again obtained. If we choose to assume that it still exists, our assumption is an unmotived one. So once more we have a cause of belief which is not a reason for belief.

Probably neither of the above-mentioned causes would have sufficed to produce an almost universal belief in survival. Both are to be regarded as interpretations of real or supposed facts in terms of this belief rather than as the original causes of it. The truth is that we have the greatest difficulty in actually envisaging the cessation of our own conscious life. It is easy enough to think of anyone else as having really ceased to exist; but it is almost impossible to give more than a cold intellectual assent to the same proposition about oneself. In making a will, *e.g.*, containing elaborate provisions for the disposal of one's property after death, it is almost impossible (unless my experience be quite exceptional) not to think of oneself as going to be conscious and able to oversee the working of one's own bequests. I at least can continually catch myself in this attitude, and I should imagine it to be quite common even among people who are intellectually persuaded of their future extinction.

Ought we to attach any weight to this primitive belief which nearly every one has in his own survival? The mere fact that it is held without reasons is no conclusive objection to it; for, unless some propositions can be known to be true without reasons, no proposition can be known to be true for reasons. We must, therefore, consider the belief on its merits without prejudice. Now it seems perfectly clear that it is not a self-evident proposition like an axiom, which becomes more certain the more carefully we inspect it. Nor can it be regarded as a postulate; *i.e.*, as a proposition which, though not self-evident and incapable of either proof or disproof by experience, has to be assumed in order to organise experience and to furnish a motive for research. Certain propositions which we use in induction seem to me to be postulates in this sense; the proposition that John Jones will survive the death of his body seems to me to be quite plainly nothing of the kind. In fact I think that the belief represents nothing more profound than an easily explicable limit of our powers of imagination. Naturally all my experience of myself has been of myself as conscious and active. There have indeed been gaps during dreamless sleep or fainting fits, but consciousness has revived and the gaps have been bridged by memory. Again, at every moment I have been obliged for practical purposes to think of myself as going to exist at later moments; it is therefore a breach with the mental habits of a lifetime to envisage a moment after which the series of my conscious states shall have finally ended. This practical difficulty, due to habit, seems the sole and sufficient explanation of our primitive belief in our own indefinite continuance; and it obviously provides no evidence for the truth of that belief.

I think then that we must conclude that a mere contemplation of the world as it appears in ordinary experience furnishes no trace of support for the belief in survival. Ought we to hold that the absence of all evidence *for* constitutes evidence *against?* This is a somewhat delicate question. Sometimes the absence of evidence for a proposition makes strongly against it, and sometimes it does not. If I look carefully round a room and, seeing no one, say: "There is no one in the room", my evidence is purely negative; but it is almost conclusive against the proposition: "There is someone in the room". But the fact that I did not see a tuberculosis bacillus in the room would be quite irrelevant to the question whether there was one there. Finding no evidence for a proposition is evidence against it only if the proposition be such that, if it were true, there ought to be some observable evidence for it.

Now the proposition: "Some men survive the death of their bodies" is not precisely in the position of either of the two quoted above. I know enough about human bodies and about tuberculosis bacilli to be sure that one of the former could hardly be present in a room without my finding it, but that one of the latter could not be seen by the naked eye even if it were present. I know very much less about the conditions under which one human spirit can make its presence known to another; but I do know something about it. I am a human spirit connected with a body, and all other spirits of whose existence I am certain are in the same position. Setting aside the phenomena treated by Psychical Research, I know that one such spirit can make its presence known to another only by moving its own body, thence agitating the air or the ether, and thence affecting another human body. My friend dies; I remain alive and connected with my body. Communication with me, therefore, presumably requires the same complex and roundabout series of material changes as before. Its very complexity and indirectness make it not unlikely that, even if my friend has survived, some necessary link in this mechanism will have broken down. Hence the absence of evidence for his survival cannot be regarded logically as very strong evidence against it.

The present position, therefore, is that at the level of ordinary experience there is not the faintest trace of evidence for survival, though there is a pretty general belief in it. The causes of this belief have been enumerated and seen not to be reasons. But the absence of evidence for the belief cannot be taken as strong evidence against it, in view of what we know about the means by which embodied human spirits have to communicate with each other.

Is there at this level any *positive* evidence *against* survival? I think that there are two sets of facts which impress common-sense and are interpreted in this direction. One is the apparently haphazard way in which men are born and die. Human beings are constantly brought into the world thoughtlessly and by mistake; many children live for a few minutes or hours and then die; many are born idiotic. The general impression produced is that the claim to permanence for creatures whose earthly lives begin and end in these trivial ways is somewhat ridiculous. An unwanted child is produced, let us say, in a drunken orgy; and in six weeks dies of neglect or is killed by its mother. Does it seem likely that a being whose earthly career is started and stopped by such causes is a permanent and indestructible part of the universe, or indeed that it survives the death of its body at all?

The second fact which is felt to bear in the same direction is the continuity between men and animals. The bodies of each begin and cease to be animated by minds through precisely similar physical and physiological causes. No doubt the mind of any living man differs, not merely quantitatively, but also qualitatively from that of any living animal; still the most primitive men can hardly have differed appreciably from the highest animals in their mental endowments. Did *Pithecanthropus erectus* and does every Australian aborigine survive the death of his body? If they do, have not the higher animals almost an equal claim? And, if you grant this for cats and monkeys, will you not be forced in the end to grant it for lice and earwigs? If, on the other hand, you deny that any animal survives, on the ground that their minds are not complex or important enough to be permanent factors in the universe, how can you be sure that any man yet born has possessed a mind complex and important enough for survival? The two facts quoted above do, I am sure, exert a considerable influence against the view that men survive the death of their bodies. I am conscious that they affect me personally more than any others. But the question remains: "Have they any logical right to exert this influence?"

I am inclined to think on reflection that the first argument is wholly fallacious. It really involves the illegitimate introduction of a judgment of value into a question of fact. And the judgment of value is itself a rather superficial one. It is thought that, because the occasioning causes of birth and death are often trivial, therefore what seems to begin with birth and to end with death cannot be important enough to survive. But (*a*) you cannot argue from the triviality of a cause to the impermanence of its effect. (*b*) The cause is trivial only in the irrelevant ethical sense that it does not involve a considered and deliberate choice by a virtuous human being. There is really no logical transition from: "This is caused by the careless or criminal action of a human being" to: "This is the kind of thing whose existence is transitory". (*c*) When we say that the cause is trivial we make the common mistake of taking for *the* cause some necessary cause-factor which happens to be specially noticeable or of special practical interest. The complete cause of the birth of a child or the death of a man must be of almost unthinkable complexity, whether the child be begotten or the man be killed carelessly or with deliberate forethought. This is true even if we confine ourselves to the material conditions; and we are not really in a position to say that the *complete* conditions of so singular an event as the manifestation of a new mind through a new body are contained in the material world.

The second argument is of course of a well-known general type. It tries to show by continuity of cases that, if a man asserts one proposition, he ought in consistency not to deny a certain other proposition which he would like to deny. Arguments of this kind can be met in one of two ways. (1) We may point out that an argument from continuity is reversible, and that the direction in which one turns it is arbitrary. We might just as well argue by continuity from the supposed immortality of men to the immortality of earwigs as from the supposed mortality of earwigs to the mortality of men. The actual direction in which the argument is used presupposes that we are *already* pretty certain that earwigs are mortal, and much more doubtful whether men are immortal. This no doubt is true. But it immediately raises the question: "Why are we practically certain that earwigs are mortal?" This question cannot be answered by considerations of continuity, but only by reflecting on the special peculiarities of earwigs. (2) When we raise this question two answers are possible. (*a*) We may find on reflection that we have no good reason for thinking that earwigs are unlikely to be immortal. In that case the argument from continuity to the case of men will prove nothing. Or (*b*) we may find that those characteristics of earwigs which make it very unlikely that they are immortal are obviously not present in men. In that case the argument from continuity will also prove nothing about men. At most it will show that it is difficult for us to say with confidence about certain intermediate forms of living being whether they are likely to be mortal or not. Let us then consider the question why we think it very unlikely that earwigs should be immortal; and let us also consider whether the reasons, whatever they may be, apply to men also.

In the first place it might be said that an earwig's mind has very little value, and therefore it is unworthy to be a permanent factor in the universe. And it might be argued that it is therefore unlikely to survive. But (*a*) this would be an ethical argument of a kind which we have already dismissed. And (*b*), even if it were valid, it is obvious that most human minds are enormously more valuable than the mind of any earwig; so that it would not be inconsistent to think it likely that human minds are immortal and unlikely that the minds of earwigs are so. All that we should be entitled to say is (*a*) that it is not certain even that any human mind is valuable enough to be immortal; and (*b*) that, if it were certain, there would be intermediate cases, *e.g.*, cats, about which the probabilities are about equally balanced.

But the differences between the minds of

men and those of the lower animals are never *mere* differences of value. Presumably an earwig's mind has very little unity, complexity, or comprehensiveness. Now it is arguable that such a very simple mind is not very likely to survive bodily death. But (*a*) I do not think that what we know of nature suggests any straightforward connexion between unity and complexity on the one hand and stability on the other. Both the very simple and the highly comprehensive seem to be fairly stable, though for different reasons. The very simple, like the electron, is stable because of its comparative indifference to changes in external conditions. The highly unified and comprehensive complex, like the solar system, tends to be stable because it contains so much within itself that there is little left over to disturb it. It is therefore quite in accordance with what we know of the order of nature to suppose that the simplicity of the earwig's mind gives it a particularly good chance of survival. (*b*) Suppose, on the other hand, that we do hold that the simplicity of the earwig's mind makes it very unlikely to survive. Then we must admit that the human mind is enormously less simple and more comprehensive and highly unified. Hence it would be perfectly consistent to hold that the human mind is likely to survive because of its unity and comprehensiveness and that the earwig's mind is unlikely to survive because of its simplicity and poverty of content. Thus on neither alternative does the argument from continuity make it unreasonable to hold that the human mind is likely to survive. As before, all that we can legitimately conclude from the argument from continuity is (*a*) that it is uncertain whether any human mind even is complex and comprehensive enough to survive; and (*b*) that, if it were certain, there would be cases of intermediate complexity, *e.g.*, cats, about which the probabilities would be nearly equally balanced.

Again, some people no doubt shrink from admitting the possibility of survival to the lower animals out of horror at the immense number of minds which there would be if none, even of the lowest kind, died with the death of their bodies. This shrinking from mere numerical vastness seems to me to be childish. We have no reason to suppose that the universe is conducted in accordance with the Law of Parsimony; and it may well be that the world exhibits a profusion in the item of minds which would horrify the inhabitants of Aberdeen. Thus I do not think that this consideration makes it specially improbable that earwigs should be immortal.

Lastly, the following argument might be used to suggest that the minds of the lower animals are very unlikely to survive the death of their bodies. The characteristic activities and experiences of animals seem to be specially and exclusively directed to preserving their own lives and those of their offspring. If we judge living things teleologically (and, in practice, it is hard to avoid doing this) it does seem that an animal accomplishes "all that is in it" when it succeeds in keeping itself alive long enough to produce young and to start them in the world. It is hard to see what "purpose" would be served by the individual survival of an earwig which dies at a reasonable age after bringing up a family of little earwigs. I do not know what weight to attach to such an argument as this. The principle of judging living beings and their parts in terms of a supposed "purpose for which they were made" is undoubtedly valuable as an heuristic method; and it is difficult to suppose that it does not in some way accord with the facts. But fortunately it is not necessary for our purpose to decide on the legitimacy of such considerations. For the position is this. (*a*) If it be not valid, the argument to show that earwigs are very unlikely to survive falls to the ground; and with it goes the argument from continuity to the probable mortality of human beings. (*b*) If, on the other hand, it be valid, the argument from continuity equally breaks down in another way. For it does seem as if human minds had many powers and faculties which are not merely directed to preserving the life of the individual and the species; and that the continued existence of certain human minds after the death of their bodies would "answer the purpose for which they seem to be made" in a way in which the continued existence of an individual earwig would not. Hence it would be perfectly consistent to hold, on the basis of this argument, that earwigs are most unlikely to be immortal and that men are quite likely to be immortal. As usual, the argument from continuity would raise a doubt only about certain intermediate cases, such as cats and dogs, where the probabilities might be about equally balanced.

To sum up. The argument from continuity makes against the probability of human survival only on two conditions. (1) There must be some reason (and not a mere prejudice) for thinking that the survival of the lower animals is very improbable. And (2) this reason must not be the presence of some characteristic in the lower animals which differentiates them sharply from human beings. For, if our only reason for thinking it very unlikely that earwigs will survive be some characteristic in which earwigs differ profoundly from men, it will be perfectly consistent to think it likely that men will survive and that earwigs will not. The existence of a continuous series of intermediate forms between earwigs and men will prove nothing except that there are certain intermediate cases in which the probabilities for and against survival are about equally balanced. And there would not be the least trace of inconsistency in the position of a man who should be practically certain that earwigs are mortal and human beings immortal but should be quite unable to make up his mind about cats or kangaroos. Now, so far as I can see, these two conditions are never both fulfilled. The alleged reasons for thinking it very unlikely that earwigs are immortal either are no reasons at all or they obviously depend on characteristics in which human beings and earwigs differ profoundly. Hence I doubt whether the argument against the probability of human survival, drawn from the continuous series of living forms between men and the lowest animals, has any logical validity. The world then, as it presents itself to common-sense and everyday experience, offers no positive reasons for and no positive reasons against human survival. The only reason against it is the utter absence of all reasons for it; and we have seen that this is not a strong argument in the present case. Let us now enquire whether the more detailed investigations of science provide us with any grounds for deciding one way or the other.

Science on the whole does not reverse, but merely amplifies and elaborates, the views of common-sense on the connexion of body and mind. We already knew that body and mind were intimately connected, and that injury to the former may gravely modify or to all appearance destroy the latter. The additional information gained from science may be summed up as follows. (i) More detailed knowledge has been got of the correlation between injuries to particular regions of the brain and defects in certain departments of mental life. Connected with this is the knowledge that many mental processes, which seem to common-sense to be almost independent of the body, have bodily correlates. (ii) We have gained the surprising information that, in spite of the apparent interaction of body and mind, the body and its material surroundings form a closed energetic system from the point of view of the Conservation of Energy. (iii) We know more about the detailed structure and general plan of the brain and nervous system. What bearing has all this on the probability of survival? We find bodies without minds; we never find minds without bodies. When we do find minds we always find a close correlation between their processes and those of their bodies. This, it is argued, strongly suggests that minds depend for their *existence* on bodies; in which case, though survival may still be abstractly possible, it is to the last degree unlikely. At death there takes place completely and permanently a process of bodily destruction which, when it occurs partially and temporarily, carries with it the destruction of part of our mental life. The inference seems only too obvious. I think it is fair to say that our ordinary scientific knowledge of the relation of body to mind most strongly suggests epiphenomenalism, though it does not necessitate it; and that epiphenomenalism is most unfavourable to the hypothesis of human survival.

It is, however, possible to put forward other theories about the mind and its relation to the body, which are consistent with ordinary experience and with scientific knowledge and are less unfavourable to survival than epiphenomenalism. I will call the first of these the "Instrumental Theory."

The Instrumental Theory

We must begin by drawing a distinction between the existence of a mind and its manifestation to other minds. On the Instrumental Theory the mind is a substance which is existentially independent of the body. It may have existed before the body began, and it may exist after the body is destroyed. For a time it is intimately connected with a certain body; and at such times it can get information about other things only by means of its body and can act on other things only by first moving its body. If the body be injured the mind may be cut off from certain sources of information about other things, and it may be prevented from expressing itself in certain ways; but otherwise it may be uninjured. It is certain that such a theory as this is consistent with a good many of the facts which are commonly held to prove the existential dependence of mind on body. Nevertheless, I think that, in this crude form, it cannot be maintained. Let us take the case of a man who is injured in a certain part of his brain, and for the time loses his power to remember certain events. It can hardly be maintained that, in any literal sense, he still remembers the events; and that all that has been damaged is his power of manifesting this knowledge to others by speech or writing. The latter case does sometimes arise, and it seems introspectively quite different from the former to the patient himself. Again, if the patient recovers these lost memories after a while, it seems to him that a change has taken place in the contents of his mind, and not merely a change in his ability to express to others what was going on in his mind before. We must suppose then that in such cases something more than the power to manifest one's knowledge to others has been injured. The only other alternative is to suppose that all such patients are lying and asserting that they cannot remember certain things which they actually are remembering. If we reject this very violent alternative we must hold that in some cases an injury to the brain does actually deprive the mind of the power to remember certain events which it formerly could remember. Could a supporter of the Instrumental Theory square the facts with his view? He might say that the general power or remembering is unchanged; and assert that all that has happened is that the injury to the body has prevented certain past events from being objects of memory, as blindfolding a man would prevent certain present objects from being perceived. But in that case the mind is reduced to something which has merely certain very general capacities, and any particular exercise of these powers seems to depend on the body.

Let us now take another example. We will suppose that a man is injured in the head; that before the injury he was of a cheerful and benevolent disposition; and that after the injury he is morose and liable to attacks of homicidal mania. Are we to say that the injury has made no difference to his mind; that this remains cheerful and benevolent; but that the change in his brain compels him to express his cheerfulness by scowling and his benevolence by attacking other people with carving-knives? This is scarcely plausible. And, if we accept it, we shall not be able to stop at this point. We shall have to conclude that it is impossible to tell what the character of anyone's mind really is. Lifelong philanthropists may be inwardly boiling with malice which some peculiar kink in their brains and nervous systems compels them to express by pensioning their poor relations and giving pennies to crossing-sweepers. Once more, the mind will be reduced to something with no definite traits of its own, such as benevolence or peevishness, but merely with certain very general powers to express itself in various ways according to the body with which it is provided. It seems to me that what is left of the mind when we try to square the Instrumental Theory with the known facts is so abstract and indefinite that it does not deserve to be called a "mind".

The Compound Theory

This suggests a modification of the Instrumental Theory, which I will call the "Compound Theory". Might not what we know as a "mind" be a compound of two factors, neither of which separately has the characteristic properties of a mind, just as salt is a compound of two substances, neither of which by itself has the characteristic properties of salt? Let us call one of these constituents the "psychic factor" and the other the "bodily factor". The psychic factor would be like some chemical element which has never been isolated; and the characteristics of a mind would depend jointly on those of the psychic factor and on those of the material organism with which it is united. This would allow of all the correlation between mind and body which could ever be discovered, and at the same time it is not open to the objections which I have pointed out in the ordinary form of the Instrumental Theory. Moreover, it is in accord with many facts which we know about other departments of nature. We know that chemical compounds have properties which cannot be deduced from those which their elements display in isolation or in other compounds. And yet the properties of these compounds are wholly dependent on those of their elements, in the sense that, given such elements in such relations, a compound necessarily arises with such and such properties. These properties do not belong to either of the elements, but only to the compound as a whole. Now this does seem to accord fairly well with what we know about minds when we reflect upon them. On the one hand, it seems a mistake to ascribe perception, reasoning, anger, love, etc., to a mere body. On the other hand, as we have seen, it is almost equally difficult to ascribe them to what is left when the bodily factor is ignored. Thus the mind, as commonly conceived, does look as if it were a compound of two factors neither of which separately is a mind. And it does look as if specifically mental characteristics belonged only to this compound substance.

It would be unwise to press the analogy to chemical compounds too far. So far as we know, when two chemical elements are united to form a chemical compound no permanent change is produced in the properties of either. It would be rash to assume that this is also true when a psychic factor is united with a bodily organism so as to give a mind. Both factors may be permanently affected by this union; so that, if they become separated again and continue to exist, their properties are characteristically different from what they were when the two first became connected with each other. Of course many different views would be antecedently possible about the supposed psychic factor. At one extreme would be the view that there is only one psychic factor for all minds. Different minds would then be compounds of this one psychic factor with different brains and nervous systems. Such a view would bear some analogy to Green's theory of the one Eternal Consciousness and the many animal organisms. But the psychic factor on our view would have no claim to be called a "Consciousness"; it would not perform those feats of relating and unifying sense-data which Green ascribed to it; and there is no reason to suppose that it would deserve honorific titles like "eternal", or be an appropriate object for those religious emotions which Green felt towards it. At the opposite extreme would be the view that there is a different psychic factor for each different mind. Then the question could be raised whether some or all of them can exist out of combination with organisms; whether some one psychic factor can combine successively with a series of different organisms to give a series of different minds; and so on. (It may be remarked that the view that the psychic factor cannot exist out of combination with organisms, and yet that the same psychic factor can be combined with a series of successive organisms, has a pretty close analogy to certain chemical facts. There are groups, such as NH_4, CH_3, etc., which are incapable of more than the most transitory independent existence. Yet one such group may pass successively from one combination to another, and may impart certain characteristic properties to each of these compounds.) Finally, there is an intermediate possibility for which there might be a good deal to be said. It might be suggested that the marked individuality of human minds indicates that there is a different psychic factor as well as a different bodily organism to each coexisting human mind. On the other hand, it might be held that there is only one psychic factor for the whole species of earwigs; and that the very trivial differences between the mind of one earwig and another are due simply to differences in their bodily organisms. It is obvious that only empirical evidence of a very special kind could help us to decide between these alternatives, even if we accepted the Compound Theory in its main outlines.

Granted that the Compound Theory is consistent with all the facts which are commonly held to prove the existential dependence of mind on body, and granted that it is in better accord with the facts than the Instrumental Theory, is there any positive evidence for it? We have a set of facts which point to the dependence of mind on body. One explanation is that mind depends on nothing but body, *i.e.*, that mental events either *are* also bodily events, or that at any rate they are all *caused* wholly by bodily events and do not in turn affect either each other or the body. The present explanation is that the mind is a compound of the body and something else, and that mental events and mental characteristics belong to this compound substance and not to its separate constituents. Both explanations fit all the normal facts equally well. But the Compound Theory is more complex than the Epiphenomenal Theory, and it would be foolish to accept it unless there were some facts which it explains and which the Epiphenomenalist Theory does not. Now I do not think that there is anything in the normal phenomena which requires us to suppose that a mind depends for its existence and functioning on anything but the body and its processes. We must therefore turn to the abnormal phenomena.

ABNORMAL AND SUPERNORMAL PHENOMENA

I think that it is very important to begin by drawing a distinction which is too commonly neglected, viz., the distinction between *Survival* and mere *Persistence*. It seems to me that a great many of the phenomena which are held to point to the survival of particular human minds point only to the persistence of some factor which was a constituent of a human mind. We are not justified in saying that the mind of John Jones has survived the death of his body unless we have reason to believe that there is still a continuous stream of conscious mental states which may be said to be "further experiences of John Jones". We must suppose that this contains conations as well as cognitions, that it puts ends before itself and tries to realise them, and that it feels elation or disappointment according to its success or failure in doing so. No doubt such a stream of consciousness would be impossible unless past experiences modified later experiences; and no doubt we should not say that John Jones had survived unless he were able to remember some events in his life in the body. But these mnemic phenomena, though necessary to survival, are certainly not by themselves sufficient to constitute survival. If they occur alone, without the continuous stream of conscious cognitions, conations, and feelings, all that we have a right to say is that "some constituent of the mind of John Jones has persisted" and not that "John Jones has survived".

Now it seems to me that the vast majority of mediumistic phenomena which are taken to suggest survival really suggest only persistence. The additional notion of survival is read into them because in our ordinary experience we do not find memories without a pretty continuous stream of consciousness filling the gaps between the memory and the event remembered. The cases that I have in mind are these. A medium goes into a trance. He is then supposed either to be in contact with the spirit of some dead man, or in rarer cases to be directly possessed by such a spirit. In either case he sometimes mentions incidents in the past life of the supposed communicator which are unknown to the sitter and can afterwards be verified. And in the latter case he sometimes exhibits in a very remarkable way some of the mannerisms and even the verbal intonations of the supposed communicator. The evidence for such phenomena is, in my opinion, good enough to make them worth serious consideration by philosophers. Now the ordinary spiritualist interprets such phenomena in terms of the Instrumental Theory; he supposes that a human mind is existentially independent of its body and just uses it as an instrument; that it leaves its body at death, goes on living its own life, and from time to time uses a medium's body for purposes of communication.

But it seems to me that, apart from the intrinsic difficulties of the Instrumental Theory, the Compound Theory fits these supernormal phenomena on the whole much better. One thing which is highly characteristic of the communications of alleged dead men is their singular reticence about their present life, occupations, and surroundings. Such observations as are made by entranced mediums on these subjects seem to me to be extraordinarily silly, and to have every appearance of being merely the crude beliefs about the spiritual world which are current in mediumistic circles. Yet this nonsense is at times mixed up with traits which are highly characteristic of the supposed communicator, and with bits of detailed information about his past life which can afterwards be verified. Now, on the Compound Theory, we can suppose that the psychic factor may persist for a time at least after the destruction of the organism with which it was united to form the compound called "John Jones's mind". This psychic factor is not itself a mind, but it may carry modifications due to experiences which happened to John Jones while he was alive. And it may become temporarily united with the organism of an entranced medium. If so, a little temporary "mind" (a "mindkin", if I may use that expression) will be formed. Since this mindkin will contain the same psychic factor as the mind of John Jones it will not be surprising if it displays some traits characteristic of John Jones, and some memories of events in his earthly life. Since the bodily factor of this mindkin is the medium's organism, which is adapted to the medium's psychic factor and not to John Jones's, it will not be surprising if it shows many traits which are characteristic of the medium. And the reason why we can get no information about the present life and experiences of John Jones is that no such mind is existing at all. When the medium is entranced the psychic factor which was a constituent of John Jones's mind forms with the medium's body a mindkin which lasts just as long as the medium remains in trance. At intermediate times, on this view, all that exists is this psychic factor; and this by itself is no more a mind than John Jones's corpse is a mind. To explain the positive part of the phenomena it is plausible to suppose that *something* has persisted, and that this something was an integral part of John Jones's mind. But it is an enormous jump from this to the conclusion that John Jones's mind has survived the death of his body. And the negative part of the phenomena strongly suggests that what has persisted is not a mind, but is at most something which in combination with a suitable organism is capable of producing a mind.

Some of the facts of multiple personality would also be neatly explained by the Compound Theory. Of course mediumistic phenomena are, in the first instance, cases of multiple personality. The peculiarity of them is that one of the personalities professes either to *be* a certain deceased human being, or more usually only to be in communication with one; and that, in some cases, there appear certain characteristic traits of this dead man, or knowledge is shown of some minute details in his past life. But ordinary multiple personality, such as that of the Beauchamp case, might be explained by supposing that the same organism can have two different psychic factors connected with it. We should then expect to find two minds having certain characteristic differences, and yet having a good deal more in common than two minds which differ in their organisms as well as in their psychic factors. Two personalities might be compared to two chemical compounds with one element in common, such as silver chloride and silver bromide; whilst two ordinary minds might be compared (say) to silver chloride and lead nitrate. I do not think, however, that ordinary multiple personality positively requires the Compound Theory for its explanation. We can never be sure that the organism is in precisely the same state when one personality is in control as it is when the other is in control. Hence it is possible that the facts could be explained on a purely epiphenomenalist theory. It is the apparent persistence of certain traces and dispositions after the destruction of the organism which seems to demand for its explanation something more than epiphenomenalism, and seems to suggest *at least* something like the Compound Theory.

We must now consider (*a*) whether there are any facts which require something *more* than the Compound Theory to explain them; and (*b*) whether the facts that I have already mentioned could be explained with something *less* than the Compound Theory. It seems to me that we should have grounds for postulating the *survival* of a *mind*, and not the mere persistence of a psychic factor, if and only if the communications showed traces of an intention which persisted between the experiments and deliberately modified and controlled each in the light of those which had preceded it. Now it is alleged that there are signs of this deliberate intention in the Cross-Correspondences which the Society for Psychical Research has been investigating for many years. If all or most of these came up to the ideal type of a Cross-Correspondence, I think we should have to admit that it looks as if a single intelligent being were deliberately trying in an extremely ingenious way to produce evidence of its continuous existence. The ideal Cross-Correspondence would be of the following form. Suppose three automatic writers in different places produce automatic scripts over a series of years. Suppose that they do not communicate with each other, but send their scripts from time to time to an impartial authority for comparison. Suppose that A, B, and C in their scripts get statements which, taken separately, are fragmentary and unintelligible to them; and suppose further that after such an unintelligible and fragmentary statement in A's script there comes an injunction to refer to what B and C are now writing or will shortly write or have written at some definite time in the past. Suppose that similar injunctions are found in B's and C's scripts after fragmentary and unintelligible passages in them. Suppose finally that when the impartial authority compares the scripts and follows the directions contained in them he finds that these separately unintelligible sentences combine to convey something which is highly characteristic of a certain deceased person who is alleged to be communicating. Then we should have a perfect instance of a Cross-Correspondence; and it would be difficult to resist the conviction that the phenomena are controlled intentionally by a single mind, which cannot be identified with the conscious part of the mind of any of the automatic writers.

Unfortunately it is not clear to me that most of the alleged Cross-Correspondences accurately exemplify this ideal type. I also cannot help feeling suspicious of the enormous amount of learning and ingenuity which the impartial authority has to exercise in order to find the key to the riddle which the scripts set. Would not the same amount of patience, learning, and ingenuity discover almost as good Cross-Correspondences between almost any set of manuscripts? I do not say that this is so; but I should need a good deal of negative evidence, *i.e.*, of failure to discover Cross-Correspondences between other manuscripts which were treated in the same way as these automatic scripts, before I was prepared to stake much on this argument for human survival. So far as I am aware, negative control experiments of this kind have not been tried. It is evident that they would be terribly laborious, and it is hardly to be expected that the same patience and ingenuity would be lavished on them as have been devoted to the interpretation of the automatic scripts in which positive results are hoped for.

There is another remark to be made on the Cross-Correspondences. Suppose that they rendered it practically certain that *some* mind other than the conscious minds of the automatists is controlling the experiments, can we feel any confidence that it is the mind of a certain deceased person who professes to be communicating? Is it not at least equally probable that it might be the unconscious part of the mind of one of the automatists or of one of the officers of the Society for Psychical Research? It would certainly be true to say that some of the automatists (in particular Mrs Verrall) were well aware of the problem of getting evidence for survival which could not be explained away by the hypothesis of telepathy between the living; that it must have occupied their thoughts a great deal; and that they must have had a permanent desire to devise some means of solving it. It is also true that the alleged communicators in the Cross-Correspondences had been well known in life to Mrs Verrall and to many prominent and active members of the Society who were not themselves automatists. Now I think that we may take the following propositions as reasonably well established. (*a*) That when a person is greatly interested in a problem this problem is often worked upon and solved by processes which are unconscious relatively to the part of the mind which is normally in control of his body. I need only mention in support of this the quite common experience of solving a problem while asleep, or the post-hypnotic calculations which I spoke of in an earlier chapter. (*b*) That it is extremely probable that telepathy can and does take place between the unconscious parts of living minds. In sittings with Mrs Leonard and other mediums I have met with clear cases of telepathy between myself and the medium when entranced. But I have noticed that these almost invariably involved past events of which I was not consciously thinking at the time.

Thus the telepathic influence must have been due to mere "traces", or at most to processes of thought going on in my mind without my being aware of them, *i.e.*, processes which were unconscious relatively to the part of my mind which normally controls my body. (*c*) That the unconscious part of the mind is often extremely willing to "oblige" the conscious part by providing "evidence" for what the conscious part wishes to believe.

Now, if these three propositions be admitted, it is not unplausible to suggest that the unconscious part of the mind of one of the automatists worked out the problem of providing "satisfactory evidence" for survival and telepathically conveyed the fragmentary messages, which were to constitute the "evidence", to the other automatists. Personally I strongly suspect the unconscious part of Mrs Verrall's mind to have accomplished this feat. I am of course quite well aware that such a theory goes far beyond anything for which we have direct evidence; for it seems to imply that the unconscious part of Mrs Verrall's mind was capable of a kind of *selective* telepathy, conveying so much and no more to one automatist and so much and no more to another automatist. But I must point out that, if we do not ascribe this power to any embodied mind, we have to ascribe it to the disembodied mind of the supposed communicator. So this much must be assumed in any case if we accept the interpretation which the investigators have put on the Cross-Correspondences. And, except on the principle of *Omne ignotum pro magnifico*, I do not see why we should think it more likely that the disembodied mind of a dead man should be able to exercise selective telepathy than that the unconscious part of the embodied mind of a living member of the Society for Psychical Research should be able to do so. In fact the hypothesis that the spirit of the late Dr Verrall is communicating involves the assumption *both* of an otherwise unknown power of selective telepathy *and* of an otherwise unknown substance, viz., a disembodied spirit, to exercise this power. The hypothesis which I tentatively put forward makes only the first of these two assumptions. It therefore has a greater intrinsic probability; and it seems equally capable of explaining the facts.

I pass now to the second question. Could the facts which we have been considering be explained by something *less* than the hypothesis of a persistent psychic factor? It will be remembered that the facts to be explained are the revelation of certain details in the past life of a certain dead man, which are unknown at the time to the sitter and can afterwards be verified; or the occurrence of certain characteristic tricks of voice and manner in the entranced medium. Now it must be admitted that it is very rare for a detail about a dead man's past life to be verifiable unless it is known or has been known to someone now living. It must therefore be admitted to be theoretically possible that these phenomena are due to telepathy from the unconscious parts of the minds of living men who are remote from the place at which the sitting is being held. But, although this is conceivable, I cannot regard it as very plausible. It is very difficult to see what can determine the medium to select just those pieces of information from distant minds which are relevant to the supposed communicator. It is true of course that the sitter has generally known the communicator; and we should have to suppose that the presence of a man who has known X causes the medium to select from other minds bits of information about X and to reject bits of information about other men. On any view some selective action on the part of the sitter must be postulated, since in the main those who are supposed to be communicating when a certain man has a sitting with a medium are people whom the sitter has known. In my own sittings with Mrs Leonard, *e.g.*, the alleged communicator has from the first been one particular man who was described with considerable accuracy and named with approximate (though not complete) accuracy at the first sitting. On the Compound Theory we should have to suppose that the presence of a certain sitter "attracts" the psychic factors of certain dead men who were known to him. On the purely telepathic theory we should have to suppose that the presence of the sitter causes the medium to "select" from various minds scattered about the world certain bits of information which are relevant to someone whom the sitter has known.

Although this hypothesis is possible, there are, I think, two arguments which make slightly against it and slightly in favour of the Compound Theory. (1) On the purely telepathic theory it is difficult to see why mediumistic communications should not be as much or more concerned with one's living friends as with those who have died. This is not found to be so. On the Compound Theory this fact is explicable; for, on this hypothesis, the psychic factor of a living mind is already attached to a certain living organism, and this would presumably make it difficult or impossible for it to enter at the same time into the same relation with the organism of the entranced medium. I think that some weight must be attached to this argument, though it is not conclusive. The main interest and expectation of both sitter and medium is to get messages which purport to come from the dead and not from those who are still alive; and this might account for the fact that the medium "selects" bits of information about dead men, even on the purely telepathic theory.

(2) The second argument is due to Dr Richard Hodgson. He used it against the hypothesis of telepathy from the sitter and in favour of the hypothesis that the messages are due to the disembodied spirits of dead men. I think that the argument can be adapted so that it can be used against the hypothesis of a more extended telepathy and in favour of the Compound Theory. The argument may be put as follows. Suppose that a number of sitters$_1$ . . . S_n sit with a certain medium, and that a number of communicators C_1 . . . C_m profess to give messages through this medium. On the Compound Theory the adequacy or inadequacy of the communications which purport to come from a certain communicator C_r through a given medium would presumably depend mainly on two things; (*a*) on the complexity of the psychic factor, and (*b*) on its adaptation to the organism of the medium. There is no obvious reason why the number and accuracy of the messages which purport to come from a given communicator through the same medium should vary much from one sitter to another; for the main function of the sitter, on this hypothesis, is simply to "attract" a certain psychic factor so that it enters into a temporary combination with the medium's organism. If this happens at all, the subsequent proceedings would seem to depend on the psychic factor and the medium rather than on the sitter. We should thus expect to find certain "communicators" who are good with most sitters, and others who are bad with most sitters; we should not expect to find certain sitters who are good with most "communicators" and others who are bad with most "communicators". On the telepathic hypothesis we should expect the opposite result. For, on this view, the sitter plays a much more active part. His thoughts and interests must determine the particular selection of information which the medium makes from a perfect rag-bag of living minds. And his power to do this would presumably depend on the peculiar endowments of his own mind and on its adaptation to the mind of the medium with whom he is sitting. On this hypothesis we should therefore expect that there would be some sitters who get good results from most alleged communicators through a given medium; and that there would be other sitters who get bad results from most alleged communicators through the same medium.

Now Dr Hodgson had an enormous amount of experience of the results of sittings with Mrs Piper extending over many years. And he carefully studied them and classified them from the above points of view. His conclusion was that certain alleged *communicators* gave copious and accurate information to *most sitters;* and that other alleged *communicators* gave fragmentary and incorrect information to *most sitters*. He did not find that certain *sitters* got copious and accurate information from *most communicators;* and that certain other *sitters* got feeble and fragmentary messages from *most communicators*. Thus, on the whole, the actual results are such as might be expected on the Compound Theory and are not such as might be expected on the theory of generalised telepathy from living minds. On the whole then I am inclined to think that there is slightly more to be said for the Compound Theory than for the other alternatives.

Conclusion

The view that the mind is existentially dependent on the organism and on nothing else is compatible with all the normal facts, and is positively suggested by them, though they do not necessitate it. And it is the simplest possible view to take. The theory that the mind merely uses the body as an instrument is difficult to reconcile with the normal facts; and it is doubtful whether there are any well-established abnormal phenomena that require it. The theory that the mind is a compound substance, whose constituents are the organism and what I have called a "psychic factor", is compatible with all the normal facts; though it is not suggested by them, and is more complex than the theory that the mind is existentially dependent on the organism and on it alone. This Compound Theory seems to be the minimum assumption that will explain certain fairly well attested abnormal phenomena. Of course, many people will unhesitatingly reject the alleged facts on which I have based the argument of the latter part of this chapter. I am pretty sure that they will be wrong in doing so; but I will confine myself to this remark for their benefit. Anyone who adopts the view that the mind is existentially dependent on the organism alone is taking up a position which is not *necessitated* by the facts which everyone admits, and which can hardly be reconciled with the very *possibility* of many alleged facts for which there is at least respectable *prima facie* evidence. Now this (I should have thought) is not a comfortable position to occupy. It compels one either to ignore all the phenomena in question, or to be continually occupied in explaining them away. The former course is not scientifically respectable; for it is certain that many people, quite as sensible as oneself and far more expert, have personally investigated these matters and have persuaded themselves of the genuineness of these phenomena and of the impossibility of explaining them completely by fraud or mistake. And the latter course may at any moment be barred by some fact which we simply cannot explain away. Now the Compound Theory has at least this merit. It is compatible with all the facts which everyone admits; it has nothing against it except a superstitious objection to dualism; and it leaves open the possibility that these debatable phenomena are genuine. At the same time it does not compel anyone to accept them. It is quite open for anyone to hold that the mind is a compound of the organism and of a psychic factor which is not itself a mind; and yet to doubt or deny that there is any conclusive evidence that a psychic factor ever persists after the destruction of the organism with which it was combined, or that if it does persist it ever combines even for a moment with the organism of some living human being to form a temporary mind. This seems to me to be the great merit of the Compound Theory. It leaves open possibilities, and allows us to investigate alleged facts without an invincible *a priori* prejudice against their possibility. And yet it allows us to be as critical as we like about each of these alleged facts, and about the evidence which is offered for each of them. . . .

Personal Identity, Memory, Survival

TERENCE PENELHUM

I propose now to say a few tentative things about the two doctrines of disembodied survival and survival in bodily form, insofar only as these matters are affected by our discussion of the relation between the memory and bodily criteria of identity. This restriction forces me to bypass many questions which are essential to any comprehensive consideration of either.[1]

DISEMBODIED SURVIVAL

A present-day advocate of the possibility of disembodied survival might wish to state his case as follows:—"Pure" experiences, i.e., experiences unaccompanied by the physical processes which are their normal conditions in life, are a logical possibility. It makes sense to say of someone, for example, that he is imagining something or seeing something, even though we deny that any of the customary brain-causes or eye-changes are taking place. It is also possible for each of us to imagine some of his experiences continuing after bodily death, e.g., the famous example of witnessing one's own funeral. So it would therefore make sense to say that each of us survives bodily death as a succession of pure experiences. The identity of such bodiless beings within themselves and with their embodied predecessors is assured by the fact that among the anticipated experiences would be memories of preceding experiences, in and out of the body.

Many objections can be and have been raised to this. It is, to begin with, not clear that one can talk of beings consisting entirely of disembodied experiences. Even though, *in exceptional cases*, we might meaningfully say of someone that he was having a pure experience in spite of the fact that there could, *ex hypothesi*, be no evidence for saying so, we would in such a case be making this assertion *about* someone who was before us, i.e., a visible and tangible human being. Saying that there might be beings consisting entirely of such experiences and totally lacking bodies is rather like saying that there would be strings of experiences with no one to have them, and it does not seem to make sense to talk of experiences which nobody has. Besides this, it is often remarked that there could in no sense be a community of disembodied beings, since they could not have any knowledge of one another's presence. Nor could embodied beings like ourselves have any knowledge that they were present. In such a situation there could be no question of memory or any other criteria being applied to them. Finally, we have seen that the bodily criterion of identity is a necessary one in our embodied life and must always be on hand for us to apply the memory-criterion; if it were subtracted, it is not clear that what we would have left could properly be described as a continuing person.

To these very substantial difficulties a reply is possible, and I shall confine myself to con-

Terence Penelhum is professor of philosophy at the University of Calgary in Canada.

From the article of the same title by Terence Penelhum, *Journal of Philosophy*, Vol. LVI, No. 22 (October 22, 1959). Reprinted by permission of the author and the *Journal of Philosophy*.

sidering it and showing why I do not think it can succeed. I do not consider this shows necessarily that no other coherent hypothesis of disembodied survival is possible.

This reply would consist in saying that these difficulties establish less than their users suppose. They establish only that disembodied beings would be solitary and not *identifiable* by other beings. But we are interested in setting up a prediction that we can *now* understand. For this it is enough to be able to say that each one of us can imagine and therefore can anticipate that his own experiences, or some of them, will continue, and can simply entertain, perhaps on the basis of some authority, the opinion that the experiences of others will continue in a similar way. However lonely and unattractive such a prospect might be, we can at least make sense of it. It could be suggested that just as the only experiences I can remember having are my own, so the only ones I can anticipate continuing to have are my own; so from the mere fact that I can imagine experiences continuing, it follows that I can anticipate myself continuing. And even if, through inability to perceive others, I eventually lost the use of the distinction between myself and them, in erecting the hypothesis now I can say that the series of experiences I imagine continuing will always be mine. It might be thought that we do not need any criterion of identity in erecting a hypothesis of disembodied survival at all, even a memory-criterion.

But although it is true that we can imagine experiences which it would be tempting to speak of in the language of disembodied survival, the question is how one is to describe such imaginative exercises. It is much too simple to answer this question by saying that, if you preface your description with the assertion that you will be dead by then, you automatically rule out the description itself. But weightier reasons can be given for the same conclusion. Let us look again at this analogy between remembering and anticipating. It is true that I can only remember experiences that I myself had. This establishes a logical connection between the *concepts* of memory and personal identity—that on certain occasions one either has to apply both or neither; it does not tell us which of these things to do on a given occasion. It is also true that if I claim to remember, or *seem* to myself or others to remember, a certain experience, it follows that I claim or seem to remember having it *myself*; but of course it does not follow that I *did* have it myself—either it did not happen at all, or it happened to somebody else and not to me, the latter being the possibility at issue in most identity cases. Shoemaker has shown us that even though on most occasions when we seem to remember something we really must, for the distinction between the two to exist at all there must be some other way of establishing whether the experience was mine, or another's, or non-existent. Let us turn to the case of anticipation. It is true that if I anticipate having an experience, I anticipate *myself* having it, and that if I *correctly* anticipate having it, *I* will have it. But an anticipation can also be incorrect, so it follows that I can *in*correctly anticipate having the experience, and this means, as in the memory-case, either that no one will have it, or that someone will but not myself. For the anticipation to be either true or false, i.e., for the hypothesis to be genuine, there must be some way of understanding a claim in it that I shall have a certain experience rather than someone else.[2] In other words, neither the fact that we rest content with a hypothesis that we alone now can entertain, nor the fact that our imaginative exercises are restricted to the persistence of *our own* experiences, obviates the need for some criterion of identity *in the hypothesis*; such a criterion serving to distinguish an experience as one person's rather than another's.

The bodily criterion is ruled out. So we are apparently forced back once more on memory. The hypothesis would have to incorporate the statement that for one being, such as myself, rather than another, to have a given predicted experience the being having it must be able to remember some earlier experience that I had.[3] But there are many problems.

1. We have to be able in the present context to make sense of the idea of the person having the experience also having the memory. Even if we could make sense of the phrase "the person having the experience" without some specifiable means of singling out the person, at least by description, other than by reference to the experience he is having (a function performed in life by reference

to bodies), we still have to specify under what conditions the person having the experience would be said to be, and under what conditions he would not be, also the person having the memory. And in such a situation the condition could not be the mere occurrence of the memory itself.

2. The same conclusion can be reached a second way. For the person having the experience to be one previous person rather than another, the memory he also has must be a *genuine* memory. For our hypothesis really to include a prediction of memory it must enable us to distinguish, in some way parallel to the way the physical facts enable us to distinguish in life, between real and apparent memories. This requires us to be able to say that the event the disembodied being seems to remember really did happen to him. And this requires some way of making sense of the concept of its happening to him rather than another, other than by reference to the fact that he seems to remember it.

3. The same point comes out a third way. For our hypothesis to be articulated it has, of course, to involve the prediction of some kind of memory-event, some experience that could be called "seeming to remember." Let us assume that we could understand such a phrase here. One of the objections to according more than secondary status to the memory-criterion was the fact that memory-claims are only forthcoming from people intermittently, whereas bodily facts about them are, in a clear sense, always available. But for the identity of a disembodied person to be articulable in terms of memory alone, it would seem that the experience of seeming (and *correctly* seeming) to remember should be available constantly in the way in which bodily facts are available constantly throughout the life of an embodied person, and I doubt if we could intelligibly describe this requirement's being met. If we are not willing to try it, then some other criterion of identity would seem to be covertly implied, at least in the hypothesis that an experience which is not conjoined with the recollection of some other experience still belongs to the same life-history as that other.

4. If one disembodied person can seem to himself to remember an event, so can another. Unless one wishes to rule out this possibility in one's hypothesis, it is clear that to make sense of the statement that one disembodied person correctly seems to remember having an experience, and the other incorrectly seems to remember it, one has to have some independent concept of how one could have the memory and the original experience also, and the other not. And without a body, it is not made clear what this would be.

So to have a coherent concept of disembodied survival there would seem to be needed some criterion of identity which would enable us to make sense of the prediction that one person (e.g., myself) rather than another person will have a particular experience. It would also seem that memory cannot serve here, and that any attempt to make it do so involves the covert appeal to some other unnamed principle. It is easy to say at this point that philosophers who try to work out such hypotheses are smuggling in by implication the very bodily identity they are supposed to have rejected. This may be true; but it does not automatically follow from this that no suitable concept can be found consistent with the denial of the existence of the body. Perhaps some concept of *physical continuity* might be invented, and perhaps, indeed, some such concept is present in such theories as Locke's doctrine of identity of consciousness. I do not intend here to explore this metaphysical possibility. It is enough in our present context to indicate that memory will not suffice.

BODILY SURVIVAL

The religiously more interesting doctrine of bodily survival, and the identity-problem that arises in connection with it, can be stated thus. It is supposed that at some future time a very large number of human beings will suddenly appear, each one clearly believing himself to be some person long since dead. Could such a claim be countenanced, or are we forced to say of such a prediction that it should be described as one in which a large number of people will arise who happen to be similar to other dead ones?

There is, first of all, no problem about criteria of identity for such people subsequent to their appearance. We can quite easily imagine both the bodily and memory criteria applying to them. In this respect, clearly, the hypothesis is much easier to articulate than that of disembodied survival, where the very idea of a multiplicity of distinct disembodied beings gives trouble apart from their identification with physical predecessors. The problem here is whether we can conceive of such future bodily people as ourselves.

Let us imagine the problem as it would face someone who had lived through the transition, and had access to records and other evidence of deceased people. Let us also insist that if there were wholesale appearances of these new beings any linguistic temptations to change, which could be resisted in isolated instances, would have to be contemplated very seriously indeed. Such a witness could learn that the new people he saw knew how to make memory claims in the manner Mr. Shoemaker says we could learn this of the cobbler-"prince." Should he, if he found that the memory-claims of the newcomers fitted the lives of the past individuals with whom they claimed to be identical, say that they *were* those people?

I have given reasons above for the view that if the memory-criterion and the bodily criterion seem to clash, we should either deny genuine memory, or abandon the memory-criterion by amending the meaning of the word "remember." What, then, would seem to follow from this in the present case? I think that however firmly one accepts such a guiding principle it does not guide us very clearly; for one has to decide, first of all, whether or not the bodily criterion is violated in this example. If we should answer that it is, then the memory-claims have all to be spurious or else only memories in some new and weaker sense; if we should answer that it is not, then we could accept the memory-claims as genuine and agree to the mass identification. But the question of whether or not to say the bodily criterion has been violated is a decision-question, involving clearly the question of how far one can contemplate adjustments in the meaning of the phrase "the same body." I shall now explore this question. If the pull of the memory-claims is very strong, as it would be, then I would suppose that it would be sufficient for the purpose if no conclusive reasons could be found for *not* extending the concept of bodily identity to cover this unique expectation.

The evidence we normally use to establish bodily identity is very various. It goes to establish bodily identity by revealing not only similarity of characteristics, which would not necessarily identify clearly enough, but also continuity in space and time. It is this which seems to be lost in our supposed case. There is in every one of the envisaged examples a gap in space and time between the last stage of the former person and the appearance of the new person. This fact would be even further marked if the new person resembled the former one not at the close of his career but at some earlier point in it.

It is already clear that making the survival bodily does not get around identity-problems in any simple way; but there are some defenses against this difficulty. First, it should be pointed out that the change contemplated in the notion of bodily identity is one of addition. There would be no need to change the criteria of identity in ordinary life merely because one elected to say that if the eventuality described took place this could be accounted the same body. Physical continuity would still be a condition of bodily identity up till physical death. Second, the discontinuity envisaged here is of a very special kind. In normal life, if there is evidence that the body before us is not spatio-temporally continuous with Smith's body, it follows that it is not Smith's body; but this follows because (unless Smith is dead) there is then some other body which is continuous with his and therefore *is* his, and because the body before us is then continuous with some other body, say Mr. Jones's, and is therefore Mr. Jones's. In our hypothesis these essential corollaries of ordinary discontinuity are absent. So a basic reason for insisting upon the retention of the normal requirement of continuity is gone. Third, it might be thought that to believe that one of these new persons could be identified with some earlier person is to commit oneself to saying that a person could go out of existence and start to exist again, which is an absurd thing to say of persons or anything else. But even supposing it is absurd, perhaps we do not have to say it: for we could say instead that we were changing the concept of a person and of a human body so that it incorporated a gap within it.[4] There are precedents in our language for this, though they are of a very different sort: certain temporal entities like tunes, or performances of plays, or march-pasts, contain observable events or objects and then pauses and then more observables; in these cases the entities do not go out of existence during the pauses, even though in a sense nothing is there—they incorporate the pauses. They continue without being continuous. We might suggest that a person could incorporate one such gap—the one between death and resurrection. This would mean that he could be said to exist during the gap even though nothing of him were there; so that the answer to the old question "What has to persist between death and resurrection for the resurrected to be the same person as the deceased?" is "Nothing."[5] Fourth, it might be suggested that there could be two people in the new world, each closely resembling some earlier person, and each having the same set of memory-claims to fit him. If such a case occurred, of course, there could be no sense to the claim that one of them really was Smith and the other was not. To admit this possibility is not to admit any internal absurdity in the hypothesis for we could just say that when this happened the two newcomers would not be identifiable with any predecessors, but would of course have their own shorter-term identities in the new world. They would be oddities, but not logical ones. Nor would it be logically odd to draw the conclusion that Smith had not survived. In any actual hypothesis it is likely that duplicated memory-claims would be ruled out in fact, which is acceptable if they are not ruled out in theory. It would also be convenient to insist in a general way that there would be no more newcomers than deceaseds.

But this brings us to a final difficulty which has to be granted much greater weight, and which at least weakens the hypothesis even if it is not fatal to it. It is a difficulty we can grasp when we see that to the above stipulations we cannot, with any confidence, add the stipulation that there are in fact to be no two newcomers both of whose bodies resemble some deceased's to the same degree.

On the view I have adopted, and tried to follow here, on the primacy of the bodily criterion of identity, the reason that the bodily criterion has to be considered satisfiable for memory to provide a criterion at all is that only thus can one envisage the possibility of checking, where doubt may exist, whether the memory-claim is true. Now for our hypothesis to masquerade as one in which the normal criteria are preserved in essentials, this essential must still be retained. This means that however compelling the memory-claims seem in a given case, there must exist at least the logical possibility of a satisfactory bodily check without reference to them. For us to be in a position to accept the Smith-like memory-claims of someone it must be possible to describe what physical tests would independently establish that this person had Smith's body, and in describing what these tests would be it is impossible to make any mention of the exactitude of the memory-claims. It is here that the gap becomes a serious logical obstacle. For, by hypothesis, the newly-appeared persons are in different times and places from the persons they claim to be, and in our present context they could not be allocated to the earlier times and places by reference to their memory-claims. But this only leaves, as bodily evidence, similarity of bodily feature. The question then arises whether this could be conclusive evidence. It seems this could only be if there were some feature in common *uniquely* between a newcomer and a former person. I do not want to insist that in the odd case this condition could not be satisfied; but on the scale necessary to accommodate the hypothesis to anything approximating to an actual religious expectation the chances against this are daunting. Our hypothesis would at best provide for survival in a small minority of cases. We also have to conclude that the more one is inclined to think of the resurrected bodies as differing from their human predecessors, the greater this difficulty becomes.

To summarize: It is incorrect to suggest that one can envisage disembodied survival without any criterion of identity, and it is also incorrect to say that the memory-criterion could be the sole one in such a case. In the belief in bodily survival, the possibility of identification depends finally upon the chances of bodily identification across a gap. Since there must be some logically possible occasions where this is done independently of reference to memory-claims, the gap itself provides reasons, though perhaps not conclusive reasons, for the belief that the hypothesis does not allow for these.

NOTES

1. In what follows I am much indebted to the writings of Professor Flew, and to discussions with Messrs. Chappel, Schneewind, and Wick of the University of Chicago, and with Professor S. Körner.

2. It might be said that I have ignored the possible hypothesis that I shall be the only survivor. But for this to make sense it is necessary for the hypothesis of multiple survival to do so.

3. I may seem to have fallen myself into the habit of talking of unowned experiences. But the point could be put equally well, though more lengthily, by saying that for me to anticipate myself (e.g.) seeing a sunset, I must be able to understand the statement that someone else will be seeing it and not myself. And the appeal to the memory-criterion could be put by saying that for it to be Penelhum who is seeing the sunset it must be possible for the person who is seeing it to remember some event in Penelhum's life.

4. See *Analysis*, Competition No. 11, June, 1957.

5. No doubt if someone could construct an intelligible hypothesis of bodiless continuance it could be used to straddle the gap if other reasons required this.

The Next World

TERENCE PENELHUM

In order to investigate the extent to which we can give content to the notion of disembodied personality we have examined the possible use of concepts of perception and agency. It was taken for granted that if a disembodied person sees or hears, what he sees or hears will be objects (things, persons) that an embodied person would see or hear; and that if a disembodied person can perform actions, these would include, in addition to mental actions, actions that bring about changes in our physical world. It seemed a matter of choice whether or not to say that his seeing things in space, or acting on them, implied his having a spatial position; but it seems natural, even so, to say that we have proceeded so far as though the disembodied survivor would inhabit the world that we inhabit. The assumption is natural enough: for how else could he have anything to perceive, or anything to do? But this assumption has only to be made explicit to be shown to be questionable. It would be a strange discussion of survival indeed that did not include some consideration of the possibility that those who survive death survive in *another* world, not in this one.

This possibility, on the other hand, runs the risk of being, for us, an empty one. For references to the Next World cannot be intelligible for us unless it is possible to use the language of our world of things and persons to describe it. And only if references to it are intelligible can we understand the claim that a survivor might perceive or act in it. So the chance of giving content to the belief that after death one survives, disembodied, in another world, depends on our being able to articulate the concept of the Next World in the language of this one.

One obvious way of doing this is to say that the Next World, though numerically distinct from this world, is nevertheless a spatial world with physical objects in it. The theory of another world that is spatial and contains physical objects, but is not in Space is dauntingly counter-intuitive, but I cannot explore its difficulties here. If we were able to overcome them, then the difficulty of articulating the notions of disembodied perception and agency and the like for *that* world would be much the same as that of articulating the same notions for *this* one. And we have already dealth with this. On the other hand, any difficulty there may be associated with the belief that one enters the Next World from this one *in* the body must be postponed until we consider the doctrine of resurrection; and it is clearly likely to be a difficulty about the identifying of the person so entering with one of us. But there is another possibility, more in accord perhaps with the general tenor of belief in disembodied survival. It is the possibility that the Next World, and the disembodied persons 'in' it, are not in space at all, either this or another.

But if the Next World is not in space, how can there be anything in the Next World to perceive or to do? How can one say at all what the Next World, so conceived, would be like? However unpromising an enterprise it might seem to be to answer this question, an answer

---

From Terence Penelhum, *Survival and Disembodied Existence*. Reprinted by permission of the publisher. New Jersey: Humanities Press, Inc.

of great ingenuity and persuasiveness has been offered by Professor H. H. Price.[1]

Failing the existence of perceptible physical objects in an environment that the disembodied survivor would occupy, the content of such a survivor's experience has to be spun from within. Whatever we say of disembodied existence, the inner activity of imagination, which has no organ, is something a survivor might very well be expected to continue. Price suggests, therefore, that our survivor who is out of space could have a life which consists in sequences of *images*. He claims that the experience of a disembodied survivor, not in our space, can contain many analogies of our ordinary perceptual experience, because of the significance that would come to be attached to certain kinds of image sequences. In his very suggestive development of this hypothesis, Price makes use of the generic notion of having images, introducing for it the term 'imaging'. Certain key elements in his account depend on the legitimacy of his doing this. He says there might be analogues of the perception of one's own body for the disembodied person: there might 'be' a cluster of appropriate 'body'-images—presumably present involuntarily. There might also be an apparent environment which might be changed voluntarily, as one changes one's imagined surroundings in day-dreams. These voluntary and involuntary experiences together form the 'world' of the survivor. He argues it would be wrong to say that the Next World, if it consisted of experiences of this kind, would be illusory; for the images would, for the survivor, *be there*, and would therefore constitute the only reality which his world could have.

Now there are at least some philosophical objections to speaking of images collectively in this way. Malcolm, for example, has argued against the very natural philosophical inference that because we dream that some events occur, there must therefore be an actual sequence of image-events that really does occur in our experience.[2] Ryle has argued against a similar inference in the case of imagining.[3] Munsat has pointed out some of the dangers that lie in wait for us if we do not distinguish one kind of imagining from another with enough care.[4] If their arguments have force (and I shall not explore them here) they would tend to make us wary of Price's last suggestion about the reality of the Next World, for this depends upon severing the talk of images from its normal connections with the language of dreaming, imagining, or hallucinating. But it is not at all clear that in speaking of having images we are saying anything more or less than that we are dreaming or imagining or hallucinating. Except, of course, that in staying with the generic expression we refrain from saying *which* of these things we are doing. This very imprecision makes it easy to be lulled into accepting the suggestion that one is doing *none* of them. Yet if one is having involuntary images and is not (*ex hypothesi*) perceiving, then one is presumably dreaming or hallucinating, whereas if one is having voluntary images, or controlling one's images at will, yet not perceiving, one is presumably imagining or daydreaming. So there can be nothing more to the suggestion that the world of images is for our survivors the *real* world than the claim that imagining or dreaming or hallucinating is, in default of there being objects in an environment to perceive, all that these survivors can do. This suggestion, though, is right enough.

It is not certain that all of these possibilities are open. In particular, the language of dreaming seems odd for a being that cannot sleep. And certain customary associations of the notions that remain would have to be abandoned—such as the suggestion that a hallucination can be combined with a genuine perception (that I have a hallucination of a pink rat on the mantelpiece which I see). But in view of the fact that such activities as imagining and hallucinating do not have organs that we do them with, as sight and hearing do, it seems pedantic to suggest that we could not intelligibly ascribe at least a reduced number of such mental performances to the survivor. If these were, for example, hallucinating (for the involuntary cases) and imagining (for the voluntary cases) we would probably have an adequate vocabulary in terms of which the language of imaging could be understood. The fact, however, that it had to be understood in these terms would serve to remind us that the survivor does not perceive, but that his world is private. We are speaking here, of course, of what *we* can properly say *about* such a survivor. It is quite in order to suggest, as Price does, that he might come to give his inherited language of perception a *new use*, to describe to himself the imaginary and hallucinatory experiences he has.

As Price explains, this could come about in the following way. There might be a cluster of persistent visual images, presumably involuntary, that came to constitute an image-body. There would be no body, indeed no environment, but the survivor might have involuntary images *of* such a body. These need not all be visual: if we allow tactile and kinaesthetic hallucinations, disembodiment might seem very like embodiment is. Furthermore, there might be involuntary images of a non-existent environment, so that although the survivor would not be in space, he might have the imaginative illusion that he was. We then have the materials necessary for the private use in this image-world of all the concepts of perception that we use now.

Price adds a further suggestion of great interest: that the Next World might be a wish-fulfilment world. Wishes for certain events might be followed, as in daydreams, by the images of those events. The wish to be at a certain place might be followed by the images of that place. In other words, in the absence of a real environment, the survivor's imagination might create its own private one. On the surface this would seem to be the place where we would make use of the concept of voluntary imaging. But in the case of deeper wish-fulfilments, where the wishes are unconscious or unacknowledged, the images would not be under *conscious* control. It might rather be that in some cases there were hallucinatory experiences generated by unconscious or unacknowledged wishes. It might be here that a survivor reaped the benefits or suffered the penalties of the character he had built up during life. The involuntary images, whether due to unconscious wishes or not, might *to him* come to be events that happened to him in his (hallucinatory) environment, whereas the sequences of images under voluntary control might *to him* come to be his actions in and upon that environment. We need not explore whether if they come to be these things to him he could still retain his normal concept of imagining. But we now, constructing this fantasy about him, can say of him only that he would be living an existence of imaginings and hallucinations.

With these provisos, there seems (again, if we put aside questions of knowledge and identity) no insuperable obstacle to the construction of a logically viable notion of disembodied survival out of space. The account we have constructed, following Price, has two difficulties.

First and far more serious, is the Next World not a solipsistic world? Although no disembodied person could perceive another, in a world in which survivors could perceive embodied persons, they would have the same reason to believe in the existence of other disembodied persons as those embodied persons had. Scanty though this seems to be, it might include allegedly paranormal manifestations of disembodied agency. But in the Next World as we have now described it the survivor could perceive no thing or person whatever. This does not mean that he could not have, among the images in his experience, images 'of' other persons, but whatever they would come to mean to him they could not be perceptions of other disembodied survivors, since those survivors could have no perceptible characteristics. It is conceivable, of course, that the images that one survivor had of other persons were closely similar to the images that certain other survivors in fact had for their image-bodies. It might not be wholly outrageous to construe this as perception; but nothing short of pre-established harmony could account for its occurrence, as Leibniz and perhaps Berkeley understood. For Smith's mind may contain images of Jones, but it cannot contain Jones himself.

It is tempting to say the same thing about the logical possibility of our disembodied survivor's perceiving embodied persons or physical things. Suppose it were the case, as we have so far assumed it is not, that some reasonably lengthy sequence of physical-object-images is interpreted by its owner as a perception of some part of our world, and that there is, by coincidence, just such a part of our world that is arranged the way the contents of his image-world look to him to be arranged? Might not this fortuitously veridical hallucination be called *seeing*? And would not some doctrine of pre-established harmony be the only way of explaining it? One must certainly answer 'Yes' to the first question, and probably to the second. But the situation envisaged in the first is the one with which we began the investigation of disembodied perception, since this is the only definition of seeing for disembodied persons open to us. At this point our former and our present accounts of the survivor's world are not clearly distinguishable. And it is important to remember that even in our account of disembodied perception where we assumed that the survivor perceived things and persons in this world, no suggestion was offered of how he could come to do so. To maintain the purity of the second hypothesis, then, the survivor must not be allowed to perceive this world from the Next one. His images, that is, must either not correspond to any vistas in this world, or not be thought by their owner to be perceptions of it.

This brings us to our second, and less serious, difficulty. In our earlier account of disembodied agency it was tacitly assumed that any interference by disembodied agents in our world would be the consequence of their perception of it. If this is not admitted into the hypothesis, then it is hard to see how any event in this world can be ascribed to someone in the Next except as an utterly mysterious cosmic accident, unknown even to its perpetrator. The inutility for physical researchers of this sort of possibility, in contrast to that which we explored before, is clear.

NOTES

1. H. H. Price, "Survival and the Idea of 'Another World,'" and "What Kind of Next World?"

2. Norman Malcolm, *Dreaming*.

3. Gilbert Ryle, *The Concept of Mind*, Chapter VIII.

4. Stanley Munsat, *The Concept of Memory*, Chapter VI.

The Resurrection of the Body

ROBERT YOUNG

In the debate about the meaningfulness of theological assertions it has been suggested that Christian theology makes empirical claims because of its dimension of eschatological verifiability (or falsifiability). It is not my intention to consider directly either the empiricist approach to meaningfulness from which the original challenge to theological assertions arose or to discuss the status of eschatological verification under such an approach, though as a matter of fact I believe that theological assertions are factually significant and truth-claiming.

It seems clearly to have been Paul's view that the whole interconnected system of Christian beliefs hinged on the truth of certain key propositions such as those about the empty tomb and Jesus' bodily resurrection.[1] It is of more than passing significance that the resurrection hope of believers was also central in first century Christian belief; this was no doubt a consequence of the emphatic concern with eschatology in primitive Christian thought.[2]

As John Hick[3] has conveniently pointed out, there are two chief issues for philosophical scrutiny in the matter of this resurrection hope. Firstly (and in his view the more important[4]) there is the issue of the relation between our world and the resurrection world, particularly the location of the latter and the proffering of epistemically unambiguous features of resurrection life which would establish beyond reasonable doubt that the Christian hope had indeed been consummated. The second issue (and in my view the primary one) is simply that of the personal identity of the resurrected persons with their counterparts who died in this world. For if only their replicas are to be raised, there is no reason for believers to concern themselves about a resurrection hope, or for non-believers to consider the possibility of being called to account for their unbelief and sins.

In this paper I intend to consider certain strategies which have been (or might conceivably be) used in relation to this second issue, to show why they founder on the matter of retaining personal identity between this life and resurrection life (though I will suggest at some points what could conceivably salvage some of these strategies), and then to develop in more detail a view which I think satisfies the identity requirements to be proposed. My hope is that this latter defence of resurrection life will show it to be a viable possibility under God[5]—a proper aim for constructive philosophical theology.

II

In considering the question of personal identity it is usually the problem of re-identification rather than of individuation that proves troublesome. In the philosophical debate of the last twenty years over this question of re-identification, perhaps the single most

Dr. Robert Young is a professor of philosophy at La Trobe University in Victoria, Australia.

Reprinted (with 1976 revisions by the author) from *Sophia*—A Journal for Discussion in Philosophical Research, Vol. IX, No. 2 (July 1970).

important point of dispute has been the necessity of bodily identity (or better, spatio-temporal continuity) in any set of criteria designed to cope with re-identification. All participants in the debate appear to be agreed that neither spatio-temporal continuity nor the cluster of memory, personality and so on can be deemed a sufficient condition of personal identity. Bernard Williams and Graham Nerlich have, however, challenged the view that there could be a set of sufficient conditions which leaves out spatio-temporal continuity and still enables us to distinguish non-vacuously mere exact similarity and true identity. They have claimed that only by taking cognizance of this fact could there be a logical guarantee against the possibility of duplication even if the duplicate be in every respect similar. They have thus stressed the one-one relation fundamental to identity. Despite the forceful arguments by C. B. Martin, Terence Penelhum and Sydney Shoemaker to the contrary, and in particular the arguments of the former two that in the penumbra cases the present concept of personal identity breaks down and conceptual decision procedures are required, I remain persuaded that the Nerlich-Williams challenge must be taken very seriously. Indeed I hope to show that failure to accept the challenge seriously is at the heart of the failure of the defences to be considered.

III

The two defences to be considered first acknowledge the need for continuity of some kind, though whether they are acceptable notions of continuity remains for consideration.

We begin with the traditional defence of resurrection hope which appeals to the soul as the continuing entity which preserves identity, the soul being considered in some dominant strands of Christian thought as the "real", even if incomplete, person.

As a preliminary point I should make it clear that the biblical view of man is not dualistic despite the dominance of this tradition. Indeed it is I think quite clear that Paul[6] argued *ad hominem* against this essentially non-Hebrew view of man in his key discussion of the resurrection hope, and further that its pervasive influence in Christian thought stems from its use for Gentile apologetic purposes.

Second, and more importantly in this paper, we must consider certain objections of a philosophical rather than biblical origin to this traditional defence.

Flew[7] has pointed out that consideration of the question of the soul as identity-preserver through death requires prior argument to show that the soul is the real person. Though I know of no such argument which is both based on reasonable premises and likely to be valid, let us allow that there is or may be one. Even making this allowance the defence still faces a barrage of problems raised particularly by C. B. Martin[8] and Terence Penelhum.[9] Martin proposed a number of situations involving the instantiation of at least two qualitatively similar experiences occurring simultaneously, with the aim of showing the difficulty (perhaps impossibility) in such situations of marking off the experiences as those of some particular disembodied soul rather than of another. Now if God is to be able to raise up bodies for disembodied souls, he must be able to both individuate and reidentify such series of disembodied experiences (souls) and this task must be in the realm of the logically possible.

Penelhum, like Martin, has grave doubts about the sense of the notion of disembodied existence. He has argued convincingly that if memory (and the cluster of associated concepts) is held to be the sole criterion for identity then we could never independently identify a disembodied person. Hence "to have a coherent concept of disembodied survival there would seem to be needed some criterion of identity which would enable us to make sense of the prediction that one person rather than another person will have a particular experience", and if memory cannot serve then there must be some other unnamed principle (p 899). In his view this could only be spatio-temporal continuity or some concept of physical continuity. Without appeal (covert or overt) to such a principle we cannot make sense of individuating an anticipated or remembered experience.[10]

In the face of these and other objections what could the believer in souls reply? He might offer the short, fideistic response that

God, being all-wise, will handle this problem which is only a problem because of our finitude. Such a response would leave no room for further discussion.

Basing his claims on the ground-work done by H. H. Price in his "Survival and the Idea of 'Another World' ", Stewart Sutherland has recently attempted to show how disembodied souls could be individuated.[11] He claims that being faced with a clearly conceivable situation of post-mortem image-experients might lead us to modify our concept of identity so that we would presume identity rather than exact similarity in this other world *in the absence of evidence to the contrary* (such as reduplication). He further suggests that image-experients in the image world of Price would be able to distinguish satisfactorily between similarity and identity in the following way (p 383):

> . . . one could think that the person with whom one communicated a short time ago is very similar to the person with whom one is now in telepathic communication, but (know) that it isn't the *same* person because that other person is in fact at this moment presenting himself as a telepathic apparition in a different area of one's image space.

We can only reply with Nerlich to the first contention about dissimilarity counting against identity and similarity for it, that "if, in a case of discontinuity, it is enough for identity that B should exactly resemble A, then we can find no room for saying even that B *might* be a different thing . . ."[12]. Against the second contention quoted above we need only reply that, in the absence of an argument showing that the mental images of disembodied souls can be spatially located, the claim does not seem viable.

A third type of response could be made along the lines Geach seems to favour.[13] He says that if we held with Aquinas, "that each disembodied human soul retained a capacity for reunion to such a body as would reconstitute a man identifiable with the man who died", this might satisfactorily account for the individuation of disembodied souls in that they would differ by being fitted for reunion with different bodies. In the light of our previous discussion I am not sure that even this puts the task of reidentification within the range of logically possible states of affairs for God, but clearly if it does, then it does the trick for those committed to belief in souls (even in Geach's sense in which it is nonsensical to ascribe sensations and feelings to the disembodied souls). However one might well ask whether there is any independent evidence to support Aquinas and Geach in their otherwise seemingly *ad hoc* (and hence question-begging) move.

We noted above Penelhum's suggestion that some concept of physical continuity for disembodied souls would overcome the individuation problem and the reidentification one (he cited Locke's doctrine of identity of consciousness as a possibility). With this in mind we might try to devise a locative criterion for distinguishing disembodied souls or minds in space-time. If this were to prove feasible souls could be uniquely identified by reference to their spatio-temporal position.[14] But the task still has (to my knowledge) not yet been accomplished.

One general consideration about these replies is that were an identity theory of mind to prove the correct one then disembodied existence might remain logically possible but empirically impossible.[15]

IV

Consonant with the popularity of parables in philosophical theology one might devise a parable to draw out the sort of idea contemplated in the next 'solution' to the identity problem for resurrected persons.

Suppose I were to make a model sand castle, then scattered its constituent parts and later remade it from the same grains of sand taking care to replace each grain of sand in exactly the same position as in the original model (the grains could be all coloured or marked individualistically). The question arises whether this would be the same or only an exactly similar castle.

Now I do not see how we could reject *a priori* the possibility of this being the same sand castle unless we are prepared to take the radical step of saying that, for any object constituted by a number of smaller parts, if the object is dismantled and later reassembled it ceases when dismantled to be capable of being the same object as it was prior to dismantling. That this would be a radical step can be seen by considering our familiarity with the idea of dismantling and reassembling the same object (e.g. the same car, house, watch, radio) when not a single part is substituted.[16] Now we may be hasty in so readily ascribing identity, but surely when it would not even *in principle* be possible to stand the "exactly similar" item next to the original there can be no real doubt that this is the same object. There is no aura of legislation about our description in this case of the object as "the same", for the case is quite distinct from the puzzle cases discussed in the literature from Locke onwards.

Now it could well be contended that there will be an historical continuity between the constituents of the earthly body at death and the resurrection body such that the identity problem is set aside by this material continuity. Though the body be in a continuous state of material change the resurrection body on this view would be the same body because made out of historically the same quantified matter into which the body disintegrated just as the model sand castle when rebuilt is the same.[17] In passing it might be well to point out that the model here is different from one rejected by Aquinas based on the re-casting of a metal statue. He says of such a re-cast statue that while the matter could be the same the form couldn't, but there is no comparable standardly identifiable particle for metals which would serve as a counterpart to the grain of sand.

The first difficulty for this defence of the resurrection is that there will be doubt (or even despair) at the identity of those whose constituent matter has been shared among others. At the simplest level we have the notorious cannibal cases, and more sophisticatedly it appears that the energy into which cells are transformed could well be shared among a number of people making it impossible for the identity of some to be preserved with the sharing of this "atomic" energy.

The thesis might be modified by claiming more weakly that enough matter is taken up into the resurrection body from the body of this life to secure identity (in conjunction of course with memory of personal life, similarity of, even if developed, character, satisfaction of anticipations and so on). Thus it might be urged, just as in earthly life we do not require every particle to be numerically the same over time in view of constant cellular replenishment, so here we would still have identity. But clearly this is a departure from the sand model case and while it may not be disputed to speak of identity there, it certainly could be here, for God could make the resurrection body before the earthly death or make more than one resurrection counterpart since he is not forced to use *all* the ingredients (as we were in the sand model case) of the earthly body in making the resurrection body.

We could make a further modification in an attempt to salvage this defence. Let us require that God in making the resurrection body must use some of the matter *cum* energy which constituted the body of this life *at the time of death*. This would remove the force of the counterfactual that the resurrected could only be replicas since God could have done the reconstituting before the death of the earthly counterpart (for obviously he is logically restricted to waiting until the death occurs). Once the counterfactual has been deposed in this way, a believer appealing to this present defence could legitimately appeal to God's nonmalicious character in order to set aside the possibility that God might make two or more replicas.

Thus so long as God could both keep track of the matter he proposed to use and also ensure that he was never required to take all the matter from one person to permit a number of others to have their identity preserved, this third modification of the "material continuity" defence would be workable.

V

The next two strategies to be considered make no appeal to any continuity at all as did in both the "soul" and "material continuity" defences. They both deliberately oppose the requirement for some spatio-temporal continuity by pitting the force of a case against the principle. Let us first consider what I call "the linguistic defence", and then in the next section "the temporal continuity defence".

In an article entitled "Puzzle Cases and Earthquakes",[18] Robert Herbert drew up an imaginative puzzle case and ranged it against the Nerlich-Williams insistence on the necessity for spatio-temporal continuity in identity attributions. He was concerned with the question of personal identity but his view lends itself to a takeover by the believer in resurrection. He argues that it is only a restricting presupposition about meaning which leads to the "philosophical or intellectual" understanding of his puzzle case that commitment to the Nerlich-Williams principle requires, rather than to his own "spiritual understanding". The difference between these two types of understanding is parallelled by being able to give for philosophical purposes an accurate *description* of a form of life and being able to *participate* in that form of life.

Thus, when in Herbert's case Volter makes identity judgments, what he is doing is bound up essentially with participating in a certain form of life. So, even though a person might clearly recognize the reminder that judgments of identity have as their ground that only one body be involved in the relevant way, according to Herbert such a person could still make what have the role, use or force of judgments of identity in his own life (or circle). Such a person would not be attempting to satisfy certain necessary or sufficient conditions[19] in using the terms "same" or "exactly similar", but would so act as to reveal that he believed there was a distinction between these terms. Herbert admits that on the Nerlich-Williams terms Volter's identity judgments are unsupported. The only clue from Herbert's view as to how one is able to participate or understand spiritually is a *post facto* one, namely does one so act as to participate in the form of life?[20] Indeed he closes his article with the following comment: ". . . who can tell whether, if he were confronted by the situation faced by Volter, he would be visited by an earthquake?"

Now the believer in resurrection might take over the substance of this view and claim that all that matters is being able to participate in resurrection life, not being able to justify to those outside the Christian circle the claim that it will be he, not his replica, who will be resurrected. In fact he will so act (toward other resurrected persons) as to show that he regards them as identical with their earthly counterparts, just as he so regards and remembers himself as the same.

The challenge to come up with a set of conditions, leaving out spatio-temporal continuity, is thus regarded as irrelevant and we have the case versus the principle. Now clearly Herbert and the "linguistic defence" are reliant on the Wittgensteinian suggestion that meaning is (determined by) the use in the lives of the users. Those who urge the fulfilment of certain criteria as a test of understanding meaning will just regard this as begging the question. According to Herbert it is one's situation in the case that determines one's probable reaction to the puzzling facts (presumably whether one has experienced the earthquake or "conversion" in one's life—otherwise this would seem to be false, since we can well imagine Volter initiating some type of restraining legal action rather than accepting "Erik" as Eino).

The only thing I would want to say of this defence is that the adopting of an attitude and the acting out of such an attitude in one's life or circle is not a necessarily justified procedure. A child's taking up a particular attitude to a replacement replica of a lost toy does not make the new toy the same one numerically as the old. Since it does not seem to be "irrelevant" to question the grounds for adopting the attitude, I consider that the believer must reject such a defence as this as inadequate for securing his resurrection hope unless he has no objection to it being possibly only a replica of himself (no matter how good a participant in the resurrection form of life) which enters into *his* resurrection joy.[21]

VI

The second of the defences to be considered which seek to oppose the Nerlich-Williams prihciple with a case of greater intuitive force than the principle, is that put forward by John Hick in the article previously cited.[22] Hick offers three progressively arranged "pictures", the possibility of which he contends is more important than their oddness. The critique will thus be offered, too, in terms of logical possibilities. Hick's first "picture" involves the disappearance of a certain academic from a meeting and the simultaneous appearance at another meeting elsewhere of an "exact replica", exactly similar as to both bodily and mental characteristics as the certain academic. There is continuity of memory, complete similarity of bodily features including even fingerprints, hair and eye coloration and stomach contents and also of beliefs, habits and mental propensities. In fact, says Hick there is everything that would lead us to identify the one who appeared with the one who disappeared, except continuity of occupancy of space. Just in passing we might note that Hick doesn't use fingerprint replication, say, as a question-begging device by saying that it guarantees identity.

Hick contends from this first picture that we would be inclined, indeed required to, and justified in *extending* our use of the term "same person". Hick is not here making a claim indistinct from that of the linguistic defence, for he is not just saying that meaning is determined by use, but that our *concept* of identity of person would need to be revised and extended in the light of such a happening. His argument gets some force from the present unlikelihood that there will be two persons exactly similar in all respects bar occupancy of space.

Since we can imagine equally well a second exactly similar academic appearing in a third meeting simultaneously with the first "replica" (used neutrally for the moment) it would be arbitrary and capricious, as Williams and Nerlich have shown, to identify the one but not the other (and therefore either) with the original academic. Furthermore Hick could not rule out *a priori* the counterfactual possibility of more than one exactly similar instantiation.

In the second picture the original academic dies in the meeting and we have his corpse, but there appears elsewhere a "replica" (still used neutrally) under the same conditions as in the first picture. Hick urges that possible legal complications and other perplexities would be outweighed by the factors inclining us to say that the one who died and the one who appeared are identical. Shorter's Junonians are very similar here to Hick's replica and indeed are subject to the same criticisms. For, in addition to the objection raised concerning the first picture, it can now be urged that, contrary to fact, it is logically possible that the replica (or if we press the first objection, replicas) could have come into existence prior to the moment of the academic's demise. If this occurred there would be no hesitation in withholding an identity ascription, and this again points up the vacuity of ascribing identity in the absence of the instantiated counterfactual. Once again it is clear that the epistemological strength of the Nerlich-Williams principle is not to be overcome by an appeal to the intuitive force of an imaginary case, for the principle simply swallows the case.

Hick's third and last supposition is that the replica appears not in another meeting from that at which the corpse is found but in the resurrection world, occupying its own distinctive space[23] inhabited by resurrected persons. One important difference in this case is that the resurrection world replica is composed of other material than physical matter as we now know it. I think this may heighten Hick's difficulties, but nevertheless we shall let it pass unquestioned.

Exactly the same criticisms may be made it seems to me about Hick's third picture as with his second. I am not sure that he can appeal to the non-malevolent purposes of God as a way of avoiding the counterfactual difficulties *without arguing against* the necessity for bodily or spatio-temporal continuity. Further, since it is not logically necessary that memories be veridical, nor that character remains unchanged, he must either face the difficulty posed by Penelhum in naming the real principle to which he appeals in claiming identity, or else he must forego the demand that we share his intuitions. Finally, I am not convinced of the viability of the notion of temporal continuity which underlies Hick's defence since according to the special theory of relativity the notions of space and time must be fused together into that of space-time. And in that case it is not clear that one can speak of temporal continuity and at the same time deny continuity of occupancy of space.

VII

We have seen how the two chief strategies employed to defend belief in bodily resurrection—appeal to either some continuous entity other than the body, or appeal to the intuitive force of puzzling happenings—

founder because they fail to take the argument for the necessity of spatio-temporal continuity in identity seriously. It is not really surprising that insistence on an epistemological guard against reduplication is resisted, since in our identity judgments we frequently disregard substantial material discontinuities and often use memory as a check on bodily identity. But these facts do not mean we can just blithely ignore the Nerlich-Williams arguments for they too recognize that these things happen.

We could argue against the universal necessity for spatio-temporal continuity as an alternative strategy, so I propose to consider one final defence of the resurrection hope which hinges on confronting this universal necessity.[24] I put this defence forward as a constructive piece of philosophical theology, as a model for consideration rather than as the last word on the problem.

If one meditates on such everyday happenings as earthquakes, thunderstorms, terms of office, wars,[25] plays, rivers, and dividing bridges one readily sees that with these and many more, we have no hesitation in ascribing identity over a space-time gap.

Thus, we do not think it vacuous to say we are dealing with the same *x* even though there is a gap such as Christmas day in Vietnam, or intermission at the theatre, or a drought which dries up the river in some but not other parts. We would, however, only be able to say "*the same x*" in reply to a query if we knew what the "*x*" was which was supposed to be identical. Thus if we thought that after intermission we were watching the same act we probably would be wrong but we could well be still watching the same play. In other words, we have to indicate the description sortal under which an item falls before we can confer identity tags. Thus when we say no two things can be in the same place at the same time we must offer further analysis, for they could be if they were described differently as, say, a rock and a monument.

Since we ground counterfactuals on behavioural generalizations about objects of the relevant kind, we are unwilling to say that it is vacuous in the sort of cases under consideration to speak of "the same *x*" where *x* incorporates some spatio-temporal gap. The counterfactual possibility of reduplication does not make it vacuous to speak of identity since we anticipate or expect the same x to appear subsequent to the gap. In fact even if we had never seen a play before but anticipated (because of advertising for example) that after intermission we would be seeing the same play (token of the type) as prior to intermission, we would have no doubt that it was the same play.

We can even imagine that after the first act the cast goes on strike and the management substitutes an entirely different supporting cast for the second act. Then when the second act commences the original cast decide to abandon their strike and two exactly similar acts of the play are performed simultaneously. In such a situation we may well not care which is "the same play", but yet on all subsequent occasions of going to the theatre have no thought when the second act of a play is performed that it is vacuous to call it the same play, since on a previous occasion an exactly similar duplicate of the second act was simultaneously performed.

Similarly we can imagine a river drying up in a drought and perhaps even changing its bed entirely after the drought breaks, but have no doubt in our mind that it is the same river, even though we know perfectly well that it isn't the same water or bed. A necessitarian theorist might claim at this point that we are just wrong to speak of the same river here or of the same *x* in gap-inclusive cases. However, if an otherwise valuable theory is forced to this resort so much the worse for this aspect of it. Or it might be said that our examples confuse the token-type distinction. I do not concede this for we certainly are speaking of the same token when discussing gap-inclusive wars, rivers, plays and so on.

It might be further objected that the move which is obviously on, namely to say that the Christian might argue that there is a sortal which in Christian theology covers the earthly life followed by a gap followed by resurrection life, makes men something different from what we have taken them to be. This objection is beside the point for the believer need only say that viewing man as the being extending in space and time from birth (or conception) to death is to view him under one sortal—a phase sortal— but not under another (and for Christian theology a more vital substance sortal). Thus death is not the end of the person but a termination of only part of his total experience of what it really is to be a person. Thus there is no need to alter our dependence on the criteria of spatio-temporal continuity when making identity judgements about men viewed under a this-worldly sortal, for it will remain a condition (probably, if not certainly, a necessary one) of ante-mortem identity. One might note the parallel with the situations in which we are aware of a gap but still make use of continuity in the sections not covered by the gap (e.g. we might use continuity to trace an act of a play even if not the whole play).

It might be objected at this point in Strawsonian vein[26] that we reidentify the same particular over against exactly similar ones by reference to other particulars and hence we should follow that general practice in the case of gap-inclusive particulars. Two things could be said here. First, ontic and epistemic considerations seem intertwined here. But even if the Strawsonian approach was urged only to solve epistemic problems, we could object secondly that it is not the case that such an approach is universally or even sufficiently generally adopted to worry us. That is, we could (with justification I think) deny the relevance of the approach in "gap-inclusive sortal" situations.

That God could counterfactually make the resurrection body prior to the death of the man in this world seems at first sight to constitute a more serious objection. However, if this were to occur, this would involve a contravention of the whole idea of the defence. Since for the defence to be a defence at all there must be a gap for the sortal to include, such a case would not come under the head of the defence being considered. God cannot be required to do what would be logically self-contradictory. Thus, no matter how infinitesimal the gap, there must be a gap; hence this counterfactual cannot be raised as an objection.

Again it might be objected that the reason why we could anticipate a play straddling a gap is because we know in advance what plays are like, but we don't know in advance that persons can straddle space-time gaps. This is a crucial objection and is important, I think, in showing something about the source of the Christian's anticipated hope, namely that at this point he will want to invoke the authority of Jesus as the one who correctly taught the nature and destiny of persons. That is, by his own resurrection from the dead testified to by the apostolic community, Jesus has grounded the believer's hope and anticipation of resurrection. The believer's hope remains at this point in principle falsifiable (i.e. he does not have to argue circularly), for the possibility remains open that we will not straddle the gap either in the way anticipated or at all. Furthermore, just as the whole Christian interpretation of the world hinges on the in-principle-falsifiable assertion that Jesus rose from the dead, so too will this particular claim.

It might be objected finally that, even if the gap is straddled, we could never know that it was really us who had been resurrected. But this objection fails, too, because it neglects the fact that we do not use criteria of personal identity for knowing who we are.[27] If this were not so then the man who was revived after clinical death, say, would forever have to rely on the testimony of doctors and nurses that he was really the same person and not just a freak who appeared at thirty-five years of age with his own set of memories and so on. There might also be the other facts which would assure us of the reality of our continuing personal awareness.

It remains to make one further comment. I would urge that the scale on which the phenomenon of bodily resurrection is anticipated by the believer to take place has to be considered as an important factor in the question of whether persons can be gap-inclusive. We might be understandably reluctant and in fact may positively resist making any description change in isolated puzzle cases of what it is to be a person. But when the claim is that a person is to be considered under a particular sortal or description, and this is considered in conjunction with the daunting scale on which bodily resurrection is anticipated, there is no more an element of linguistic change involved in our ascribing the epithet "same person" to the resurrected than there is in saying "same play", "same thunderstorm", "same war" and so on, where these terms cover situations involving spatio-temporal discontinuities. All that will have happened is that our conceptual scheme will have been improved.

POSTCRIPT, 1976

In the years since the publication of my paper a number of powerful attacks have been directed against the necessity of spatio-temporal continuity in underwriting judgments of personal identity. These attacks provide welcome support for what I attempted to do in section VII of "The Resurrection of the Body". At the same time such attacks also tend to undercut the strategy I adopted in several places in my paper (e.g., section VI) of using the failure to offer any argument against the necessity of spatio-temporal continuity for identity as a ground for criticizing alternative defences of the resurrection hope. While there was real point, I believe, in urging people to see that the necessitarian view had to be *argued* against and in trying to start that process by pointing to the fact that the concept of identity did not preclude gap-inclusiveness, the availability now of strong arguments against the necessitarian would require me to write my article rather differently were I doing so now for the first time. For those who would like to follow up some of the recent discussions the following papers are of major importance:

Derek Parfit, "Personal Identity", *Philosophical Review* 80 (1971), pp. 3-27;

Derek Parfit, "On 'The Importance of Self-Identity'", *Journal of Philosophy* 68 (1971), pp. 683-690;

Bruce Langtry, "Similarity, Continuity and Survival", *Australasian Journal of Philosophy* 53 (1975), pp. 3-18.

NOTES

1. I Corinthians 15 esp. vv 17 ff (*pace* the aberrations of theological reductivists).

2. John 5:29; I Corinthians 15:32.

3. "Theology and Verification" reprinted in Hick (ed) *The Existence of God* p. 263.

4. So, too, it would seem for Paul Edwards in "Difficulties in the Idea of God", reprinted in E. Madden, R. Handy and M. Faber (eds.) *The Idea of God*, pp 63 ff.

5. The epistemological difficulties involved in getting to the point of affirming belief in God have not gone unnoticed but are beyond the scope of this paper.

6. I Corinthians 15.

7. A. G. N. Flew, "Body, Mind, and Death", p. 5.

8. *Religious Belief*, pp. 112-116.

9. "Personal Identity, Memory and Survival", *Journal of Philosophy*, 1959, pp 895 ff.

10. Nerlich also draws attention to anticipations in his "Sameness, Difference and Continuity", *Analysis*, 1958, p 145.

11. S. R. Sutherland, "Immortality and Resurrection", *Religious Studies*, 1967, pp 377-389.

12. op. cit., p. 149.

13. *God and the Soul*, esp. pp. 22-3.

14. Something like this may be in J. Shaffer's mind, "Recent Work on the Mind-Body Problem", *American Phil. Quarterly*, 1965, pp. 97-8, and in an unpublished paper by C. A. Hooker "Concerning Defensible Dualisms" read in University of Sydney, 1967.

15. cf. D. M. Armstrong "A Materialist Theory of Mind", pp. 19, 91. He claims that any acceptable theory of mind must keep open the logical possibility of disembodied existence. His own argument for this (p. 19) is somewhat truncated and may be inadequate in the light of the claims by Martin and Penelhum (above) that the inability to give point to numerical distinctness and identity for the disembodied casts doubt on the sense of the notion of disembodied existence itself.

16. Compare Hobbes' case of the ship completely repaired and renovated by the Athenians.

17. This view and the modifications considered probably depends on the truth of atomist theories of matter (that is, the view that matter consists of permanent incorruptible atoms or particles which remain the same under processes of change).

18. *Analysis*, January 1968, pp. 78-89.

19. The Williams-Nerlich view that the meaning of "same" requires adherence to a necessary condition is viewed by Herbert as a *supposition*.

20. Nevertheless he talks (p. 88) as if both insiders and outsiders to the form of life have mutually exclusive explanations of their positions. At best there is need for clarification of his position on this question.

21. I have intentionally omitted the criticism that Herbert's view depends on dualistic presuppositions, not because I think it irrelevant but because I think the defence fails for more significant reasons from our point of view.

22. There are a number of points of similarity

with an article by J. M. Shorter "More About Bodily Continuity", *Analysis*, 1962; pp. 79-85 in Hick's paper.

23. See on this possibility A. M. Quinton, "Spaces and Times", in *Philosophy*, 1962.

24. In neither of two most significant recent discussions, D. Wiggins, *Identity and Spatio-Temporal Continuity* and J. J. McIntosh, "Memory and Personal Identity", reprinted in J. J. McIntosh and S. Coval (eds.) *The Business of Reason*, pp. 150-167, is such a direct confrontation made. While Wiggins argues against the criterion of straight-forward bodily identity as necessary it is only to supersede it with a more acceptable notion of spatiotemporal continuity. McIntosh argues that memory is a necessary condition but concedes the necessity of bodily continuity for strict identity even though it might be empirically unnecessary.

25. Compares Hobbes' classic account of war (*Leviathan*, Pt. 1, Ch. 13) ".....Warre consisteth not in battell onely, or in the act of fighting; but in a tract of time, wherein the will to contend by Battell is sufficiently known; and therefore the notion of time, is to be considered in the nature of Warre as it is in the nature of Weather.....So the nature of Warre consisteth not in actual fighting; but in the known disposition thereto, during all the time there is no assurance to the contrary."

26. *Individuals*, p. 17.

27. This issue is independent of the amnesia or paramnesia problems which relate to knowing *what we have done*, not personal awareness of self-identity.

FURTHER READINGS

Ducase, C. J. *The Belief in Life After Death*. Springfield, Ill.: Charles C. Thomas, 1961.

Flew, Antony. "Immortality." In *Encyclopedia of Philosophy*, edited by Paul Edwards. New York: Macmillan, 1967.

Maritain, J. "The Immortality of the Soul" in *The Range of Reason*. New York: Scribner's, 1952.

Martin, C. B. *Religious Belief*, chap. VI. Ithaca, N. Y.: Cornell University Press, 1959.

Penelhum, T., ed. *Immortality*. Belmont, Calif.: Wadsworth Publishing Co., 1973.

Penelhum, T. *Survival and Disembodied Existence*. London: Routledge and Kegan Paul, 1970.

Phillips, D. Z. *Death and Immortality*. London: Macmillan, 1970.

Puccetti, R. *Persons*. London: Macmillan, 1968.

Taylor, A. E. *The Christian Hope of Immortality*. New York: Macmillan, 1947.

Williams, Bernard. *Problems of the Self*. Cambridge: Cambridge University Press, 1973.

PART FIVE

Ethics

Introduction

HAROLD MOORE

How should I live? Which principles, of the many available ones, should man live by? Is there any justification for choosing one set of principles over and above another? The study of such questions is the concern of ethics or moral philosophy.

To be sure, we make moral judgments all the time without having comprehensive understanding of moral theory. But it is of considerable theoretical and practical interest to know if these pre-analytic judgments have any rational backing. If they do have such backing, how is it to be analyzed? If moral judgment is not defensible on rational grounds, why is this so? The study of such questions is as important as it is inescapable for any rational man. And the only way to make progress on such issues is to philosophically examine fundamental moral concepts and theories of conduct.

How should I live? What sorts of considerations, if any, are relevant to adjudicating such an issue? The question is primarily a question about value and consequently our problem is concerned with how it is that one justifies a value judgment about conduct. Any rational person knows what it means for example to say that someone stole money or what it would mean to say that another individual was generally honest, kept his promises and so on. But how do we move from these claims, which seem to present no interesting problem at all, to claims like "stealing is bad" and "individuals ought to keep their promises?" To answer this question, we can briefly examine four proposed generalized answers to it: emotivism, relativism, utilitarianism, and Kantianism.

Emotivism is a version of what we may call ethical 'noncognitivism', a view that claims that ethical sentences do not express genuine (cognitive) propositions at all and hence are 'cognitively meaningless'. In the noncognitivist account, a sentence like "Jones stole the money" is a perfectly meaningful expression while an expression like "Jones' stealing the money is wrong" expresses no proposition and is not used to *assert* anything by the person who utters it. Genuine assertions have a truth value, ethical judgments do not. Any rational person knows how to assign a truth value to "Jones stole the money," but it makes no sense to assign a truth value to "Jones' stealing is wrong," and if ethical judgments have no truth values they cannot express genuine propositions. And if this is so, then ethical discourse must be analyzed as 'noncognitive'.

At this stage, the distinctive feature of emotivism can be clarified, for if ethical judgments are not genuine assertions, what are they? According to the emotivist, the role of ethical "judgment" is primarily the expression of feelings or emotion. Moral statements, like grunts, groans, burps, and the like, have primarily an expressive, and not an assertive function. What could it mean to say, for example, that a groan was true or false? Expressions of emotion then are taken as the model for moral concepts and like emotive expressions moral concepts are analyzed in a noncognitive way. If this account is correct, of course, our original question concerning how a man ought to live will not be capable of any cognitive resolution.

The success of emotivism as a theory depends directly on the account rendered of what is 'cognitive' and 'noncognitive'. Unfortunately many emotivists have made this distinction by presupposing some version of the verifiability principle of meaning. On this account, the reason that "stealing money is wrong" is cognitively meaningless is that there are no observations that entail our moral judgment and hence such judgments are excluded from the domain of meaningful expressions. But far from giving us a reason for rejecting moral judgment, we have yet another reason for rejecting the verifiability principle. For the task of a theory of meaning is to at least capture our pre-analytic intuitions about what is and what is not meaningful. And certainly it does seem that judgments like "stealing is wrong" are perfectly meaningful. Nor is it clear that such moral judgments can be analyzed into expressions of emotion. Certainly, a claim like "stealing is wrong" *looks* like a meaningful claim, it at least purports to say something that is not captured by 'boo' or 'hooray'. What we need is an account of moral concepts independent of the proposed theory of meaning that possesses the analytical resources for demonstrating why our pre-analytic intuitions should be revised in the way the emotivist suggests. But if we don't hold some version of the verifiability principle, there is no reason we should even try.

A second account of moral judgment is given by the so-called relativist. On this account, moral judgments are not just expressions of emotion, and are not to be analyzed in a noncognitive way. Rather there are norms for assessing behavior, but these norms are relative to a particular cultural or social group. Sometimes a relativist means only to assert what we might call 'sociological relativism', according to which as a *matter of fact* different cultural groups *have* different norms. There is another kind of relativism which we may term 'ethical relativism', according to which, if there are two cultural groups, and one group believes that a certain practice is correct and the other group believes that the same practice is wrong, they are *both* right. The practice is morally right in the one society and morally wrong in the other. For example, since most Americans believe that killing one's parents is wrong, it is wrong—in American society. Since, there are other cultural groups, (say, the Eskimos) that believe that it is right sometimes to kill one's parents, it is right—in that society.

The first kind of relativism is an empirical claim that is, in all likelihood true; different cultural groups do seem to have different norms. The second kind of relativism is a philosophical claim that is much more troublesome. Why should the justifiability of a belief be analyzed solely in terms of the *number* of people who hold it? How can the rational acceptability of a belief be settled by counting heads? At one time, a majority of people believed the earth flat. A majority of people even now might not believe the theory of evolution, but why should this be at all related to its rational acceptability? Granted that different cultures might sometimes have different norms, what the ethical relativist needs to show is that there is nothing to choose between the different norms. And this is a difficult task indeed.

A third account of moral judgment is given by utilitarian theorists. Like the relativist, the utilitarian believes that there are relevant standards available for justifying moral beliefs, but unlike the relativist, the utilitarian believes that there is one such standard: perform the action which will bring about the greatest good possible. An action is morally judged in this account by the consequences it produces and the 'consequences' mentioned here are to be interpreted in a broad sense; not just one's own good should be considered, but the good of everyone affected by the action.

The principle has some plausibility, but when pressed all kinds of problems arise. How are we to *know* what the consequences of performing a given action are? Granted that there are instances where a reasonable and prudent man does know the consequences of a given action, there are just as plainly cases where we do not have such knowledge, what guides to conduct do we have in the latter case? How are we to interpret *total* good? Suppose a given amount of goodness can be showed equally or the same amount of goodness shared disproportionately, what utilitarian reason can be given for preferring the former distribution? Or does it even make sense to speak of 'amount of goodness', presupposing, as it seems to, that there is something here that can be measured? Or what of goodness itself, how are we to understand it? On Mill's account goodness is analyzed ultimately to a kind of pleasure and Mill even attempts to make a distinction that will mark qualitatively different *kinds* of pleasure: better, says Mill, to be "Socrates dissatisfied than a fool satisfied." This may afford a way around some of the problems involved with the measurement of pleasure, but it also seems to introduce a nonutilitarian method of evaluation. If so, then why should utilitarianism be the preferred moral standard?

The real problem with utilitarianism, however, is that it seems to justify actions that are morally outrageous. Murder of the innocent and punishment of people who haven't done anything wrong, for example, could conceivably have consequences that justify such actions on this kind of model of moral reasoning. If so, then utilitarianism hardly seems plausible. Mill tried to block such consequences, arguing, for example, that the maintenance of an impartial system of justice was so important to the general happiness that virtually any deviation from such a system would have harmful consequences and hence would not have a good utilitarian justification. But now the thesis is in danger of becoming uninformative as a guide to action. How can we tell when deviations from our "normal" moral ways of treating people fairly, impartially, justly, are justified by consequential reasoning? If there is a decision procedure here, then what is it? If there is not, then why do we need utilitarianism as an account of moral reasoning?

Utilitarianism is a teleological theory of ethics, actions are justified in terms of the consequences they bring about. There is another general kind of moral theory, so-called 'deontological' ethics, according to which the rightness of an action has nothing to do with the consequences it produces. The chief architect of this theory is Kant. In the *Foundations of the Metaphysics of Morals*, Kant claims that the only item of unqualified worth is the human will and that what determines the moral quality of an action is the reason for which it is done and not the results it will bring about. It might be true that being a moral person will, in general, have beneficial conquences and perhaps, in general, being immoral will not; no matter says Kant, the morality of an action is determined by the intention with which it is formed and not because of what it brings about.

Consider the distinction, for example, between morality and prudence or the distinction between someone who acts out of interest and someone who acts out of commitment to principle. A man who does something simply out of self-interest, simply in terms of what the action will produce for him does not seem to deserve any straightforward moral praise. Consider someone who gives money to charity simply because he wants to help the poor and someone who also donates money but does it because of the tax benefits he can derive. Surely we would want to mark some difference here between the operative action guiding principles.

But what kind of principle, rule or imperative for action can the will adopt? If the morality of a proposed rule of conduct derives not from the consequences, and not from self-interest, what does it derive from? For Kant, the answer lies in the *form* of the rule or imperative being considered. Kant asks us to contrast two kinds of rules.

A. *Hypothetical Imperatives* which command us to adopt a certain means to an end which we have already adopted. "*If* you *want* to be a doctor, then you must take organic chemistry," that is, given that you have adopted a certain goal then it is prudent or required that you adopt the appropriate means to the end.

B. *Categorical Imperatives* which command in virture of their claim on the rationality of any man qua man and not in terms of any goal which has been adopted by a particular individual. On Kant's account, only categorical imperatives have binding force.

Why does Kant make the rather stark claim for the second kind of imperatives, why is this the only imperative with binding moral force? Aren't the hypothetical imperatives of prudence also universal? Don't all men desire happiness? To see why Kant restricts moral worth to the categorical imperative is to arrive at the core of his theory. It might be true that all men desire happiness, but imperatives of this sort make implicit appeal to circumstance, time, place and sentiment, as these vary, the imperatives vary. And what Kant is seeking is a rule that applies to *all* moral agents *regardless* of their particular situation. To reduce moral worth to contingent circumstances is to invite all the utilitarian difficulties. The only way to secure moral worth is to anchor it independent of such contingency.

To quickly regroup, the requisite action guiding principles should have two features: first, they must not contain any appeal to interest; second, they must apply to all rational beings. Hence, any morally acceptable principle is implicitly general; if it applies in any one particular occasion, it must apply on any similar occasion. With these constraints, Kant then formulates the appropriate rule, the first form of the categorical imperative "act only according to that maxim by which you can at the same time will that it should become a universal law." What Kant is suggesting here is a necessary condition—the universalizability criterion—for any principle to be a morally acceptable one. Before you do something, you are to ask yourself if the proposed rule under consideration could be adopted by any person, and not just yourself.

Consider proposed rules like "be a parasite" or "break a promise whenever it is convenient to do so." Both rules self-destruct on Kant's model, for they cannot consistently be applied to all moral agents. And since they cannot, they are not acceptable moral rules, an acceptable rule must apply to all individuals: if it is permissible for you to adopt a particular moral rule, then it must be permissible for others to adopt it also. What must not be permitted in adopting the moral point of view, what must systematically be factored out of every proposed moral rule is self-interest, and the conceptual constraint that plays this role is the universalizability condition, for it guarantees the impartiality requisite for the moral point of view.

The categorical imperative is still troublesome in the sense that it does not render sufficient substantial guidance for the evaluation of particular rules. There are any number of universalizable maxims that don't seem to be of significant moral interest. Nor is it clear how to use the principle to deal with fanatics who might be willing to have all sorts of bizarre acts universalized.

But no matter, for Kant's theory moves in a direction that is essential for any acceptable moral theory. For in analyzing the concept of morality, Kant has given great prominence to the concept of the worth of each individual qua individual, claiming that genuine moral worth derives not from any talent or skill, but simply in virtue of being a human, that each person has a *right* to a certain kind of treatment simply because they are human. And surely any moral theory that cannot underwrite such a commitment is deficient in a very basic respect.

Ethical Relativity

RUTH F. BENEDICT

Modern social anthropology has become more and more a study of the varieties and common elements of cultural environment and the consequences of these in human behavior. For such a study of diverse social orders primitive peoples fortunately provide a laboratory not yet entirely vitiated by the spread of a standardized worldwide civilization. Dyakes and Hopis, Fijians and Yakuts are significant for psychological and sociological study because only among these simpler peoples has there been sufficient isolation to give opportunity for the development of localized social forms. In the higher cultures the standardization of custom and belief over a couple of continents has given a false sense of the inevitability of the particular forms that have gained currency, and we need to turn to a wider survey in order to check the conclusions we hastily base upon this near-universality of familiar customs. Most of the simpler cultures did not gain the wide currency of the one which, out of our experience, we identify with human nature, but this was for various historical reasons, and certainly not for any that gives us as its carriers a monopoly of social good or of social sanity. Modern civilization, from this point of view, becomes not a necessary pinnacle of human achievement but one entry in a long series of possible adjustments.

These adjustments, whether they are in mannerisms like the ways of showing anger, or joy, or grief in any society, or in major human drives like those of sex, prove to be far more variable than experience in any one culture would suggest. In certain fields, such as that of religion or of formal marriage arrangements, these wide limits of variability are well known and can be fairly described. In others it is not yet possible to give a generalized account, but that does not absolve us of the task of indicating the significance of the work that has been done and of the problems that have arisen.

One of these problems relates to the customary modern normal-abnormal categories and our conclusions regarding them. In how far are such categories culturally determined, or in how far can we with assurance regard them as absolute? In how far can we regard inability to function socially as diagnostic of abnormality, or in how far is it necessary to regard this as a function of the culture? . . .

The most spectacular illustrations of the extent to which normality may be culturally defined are those cultures where an abnormality of our culture is the cornerstone of their social structure. It is not possible to do justice to these possibilities in a short discussion. A recent study of an island of northwest Melanesia by *Fortune* describes a society built upon traits which we regard as beyond the border of paranoia. In this tribe the exogamic groups look upon each other as prime manipulators of black magic, so that one marries always into an enemy group which remains for life one's deadly and unap-

---

Ruth F. Benedict (1887-1948) was professor of anthropology at Columbia University.

From Ruth Fulton Benedict, "Anthropology and the Abnormal," *Journal of General Psychology* X (1934), pp. 59-80. Reprinted by permission of The Journal Press, Provincetown, Mass.

peasable foes. They look upon a good garden crop as a confession of theft, for everyone is engaged in making magic to induce into his garden the productiveness of his neighbor's; therefore no secrecy in the island is so rigidly insisted upon as the secrecy of a man's harvesting of his yams. Their polite phrase at the acceptance of a gift is, "And if you now poison me, how shall I repay you this present?" Their preoccupation with poisoning is constant; no woman ever leaves her cooking pot for a moment unattended. Even the great affinal economic exchanges that are characteristic of this Melanesian culture area are quite altered in Dobu since they are incompatible with this fear and distrust that pervades the culture. . . . They go farther and people the whole world outside their own quarters with such malignant spirits that all-night feasts and ceremonials simply do not occur here. They have even religiously enforced customs that forbid the sharing of seed even in one family group. Anyone else's food is deadly poison to you, so that communality of stores is out of the question. For some months before harvest the whole society is on the verge of starvation, but if one falls to the temptation and eats up one's seed yams, one is an outcast and a beachcomber for life. There is no coming back. It involves, as a matter of course, divorce and the breaking of all social ties.

Now in this society where no one may work with another and no one may share with another, *Fortune* describes the individual who was regarded by all his fellows as crazy. He was not one of those who periodically ran amok and, beside himself and frothing at the mouth, fell with a knife upon anyone he could reach. Such behavior they did not regard as putting anyone outside the pale. They did not even put the individuals who were known to be liable to these attacks under any kind of control. They merely fled when they saw the attack coming on and kept out of the way. "He would be all right tomorrow." But there was one man of sunny, kindly disposition who liked work and liked to be helpful. The compulsion was too strong for him to repress it in favor of the opposite tendencies of his culture. Men and women never spoke of him without laughing; he was silly and simple and definitely crazy. Nevertheless, to the ethnologist used to a culture that has, in Christianity, made his type the model of all virture, he seemed a pleasant fellow.

An even more extreme example, because it is of a culture that has built itself upon a more complex abnormality, is that of the North Pacific Coast of North America. The civilization of the Kwakiutl, at the time when it was first recorded in the last decades of the nineteenth century, was one of the most vigorous in North America. It was built up on an ample economic supply of goods, the fish which furnished their food staple being practically inexhaustible and obtainable with comparatively small labor, and the wood which furnished the material for their houses, their furnishings, and their arts being, with however much labor, always procurable. They lived in coastal villages that compared favorably in size with those of any other American Indians and they kept up constant communication by means of sea-going dugout canoes.

It was one of the most vigorous and zestful of the aboriginal cultures of North America, with complex crafts and ceremonials, and elaborate and striking arts. It certainly had none of the earmarks of a sick civilization. The tribes of the Northwest Coast had wealth, and exactly in our terms. That is, they had not only a surplus of economic goods, but they made a game of the manipulation of wealth. It was by no means a mere direct transcription of economic needs and the filling of those needs. It involved the idea of capital, of interest, and of conspicuous waste. It was a game with all the binding rules of a game, and a person entered it as a child. His father distributed wealth for him, according to his ability, at a small feast or potlatch, and each gift the receiver was obliged to accept and to return after a short interval with interest that ran to about 100 per cent a year. By the time the child was grown, therefore, he was well launched, a larger potlatch had been given for him on various occasions of exploit or initiation, and he had wealth either out at usury or in his own possession. Nothing in the civilization could be enjoyed without validating it by the distribution of this wealth. Everything that was valued, names and songs as well as material objects were passed down in family lines, but they were always publicly assumed with accompanying sufficient distributions of property. It was the game of validating and exercising all the privileges one could accumulate from one's various forebears, or by gift, or by marriage, that made the chief interest of the culture. Eveyone in his degree took part in it, but many, of course, mainly as spectators. In its highest form it was played out between rival chiefs representing not only themselves and their family lines but their communities, and the object of the contest was to glorify oneself and to humiliate one's opponent. On this level of greatness the property involved was no longer represented by blankets, so many thousand of them to a potlatch, but by higher units of value. These higher units were like our bank notes. They were incised copper tablets, each of them named, and having a value that depended upon their illustrious history. This was as high as ten thousand blankets, and to possess one of them, still more to enhance its value at a great potlatch, was one of the greatest glories within the compass of the chiefs of the Northwest Coast. . . .

Every contingency of life was dealt with in . . . two traditional ways. To them the two were equivalent. Whether one fought with weapons or "fought with property," as they say, the same idea was at the bottom of both. In the olden times, they say, they fought with spears, but now they fight with property. One overcomes one's opponents in equivalent fashion in both, matching forces and seeing that one comes out ahead, and one can thumb one's nose at the vanquished rather more satisfactorily at a potlatch than on a battlefield. Every occasion in life was noticed, not in its own terms, as a stage in the sex life of the individual or as a climax of joy or of grief, but as furthering this drama of consolidating one's own prestige and bringing shame to one's guests. Whether it was the occasion of the birth of a child, or a daughter's adolescence, or of the marriage of one's son, they were all equivalent raw material for the culture to use for this one traditionally selected end. They were all to raise one's own personal status and to entrench oneself by the humiliation of one's fellows. A girl's adolescence among the Nootka was an event for which her father gathered property from the time she was first able to run about. When she was adolescent he would demonstrate his greatness by an unheard of distribution of these goods, and put down all his rivals. It was not as a fact of the girl's sex life that it figured in their culture, but as the occasion for a major move in the great game of vindicating one's own greatness and humiliating one's associates.

In their behavior at great bereavements this set of the culture comes out most strongly. Among the Kwakiutl it did not matter whether a relative had died in bed of disease, or by the hand of an enemy; in either case death was an affront to be wiped out by the death of another person. The fact that one had been caused to mourn was proof that one had been put upon. A chief's sister and her daughter had gone up to Victoria, and either because they drank bad whiskey or because their boat capsized they never came back. The chief called together his warriors. "Now, I ask you, tribes, who shall wail? Shall I do it or shall another?" The spokesman answered, of course, "Not you, Chief. Let some other of the tribes." Immediately they set up the war pole to announce their intention of wiping out the injury, and gathered a war party. They set out, and found seven men and two children asleep and killed them. "Then they felt good when they arrived at Sebaa in the evening."

The point which is of interest to us is that in our society those who on that occasion would feel good when they arrived at Sebaa that evening would be the definitely abnormal. There would be some, even in our society, but it is not a recognized and approved mood under the circumstances. On the Northwest Coast those are favored and fortunate to whom that mood under those circumstances is congenial, and those to whom it is repugnant are unlucky. This latter minority can register in their own culture only by doing violence to their congenial responses and acquiring others that are difficult for them. The person, for instance, who, like a Plains Indian whose wife has been taken from him, is too proud to fight, can deal with the Northwest Coast civilization only by ignoring its strongest bents. If he cannot achieve it, he is the deviant in that culture, their instance of abnormality.

This head-hunting that takes place on the Northwest Coast after a death is no matter of blood revenge or of organized vengeance. There is no effort to tie up the subsequent killing with any responsibility on the part of the victim for the death of the person who is being mourned. A chief whose son has died goes visiting wherever his fancy dictates, and he says to his host, "My prince has died today, and you go with him." Then he kills him. In this, according to their interpretation, he acts nobly because he has not been downed. He has thrust back in return. The whole procedure is meaningless without the fundamental paranoid reading of bereavement. Death, like all the other untoward accidents of existence, confounds man's pride and can only be handled in the category of insults. . . .

These illustrations, which it has been possible to indicate only in the briefest manner, force upon us the fact that normality is culturally defined. An adult shaped to the drives and standards of either of these cultures, if he were transported into our civilization, would fall into our categories of abnormality. He would be faced with the psychic dilemmas of the socially unavailable. In his own culture, however, he is the pillar of society, the end result of socially inculcated mores, and the problem of personal instability in his case simply does not arise.

No one civilization can possibly utilize in its mores the whole potential range of human behavior. Just as there are great numbers of possible phonetic articulations, and the possiblity of language depends on a selection and standardization of a few of these in order that speech communication may be possible at all, so the possibility of organized behavior of every sort, from the fashions of local dress and houses to the dicta of a people's ethics and religion, depends upon a similar selection among the possible behavior traits. In the field of recognized economic obligations or sex tabus this selection is as nonrational and subconscious a process as it is in the field of phonetics. It is a process which goes on in the group for long periods of time and is historically conditioned by innumerable accidents of isolation or of contact of peoples. In any comprehensive study of psychology, the selection that different cultures have made in the course of history within the great circumference of potential behavior is of great significance.

Every society, beginning with some slight inclination in one direction or another, carries its preference farther and farther, integrating itself more and more completely upon its chosen basis, and discarding those types of behavior that are uncongenial. Most of those organizations of personality that seem to us most incontrovertibly abnormal have been used by different civilizations in the very foundations of their institutional life. Conversely the most valued traits of our normal individuals have been looked on in differently organized cultures as aberrant. Normality, in short, within a very wide range, is culturally defined. It is primarily a term for the socially elaborated segment of human behavior in any culture; and abnormality, a term for the segment that that particular civilization does not use. The very eyes with which we see the problem are conditioned by the long traditional habits of our own society.

It is a point that has been made more often in relation to ethics than in relation to psychiatry. We do not any longer make the mistake of deriving the morality of our own locality and decade directly from the inevitable constitution of human nature. We do not elevate it to the dignity of a first principle. We recognize that morality differs in every society, and is a convenient term for socially approved habits. Mankind has always preferred to say, "It is morally good," rather than "It is habitual," and the fact of this preference is matter enough for a critical science of ethics. But historically the two phases are synonymous.

The concept of the normal is properly a variant of the concept of the good. It is that which society has approved. A normal action is one which falls well within the limits of expected behavior for a particular society. Its variability among different peoples is essentially a function of the variability of the behavior patterns that different societies have created for themselves, and can never be wholly divorced from a consideration of culturally institutionalized types of behavior.

Each culture is a more or less elaborate working-out of the potentialities of the segment it has chosen. In so far as a civilization is well integrated and consistent within itself, it will tend to carry farther and farther, according to its nature, its initial impulse toward a particular type of action, and from the point of view of any other culture those elaborations will include more and more extreme and aberrant traits.

Each of these traits, in proportion as it reinforces the chosen behavior patterns of that culture, is for that culture normal. Those individuals to whom it is congenial either congenitally, or as the result of childhood sets, are accorded prestige in that culture, and are not visited with the social contempt or disapproval which their traits would call down upon them in a society that was differently organized. On the other hand, those individuals whose characteristics are not congenial to the selected type of human behavior in that community are the deviants, no matter how valued their personality traits may be in a contrasted civilization. . . .

The problem of understanding abnormal human behavior in any absolute sense independent of cultural factors is still far in the future. The categories of borderline behavior which we derive from the study of the neuroses and psychoses of our civilization are categories of prevailing local types of instability. They give much information about the stresses and strains of Western civilization, but no final picture of inevitable human behavior. Any conclusions about such behavior must await the collection by trained observers of psychiatric data from other cultures. Since no adequate work of the kind has been done at the present time, it is impossible to say what core of definition of abnormality may be found valid from the comparative material. It is as it is in ethics; all our local conventions of moral behavior and of immoral are without absolute validity, and yet it is quite possible that a modicum of what is considered right and what wrong could be disentangled that is shared by the whole human race. When data are available in psychiatry, this minimum definition of abnormal human tendencies will be probably quite unlike our culturally conditioned, highly elaborated psychoses such as those that are described, for instance, under the terms of schizophrenia and manic-depressive.

Science and Ethics

BERTRAND RUSSELL

Those who maintain the insufficiency of science, as we have seen in the last two chapters, appeal to the fact that science has nothing to say about "values." This I admit; but when it is inferred that ethics contains truths which cannot be proved or disproved by science, I disagree. The matter is one of which it is not altogether easy to think clearly, and my own views on it are quite different from what they were thirty years ago. But it is necessary to be clear about it if we are to appraise such arguments as those in support of Cosmic Purpose. As there is no consensus of opinion about ethics, it must be understood that what follows is my personal belief, not the dictum of science.

The study of ethics, traditionally, consists of two parts, one concerned with moral rules, the other with what is good on its own account. Rules of conduct, many of which have a ritual origin, play a great part in the lives of savages and primitive peoples. It is forbidden to eat out of the chief's dish, or to seethe the kid in its mother's milk; it is commanded to offer sacrifices to the gods, which, at a certain stage of development, are thought most acceptable if they are human beings. Other moral rules, such as the prohibition of murder and theft, have a more obvious social utility, and survive the decay of the primitive theological systems with which they were originally associated. But as men grow more reflective there is a tendency to lay less stress on rules and more on states of mind. This comes from two sources—philosophy and mystical religion. We are all familiar with passages in the prophets and the gospels, in which purity of heart is set above meticulous observance of the Law; and St. Paul's famous praise of charity, or love, teaches the same principle. The same thing will be found in all great mystics, Christian and non-Christian: what they value is a state of mind, out of which, as they hold, right conduct must ensue; rules seem to them external, and insufficiently adaptable to circumstances.

One of the ways in which the need of appealing to external rules of conduct has been avoided has been the belief in "conscience," which has been especially important in Protestant ethics. It has been supposed that God reveals to each human heart what is right and what is wrong, so that, in order to avoid sin, we have only to listen to the inner voice. There are, however, two difficulties in this theory: first, that conscience says different things to different people; secondly, that the study of the unconscious has given us an understanding of the mundane causes of conscientious feelings.

As to the different deliverances of conscience: George III's conscience told him that he must not grant Catholic Emancipation, as, if he did, he would have committed perjury in taking the Coronation Oath, but later monarchs have had no such scruples. Conscience leads some to condemn the spoliation of the rich by the poor, as advocated by communists; and others to condemn exploitation of the poor by the rich, as practised by

---

Bertrand Russell (1872-1970) was an extremely influential modern thinker.

From *Religion and Science* by Bertrand Russell, published by Oxford University Press.

capitalists. It tells one man that he ought to defend his country in case of invasion, while it tells another that all participation in warfare is wicked. During the War, the authorities, few of whom had studied ethics, found conscience very puzzling, and were led to some curious decisions, such as that a man might have conscientious scruples against fighting himself, but not against working on the fields so as to make possible the conscription of another man. They held also that, while conscience might disapprove of all war, it could not, failing that extreme position, disapprove of the war then in progress. Those who, for whatever reason, thought it wrong to fight, were compelled to state their position in terms of this somewhat primitive and unscientific conception of "conscience."

The diversity in the deliverances of conscience is what is to be expected when its origin is understood. In early youth, certain classes of acts meet with approval, and others with disapproval; and by the normal process of association, pleasure and discomfort gradually attach themselves to the acts, and not merely to the approval and disapproval respectively produced by them. As time goes on, we may forget all about our early moral training, but we shall still feel uncomfortable about certain kinds of actions, while others will give us a glow of virtue. To introspection, these feelings are mysterious, since we no longer remember the circumstances which originally caused them; and therefore it is natural to attribute them to the voice of God in the heart. But in fact conscience is a product of education, and can be trained to approve or disapprove, in the great majority of mankind, as educators may see fit. While, therefore, it is right to wish to liberate ethics from external moral rules, this can hardly be satisfactorily achieved by means of the notion of "conscience."

Philosophers, by a different road, have arrived at a different position in which, also, moral rules of conduct have a subordinate place. They have framed the concept of the Good, by which they mean (roughly speaking) that which, in itself and apart from its consequences, we should wish to see existing—or, if they are theists, that which is pleasing to God. Most people would agree that happiness is preferable to unhappiness, friendliness to unfriendliness, and so on. Moral rules, according to this view, are justified if they promote the existence of what is good on its own account, but not otherwise. The prohibition of murder, in the vast majority of cases, can be justified by its effects, but the practice of burning widows on their husband's funeral pyre cannot. The former rule, therefore, should be retained, but not the latter. Even the best moral rules, however, will have *some* exceptions, since no class of actions *always* has bad results. We have thus three different senses in which an act may be ethically commendable: (1) it may be in accordance with the received moral code; (2) it may be sincerely intended to have good effects; (3) it may in fact have good effects. The third sense, however, is generally considered inadmissible in morals. According to orthodox theology, Judas Iscariot's act of betrayal had good consequences, since it was necessary for the Atonement; but it was not on this account laudable.

Different philosophers have formed different conceptions of the Good. Some hold that it consists in the knowledge and love of God; others in universal love; others in the enjoyment of beauty; and yet others in pleasure. The Good once defined, the rest of ethics follows: we ought to act in the way we believe most likely to create as much good as possible, and as little as possible of its correlative evil. The framing of moral rules, so long as the ultimate Good is supposed known, is matter for science. For example: should capital punishment be inflicted for theft, or only for murder, or not at all? Jeremy Bentham, who considered pleasure to be the Good, devoted himself to working out what criminal code would most promote pleasure, and concluded that it ought to be much less severe than that prevailing in his day. All this, except the proposition that pleasure is the Good, comes within the sphere of science.

But when we try to be definite as to what we mean when we say that this or that is "the Good," we find ourselves involved in very great difficulties. Bentham's creed that pleasure is the Good roused furious opposition, and was said to be a pig's philosophy. Neither he nor his opponents could advance any argument. In a scientific question, evidence can be adduced on both sides, and in the end one side is seen to have the better case—or, if this does not happen, the question is left undecided. But in a question as to whether this or that is the ultimate Good, there is no evidence either way; each disputant can only appeal to his own emotions, and employ such rhetorical devices as shall rouse similar emotions in others.

Take for example, a question which has come to be important in practical politics. Bentham held that one man's pleasure has the same ethical importance as another man's, provided the quantities are equal; and on this ground he was led to advocate democracy. Nietzsche, on the contrary, held that only the great man can be regarded as important on his own account, and that the bulk of mankind are only means to his well-being. He viewed ordinary men as many people view animals: he thought it justifiable to make use of them, not for their own good, but for that of the superman, and this view has since been adopted to justify the abandonment of democracy. We have here a sharp disagreement of great practical importance, but we have absolutely no means, of a scientific or intellectual kind, by which to persuade either party that the other is in the right. There are, it is true, ways of altering men's opinions on such subjects, but they are all emotional, not intellectual.

Questions as to "values"—that is to say, as to what is good or bad on its own account, independently of its effects—lie outside the domain of science, as the defenders of religion emphatically assert. I think that in this they are right, but I draw the further conclusion, which they do not draw, that questions as to "values" lie wholly outside the domain of knowledge. That is to say, when we assert that this or that has "value," we are giving expression to our own emotions, not to a fact which would still be true if our personal feelings were different. To make this clear, we must try to analyse the conception of the Good.

It is obvious, to begin with, that the whole idea of good and bad has some connection with *desire*. *Prima facie*, anything that we all desire is "good," and anything that we all dread is "bad." If we all agreed in our desires, the matter could be left there, but unfortunately our desires conflict. If I say "what I want is good," my neighbour will say "No, what *I* want." Ethics is an attempt—though not, I think, a successful one—to escape from this subjectivity. I shall naturally try to show, in my dispute with my neighbour, that my desires have some quality which makes them more worthy of respect than his. If I want to preserve a right of way, I shall appeal to the landless inhabitants of the district; but he, on his side, will appeal to the landowners. I shall say: "What use is the beauty of the countryside if no one sees it?" He will retort: "What beauty will be left if trippers are allowed to spread devastation?" Each tries to enlist allies by showing that his own desires harmonize with those of other people. When this is obviously impossible, as in the case of a burglar, the man is condemned by public opinion, and his ethical status is that of a sinner.

Ethics is thus closely related to politics: it is an attempt to bring the collective desires of a group to bear upon individuals; or, conversely, it is an attempt by an individual to cause his desires to become those of his group. This latter is, of course, only possible if his desires are not too obviously opposed to the general interest: the burglar will hardly attempt to persuade people that he is doing them good, though plutocrats make similar attempts, and often succeed. When our desires are for things which all can enjoy in common, it seems not unreasonable to hope that others may concur; thus the philosopher who values Truth, Goodness and Beauty seems, to himself, to be not merely expressing his own desires, but pointing the way to the welfare of all mankind. Unlike the burglar, he is able to believe that his desires are for something that has value in an impersonal sense.

Ethics is an attempt to give universal, and not merely personal, importance to certain of our desires. I say "certain" of our desires, because in regard to some of them this is obviously impossible, as we saw in the case of the burglar. The man who makes money on the Stock Exchange by means of some secret knowledge does not wish others to be equally well informed: Truth (in so far as he values it) is for him a private possession, not the general human good that it is for the philosopher. The philosopher may, it is true, sink to the level of the stock-jobber, as when he claims priority for a discovery. But this is a lapse: in his purely philosophic capacity, he wants only to enjoy the contemplation of Truth, in doing which he in no way interferes with others who wish to do likewise.

To seem to give universal importance to our desires—which is the business of ethics—may be attempted from two points of view, that of the legislator, and that of the preacher. Let us take the legislator first.

I will assume, for the sake of argument, that the legislator is personally disinterested. That is to say, when he recognizes one of his desires as being concerned only with his own welfare, he does not let it influence him in framing the laws; for example, his code is not designed to increase his personal fortune. But he has other desires which seem to him impersonal. He may believe in an ordered hierarchy from king to peasant, or from mine-owner to black indentured labourer. He may believe that women should be submissive to men. He may hold that the spread of knowledge in the lower classes is dangerous. And so on and so on. He will then, if he can, so construct his code that conduct promoting the ends which he values shall, as far as possible, be in accordance with individual self-interest; and he will establish a system of moral instruction which will, where it succeeds, make men feel wicked if they pursue other purposes than his.[1] Thus "virtue" will come to be in fact, though not in subjective estimation, subservience to the desires of the legislator, in so far as he himself considers these desires worthy to be universalized.

The standpoint and method of the preacher are necessarily somewhat different, because he does not control the machinery of the State, and therefore cannot produce an artificial harmony between his desires and those of others. His only method is to try to rouse in others the same desires that he feels himself, and for this purpose his appeal must be to the emotions. Thus Ruskin caused people to like Gothic architecture, not by argument, but by the moving effect of rhythmical prose. *Uncle Tom's Cabin* helped to make people think slavery an evil by causing them to imagine themselves as slaves. Every attempt to persuade people that something is good (or bad) in itself, and not merely in its effects, depends upon the art of rousing feelings, not upon an appeal to evidence. In every case the preacher's skill consists in creating in others emotions similar to his own—or dissimilar, if he is a hypocrite. I am not saying this as a criticism of the preacher, but as an analysis of the essential character of his activity.

When a man says "this is good in itself," he *seems* to be making a statement, just as much as if he said "this is square" or "this is sweet." I believe this to be a mistake. I think that what the man really means is: "I wish everybody to desire this," or rather "Would that everybody desired this." If what he says is interpreted as a statement, it is merely an affirmation of his own personal wish; if, on the other hand, it is interpreted in a general way, it states nothing, but merely desires something. The wish, as an occurrence, is personal, but what it desires is universal. It is, I think, this curious interlocking of the particular and the universal which has caused so much confusion in ethics.

The matter may perhaps become clearer by contrasting an ethical sentence with one which makes a statement. If I say "all Chinese are Buddhists," I can be refuted by the production of a Chinese Christian or Mohammedan. If I say "I believe that all Chinese are Buddhists," I cannot be refuted by any evidence from China, but only by evidence that I do not believe what I say; for what I am asserting is only something about my own state of mind. If, now, a philosopher says "Beauty is good," I may interpret him as meaning either "Would that everybody loved the beautiful" (which corresponds to "all Chinese are Buddhists") or "I wish that everybody loved the beautiful" (which corresponds to "I believe that all Chinese are Buddhists"). The first of these makes no assertion, but expresses a wish; since it affirms nothing, it is logically impossible that there should be evidence for or against it, or for it to possess either truth or falsehood. The second sentence, instead of being merely optative, does make a statement, but it is one about the philosopher's state of mind, and it could only be refuted by evidence that he does not have the wish that he says he has. This second sentence does not belong to ethics, but to psychology or biography. The first sentence, which does belong to ethics, expresses a desire for something, but asserts nothing.

Ethics, if the above analysis is correct, contains no statements, whether true or false, but consists of desires of a certain general kind, namely such as are concerned with the desires of mankind in general—and of gods, angels, and devils, if they exist. Science can discuss the causes of desires, and the means for realizing them, but it cannot contain any genuinely ethical sentences, because it is concerned with what is true or false.

The theory which I have been advocating is a form of the doctrine which is called the "subjectivity" of values. This doctrine consists in maintaining that, if two men differ about values, there is not a disagreement as to any kind of truth, but a difference of taste. If one man says "oysters are good" and another says "*I* think they are bad," we recognize that there is nothing to argue about. The theory in question holds that all differences as to values are of this sort, although we do not naturally think them so when we are dealing with matters that seem to us more exalted than oysters. The chief ground for adopting this view is the complete impossibility of finding any arguments to prove that this or that has intrinsic value. If we all agreed, we might hold that we know values by intuition. We cannot *prove*, to a colour-blind man, that grass is green and not red. But there are various ways of proving to him that he lacks a power of discrimination which most men possess, whereas in the case of values there are no such ways, and disagreements are much more frequent than in the case of colours. Since no way can be even imagined for deciding a difference as to values, the conclusion is forced upon us that the difference is one of tastes, not one as to any objective truth.

The consequences of this doctrine are considerable. In the first place, there can be no such thing as "sin" in any absolute sense; what one man calls "sin" another may call "virtue," and though they may dislike each other on account of this difference, neither can convict the other of intellectual error. Punishment cannot be justified on the ground that the criminal is "wicked," but only on the ground that he has behaved in a way which others wish to discourage. Hell, as a place of punishment for sinners, becomes quite irrational.

In the second place, it is impossible to uphold the way of speaking about values which is common among those who believe in Cosmic Purpose. Their argument is that certain things which have been evolved are "good," and therefore the world must have had a purpose which was ethically admirable. In the language of subjective values, this argument becomes: "Some things in the world are to our liking, and therefore they must have been created by a Being with our tastes, Whom, therefore, we also like, and Who, consequently, is good." Now it seems fairly evident that, if creatures having likes and dislikes were to exist at all, they were pretty sure to like *some* things in their environment, since otherwise they would find life intolerable. Our values have been evolved along with the rest of our constitution, and nothing as to any original purpose can be inferred from the fact that they are what they are.

Those who believe in "objective" values often contend that the view which I have been advocating has immoral consequences. This seems to me to be due to faulty reasoning. There are, as has already been said, certain ethical consequences of the doctrine of subjective values, of which the most important is the rejection of vindictive punishment and the notion of "sin." But the more general consequences which are feared, such as the decay of all sense of moral obligation, are not to be logically deduced. Moral obligation, if it is to influence conduct, must consist not merely of a belief, but of a desire. The desire, I may be told, is the desire to be "good" in a sense which I no longer allow. But when we analyse the desire to be "good" it generally resolves itself into a desire to be approved, or, alternatively, to act so as to bring about certain general consequences which we desire. We have wishes which are not purely personal, and, if we had not, no amount of ethical teaching would influence our conduct except through fear of disapproval. The sort of life that most of us admire is one which is guided by large impersonal desires; now such desires can, no doubt, be encouraged by example, education, and knowledge, but they can hardly be created by the mere abstract belief that they are good, nor discouraged by an analysis of what is meant by the word "good."

When we contemplate the human race, we may desire that it should be happy, or healthy, or intelligent, or warlike, and so on. Any one of these desires, if it is strong, will produce its own morality; but if we have no such general desires, our conduct, whatever our ethic may be, will only serve social purposes in so far as self-interest and the interests of society are in harmony. It is the business of wise institutions to create such harmony as far as possible, and for the rest, whatever may be our theoretical definition of value, we must depend upon the existence of impersonal desires. When you meet a man with whom you have a fundamental ethical disagreement—for example, if you think that all men count equally, while he selects a class as alone important—you will find yourself no better able to cope with him if you believe in objective values than if you do not. In either case, you can only influence his conduct through influencing his desires: if you succeed in that, his ethic will change, and if not, not.

Some people feel that if a general desire, say for the happiness of mankind, has not the sanction of absolute good, it is in some way irrational. This is due to a lingering belief in objective values. A desire cannot, in itself, be either rational or irrational. It may conflict with other desires, and therefore lead to unhappiness; it may rouse opposition in others, and therefore be incapable of gratification. But it cannot be considered "irrational" merely because no reason can be given for feeling it. We may desire A because it is a means to B, but in the end, when we have done with mere means, we must come to something which we desire for no reason, but not on that account "irrationally." All systems of ethics embody the desires of those who advocate them, but this fact is concealed in a mist of words. Our desires are, in fact, more general and less purely selfish than many moralists imagine; if it were not so, no theory of ethics would make moral improvement possible. It is, in fact, not by ethical theory, but by the cultivation of large and generous desires through intelligence, happiness, and freedom from fear, that men can be brought to act more than they do at present in a manner that is consistent with the general happiness of mankind. Whatever our definition of the "Good," and whether we believe it to be subjective or objective, those who do not desire the happiness of mankind will not endeavour to further it, while those who do desire it will do what they can to bring it about.

I conclude that, while it is true that science cannot decide questions of value, that is because they cannot be intellectually decided at all, and lie outside the realm of truth and falsehood. Whatever knowledge is attainable, must be attained by scientific methods; and what science cannot discover, mankind cannot know.

NOTES

1. Compare the following advice by a contemporary of Aristotle (Chinese, not Greek): "A ruler should not listen to those who believe in people having opinions of their own and in the importance of the individual. Such teachings cause men to withdraw to quiet places and hide away in caves or on mountains, there to rail at the prevailing government, sneer at those in authority, belittle the importance of rank and emoluments, and despise all who hold official posts." Waley, *The Way and its Power*, p. 37.

The New Subjectivism in Ethics

BRAND BLANSHARD

By the new subjectivism in ethics I mean the view that when anyone says "this is right" or "this is good," he is only expressing his own feeling; he is not asserting anything true or false, because he is not asserting or judging at all; he is really making an exclamation that expresses a favorable feeling.

This view has recently come into much favor. With variations of detail, it is being advocated by Russell, Wittgenstein and Ayer in England, and by Carnap, Stevenson, Feigl, and others, in this country. Why is it that the theory has come into so rapid a popularity? Is it because moralists of insight have been making a fresh and searching examination of moral experience and its expression? No, I think not. A consideration of the names just mentioned suggests a truer reason. All these names belong, roughly speaking, to a single school of thought in the theory of knowledge. If the new view has become popular in ethics, it is because certain persons who were at work in the theory of knowledge arrived at a new view *there*, and found, on thinking it out, that it required the new view in ethics; the view comes less from ethical analysis than from logical positivism.

As positivists, these writers held that every judgment belongs to one or other of two types. On the one hand, it may be *a priori* or necessary. But then it is always analytic, i.e., it unpacks in its predicate part or all of its subject. Can we safely say that 7 +5 make 12? Yes, because 12 is what we mean by "7 +5." On the other hand, the judgment may be empirical, and then, if we are to verify it, we can no longer look to our meanings only; it refers to sense experience and there we must look for its warrant. Having arrived at this division of judgments, the positivists raised the question where value judgments fall. The judgment that knowledge is good, for example, did not seem to be analytic; the value that knowledge might have did not seem to be part of our concept of knowledge. But neither was the statement empirical, for goodness was not a quality like red or squeaky that could be seen or heard. What were they to do, then, with these awkward judgments of value? To find a place for them in their theory of knowledge would require them to revise the theory radically, and yet that theory was what they regarded as their most important discovery. It appeared that the theory could be saved in one way only. If it could be shown that judgments of good and bad were not judgments at all, that they asserted nothing true or false, but merely expressed emotions like "Hurrah" or "Fiddlesticks," then these wayward judgments would cease from troubling and weary heads could be at rest. This is the course the positivists took. They explained value judgments by explaining them away.

Now I do not think their view will do. But before discussing it, I should like to record one vote of thanks to them for the clarity with which they have stated their case. It has been said of John Stuart Mill that he wrote so clearly that he could be found out. This theory

---

Brand Blanshard is professor emeritus at Yale University.

Reprinted by permission from *Philosophy and Phenomenological Research,* Vol. IX, No. 3 (March 1949), pp. 504-511.

has been put so clearly and precisely that it deserves criticism of the same kind, and this I will do my best to supply. The theory claims to show by analysis that when we say, "That is good," we do not mean to assert a character of the subject of which we are thinking. I shall argue that we do mean to do just that.

Let us work through an example, and the simpler and commoner the better. There is perhaps no value statement on which people would more universally agree than the statement that intense pain is bad. Let us take a set of circumstances in which I happen to be interested on the legislative side and in which I think every one of us might naturally make such a statement. We come upon a rabbit that has been caught in one of the brutal traps in common use. There are signs that it has struggled for days to escape and that in a frenzy of hunger, pain, and fear, it has all but eaten off its own leg. The attempt failed: the animal is now dead. As we think of the long and excruciating pain it must have suffered, we are very likely to say: "It was a bad thing that the little animal should suffer so." The positivist tells us that when we say this we are only expressing our present emotion. I hold, on the contrary, that we mean to assert something of the pain itself, namely, that it was bad—bad when and as it occurred.

Consider what follows from the positivist view. On that view, nothing good or bad happened in the case until I came on the scene and made my remark. For what I express in my remark is something going on in me at the time, and that of course did not exist until I did come on the scene. The pain of the rabbit was not itself bad; nothing evil was happening when that pain was being endured; badness, in the only sense in which it is involved at all, waited for its appearance till I came and looked and felt. Now that this is at odds with our meaning may be shown as follows. Let us put to ourselves the hypothesis that we had not come on the scene and that the rabbit never was discovered. Are we prepared to say that in that case nothing bad occurred in the sense in which we said it did? Clearly not. Indeed we should say, on the contrary, that the accident of our later discovery made no difference whatever to the badness of the animal's pain, that it would have been every whit as bad whether a chance passer-by happened later to discover the body and feel repugnance or not. If so, then it is clear that in saying the suffering was bad we are not expressing our feelings only. We are saying that the pain was bad when and as it occurred and before anyone took an attitude toward it.

The first argument is thus an ideal experiment in which we use the method of difference. It removes our present expression and shows that the badness we meant would not be affected by this, whereas on positivist grounds it should be. The second argument applies the method in the reverse way. It ideally removes the past event, and shows that this would render false what we mean to say, whereas on positivist grounds it should not. Let us suppose that the animal did not in fact fall into the trap and did not suffer at all, but that we mistakenly believe it did, and say as before that its suffering was an evil thing. On the positivist theory, everything I sought to express by calling it evil in the first case is still present in the second. In the only sense in which badness is involved at all, whatever was bad in the first case is still present in its entirety, since all that is expressed in either case is a state of feeling, and that feeling is still there. And our question is, is such an implication consistent with what we meant? Clearly it is not. If anyone asked us, after we made the remark that the suffering was a bad thing, whether we should think it was relevant to what we said to learn that the incident had never occurred and no pain had been suffered at all, we should say that it made all the difference in the world, that what we were asserting to be bad was precisely the suffering we thought had occurred back there, that if this had not occurred, there was nothing left to be bad, and that our assertion was in that case mistaken. The suggestion that in saying something evil had occurred we were after all making no mistake, because we had never meant anyhow to say anything about the past suffering, seems to me merely frivolous. If we did not mean to say this, why should we be so relieved on finding that the suffering had not occurred? On the theory before us, such relief would be groundless, for in that suffering itself there was nothing bad at all, and hence in its non-occurrence there would be nothing to be relieved about. The positivist theory would here distort our meaning beyond recognition.

So far as I can see, there is only one way out for the positivist. He holds that goodness and badness lie in feelings of approval or disapproval. And there is a way in which he might hold that badness did in this case precede our own feeling of disapproval without belonging to the pain itself. The pain in itself was neutral; but unfortunately the rabbit, on no grounds at all, took up toward this neutral object an attitude of disapproval, and that made it for the first time, and in the only intelligible sense, bad. This way of escape is theoretically possible, but since it has grave difficulties of its own and has not, so far as I know, been urged by positivists, it is perhaps best not to spend time over it.

I come now to a third argument, which again is very simple. When we come upon the rabbit and make our remark about its suffering being a bad thing, we presumably make it with some feeling; the positivists are plainly right in saying that such remarks do usually express feeling. But suppose that a week later we revert to the incident in thought and make our statement again. And suppose that the circumstances have now so changed that the feeling with which we made the remark in the first place has faded. The pathetic evidence is no longer before us; and we are now so fatigued in body and mind that feeling is, as we say, quite dead. In these circumstances, since what was expressed by the remark when first made is, on the theory before us, simply absent, the remark now expresses nothing. It is as empty as the word "Hurrah" would be when there was no enthusiasm behind it. And this seems to me untrue. When we repeat the remark that such suffering was a bad thing, the feeling with which we made it last week may be at or near the vanishing point, but if we were asked whether we meant to say what we did before, we should certainly answer Yes. We should say that we made our point with feeling the first time and little or no feeling the second time, but that it was the same point we were making. And if we can see that what we meant to say remains the same, while the feeling varies from intensity to near zero, it is not the feeling that we primarily meant to express.

I come now to a fourth consideration. We all believe that toward acts or effects of a certain kind one attitude is fitting and another not; but on the theory before us such a belief would not make sense. Broad and Ross have lately contended that this fitness is one of the main facts of ethics, and I suspect they are right. But that is not exactly my point. My point is this: whether there is such fitness or not, we all assume that there is, and if we do, we express in moral judgments more than the subjectivists say we do. Let me illustrate.

In his novel *The House of the Dead*, Dostoevsky tells of his experiences in a Siberian prison camp. Whatever the unhappy inmates of such camps are like today, Dostoevsky's companions were about as grim a lot as can be imagined. "I have heard stories," he writes, "of the most terrible, the most unnatural actions, of the most monstrous murders, told with the most spontaneous, childishly merry laughter." Most of us would say that in this delight at the killing of others or the causing of suffering there is something very unfitting. If we were asked why we thought so, we should say that these things involve great evil and are wrong, and that to take delight in what is evil or wrong is plainly unfitting. Now on the subjectivist view, this answer is ruled out. For before someone takes up an attitude toward death, suffering, or their infliction, they have no moral quality at all. There is therefore nothing about them to which an attitude of approval or condemnation could be fitting. They are in themselves neutral, and, so far as they get a moral quality, they get it only through being invested with it by the attitude of the onlooker. But if that is true, why is any attitude more fitting than any other? Would applause, for example, be fitting if, apart from the applause, there were nothing good to applaud? Would condemnation be fitting if, independently of the condemnation, there were nothing bad to condemn? In such a case, any attitude would be as fitting or unfitting as any other, which means that the notion of fitness has lost all point.

Indeed we are forced to go much farther. If goodness and badness lie in attitudes only and hence are brought into being by them, those men who greeted death and misery with childishly merry laughter are taking the only sensible line. If there is nothing evil in these things, if they get their moral complexion only from our feeling about them, why shouldn't they be greeted with a cheer? To greet them with repulsion would turn what before was neutral into something bad; it would needlessly bring badness into the world; and even on subjectivist assumptions that does not seem very bright. On the other hand, to greet them with delight would convert what before was neutral into something good; it would bring goodness into the world. If I have murdered a man and wish to remove the stain, the way is clear. It is to cry, "Hurrah for murder."

What is the subjectivist to reply? I can only guess. He may point out that the inflicting of death is *not* really neutral before the onlooker takes his attitude, for the man who inflicted the death no doubt himself took an attitude, and thus the act had a moral quality derived from this. But that makes the case more incredible still, for the man who did the act presumably approved it, and if so it was good in the only sense in which anything is good, and then our conviction that the laughter is unfit is more unaccountable still. It may be replied that the victim, too, had his attitude and that since this was unfavorable, the act was not unqualifiedly good. But the answer is plain. Let the killer be expert at his job; let him despatch his victim instantly before he has time to take an attitude, and then gloat about his perfect crime without ever telling anyone. Then, so far as I can see, his act will be good without any qualification. It would become bad only if someone found out about it and disliked it. And that would be a curiously irrational procedure, since the man's approving of his own killing is in itself as neutral as the killing that it approves. Why then should anyone dislike it?

It may be replied that we can defend our dislike on this ground that, if the approval of killing were to go unchecked and spread, most men would have to live in insecurity and fear, and these things are undesirable. But surely this reply is not open; these things are not, on the theory, undesirable, for nothing is; in themselves they are neutral. Why then should I disapprove men's living in this state? The answer may come that if other men live in insecurity and fear, I shall in time be infected myself. But even in my own insecurity and fear there is, on the theory before us, nothing bad whatever, and therefore, if I disapprove them, it is without a shadow of ground and with no more fitness in my attitude than if I cordially cheered them. The theory thus conflicts with our judgments of fitness all along the line.

I come now to a fifth and final difficulty with the theory. It makes mistakes about values impossible. There is a whole nest of inter-connected criticisms here, some of which have been made so often that I shall not develop them again, such as that I can never agree or disagree in opinion with anyone else about an ethical matter, and that in these matters I can never be inconsistent with others or with myself. I am not at all content with the sort of analysis which says that the only contradictions in such cases have regard to facts and that contradictions about value are only differences of feeling. I think that if anyone tells me that having a bicuspid out without an anaesthetic is not a bad experience and I say it is a very nasty experience indeed, I am differing with him in opinion, and differing about the degrees of badness of the experience. But without pressing this further, let me apply the argument in what is perhaps a fresh direction.

There is an old and merciful distinction that moralists have made for many centuries about conduct—the distinction between what is subjectively and what is objectively right. They have said that in any given situation there is some act which, in view of all the circumstances, would be the best act to do; and this is what would be objectively right. The notion of an objectively right act is the ground of our notion of duty: our duty is always to find and do this act if we can. But of course we often don't find it. We often hit upon and do acts that we think are the right ones, but we are mistaken; and then our act is only subjectively right. Between these two acts the disparity may be continual; Professor Prichard suggested that probably few of us in the course of our lives ever succeed in doing *the* right act.

Now so far as I can see, the new subjectivism would abolish this difference at a stroke. Let us take a case. A boy abuses his small brother. We should commonly say, "That is wrong, but perhaps he doesn't know any better. By reason of bad teaching and a feeble imagination, he may see nothing wrong in what he is doing, and may even be proud of it. If so, his act may be subjectively right, though it is miles away from what is objectively right." What concerns me about the new subjectivism is that it prohibits this distinction. If the boy feels this way about his act, then it is right in the only sense in which anything is right. The notion of an objective right lying beyond what he has discovered, and which he ought to seek and do is meaningless. There might, to be sure, be an act that would more generally arouse favorable feelings in others, but that would not make it right for him unless he thought of it and approved it, which he doesn't. Even if he did think of it, it would not be obligatory for him to feel about it in any particular way, since there is nothing in any act, as we have seen, which would make any feeling more suitable than any other.

Now if there is no such thing as an objectively right act, what becomes of the idea of duty? I have suggested that the idea of duty rests on the idea of such an act, since it is always our duty to find that act and do it if we can. But if whatever we feel approval for at the time is right, what is the point of doubting and searching further? Like the little girl in Boston who was asked if she would like to travel, we can answer, "Why should I travel when I'm already there?" If I am reconciled in feeling to my present act, no act I could discover by reflection could be better, and therefore why reflect or seek at all? Such a view seems to me to break the mainspring of duty, to destroy the motive for self-improvement, and to remove the ground for self-criticism. It may be replied that by further reflection I can find an act that would satisfy my feelings more widely than the present one, and that this is the act I should seek. But this reply means either that such general satisfaction is objectively better, which would contradict the theory, or else that, if at the time I don't feel it better, it isn't better, in which case I have no motive for seeking it. When certain self-righteous persons took an inflexible line with Oliver Cromwell, his very Cromwellian reply was, "Bethink ye, gentlemen, by the bowels of Christ, that ye may be mistaken." It was good advice. I hope nobody will take from me the privilege of finding myself mistaken. I should be sorry to think that the self of thirty years ago was as far along the path as the self of today, merely because he was a smug young jackanapes, or even that the paragon of today has as little room for improvement as would be allowed by his myopic complacency.

One final remark. The great problems of the day are international problems. Has the new subjectivism any bearing upon these problems? I think it has, and a somewhat sinister bearing. I would not suggest, of course, that those who hold the theory are one whit less public-spirited than others; surely there are few who could call themselves citizens of the world with more right (if "rights" have meaning any longer) than Mr. Russell. But Mr. Russell has confessed himself discontented with his ethical theory, and in view of his breadth of concern, one cannot wonder. For its general acceptance would, so far as one can see, be an international disaster. The assumption behind the old League and the new United Nations was that there is such a thing as right and wrong in the conduct of a nation, a right and wrong that do not depend on how it happens to feel at the time. It is implied, for example, that when Japan invaded Manchuria in 1931 she might be wrong, and that by discussion and argument she might be shown to be wrong. It was implied that when the Nazis invaded Poland they might be wrong, even though German public sentiment overwhelmingly approved it. On the theory before us, it would be meaningless to call these nations mistaken; if they felt approval for what they did, then it was right with as complete a justification as could be supplied for the disapproval felt by the rest of the world. In the present dispute between Russia and our own country over southeast Europe, it is nonsense to speak of the right or rational course for either of us to take; if with all the facts before the two parties, each feels approval for its own course, both attitudes are equally justified or unjustified; neither is mistaken; there is no common reason to which they can take an appeal; there are no principles by which an international court could pronounce on the matter; nor would there be any obligation to obey the pronouncement if it were made. This cuts the ground from under any attempt to establish one's case as right or anyone else's case as wrong. So if our friends the subjectivists still hold their theory after I have applied my little ruler to their knuckles, which of course they will, I have but one request to make of them: Do keep it from Mr. Molotov and Mr. Vishinsky.

What Utilitarianism Is

JOHN STUART MILL

A passing remark is all that needs be given to the ignorant blunder of supposing that those who stand up for utility as the test of right and wrong use the term in that restricted and merely colloquial sense in which utility is opposed to pleasure. An apology is due to the philosophical opponents of utilitarianism for even the momentary appearance of confounding them with anyone capable of so absurd a misconception; which is the more extraordinary, inasmuch as the contrary accusation, of referring everything to pleasure, and that, too, in its grossest form, is another of the common charges against utilitarianism: and, as has been pointedly remarked by an able writer, the same sort of persons, and often the very same persons, denounce the theory "as impracticably dry when the word 'utility' precedes the word 'pleasure,' and as too practicably voluptuous when the word 'pleasure' precedes the word 'utility.'" Those who know anything about the matter are aware that every writer, from Epicurus to Bentham, who maintained the theory of utility meant by it, not something to be contradistinguished from pleasure, but pleasure itself, together with exemption from pain; and instead of opposing the useful to the agreeable or the ornamental, have always declared that the useful means these, among other things. Yet the common herd, including the herd of writers, not only in newspapers and periodicals, but in books of weight and pretension, are perpetually falling into this shallow mistake. Having caught up the word "utilitarian," while knowing nothing whatever about it but its sound, they habitually express by it the rejection or the neglect of pleasure in some of its forms: of beauty, of ornament, or of amusement. Nor is the term thus ignorantly misapplied solely in disparagement, but occasionally in compliment, as though it implied superiority to frivolity and the mere pleasures of the moment. And this perverted use is the only one in which the word is popularly known, and the one from which the new generation are acquiring their sole notion of its meaning. Those who introduced the word, but who had for many years discontinued it as a distinctive appellation, may well feel themselves called upon to resume it if by doing so they can hope to contribute anything toward rescuing it from this utter degradation.[1]

The creed which accepts as the foundation of morals "utility" or the "greatest happiness principle" holds that actions are right in proportion as they tend to promote happiness; wrong as they tend to produce the reverse of happiness. By happiness is intended pleasure and the absence of pain; by unhappiness, pain and the privation of pleasure. To give a clear view of the moral standard set up by the theory, much more requires to be said; in particular, what things it includes in the ideas of pain and pleasure, and to what extent this is left an open question. But these supplementary explanations do not affect the theory of life on which this theory of morality is grounded—namely, that pleasure and freedom from pain are the only things desirable as

---

John Stuart Mill (1806-1873) was a prominent British philosopher. He wrote in virtually every area of philosophy.

From Mill's *Utilitarianism* (1863).

ends; and that all desirable things (which are as numerous in the utilitarian as in any other scheme) are desirable either for pleasure inherent in themselves or as means to the promotion of pleasure and the prevention of pain.

Now such a theory of life excites in many minds, and among them in some of the most estimable in feeling and purpose, inveterate dislike. To suppose that life has (as they express it) no higher end than pleasure—no better and nobler object of desire and pursuit—they designate as utterly mean and groveling, as a doctrine worthy only of swine, to whom the followers of Epicurus were, at a very early period, contemptuously likened; and modern holders of the doctrine are occasionally made the subject of equally polite comparisons by its German, French, and English assailants.

When thus attacked, the Epicureans have always answered that it is not they, but their accusers, who represent human nature in a degrading light, since the accusation supposes human beings to be capable of no pleasures except those of which swine are capable. If this supposition were true, the charge could not be gainsaid, but would then be no longer an imputation; for if the sources of pleasure were precisely the same to human beings and to swine, the rule of life which is good enough for the one would be good enough for the other. The comparison of the Epicurean life to that of beasts is felt as degrading, precisely because a beast's pleasures do not satisfy a human being's conceptions of happiness. Human beings have faculties more elevated than the animal appetites and, when once made conscious of them, do not regard anything as happiness which does not include their gratification. I do not, indeed, consider the Epicureans to have been by any means faultless in drawing out their scheme of consequences from the utilitarian principle. To do this in any sufficient manner, many Stoic, as well as Christian, elements require to be included. But there is no known Epicurean theory of life which does not assign to the pleasures of the intellect, of the feelings and imagination, and of the moral sentiments a much higher value as pleasures than to those of mere sensation. It must be admitted, however, that utilitarian writers in general have placed the superiority of mental over bodily pleasures chiefly in the greater permanency, safety, uncostliness, etc., of the former—that is, in their circumstantial advantages rather than in their intrinsic nature. And on all these points utilitarians have fully proved their case; but they might have taken the other and, as it may be called, higher ground with entire consistency. It is quite compatible with the principle of utility to recognize the fact that some kinds of pleasure are more desirable and more valuable than others. It would be absurd that, while in estimating all other things quality is considered as well as quantity, the estimation of pleasure should be supposed to depend on quantity alone.

If I am asked what I mean by difference of quality in pleasures, or what makes one pleasure more valuable than another, merely as a pleasure, except its being greater in amount, there is but one possible answer. Of two pleasures, if there be one to which all or almost all who have experience of both give a decided preference, irrespective of any feeling of moral obligation to prefer it, that is the more desirable pleasure. If one of the two is, by those who are competently acquainted with both, placed so far above the other that they prefer it, even though knowing it to be attended with a greater amount of discontent, and would not resign it for any quantity of the other pleasure which their nature is capable of, we are justified in ascribing to the preferred enjoyment a superiority in quality so far outweighing quantity as to render it, in comparison, of small account.

Now it is an unquestionable fact that those who are equally acquainted with and equally capable of appreciating and enjoying both do give a most marked preference to the manner of existence which employs their higher faculties. Few human creatures would consent to be changed into any of the lower animals for a promise of the fullest allowance of a beast's pleasures; no intelligent human being would consent to be a fool, no instructed person would be an ignoramus, no person of feeling and conscience would be selfish and base, even though they should be persuaded that the fool, the dunce, or the rascal is better satisfied with his lot than they are with theirs. They would not resign what they possess more than he for the most complete satisfaction of all the desires which they have in common with him. If they ever fancy they would, it is only in cases of unhappiness so extreme that to escape from it they would exchange their lot for almost any other, however undesirable in their own eyes. A being of higher faculties requires more to make him happy, is capable probably of more acute suffering, and certainly accessible to it at more points, than one of an inferior type; but in spite of these liabilities, he can never really wish to sink into what he feels to be a lower grade of existence. We may give what explanation we please of this unwillingness; we may attribute it to pride, a name which is given indiscriminately to some of the most and to some of the least estimable feelings of which mankind are capable; we may refer it to the love of liberty and personal independence, an appeal to which was with the Stoics one of the most effective means for the inculcation of it; to the love of power or to the love of excitement, both of which do really enter into and contribute to it; but its most appropriate appellation is a sense of dignity, which all human beings possess in one form or other, and in some, though by no means in exact, proportion to their higher faculties, and which is so essential a part of the happiness of those in whom it is strong that nothing which conflicts with it could be otherwise than momentarily an object of desire to them. Whoever supposes that this preference takes place at a sacrifice of happiness—that the superior being, in anything like equal circumstances, is not happier than the inferior—confounds the two very different ideas of happiness and content. It is indisputable that the being whose capacities of enjoyment are low has the greatest chance of having them fully satisfied; and a highly endowed being will always feel that any happiness which he can look for, as the world is constituted, is imperfect. But he can learn to bear its imperfections, if they are at all bearable; and they will not make him envy the being who is indeed unconscious of the imperfections, but only because he feels not at all the good which those imperfections qualify. It is better to be a human being dissatisfied than a pig satisfied; better to be Socrates dissatisfied than a fool satisfied. And if the fool, or the pig, are of a different opinion, it is because they only know their own side of the question. The other party to the comparison knows both sides.

It may be objected that many who are capable of the higher pleasures occasionally, under the influence of temptation, postpone them to the lower. But this is quite compatible with a full appreciation of the intrinsic superiority of the higher. Men often, from infirmity of character, make their election for the nearer good, though they know it to be the less valuable; and this no less when the choice is between two bodily pleasures than when it is between bodily and mental. They pursue sensual indulgences to the injury of health, though perfectly aware that health is the greater good. It may be further objected that many who begin with youthful enthusiasm for everything noble, as they advance in years, sink into indolence and selfishness. But I do not believe that those who undergo this very common change voluntarily choose the lower description of pleasures in preference to the higher. I believe that, before they devote themselves exclusively to the one, they have already become incapable of the other. Capacity for the nobler feelings is in most natures a very tender plant, easily killed, not only by hostile influences, but by mere want of sustenance; and in the majority of young persons it speedily dies away if the occupations to which their position in life has devoted them, and the society into which it has thrown them, are not favorable to keeping that higher capacity in exercise. Men lose their high aspirations as they lose their intellectual tastes, because they have not time or opportunity for indulging them; and they addict themselves to inferior pleasures, not because they deliberately prefer them, but because they are either the only ones to which they have access or the only ones which they are any longer capable of enjoying. It may be questioned whether anyone who has remained equally susceptible to both classes of pleasures ever knowingly and calmly preferred the lower, though many, in all ages, have broken down in an ineffectual attempt to combine both.

From this verdict of the only competent judges, I apprehend there can be no appeal. On a question which is the best worth having of two pleasures, or which of two modes of existence is the most grateful to the feelings, apart from its moral attributes and from its consequences, the judgment of those who are qualified by knowledge of both, or, if they differ, that of the majority among them, must be admitted as final. And there needs be the less hesitation to accept this judgment respecting the quality of pleasures, since there is no other tribunal to be referred to even on the question of quantity. What means are there of determining which is the acutest of two pains, or the intensest of two pleasurable sensations, except the general suffrage of those who are familiar with both? Neither pains nor pleasures are homogeneous, and pain is always heterogeneous with pleasure. What is there to decide whether a particular pleasure is worth purchasing at the cost of a particular pain, except the feelings and judgment of the experienced? When, therefore, those feelings and judgment declare the pleasures derived from the higher faculties to be preferable *in kind*, apart from the question of intensity, to those of which the animal nature, disjoined from the higher faculties, is susceptible, they are entitled on this subject to the same regard.

I have dwelt on this point as being a necessary part of a perfectly just conception of utility or happiness considered as the directive rule of human conduct. But it is by no means an indispensable condition to the acceptance of the utilitarian standard; for that standard is not the agent's own greatest happiness, but the greatest amount of happiness altogether; and if it may possibly be doubted whether a noble character is always the happier for its nobleness, there can be no doubt that it makes other people happier, and that the world in general is immensely a gainer by it. Utilitarianism, therefore, could only attain its end by the general cultivation of nobleness of character, even if each individual were only benefited by the nobleness of others, and his own, so far as happiness is concerned, were a sheer deduction from the benefit. But the bare enunciation of such an absurdity as this last renders refutation superfluous.

According to the greatest happiness principle, as above explained, the ultimate end, with reference to and for the sake of which all other things are desirable—whether we are considering our own good or that of other people—is an existence exempt as far as possible from pain, and as rich as possible in enjoyments, both in point of quantity and quality; the test of quality and the rule for measuring it against quantity being the preference felt by those who, in their opportunities of experience, to which must be added their habits of self-consciousness and self-observation, are best furnished with the means of comparison. This, being according to the utilitarian opinion the end of human action, is necessarily also the standard of morality, which may accordingly be defined "the rules and precepts for human conduct," by the observance of which an existence such as has been described might be, to the greatest extent possible, secured to all mankind; and not to them only, but, so far as the nature of things admits, to the whole sentient creation.

Against this doctrine, however, arises another class of objectors who say that happiness, in any form, cannot be the rational purpose of human life and action; because, in the first place, it is unattainable; and they contemptuously ask, What right has thou to be happy?—a question which Mr. Carlyle clinches by the addition, What right, a short time ago, hadst thou even *to be*? Next they say that men can do *without* happiness; that all noble human beings have felt this, and could not have become noble but by learning the lesson of *Entsagen*, or renunciation; which lesson, thoroughly learned and submitted to, they affirm to be the beginning and necessary condition of all virtue.

The first of these objections would go to the root of the matter were it well founded; for if no happiness is to be had at all by human beings, the attainment of it cannot be the end of morality or of any rational conduct. Though, even in that case, something might still be said for the utilitarian theory, since utility includes not solely the pursuit of happiness, but the prevention or mitigation of unhappiness; and if the former aim be chimerical, there will be all the greater scope and more imperative need for the latter, so long at least as mankind think fit to live and do not take refuge in the simultaneous act of suicide recommended under certain conditions by Novalis. When, however, it is thus positively asserted to be impossible that human life should be happy, the assertion, if not something like a verbal quibble, is at least an exaggeration. If by happiness be meant a continuity of highly pleasurable excitement, it is evident enough that this is impossible. A state of exalted pleasure lasts only moments or in some cases, and with some intermissions, hours or days, and is the occasional brilliant flash of enjoyment, not its permanent and steady flame. Of this the philosophers who have taught that happiness is the end of life were as fully aware as those who taunt them. The happiness which they meant was not a life of rapture, but moments of such, in an existence made up of few and transitory pains, many and various pleasures, with a decided predominance of the active over the passive, and having as the foundation of the whole not to expect more from life than it is capable of bestowing. A life thus composed, to those who have been fortunate enough to obtain it, has always appeared worthy of the name of happiness. And such an existence is even now the lot of many during some considerable portion of their lives. The present wretched education and wretched social arrangements are the only real hindrance to its being attainable by almost all.

The objectors perhaps may doubt whether human beings, if taught to consider happiness as the end of life, would be satisfied with such a moderate share of it. But great numbers of mankind have been satisfied with much less. The main constituents of a satisfied life appear to be two, either of which by itself is often found sufficient for the purpose: tranquillity and excitement. With much tranquillity, many find that they can be content with very little pleasure; with much excitement, many can reconcile themselves to a considerable quantity of pain. There is assuredly no inherent impossibility of enabling even the mass of mankind to unite both, since the two are so far from being incompatible that they are in natural alliance, the prolongation of either being a preparation for, and exciting a wish for, the other. It is only those in whom indolence amounts to a vice that do not desire excitement after an interval of repose; it is only those in whom the need of excitement is a disease that feel the tranquillity which follows excitement dull and insipid, instead of pleasurable in direct proportion to the excitement which preceded it. When people who are tolerably fortunate in their outward lot do not find in life sufficient enjoyment to make it valuable to them, the cause generally is caring for nobody but themselves. To those who have neither public nor private affections, the excitements of life are much curtailed, and in any case dwindle in value as the time approaches when all selfish interests must be terminated by death; while those who leave after them objects of personal affection, and especially those who have also cultivated a fellow-feeling with the collective interests of mankind, retain as lively an interest in life on the eve of death as in the vigor of youth and health. Next to selfishness, the principal cause which makes life unsatisfactory is want of mental cultivation. A cultivated mind—I do not mean that of a philosopher, but any mind to which the fountains of knowledge have been opened, and which has been taught, in any tolerable degree, to exercise its faculties—finds sources of inexhaustible interest in all that surrounds it: in the objects of nature, the achievements of art, the imaginations of poetry, the incidents of history, the ways of mankind, past and present, and their prospects in the future. It is possible, indeed, to become indifferent to all this, and that too without having exhausted a thousandth part of it, but only when one has had from the beginning no moral or human interest in these things and has sought in them only the gratification of curiosity.

Now there is absolutely no reason in the nature of things why an amount of mental culture sufficient to give an intelligent interest in these objects of contemplation should not be the inheritance of everyone born in a civilized country. As little is there an inherent necessity that any human being should be a selfish egotist, devoid of every feeling or care but those which center in his own miserable individuality. Something far superior to this is sufficiently common even now, to give ample earnest of what the human species may be made. Genuine private affections and a sincere interest in the public good are possible, though in unequal degrees, to every rightly brought up human being. In a world in which there is so much to interest, so much to enjoy, and so much also to correct and improve, everyone who has this moderate amount of moral and intellectual requisites is capable of an existence which may be called enviable; and unless such a person, through bad laws or subjection to the will of others, is denied the liberty to use the sources of happiness within his reach, he will not fail to find this enviable existence, if he escape the positive evils of life, the great sources of physical and mental suffering—such as indigence, disease, and the unkindness, worthlessness, or premature loss of objects of affection. The main stress of the problem lies, therefore, in the contest with these calamities from which it is a rare good fortune entirely to escape; which, as things now are, cannot be obviated, and often cannot be in any material degree mitigated. Yet no one whose opinion deserves a moment's consideration can doubt that most of the great positive evils of the world are in themselves removable, and will, if human affairs continue to improve, be in the end reduced within narrow limits. Poverty, in any sense implying suffering, may be completely extinguished by the wisdom of society combined with the good sense and providence of individuals, Even that most intractable of enemies, disease, may be indefinitely reduced in dimensions by good physical and moral education and proper control of noxious influences, while the progress of science holds out a promise for the future of still more direct conquests over this detestable foe. And every advance in that direction relieves us from some, not only of the chances which cut short our own lives, but, what concerns us still more, which deprive us of those in whom our happiness is wrapt up. As for vicissitudes of fortune and other disappointments connected with worldly circumstances, these are principally the effect either of gross imprudence, of ill-regulated desires, or of bad or imperfect social institutions. All the grand sources, in short, of human suffering are in a great degree, many of them almost entirely, conquerable by human care and effort; and though their removal is grievously slow—though a long succession of generations will perish in the breach before the conquest is completed, and this world becomes all that, if will and knowledge were not wanting, it might easily be made—yet every mind sufficiently intelligent and generous to bear a part, however small and inconspicuous, in the endeavor will draw a noble enjoyment from the contest itself, which he would not for any bribe in the form of selfish indulgence consent to be without.

And this leads to the true estimation of what is said by the objectors concerning the possibility and the obligation of learning to do without happiness. Unquestionably it is possible to do without happiness; it is done involuntarily by nineteen-twentieths of mankind, even in those parts of our present world which are least deep in barbarism; and it often has to be done voluntarily by the hero or the martyr, for the sake of something which he prizes more than his individual happiness. But this something, what is it, unless the happiness of others or some of the requisites of happiness? It is noble to be capable of resigning entirely one's own portion of happiness, or chances of it; but, after all, this self-sacrifice must be for some end; it is not its own end; and if we are told that its end is not happiness but virtue, which is better than happiness, I ask, would the sacrifice be made if the hero or martyr did not believe that it would earn for others immunity from similar sacrifices? Would it be made if he thought that his renunciation of happiness for himself would produce no fruit for any of his fellow creatures, but to make their lot like his and place them also in the condition of persons who have renounced happiness? All honor to those who can abnegate for themselves the personal enjoyment of life when by such renunciation they contribute worthily to increase the amount of happiness in the world; but he who does it or professes to do it for any other purpose is no more deserving of admiration than the ascetic mounted on his pillar. He may be an inspiriting proof of what men *can* do, but assuredly not an example of what they *should*.

Though it is only in a very imperfect state of the world's arrangements that anyone can best serve the happiness of others by the absolute sacrifice of his own, yet, so long as the world is in that imperfect state, I fully acknowledge that the readiness to make such a sacrifice is the highest virtue which can be found in man. I will add that in this condition of the world, paradoxical as the assertion may be, the conscious ability to do without happiness gives the best prospect of realizing such happiness as is attainable. For nothing except that consciousness can raise a person above the chances of life by making him feel that, let fate and fortune do their worst, they have not power to subdue him; which, once felt, frees him from excess of anxiety concerning the evils of life and enables him, like many a Stoic in the worst times of the Roman Empire, to cultivate in tranquillity the sources of satisfaction accessible to him, without concerning himself about the uncertainty of their duration any more than about their inevitable end.

Meanwhile, let utilitarians never cease to claim the morality of self-devotion as a possession which belongs by as good a right to them as either to the Stoic or to the Transcendentalist. The utilitarian morality does recognize in human beings the power of sacrificing their own greatest good for the good of others. It only refuses to admit that the sacrifice is itself a good. A sacrifice which does not increase or tend to increase the sum total of happiness, it considers as wasted. The only self-renunciation which it applauds is devotion to the happiness, or to some of the means of happiness, of others, either of mankind collectively or of individuals within the limits imposed by the collective interests of mankind.

I must again repeat what the assailants of utilitarianism seldom have the justice to acknowledge, that the happiness which forms the utilitarian standard of what is right in conduct is not the agent's own happiness but that of all concerned. As between his own happiness and that of others, utilitarianism requires him to be as strictly impartial as a disinterested and benevolent spectator. In the golden rule of Jesus of Nazareth, we read the complete spirit of the ethics of utility. "To do as you would be done by," and "to love your neighbor as yourself," constitute the ideal perfection of utilitarian morality. As the means of making the nearest approach to this ideal, utility would enjoin, first, that laws and social arrangements should place the happiness or (as, speaking practically, it may be called) the interest of every individual as nearly as possible in harmony with the interest of the whole; and, secondly, that education and opinion, which have so vast a power over human character, should so use that power as to establish in the mind of every individual an indissoluble association between his own happiness and the good of the whole, especially between his own happiness and the practice of such modes of conduct, negative and positive, as regard for the universal happiness prescribes; so that not only he may be unable to conceive the possibility of happiness to himself, consistently with conduct opposed to the general good, but also that a direct impulse to promote the general good may be in every individual one of the habitual motives of action, and the sentiments connected therewith may fill a large and prominent place in every human being's sentient existence. If the impugners of the utilitarian morality represented it to their own minds in this its true character. I know not what recommendation possessed by any other morality they could possibly affirm to be wanting to it; what more beautiful or more exalted developments of human nature any other ethical system can be supposed to foster, or what springs of action, not accessible to the utilitarian, such systems rely on for giving effect to their mandates.

The objectors to utilitarianism cannot always be charged with representing it in a discreditable light. On the contrary, those among them who entertain anything like a just idea of its disinterested character sometimes find fault with its standard as being too high for humanity. They say it is exacting too much to require that people shall always act from the inducement of promoting the general interests of society. But this is to mistake the very meaning of a standard of morals and confound the rule of action with the motive of it. It is the business of ethics to tell us what are our duties, or by what test we may know them; but no system of ethics requires that the sole motive of all we do shall be a feeling of duty; on the contrary, ninety-nine hundredths of all our actions are done from other motives, and rightly so done if the rule of duty does not condemn them. It is the more unjust to utilitarianism that this particular misapprehension should be made a ground of objection to it, inasmuch as utilitarian moralists have gone beyond almost all others in affirming that the motive has nothing to do with the morality of the action, though much with the worth of the agent. He who saves a fellow creature from drowning does what is morally right, whether his motive be duty or the hope of being paid for his trouble; he who betrays the friend that trusts him is guilty of a crime, even if his object be to serve another friend to whom he is under greater obligations. But to speak only of actions done from the motive of duty, and in direct obedience to principle: it is a misapprehension of the utilitarian mode of thought to conceive it as implying that people should fix their minds upon so wide a generality as the world, or society at large. The great majority of good actions are intended not for the benefit of the world, but for that of individuals, of which the good of the world is made up; and the thoughts of the most virtuous man need not on these occasions travel beyond the particular persons concerned, except so far as is necessary to assure himself that in benefiting them he is not violating the rights, that is, the legitimate and authorized expectations, of anyone else. The multiplication of happiness is, according to the utilitarian ethics, the object of virtue: the occasions on which any person (except one in a thousand) has it in his power to do this on an extended scale—in other words, to be a public benefactor—are but exceptional; and on these occasions alone is he called on to consider public utility; in every other case, private utility, the interest or happiness of some few persons, is all he has to attend to. Those alone the influence of whose actions extends to society in general need concern themselves habitually about so large an object. In the case of abstinences indeed—of things which people forbear to do from moral considerations, though the consequences in the particular case might be beneficial—it would be unworthy of an intelligent agent not to be consciously aware that the action is of a class which, if practiced generally, would be generally injurious, and that this is the ground of the obligation to abstain from it. The amount of regard for the public interest implied in this recognition is no greater than is demanded by every system of morals, for they all enjoin to abstain from whatever is manifestly pernicious to society.

The same considerations dispose of another reproach against the doctrine of utility, founded on a still grosser misconception of the purpose of a standard of morality and of the very meaning of the words "right" and "wrong." It is often affirmed that utilitarianism renders men cold and unsympathizing; that it chills their moral feelings toward individuals; that it makes them regard only the dry and hard consideration of the consequences of actions, not taking into their moral estimate the qualities from which those actions emanate. If the assertion means that they do not allow their judgment respecting the rightness or wrongness of an action to be influenced by their opinion of the qualities of the person who does it, this is a complaint not against utilitarianism, but against any standard of morality at all; for certainly no known ethical standard decides an action to be good or bad because it is done by a good or a bad man, still less because done by an amiable, a brave, or a benevolent man, or the contrary. These considerations are relevant, not to the estimation of actions, but of persons; and there is nothing in the utilitarian theory inconsistent with the fact that there are other things which interest us in persons besides the rightness and wrongness of their actions. The Stoics, indeed, with the paradoxical misuse of language which was part of their system, and by which they strove to raise themselves above all concern about anything but virtue, were fond of saying that he who has that has everything; that he, and only he, is rich, is beautiful, is a king. But no claim of this description is made for the virtuous man by the utilitarian doctrine. Utilitarians are quite aware that there are other desirable possessions and qualities besides virtue, and are perfectly willing to allow to all of them their full worth. They are also aware that a right action does not necessarily indicate a virtuous character, and that actions which are blamable often proceed from qualities entitled to praise. When this is apparent in any particular case, it modifies their estimation, not certainly of the act, but of the agent. I grant that they are, notwithstanding, of opinion that in the long run the best proof of a good character is good actions; and resolutely refuse to consider any mental disposition as good of which the predominant tendency is to produce bad conduct. This makes them unpopular with many people, but it is an unpopularity which they must share with everyone who regards the distinction between right and wrong in a serious light; and the reproach is not one which a conscientious utilitarian need be anxious to repel.

If no more be meant by the objection than that many utilitarians look on the morality of actions, as measured by the utilitarian standards, with too exclusive a regard, and do not lay sufficient stress upon the other beauties of character which go toward making a human being lovable or admirable, this may be admitted. Utilitarians who have cultivated their moral feelings, but not their sympathies, nor their artistic perceptions, do fall into this mistake; and so do all other moralists under the same conditions. What can be said in excuse for other moralists is equally available for them, namely, that, if there is to be any error, it is better that it should be on that side. As a matter of fact, we may affirm that among utilitarians, as among adherents of other systems, there is every imaginable degree of rigidity and of laxity in the application of their standard; some are even puritanically rigorous, while others are as indulgent as can possibly be desired by sinner or by sentimentalist. But on the whole, a doctrine which brings prominently forward the interest that mankind have in the repression and prevention of conduct which violates the moral law is likely to be inferior to no other in turning the sanctions of opinion against such violations. It is true, the question "What does violate the moral law?" is one on which those who recognize different standards of morality are likely now and then to differ. But difference of opinion on moral questions was not first introduced into the world by utilitarianism, while that doctrine does supply, if not always an easy, at all events a tangible and intelligible, mode of deciding such differences.

It may not be superfluous to notice a few more of the common misapprehensions of utilitarian ethics, even those which are so obvious and gross that it might appear impossible for any person of candor and intelligence to fall into them; since persons, even of considerable mental endowment, often give themselves so little trouble to understand the bearings of any opinion against which they entertain a prejudice, and men are in general so little conscious of this voluntary ignorance as a defect that the vulgarest misunderstandings of ethical doctrines are continually met with in the deliberate writings of persons of the greatest pretensions both to high principle and to philosophy. We not uncommonly hear the doctrine of utility inveighed against as a *godless* doctrine. If it be necessary to say anything at all against so mere an assumption, we may say that the question depends upon what idea we have formed of the moral character of the Deity. If it be a true belief that God desires, above all things, the happiness of his creatures, and that this was his purpose in their creation, utility is not only not a godless doctrine, but more profoundly religious than any other. If it be meant that utilitarianism does not recognize the revealed will of God as the supreme law of morals, I answer that a utilitarian who believes in the perfect goodness and wisdom of *God* necessarily believes that whatever God has thought fit to reveal on the subject of morals must fulfill the requirements of utility in a supreme degree. But others besides utilitarians have been of opinion that the Christian revelation was intended, and is fitted, to inform the hearts and minds of mankind with a spirit which should enable them to find for themselves what is right, and incline them to do it when found, rather than to tell them, except in a very general way, what it is; and that we need a doctrine of ethics, carefully followed out, to *interpret* to us the will of God. Whether this opinion is correct or not, it is superfluous here to discuss; since whatever aid religion, either natural or revealed, can afford to ethical investigation is as open to the utilitarian moralist as to any other. He can use it as the testimony of God to the usefulness or hurtfulness of any given course of action by as good a right as others can use it for the indication of a transcendental law having no connection with usefulness or with happiness.

Again, utility is often summarily stigmatized as an immoral doctrine by giving it the name of "expediency," and taking advantage of the popular use of that term to contrast it with principle. But the expedient, in the sense in which it is opposed to the right, generally means that which is expedient for the particular interest of the agent himself; as when a minister sacrifices the interests of his country to keep himself in place. When it means anything better than this, it means that which is expedient for some immediate object, some temporary purpose, but which violates a rule whose observance is expedient in a much higher degree. The expedient, in this sense, instead of being the same thing with the useful, is a branch of the hurtful. Thus it would often be expedient, for the purpose of getting over some momentary embarrassment, or attaining some object immediately useful to ourselves or others, to tell a lie. But inasmuch as the cultivation in ourselves of a sensitive feeling on the subject of veracity is one of the most useful, and the enfeeblement of that feeling one of the most hurtful, things to which our conduct can be instrumental; and inasmuch as any, even unintentional, deviation from truth does that much toward weakening the trustworthiness of human assertion, which is not only the principal support of all present social well-being, but the insufficiency of which does more than any one thing that can be named to keep back civilization, virtue, everything on which human happiness on the largest scale depends—we feel that the violation, for a present advantage, of a rule of such transcendent expediency is not expedient, and that he who, for the sake of convenience to himself or to some other individual, does what depends on him to deprive mankind of the good, and inflict upon them the evil, involved in the greater or less reliance which they can place in each other's word, acts the part of one of their worst enemies. Yet that even this rule, sacred as it is, admits of possible exceptions is acknowledged by all moralists; the chief of which is when the withholding of some fact (as of information from a malefactor, or of bad news from a person dangerously ill) would save an individual (especially an individual other than oneself) from great and unmerited evil, and when the withholding can only be effected by denial. But in order that the exception may not extend itself beyond the need, and may have the least possible effect in weakening reliance on veracity, it ought to be recognized and, if possible, its limits defined; and, if the principle of utility is good for anything, it must be good for weighing these conflicting utilities against one another and marking out the region within which one or the other preponderates.

Again, defenders of utility often find themselves called upon to reply to such objections as this—that there is not time, previous to action, for calculating and weighing the effects of any line of conduct on the general happiness. This is exactly as if anyone were to say that it is impossible to guide our conduct by Christianity because there is not time, on every occasion on which anything has to be done, to read through the Old and New Testaments. The answer to the objection is that there has been ample time, namely, the whole past duration of the human species. During all that time mankind have been learning by experience the tendencies of actions; on which experience all the prudence as well as all the morality of life are dependent. People talk as if the commencement of this course of experience had hitherto been put off, and as if, at the moment when some man feels tempted to meddle with the property or life of another, he had to begin considering for the first time whether murder and theft are injurious to human happiness. Even then I do not think that he would find the question very puzzling; but, at all events, the matter is now done to his hand. It is truly a whimsical supposition that, if mankind were agreed in considering utility to be the test of morality, they would remain without any agreement as to what *is* useful, and would take no measures for having their notions on the subject taught to the young and enforced by law and opinion. There is no difficulty in proving any ethical standard whatever to work ill if we suppose universal idiocy to be conjoined with it; but on any hypothesis short of that, mankind must by this time have acquired positive beliefs as to the effects of some actions on their happiness; and the beliefs which have thus come down are the rules of morality for the multitude, and for the philosopher until he has succeeded in finding better. That philosophers might easily do this, even now, on many subjects; that the received code of ethics is by no means of divine right; and that mankind have still much to learn as to the effects of actions on the general happiness, I admit or rather earnestly maintain. The corollaries from the principle of utility, like the precepts of every practical art, admit of indefinite improvement, and, in a progressive state of the human mind, their improvement is perpetually going on. But to consider the rules of morality as improvable is one thing; to pass over the intermediate generalization entirely and endeavor to test each individual action directly by the first principle is another. It is a strange notion that the acknowledgment of a first principle is inconsistent with the admission of secondary ones. To inform a traveler respecting the place of his ultimate destination is not to forbid the use of landmarks and direction-posts on the way. The proposition that happiness is the end and aim of morality does not mean that no road ought to be laid down to that goal, or that persons going thither should not be advised to take one direction rather than another. Men really ought to leave off talking a kind of nonsense on this subject, which they would neither talk nor listen to on other matters of practical concernment. Nobody argues that the art of navigation is not founded on astronomy because sailors cannot wait to calculate the Nautical Almanac. Being rational creatures, they go to sea with it ready calculated; and all rational creatures go out upon the sea of life with their minds made up on the common questions of right and wrong, as well as on many of the far more difficult questions of wise and foolish. And this, as long as foresight is a human quality, it is to be presumed they will continue to do. Whatever we adopt as the fundamental principle of morality, we require subordinate principles to apply it by; the impossibility of doing without them, being common to all systems, can afford no argument against any one in particular; but gravely to argue as if no such secondary principles could be had, and as if mankind had remained till now, and always must remain, without drawing any general conclusions from the experience of human life is as high a pitch, I think, as absurdity has ever reached in philosophical controversy.

The remainder of the stock arguments against utilitarianism mostly consist in laying to its charge the common infirmities of human nature, and the general difficulties which embarrass conscientious persons in shaping their course through life. We are told that a utilitarian will be apt to make his own particular case an exception to moral rules, and, when under temptation, will see a utility in the breach of a rule, greater than he will see in its observance. But is utility the only creed which is able to furnish us with excuses for evil-doing and means of cheating our own conscience? They are afforded in abundance by all doctrines which recognize as a fact in morals the existence of conflicting considerations, which all doctrines do that have been believed by sane persons. It is not the fault of any creed, but of the complicated nature of human affairs, that rules of conduct cannot be so framed as to require no exceptions, and that hardly any kind of action can safely be laid down as either always obligatory or always condemnable. There is no ethical creed which does not temper the rigidity of its laws by giving a certain latitude, under the moral responsibility of the agent, for accommodation to peculiarities of circumstances; and under every creed, at the opening thus made, self-deception and dishonest casuistry get in. There exists no moral system under which there do not arise unequivocal cases of conflicting obligation. These are the real difficulties, the knotty points both in the theory of ethics and in the conscientious guidance of personal conduct. They are overcome practically, with greater or with less success, according to the intellect and virtue of the individual; but it can hardly be pretended that anyone will be the less qualified for dealing with them, from possessing an ultimate standard to which conflicting rights and duties can be referred. If utility is the ultimate source of moral obligations, utility may be invoked to decide between them when their demands are incompatible. Though the application of the standard may be difficult, it is better than none at all; while in other systems, the moral laws all claiming independent authority, there is no common umpire entitled to interfere between them; their claims to precedence one over another rest on little better than sophistry, and, unless determined, as they generally are, by the unacknowledged influence of consideration of utility, afford a free scope for the action of personal desires and partialities. We must remember that only in these cases of conflict between secondary principles is it requisite that first principles should be appealed to. There is no case of moral obligation in which some secondary principle is not involved; and if only one, there can seldom be any real doubt which one it is, in the mind of any person by whom the principle itself is recognized.

NOTES

1. The author of this essay has reason for believing himself to be the first person who brought the word "utilitarian" into use. He did not invent it, but adopted it from a passing expression in Mr. Galt's *Annals of the Parish*. After using it as a designation for several years, he and others abandoned it from a growing dislike to anything resembling a badge or watchword of sectarian distinction. But as a name for one single opinion, not a set of opinions—to denote the recognition of utility as a standard, not any particular way of applying it—the term supplies a want in the language, and offers, in many cases, a convenient mode of avoiding tiresome circumlocution.

Of What Sort of Proof the Principle of Utility Is Susceptible

JOHN STUART MILL

It has already been remarked that questions of ultimate ends do not admit of proof, in the ordinary acceptation of the term. To be incapable of proof by reasoning is common to all first principles, to the first premises of our knowledge, as well as to those of our conduct. But the former, being matters of fact, may be the subject of a direct appeal to the faculties which judge of fact—namely, our senses and our internal consciousness. Can an appeal be made to the same faculties on questions of practical ends? Or by what other faculty is cognizance taken of them?

Questions about ends are, in other words, questions what things are desirable. The utilitarian doctrine is that happiness is desirable, and the only thing desirable, as an end; all other things beings only desirable as means to that end. What ought to be required of this doctrine, what conditions is it requisite that the doctrine should fulfill—to make good its claim to be believed?

The only proof capable of being given that an object is visible is that people actually see it. The only proof that a sound is audible is that people hear it; and so of the other sources of our experience. In like manner, I apprehend, the sole evidence it is possible to produce that anything is desirable is that people do actually desire it. If the end which the utilitarian doctrine proposes to itself were not, in theory and in practice, acknowledged to be an end, nothing could ever convince any person that it was so. No reason can be given why the general happiness is desirable, except that each person, so far as he believes it to be attainable, desires his own happiness. This, however, being a fact, we have not only all the proof which the case admits of, but all which it is possible to require, that happiness is a good, that each person's happiness is a good to that person, and the general happiness, therefore, a good to the aggregate of all persons. Happiness has made out its title as *one* of the ends of conduct and, consequently, one of the criteria of morality.

But it has not, by this alone, proved itself to be the sole criterion. To do that, it would seem, by the same rule, necessary to show, not only that people desire happiness, but that they never desire anything else. Now it is palpable that they do desire things which, in common language, are decidedly distinguished from happiness. They desire, for example, virtue and the absence of vice no less really than pleasure and the absence of pain. The desire of virtue is not as universal, but it is as authentic a fact as the desire of happiness. And hence the opponents of the utilitarian standard deem that they have a right to infer that there are other ends of human action besides happiness, and that happiness is not the standard of approbation and disapprobation.

But does the utilitarian doctrine deny that people desire virtue, or maintain that virtue is not a thing to be desired? The very reverse. It maintains not only that virtue is to be desired,

---

From Mill's *Utilitarianism* (1863).

but that it is to be desired disinterestedly, for itself. Whatever may be the opinion of utilitarian moralists as to the original conditions by which virtue is made virtue, however they may believe (as they do) that actions and dispositions are only virtuous because they promote another end than virtue, yet this being granted, and it having been decided, from considerations of this description, what *is* virtuous, they not only place virtue at the very head of the things which are good as means to the ultimate end, but they also recognize as a psychological fact the possibility of its being, to the individual, a good in itself, without looking to any end beyond it; and hold that the mind is not in a right state, not in a state conformable to utility, not in the state most conducive to the general happiness, unless it does love virtue in this manner—as a thing desirable in itself, even although, in the individual instance, it should not produce those other desirable consequences which it tends to produce, and on account of which it is held to be virtue. This opinion is not, in the smallest degree, a departure from the happiness principle. The ingredients of happiness are very various, and each of them is desirable in itself, and not merely when considered as swelling an aggregate. The principle of utility does not mean that any given pleasure, as music, for instance, or any given exemption from pain, as for example health, is to be looked upon as means to a collective something termed happiness, and to be desired on that account. They are desired and desirable in and for themselves; besides being means, they are a part of the end. Virtue, according to the utilitarian doctrine, is not naturally and originally part of the end, but it is capable of becoming so; and in those who live it disinterestedly it has become so, and is desired and cherished, not as a means to happiness, but as a part of their happiness.

To illustrate this further, we may remember that virtue is not the only thing originally a means, and which if it were not a means to anything else would be and remain indifferent, but which by association with what it is a means to comes to be desired for itself, and that too with the utmost intensity. What, for example, shall we say of the love of money? There is nothing originally more desirable about money than about any heap of glittering pebbles. Its worth is solely that of the things which it will buy; the desires for other things than itself, which it is a means of gratifying. Yet the love of money is not only one of the strongest moving forces of human life, but money is, in many cases, desired in and for itself; the desire to possess it is often stronger than the desire to use it, and goes on increasing when all the desires which point to ends beyond it, to be compassed by it, are falling off. It may, then, be said truly that money is desired not for the sake of an end, but as part of the end. From being a means to happiness, it has come to be itself a principal ingredient of the individual's conception of happiness. The same may be said of the majority of the great objects of human life: power, for example, or fame, except that to each of these there is a certain amount of immediate pleasure annexed, which has at least the semblance of being naturally inherent in them—a thing which cannot be said of money. Still, however, the strongest natural attraction, both of power and of fame, is the immense aid they give to the attainment of our other wishes; and it is the strong association thus generated between them and all our objects of desire which gives to the direct desire of them the intensity it often assumes, so as in some characters to surpass in strength all other desires. In these cases the means have become a part of the end, and a more important part of it than any of the things which they are means to. What was once desired as an instrument for the attainment of happiness has come to be desired for its own sake. In being desired for its own sake it is, however, desired as *part* of happiness. The person is made, or thinks he would be made, happy by its mere possession; and is made unhappy by failure to obtain it. The desire of it is not a different thing from the desire of happiness any more than the love of music or the desire of health. They are included in happiness. They are some of the elements of which the desire of happiness is made up. Happiness is not an abstract idea but a concrete whole; and these are some of its parts. And the utilitarian standard sanctions and approves their being so. Life would be a poor thing, very ill provided with sources of happiness, if there were not this provision of nature by which things originally indifferent, but conducive to, or otherwise associated with, the satisfaction of our primitive desires, become in themselves sources of pleasure more valuable than the primitive pleasures, both in permanency, in the space of human existence that they are capable of covering, and even in intensity.

Virtue, according to the utilitarian conception, is a good of this description. There was no original desire of it, or motive to it, save its conduciveness to pleasure, and especially to protection from pain. But through the association thus formed it may be felt a good in itself, and desired as such with as great intensity as any other good; and with this difference between it and the love of money, of power, or of fame—that all of these may, and often do, render the individual noxious to the other members of the society to which he belongs, whereas there is nothing which makes him so much a blessing to them as the cultivation of the disinterested love of virtue. And consequently, the utilitarian standard, while it tolerates and approves those other acquired desires, up to the point beyond which they would be more injurious to the general happiness than promotive of it, enjoins and requires the cultivation of the love of virtue up to the greatest strength possible, as being above all things important to the general happiness.

It results from the preceding considerations that there is in reality nothing desired except happiness. Whatever is desired otherwise than as a means to some end beyond itself, and ultimately to happiness, is desired as itself a part of happiness, and is not desired for itself until it has become so. Those who desire virtue for its own sake desire it either because the consciousness of it is a pleasure, or because the consciousness of being without it is a pain, or for both reasons united; as in truth the pleasure and pain seldom exist separately, but almost always together—the same person feeling pleasure in the degree of virtue attained, and pain in not having attained more. If one of these gave him no pleasure, and the other no pain, he would not love or desire virtue, or would desire it only for the other benefits which it might produce to himself or to persons whom he cared for.

We have now, then, an answer to the question of what sort of proof the principle of utility is susceptible. If the opinion which I have now stated is psychologically true—if human nature is so constituted as to desire nothing which is not either a part of happiness or a means of happiness—we can have no other proof, and we require no other, that these are the only things desirable. If so, happiness is the sole end of human action, and the promotion of it the test by which to judge of all human conduct; from whence it necessarily follows that it must be the criterion of morality, since a part is included in the whole.

And now to decide whether this is really so, whether mankind do desire nothing for itself but that which is a pleasure to them, or of which the absence is a pain, we have evidently arrived at a question of fact and experience, dependent, like all similar questions, upon evidence. It can only be determined by practiced self-consciousness and self-observation, assisted by observation of others. I believe that these sources of evidence, impartially consulted, will declare that desiring a thing and finding it pleasant, aversion to it and thinking of it as painful, are phenomena entirely inseparable or, rather, two parts of the same phenomenon—in strictness of language, two different modes of naming the same psychological fact; that to think of an object as desirable (unless for the sake of its consequences) and to think of it as pleasant are one and the same thing; and that to desire anything except in proportion as the idea of it is pleasant is a physical and metaphysical impossibility.

So obvious does this appear to me that I expect it will hardly be disputed; and the objection made will be, not that desire can possibly be directed to anything ultimately except pleasure and exemption from pain, but that the will is a different thing from desire; that a person of confirmed virtue or any other person whose purposes are fixed carries out his purposes without any thought of the pleasure he has in contemplating them or expects to derive from their fulfillment, and persists in acting on them, even though these pleasures are much diminished by changes in his character or decay of his passive sensibilities, or are out-weighed by the pains which the pursuit of the purposes may bring upon him. All this I fully admit and have stated it elsewhere as positively and emphatically as anyone. Will, the active phenomenon, is a different thing from desire, the state of passive sensibility, and, though originally an offshoot from it, may in time take root and detach itself from the parent stock, so much so that in the case of a habitual purpose, instead of willing the thing because we desire it, we often desire it only because we will it. This, however, is but an instance of that familiar fact, the power of habit, and is nowise confined to the case of virtuous actions. Many indifferent things which men originally did from a motive of some sort they continue to do from habit. Sometimes this is done unconsciously, the consciousness coming only after the action; at other times with conscious volition, but volition which has become habitual and is put in operation by the force of habit, in opposition perhaps to the deliberate preference, as often happens with those who have contracted habits of vicious or hurtful indulgence. Third and last comes the case in which the habitual act of will in the individual instance is not in contradiction to the general intention prevailing at other times, but in fulfillment of it, as in the case of the person of confirmed virtue and of all who pursue deliberately and consistently any determinate end. The distinction between will and desire thus understood is an authentic and highly important psychological fact; but the fact consists solely in this—that will, like all other parts of our constitution, is amenable to habit, and that we may will from habit what we no longer desire for itself, or desire only because we will it. It is not the less true that will, in the beginning, is entirely produced by desire, including in that term the repelling influence of pain as well as the attractive one of pleasure. Let us take into consideration no longer the person who has a confirmed will to do right, but him in whom that virtuous will is still feeble, conquerable by temptation, and not to be fully relied on; by what means can it be strengthened? How can the will to be virtuous, where it does not exist in sufficient force, be implanted or awakened? Only by making the person *desire* virtue—by making him think of it in a pleasurable light, or of its absence in a painful one. It is by associating the doing right with pleasure, or the wrong with pain, or by eliciting and impressing and bringing home to the person's experience the pleasure naturally involved in the one or the pain in the other, that it is possible to call forth that will to be virtuous which, when confirmed, acts without any thought of either pleasure or pain. Will is the child of desire, and passes out of the dominion of its parent only to come under that of habit. That which is the result of habit affords no presumption of being intrinsically good; and there would be no reason for wishing that the purpose of virtue should become independent of pleasure and pain were it not that the influence of the pleasurable and painful associations which prompt to virtue is not sufficiently to be depended on for unerring constancy of action until it has acquired the support of habit. Both in feeling and in conduct, habit is the only thing which imparts certainty; and it is because of the importance to others of being able to rely absolutely on one's feelings and conduct, and to oneself of being able to rely on one's own, that the will to do right ought to be cultivated into this habitual independence. In other words, this state of the will is a means to good, not intrinsically a good; and does not contradict the doctrine that nothing is a good to human beings but in so far as it is either itself pleasurable or a means of attaining pleasure or averting pain.

But if this doctrine be true, the principle of utility is proved. Whether it is so or not must now be left to the consideration of the thoughtful reader.

Moral Worth

IMMANUEL KANT

Nothing can possibly be conceived in the world, or even out of it, which can be called good without qualification, except a *good will*. Intelligence, wit, judgment, and the other *talents* of the mind, however they may be named, or courage, resolution, perseverance, as qualities of temperament, are undoubtedly good and desirable in many respects; but these gifts of nature may also become extremely bad and mischievous if the will which is to make use of them, and which, therefore, constitutes what is called *character*, is not good. It is the same with the *gifts of fortune*. Power, riches, honor, even health, and the general well-being and contentment with one's condition which is called *happiness*, inspire pride, and often presumption, if there is not a good will to correct the influence of these on the mind, and with this also to rectify the whole principle of acting, and adapt it to its end. The sight of a being who is not adorned with a single feature of a pure and good will, enjoying unbroken prosperity, can never give pleasure to an impartial rational spectator. Thus a good will appears to constitute the indispensable condition even of being worthy of happiness.

There are even some qualities which are of service to this good will itself, and may facilitate its action, yet which have no intrinsic unconditional value, but always presuppose a good will, and this qualifies the esteem that we justly have for them, and does not permit us to regard them as absolutely good. Moderation in the affections and passions, self-control, and calm deliberation are not only good in many respects, but even seem to constitute part of the intrinsic worth of the person; but they are far from deserving to be called good without qualification, although they have been so unconditionally praised by the ancients. For without the principles of a good will, they may become extremely bad; and the coolness of a villain not only makes him far more dangerous, but also directly makes him more abominable in our eyes than he would have been without it.

A good will is good not because of what it performs or effects, not by its aptness for the attainment of some proposed end, but simply by virtue of the volition—that is, it is good in itself, and considered by itself is to be esteemed much higher than all that can be brought about by it in favor of any inclination, nay, even of the sum-total of all inclinations. Even if it should happen that, owing to special disfavor of fortune, or the niggardly provision of a step-motherly nature, this will should wholly lack power to accomplish its purpose, if with its greatest efforts it should yet achieve nothing, and there should remain only the good will (not, to be sure, a mere wish, but the summoning of all means in our power), then, like a jewel, it would still shine by its own light, as a thing which has its whole value in itself. Its usefulness or fruitlessness can neither add to nor take away anything from this value. It would be, as it were, only the setting to enable us to handle it the more

---

Immanuel Kant (1724-1804) is perhaps the most influential philosopher of the modern period.

From Kant's *Foundations of the Metaphysics of Morals* (1787), trans. T. Abbott.

conveniently in common commerce, or to attract to it the attention of those who are not yet connoisseurs, but not to recommend it to true connoisseurs, or to determine its value.

There is, however, something so strange in this idea of the absolute value of the mere will, in which no account is taken of its utility, that notwithstanding the thorough assent of even common reason to the idea, yet a suspicion must arise that may perhaps really be the product of mere high-flown fancy, and that we may have misunderstood the purpose of nature in assigning reason as the governor of our will. Therefore we will examine this idea from this point of view.

In the physical constitution of an organized being, that is, a being adapted suitably to the purposes of life, we assume it as a fundamental principle that no organ for any purpose will be found but what is also the fittest and best adapted for that purpose. Now in a being which has reason and a will, if the proper object of nature were its *conservation*, its *welfare*, in a word, its *happiness*, then nature would have hit upon a very bad arrangement in selecting the reason of the creature to carry out this purpose. For all the actions which the creature has to perform with a view to this purpose, and the whole rule of its conduct, would be far more surely prescribed to it by instinct, and that end would have been attained thereby much more certainly than it ever can be by reason. Should reason have been communicated to this favored creature over and above, it must only have served it to contemplate the happy constitution of its nature, to admire it, to congratulate itself thereon, and to feel thankful for it to the beneficent cause, but not that it should subject its desires to that weak and delusive guidance, and meddle bunglingly with the purpose of nature. In a word, nature would have taken care that reason should not break forth into *practical exercise*, nor have the presumption, with its weak insight, to think out for itself the plan of happiness and of the means of attaining it. Nature would not only have taken on herself the choice of the ends but also of the means, and with wise foresight would have entrusted both to instinct.

And, in fact, we find that the more a cultivated reason applies itself with deliberate purpose to the enjoyment of life and happiness, so much the more does the man fail of true satisfaction. And from this circumstance there arises in many, if they are candid enough to confess it, a certain degree is *misology*, that is, hatred of reason, especially in the case of those who are most experienced in the use of it, because after calculating all the advantages they derive—I do not say from the invention of all the arts of common luxury, but even from the sciences (which seem to them to be after all only a luxury of the understanding)—they find that they have, in fact, only brought more trouble on their shoulders rather than gained in happiness; and they end by envying rather than despising the more common stamp of men who keep closer to the guidance of mere instinct, and do not allow their reason much influence on their conduct. And this we must admit, that the judgment of those who would very much lower the lofty eulogies of the advantages which reason gives us in regard to the happiness and satisfaction of life, or who would even reduce them below zero, is by no means morose or ungrateful to the goodness with which the world is governed, but that there lies at the root of these judgments the idea that our existence has a different and far nobler end, for which, and not for happiness, reason is properly intended, and which must, therefore, be regarded as the supreme condition to which the private ends of man must, for the most part, be postponed.

For as reason is not competent to guide the will with certainty in regard to its objects and the satisfaction of all our wants (which it to some extent even multiplies), this being an end to which an implanted instinct would have led with much greater certainty; and since, nevertheless, reason is imparted to us as a practical faculty, that is, as one which is to have influence on the *will*, therefore, admitting that nature generally in the distribution of her capacities has adapted the means to the end, its true destination must be to produce a *will*, not merely good as a *means* to something else, but *good in itself*, for which reason was absolutely necessary. This will then, though not indeed the sole and complete good, must be the supreme good and the condition of every other, even of the desire of happiness. Under these circumstances, there is nothing inconsistent with the wisdom of nature in the fact that the cultivation of the reason, which is requisite for the first and unconditional purpose, does in many ways interfere, at least in this life, with the attainment of the second, which is always conditional—namely, happiness. Nay, it may even reduce it to nothing, without nature thereby failing of her purpose. For reason recognizes the establishment of a good will as its highest practical destination, and in attaining this purpose is capable only of a satisfaction of its own proper kind, namely, that from the attainment of an end, which end again is determined by reason only, notwithstanding that this may involve many a disappointment to the ends of inclination.

We have then to develop the notion of a will which deserves to be highly esteemed for itself, and is good without a view to anything further, a notion which exists already in the sound natural understanding, requiring rather to be cleared up than to be taught, and which in estimating the value of our actions always takes the first place and constitutes the condition of all the rest. In order to do this, we will take the notion of duty, which includes that of a good will, although implying certain subjective restrictions and hindrances. These, however, far from concealing it or rendering it unrecognizable, rather bring it out by contrast and make it shine forth so much the brighter.

I omit here all actions which are already recognized as inconsistent with duty, although they may be useful for this or that purpose, for with these the question whether they are done *from duty* cannot arise at all, since they even conflict with it. I also set aside those actions which really conform to duty, but to which men have *no* direct *inclination*, performing them because they are impelled thereto by some other inclination. For in this case we can readily distinguish whether the action which agrees with duty is done *from duty* or from a selfish view. It is much harder to make this distinction when the action accords with duty, and the subject has besides a *direct* inclination to it. For example, it is always a matter of duty that a dealer should not overcharge an inexperienced purchaser; and wherever there is much commerce the prudent tradesman does not overcharge, but keeps a fixed price for everyone, so that a child buys of him as well as any other. Men are thus *honestly* served; but this is not enough to make us believe that the tradesman has so acted from duty and from principles of honesty; his own advantage required it; it is out of the question in this case to suppose that he might besides have a direct inclination in favor of the buyers, so that, as it were, from love he should give no advantage to one over another. Accordingly the action was done neither from duty nor from direct inclination, but merely with a selfish view.

On the other hand, it is a duty to maintain one's life; and, in addition, everyone has also a direct inclination to do so. But on this account the often anxious care which most men take for it has no intrinsic worth, and their maxim has no moral import. They preserve their life *as duty requires*, no doubt, but not *because duty requires*. On the other hand, if adversity and hopeless sorrow have completely taken away the relish for life, if the unfortunate one, strong in mind, indignant at his fate rather than desponding or dejected, wishes for death, and yet preserves his life without loving it—not from inclination or fear, but from duty—then his maxim has a moral worth.

To be beneficent when we can is a duty; and besides this, there are many minds so sympathetically constituted that, without any other motive of vanity or self-interest, they find a pleasure in spreading joy around them, and can take delight in the satisfaction of others so far as it is their own work. But I maintain that in such a case an action of this kind, however proper, however amiable it may be, has nevertheless no true moral worth, but is on a level with other inclinations, for example, the inclination to honor, which, if it is happily directed to that which is in fact of public utility and accordant with duty, and consequently honorable, deserves praise and encouragement, but not esteem. For the maxim lacks the moral import, namely, that such actions be done *from duty*, not from inclination. Put the case that the mind of that philanthropist was clouded by sorrow of his own, extinguishing all sympathy with the lot of others, and that while he still has the power to benefit others in distress, he is not touched by their trouble because he is absorbed with his own; and now suppose that he tears himself out of this dead insensibility and performs the action without any inclination to it, but simply from duty, then first has his action its genuine moral worth. Further still, if nature has put little sympathy in the heart of this or that man, if he, supposed to be an upright man, is by temperament cold and indifferent to the sufferings of others, perhaps because in respect of his own he is provided with the special gift of patience and fortitude, and supposes, or even requires, that others should have the same—and such a man would certainly not be the meanest product of nature—but if nature had not specially framed him for a philanthropist, would he not still find in himself a source from whence to give himself a far higher worth than that of a good-natured temperament could be? Unquestionably. It is just in this that the moral worth of the character is brought out which is incomparably the highest of all, namely, that he is beneficient, not from inclination, but from duty.

To secure one's own happiness is a duty, at least indirectly; for discontent with one's condition, under a pressure of many anxieties and amidst unsatisfied wants, might easily become a great *temptation to transgression of duty*. But here again, without looking to duty, all men have already the strongest and most intimate inclination to happiness, because it is just in this idea that all inclinations are combined in one total. But the precept of happiness is often of such a sort that it greatly interferes with some inclinations, and yet a man cannot form any definite and certain conception of the sum of satisfaction of all of them which is called happiness. It is not then to be wondered at that a single inclination, definite both as to what it promises and as to the time within which it can be gratified, is often able to overcome such a fluctuating idea, and that a gouty patient, for instance, can choose to enjoy what he likes, and to suffer what he may, since, according to his calculation, on this occasion at least, he has [only] not sacrificed the enjoyment of the present moment to a possibly mistaken expectation of a happiness which is supposed to be found in health. But even in this case, if the general desire for happiness did not influence his will, and supposing that in his particular case health was not a necessary element in this calculation, there yet remains in this, as in all other cases, this law—namely, that he should promote his happiness not from inclination but from duty, and by this would his conduct first acquire true moral worth.

It is in this manner, undoubtedly, that we are to understand those passages of Scripture also in which we are commanded to love our neighbor, even our enemy. For love, as an affection, cannot be commanded, but beneficence for duty's sake may, even though we are not impelled to it by any inclination—nay, are even repelled by a natural and unconquerable aversion. This is *practical* love, and not *pathological*—a love which is seated in the will, and not in the propensions of sense—in principles of action and not of tender sympathy; and it is this love alone which can be commanded.

The second proposition is: That an action done from duty derives its moral worth; *not from the purpose* which is to be attained by it, but from the maxim by which it is determined, and therefore does not depend on the realization of the object of the action, but merely on the *principle of volition* by which the action has taken place, without regard to any object of desire. It is clear from what precedes that the purposes which we may have in view in our actions, or their effects regarded as ends and springs of the will, cannot give to actions any unconditional or moral worth. In what, then, can their worth lie if it is not to consist in the will and in reference to its expected effect? It cannot lie anywhere but in the *principle of the will* without regard to the ends which can be attained by the action. For the will stands between its *a priori* principle, which is formal, and its *a posteriori* spring, which is material, as between two roads, and as it must be determined by something, it follows that it must be determined by the formal principle of volition when an action is done from duty, in which case every material principle has been withdrawn from it.

The third proposition, which is a consequence of the two preceding, I would express thus: *Duty is the necessity of acting from respect for the law*. I may have *inclination* for an object as the effect of my proposed action, but I cannot have *respect* for it just for this reason that it is an effect and not an energy of will. Similarly, I cannot have respect for inclination, whether my own or another's; I can at most, if my own, approve it; if another's, sometimes even love it, that is, look on it as favorable to my own interest. It is only what is connected with my will as a principle, by no means as an effect—what does not subserve my inclination, but overpowers it, or at least in case of choice excludes it from its calculation—in other words, simply the law of itself, which can be an object of respect, and hence a command. Now an action done from duty must wholly exclude the influence of inclination, and with it every object of the will, so that nothing remains which can determine the will except objectively the *law*, and subjectively *pure respect* for this practical law, and consequently the maxim[1] that I should follow this law even to the thwarting of all my inclinations.

Thus the moral worth of an action does not lie in the effect expected from it, nor in any principle of action which requires to borrow its motive from this expected effect. For all these effects—agreeableness of one's condition, and even the promotion of the happiness of others—could have been also brought about by other causes, so that for this there would have been no need of the will of a rational being; whereas it is in this alone that the supreme and unconditional good can be found. The pre-eminent good which we call moral can therefore consist in nothing else than *the conception of law* in itself, *which certainly is only possible in a rational being*, in so far as this conception, and not the expected effect, determines the will. This is a good which is already present in the person who acts accordingly, and we have not to wait for it to appear first in the result.[2]

But what sort of law can that be the conception of which must determine the will, even without paying any regard to the effect expected from it, in order that this will may be called good absolutely and without qualification? As I have deprived the will of every impulse which could arise to it from obedience to any law, there remains nothing but the universal conformity of its actions to law in general, which alone is to serve the will as a principle, that is, I am never to act otherwise than so *that I could also will that my maxim should become a universal law*. Here, now, it is the simple conformity to law in general, without assuming any particular law applicable to certain actions, that serves the will as its principle, and must so serve it if duty is not to be a vain delusion and a chimerical notion. The common reason of men in its practical judgments perfectly coincides with this, and always has in view the principle here suggested. Let the question be, for example: May I when in distress make a promise with the intention not to keep it? I readily distinguish here between the two significations which the question may have: whether it is prudent or whether it is right to make a false promise? The former may undoubtedly often be the case. I see clearly indeed that it is not enough to extricate myself from a present difficulty by means of this subterfuge, but it must be well considered whether there may not hereafter spring from this lie much greater inconvenience than that from which I now free myself, and as, with all my supposed *cunning*, the consequences cannot be so easily foreseen but that credit once lost may be much more injurious to me than any mischief which I seek to avoid at present, it should be considered whether it would not be more *prudent* to act herein according to a universal maxim, and to make it a habit to promise nothing except with the intention of keeping it. But it is soon clear to me that such a maxim will still only be based on the fear of consequences. Now it is a wholly different thing to be truthful from duty, and to be so from apprehension of injurious consequences. In the first case, the very notion of the action already implies a law for me; in the second case, I must first look about elsewhere to see what results may be combined with it which would affect myself. For to deviate from the principle of duty is beyond all doubt wicked; but to be unfaithful to my maxim of prudence may often be very advantageous to me, although to abide by it is certainly safer. The shortest way, however, and an unerring one, to discover the answer to this question whether a lying promise is consistent with duty, is to ask myself, Should I be content that my maxim (to extricate myself from difficulty by a false promise) should hold good as a universal law, for myself as well as for others; and should I be able to say to myself, "Every one may make a deceitful promise when he finds himself in a difficulty from which he cannot otherwise extricate himself"? Then I presently become aware that, while I can will the lie, I can by no means will that lying should be a universal law. For with such a law there would be no promises at all, since it would be in vain to allege my intention in regard to my future actions to those who would not believe this allegation, or if they over-hastily did so, would pay me back in my own coin. Hence my maxim, as soon as it should be made a universal law, would necessarily destroy itself.

I do not, therefore, need any far-reaching penetration to discern what I have to do in order that my will may be morally good. Inexperienced in the course of the world, incapable of being prepared for all its contingencies, I only ask myself: Canst thou also will that thy maxim should be a universal law? If not, then it must be rejected, and that not because of a disadvantage accruing from it to myself or even to others, but because it cannot enter as a principle into a possible universal legislation, and reason extorts from me immediate respect for such legislation. I do not indeed as yet *discern* on what this respect is based (this the philosopher may inquire), but at least I understand this—that it is an estimation of the worth which far outweighs all worth of what is recommended by inclination, and that the necessity of acting from *pure* respect for the practical law is what constitutes duty, to which every other motive must give place because it is the condition of a will being good *in itself*, and the worth of such a will is above everything.

Thus, then, without quitting the moral knowledge of common human reason, we have arrived at its principle. And although, no doubt, common men do not conceive it in such an abstract and universal form, yet they always have it really before their eyes and use it as the standard of their decision. Here it would be easy to show how, with this compass in hand, men are well able to distinguish, in every case that occurs, what is good, what bad, conformably to duty or inconsistent with it, if, without in the least teaching them anything new, we only, like Socrates, direct their attention to the principle they themselves employ; and that, therefore, we do not need science and philosophy to know what we should do to be honest and good, yea, even wise and virtuous. Indeed we might well have conjectured beforehand that the knowledge of what every man is bound to do, and therefore also to know, would be within the reach of every man, even the commonest. Here we cannot forbear admiration when we see how great an advantage the practical judgment has over the theoretical in the common understanding of men. In the latter, if common reason ventures to depart from the laws of experience and from the perceptions of the senses, it falls into mere inconceivabilities and self-contradictions, at least into a chaos of uncertainty, obscurity, and instability. But in the practical sphere it is just when the common understanding excludes all sensible springs from practical laws that its power of judgment begins to show itself to advantage. It then becomes even subtle, whether it be that it chicanes with its own conscience or with other claims respecting what is to be called right, or whether it desires for its own instruction to determine honestly the worth of actions; and, in the latter case, it may even have as good a hope of hitting the mark as any philosopher whatever can promise himself. Nay, it is almost more sure of doing so, because the philosopher cannot have any other principle, while he may easily perplex his judgment by a multitude of considerations foreign to the matter, and so turn aside from the right way. Would it not therefore be wiser in moral concerns to acquiesce in the judgment of common reason, or at most only to call in philosophy for the purpose of rendering the system of morals more complete and intelligible, and its rules more convenient for use (especially for disputation), but not so as to draw off the common understanding from its happy simplicity, or to bring it by means of philosophy into a new path of inquiry and instruction?

Innocence is indeed a glorious thing; only, on the other hand, it is very sad that it cannot well maintain itself, and is easily seduced. On this account even wisdom—which otherwise consists more in conduct than in knowledge—yet has need of science, not in order to learn from it, but to secure for its precepts admission and permanence. Against all the commands of duty which reason represents to man as so deserving of respect, he feels in himself a powerful counterpoise in his wants and inclinations, the entire satisfaction of which he sums up under the name of happiness. Now reason issues its commands unyieldingly, without promising anything to the inclinations, and, as it were, with disregard and contempt for these claims, which are so impetuous and at the same time so plausible, and which will not allow themselves to be suppressed by any command. Hence there arises a natural *dialectic*, that is, a disposition to argue against these strict laws of duty and to question their validity, or at least their purity and strictness; and, if possible, to make them more accordant with our wishes and inclinations, that is to say, to corrupt them at their very source and entirely to destroy their worth—a thing which even common practical reason cannot ultimately call good. . . .

When we add further that, unless we deny that the notion of morality has any truth or reference to any possible object, we must admit that its law must be valid, not merely for men, but for all *rational creatures generally*, not merely under certain contingent conditions or with exceptions, but *with absolute necessity*, then it is clear that no experience could enable us to infer even the possibility of such apodictic laws. For with what right could we bring into unbounded respect as a universal precept for every rational nature that which perhaps holds only under the contingent conditions of humanity? Or how could laws of the determination of *our* will be regarded as laws of the determination of the will of rational beings generally, and for us only as such, if they were merely empirical and did not take their origin wholly *a priori* from pure but practical reason?

Nor could anything be more fatal to morality than that we should wish to derive it from examples. For every example of it that is set before me must be first itself tested by principles of morality, whether it is worthy to serve as an original example, that is, as a pattern, but by no means can it authoritatively furnish the conception of morality. Even the Holy One of the Gospels must first be compared with our ideal of moral perfection before we can recognize Him as such; and so He says of Himself, "Why call ye Me [whom you see] good; none is good [the model of good] but God only [whom ye do not see]?" But whence have we the conception of God as the supreme good? Simply from the *idea* of moral perfection, which reason frames *a priori* and connects inseparably with the notion of a free will. Imitation finds no place at all in morality, and examples serve only for encouragement, that is, they put beyond doubt the feasibility of what the law commands, they make visible that which the practical rule expresses more generally, but they can never authorize us to set aside the true original which lies in reason, and to guide ourselves by examples. . . .

From what has been said, it is clear that all moral conceptions have their seat and origin completely *a priori* in the reason, and that, moreover, in the commonest reason just as truly as in that which is in the highest degree speculative; that they cannot be obtained by abstraction from any empirical, and therefore merely contingent, knowledge; that it is just this purity of their origin that makes them worthy to serve as our supreme practical principle, and that just in proportion as we add anything empirical, we detract from their genuine influence and from the absolute value of actions; that it is not only of the greatest necessity, in a purely speculative point of view, but is also of the greatest practical importance, to derive these notions and laws from pure reason, to present them pure and unmixed, and even to determine the compass of this practical or pure rational knowledge, that is, to determine the whole faculty of pure practical reason; and, in doing so, we must not make its principles dependent on the particular nature of human reason, though in speculative philosophy this may be permitted, or may even at times be necessary; but since moral laws ought to hold good for every rational creature, we must derive them from the general concept of a rational being. In this way, although for its *application* to man morality has need of anthropology, yet, in the first instance, we must treat it independently as pure philosophy, that is, as metaphysic, complete in itself (a thing which in such distinct branches of science is easily done); knowing well that, unless we are in possession of this, it would not only be vain to determine the moral element of duty in right actions for purposes of speculative criticism, but it would be impossible to base morals on their genuine principles, even for common practical purposes, especially of moral instruction, so as to produce pure moral dispositions, and to engraft them on men's minds to the promotion of the greatest possible good in the world.

But in order that in this study we may not merely advance by the natural steps from the common moral judgment (in this case very worthy of respect) to the philosophical, as has been already done, but also from a popular philosophy, which goes no further than it can reach by groping with the help of examples, to metaphysic (which does not allow itself to be checked by anything empirical and, as it must measure the whole extent of this kind of rational knowledge, goes as far as ideal conceptions, where even examples fail us), we must follow and clearly describe the practical faculty of reason, from the general rules of its determination to the point where the notion of duty springs from it.

Everything in nature works according to laws. Rational beings alone have the faculty of acting according *to the conception* of laws—that is, according to principles, that is, have a *will*. Since the deduction of actions from principles requires *reason*, the will is nothing but practical reason. If reason infallibly determines the will, then the actions of such a being which are recognized as objectively necessary are subjectively necessary also, that is, the will is a faculty to choose *that only* which reason independent on inclination recognizes as practically necessary, that is, as good. But if reason of itself does not sufficiently determine the will, if the latter is subject also to subjective conditions (particular impulses) which do not always coincide with the objective conditions, in a word, if the will does not *in itself* completely accord with reason (which is actually the case with men), then the actions which objectively are recognized as necessary are subjectively contingent, and the determination of such a will according to objective laws is *obligation*, that is to say, the relation of the objective laws to a will that is not thoroughly good is conceived as the determination of the will of a rational being by principles of reason, but which the will from its nature does not of necessity follow.

The conception of an objective principle, in so far as it is obligatory for a will, is called a command (of reason), and the formula of the command is called an Imperative.

All imperatives are expressed by the word *ought* [or *shall*], and thereby indicate the relation of an objective law of reason to a will which from its subjective constitution is not necessarily determined by it (an obligation). They say that something would be good to do or to forbear, but they say it to a will which does not always do a thing because it is conceived to be good to do it. That is practically *good*, however, which determines the will by means of the conceptions of reason, and consequently not from subjective causes, but objectively, that is, on principles which are valid for every rational being as such. It is distinguished from the *pleasant* as that which influences the will only by means of sensation from merely subjective causes, valid only for the sense of this or that one, and not as a principle of reason which holds for every one.

A perfectly good will would therefore be equally subject to objective laws (viz., laws of good), but could not be conceived as *obliged* thereby to act lawfully, because of itself from its subjective constitution it can only be determined by the conception of good. Therefore no imperatives hold for the Divine will, or in general for a *holy* will; *ought* is here out of place because the volition is already of itself necessarily in unison with the law. Therefore imperatives are only formulae to express the relation of objective laws of all volition to the subjective imperfection of the will of this or that rational being, for example, the human will.

Now all *imperatives* command either *hypothetically* or *categorically*. The former represent the practical necessity of a possible action as means to something else that is willed (or at least which one might possibly will). The categorical imperative would be that which represented an action as necessary of itself without reference to another end, that is, as objectively necessary.

Since every practical law represents a possible action as good, and on this account, for a subject who is practically determinable by reason as necessary, all imperatives are formulae determining an action which is necessary according to the principle of a will good in some respects. If now the action is good only as a means *to something else*, then the imperative is *hypothetical*; if it is conceived as good *in itself* and consequently as being necessarily the principle of a will which of itself conforms to reason, then it is *categorical*.

Thus the imperative declares what action possible by me would be good, and presents the practical rule in relation to a will which does not forthwith perform an action simply because it is good, whether because the subject does not always know that it is good, or because, even if it knows this, yet its maxims might be opposed to the objective principles of practical reason.

Accordingly the hypothetical imperative only says that the action is good for some purpose, *possible* or *actual*. In the first case it is a *problematical*, in the second an *assertorial* practical principle. The categorical imperative which declares an action to be objectively necessary in itself without reference to any purpose, that is, without any other end, is valid as an *apodictic* (practical) principle.

Whatever is possible only by the power of some rational being may also be conceived as a possible purpose of some will; and therefore the principles of action as regards the means necessary to attain some possible purpose are in fact infinitely numerous. All sciences have a practical part consisting of problems expressing that some end is possible for us, and of imperatives directing how it may be attained. These may, therefore, be called in general imperatives of *skill*. Here there is no question whether the end is rational and good, but only what one must do in order to attain it. The precepts for the physician to make his patient thoroughly healthy, and for a poisoner to ensure certain death, are of equal value in this respect, that each serves to effect its purpose perfectly. Since in early youth it cannot be known what ends are likely to occur to us in the course of life, parents seek to have their children taught a *great many things*, and provide for their *skill* in the use of means for all sorts of arbitrary ends, of none of which can they determine whether it may not perhaps hereafter be an object to their pupil, but which it is at all events *possible* that he might aim at; and this anxiety is so great that they commonly neglect to form and correct their judgment on the value of the things which may be chosen as ends.

There is *one* end, however, which may be assumed to be actually such to all rational beings (so far as imperatives apply to them, viz., as dependent beings), and, therefore, one purpose which they not merely *may* have, but which we may with certainty assume that they all actually *have* by a natural necessity, and this is *happiness*. The hypothetical imperative which expresses the practical necessity of an action as means to the advancement of happiness is *assertorial*. We are not to present it as necessary for an uncertain and merely possible purpose, but for a purpose which we may presuppose with certainty and *a priori* in every man, because it belongs to his being. Now skill in the choice of means to his own greatest well-being may be called *prudence*, in the narrowest sense. And thus the imperative which refers to the choice of means to one's own happiness, that is, the precept of prudence, is still always *hypothetical*; the action is not commanded absolutely, but only as means to another purpose.

Finally, there is an imperative which commands a certain conduct immediately, without having as its condition any other purpose to be attained by it. This imperative is *categorical*. It concerns not the matter of the action, or its intended result, but its form and the principle of which it is itself a result; and what is essentially good in it consists in the mental disposition, let the consequence be what it may. This imperative may be called that of *morality*.

There is a marked distinction also between the volitions on these three sorts of principles in the *dissimilarity* of the obligation of the will. In order to mark this difference more clearly, I think they would be most suitably named in their order if we said they are either *rules* of skill, or *counsels* of prudence, or *commands (laws)* of morality. For it is *law* only that involves the conception of an *unconditional* and objective necessity, which is consequently universally valid; and commands are laws which must be obeyed, that is, must be followed, even in opposition to inclination. *Counsels*, indeed, involve necessity, but one which can only hold under a contingent subjective condition, viz., they depend on whether this or that man reckons this or that as part of his happiness; the categorical imperative, on the contrary, is not limited by any condition, and as being absolutely, although practically, necessary may be quite properly called a command. We might also call the first kind of imperatives *technical* (belonging to art), the second *pragmatic* (belonging to welfare), the third *moral* (belonging to free conduct generally, that is, to morals).

Now arises the question, how are all these imperatives possible? This question does not seek to know how we can conceive the accomplishment of the action which the imperative ordains, but merely how we can conceive the obligation of the will which the imperative expresses. No special explanation is needed to show how an imperative of skill is possible. Whoever wills the end wills also (so far as reason decides his conduct) the means in his power which are indespensably necessary thereto. This proposition is, as regards the volition, analytical; for in willing an object as my effect there is already thought the causality of myself as an acting cause, that is to say, the use of the means; and the imperative educes from the conception of volition of an end the conception of actions necessary to this end. Synthetical propositions must no doubt be employed in defining the means to a proposed end; but they do not concern the principle, the act of the will, but the object and its realization. For example, that in order to bisect a line on an unerring principle I must draw from its extremities two intersecting arcs; this no doubt is taught by mathematics only in synthetical propositions; but if I know that it is only by this process that the intended operation can be performed, then to say that if I fully will the operation, I also will the action required for it, is an analytical proposition; for it is one and the same thing to conceive something as an effect which I can produce in a certain way, and to conceive myself as acting in this way.

If it were only equally easy to give a definite conception of happiness, the imperatives of prudence would correspond exactly with those of skill, and would likewise be analytical. For in this case as in that, it could be said whoever wills the end wills also (according to the dictate of reason necessarily) the indispensable means thereto which are in his power. But, unfortunately, the notion of happiness is so indefinite that although every man wishes to attain it, yet he never can say definitely and consistently what it is that he really wishes and wills. The reason of this is that all the elements which belong to the notion of happiness are altogether empirical, that is, they must be borrowed from experience, and nevertheless the idea of happiness requires an absolute whole, a maximum of welfare in my present and all future circumstances. Now it is impossible that the most clear-sighted and at the same time most powerful being (supposed finite) should frame to himself a definite conception of what he really wills in this. Does he will riches, how much anxiety, envy, and snares might he not thereby draw upon his shoulders? Does he will knowledge and discernment, perhaps it might prove to be only an eye so much the sharper to show him so much the more fearfully the evils that are now concealed from him and that cannot be avoided, or to impose more wants on his desires, which already give him concern enough. Would he have long life? Who guarantees to him that it would not be a long misery? Would he at least have health? How often has uneasiness of the body restrained from excesses into which perfect health would have allowed one to fall, and so on? In short, he is unable, on any principle, to determine with certainty what would make him truly happy; because to do so he would need to be omniscient. We cannot therefore act on any definite principles to secure happiness, but only on empirical counsels, for example, of regimen, frugality, courtesy, reserve, etc., which experience teaches do, on the average, most promote well-being. Hence it follows that the imperatives of prudence do not, strictly speaking, command at all, that is, they cannot present actions objectively as practically *necessary*; that they are rather to be regarded as counsels than precepts of reason, that the problem to determine certainly and universally what action would promote the happiness of a rational being is completely insoluble, and consequently no imperative respecting it is possible which should, in the strict sense, command to do what makes happy; because happiness is not an ideal of reason but of imagination, resting solely on empirical grounds, and it is vain to expect that these should define an action by which one could attain the totality of a series of consequences which is really endless. This imperative of prudence would, however, be an analytical proposition if we assume that the means to happiness could be certainly assigned; for it is distinguished from the imperative of skill only by this that in the latter the end is merely *possible*, in the former it is *given*; as, however, both only ordain the means to that which we suppose to be willed as an end, it follows that the imperative which ordains the willing of the means to him who wills the end is in both cases analytical. Thus there is no difficulty in regard to the possibility of an imperative of this kind either. . . .

When I conceive a hypothetical imperative, in general I do not know beforehand what it will contain until I am given the condition. But when I conceive a categorical imperative, I know at once what it contains. For as the imperative contains besides the law only the necessity that the maxims[3] shall conform to this law, while the law contains no conditions restricting it, there remains nothing but the general statement that the maxim of the action should conform to a universal law, and it is this conformity alone that the imperative properly represents as necessary.

There is therefore but one categorical imperative, namely, this: *Act only on that maxim whereby thou canst at the same time will that it should become a universal law.*

Now if all imperatives of duty can be deduced from this one imperative as from their principle, then, although it should remain undecided whether what is called duty is not merely a vain notion, yet at least we shall be able to show what we understand by it and what this notion means.

Since the universality of the law according to which effects are produced constitutes what is properly called *nature* in the most general sense (as to form)—that is, the existence of things so far as it is determined by general laws—the imperative of duty may be expressed thus: *Act as if the maxim of thy action were to become by thy will a universal law of nature.*

We will now enumerate a few duties, adopting the usual division of them into duties to ourselves and to others, and into perfect and imperfect duties.

1. A man reduced to despair by a series of misfortunes feels wearied of life, but is still so far in possession of his reason that he can ask himself whether it would not be contrary to his duty to himself to take his own life. Now he inquires whether the maxim of his action could become a universal law of nature. His maxim is: From self-love I adopt it as a principle to shorten my life when its longer duration is likely to bring more evil than satisfaction. It is asked then simply whether this principle founded on self-love can become a universal law of nature. Now we see at once that a system of nature of which it should be a law to destroy life by means of the very feeling whose special nature it is to impel to the improvement of life would contradict itself, and therefore could not exist as a system of nature; hence that maxim cannot possibly exist as a universal law of nature, and consequently would be wholly inconsistent with the supreme principle of all duty.

2. Another finds himself forced by necessity to borrow money. He knows that he will not be able to repay it, but sees also that nothing will be lent to him unless he promises stoutly to repay it in a definite time. He desires to make this promise, but he has still so much conscience as to ask himself: Is it not unlawful and inconsistent with duty to get out of a difficulty in this way? Suppose, however, that he resolves to do so, then the maxim of his action would be expressed thus: When I think myself in want of money, I will borrow money and promise to repay it, although I know that I never can do so. Now this principle of self-love or of one's own advantage may perhaps be consistent with my whole future welfare; but the question now is, Is it right? I change then the suggestion of self-love into a universal law, and state the question thus: How would it be if my maxim were a universal law? Then I see at once that it could never hold as a universal law of nature, but would necessarily contradict itself. For supposing it to be a universal law that everyone when he thinks himself in a difficulty should be able to promise whatever he pleases, with the purpose of not keeping his promise, the promise itself would become impossible, as well as the end that one might have in view in it, since no one would consider that anything was promised to him, but would ridicule all such statements as vain pretenses.

3. A third finds in himself a talent which with the help of some culture might make him a useful man in many respects. But he finds

himself in comfortable circumstances and prefers to indulge in pleasure rather than to take pains in enlarging and improving his happy natural capacities. He asks, however, whether his maxim of neglect of his natural gifts, besides agreeing with his inclination to indulgence, agrees also with what is called duty. He sees then that a system of nature could indeed subsist with such a universal law, although men (like the South Sea islanders) should let their talents rest and resolve to devote their lives merely to idleness, amusement, and propagation of their species—in a word, to enjoyment; but he cannot possibly *will* that this should be a universal law of nature, or be implanted in us as such by a natural instinct. For, as a rational being, he necessarily wills that his faculties be developed, since they serve him, and have been given him, for all sorts of possible purposes.

4. A fourth, who is in prosperity, while he sees that others have to contend with great wretchedness and that he could help them, thinks: What concern is it of mine? Let everyone be as happy as Heaven pleases, or as he can make himself; I will take nothing from him nor even envy him, only I do not wish to contribute anything to his welfare or to his assistance in distress! Now no doubt, if such a mode of thinking were a universal law, the human race might very well subsist, and doubtless even better than in a state in which everyone talks of sympathy and good-will, or even takes care occasionally to put it into practice, but, on the other side, also cheats when he can, betrays the rights of men, or otherwise violates them. But although it is possible that a universal law of nature might exist in accordance with that maxim, it is impossible to *will* that such a principle should have the universal validity of a law of nature. For a will which resolved this would contradict itself, inasmuch as many cases might occur in which one would have need of the love and sympathy of others, and in which, by such a law of nature, sprung from his own will, he would deprive himself of all hope of the aid he desires.

These are a few of the many actual duties, or at least what we regard as such, which obviously fall into two classes on the one principle that we have laid down. We must be *able to will* that a maxim of our action should be a universal law. This is the canon of the moral appreciation of the action generally. Some actions are of such a character that their maxim cannot without contradiction be even *conceived* as a universal law of nature, far from it being possible that we should *will* that it *should* be so. In others, this intrinsic impossibility is not found, but still it is impossible to *will* that their maxim should be raised to the universality of a law of nature, since such a will would contradict itself. It is easily seen that the former violate strict or rigorous (inflexible) duty; the latter only laxer (meritorious) duty. Thus it has been completely shown by these examples how all duties depend as regards the nature of the obligation (not the object of the action) on the same principle.

If now we attend to ourselves on occasion of any transgression of duty, we shall find that we in fact do not will that our maxim should be a universal law, for that is impossible for us; on the contrary, we will that the opposite should remain a universal law, only we assume the liberty of making an *exception* in our own favor or (just for this time only) in favor of our inclination. Consequently, if we considered all cases from one and the same point of view, namely, that of reason, we should find a contradiction in our own will, namely, that a certain principle should be objectively necessary as a universal law, and yet subjectively should not be universal, but admit of exceptions. As, however, we at one moment regard our action from the point of view of a will wholly conformed to reason, and then again look at the same action from the point of view of a will affected by inclination, there is not really any contradiction, but an antagonism of inclination to the precept of reason, whereby the universality of the principle is changed into a mere generality, so that the practical principle of reason shall meet the maxim half way. Now, although this cannot be justified in our own impartial judgment, yet it proves that we do really recognize the validity of the categorical imperative and (with all respect for it) only allow ourselves a few exceptions which we think unimportant and forced from us.

We have thus established at least this much—that if duty is a conception which is to have any import and real legislative authority for our actions, it can only be expressed in categorical, and not at all in hypothetical, imperatives. We have also, which is of great importance, exhibited clearly and definitely for every practical application the content of the categorical imperative, which must contain the principle of all duty if there is such a thing at all. We have not yet, however, advanced so far as to prove *a priori* that there actually is such an imperative, that there is a practical law which commands absolutely of itself and without any other impulse, and that the following of this law is duty.

With the view of attaining to this it is of extreme importance to remember that we must not allow ourselves to think of deducing the reality of this principle from the *particular attributes of human nature*. For duty is to be a practical, unconditional necessity of action; it must therefore hold for all rational beings (to whom an imperative can apply at all), and *for this reason only* be also a law for all human wills. On the contrary, whatever is deduced from certain feelings and propensions, nay, even, if possible, from any particular tendency proper to human reason, and which need not necessarily hold for the will of every rational being—this may indeed supply us with a maxim but not with a law; with a subjective principle on which we may have a propension and inclination to act, but not with an objective principle on which we should be *enjoined* to act, even though all our propensions, inclinations, and natural dispositions were opposed to it. In fact, the sublimity and intrinsic dignity of the command in duty are so much the more evident, the less the subjective impulses favor it and the more they oppose it, without being able in the slightest degree to weaken the obligation of the law or to diminish its validity.

Here then we see philosophy brought to a critical position, since it has to be firmly fixed, notwithstanding that it has nothing to support it in heaven or earth. Here it must show its purity as absolute director of its own laws, not the herald of those which are whispered to it by an implanted sense or who knows what tutelary nature. Although these may be better than nothing, yet they can never afford principles dictated by reason, which must have their source wholly *a priori* and thence their commanding authority, expecting everything from the supremacy of the law and the due respect for it, nothing from inclination, or else condemning the man to self-contempt and inward abhorrence.

Thus every empirical element is not only quite incapable of being an aid to the principle of morality, but is even highly prejudicial to the purity of morals; for the proper and inestimable worth of an absolutely good will consists just in this that the principle of action is free from all influence of contingent grounds, which alone experience can furnish. We cannot too much or too often repeat our warning against this lax and even mean habit of thought which seeks for its principle among empirical motives and laws; for human reason in its weariness is glad to rest on this pillow, and in a dream of sweet illusions (in which, instead of Juno, it embraces a cloud) it substitutes for morality a bastard patched up from limbs of various derivation, which looks like anything one chooses to see in it; only not like virtue to one who has once beheld her in her true form.[4]

The question then is this: Is it a necessary law *for all rational beings* that they should always judge of their actions by maxims of which they can themselves will that they should serve as universal laws? If it is so, then it must be connected (altogether *a priori*) with the very conception of the will of a rational being generally. But in order to discover this connection we must, however reluctantly, take a step into metaphysic, although into a domain of it which is distinct from speculative philosophy—namely, the metaphysic of morals. In a practical philosophy, where it is not the reasons of what *happens* that we have to ascertain, but the laws of what *ought to happen*, even although it never does, that is, objective practical laws, there it is not necessary to inquire into the reasons why anything pleases or displeases, how the pleasure of mere sensation differs from taste, and whether the latter is distinct from a general satisfaction of reason; on what the feeling of pleasure or pain rests, and how from it desires and inclinations arise, and from these again maxims by the cooperation of reason; for all this belongs to an empirical psychology, which would constitute the second part of physics, if we regard physics as the *philosophy* of nature, so far as it is based on *empirical laws*. But here we are concerned with objective practical laws, and consequently with the relation of the will to itself so far as it is determined by reason alone, in which case whatever has reference to anything empirical is necessarily excluded; since if *reason of itself alone* determines the conduct (and it is the possibility of this that we are now investigating), it must necessarily do so *a priori*.

The will is conceived as a faculty of determining oneself to action *in accordance with the conception of certain laws*. And such a faculty can be found only in rational beings. Now that which serves the will as the objective ground of its self-determination is the *end*, and if this is assigned by reason alone, it must hold for all rational beings. On the other hand, that which merely contains the ground of possibility of the action of which the effect is the end, this is called the *means*. The subjective ground of the desire is the *spring*, the objective ground of the volition is the *motive*; hence the distinction between subjective ends which rest on springs, and objective ends which depend on motives valid for every rational being. Practical principles are *formal* when they abstract from all subjective ends; they are *material* when they assume these, and therefore particular, springs of action. The ends which a rational being proposes to himself at pleasure as *effects* of his actions (material ends) are all only relative, for it is only their relation to the particular desires of the subject that gives them their worth, which therefore cannot furnish principles universal and necessary for all rational beings and for every volition, that is to say, practical laws. Hence all these relative ends can give rise only to hypothetical imperatives.

Supposing, however, that there were something *whose existence* has *in itself* an absolute worth, something which, being *an end in itself*, could be a source of definite laws, then in this and this alone would lie the source of a possible categorical imperative, that is, a practical law.

Now I say: man and generally any rational being *exists* as an end in himself, *not merely as a means* to be arbitrarily used by this or that will, but in all his actions, whether they concern himself or other rational beings, must be always regarded at the same time as an end. All objects of the inclinations have only a conditional worth; for if the inclinations and the wants founded on them did not exist, then their object would be without value. But the inclinations themselves, being sources of want, are so far from having an absolute worth for which they should be desired that, on the contrary, it must be the universal wish of every rational being to be wholly free from them. Thus the worth of any object which is *to be acquired* by our action is always conditional. Beings whose existence depends not on our will but on nature's, have nevertheless, if they are nonrational beings, only a relative value as means, and are therefore called *things*; rational beings, on the contrary, are called *persons*, because their very nature points them out as ends in themselves, that is, as something which must not be used merely as means, and so far therefore restricts freedom of action (and is an object of respect). These, therefore, are not merely subjective ends whose existence has a worth *for us* as an effect of our action, but *objective ends*, that is, things whose existence is an end in itself—an end, moreover, for which no other can be substituted, which they should subserve *merely* as means, for otherwise nothing whatever would possess *absolute worth*; but if all worth were conditioned and therefore contingent, then there would be no supreme practical principle of reason whatever.

If then there is a supreme practical principle or, in respect of the human will, a categorical imperative, it must be one which, being drawn from the conception of that which is necessarily an end for everyone because it is *an end in itself*, constitutes an *objective* principle of will, and can therefore serve as a universal practical law. The foundation of this principle is: *rational nature exists as an end in itself*. Man necessarily conceives his own existence as being so; so far then this is a *subjective* principle of human actions. But every other rational being regards its existence similarly, just on the same rational principle that holds for me; so that it is at the same time an objective principle from which as a supreme practical law all laws of the will must be capable of being deduced. Accordingly the practical imperative will be as follows: *So act as to treat humanity, whether in thine own person or in that of any other, in every case as an end withal, never as means only*. We will now inquire whether this can be practically carried out.

To abide by the previous examples:

First, under the head of necessary duty to oneself: He who contemplates suicide should ask himself whether his action can be consistent with the idea of humanity *as an end in itself*. If he destroys himself in order to escape from painful circumstances, he uses a person merely as *a mean* to maintain a tolerable condition up to the end of life. But a man is not a thing, that is to say, something which can be used merely as means, but must in all his actions be always considered as an end in himself: I cannot, therefore, dispose in any way of a man in my own person so as to mutilate him, to damage or kill him. (It belongs to ethics proper to define this principle more precisely, so as to avoid all misunderstanding, for example, as to the amputation of the limbs in order to preserve myself; as to exposing my life to danger with a view to preserve it, etc. This question is therefore omitted here.)

Secondly, as regards necessary duties, or those of strict obligation, towards others: He who is thinking of making a lying promise to others will see at once that he would be using another man *merely as a mean*, without the latter containing at the same time the end in himself. For he whom I propose by such a promise to use for my own purposes cannot possibly assent to my mode of acting towards him, and therefore cannot himself contain the end of this action. This violation of the principle of humanity in other men is more obvious if we take in examples of attacks on the freedom and property of others. For then it is clear that he who transgresses the rights of men intends to use the person of others merely as means, without considering that as rational beings they ought always to be esteemed also as ends, that is, as beings who must be capable of containing in themselves the end of the very same action.

Thirdly, as regards contingent (meritorious) duties to oneself: It is not enough that the action does not violate humanity in our own person as an end in itself, it must also *harmonize with* it. Now there are in humanity capacities of greater perfection which belong to the end that nature has in view in regard to humanity in ourselves as the subject; to neglect these might perhaps be consistent with the *maintenance* of humanity as an end in itself, but not with the *advancement* of this end.

Fourthly, as regards meritorious duties towards others: The natural end which all men have is their own happiness. Now humanity might indeed subsist although no one should contribute anything to the happiness of others, provided he did not intentionally withdraw anything from it; but after all, this would only harmonize negatively, not positively, with *humanity as an end in itself*, if everyone does not also endeavor, as far as in him lies, to forward the ends of others. For the ends of any subject which is an end in himself ought as far as possible to be *my* ends also, if that conception is to have its *full* effect with me. . . .

NOTES

1. A *maxim* is the subjective principle of volition. The objective principle (i.e., that which would also serve subjectively as a practical principle to all rational beings if reason had full power over the faculty of desire) is the practical *law*.

2. It might be here objected to me that I take refuge behind the word *respect* in an obscure feeling, instead of giving a distinct solution of the question by a concept of the reason. But although respect is a feeling, it is not a feeling *received* through influence, but is *self-wrought* by a rational concept, and, therefore, is specifically distinct from all feelings of the former kind, which may be referred either to inclination or fear. What I recognize immediately as a law for me, I recognize with respect. This merely signifies the consciousness that my will is *subordinate* to a law, without the intervention of other influences on my sense. The immediate determination of the will by the law, and the consciousness of this, is called *respect*, so that this is regarded as an *effect* of the law on the subject, and not as the *cause* of it. Respect is properly the conception of a worth which thwarts my self-love. Accordingly it is something which is considered neither as an object of inclination nor of fear, although it has something analogous to both.

The *object* of respect is the *law* only, that is, the law which we impose on *ourselves*, and yet recognize as necessary in itself. As a law, we are subjected to it without consulting self-love; as imposed by us on ourselves, it is a result of our will. In the former aspect it has an analogy to fear, in the latter to inclination. Respect for a person is properly only respect for the law (of honesty, etc.) of which he gives us an example. Since we also look on the improvement of our talents as a duty, we consider that we see in a person of talents, as it were, the *example of a law* (viz., to become like him in this by exercise), and this constitutes our respect. All so-called moral *interest* consists simply in *respect* for the law.

3. A "maxim" is a subjective principle of action, and must be distinguished from the *objective principle*, namely, practical law. The former contains the practical rule set by reason according to the conditions of the subject (often its ignorance or its inclinations), so that it is the principle on which the subject *acts*; but the law is the objective principle valid for every rational being, and is the principle on which it *ought to act*—that is an imperative.

4. To behold virtue in her proper form is nothing else but to contemplate morality stripped of all admixture of sensible things and of every spurious ornament of reward or self-love. How much she then eclipses everything else that appears charming to the affections, every one may readily perceive with the least exertion of his reason, if it be not wholly spoiled for abstraction.

Existentialism

JEAN-PAUL SARTRE

What is meant by the term *existentialism*?

Most people who use the word would be rather embarrassed if they had to explain it, since now that the word is all the rage, even the work of a musician or painter is being called existentialist. . . . It seems that for want of an advance-guard doctrine analogous to surrealism, the kind of people who are eager for scandal and flurry turn to this philosophy which in other respects does not at all serve their purposes in this sphere.

Actually, it is the least scandalous, the most austere of doctrines. It is intended strictly for specialists and philosophers. Yet it can be defined easily. What complicates matters is that there are two kinds of existentialist; first, those who are Christian, among whom I would include Jaspers and Gabriel Marcel, both Catholic; and on the other hand, the atheistic existentialists, among whom I class Heidegger, and then the French existentialists and myself. What they have in common is that they think that existence precedes essence, or, if you prefer, that subjectivity must be the starting point.

Just what does that mean? Let us consider some object that is manufactured, for example, a book or a paper-cutter: here is an object which has been made by an artisan whose inspiration came from a concept. He referred to the concept of what a paper-cutter is and likewise to a known method of production, which is part of the concept, something which is, by and large, a routine. Thus, the paper-cutter is at once an object produced in a certain way and, on the other hand, one having a specific use; and one cannot postulate a man who produces a paper-cutter but does not know what it is used for. Therefore, let us say that, for the paper-cutter, essence—that is, the ensemble of both the production routines and the properties which enable it to be both produced and defined—precede existence. Thus, the presence of the paper-cutter or book in front of me is determined. Therefore, we have here a technical view of the world whereby it can be said that production precedes existence.

When we conceive God as the Creator, He is generally thought of as a superior sort of artisan. Whatever doctrine we may be considering, whether one like that of Descartes or that of Leibnitz, we always grant that will more or less follows understanding or, at the very least, accompanies it, and that when God creates He knows exactly what He is creating. Thus, the concept of man in the mind of God is comparable to the concept of paper-cutter in the mind of the manufacturer, and, following certain techniques and a conception, God produces man, just as the artisan, following a definition and a technique, makes a paper-cutter. Thus, the individual man is the realization of a certain concept in the divine intelligence.

In the eighteenth century, the atheism of the *philosophes* discarded the idea of God, but

---

Jean-Paul Sartre (1905—   ) is a contemporary French philosopher and novelist.

not so much for the notion that essence precedes existence. To a certain extent, this idea is found everywhere; we find it in Diderot, in Voltaire, and even in Kant. Man has a human nature: this human nature, which is the concept of the human, is found in all men, which means that each man is a particular example of a universal concept, man. In Kant, the result of this universality is that the wild-man, the natural man, as well as the bourgeois, are circumscribed by the same definition and have the same basic qualities. Thus, here too the essence of man precedes the historical existence that we find in nature.

Atheistic existentialism, which I represent is more coherent. It states that if God does not exist, there is at least one being in whom existence precedes essence, a being who exists before he can be defined by any concept, and that this being is man, or as Heidegger says, human reality. What is meant here by saying that existence precedes essence? It means that, first of all, man exists, turns up, appears on the scene, and, only afterwards, defines himself. If man, as the existentialist conceives him, is indefinable, it is because at first he is nothing. Only afterward will he be something, and he himself will have made what he will be. Thus, there is no human nature, since there is no God to conceive it. Not only is man what he conceives himself to be, but he is also only what he wills himself to be after his thrust toward existence.

Man is nothing else but what he makes of himself. Such is the first principle of existentialism. It is also what is called subjectivity, the name we are labeled with when charges are brought against us. But what do we mean by this, if not that man has a greater dignity than a stone or table? For we mean that man first exists, that is, that man first of all is the being in the future. Man is at the start a plan which is aware of itself, rather than a patch of moss, a piece of garbage, or a cauliflower; nothing exists prior to this plan; there is nothing in heaven; man will be what he will have planned to be. Not what he will want to be. Because by the word "will" we generally mean a conscious decision, which is subsequent to what we have already made of ourselves. I may want to belong to a political party, write a book, get married; but all that is only a manifestation of an earlier, more spontaneous choice that is called "will." But if existence really does precede essence, man is responsible for what he is. Thus, existentialism's first move is to make every man aware of what he is and to make the full responsibility of his existence rest on him. And when we say that a man is responsible for himself, we do not only mean that he is responsible for his own individuality, but that he is responsible for all men.

The word subjectivism has two meanings, and our opponents play on the two. Subjectivism means, on the one hand, that an individual chooses and makes himself; and, on the other, that it is impossible for man to transcend human subjectivity. The second of these is the essential meaning of existentialism. When we say that man chooses his own self, we mean that every one of us does likewise; but we also mean by that that in making this choice he also chooses all men. In fact, in creating the man that we want to be, there is not a single one of our acts which does not at the same time create an image of man as we think he ought to be. To choose to be this or that is to affirm at the same time the value of what we choose, because we can never choose evil. We always choose the good, and nothing can be good for us without being good for all.

If, on the other hand, existence precedes essence, and if we grant that we exist and fashion our image at one and the same time, the image is valid for everybody and for our whole age. Thus, our responsibility is much greater than we might have supposed, because it involves all mankind. If I am a workingman and choose to join a Christian trade-union rather than be a communist, and if by being a member I want to show that the best thing for man is resignation, that the kingdom of man is not of this world, I am not only involving my own case—I want to be resigned for everyone. As a result, my action has involved all humanity. To take a more individual matter, if I want to marry, to have children; even if this marriage depends solely on my own circumstances or passion or wish, I am involving all humanity in monogamy and not merely myself. Therefore, I am responsible for myself and for everyone else. I am creating a certain image of man of my own choosing. In choosing myself, I choose man.

This helps us understand what the actual content is of such rather grandiloquent words as anguish, forlornness, despair. As you will see, it's all quite simple.

First, what is meant by anguish? The existentialists say at once that man is anguish. What that means is this: the man who involves himself and who realizes that he is not only the person he chooses to be, but also a lawmaker who is, at the same time, choosing all mankind as well as himself, cannot help escape the feeling of his total and deep responsibility. Of course, there are many people who are not anxious; but we claim that they are hiding their anxiety, that they are fleeing from it. Certainly, many people believe that when they do something, they themselves are the only ones involved, and when someone says to them, "What if everyone acted that way?" they shrug their shoulders and answer, "Everyone doesn't act that way." But really, one should always ask himself, "What would happen if everybody looked at things that way?" There is no escaping this disturbing thought except by a kind of double-dealing. A man who lies and makes excuses for himself by saying "not everybody does that," is someone with an uneasy conscience, because the act of lying implies that a universal value is conferred upon the lie.

Anguish is evident even when it conceals itself. This is the anguish that Kierkegaard called the anguish of Abraham. You know the story: an angel has ordered Abraham to sacrifice his son; if it really were an angel who has come and said, "You are Abraham, you shall sacrifice your son," everything would be all right. But everyone might first wonder, "Is it really an angel, and am I really Abraham? What proof do I have? . . .

Now, I'm not being singled out as an Abraham, and yet at every moment I'm obliged to perform exemplary acts. For every man, everything happens as if all mankind had its eyes fixed on him and were guiding itself by what he does. And every man ought to say to himself, "Am I really the kind of man who has the right to act in such a way that humanity might guide itself by my actions?" And if he does not say that to himself, he is masking his anguish.

There is no question here of the kind of anguish which would lead to quietism, to inaction. It is a matter of a simple sort of anguish that anybody who has had responsibilities is familiar with. For example, when a military officer takes the responsibility for an attack and sends a certain number of men to death, he chooses to do so, and in the main he alone makes the choice. Doubtless, orders come from above, but they are too broad; he interprets them, and on this interpretation depend the lives of ten or fourteen or twenty men. In making a decision he cannot help having a certain anguish. All leaders know this anguish. That doesn't keep them from acting; on the contrary, it is the very condition of their action. For it implies that they envisage a number of possibilities, and when they choose one, they realize that it has value only because it is chosen. We shall see that this kind of anguish, which is the kind that existentialism describes, is explained, in addition, by a direct responsibility to the other men whom it involves. It is not a curtain separating us from action, but is part of action itself.

When we speak of forlornness, a term Heidegger was fond of, we mean only that God does not exist and that we have to face all the consequences of this. The existentialist is strongly opposed to a certain kind of secular ethics which would like to abolish God with the least possible expense. About 1880, some French teachers tried to set up a secular ethics which went something like this: God is a useless and costly hypothesis; we are discarding it; but, meanwhile, in order for there to be an ethics, a society, a civilization, it is essential that certain values be taken seriously and that they be considered as having an *a priori* existence. It must be obligatory, *a priori*, to be honest, not to lie, not to beat your wife, to have children, etc., etc. So we're going to try a little device which will make it possible to show that values exist all the same, inscribed in a heaven of ideas, though otherwise God does not exist. In other words—and this, I believe, is the tendency of everything called reformism in France—nothing will be changed if God does not exist. We shall find ourselves with the same norms of honesty, progress, and humanism, and we shall have made of God an outdated hypothesis which will peacefully die off by itself.

The existentialist, on the contrary, thinks it

very distressing that God does not exist, because all possibility of finding values in a heaven of ideas disappear along with Him; there can no longer be an *a priori* Good, since there is no infinite and perfect consciousness to think it. Nowhere is it written that the Good exists, that we must be honest, that we must not lie; because the fact is we are on a plane where there are only men. Dostoievsky said, "If God didn't exist, everything would be possible." That is the very starting point of existentialism. Indeed, everything is permissible if God does not exist, and as a result man is forlorn, because neither within him nor without does he find anything to cling to. He can't start making excuses for himself.

If existence really does precede essence, there is no explaining things away by reference to a fixed and given human nature. In other words, there is no determinism, man is free, man is freedom. On the other hand, if God does not exist, we find no values or commands to turn to which legitimize our conduct. So, in the bright realm of values, we have no excuse behind us, no justification before us. We are alone, with no excuses.

That is the idea I shall try to convey when I say that man is condemned to be free. Condemned, because he did not create himself, yet, in other respects is free; because, once thrown into the world, he is responsible for everything he does. The existentialist does not believe in the power of passion. He will never agree that a sweeping passion is a ravaging torrent which fatally leads a man to certain acts and is therefore an excuse. He thinks that man is responsible for his passion.

The existentialist does not think that man is going to help himself by finding in the world some omen by which to orient himself. Because he thinks that man will interpret the omen to suit himself. Therefore, he thinks that man, with no support and no aid, is condemned every moment to invent man. Ponge, in a very fine article, has said, "Man is the future of man." That's exactly it. But if it is taken to mean that this future is recorded in heaven, that God sees it, then it is false, because it would really no longer be a future. If it is taken to mean that, whatever a man may be, there is a future to be forged, a virgin future before him, then this remark is sound. But then we are forlorn.

To give you an example which will enable you to understand forlornness better, I shall cite the case of one of my students who came to see me under the following circumstances: his father was on bad terms with his mother, and, moreover, was inclined to be a collaborationist; his older brother had been killed in the German offensive of 1940, and the young man, with somewhat immature but generous feelings, wanted to avenge him. His mother lived alone with him, very much upset by the half-treason of her husband and the death of her older son; the boy was her only consolation.

The boy was faced with the choice of leaving for England and joining the Free French Forces—that is, leaving his mother behind—or remaining with his mother and helping her to carry on. He was fully aware that the woman lived only for him and that his going-off—and perhaps his death—would plunge her into despair. He was also aware that every act that he did for his mother's sake was a sure thing, in the sense that it was helping her to carry on, whereas every effort he made toward going off and fighting was an uncertain move which might run aground and prove completely useless; for example, on his way to England he might, while passing through Spain, be detained indefinitely in a Spanish camp; he might reach England or Algiers and be stuck in an office at a desk job. As a result, he was faced with two very different kinds of action: one, concrete, immediate, but concerning only one individual; the other concerned an incomparably vaster group, a national collectivity, but for that very reason was dubious, and might be interrupted en route. And, at the same time, he was wavering between two kinds of ethics. On the one hand, an ethics of sympathy, of personal devotion; on the other, a broader ethics, but one whose efficacy was more dubious. He had to choose between the two.

Who could help him choose? Christian doctrine? No. Christian doctrine says, "Be charitable, love your neighbor, take the more rugged path, etc., etc." But which is the more rugged path? Whom should he love as a brother? The fighting man or his mother? Which does the greater good, the vague act of fighting in a group, or the concrete one of helping a particular human being to go on living? Who can decide *a priori*? Nobody. No book of ethics can tell him. The Kantian ethics says, "Never treat any person as a means, but as an end." Very well, if I stay with my mother, I'll treat her as an end and not as a means; but by virtue of this very fact, I'm running the risk of treating the people around me who are fighting, as means, and, conversely, if I go to join those who are fighting, I'll be treating them as an end, and, by doing that, I run the risk of treating my mother as a means.

If values are vague, and if they are always too broad for the concrete and specific case that we are considering, the only thing left for us is to trust our instincts. That's what this young man tried to do; and when I saw him, he said, "In the end, feeling is what counts. I ought to choose whichever pushes me in one direction. If I feel that I love my mother enough to sacrifice everything else for her—my desire for vengeance, for action, for adventure—then I'll stay with her. If, on the contrary, I feel that my love for my mother isn't enough, I'll leave."

But how is the value of a feeling determined? What gives his feeling for his mother value? Precisely the fact that he remained with her. I may say that I like so-and-so well enough to sacrifice a certain amount of money for him, but I may say so only if I've done it. I may say, "I love my mother well enough to remain with her" if I have remained with her. The only way to determine the value of this affection is, precisely, to perform an act which confirms and defines it. But, since I require this affection to justify my act, I find myself caught in a vicious circle. . . .

As for despair, the term has a very simple meaning. It means that we shall confine ourselves to reckoning only with what depends upon our will, or on the ensemble of probabilities which make our action possible. When we want something, we always have to reckon with probabilities. I may be counting on the arrival of a friend. The friend is coming by rail or streetcar; this supposes that the train will arrive on schedule, or that the streetcar will not jump the track. I am left in the realm of possibility; but possibilities are to be reckoned with only to the point where my action comports with the ensemble of these possibilities, and no further. The moment the possibilities I am considering are not rigorously involved by my action, I ought to disengage myself from them, because no God, no scheme, can adapt the world and its possibilities to my will. When Descartes said, "Conquer yourself rather than the world," he meant essentially the same thing.

The Marxists to whom I have spoken reply, "You can rely on the support of others in your action, which obviously has certain limits because you're not going to live forever. That means: rely on both what others are doing elsewhere to help you, in China, in Russia, and what they will do later on, after your death, to carry on the action and lead it to its fulfillment, which will be the revolution. You even *have* to rely upon that, otherwise you're immoral." I reply at once that I will always rely on fellow fighters insofar as these comrades are involved with me in a common struggle, in the unity of a party or a group in which I can more or less make my weight felt; that is, one whose ranks I am in as a fighter and whose movements I am aware of at every moment. In such a situation, relying on the unity and will of the party is exactly like counting on the fact that the train will arrive on time or that the car won't jump the track. But, given that man is free and that there is no human nature for me to depend on, I cannot count on men whom I do not know by relying on human goodness or man's concern for the good of society. I don't know what will become of the Russsian revolution; I may make an example of it to the extent that at the present time it is apparent that the proletariat plays a part in Russia that it plays in no other nation. But I can't swear that this will inevitably lead to a triumph of the proletariat. I've got to limit myself to what I see.

Given that men are free, and that tomorrow they will freely decide what man will be, I cannot be sure that, after my death, fellow fighters will carry on my work to bring it to its maximum perfection. Tomorrow, after my death, some men may decide to set up Fascism, and the others may be cowardly and muddled enough to let them do it. Fascism will then be the human reality, so much the worse for us.

Actually, things will be as man will have decided they are to be. Does that mean that I should abandon myself to quietism? No.

First, I should involve myself; then, act on the old saw, "Nothing ventured, nothing gained." Nor does it mean that I shouldn't belong to a party, but rather that I shall have no illusions and shall do what I can. For example, suppose I ask myself, "Will socialization, as such, ever come about?" I know nothing about it. All I know is that I'm going to do everything in my power to bring it about. Beyond that, I can't count on anything. Quietism is the attitude of people who say, "Let others do what I can't do." The doctrine I am presenting is the very opposite of quietism, since it declares, "There is no reality except in action." Moreover, it goes further, since it adds, "Man is nothing else than his plan; he exists only to the extent that he fulfills himself; he is, therefore, nothing else than the ensemble of his acts, nothing else than his life."

FURTHER READINGS

Brandt, R. B. *Ethical Theory*, Englewood Cliffs, N. J.: Prentice-Hall, 1959.

Brandt, R. B., ed. *Value and Obligation*. New York: Harcourt Brace and World, 1961.

Edwards, Paul, editor-in-chief. *The Encyclopedia of Philosophy*. New York: Macmillan, 1967.

Frankena, William. *Ethics*. Englewood Cliffs, N.J.: Prentice Hall, 1963.

Hospers, John. *Human Conduct*. New York: Harcourt Brace, 1961.

Murphy, Jeffrie. *Kant: The Philosophy of Right*. New York: St. Martin's, 1970.

Sellars, Wilfrid, and Hospers, John, eds. *Readings in Ethical Theory*. New York: Appleton Century Crofts, 1952.

PART SIX

Political Philosophy

Introduction

HAROLD MOORE

In many ways, political philosophy is the most "practical" part of philosophy. Unlike at least some parts of the philosophical enterprise, which sometimes tend to be remote and unrelated to the concerns of everyday life, political problems often impinge on our lives in direct and immediate ways: in ways that demand reflective attention and, where possible, satisfactory resolution. Any adequate understanding of the "problems of politics," however, must be philosophical in basic character. This is so for at least two basic reasons.

First, our perception of the problems and goals of political theory are directly tied to basic and far-ranging assumptions about the nature of man and the nature of human community and how each is to be related to the other. Democratic theorists tend to hold certain doctrines about the nature and importance of individuality and liberty. Marxists tend to deny just such claims; consequently any adequate comprehension of what is at issue between the democrat and the Marxist waits on an understanding of the rationale behind their differing philosophical conceptions of what a man is. Attempts to understand such debates that do not explicitly address the philosophical issues somewhere are bound to be superficial and question begging.

Second, the parameters of political debate are often *moral* ones. Consider claims like: "Capital punishment is unjust." "Property is crime." "The function of government is the preservation of property." "Draft laws are immoral." "American society is oppresive and racist." Each claim systematically presupposes some standard that can be employed to judge the moral adequacy of either a society or a given social practice. Without such a standard, the claims themselves are meaningless and hence uninteresting. But surely anyone who uses such discourse is using language in a perfectly meaningful way. If so, then what standards is he using? Are they rationally defensible? Are they morally defensible assumptions? But again, to answer their questions, a philosophical account of how such standards are justified is required.

The basic problem of political philosophy is the problem of the justification of authority, for the basic concepts of much of political theory, for example, the concept of 'right', the concept of 'obligation', have no straightforward determinate sense unless the notion of authority can be given some substance. In short, the extent and scope of the political bond all revolve around how the concept of authority is analyzed. Extensive and strong accounts of authority generate an extensive and strong sort of state, weaker accounts of authority generate weaker kinds of states.

The most basic issue of political philosophy, however, is whether *any* claim to have political authority is justified. The point can be explored by examining the claims of Robert Paul Wolff,[1] a contemporary political philosopher who is an anarchist; that is, Wolff denies that authority can be justified. An anarchist usually begins his argument by making a basic distinction between two kinds of authority:

(1) *De facto authority*. This sort of authority is simply the *ability* to have one's commands obeyed. Force, power, threat, violence are

all possible ways of establishing *de facto* authority.

(2) *De jure authority*. This sort of authority is the *right* to have one's commands obeyed *because* they issue from a justified authority.

Any number of governments can meet (1), all it requires is the means to get its dictates obeyed and enforced. The mere ability to have one's commands obeyed, however, is not yet to justify them, to show they are morally acceptable. Granted then that it is sometimes possible to enforce one's commands, what is the justification for so enforcing them? An acceptable answer to this question would count as an answer to the problem of authority and hence to the basic problem of political philosophy. And the precise reason that the anarchist is interesting at this stage of the argument is that he claims that states might possess *de facto* authority, but never *de jure* authority. Wolff's argument for this claim is straightforward; (2) which is needed for the establishment of authority entails, claims Wolff:

(3) The commands of a *de jure* state are to be obeyed *because* they are made by an *authority*.

But (3) is unacceptable to any moral agent, for to be a moral agent, claims Wolff, is to be morally autonomous, that is, each individual must act for reasons that *he* acknowledges as morally persuasive ones, but this is to say that the individual, and not the state, is the final authority in determining a particular course of action. But if (2) entails (3) and if (3) is false, then (2) is false. No account of *de jure* authority is acceptable to a moral agent.

Even if one finds Wolff's account of morality puzzling or dubious, the problem can be generated in other ways. To have a state is to have power. To claim to have a justified state is to claim to be able to justify, at least sometimes, the use of power to achieve certain social ends. But what justifies this? What justifies coercion, if it is required? At a minimum, a moral agent needs an account of political authority, that is consistent with his basic moral committments.

The only way to make substantial progress on the concept of 'legitimacy' is to examine the methods, arguments, and assumptions of the Western political tradition. For present purposes, we can proceed by generating four models of legitimacy that have been important and influential. The models are neither exhaustive nor well-defined, their justification is the methodological one of simplicity. The same models, moreover, can be utilized to get some slight perspective on the vast historical data from which the political theorist derives his concepts. Our models are: the classical approach of Greek and medieval political theory, the contractarian approach of Locke and Hobbes, the utilitarian model of the liberal tradition, best embodied by Mill and the Marxist critique of and alternative to the liberal tradition.

Plato and Aristotle would scarcely know how to cope with the claims of an anarchist, for the anarchist "invitation" to life without government would strike them as barely intelligible. To be *human* is to live in the *polis*, the basic unit of social life, and the ungoverned *polis* borders on the incoherent. Perhaps the best way to understand *polis* is in terms of community and correspondingly political theory is the art of directing or controlling designing the community in the proper way. The primary social bond is the political one that defines the relationship between the individual and the polis. The primary purpose of the political theory is irreducibly moral: the best polis is one governed with an eye on the development of human nature, seeing to it that the right kind of character is developed.

The coherence of the concept of 'right kind of character', of course, depends on the ability of the political theorist to develop and defend in detail the particular account of excellence in human character his particular political theory is modelled on. And unfortunately the account of human nature presupposed by many classical accounts of the state (Plato, Aristotle, Augustine, and Aquinas are typical) *themselves* involve analytically suspect notions or highly speculative theories. If so, it is unlikely that the difficult questions of normative political theory will be substantially illuminated by tying their adequate conceptual explication to the successful completion of a particular speculative program. To the extent that political theory must rely on philosophical theory, it is reasonable to search for a set of philosophical assumptions no stronger than those needed to generate the political theory; assumptions richer in philosophical commitment, while their analysis is important for other reasons, only weaken the political theory.

By the time of the seventeenth century, many of the classical accounts of human nature had been severely challenged. At the same time, a new model for knowledge—the scientific model—was being developed. Could a "scientific" account of the state provide a model for the resolution of the problems of political philosophy? In a very broad sense, this is what Hobbes tried to do.

Philosophically, Hobbes was an empiricist who rejected the degenerate Aristotelianism then taught in the universities of Europe. Rather than appealing to Aristotle, the church, or history as the justification for his political theory, Hobbes appealed to a new authority: the scientific authority of the method of Galileo. The basic methodological move Hobbes takes the new scientists to be making is alarmingly simplistic, almost trivial: resolve the complex components of a situation into its simplest elements and then reconstruct (deduce) the characteristics of the whole from the characteristics of the primitive elements. For our purposes, Hobbes takes the primitive unit of society to be the *individual*, and he will attempt to explain the generation of authority in the society in terms of the coming together of individuals.

From the perspective of the value constraints on the political theorist, similar desired constraints are met with this scheme. For as a substitute for the metaphysically and theologically grounded accounts of human nature of the classical and medieval theories, Hobbes offers the empirically based description of what individuals actually desire, and can use this as the basis for the story of how authority is generated. At the same time the methodological and normative dimensions of Hobbes' theory are consistent with the values of the emerging individualism and secularization of Western Europe.

On this account, man is a passionate, self-interested being who is naturally interested in the satisfaction of his desires. If this is so, then life without some rational method of conflict resolution, would be impossible; life in this "state of nature" would indeed be "nasty, brutish, and short." It is only rational, then, that individuals should forego the satisfaction of some of these desires simply and basically for *reasons of self-interest*. And it is here that Hobbes introduces the device of the social contract. Self-interested individuals come together and, for reasons that can be entirely selfish, voluntarily agree to a certain set of procedural rules (the contract) for adjudicating conflict. Such consent constitutes legitimacy and hence answers the basic problem of political theory. Consent to the contract legitimates and defines the state as a means to an end, not as an expression of man's communal nature or as an extension of divine law, but simply as a means to the end of the resolution of conflict, a goal necessary for even the most minimal condition of civilized life and hence acceptable to any rational man. Quite simply the contract is the artificial construction that satisfies all the methodological constraints Hobbes labored with.

If there is a difficulty with Hobbes' overall approach it surely lies in the direction of what individuals give up in consenting to the contract. Hobbes perhaps overemphasized the role that law and order might play in civilized life. As Hobbes wrote during the English civil war, this attitude is perfectly understandable, yet most people would argue that Hobbes' theory invests far too much power in the sovereign, for he argued that the "covenant without the sword" is empty. Or quite simply, human nature being what it is, driven by passion, desire, and greed, individuals will revert to a state of nature situation unless the conditions of the contract can *be enforced*. The meaning of government is power; a state that cannot enforce its commands is no longer a state. Hobbes argued that the best way to ensure that this necessary condition was met was to invest virtually all power in a monarch. His power, in this scheme, was virtually limitless. The only way for him to lose it was to be unable to defend or protect his subjects. Aside from the right of self-defense and kindred notions, there are few nontransferable rights retained by the citizenry, provided of course that the sovereign succeeds in protecting and defending the state. Hobbes' theory, then, presumably justifies too much.

A second, perhaps the most basic difficulty for Hobbes is his equation of the *pre-political with the pre-social*. Moral concepts for Hobbes are definable in an interesting way only with respect to the state and the commands of the soverign. 'Injustice', for example, is defined as nonperformance of contract; the commands of the monarch constitute, with little exception, what justice is. In the precontract, state-of-nature situation, moral concepts, having moral reasons for acting in a certain way, do not apply. In the situation as described by Hobbes, it is extremely difficult to see how a rational person *could begin* to apply moral concepts to his actions, that is, if the contract between the state of nature and civilization is as stark as Hobbes claims, then it is not clear how individuals in the one situation could ever arrive at the other. The point here is not just the empirical one of complexity and difficulty; rather the point is that the conceptual conditions for making sense of the notion of 'contract'—shared values, language, mutual understanding—are absent from Hobbes' account of the state of nature. It is not clear, then, that Hobbes' account could possibly be an acceptable answer to the problem of authority.

Locke's account of obligation is an attempt to go beyond Hobbes' account of the state of nature, while remaining in the general contractarian tradition. Having rejected the assumptions of the classical and medieval accounts, there is really only one answer Locke can give: consent, that is, once the situation has been defined in terms of individuals coming together to form a society, it is hard to see how to conceive of the problem of authority without introducing this notion at some very basic level of the problem. The answer to our basic problem then is this: individuals are bound by law because they have consented to be bound by it. The emphasis on consent once again should be taken as a symptom of the methodological and normative significance of the individual: key elements in the development of democratic theory.

Much more needs to be filled in of course. For unlike Hobbes, Locke does not equate the pre-political with the pre-social. Man is not, on this account, merely a being driven by passion and appetite, he is at least that, but he is more; in particular, man is primarily a moral being endowed with *natural* and not merely social rights. Hobbes' account is turned upside down: justice is not defined in terms of the acts of the sovereign, rather, the acts of the sovereign can be *judged* with respect to an external standard: the natural rights each man possesses merely in virtue of being human. Insofar as these rights are systematically transgressed by a sovereign, one has a prima-facie basis for noncompliance or revolution. To be sure the basic justification is still in terms of consent, and the "inconvenience of the state of nature" is what renders the consent rational. Unlike Hobbes, however, a moral element has been reintroduced: the concept of 'natural right' and hence there is now an external limit on what that consent authorizes. The *point* of the social contract is the defense and enhancement of the exercise of one's natural rights; the state and hence the exercise of power is primarily a means to that end. When those rights are transgressed, the state loses whatever moral authority it might have had. We now have a democratic answer to our original problem: authority results from the free exercise of the rights of an individual moral agent.

Locke's version may well be an advance on the Hobbesian version of the contract. There are, however, a number of outstanding problems involved with this particular account. What, in particular, is a natural right? How do we come to have them? What is their scope? How does one handle conflicts of rights? Locke's answers to such questions are unspecific and questionable. Natural right is based on natural law which in turn is simply the "right rule of reason." Locke interprets this to mean that there is a *naturally based* moral equality and liberty in the state of nature. Each person should be free to live out his life plan, in this scheme, free from the arbitrary imposition of another's will on his own. Each person is free to exercise his natural rights provided that such exercise does not infringe or impose on the rights of others.

This seems to generate an extremely negative conception of what a state is. The function of the state is basically to *preserve* the individual's life, liberty, and property. And hence Locke claims the chief end of government is "preservation of property." An individual has the rights in the state of nature and does not relinquish them on entering society. In fact, insofar as the state systematically infringes on such rights, it loses its right to rule.

But if this is so, then there is little or no positive role that a state can play toward creating a morally better society. Locke's theory, moreover, seems to legitimate the worst forms of degradation and exploitation. For though initially a man has a right only to the property that *his own* labor has created, he may use this "initial" wealth to generate even more income, and there seems to be no straightforward way to put *any* moral upper bound on what that income might be. Hence, Locke's theory seems to be consistent with wildly disproportionate distributions of income. This seems to be blatantly immoral and an unacceptable consequence of Locke's theory.

The issues here, of course, are extremely complicated. The key issue though is this: it seems arbitrary, morally arbitrary, to permit the spread of income that seems to typify capitalist economics. Surely, it is relevant to press here for some morally independent criterion to justify this state of affairs. Perhaps some utilitarian or pragmatic argument might be appealed to (e.g., that all other things being equal, this is the best economic distribution possible under the circumstances) in order to save Locke's theory, but surely no mere claim to the alleged abstract natural right to property will do here as a morally adequate justification.

There is perhaps a way around some of these problems and we may conveniently regard John Stuart Mill as providing one kind of solution. The consent of individuals is the abstract model for legitimating authority in democratic theory. Instead of attempting to explicate consent in Locke's way by introducing the notion of 'natural right', Mill tries another route. The democratic preservation of individual liberty and individual rights is justified not by any abstract model of consent, but by the *consequences* of such a social arrangement. What justifies the political and social autonomy of individuals is the "permanent interest of man as a progressive being." It is because libertarian social arrangements best advance such interests that they are justifiable.

Both Locke and Mill give us *some* handle on the problem of obligation. Certainly there are problems with both accounts but if we can model obligation on consent or if Mill's claim about the "permanent interest of man as a progressive being" can be sustained, then we can give some good moral reason for accepting political authority. But there is a fundamental challenge that still must be explored: the challenge of Marxism.

Marxism is an extremely complicated social theory; its complexities stem from both the inner elegance and coherence of the theory and from the range of input from external sources—philosophy, politics, economics, and history—into the theory. In terms of the development we have given to issue, Marx is squarely in the tradition of Plato, Aristotle, and Aquinas and fundamentally opposed to the ideas of Hobbes and Locke. For, like the thinkers of the classical tradition. Marx agrees that the purpose of the state is profoundly a moral one: the state has a positive, if not a primary, role in developing individuals into all they can be. But Marx seemingly has a way around the methodological difficulties implicit in classical political theory, for unlike those thinkers, Marx's "moral imperative," his program for the reform of society, is based on (allegedly) empirical evidence. Hence, his political theory is based on a "scientifically grounded" account of human nature, and the concerns of classical political theory—the moral nature of community, the primacy of the social bond, the nature of man—are once again viable concerns of the political theorist.

A good point of departure for understanding the Marxist synthesis is the critique of the individualism of the contractarian models. The atomistic notion of societies being formed by individuals is an abstraction having no possible reference to the real nature of social behavior. The social is the irreducible unit; political behavior can only be analyzed in terms of it and not in terms of any "deeper" level of individual behavior. Individualism has the truth of the matter reversed: the social determines of the individual and the latter notion cannot be analyzed in an illuminating way independent of its parent concept. The assumptions made about man by Hobbes and Locke, then, are not descriptive of human nature. Man is not necessarily a being driven by greed, passion, and the desire to possess. They are simply required by capitalist economic theory, and the assumptions about man are simply assumptions of the economic theory. As Marx sees it, it is at least reasonable to reach for a better set of assumptions.

The key to the search for these better assumptions is Marx's theory of alienation. 'Alienation' is an abused concept, overemployed to the point where it has a variety of meanings. Existential analysts use it to mean 'feeling of hostility'; it may refer to group or individual traits or dispositions; the list could be carried on indefinitely. For Marx, however, 'alienation' was primarily a concept that was to be employed for understanding social relationships, not subjective feelings. First, when someone is alienated, he is cut off or blocked from being something or reaching something that he can be, that he was designed to be. The alienation need *not* be conscious, on Marx's account an important feature of capitalist society is that there is a certain sense in which 'alienation' *cannot,* logically cannot, be acknowledged by all the members of the society. Second, the 'cutting off' must involve the notion of 'loss' in the sense of 'wrong', that is, the separation or alienation can be analyzed as involving some sort of harm. Third, individuals are not to be held primarily responsible for the alienation at least if this notion is interpreted as meaning that an individual could *overcome* his sense of alienation by changing his attitude or making an act of will. The reason such internal changes will not work is that alienation is itself the result of factors, social and economic, that are not, at least in the "normal" course of events, under the control of an individual.

Marx fleshed out these notions as follows. Man is primarily a species being, a social animal designed for community, man's labor primarily a social, cooperative enterprise. If the reader finds this an implausible notion, reflect on Hobbes' equation of the pre-political with the pre-social, Marx's claim can be plausibly reinterpreted as a denial of Hobbes basic thesis: a denial, which we have seen, has solid conceptual underpinning. But in capitalist society, man cannot act in accordance with his fundamental nature as a species being. In general, competition and exploitation are acceptable components of the capitalist scheme. If so then the development of any genuine sense of community—one based on cooperation, not competition—must wait the overthrow of capitalism. At any rate, if this is right, the first condition for alienation seems to be met.

What, in particular, constitutes the wrongness of alienation? Marx argues that man has lost something absolutely essential to his self-identity: his labor. For instead of his labor being an expression of the satisfaction of natural human needs and desires, labor is devoted to the maximization of profit and property. And it is this that constitutes the economic scheme of capitalist society. Human creativity can be perverted and twisted into the continuous generation of artificial needs in the name of profit. Man's labor, his making, his production then are all governed by goals *external* to the activity. Action is transformed from the expression of the distinctively human into a means to an external end: the acquisition of private property. Hence, the second condition also seems to be satisfied.

Now there are any number of thinkers who might agree with substantial parts of this critique: Rousseau, Hegel, perhaps Plato. The distinctively Marxist contribution is the analysis of the third factor, what produces alienation? Marx claims that alienation is the necessary product, the inevitable consequence, of *any* capitalist society. The social relationships of a society are determined, claims Marx, by the mode of economic production of the society. But the social relationships of capitalist society amount to alienation, and if Marx is right there is no way of modifying those relationships without altering the economic substructure of the society. Consequently, capitalist society cannot be reformed internally, rather, the only hope for the development of a truly human society consists in the revolutionary overthrow of capitalism.

It is difficult to assess the Marxist contribution without begging all sorts of fundamental questions. And even if one does not ultimately accept the elements of the Marxist synthesis, there is much that democratic theory can absorb from Marx, for Marx is perhaps at his best as a critic, especially a moral critic, of the tendencies and assumptions of democratic theory. Perhaps the best way to assess Marxism, for present purposes at any rate, is to reflect on the third issue: the relationship between capitalism and alienation. It is this relationship that allegedly gives Marxism a scientific status; and hence affords it a path for circumventing some of the problems of classical political theory.

And yet in terms of the available empirical evidence, Marxism seems to be a relatively weak theory. To be sure, the empirical assessment of any theory, especially one as comprehensive as Marxism, is difficult, nonetheless it does not seem to be an acceptable empirical account of the market economy, for it has systematically underestimated the adaptability of such economies to new situations. Virtually no, or few at any rate, market economists hold the assumptions of nineteenth century capitalism: some measure of government control is now accepted and even welcomed. On Marxist theory, such developments *cannot* be analyzed as adaptive changes of a well-functioning society, but rather as expressions of an inherently unstable social situation. This conclusion, however, is wildly at variance with even the most charitable interpretation of the empirical evidence. A Marxist might then argue that evidence of whatever sort is simply irrelevant because alienation is to be *defined* in terms of capitalistic economies, but this would be a Pyrrhic victory because it renders the Marxist claim definitional and hence trivial. The concept of alienation—which had been taken to be a key concept for interpreting social relationships—is rendered into a tautology.

To be sure, any democratic theorist can learn a great deal from Marxist accounts of society, but in the last analysis, its scientific status is extremely dubious, and since the alleged scientific character of Marxism is an essential part of its justification, then it seems that Marxism is an implausible account of society. If we are to improve on Locke and Mill, perhaps we should look elsewhere.

We can use the laws of the democratic tradition—as exemplified by Locke and Mill—to show what is wrong with the basic anarchist claim. The obligation to obey the state is a *prima facie* obligaton justified by reference to certain moral conditions and what can be rationally deduced from such conditions. Disagreements about the employment and extent of political power doubtless remain, and perhaps under certain conditions civil disobedience might even be obligatory. The problems involved in adjudicating these issues are quite complicated and still hotly debated. But the anarchist analysis can certainly now be regarded for what it is: an oversimplification, for it is not a case of a moral agent obeying the dictates of a state *because* they are dictates of that state. If this were so, then anarchism would be the only account acceptable to a morally conscientious person. Rather, a *prima facie* obligation exists only because certain procedures are regarded as morally acceptable ones. Political authority, such as it is, stems from the acceptance of certain decision procedures. Any serious disproportion between political authority and what those decision procedures warrant thereby weakens the claim to possess morally justifiable political authority. Political scepticism, like its twin moral skepticism, turns out to be too stark a notion to illuminate the logic of our practical reasoning.

NOTES

1. R. P. Wolff, *In Defense of Anarchism* (New York: Harper and Row, 1971).

Crito

PLATO

Why have you come at this hour, Crito? it must be quite early?

CRITO: Yes, certainly.

SOCRATES: What is the exact time?

CRITO: The dawn is breaking.

SOCRATES: I wonder that the keeper of the prison would let you in.

CRITO: He knows me, because I often come, Socrates; moreover, I have done him a kindness.

SOCRATES: And are you only just arrived?

CRITO: No, I came some time ago.

SOCRATES: Then why did you sit and say nothing, instead of at once awakening me?

CRITO: I should not have liked myself, Socrates, to be in such great trouble and unrest as you are—indeed I should not: I have been watching with amazement your peaceful slumbers; and for that reason I did not awake you, because I wished to minimize the pain. I have always thought you to be of a happy disposition; but never did I see anything like the easy, tranquil manner in which you bear this calamity.

SOCRATES: Why, Crito, when a man has reached my age he ought not be repining at the approach of death.

CRITO: And yet other old men find themselves in similar misfortunes, and age does not prevent them from repining.

SOCRATES: That is true. But you have not told me why you come at this early hour.

CRITO: I come to bring you a message which is sad and painful; not, as I believe, to yourself, but to all of us who are your friends, and saddest of all to me.

SOCRATES: What? Has the ship come from Delos, on the arrival of which I am to die?

CRITO: No, the ship has not actually arrived, but she will probably be here today, as persons who have come from Sunium tell me that they left her there; and therefore tomorrow, Socrates, will be the last day of your life.

SOCRATES: Very well, Crito; if such is the will of God, I am willing; but my belief is that there will be a delay of a day.

CRITO: Why do you think so?

SOCRATES: I will tell you. I am to die on the day after the arrival of the ship.

CRITO: Yes, that is what the authorities say.

SOCRATES: But I do not think that the ship will be here until tomorrow; this I infer from a vision which I had last night, or rather only just now, when you fortunately allowed me to sleep.

CRITO: And what was the nature of the vision?

SOCRATES: There appeared to me the likeness of a woman, fair and comely, clothed in bright raiment, who called to me and said: O Socrates,

The third day hence to fertile Phthia shalt thou go.[1]

CRITO: What a singular dream, Socrates!

SOCRATES: There can be no doubt about the meaning, Crito, I think.

CRITO: Yes, the meaning is only too clear. But, oh! my beloved Socrates, let me entreat

---

Plato (426-327 B.C.) is considered by many the greatest thinker in the western philosophical tradition.

From *The Dialogues of Plato,* trans. B. Jowett (Macmillan, 1892).

you once more to take my advice and escape. For if you die I shall not only lose a friend who can never be replaced, but there is another evil: people who do not know you and me will believe that I might have saved you if I had been willing to give money, but that I did not care. Now, can there be a worse disgrace than this—that I should be thought to value money more than the life of a friend? For the many will not be persuaded that I wanted you to escape, and that you refused.

SOCRATES: But why, my dear Crito, should we care about the opinion of the many? Good men, and they are the only persons who are worth considering, will think of these things truly as they occurred.

CRITO: But you see, Socrates, that the opinion of the many must be regarded, for what is now happening shows that they can do the greatest evil to anyone who has lost their good opinion.

SOCRATES: I only wish it were so, Crito; and that the many could do the greatest evil; for then they would also be able to do the greatest good—and what a fine thing this would be! But in reality they can do neither; for they cannot make a man either wise or foolish; and whatever they do is the result of chance.

CRITO: Well, I will not dispute with you; but please to tell me, Socrates, whether you are not acting out of regard to me and your other friends: are you not afraid that if you escape from prison we may get into trouble with the informers for having stolen you away, and lose either the whole or a great part of our property; or that even a worse evil may happen to us? Now, if you fear on our account, be at ease; for in order to save you, we ought surely to run this, or even a greater risk; be persuaded, then, and do as I say.

SOCRATES: Yes, Crito, that is one fear which you mention, but by no means the only one.

CRITO: Fear not—there are persons who are willing to get you out of prison at no great cost; and as for the informers, they are far from being exorbitant in their demands—a little money will satisfy them. My means, which are certainly ample, are at your service, and if you have a scruple about spending all mine, here are strangers who will give you the use of theirs; and one of them, Simmias the Theban,[2] has brought a large sum of money for this very purpose; and Cebes and many others are prepared to spend their money in helping you to escape. I say, therefore, do not hesitate on our account, and do not say, as you did in the court, that you will have a difficulty in knowing what to do with yourself anywhere else. For men will love you in other places to which you may go, and not in Athens only; there are friends of mine in Thessaly,[3] if you like to go to them, who will value and protect you, and no Thessalian will give you any trouble. Nor can I think that you are at all justified, Socrates, in betraying your own life when you might be saved; in acting thus you are playing into the hands of your enemies, who are hurrying on your destruction. And further I should say that you are deserting your own children; for you might bring them up and educate them; instead of which you go away and leave them, and they will have to take their chance; and if they do not meet with the usual fate of orphans, there will be small thanks to you. No man should bring children into the world who is unwilling to perservere to the end in their nurture and education. But you appear to be choosing the easier part, not the better and manlier, which would have been more becoming in one who professes to care for virtue in all his actions, like yourself. And indeed, I am ashamed not only of you, but of us who are your friends, when I reflect that the whole business will be attributed entirely to our want of courage. The trial need never have come on, or might have been managed differently; and this last act, or crowning folly, will seem to have occurred through our negligence and cowardice, who might have saved you, if we had been good for anything; and you might have saved yourself, for there was no difficulty at all. See now, Socrates, how sad and discreditable are the consequences, both to us and you. Make up your mind then, or rather have your mind already made up, for the time of deliberation is over, and there is only one thing to be done, which must be done this very night, and, if we delay at all, will be no longer practicable or possible; I beseech you therefore, Socrates, be persuaded by me, and do as I say.

SOCRATES: Dear Crito, your zeal is invaluable, if a right one; but if wrong, the greater the zeal the greater the danger; and therefore we ought to consider whether I shall or shall not do as you say. For I am and always have been one of those natures who must be guided by reason, whatever the reason may be which upon reflection appears to me to be the best; and now that this chance has befallen me, I cannot repudiate my own words: the principles which I have hitherto honored and revered I still honor, and unless we can at once find other and better principles, I am certain not to agree with you; no, not even if the power of the multitude could inflict many more imprisonments, confiscations, deaths, frightening us like children with hobgoblin terrors. What will be the fairest way of considering the question? Shall I return to your old argument about the opinions of men?—we were saying that some of them are to be regarded, and others not. Now were we right in maintaining this before I was condemned? And has the argument which was once good now proved to be talk for the sake of talking—mere childish nonsense? That is what I want to consider with your help, Crito: whether, under my present circumstances, the argument appears to be in any way different or not; and is to be allowed by me or disallowed. That argument, which, as I believe, is maintained by many persons of authority, was to the effect, as I was saying, that the opinions of some men are to be regarded, and of other men not to be regarded. Now you, Crito, are not going to die tomorrow—at least, there is no human probability of this—and therefore you are disinterested and not liable to be deceived by the circumstances in which you are placed. Tell me then, whether I am right in saying that some opinions, and the opinions of some men only, are to be valued, and that other opinions, and the opinions of other men, are not to be valued. I ask you whether I was right in maintaining this?

CRITO: Certainly.

SOCRATES: The good are to be regarded, and not the bad?

CRITO: Yes.

SOCRATES: And the opinions of the wise are good, and the opinions of the unwise are evil?

CRITO: Certainly.

SOCRATES: And what was said about another matter? Is the pupil who devotes himself to the practice of gymnastics supposed to attend to the praise and blame and opinion of every man, or of one man only—his physician or trainer, whoever he may be?

CRITO: Of one man only.

SOCRATES: And he ought to fear the censure and welcome the praise of that one only, and not of the many?

CRITO: Clearly so.

SOCRATES: And he ought to act and train, and eat and drink in the way which seems good to his single master who has understanding, rather than according to the opinion of all other men put together?

CRITO: True.

SOCRATES: And if he disobeys and disregards the opinion and approval of the one, and regards the opinion of the many who have no understanding, will he not suffer evil?

CRITO: Certainly he will.

SOCRATES: And what will the evil be, whither tending and what affecting, in the disobedient person?

CRITO: Clearly, affecting the body; that is what is destroyed by the evil.

SOCRATES: Very good; and is not this true, Crito, of other things which we need not separately enumerate? In questions of just and unjust, fair and foul, good and evil, which are the subjects of our present consultation, ought we to follow the opinion of the many and to fear them; or the opinion of the one man who has understanding? ought we not to fear and reverence him more than all the rest of the world: and if we desert him shall we not destroy and injure that principle in us which may be assumed to be improved by justice and deteriorated by injustice—there is such a principle?

CRITO: Certainly there is, Socrates.

SOCRATES: Take a parallel instance: if, acting under the advice of those who have no understanding, we destroy that which is improved by health and is deteriorated by disease, would life be worth having? And that which has been destroyed is—the body?

CRITO: Yes.

SOCRATES: Could we live, having an evil and corrupted body?

CRITO: Certainly not.

SOCRATES: And will life be worth having, if that higher part of man be destroyed, which is improved by justice and depraved by injustice? Do we suppose that principle, whatever it may be in man, which has to do with justice and injustice, to be inferior to the body?

CRITO: Certainly not.

SOCRATES: More honorable than the body?

CRITO: Far more.

SOCRATES: Then, my friend, we must not regard what the many say of us; but what he, the one man who has understanding of just and unjust, will say, and what the truth will say. And therefore you begin in error when you advise that we should regard the opinion of the many about just and unjust, good and evil, honorable and dishonorable.—"Well," someone will say, "but the many can kill us."

CRITO: Yes, Socrates; that will clearly be the answer.

SOCRATES: And it is true: but still I find with surprise that the old argument is unshaken as ever. And I should like to know whether I may say the same of another proposition—that not life, but a good life, is to be chiefly valued?

CRITO: Yes, that also remains unshaken.

SOCRATES: And a good life is equivalent to a just and honorable one—that holds also?

CRITO: Yes, it does.

SOCRATES: From these premises I proceed to argue the question whether I ought or ought not to try and escape without the consent of the Athenians: and if I am clearly right in escaping, then I will make the attempt; but if not, I will abstain. The other considerations which you mention, of money and loss of character and the duty of educating one's children, are, I fear, only the doctrines of the multitude, who would be as ready to restore people to life, if they were able, as they are to put them to death—and with as little reason. But now, since the argument has thus far prevailed, the only question which remains to be considered is whether we shall do rightly either in escaping or in suffering others to aid in our escape and paying them in money and thanks, or whether in reality we shall not do rightly; and if the latter, then death or any other calamity which may ensue on my remaining here must not be allowed to enter into the calculation.

CRITO: I think that you are right, Socrates; how then shall we proceed?

SOCRATES: Let us consider the matter together, and do you either refute me if you can, and I will be convinced; or else cease, my dear friend, from repeating to me that I ought to escape against the wishes of the Athenians: for I highly value your attempts to persuade me to do so, but I may not be persuaded against my own better judgment. And now please to consider my first position, and try how you can best answer me.

CRITO: I will.

SOCRATES: Are we to say that we are never intentionally to do wrong, or that in one way we ought and in another way we ought not to do wrong, or is doing wrong always evil and dishonorable, as I was just now saying, and as has been already acknowledged by us? Are all our former admissions which were made within a few days to be thrown away? And have we, at our age, been earnestly discoursing with one another all our life long only to discover that we are no better than children? Or, in spite of the opinion of the many, and in spite of consequences whether better or worse, shall we insist on the truth of what was then said, that injustice is always an evil and dishonor to him who acts unjustly? Shall we say so or not?

CRITO: Yes.

SOCRATES: Then we must do no wrong?

CRITO: Certainly not.

SOCRATES: Nor, when injured, injure in return, as the many imagine; for we must injure no one at all?

CRITO: Clearly not.

SOCRATES: Again, Crito, may we do evil?

CRITO: Surely not, Socrates.

SOCRATES: And what of doing evil in return for evil, which is the morality of the many—is that just or not?

CRITO: Not just.

SOCRATES: For doing evil to another is the same as injuring him?

CRITO: Very true.

SOCRATES: Then we ought not to retaliate or render evil for evil to anyone, whatever evil we may have suffered from him. But I would have you consider, Crito, whether you really mean what you are saying. For this opinion has never been held, and never will be held, by any considerable number of persons; and those who are agreed and those who are not agreed upon this point have no common ground, and can only despise one another when they see how widely they differ. Tell me, then, whether you agree with and assent to my first principle, that neither injury nor retaliation nor warding off evil by evil is ever right. And shall that be the premise of our agrument? Or do you decline and dissent from this? For so I have ever thought, and continue to think; but, if you are of another opinion, let me hear what you have to say. If however, you remain of the same mind as formerly, I will proceed to the next step.

CRITO: You may proceed, for I have not changed my mind.

SOCRATES: Then I will go on to the next point, which may be put in the form of a question: Ought a man to do what he admits to be right, or ought he to betray the right?

CRITO: He ought to do what he thinks right.

SOCRATES: But if this is true, what is the application? In leaving the prison against the will of the Athenians, do I wrong any? or rather do I not wrong those whom I ought least to wrong? Do I not desert the principles which were acknowledged by us to be just—what do you say?

CRITO: I cannot tell, Socrates; for I do not know.

SOCRATES: Then consider the matter in this way: Imagine that I am about to play truant (you may call the proceeding by any name which you like), and the laws and the government come and interrogate me: "Tell us, Socrates," they say: "what are you about? are you not going by an act of yours to overturn us—the laws, and the whole state, as far as in you lies? Do you imagine that a state can subsist and not be overthrown, in which the decisions of law have no power, but are set aside and trampled upon by individuals?"—What will be our answer, Crito, to these and the like words? Anyone, and especially a rhetorician, will have a good deal to say on behalf of the law which requires a sentence to be carried out. He will argue that this law should not be set aside; and shall we reply, "Yes; but the state has injured us and given an unjust sentence." Suppose I say that?

CRITO: Very good, Socrates.

SOCRATES: "And was that our agreement with you?" the law would answer; "or were you to abide by the sentence of the state?" And if I were to express my astonishment at their words, the law would probably add: "Answer, Socrates, instead of opening your eyes: you are in the habit of asking and answering questions. Tell us: What complaint have you to make against us which justifies you in attempting to destroy us and the state? In the first place did we not bring you into existence? Your father married your mother by our aid and begat you. Say whether you have any objection to urge against those of us who regulate marriage?" None, I should reply. "Or against those of us who after birth regulate the nurture and education of children, in which you also were trained? Were not the laws, which have the charge of education, right in commanding your father to train you in music and gymnastic?" Right, I should reply. "Well then, since you were brought into the world and nurtured and educated by us, can you deny in the first place that you are our child and slave, as your fathers were before you? And if this is true you are not on equal terms with us; nor can you think that you have a right to do to us what we are doing to you. Would you have any right to strike or revile or do any other evil to your father or your master, if you had one, because you have been struck or reviled by him, or received some other evil at his hands? You would not say this. And because we think right to destroy you, do you think that you have any right to destroy us in return, and your country as far as in you lies? Will you, O professor of true virtue, pretend that you are justified in this? Has a philosopher like you failed to discover that our country is more to be valued and higher and holier far than mother or father or any ancestor, and more to be regarded in the eyes of the gods and of men of understanding? also to be soothed, and gently and reverently entreated when angry, even more than a father, and either to be persuaded, or if not persuaded, to be obeyed? And when we are punished by her, whether with imprisonment or stripes, the punishment is to be endured in silence; and if she lead us to wounds or death in battle, thither we follow as is right; neither may anyone yield or retreat or leave his rank, but whether in battle or in a court of law, or in any other place, he must do what his city and his country order him; or he must change their view of what is just: and if he may do no violence to his father or mother, much less may he do violence to his country." What answer shall we make to this, Crito? Do the laws speak truly, or do they not?

CRITO: I think that they do.

SOCRATES: Then the laws will say: "Consider, Socrates, if we are speaking truly that in your present attempt you are going to do us an injury. For, having brought you into the world, and nurtured and educated you, and given you and every other citizen a share in every good which we had to give, we further proclaim to any Athenian by the liberty which we allow him, that if he does not like us when he has become of age and has seen the ways of the city, and made our acquaintance, he may go where he pleases and take his goods with him. None of us laws will forbid him or interfere with him. Anyone who does not like us and the city, and who wants to emigrate to a colony or to any other city, may go where he likes, retaining his property. But he who has experience of the manner in which we order justice and administer the state, and still remains, has entered into an implied contract that he will do as we command him. And he who disobeys us is, as we maintain, thrice wrong; first, because in disobeying us he is disobeying his parents; secondly, because we are the authors of his education; thirdly, because he has made an agreement with us that he will duly obey our commands; and he neither obeys them nor convinces us that our commands are unjust; and we do not rudely impose them, but give him the alternative of obeying or convincing us; that is what we offer, and he does neither. These are the sort of accusations to which, as we were saying, you, Socrates, will be exposed if you accomplish your intentions; you, above all other Athenians."

Suppose now I ask, why I rather than anybody else? They will justly retort upon me that I above all other men have acknowledged the agreement. "There is clear proof," they will say, "Socrates, that we and the city were not displeasing to you. Of all Athenians you have been the most constant resident in the city, which, as you never leave, you may be supposed to love. For you never went out of the city either to see the games, except once when you went to the Isthmus,[4] or to any other place unless when you were on military service; nor did you travel as other men do. Nor had you any curiosity to know other states or their laws: your affections did not go beyond us and our state; we were your special favorites, and you acquiesced in our government of you; and here in this city you begat your children, which is a proof of your satisfaction. Moreover you might in the course of the trial, if you had liked, have fixed the penalty at banishment; the state which refuses to let you go now would have let you go then. But you pretended that you preferred death to exile,[5] and that you were not unwilling to die. And now you have forgotten these fine sentiments, and pay no respect to us, the laws, of whom you are the destroyer; and are doing what only a miserable slave would do, running away and turning your back upon the compacts and agreements which you made as a citizen. And, first of all, answer this very question: Are we right in saying that you agreed to be governed according to us in deed, and not in word only? Is that true or not?" How shall we answer, Crito? Must we not assent?

CRITO: We cannot help it, Socrates.

SOCRATES: Then will they not say: "You, Socrates, are breaking the covenants and agreements which you made with us at your leisure, not in any haste or under any compulsion or deception, but after you have had seventy years to think of them, during which time you were at liberty to leave the city, if we were not to your mind, or if our covenants appeared to you to be unfair. You had your choice, and might have gone either to Lacedaemon[6] or Crete, both which states are often praised by you for their good government, or to some other Hellenic or foreign state. Whereas you, above all other Athenians, seemed to be so fond of the state, or, in other words, of us, her laws (and who would care about a state which has no laws?), that you never stirred out of her; the halt, the blind, the maimed were not more stationary in her than you were. And now you run away and forsake your agreements. Not so, Socrates, if you will take our advice; do not make yourself ridiculous by escaping out of the city.

"For just consider, if you transgress and err in this sort of way, what good will you do either to yourself or to your friends? That your friends will be driven into exile and deprived of citizenship, or will lose their property, is tolerably certain; and you yourself, if you fly to one of the neighboring cities, as, for example, Thebes or Megara, both of which are well governed, will come to them as an enemy, Socrates, and their government will be against you, and all patriotic citizens will cast an evil eye upon you as a subverter of the laws, and you will confirm in the minds of the judges the justice of their own condemnation of you. For he who is a corrupter of the laws is more than likely to be a corrupter of the young and foolish portion of mankind. Will you then flee from well-ordered cities and virtuous men? and is existence worth having on these terms? Or will you go to them without shame, and talk to them, Socrates? And what will you say to them? What you say here about virtue and justice and institutions and laws being the best things among men? Would that be decent of you? Surely not. But if you go away from well-governed states to Crito's friends in Thessaly, where there is great disorder and license, they will be charmed to hear the tale of your escape from prison, set off with ludicrous particulars of the manner in which you were wrapped in a goatskin or some other disguise, and metamorphosed as the manner is of runaways; but will there be no one to remind you that in your old age you were not ashamed to violate the most sacred laws from a miserable desire of a little more life? Perhaps not, if you keep them in a good temper; but if they are out of temper you will hear many degrading things; you will live, but how?—as the flatterer of all men, and the servant of all men: and doing what?—eating and drinking in Thessaly, having gone abroad in order that you may get a dinner. And where will be your fine sentiments about justice and virtue? Say that you wish to live for the sake of your children—you want to bring them up and educate them—will you take them into Thessaly and deprive them of Athenian citizenship? Is this the benefit which you will confer upon them? Or are you under the impression that they will be better cared for and educated here if you are still alive, although absent from them; for your friends will take care of them? Do you fancy that if you are an inhabitant of Thessaly they will take care of them, and if you are an inhabitant of the other world that they will not take care of them? Nay; but if they who call themselves friends are good for anything, they will—to be sure they will.

"Listen, then, Socrates, to us who have brought you up. Think not of life and children first, and of justice afterwards, but of justice first, that you may be justified before the princes of the world below. For neither will you nor any that belong to you be happier or holier or juster in this life, or happier in another, if you do as Crito bids. Now you depart in innocence, a sufferer and not a doer of evil; a victim, not of the laws, but of men. But if you go forth, returning evil for evil, and injury for injury, breaking the covenants and agreements which you have made with us, and wronging those whom you ought least of all to wrong, that is to say, yourself, your friends, your country, and us, we shall be angry with you while you live, and our brethren, the laws in the world below, will receive you as an enemy; for they will know that you have done your best to destroy us. Listen, then, to us and not to Crito."

This, dear Crito, is the voice which I seem to hear murmuring in my ears, like the sound of the flute in the ears of the mystic; that voice, I say, is humming in my ears, and prevents me from hearing any other. And I know that anything more which you may say will be vain. Yet speak, if you have anything to say.

CRITO: I have nothing to say, Socrates.

SOCRATES: Leave me then, Crito, to fulfill the will of God, and to follow whither he leads.

NOTES

1. *Iliad*, IX, 363.

2. Simmias and his friend Cebes, pupils of Socrates from the nearby city of Thebes, figure largely in the next dialogue, the *Phaedo*.

3. A province of northern Greece.

4. The Isthmian games, held on the Isthmus of Corinth in honor of the sea god Poseidon, were almost as famous as the Olympian games in honor of Zeus.

5. See *Apology*.

6. Another name for Sparta.

On Violence

ROBERT PAUL WOLFF

Everything I shall say in this essay has been said before, and much of it seems to me to be obvious as well as unoriginal. I offer two excuses for laying used goods before you. In the first place, I think that what I have to say about violence is true. Now, there are many ways to speak falsehood and only one way to speak truth. It follows, as Kierkegaard pointed out, that the truth is likely to become boring. On a subject as ancient and much discussed as ours today, we may probably assume that a novel—and, hence, interesting—view of violence is likely to be false.

But truth is not my sole excuse, for the subject before us suffers from the same difficulty that Kant discerned in the area of metaphysics. After refuting the various claims that had been made to transcendent rational knowledge of things-in-themselves, Kant remarked that the refutations had no lasting psychological effect on true believers. The human mind, he concluded, possessed a natural disposition to metaphysical speculation, which philosophy must perpetually keep in check. Somewhat analogously, men everywhere are prone to certain beliefs about the legitimacy of political authority, even though their beliefs are as groundless as metaphysical speculations. The most sophisticated of men persist in supposing that some valid distinction can be made between legitimate and illegitimate commands, on the basis of which they can draw a line, for example, between mere violence and the legitimate use of force. This lingering superstition is shared by those dissenters who call police actions or ghetto living conditions "violent"; for they are merely advancing competing legitimacy claims.

I shall set forth and defend *three* propositions about violence:

First: The concept of violence is inherently confused, as is the correlative concept of nonviolence; these and related concepts depend for their meaning in political discussions on the fundamental notion of legitimate authority, which is also inherently incoherent.

Second: It follows that a number of familiar questions are also confusions to which no coherent answers could ever be given, such as: when it is permissible to resort to violence in politics; whether the black movement and the student movement should be nonviolent; and whether anything good in politics is ever accomplished by violence.

Finally: The dispute over violence and nonviolence in contemporary American politics is ideological rhetoric designed either to halt change and justify the existing distribution of power and privilege or to slow change and justify some features of the existing distribution of power and privilege or else to hasten change and justify a total redistribution of power and privilege.

Let us begin with the first proposition, which is essential to my entire discussion.

Robert Paul Wolff is professor of philosophy at the University of Massachusetts.

From the *Journal of Philosophy* LXVI, No. 19 (Oct. 2, 1969). Reprinted by permission of the author and the *Journal of Philosophy*.

I

The fundamental concepts of political philosophy are the concepts of power and authority.[1] Power in general is the ability to make and enforce decisions. Political power is the ability to make and enforce decisions about matters of major social importance. Thus the ability to dispose of my private income as I choose is a form of power, whereas the ability to make and enforce a decision about the disposition of some sizable portion of the tax receipts of the federal government is a form of *political* power. (So too is the ability to direct the decisions of a large private corporation; for the exercise of political power is not confined to the sphere of government.) A complete analysis of the concept of political power would involve a classification both of the means employed in the enforcing of decisions and of the scope and variety of questions about which decisions can be made.[2] It would also require an examination of the kinds of opposition against which the decision could be enforced. There is a very considerable difference between the ability a parliamentary majority has to enforce its decisions against the will of the minority and the ability of a rebel military clique to enforce its decisions against the Parliament as a whole.

Authority, by contrast with power, is not an ability but a right. It is the right to command and, correlatively, the right to be obeyed. Claims to authority are made in virtually every area of social life, and, in a remarkably high proportion of cases, the claims are accepted and acquiesced in by those over whom they are made. Parents claim the right to be obeyed by their children; husbands until quite recently claimed the right to be obeyed by their wives; popes claim the right to be obeyed by the laity and clergy; and of course, most notably, virtually all existing governments claim the right to be obeyed by their subjects.

A claim to authority must be sharply differentiated both from a threat or enticement and from a piece of advice. When the state commands, it usually threatens punishment for disobedience, and it may even on occasion offer a reward for compliance, but the command cannot be reduced to the mere threat or reward. What characteristically distinguishes a state from an occupying army or private party is its insistence, either explicit or implicit, on its *right* to be obeyed. By the same token, an authoritative command is not a mere recommendation. Authority says, "Do this!" not, "Let me suggest this for your consideration."

Claims to authority have been defended on a variety of grounds, most prominent among which are the appeal to God, to tradition, to expertise, to the laws of history, and to the consent of those commanded. We tend to forget that John Locke thought it worth while to devote the first of his *Two Treatises on Civil Government* to the claim that Europe's monarchs held their authority by right of primogenitural descent from Adam. It is common today to give lip service to the theory that authority derives from the consent of the governed, but most of us habitually accord *some* weight to any authority claim issuing from a group of men who regularly control the behavior of a population in a territory, particularly if the group tricks itself out with flags, uniforms, courts of law, and printed regulations.

Not all claims to authority are justified. Indeed, I shall suggest shortly that few if any are. Nevertheless, men regularly accept the authority claims asserted against them, and so we must distinguish a descriptive from a normative sense of the term. Let us use the term '*de facto* authority' to refer to *the ability to get one's authority claims accepted by those against whom they are asserted*. '*De jure* authority', then, will refer to *the right to command and to be obeyed*. Obviously, the concept of *de jure* authority is primary, and the concept of *de facto* authority is derivative.

Thus understood, *de facto* authority is a form of power, for it is a means by which its possessor can enforce his decisions. Indeed, as Max Weber—from whom much of this analysis is taken—has pointed out, *de facto* authority is the *principal* means on which states rely to carry out their decisions. Threats and inducements play an exceedingly important role in the enforcement of political decisions, to be sure, but a state that must depend upon them entirely will very soon suffer a crippling reduction in its effectiveness, which is to say, in its political power. Modern states especially require for the successful prosecution of their programs an extremely high level of coordination of the behavior of large numbers of individuals. The myth of legitimacy is the only efficient means available to the state for achieving that coordination.

Force is the ability to work some change in the world by the expenditure of physical effort. A man may root up a tree, move a stalled car, drive a nail, or restrain another man, *by force*. Force, in and of itself, is morally neutral. Physically speaking, there may be very little difference between the physical effort of a doctor who resets a dislocated shoulder and that of the ruffian who dislocated it. Sometimes, of course, force is used to work some change in the body of another man—to punch him, shoot him, take out his appendix, hold his arms, or cut his hair. But there is in principle no significant distinction between these uses of force and those uses which involve changing some other part of the world about which he cares. A man who slips into a parking place for which I am heading inflicts an injury on me roughly as great as if he had jostled me in a crowd or stepped on my toe. If he destroys a work of art on which I have lavished my most intense creative efforts, he may harm me more than a physical assault would.

Force is a means to power, but it is not of course a guarantee of power. If I wish to elicit hard work from my employees, I can threaten them with the lash or tempt them with bonuses—both of which are employments of force—but if my workers prefer not to comply, my threats and inducements may be fruitless. It is a commonplace both of domestic and of international politics that the mere possession of a monopoly of force is no guarantee of political power. Those who fail to grasp this truth are repeatedly frustrated by the baffling inability of the strong to impose their will upon the weak.

There are, so far as I can see, *three* means or instruments by which power is exercised—three ways, that is to say, in which men enforce or carry out their social decisions. The first is *force,* the ability to rearrange the world in ways that other men find appealing or distasteful. In modern society, money is of course the principal measure, exchange medium, and symbol of force. The second instrument of power is *de facto* authority—the ability to elicit obedience, as opposed to mere compliance, from others. *De facto* authority frequently accrues to those with a preponderance of force, for men are fatally prone to suppose that he who can compel compliance deserves obedience. But *de facto* authority does not reduce to the possession of a preponderance of force, for men habitually obey commands they know could not effectively be enforced. The third instrument of power is social opinion, or what might be called the "symbolic" use of force. When a runner competes in a race, he may want the first-prize money or the commercial endorsements that will come to the winner, or he may even just like blue ribbons—but he may also want the acclaim of the fans. Now, that acclaim is expressed by certain uses of force—by clapping of hands and cheering, which are physical acts. But its value to the runner is symbolic; he cherishes it as an expression of approval, not merely as a pleasing sound. To say that man is a social creature is not merely to say that he hangs out in groups, nor even to say that he engages in collective and cooperative enterprises for self-interested purposes; it is most importantly to say that he values symbolic interactions with other men and is influenced by them as well as by the ordinary exercise of force and by claims of authority. This point is important for our discussion, for, as we shall see, many persons who shrink from the use of force as an instrument of political power have no compunctions about the use of social opinion or what I have called the "symbolic" use of force. Anyone who has observed a progressive classroom run by a teacher with scruples of this sort will know that a day "in coventry" can be a far crueler punishment for an unruly ten-year old than a sharp rap on the knuckles with a ruler.

We come, finally, to the concept of violence. Strictly speaking, *violence is the illegitimate or unauthorized use of force to effect decisions against the will or desire of others*. Thus, murder is an act of violence, but capital punishment *by a legitimate state* is not; theft or extortion is violent, but the collection of taxes *by a legitimate state* is not. Clearly, on this interpretation the concept of violence is normative as well as descriptive, for it involves an implicit appeal to the principle of *de jure* legitimate authority. There is an associated sense of the term which is purely descriptive, relying on the descriptive notion of *de facto* authority. Violence in this latter sense is the use of force in ways that are proscribed or unauthorized by those who are generally accepted as the legitimate authorities in the territory. Descriptively speaking, the attack on Hitler's life during the second World War was an act of violence, but one might perfectly well deny that it was violent in the strict sense, on the grounds that Hitler's regime was illegitimate. On similar grounds, it is frequently said that police behavior toward workers or ghetto dwellers or demonstrators is violent even when it is clearly within the law, for the authority issuing the law is illegitimate.

It is common, but I think wrong-headed, to restrict the term 'violence' to uses of force that involve bodily interference or the direct infliction of physical injury. Carrying a dean out of his office is said to be violent, but not seizing his office when he is absent and locking him out. Physically tearing a man's wallet from his pocket is "violent," but swindling him out of the same amount of money is not. There is a natural enough basis for this distinction. Most of us value our lives and physical well-being above other goods that we enjoy, and we tend therefore to view attacks or threats on our person as different in kind from other sorts of harm we might suffer. Nevertheless, the distinction is not sufficiently sharp to be of any analytical use, and, as we shall see later, it usually serves the ideological purpose of ruling out, as immoral or politically illegitimate, the only instrument of power that is available to certain social classes.

In its strict or normative sense, then, the concept of political violence depends upon the concept of *de jure*, or legitimate authority. If there is no such thing as legitimate political authority, then it is impossible to distinguish between legitimate and illegitimate uses of force. Now, of course, under any circumstances, we can distinguish between right and wrong, justified and unjustified, uses of force. Such a distinction belongs to moral philosophy in general, and our choice of the criteria by which we draw the distinction will depend on our theory of value and obligation. But the distinctive political concept of violence can be given a coherent meaning *only* by appeal to a doctrine of legitimate political authority.

On the basis of a lengthy reflection upon the concept of *de jure* legitimate authority, I have come to the conclusion that philosophical anarchism is true. That is to say, I believe that there is not, and there could not be, a state that has a right to command and whose subjects have a binding obligation to obey. I have defended this view in detail elsewhere, and I can only indicate here the grounds of my conviction.[3] Briefly, I think it can be shown that every man has a fundamental duty to be autonomous, in Kant's sense of the term. Each of us must make himself the author of his actions and take responsibility for them by refusing to act save on the basis of reasons he can see for himself to be good. Autonomy, thus understood, is in direct opposition to obedience, which is submission to the will of another, irrespective of reasons. Following Kant's usage, political obedience is heteronymy of the will.

Now, political theory offers us one great argument designed to make the autonomy of the individual compatible with submission to the putative authority of the state. In a democracy, it is claimed, the citizen is both lawgiver and law-obeyer. Since he shares in the authorship of the laws, he submits to his own will in obeying them, and hence is autonomous, not heteronymous.

If this argument were valid, it would provide a genuine ground for a distinction between violent and nonviolent political actions. Violence would be a use of force proscribed by the laws or executive authority of a genuinely democratic state. The only possible justification of illegal or extralegal political acts would be a demonstration of the illegitimacy of the state, and this in turn would involve showing that the commands of the state were not expressions of the will of the people.

But the classic defense of democracy is *not* valid. For a variety of reasons, neither majority rule nor any other method of making decisions in the absence of unanimity can be shown to preserve the autonomy of the individual citizens. In a democracy, as in any state, obedience is heteronymy. The autonomous man is of necessity an anarchist.

Consequently, there is no valid *political* criterion for the justified use of force. Legality is, by itself, no justification. Now, of course, there are all manner of utilitarian arguments for submitting to the state and its agents, even if the state's claim to legitimacy is unfounded. The laws may command actions that are in fact morally obligatory or whose effects promise to be beneficial. Widespread submission to law may bring about a high level of order, regularity, and predictability in social relationships which is valuable independently of the particular character of the acts commanded. But in and of themselves, the acts of police and the commands of legislatures have no peculiar legitimacy or sanction. Men everywhere and always impute authority to established governments, and they are always wrong to do so.

II

The foregoing remarks are quite banal, to be sure. Very few serious students of politics will maintain either the democratic theory of legitimate authority or any alternatives to it. Nevertheless, like post-theological, demythologized Protestants who persist in raising prayers to a God they no longer believe in, modern men go on exhibiting a superstitious belief in the authority of the state. Consider, for example, a question now much debated: When is it permissible to resort to violence in politics? If 'violence' is taken to mean an *unjustified* use of force, then the answer to the question is obviously *never*. If the use of force were permissible, it would not, by definition, be violence, and if it were violent, it would not, by definition, be permissible. If 'violence' is taken in the strict sense to mean "an illegitimate or unauthorized use of force," then *every* political act, whether by private parties or by agents of the state, is violent, for there is no such thing as legitimate authority. If 'violence' is construed in the restricted sense as "bodily interference or the direct infliction of physical harm," then the obvious but correct rule is to resort to violence when less harmful or costly means fail, providing always that the balance of good and evil produced is superior to that promised by any available alternative.

These answers are all trivial, but that is precisely my point. Once the concept of violence is seen to rest on the unfounded distinction between legitimate and illegitimate political authority, the question of the appropriateness of violence simply dissolves. It is mere superstition to describe a policeman's beating of a helpless suspect as "an excessive use of force" while characterizing an attack by a crowd on the policeman as "a resort to violence." The implication of such a distinction is that the policeman, as the duly appointed representative of a legitimate government, has a right to use physical force, although no right to use "excessive" force, whereas the crowd of private citizens has no right at all to use even moderate physical force. But there are no legitimate governments, hence no special rights attaching to soldiers, policemen, magistrates, or other law-enforcement agents, hence no coherent distinction between violence and the legitimate use of force.

Consider, as a particular example, the occupation of buildings and the student strike at Columbia University during April and May of 1968. The consequences of those acts have not yet played themselves out, but I think certain general conclusions can be drawn. First, the total harm done by the students and their supporters was very small in comparison with the good results that were achieved. A month of classwork was lost, along with many tempers and a good deal of sleep. Someone—it is still not clear who—burned the research notes of a history professor, an act which, I am happy to say, produced a universal revulsion shared even by the SDS. In the following year, a number of classes were momentarily disrupted by SDS activists in an unsuccessful attempt to repeat the triumph of the previous spring.

Against this, what benefits flowed from the protest? A reactionary and thoroughly unresponsive administration was forced to resign; an all-university Senate of students, professors, and administrators was created, the first such body at Columbia. A callous and antisocial policy of university expansion into the surrounding neighborhood was reversed; some at least of the university's ties with the military were loosened or severed; and an entire community of students and professors were forced to confront moral and political issues which till then they had managed to ignore.

Could these benefits have been won at less cost? Considering the small cost of the uprising, the question seems to me a bit finicky; nevertheless, the answer is clearly, No. The history of administrative intransigence and faculty apathy at Columbia makes it quite clear that nothing short of a dramatic act such as the seizure of buildings could have deposed the university administration and produced a university senate. In retrospect, the affair seems to have been a quite prudent and restrained use of force.

Assuming this assessment to be correct, it is tempting to conclude, "In the Columbia case, violence was justified." But this conclusion is *totally wrong*, for it implies that a line can be drawn between legitimate and illegitimate forms of protest, the latter being justified only under special conditions and when all else has failed. We would all agree, I think, that, under a dictatorship, men have the right to defy the state or even to attack its representatives when their interests are denied and their needs ignored—the only rule that binds them is the general caution against doing more harm than they accomplish good. My purpose here is simply to argue that a modern industrial democracy, whatever merits it may have, is in this regard no different from a dictatorship. No special authority attaches to the laws of a representative, majoritarian state; it is only superstition and the myth of legitimacy that invests the judge, the policeman, or the official with an exclusive right to the exercise of certain kinds of force.

In the light of these arguments, it should be obvious that I see no merit in the doctrine of nonviolence, nor do I believe that any special and complex justification is needed for what is usually called "civil disobedience." A commitment to nonviolence can be understood in two different senses, depending on the interpretation given to the concept of violence. If violence is understood in the strict sense as the political use of force in ways proscribed by a lègitimate government, then of course the doctrine of nonviolence depends upon the assumption that there *are* or *could be* legitimate governments. Since I believe this assumption to be false, I can attribute no coherent meaning to this first conception of nonviolence.

If violence is understood, on the other hand, as the use of force to interfere with someone in a direct, bodily way or to injure him physically, then the doctrine of nonviolence is merely a subjective queasiness having no moral rationale. When you occupy the seats at a lunch counter for hours on end, thereby depriving the proprietor of the profits he would have made on ordinary sales during that time, you are taking money out of his pocket quite as effectively as if you had robbed his till or smashed his stock. If you persist in the sit-in until he goes into debt, loses his lunch counter, and takes a job as a day laborer, then you have done him a much greater injury than would be accomplished by a mere beating in a dark alley. He may deserve to be ruined, of course, but, if so, then he probably also deserves to be beaten. A penchant for such indirect coercion as a boycott or a sit-in is morally questionable, for it merely leaves the dirty work to the bank that forecloses on the mortgage or the policeman who carries out the eviction. Emotionally, the commitment to nonviolence is frequently a severely repressed expression of extreme hostility akin to the mortifications and self-flagellations of religious fanatics. Enough testimony has come from Black novelists and psychiatrists to make it clear that the philosophy of nonviolence is, for the American Negro, what Nietzsche called a "slave morality"—the principal difference is that, in traditional Christianity, God bears the guilt for inflicting pain on the wicked; in the social gospel, the law acts as the scourge.

The doctrine of civil disobedience is an American peculiarity growing out of the conflict between the authority claims of the state and the directly contradictory claims of individual conscience. In a futile attempt to deny and affirm the authority of the state simultaneously, a number of conscientious dissenters have claimed the right to disobey what they believe to be immoral laws, so long as they are prepared to submit to punishment by the state. A willingness to go to jail for one's beliefs is widely viewed in this country as evidence of moral sincerity, and even as a sort of argument for the position one is defending.

Now, tactically speaking, there is much to be said for legal martyrdom. As tyrannical governments are perpetually discovering, the sight of one's leader nailed to a cross has a marvelously bracing effect on the faithful members of a dissident sect. When the rulers are afflicted by the very principles they are violating, even the *threat* of self-sacrifice may force a government to its knees. But leaving tactics aside, no one has any moral obligation whatsoever to resist an unjust government openly rather than clandestinely. Nor has anyone a duty to invite and then to suffer unjust punishment. The choice is simple: if the law is right, follow it. If the law is wrong, evade it.

I think it is possible to understand why conscientious and morally concerned men should feel a compulsion to seek punishment for acts they genuinely believe to be right. Conscience is the echo of society's voice within us. The men of strongest and most independent conscience are, in a manner of speaking, just those who have most completely internalized this social voice, so that they hear and obey its commands even when no policeman compels their compliance. Ironically, it is these same men who are most likely to set themselves against the government in the name of ideals and principles to which they feel a higher loyalty. When a society violates the very principles it claims to hold, these men of conscience experience a terrible conflict. They are deeply committed to the principles society has taught them, principles they have truly come to believe. But they can be true to their beliefs only by setting themselves against the laws of the very society that has been their teacher and with whose authority they identify themselves. Such a conflict never occurs in men of weak conscience, who merely obey the law, however much it violates the moral precepts they have only imperfectly learned.

The pain of the conflict is too great to be borne; somehow, it must be alleviated. If the commitment to principle is weak, the individual submits, though he feels morally unclean for doing so. If the identification with society is weak, he rejects the society and becomes alienated, perhaps identifying with some other society. But if both conscience and identification are too strong to be broken, the only solution is to expiate the guilt by seeking social punishment for the breach of society's laws. Oddly enough, the expiation, instead of bringing them back into the fold of law-obeyers, makes it psychologically all the easier for them to continue their defiance of the state.

III

The foregoing conclusions seem to reach far beyond what the argument warrants. The classical theory of political authority may indeed be inadequate; it may even be that the concept of legitimate authority is incoherent; but surely *some* genuine distinction can be drawn between a politics of reason, rules, and compromise on the one hand, and the resort to violent conflict on the other! Are the acts of a rioting mob different only in degree from the calm and orderly processes of a duly constituted court of law? Such a view partakes more of novelty than of truth!

Unless I very much misjudge my audience, most readers will respond roughly in this manner. There may be a few still willing to break a lance for sovereignty and legitimate authority, and a few, I hope, who agree immediately with what I have said, but the distinction between violence and nonviolence in politics is too familiar to be so easily discarded. In this third section of my essay, therefore, I shall try to discover what makes the distinction so plausible, even though it is—I insist—unfounded.

The customary distinction between violent and nonviolent modes of social interaction seems to me to rest on *two* genuine distinctions: the first is the *subjective* distinction between the regular or accepted and the irregular or unexpected uses of force; the second is the *objective* distinction between those interests which are central or vital to an individual and those which are secondary or peripheral.

Consider first the subjective distinction between regular and irregular uses of force in social interactions. It seems perfectly appropriate to us that a conflict between two men who desire the same piece of land should be settled in favor of the one who can pull more money out of his pocket. We consider it regular and orderly that the full weight of the police power of the state be placed behind that settlement in order to ensure that nothing upset it. On the other hand, we consider it violent and disorderly to resolve the dispute by a fist fight or a duel. Yet what is the difference between the use of money, which is one kind of force, and the use of fists, which is another? Well, if we do not appeal to the supposed legitimacy of financial transactions or to the putative authority of the law, then the principal difference is that we are accustomed to settling disputes with dollars and we are no longer accustomed to settling them with fists.

Imagine how barbaric, how unjust, how *violent*, it must seem, to someone unfamiliar with the beauties of capitalism, that a man's ability to obtain medical care for his children should depend solely on the contingency that some other man can make a profit from his productive labor! Is the Federal Government's seizure of my resources for the purpose of killing Asian peasants less violent than a bandit's extortion of tribute at gunpoint? Yet we are accustomed to the one and unaccustomed to the other.

The objective distinction between central and peripheral interests also shapes our conception of what is violent in politics. When my peripheral or secondary interests are at stake in a conflict, I quite naturally consider only a moderate use of force to be justified. Anything more, I will probably call "violence." What I tend to forget, of course, is that other parties to the conflict may find their primary interests challenged and, hence, may have a very different view of what is and is not violent. In the universities, for example, most of the student challenges have touched only on the peripheral interests of professors. No matter what is decided about ROTC, curriculum, the disposition of the endowment, or Black studies, the typical philosophy professor's life will be largely unchanged. His tenure, salary, working conditions, status, and family life remain the same. Hence he is likely to take a tolerant view of building seizures and sit-ins. But let a classroom be disrupted, and he cries out that violence has no place on campus. What he means is that force has been used in a way that touches one of his deeper concerns.

The concept of violence serves as a rhetorical device for proscribing those political uses of force which one considers inimical to one's central interests. Since different social groups have different central interests and can draw on different kinds of force, it follows that there are conflicting definitions of violence. Broadly speaking, in the United States today, there are four conceptions of violence corresponding to four distinct socioeconomic classes.

The first view is associated with the established financial and political interests in the country. It identifies the violent with the illegal, and condemns all challenges to the authority of the state and all assaults on the rights of property as beyond the limits of permissible politics. The older segments of the business community adopt this view, along with the military establishment and the local elites of middle America. Robert Taft was once a perfect symbol of this sector of opinion.

The second view is associated with the affluent, educated, technical and professional middle class in America, together with the new, rapidly growing, future-oriented sectors of the economy, such as the communications industry, electronics, etc. They accept, even welcome, dissent, demonstration, ferment, and—within limits—attacks on property in ghetto areas. They look with favor on civil disobedience and feel at ease with extralegal tactics of social change. Their interests are identified with what is new in American society, and they are confident of coming out on top in the competition for wealth and status within an economy built on the principle of reward for profitable performance.

The "liberals," as this group is normally called, can afford to encourage modes of dissent or disruption that do not challenge the economic and social arrangements on which their success is based. They will defend rent strikes, grape boycotts, or lunch-counter sit-ins with the argument that unemployment and starvation are a form of violence also. Since they are themselves in competition with the older elite for power and prestige, they tend to view student rebels and black militants as their allies, up to the point at which their own interests are attacked. But when tactics are used that threaten their positions in universities, in corporations, or in affluent suburbs, then the liberals cry *violence* also, and call for the police. A poignant example of this class is the liberal professor who cheers the student rebels as they seize the Administration building and then recoils in horror at the demand that he share his authority to determine curriculum and decide promotions.

The third view of violence is that held by working-class and lower-middle-class Americans, those most often referred to as the "white backlash." They perceive the principal threat to their interests as coming from the bottom class of ghetto dwellers, welfare clients, and nonunionized laborers who demand more living space, admission to union jobs with union wages, and a larger share of the social product. To this hard-pressed segment of American society, 'violence' means street crime, ghetto riots, civil-rights marches into all-white neighborhoods, and antiwar attacks on the patriotic symbols of constituted authority with which backlash America identifies. Studies of the petty bourgeoisie in Weimar Germany suggest, and George Wallace's presidential campaign of 1968 confirms, that the lower middle class, when it finds itself pressed between inflationary prices and demands from the lower class, identifies its principal enemy as the lower class. So we find the classic political alliance of old established wealth with right-wing populist elements, both of which favor a repressive response to attacks on authority and a strong governmental policy toward the "violence" of demands for change.

The fourth view of violence is the revolutionary counterdefinition put forward by the outclass and its sympathizers within the liberal wing of the established order. Two complementary rhetorical devices are employed. First, the connotation of the term 'violence' is accepted, but the application of the term is reversed: police are violent, not rioters; employers, not strikers; the American army, not the enemy. In this way, an attack is mounted on the government's claim to possess the right to rule. Secondly, the denotation of the term is held constant and the connotation reversed. Violence is good, not bad; legitimate, not illegitimate. It is, in Stokely Carmichael's great rhetorical flourish, "as American as cherry pie." Since the outclass of rebels has scant access to the instruments of power used by established social classes—wealth, law, police power, legislation—it naturally seeks to legitimize the riots, harassments, and street crime which are its only weapons. Equally naturally, the rest of society labels such means "violent" and suppresses them.

In the complex class struggle for wealth and power in America, each of us must decide for himself which group he will identify with. It is not my purpose here to urge one choice rather than another. My sole aim is to argue that the concept of violence has no useful role to play in the deliberations leading to that choice. Whatever other considerations of utility and social justice one appeals to, no weight should be given to the view that *some* uses of force are prima facie ruled out as illegitimate and hence "violent" or that other uses of force are prima facie ruled in as legitimate, or legal. Furthermore, in the advancement of dissenting positions by illegal means, no special moral merit attaches to the avoiding, as it were, of body contact. Physical harm may be among the most serious injuries that can be done to an opponent, but, if so, it differs only in degree and not in kind from the injuries inflicted by so-called "non-violent" techniques of political action.

IV

The myth of legitimate authority is the secular reincarnation of that religious superstition which has finally ceased to play a significant role in the affairs of men. Like Christianity, the worship of the state has its fundamentalists, its revisionists, its ecumenicists (or world-Federalists), and its theological rationale. The philosophical anarchist is the atheist of politics. I began my discussion with the observation that the belief in legitimacy, like the penchant for transcendent metaphysics, is an ineradicable irrationality of the human experience. However, the slow extinction of religious faith over the past two centuries may encourage us to hope that in time anarchism, like atheism, will become the accepted conviction of enlightened and rational men.

NOTES

1. What follows is a summary of analyses I have published elsewhere. The concept of political power is treated in Chapter III of *The Poverty of Liberalism* (Boston: Beacon Press, 1968). The concepts of legitimacy and authority are analyzed in my essay on "Political Philosophy" in Arthur Danto, ed., *The Harper Guide to Philosophy* (New York: Harper & Row, 1970).

2. See Robert A. Dahl, "The Concept of Power," *Behavioral Science* (July 1957), for just such a classification.

3. See "Political Philosophy," in Danto, *op. cit.*

The Justification of Authority

THOMAS HOBBES

OF POWER, WORTH, DIGNITY, HONOUR, AND WORTHINESS

The power *of a Man*, (to take it Universally,) is his present means, to obtain some future apparent Good. And is either *Originall*, or *Instrumentall*.

Naturall Power, is the eminence of the Faculties of Body, or Mind: as extraordinary Strength, Forme, Prudence, Arts, Eloquence, Liberality, Nobility. *Instrumentall* are those Powers, which acquired by these, or by fortune, are means and Instruments to acquire more: as Riches, Reputation, Friends, and the secret working of God, which men call Good Luck. For the nature of Power, is in this point, like to Fame, increasing as it proceeds; or like the motion of heavy bodies, which the further they go, make still the more hast. . . . absolute; but a thing dependant on the need and judgement of another. An able conductor of Souldiers, is of great Price in time of War present, or imminent; but in Peace not so. A learned and uncorrupt Judge, is much Worth in time of Peace; but not so much in War. And as in other things, so in men, not the seller, but the buyer determines the Price. For let a man (as most men do,) rate themselves as the highest Value they can; yet their true Value is no more than it is esteemed by others.

The manifestation of the Value we set on one another, is that which is commonly called Honouring, and Dishonouring. To Value a man at a high rate, is to *Honour* him; at a low rate, is to *Dishonour* him. But high, and low, in this case, is to be understood by comparison to the rate that each man setteth on himselfe. . . .

OF THE DIFFERENCE OF MANNERS

By Manners, I mean not here, Decency of behaviour; as how one man should salute another, or how a man should wash his mouth, or pick his teeth before company, and such other points of the *Small Moralls*; But those qualities of man-kind, that concern their living together in Peace, and Unity. To which end we are to consider, that the Felicity of this life, consisteth not in the repose of a mind satisfied. For there is no such *Finis ultimus*, (utmost ayme,) nor *Summum Bonum*, (greatest Good,) as is spoken of in the Books of the old Morall Philosophers. Nor can a man any more live, whose Desires are at an end, than he, whose Senses and Imaginations are at a stand. Felicity is a continuall progresse of the desire, from one object to another; the attaining of the former, being still but the way to the later. The cause whereof is, That the object of mans desire, is not to enjoy once onely, and for one instant of time; but to assure for ever, the way of his future desire. And therefore the voluntary actions, and inclinations of all men, tend, not only to the procuring, but also to the assuring of a contented life; and differ onely in the way: which ariseth partly from the diversity of passions, in divers men; and partly from the difference

---

Thomas Hobbes (1588-1679) was an English philosopher who defended an original and distinctive version of the social contract theory.

From Hobbes's *Leviathan* (1651).

of the knowledge, or opinion each one has of the causes, which produce the effect desired.

So that in the first place, I put for a generall inclination of all mankind, a perpetuall and restlesse desire of Power after power, that ceaseth onely in Death. And the cause of this, is not alwayes that a man hopes for a more intensive delight, than he has already attained to; or that he cannot be content with a moderate power: but because he cannot assure the power and means to live well, which he hath present, without the acquisition of more. And from hence it is, that Kings, whose power is greatest, turn their endeavours to the assuring it at home by Lawes, or abroad by Wars: and when that is done, there succeedeth a new desire; in some, of Fame from new Conquest; in others, of ease and sensuall pleasure; in others, of admiration, or being flattered for excellence in some art, or other ability of the mind.

Competition of Riches, Honour, Command, or other power, enclineth to Contention, Enmity, and War: Because the way of one Competitor, to the attaining of his desire, is to kill, subdue, supplant, or repell the other. Particularly, competition of praise, enclineth to a reverence of Antiquity. For men contend with the living, not with the dead; to these ascribing more than due, that they may obscure the glory of the other.

Desire of Ease, and sensuall Delight, disposeth men to obey a common Power: Because by such Desires, a man doth abandon the protection might be hoped for from his own Industry, and labour. Fear of Death, and Wounds, disposeth to the same; and for the same reason. On the contrary, needy men, and hardy, not contented with their present condition; as also, all men that are ambitious of Military command, are enclined to continue the causes of warre; and to stirre up trouble and sedition: for there is no honour Military but by warre; nor any such hope to mend an ill game, as by causing a new shuffle.

Desire of Knowledge, and Arts of Peace, enclineth men to obey a common Power: For such Desire, containeth a desire of leasure; and consequently protection from some other Power than their own.

Desire of Praise, disposeth to laudable actions, such as please them whose judgement they value; for of those men whom we contemn, we contemn also the Praises. Desire of Fame after death does the same. And though after death, there be no sense of the praise given us on Earth, as being joyes, that are either swallowed up in the unspeakable joyes of Heaven, or extinguished in the extreme torments of Hell: yet is not such Fame vain; because men have a present delight therein, from the foresight of it, and of the benefit that may rebound thereby to their posterity: which though they now see not, yet they imagine; and anything that is pleasure in the sense, the same also is pleasure in the imagination. . . .

OF THE NATURALL CONDITION OF MANKIND, AS CONCERNING THEIR FELICITY, AND MISERY

Nature hath made men so equall, in the faculties of body, and mind; as that though there bee found one man sometimes manifestly stronger in body, or of quicker mind then another; yet when all is reckoned together, the difference between man, and man, is not so considerable, as that one man can thereupon claim to himselfe any benefit, to which another may not pretend, as well as he. For as to the strength of body, the weakest has strength enough to kill the strongest, either by secret machination, or by confederacy with others, that are in the same danger with himselfe.

And as to the faculties of the mind, (setting aside the arts grounded upon words, and especially that skill of proceeding upon generall, and infallible rules, called Science; which very few have, and but in few things; as being not a native faculty, born with us; nor attained, (as Prudence,) while we look after somewhat els,) I find yet a greater equality amongst men, than that of strength. For Prudence, is but Experience; which equall time, equally bestowes on all men, in those things they equally apply themselves unto. That which may perhaps make such equality incredible, is but a vain conceipt of ones owne wisdome, which almost all men think they have in a greater degree, than the Vulgar; that is, than all men but themselves, and a few others, whom by Fame, or for concurring with themselves, they approve. For such is the nature of men, that howsoever they may acknowledge many others to be more witty, or more eloquent, or more learned; Yet they will hardly believe there be many so wise as themselves: For they see their own wit at hand, and other mens at a distance. But this proveth rather that men are in that point equall, than unequall. For there is not ordinarily a greater signe of the equall distribution of any thing, than that every man is contented with his share.

From this equality of ability, ariseth equality of hope in the attaining of our Ends. And therefore if any two men desire the same thing, which neverthelesse they cannot both enjoy, they become enemies; and in the way to their End, (which is principally their owne conservation, and sometimes their delectation only,) endeavour to destroy, or subdue one an other. And from hence it comes to passe, that where an Invader hath no more to feare, than an other mans single power; if one plant, sow, build, or possesse a convenient Seat, others may probably be expected to come prepared with forces united, to dispossesse, and deprive him, not only of the fruit of his labour, but also of his life, or liberty. And the Invader again is in the like danger of another.

And from this diffidence of one another, there is no way for any man to secure himselfe, so reasonable, as Anticipation; that is, by force, or wiles, to master the persons of all men he can, so long, till he see no other power great enough to endanger him: And this is no more than his own conservation requireth, and is generally allowed. Also because there be some, that taking pleasure in contemplating their own power in the acts of conquest, which they pursue farther than their security requires; if others, that otherwise would be glad to be at ease within modest bounds, should not by invasion increase their power, they would not be able, long time, by standing only on their defence, to subsist. And by consequence, such augmentation of dominion over men, being necessary to a mans conservation, it ought to be allowed him.

Againe, men have no pleasure, (but on the contrary a great deale of griefe) in keeping company, where there is no power able to over-awe them all. For every man looketh that his companion should value him, at the same rate he sets upon himselfe: And upon all signes of contempt, or undervaluing, naturally endeavours, as far as he dares (which amongst them that have no common power, to keep them in quiet, is far enough to make them destroy each other,) to extort a greater value from his contemners, by dommage; and from others, by the example.

So that in the nature of man, we find three principall causes of quarrell. First, Competition; Secondly, Diffidence; Thirdly, Glory.

The first, maketh men invade for Gain; the second, for Safety; and the third, for Reputation. The first use Violence, to make themselves Masters of other mens persons, wives, children, and cattell; the second, to defend them; the third, for trifles, as a word, a smile, a different opinion, and any other signe of undervalue, either direct in their Persons, or by reflexion in their Kindred, their Friends, their Nation, their Profession, or their Name.

Hereby it is manifest, that during the time men live without a common Power to keep them all in awe, they are in that condition which is called Warre; and such a warre, as is of every man, against every man. For WARRE, consisteth not in Battell onely, or the act of fighting; but in a tract of time, wherein the Will to contend by Battell is sufficiently known: and therefore the notion of *Time*, is to be considered in the nature of Warre; as it is in the nature of Weather. For as the nature of Foule weather, lyeth not in a showre or two of rain; but in an inclination thereto of many dayes together: So the nature of War, consisteth not in actuall fighting; but in the known disposition thereto, during all the time there is no assurance to the contrary. All other time is PEACE.

Whatsoever therefore is consequent to a time of Warre, where every man is Enemy to every man; the same is consequent to the time, wherein men live without other security, than what their own strength, and their own invention shall furnish them withall. In such condition, there is no place for Industry; because the fruit thereof is uncertain: and consequently no Culture of the Earth; no Navigation, nor use of the commodities that may be imported by Sea; no commodious Building; no Instruments of moving, and removing such things as require much force; no Knowledge of the face of the Earth; no account of Time; no Arts; no Letters; no Society; and which is worst of all, continuall feare, and danger of violent death; And the life of man, solitary, poore, nasty, brutish, and short.

It may seem strange to some man, that has not well weighed these things; that Nature should thus dissociate, and render men apt to invade, and destroy one another: and he may therefore, not trusting to this Inference, made from the Passions, desire perhaps to have the same confirmed by Experience. Let him therefore consider with himselfe, when taking a journey, he armes himselfe, and seeks to go well accompanied; when going to sleep, he locks his dores; when even in his house he locks his chests; and this when he knows there bee Lawes, and publike Officers, armed, to revenge all injuries shall bee done him; what opinion he has of his fellow subjects, when he rides armed; of his fellow Citizens, when he locks his dores; and of his children, and servants, when he locks his chests. Does he not there as much accuse mankind by his actions, as I do by my words? But neither of us accuse mans nature in it. The Desires, and other Passions of man, are in themselves no Sin. No more are the Actions, that proceed from those Passions, till they know a Law that forbids them: which till Lawes be made they cannot know: nor can any Law be made, till they have agreed upon the Person that shall make it.

It may peradventure be thought, there was never such a time, nor condition of warre as this; and I believe it was never generally so, over all the world: but there are many places, where they live so now. For the savage people in many places of *America,* except the government of small Families, the concord whereof dependeth on naturall lust, have no government at all; and live at this day in that brutish manner, as I said before. Howsoever, it may be perceived what manner of life there would be, where there were no common Power to feare; by the manner of life, which men that have formerly lived under a peacefull government, use to degenerate into, in a civill Warre.

But though there had never been any time, wherein particular men were in a condition of warre one against another; yet in all times, Kings, and Persons of Soveraigne authority, because of their Independency, are in continuall jealousies, and in the state and posture of Gladiators; having their weapons pointing, and their eyes fixed on one another; that is, their Forts, Garrisons, and Guns upon the Frontiers of their Kingdomes; and continuall Spyes upon their neighbours; which is a posture of War. But because they uphold thereby, the Industry of their Subjects; there does not follow from it, that misery, which accompanies the Liberty of particular men.

To this warre of every man against every man, this also is consequent; that nothing can be Unjust. The notions of Right and Wrong, Justice and Injustice have there no place. Where there is no common Power, there is no Law: where no Law, no Injustice. Force, and Fraud, are in warre the two Cardinall vertues. Justice, and Injustice are none of the Faculties neither of the Body, nor Mind. If they were, they might be in a man that were alone in the world, as well as his Senses, and Passions. They are Qualities, that relate to men in Society, not in Solitude. It is consequent also to the same condition, that there be no Propriety, no Dominion, no *Mine* and *Thine* distinct; but onely that to be every mans that he can get; and for so long, as he can keep it. And thus much for the ill condition, which man by meer Nature is actually placed in; though with a possibility to come out of it, consisting partly in the Passions, partly in his Reason.

The Passions that encline men to Peace, are Feare of Death; Desire of such things as are necessary to commodious living; and a Hope by their Industry to obtain them. And Reason suggesteth convenient Articles of Peace, upon which men may be drawn to agreement. These Articles, are they, which otherwise are called the Lawes of Nature: whereof I shall speak more particularly, in the two following Chapters.

OF THE FIRST AND SECOND NATURALL LAWES, AND OF CONTRACTS

The RIGHT OF NATURE, which Writers commonly call *Jus Naturale*, is the Liberty each man hath, to use his own power, as he will himselfe, for the preservation of his own Nature; that is to say, of his own Life; and consequently, of doing any thing, which in his own Judgement, and Reason, hee shall conceive to be the aptest means thereunto.

By LIBERTY, is understood, according to the proper signification of the word, the absence of externall Impediments: which Impediments, may oft take away part of a mans power to do what hee would; but cannot hinder him from using the power left him, according as his judgement, and reason shall dictate to him.

A LAW OF NATURE, (*Lex Naturalis*,) is a Precept, or generall Rule, found out by Reason, by which a man is forbidden to do, that, which is destructive of his life, or taketh away the means of preserving the same; and to omit, that, by which he thinketh it may be best preserved. For though they that speak of this subject, use to confound *Jus*, and *Lex*, *Right* and *Law*; yet they ought to be distinguished; because RIGHT, consisteth in liberty to do, or to forbeare; Whereas LAW, determineth, and bindeth to one of them: so that Law, and Right, differ as much, as Obligation, and Liberty; which in one and the same matter are inconsistent.

And because the condition of Man, (as hath been declared in the precedent Chapter) is a condition of Warre of every one against every one; in which case every one is governed by his own Reason; and there is nothing he can make use of, that may not be a help unto him, in preserving his life against his enemyes; It followeth, that in such a condition, every man has a Right to every thing; even to one anothers body. And therefore, as long as this naturall Right of every man to every thing endureth, there can be no security to any man, (how strong or wise soever he be,) of living out the time, which Nature ordinarily alloweth men to live. And consequently it is a precept, or generall rule of Reason, *That every man, ought to endeavour Peace, as farre as he has hope of obtaining it; and when he cannot obtain it, that he may seek, and use, all helps, and advantages of Warre*. The first branch of which Rule, containeth the first, and Fundamentall Law of Nature; which is, *to seek Peace, and follow it*. The Second, the summe of the Right of Nature; which is, *By all means we can, to defend our selves*.

From this Fundamentall Law of Nature, by which men are commanded to endeavour Peace, is derived this second Law; *That a man be willing, when others are so too, as farre-forth, as for Peace, and defence of himselfe he shall think it necessary, to lay down this right to all things; and be contented with so much liberty against other men, as he would allow other men against himselfe*. For as long as every man holdeth this Right, of doing any thing he liketh; so long are all men in the condition of Warre. But if other men will not lay down their Right, as well as he; then there is no Reason for any one, to devest himselfe of his: For that were to expose himselfe to Prey, (which no man is bound to) rather than to dispose himselfe to Peace. This is that Law of the Gospell; *Whatsoever you require that others should do to you, that do ye to them*. And that Law of all men, *Quod tibi fieri non vis, alteri ne feceris*.

To *lay downe* a mans *Right* to any thing, is to *devest* himselfe of the *Liberty*, of hindring another of the benefit of his own Right to the same. For he that renounceth, or passeth away his Right, giveth not to any other man a Right which he had not before; because there is nothing to which every man had not Right by Nature: but onely standeth out of his way, that he may enjoy his own originall Right, without hindrance from him; not without hindrance from another. So that the effect which redoundeth to one man, by another mans defect of Right, is but so much diminution of impediments to the use of his own Right originall.

Right is layd aside, either by simply Renouncing it; or by Transferring it to another. By *Simply* RENOUNCING; when he cares not to whom the benefit thereof redoundeth. By TRANSFERRING; when he intendeth the benefit thereof to some certain person, or persons. And when a man hath in either manner abandoned, or granted away his Right; then is he said to be OBLIGED, or BOUND, not to hinder those, to whom such Right is granted, or abandoned, from the benefit of it: and that he *Ought*, and it is his DUTY, not to make voyd that voluntary act of his own: and that such hindrance is INJUSTICE, and INJURY, as being *Sine Jure*; the Right being before renounced, or transferred. So that *Injury*, or *Injustice*, in the controversies of the world, is somewhat like to that, which in the disputations of Scholers is called *Absurdity*. For as it is there called an Absurdity, to contradict what one maintained in the Beginning: so in the world, it is called Injustice, and Injury, voluntarily to undo that, which from the beginning he had voluntarily done. The way by which a man either simply Renounceth, or Transferreth his Right, is a Declaration, or Signification, by some voluntary and sufficient signe, or signes, that he doth so Renounce, or Transferre; or hath so Renounced, or Transferred the same, to him that accepteth it. And these Signes are either Words onely, or Actions onely; or (as it happeneth most often) both Words and Actions. And the same are the BONDS, by which men are bound, and obliged: Bonds, that have their strength, not from their own Nature, (for nothing is more easily broken then a mans word,) but from Feare of some evill consequence upon the rupture.

Whensoever a man Transferreth his Right, or Renounceth it; it is either in consideration of some Right reciprocally transferred to himselfe; or for some other good he hopeth for thereby. For it is a voluntary act: and of the voluntary acts of every man, the object is some *Good to himselfe*. And therefore there be some Rights, which no man can be understood by any words, or other signes, to have abandoned, or transferred. As first a man cannot lay down the right of resisting them, that assault him by force, to take away his life; because he cannot be understood to ayme thereby, at any Good to himselfe. The same may be sayd of Wounds, and Chayns, and Imprisonment; both because there is no benefit consequent to such patience; as there is to the patience of suffering another to be wounded, or imprisoned: as also because a man cannot tell, when he seeth men proceed against him by violence, whether they intend his death or not. And lastly the motive, and end for which this renouncing, and transferring of Right is introduced, is nothing else but the security of a mans person, in his life, and in the means of so preserving life, as not to be weary of it. And therefore if a man by words, or other signes, seem to despoyle himselfe of the End, for which those signes were intended; he is not to be understood as if he meant it, or that it was his will; but that he was ignorant of how such words and actions were to be interpreted.

The mutuall transferring of Right, is that which men call CONTRACT. . . .

OF THE CAUSES, GENERATION, AND DEFINITION OF A COMMON-WEALTH

The finall Cause, End, or Designe of men, (who naturally love Liberty, and Dominion over others,) in the introduction of that restraint upon themselves, (in which wee see them live in Common-wealths,) is the foresight of their own preservation, and of a more contented life thereby; that is to say, of getting themselves out from that miserable condition of Warre, which is necessarily consequent (as hath been shewn) to the naturall Passions of men, when there is no visible Power to keep them in awe, and tye them by feare of punishment to the performance of their Covenants, and observation of those Lawes of Nature set down in the fourteenth and fifteenth Chapters.

For the Lawes of Nature (as *Justice, Equity, Modesty, Mercy*, and (in summe) *doing to others, as wee would be done to*,) of themselves, without the terrour of some Power, to cause them to be observed, are contrary to our naturall Passions, that carry us to Partiality, Pride, Revenge, and the like. And Covenants, without the Sword, are but Words, and of no strength to secure a man at all. Therefore notwithstanding the Lawes of Nature, (which every one hath then kept, when he has the will to keep them, when he can do it safely,) if there be no Power erected, or not great enough for our security; every man will and may lawfully rely on his own strength and art, for caution against all other men. And in all places, where men have lived by small Families, to robbe and spoyle one another, has been a Trade, and so farre from being reputed against the Law of Nature, that the greater spoyles they gained, the greater was their honour; and men observed no other Lawes therein, but the Lawes of Honour; that is, to abstain from cruelty, leaving to men their lives, and instruments of husbandry. And as small Familyes did then; so now do Cities and Kingdomes which are but greater Families (for their own security) enlarge their Dominions, upon all pretences of danger, and fear of Invasion, or assistance that may be given to Invaders, endeavour as much as they can, to subdue, or weaken their neighbours, by open force, and secret arts, for want of other Caution, justly; and are remembred for it in after ages with honour.

Nor is it the joyning together of a small number of men, that gives them this security; because in small numbers, small additions on the one side or the other, make the advantage of strength so great, as is sufficient to carry the Victory; and therefore gives encouragement to an Invasion. The Multitude sufficient to confide in for our Security, is not determined by any certain number, but by comparison with the Enemy we feare; and is then sufficient, when the odds of the Enemy is not of so visible and conspicuous moment, to determine the event of warre, as to move him to attempt.

And be there never so great a Multitude; yet if their actions be directed according to their particular judgements, and particular appetites, they can expect thereby no defence, nor protection, neither against a Common enemy, nor against the injuries of one another. For being distracted in opinions concerning the best use and application of their strength, they do not help, but hinder one another; and reduce their strength by mutuall opposition to nothing: whereby they are easily, not onely subdued by a very few that agree together; but also when there is no common enemy, they make warre upon each other, for their particular interests. For if we could suppose a great Multitude of men to consent in the observation of Justice, and other Lawes of Nature, without a common Power to keep them all in awe; we might as well suppose all Man-kind to do the same; and then there neither would be, nor need to be any Civill Government, or Common-wealth at all; because there would be Peace without subjection.

Nor is it enough for the security, which men desire should last all the time of their life, that they be governed, and directed by one judgement, for a limited time; as in one Battell, or one Warre. For though they obtain a Victory by their unanimous endeavour against a forraign enemy; yet afterwards, when either they have no common enemy, or he that by one part is held for an enemy, is by another part held for a friend, they must needs by the difference of their interests dissolve, and fall again into a Warre amongst themselves.

It is true, that certain living creatures, as Bees, and Ants, live sociably one with another, (which are therefore by *Aristotle* numbred amongst Politicall creatures;) and yet have no other direction, than their particular judgements and appetites; nor speech, whereby one of them can signifie to another, what he thinks expedient for the common benefit: and therefore some man may perhaps desire to know, why Man-kind cannot do the same. To which I answer,

First, that men are continually in competition for Honour and Dignity, which these creatures are not; and consequently amongst men there ariseth on that ground, Envy and Hatred, and finally Warre; but amongst these not so.

Secondly, that amongst these creatures, the Common good differeth not from the Private; and being by nature enclined to their private, they procure thereby the common benefit. But man, whose Joy consisteth in comparing himselfe with other men, can relish nothing but what is eminent.

Thirdly, that these creatures, having not (as man) the use of reason, do not see, nor think they see any fault, in the administration of their common businesse: whereas amongst men, there are very many, that thinke themselves wiser, and abler to govern the Publique, better than the rest; and these strive to reforme and innovate, one this way, another that way; and thereby bring it into Distraction and Civill warre.

Fourthly, that these creatures, though they have some use of voice, in making knowne to one another their desires, and other affections; yet they want that art of words, by which some men can represent to others, that which is Good, in the likenesse of Evill; and Evill, in the likenesse of Good; and augment, or diminish the apparent greatnesse of Good and Evill; discontenting men, and troubling their Peace at their pleasure.

Fiftly, irrationall creatures cannot distinguish betweene *Injury*, and *Dammage*; and therefore as long as they be at ease, they are not offended with their fellowes: whereas Man is then most troublesome, when he is most at ease: for then it is that he loves to shew his Wisdome, and controule the Actions of them that governe the Common-wealth.

Lastly, the agreement of these creatures is Naturall; that of men, is by Covenant only, which is Artificiall: and therefore it is no wonder if there be somewhat else required (besides Covenant) to make their Agreement constant and lasting; which is a Common Power, to keep them in awe, and to direct their actions to the Common Benefit.

The only way to erect such a Common Power, as may be able to defend them from the invasion of Forraigners, and the injuries of one another, and thereby to secure them in such sort, as that by their owne industrie, and by the fruites of the Earth, they may nourish themselves and live contentedly; is, to conferre all their power and strength upon one Man, or upon one Assembly of men, that may reduce all their Wills, by plurality of voices, unto one Will: which is as much as to say, to appoint one man, or Assembly of men, to beare their Person; and every one to owne, and acknowledge himselfe to be Author of whatsoever he that so beareth their Person, shall Act, or cause to be Acted, in those things which concerne the Common Peace and Safetie; and therein to submit their Wills, every one to his Will, and their Judgements, to his Judgment. This is more than Consent, or Concord; it is a reall Unitie of them all, in one and the same Person, made by Covenant of every man with every man, in such manner, as if every man should say to every man, *I Authorise and give up my Right of Governing my selfe, to this Man, or to this Assembly of men, on this condition, that thou give up thy Right to him, and Authorise all his Actions in like manner*. This done, the Multitude so united in one Person, is called a COMMON-WEALTH, in latine CIVITAS. This is the Generation of that great LEVIATHAN, or rather (to speake more reverently) of that *Mortall God*, to which wee owe under the *Immortall God*, our peace and defence. For by this Authoritie, given him by every particular man in the Common-Wealth, he hath the use of so much Power and Strength conferred on him, that by terror thereof, he is inabled to forme the wills of them all, to Peace at home, and mutuall ayd against their enemies abroad. And in him consisteth the Essence of the Common-wealth; which (to define it,) is *One Person, of whose Acts a great Multitude, by mutuall Covenants one with another, have made themselves every one the Author, to the end he may use the strength and means of them all, as he shall think expedient, for their Peace and Common Defence*.

And he that carryeth this Person, is called SOVERAIGNE, and said to have *Soveraigne Power*; and every one besides, his SUBJECT.

The attaining to this Soveraigne Power, is by two wayes. One, by Naturall force; as when a man maketh his children, to submit themselves, and their children to his government, as being able to destroy them if they refuse; or by Warre subdueth his enemies to his will, giving them their lives on that condition. The other, is when men agree amongst themselves, to submit to some Man, or Assembly of men, voluntarily, on confidence to be protected by him against all others. This later, may be called a Political Common-wealth or Common-wealth by *Institution*; and the former, a Common-wealth by *Acquisition*. And first, I shall speak of a Common-wealth by Institution.

OF THE RIGHTS OF SOVERAIGNES BY INSTITUTION

A *Common-wealth* is said to be *Instituted*, when a *Multitude* of men do Agree, and *Covenant, every one, with every one,* that to whatsoever *Man*, or *Assembly of Men*, shall be given by the major part, the *Right* to *Present* the Person of them all, (that is to say, to be their *Representative*;) every one, as well he that *Voted for it*, as he that *Voted against it*, shall *Authorise* all the Actions and Judgements, of that Man, or Assembly of men, in the same manner, as if they were his own, to the end, to live peaceably amongst themselves, and be protected against other men.

From this Institution of a Common-wealth are derived all the *Rights*, and *Facultyes* of him, or them, on whom the Soveraigne Power is conferred by the consent of the People assembled.

First, because they Covenant, it is to be understood, they are not obliged by former Covenant to any thing repugnant hereunto. And Consequently they that have already Instituted a Common-wealth, being thereby bound by Covenant, to own the Actions, and Judgements of one, cannot lawfully make a new Covenant, amongst themselves, to be obedient to any other, in any thing whatsoever, without his permission. And therefore, they that are subjects to a Monarch, cannot without his leave cast off Monarchy, and return to the confusion of a disunited Multitude; nor transferre their Person from him that beareth it, to another Man, or other Assembly of men: for they are bound, every man to every man, to Own, and be reputed Author of all, that he that already is their Soveraigne, shall do, and judge fit to be done: so that any one man dissenting, all the rest should break their Covenant made to that man, which is injustice: and they have also every man given the Soveraignty to him that beareth their Person; and therefore if they depose him, they take from him that which is his own, and so again it is injustice. Besides, if he that attempteth to depose his Soveraign, be killed, or punished by him for such attempt, he is author of his own punishment, as being by the Institution, Author of all his Soveraign shall do: And because it is injustice for a man to do any thing, for which he may be punished by his own authority, he is also upon that title, unjust. And whereas some men have pretended for their disobedience to their Soveraign, a new Covenant, made, not with men, but with God; this also is unjust: for there is no Covenant with God, but by mediation of some body that representeth Gods Person; which none doth but Gods Lieutenant, who hath the Soveraignty under God. But this pretence of Covenant with God, is so evident a lye, even in the pretenders own consciences, that it is not onely an act of an unjust, but also of a vile, and unmanly disposition.

Secondly, Because the Right of bearing the Person of them all, is given to him they make Soveraigne, by Covenant onely of one to another, and not of him to any of them; there can happen no breach of Covenant on the part of the Soveraigne; and consequently none of his Subjects, by any pretence of forfeiture, can be freed from his Subjection. That he which is made Soveraigne maketh no Covenant with his Subjects beforehand, is manifest; because either he must make it with the whole multitude, as one party to the Covenant; or he must make a severall Covenant with every man. With the whole, as one party, it is impossible; because as yet they are not one Person: and if he make so many severall Covenants as there be men, those Covenants after he hath the Soveraignty are voyd, because what act soever can be pretended by any one of them for breach thereof, is the act both of himselfe, and of all the rest, because done in the Person, and by the Right of every one of them in particular. Besides, if any one, or more of them, pretend a breach of the Covenant made by the Soveraigne at his Institution; and others, or one other of his Subjects, or himselfe alone, pretend there was no such breach, there is in this case, no Judge to decide the controversie: it returns therefore to the Sword again; and every man recovereth the right of Protecting himselfe by his own strength, contrary to the designe they had in the Institution. It is therefore in vain to grant Soveraignty by way of precedent Covenant. The opinion that any Monarch receiveth his Power by Covenant, that is to say on Condition, proceedeth from want of understanding this easie truth, that Covenants being but words, and breath, have no force to oblige, contain, constrain, or protect any man, but what it has from the publique Sword; that is, from the untyed hands of that Man, or Assembly of men that hath the Soveraignty, and whose actions are avouched by them all, and performed by the strength of them all, in him united. But when an Assembly of men is made Soveraigne; then no man imagineth any such Covenant to have past in the Institution; for no man is so dull as to say, for example, the People of *Rome*, made a Covenant with the Romans, to hold the Soveraignty on such or such conditions; which not performed, the Romans might lawfully depose the Roman People. That men see not the reason to be alike in a Monarchy, and in a Popular Government, proceedeth from the ambition of some, that are kinder to the government of an Assembly, whereof they may hope to participate, than of Monarchy, which they despair to enjoy.

Thirdly, because the major part hath by consenting voices declared a Soveraigne; he that dissented must now consent with the rest; that is, be contented to avow all the actions he shall do, or else justly be destroyed by the rest. For if he voluntarily entered into the Congregation of them that were assembled, be sufficiently declared thereby his will (and therefore tacitely covenanted) to stand to what the major part should ordayne: and therefore if he refuse to stand thereto, or make Protestation against any of their Decrees, he does contrary to his Covenant, and therfore unjustly. And whether he be of the Congregation, or not; and whether his consent be asked, or not, he must either submit to their decrees, or be left in the condition of warre he was in before; wherein he might without injustice be destroyed by any man whatsoever.

Fourthly, because every Subject is by this Institution Author of all the Actions, and Judgments of the Soveraigne Instituted; it followes, that whatsoever he doth, it can be no injury to any of his Subjects; nor ought he to be by any of them accused of Injustice. For he that doth any thing by authority from another, doth therein no injury to him by whose authority he acteth: But by this Institution of a Common-wealth, every particular man is Author of all the Soveraigne doth; and consequently he that complaineth of injury from his Soveraigne, complaineth of that whereof he himselfe is Author; and therefore ought not to accuse any man but himselfe; no nor himselfe of injury; because to do injury to ones selfe, is impossible. It is true that they that have Soveraigne power, may commit Iniquity; but not Injustice, or Injury in the proper signification.

Fiftly, and consequently to that which was sayd last, no man that hath Soveraigne power can justly be put to death, or otherwise in any manner by his Subjects punished. For seeing every Subject is Author of the actions of his Soveraigne; he punisheth another, for the actions committed by himselfe.

And because the End of this Institution, is the Peace and Defence of them all; and whosoever has right to the End, has right to the Means; it belongeth of Right, to whatsoever Man, or Assembly that hath the Soveraignty, to be Judge both of the meanes of Peace and Defence; and also of the hindrances, and disturbances of the same; and to do whatsoever he shall think necessary to be done, both before hand, for the preserving of Peace and Security, by prevention of Discord at home and Hostility from abroad; and, when Peace and Security are lost, for the recovery of the same. And therefore,

Sixtly, it is annexed to the Soveraignty, to be Judge of what Opinions and Doctrines are averse, and what conducing to Peace; and consequently, on what occasions, how farre, and what, men are to be trusted withall, in speaking to Multitudes of people; and who shall examine the Doctrines of all bookes before they be published. For the Actions of men proceed from their Opinions; and in the wel governing of Opinions, consisteth the well governing of mens Actions, in order to their Peace, and Concord. And though in matter of Doctrine, nothing ought to be regarded but the Truth; yet this is not repugnant to regulating of the same by Peace. For Doctrine repugnant to Peace, can no more be True, than Peace and Concord can be against the Law of Nature. It is true, that in a Commonwealth, where by the negligence, or unskilfullnesse of Governours, and Teachers, false Doctrines are by time generally received; the contrary Truths may be generally offensive: Yet the most sudden, and rough busling in of a new Truth, that can be, does never breake the Peace, but only somtimes awake the Warre. For those men that are so remissely governed, that they dare take up Armes, to defend, or introduce an Opinion, are still in Warre; and their condition not Peace, but only a Cessation of Armes for feare of one another; and they live as it were, in the procincts of battaile continually. It belongeth therefore to him that hath the Soveraign Power, to be Judge, or constitute all Judges of Opinions and Doctrines, as a thing necessary to Peace, thereby to prevent Discord and Civill Warre.

Seventhly, is annexed to the Soveraigntie, the whole power of prescribing the Rules, whereby every man may know, what Goods he may enjoy and what Actions he may doe, without being molested by any of his fellow Subjects: And this is it men call *Propriety*. For before constitution of Soveraign Power (as hath already been shewn) all men had right to all things; which necessarily causeth Warre: and therefore this Proprietie, being necessary to Peace, and depending on Soveraign Power, is the Act of that Power, in order to the publique peace. These Rules of Propriety (or *Meum* and *Tuum*) and of *Good, Evill, Lawfull*, and *Unlawfull* in the actions of Subjects, are the Civill Lawes, that is to say, the Lawes of each Common-wealth in particular; though the name of Civill Law be now restrained to the antient Civill Lawes of the City of *Rome*;

which being the head of a great part of the World, her Lawes at that time were in these parts the Civill Law. . . .

But a man may here object, that the Condition of Subjects is very miserable; as being obnoxious to the lusts, and other irregular passions of him, or them that have so unlimited a Power in their hands. And commonly they that live under a Monarch, think it the fault of Monarchy; and they that live under the government of Democracy, or other Soveraign Assembly, attribute all the inconvenience to that forme of Common-wealth; whereas the Power in all formes, if they be perfect enough to protect them, is the same; not considering that the estate of Man can never be without some incommodity or other; and that the greatest, that in any forme of Government can possibly happen to the people in generall, is scarce sensible, in respect of the miseries, and horrible calamities, that accompany a Civill Warre; or that dissolute condition of masterlesse men, without subjection to Lawes, and a coërcive Power to tye their hands from rapine, and revenge: nor considering that the greatest pressure of Soveraign Governours, proceedeth not from any delight, or profit they can expect in the dammage, or weakening of their Subjects, in whose vigor, consisteth their own strength and glory; but in the restiveness of themselves, that unwillingly contributing to their own defence, make it necessary for their Governours to draw from them what they can in time of Peace, that they may have means on any emergent occasion, or sudden need, to resist, or take advantage on their Enemies. For all men are by nature provided of notable multiplying glasses, (that is their Passions and Self-love,) through which, every little payment appeareth a great grievance; but are destitute of those prospective glasses, (namely Morall and Civill Science,) to see a farre off the miseries that hang over them, and cannot without such payments be avoyded.

The Obligation of Subjects to the Soveraign, is understood to last as long, and no longer, than the power lasteth, by which he is able to protect them. For the right men have by Nature to protect themselves, when none else can protect them, can by no Covenant be relinquished. The Soveraignty is the Soule of the Common-wealth; which once departed from the Body, the members doe no more receive their motion from it. The end of Obedience is Protection; which, wheresoever a man seeth it, either in his own, or in anothers sword, Nature applyeth his obedience to it, and his endeavour to maintaine it. And though Soveraignty, in the intention of them that make it, be immortall; yet is it in its own nature, not only subject to violent death, by forreign war; but also through the ignorance, and passions of men, it hath in it, from the very institution, many seeds of a naturall mortality, by Intestine Discord.

Consent and Natural Law

JOHN LOCKE

To understand political power right and derive it from its original, we must consider what state all men are naturally in, and that is a state of perfect freedom to order their actions and dispose of their possessions and persons as they think fit, within the bounds of the law of nature, without asking leave or depending upon the will of any other man.

A state also of equality, wherein all the power and jurisdiction is reciprocal, no one having more than another; there being nothing more evident than that creatures of the same species and rank, promiscuously born to all the same advantages of nature and the use of the same faculties, should also be equal one amongst another without subordination or subjection; unless the lord and master of them all should, by any manifest declaration of his will, set one above another, and confer on him by an evident and clear appointment an undoubted right to dominion and sovereignty.

This equality of men by nature the judicious Hooker looks upon as so evident in itself and beyond all question that he makes it the foundation of that obligation to mutual love amongst men on which he builds the duties we owe one another, and from whence he derives the great maxims of justice and charity. His words are:

> The like natural inducement hath brought men to know that it is no less their duty to love others than themselves; for seeing those things which are equal must needs all have one measure; if I cannot but wish to receive good, even as much at every man's hands as any man can wish unto his own soul, how should I look to have any part of my desire herein satisfied unless myself be careful to satisfy the like desire, which is undoubtedly in other men, being of one and the same nature? To have anything offered them repugnant to this desire must needs in all respects grieve them as much as me; so that, if I do harm, I must look to suffer, there being no reason that others should show greater measure of love to me than they have by me showed unto them; my desire therefore to be loved of my equals in nature, as much as possibly may be, imposeth upon me a natural duty of bearing to them-ward fully the like affection; from which relation of equality between ourselves and them that are as ourselves. what several rules and canons natural reason hath drawn, for direction of life, no man is ignorant (*Eccl. Pol.* lib. i.).

But though this be a state of liberty, yet it is not a state of license; though man in that state have an uncontrollable liberty to dispose of his person or possessions, yet he has not liberty to destroy himself, or so much as any creature in his possession, but where some nobler use than its bare preservation calls for it. The state of nature has a law of nature to govern it, which obliges every one; and reason, which is that law, teaches all mankind who will but consult it that, being all equal and independent, no one ought to harm another in his life, health, liberty, or possessions; for men being all the workmanship of one omnipotent and infinitely wise Maker—all the servants of one sovereign master, sent into the world by his order, and about his business—they are his property whose

---

John Locke (1632-1704) was an English philosopher best known for his work in political philosophy and theory of knowledge.

Excerpted from Locke's *Second Treatise on Government* (1689).

workmanship they are, made to last during his, not one another's, pleasure; and being furnished with like faculties, sharing all in one community of nature, there cannot be supposed any such subordination among us that may authorize us to destroy another, as if we were made for one another's uses as the inferior ranks of creatures are for ours. Every one, as he is bound to preserve himself and not to quit his station wilfully, so by the like reason, when his own preservation comes not in competition, ought he, as much as he can, to preserve the rest of mankind, and may not, unless it be to do justice to an offender, take away or impair the life, or what tends to the preservation of the life, the liberty, health, limb, or goods of another.

And that all men may be restrained from invading others' rights and from doing hurt to one another, and the law of nature be observed, which wills the peace and preservation of all mankind, the execution of the law of nature is, in that state, put into every man's hands, whereby everyone has a right to punish the transgressors of that law to such a degree as may hinder its violation; for the law of nature would, as all other laws that concern men in this world, be in vain if there were nobody that in that state of nature had a power to execute that law and thereby preserve the innocent and restrain offenders. And if anyone in the state of nature may punish another for any evil he has done, everyone may do so; for in that state of perfect equality, where naturally there is no superiority or jurisdiction of one over another, what any may do in prosecution of that law, everyone must needs have a right to do.

And thus in the state of nature one man comes by a power over another; but yet no absolute or arbitrary power to use a criminal, when he has got him in his hands, according to the passionate heats or boundless extravagance of his own will; but only to retribute to him, so far as calm reason and conscience dictate, what is proportionate to his transgression, which is so much as may serve for reparation and restraint; for these two are the only reasons why one man may lawfully do harm to another, which is that we call punishment. In transgressing the law of nature, the offender declares himself to live by another rule than that of reason and common equity, which is that measure God has set to the actions of men for their mutual security; and so he becomes dangerous to mankind, the tie which is to secure them from injury and violence being slighted and broken by him. Which being a trespass against the whole species and the peace and safety of it provided for by the law of nature, every man upon this score, by the right he has to preserve mankind in general, may restrain, or, where it is necessary, destroy things noxious to them, and so may bring such evil on any one who has transgressed that law, as may make him repent the doing of it and thereby deter him, and by his example others, from doing the like mischief. And in this case, and upon this ground, *every man has a right to punish the offender and be executioner of the law of nature*. . . .

OF PROPERTY

Whether we consider natural reason, which tells us that men, being once born, have a right to their preservation, and consequently to meat and drink and such other things as nature affords for their subsistence; or revelation, which gives us an account of those grants God made of the world to Adam, and to Noah and his sons; it is very clear that God, as King David says (Psalm cxv. 16), "has given the earth to the children of men," given it to mankind in common. But this being supposed, it seems to some a very great difficulty how any one should ever come to have a property in anything. I will not content myself to answer that if it be difficult to make out property upon a supposition that God gave the world to Adam and his posterity in common, it is impossible that any man but one universal monarch should have any property upon a supposition that God gave the world to Adam and his heirs in succession, exclusive of all the rest of his posterity. But I shall endeavor to show how men might come to have a property in several parts of that which God gave to mankind in common, and that without any express compact of all the commoners.

God, who has given the world to men in common, has also given them reason to make use of it to the best advantage of life and convenience. The earth and all that is therein is given to men for the support and comfort of their being. And though all the fruits it naturally produces and beasts it feeds belong to mankind in common, as they are produced by the spontaneous hand of nature; and nobody has originally a private dominion exclusive of the rest of mankind in any of them, as they are thus in their natural state; yet, being given for the use of men, there must of necessity be a means to appropriate them some way or other before they can be of any use or at all beneficial to any particular man. The fruit or venison which nourishes the wild Indian, who knows no enclosure and is still a tenant in common, must be his, and so his, i. e., a part of him, that another can no longer have any right to it before it can do him any good for the support of his life.

Though the earth and all inferior creatures be common to all men, yet every man has a property in his own person; this nobody has any right to but himself. The labor of his body and the work of his hands, we may say, are properly his. Whatsoever then he removes out of the state that nature has provided and left it in, he has mixed his labor with, and joined to it something that is his own, and thereby makes it his property. It being by him removed from the common state nature has placed it in, it has by this labor something annexed to it that excludes the common right of other men. For this labor being the unquestionable property of the laborer, no man but he can have a right to what that is once joined to, at least where there is enough and as good left in common for others.

He that is nourished by the acorns he picked up under an oak, or the apples he gathered from the trees in the wood, has certainly appropriated them to himself. Nobody can deny but the nourishment is his. I ask, then, When did they begin to be his? When he digested or when he ate or when he boiled or when he brought them home? Or when he picked them up? And it is plain, if the first gathering made them not his, nothing else could. That labor put a distinction between them and common; that added something to them more than nature, the common mother of all, had done; and so they became his private right. And will anyone say he had no right to those acorns or apples he thus appropriated because he had not the consent of all mankind to make them his? Was it a robbery thus to assume to himself what belonged to all in common? If such a consent as that was necessary, man had starved, notwithstanding the plenty God had given him. We see in commons, which remain so by compact, that it is the taking any part of what is common and removing it out of the state nature leaves it in which begins the property, without which the common is of no use. And the taking of this or that part does not depend on the express consent of all the commoners. Thus the grass my horse has bit, the turfs my servant has cut, and the ore I have digged in any place where I have a right to them in common with others, become my property without the assignation or consent of anybody. The labor that was mine, removing them out of that common state they were in, has fixed my property in them. . . .

It will perhaps be objected to this that "if gathering the acorns, or other fruits of the earth, etc., makes a right to them, then any one may engross as much as he will." To which I answer: not so. The same law of nature that does by this means give us property does also bound that property, too. "God has given us all things richly" (I Tim. vi. 17), is the voice of reason confirmed by inspiration. But how far has he given it us? To enjoy. As much as any one can make use of to any advantage of life before it spoils, so much he may by his labor fix a property in; whatever is beyond this is more than his share and belongs to others. Nothing was made by God for man to spoil or destroy. And thus considering the plenty of natural provisions there was a long time in the world, and the few spenders, and to how small a part of that provision the industry of one man could extend itself and engross it to the prejudice of others, especially keeping within the bounds set by reason of what might serve for his use, there could be then little room for quarrels or contentions about property so established.

But the chief matter of property being now not the fruits of the earth and the beasts that subsist on it, but the earth itself, as that which takes in and carries with it all the rest, I think it is plain that property in that, too, is acquired as the former. As much land as a man tills, plants, improves, cultivates, and can use the product of, so much is his property. He by his labor does, as it were, enclose it from the common. Nor will it invalidate his right to say everybody else has an equal title to it, and therefore he cannot appropriate, he cannot enclose, without the consent of all his fellow commoners—all mankind. God, when he gave the world in common to all mankind, commanded man also to labor, and the penury of his condition required it of him. God and his reason commanded him to subdue the earth, i. e., improve it for the benefit of life, and therein lay out something upon it that was his own, his labor. He that in obedience to this command of God subdued, tilled, and sowed any part of it, thereby annexed to it something that was his property, which another had no title to, nor could without injury take from him.

Nor was this appropriation of any parcel of land by improving it any prejudice to any other man, since there was still enough and as good left, and more than the yet unprovided could use. So that, in effect, there was never the less left for others because of his enclosure for himself; for he that leaves as much as another can make use of does as good as take nothing at all. Nobody could think himself injured by the drinking of another man, though he took a good draught, who had a whole river of the same water left him to quench his thirst; and the case of land and water, where there is enough for both, is perfectly the same.

God gave the world to men in common; but since he gave it them for their benefit and the greatest conveniences of life they were capable to draw from it, it cannot be supposed he meant it should always remain common and uncultivated. He gave it to the use of the industrious and rational—and labor was to be his title to it—not to the fancy or covetousness of the quarrelsome and contentious. He that had as good left for his improvement as was already taken up needed not complain, ought not to meddle with what was already improved by another's labor; if he did, it is plain he desired the benefit of another's pains which he had no right to, and not the ground which God had given him in common with others to labor on, and whereof there was as good left as that already possessed, and more than he knew what to do with, or his industry could reach to. . . .

EQUALITY

Though I have said above (Chap. II) that all men by nature are equal, I cannot be supposed to understand all sorts of equality. Age or virtue may give men a just precedence; excellence of parts and merit may place others above the common level; birth may subject some, and alliance or benefits others, to pay an observance to those whom nature, gratitude, or other respects may have made it due; and yet all this consists with the equality which all men are in, in respect of jurisdiction or dominion one over another, which was the equality I there spoke of as proper to the business in hand, being that equal right that every man has to his natural freedom, without being subjected to the will or authority of any other man. . . .

OF THE BEGINNING OF POLITICAL SOCIETIES

Men being, as has been said, by nature all free, equal, and independent, no one can be put out of this estate and subjected to the political power of another without his own consent. The only way whereby any one divests himself of his natural liberty and puts on the bonds of civil society is by agreeing with other men to join and unite into a community for their comfortable, safe, and peaceable living one amongst another, in a secure enjoyment of their properties and a greater security against any that are not of it. This any number of men may do, because it injures not the freedom of the rest; they are left as they were in the liberty of the state of nature. When any number of men have so consented to make one community or government, they are thereby presently incorporated and make one body politic wherein the majority have a right to act and conclude the rest.

For when any number of men have, by the consent of every individual, made a community, they have thereby made that community one body, with a power to act as one body, which is only by the will and determination of the majority; for that which acts any community being only the consent of the individuals of it, and it being necessary to that which is one body to move one way, it is necessary the body should move that way whither the greater force carries it, which is the consent of the majority; or else it is impossible it should act or continue one body, one community, which the consent of every individual that united into it agreed that it should; and so every one is bound by that consent to be concluded by the majority. And therefore we see that in assemblies impowered to act by positive laws, where no number is set by that positive law which impowers them, the act of the majority passes for the act of the whole and, of course, determines, as having by the law of nature and reason the power of the whole.

And thus every man, by consenting with others to make one body politic under one government, puts himself under an obligation to every one of that society to submit to the determination of the majority and to be concluded by it; or else this original compact, whereby he with others incorporates into one society, would signify nothing, and be no compact, if he be left free and under no other ties than he was in before in the state of nature. For what appearance would there be of any compact? What new engagement if he were no further tied by any decrees of the society than he himself thought fit and did actually consent to? This would be still as great a liberty as he himself had before his compact, or any one else in the state of nature has who may submit himself and consent to any acts of it if he thinks fit.

For if the consent of the majority shall not in reason be received as the act of the whole and conclude every individual, nothing but the consent of every individual can make anything to be the act of the whole; but such a consent is next to impossible ever to be had if we consider the infirmities of health and avocations of business which in a number, though much less than that of a commonwealth, will necessarily keep many away from the public assembly. To which, if we add the variety of opinions and contrariety of interests which unavoidably happen in all collections of men, the coming into society upon such terms would be only like Cato's coming into the theatre only to go out again. Such a constitution as this would make the mighty leviathan of a shorter duration than the feeblest creatures, and not let it outlast the day it was born in; which cannot be supposed till we can think that rational creatures should desire and constitute societies only to be dissolved; for where the majority cannot conclude the rest, there they cannot act as one body, and consequently will be immediately dissolved again.

Whosoever, therefore, out of a state of nature unite into a community must be understood to give up all the power necessary to the ends for which they unite into society to the majority of the community, unless they expressly agreed in any number greater than the majority. And this is done by barely agreeing to unite into one political society, which is all the compact that is, or needs be, between the individuals that enter into or make up a commonwealth. And thus that which begins and actually constitutes any political society is nothing but the consent of any number of freemen capable of a majority to unite and incorporate into such a society. And this is that, and that only, which did or could give beginning to any lawful government in the world. . . .

CONSENT

Every man being, as has been shown, naturally free, and nothing being able to put him into subjection to any earthly power but only his own consent, it is to be considered what shall be understood to be a sufficient declaration of a man's consent to make him subject to the laws of any government. There is a common distinction of an express and a tacit consent which will concern our present case. Nobody doubts but an express consent of any man entering into any society makes him a perfect member of that society, a subject of that government. The difficulty is, what ought to be looked upon as a tacit consent, and how far it binds—i. e., how far any one shall be looked upon to have consented and thereby submitted to any government, where he has made no expressions of it at all. And to this I say that every man that has any possessions or enjoyment of any part of the dominions of any government does thereby give his tacit consent and is as far forth obliged to obedience to the laws of that government, during such enjoyment, as anyone under it; whether this his possession be of land to him and his heirs for ever, or a lodging only for a week, or whether it be barely traveling freely on the highway; and, in effect, it reaches as far as the very being of anyone within the territories of that government. . . .

But since the government has a direct jurisdiction only over the land, and reaches the possessor of it—before he has actually incorporated himself in the society—only as he dwells upon and enjoys that, the obligation anyone is under by virtue of such enjoyment, to submit to the government, begins and ends with the enjoyment; so that whenever the owner, who has given nothing but such a tacit consent to the government, will, by donation, sale, or otherwise, quit the said possession, he is at liberty to go and incorporate himself into any other commonwealth, or to agree with others to begin a new one *in vacuis locis*, in any part of the world they can find free and unpossessed. Whereas he that has once, by actual agreement and any express declaration, given his consent to be of any commonwealth is perpetually and indispensably obliged to be and remain unalterably a subject to it, and can never be again in the liberty of the state of nature, unless by any calamity the government he was under comes to be dissolved, or else, by some public act, cuts him off from being any longer a member of it.

But submitting to the laws of any country, living quietly and enjoying privileges and protection under them, makes not a man a member of that society; this is only a local protection and homage due to and from all those who, not being in a state of war, come within the territories belonging to any government, to all parts whereof the force of its laws extends. But this no more makes a man a member of that society, a perpetual subject of that commonwealth, than it would make a man a subject to another in whose family he found it convenient to abide for some time, though, while he continued in it, he were obliged to comply with the laws and submit to the government he found there. And thus we see that foreigners, by living all their lives under another government and enjoying the privileges and protection of it, though they are bound, even in conscience, to submit to its administration as far forth as any denizen, yet do not thereby come to be subjects or members of that commonwealth. Nothing can make any man so but his actually entering into it by positive engagement and express promise and compact. That is that which I think concerning the beginning of political societies and that consent which makes any one a member of any commonwealth.

OF THE ENDS OF POLITICAL SOCIETY AND GOVERNMENT

If man in the state of nature be so free, as has been said, if he be absolute lord of his own person and possessions, equal to the greatest, and subject to nobody, why will he part with his freedom, why will he give up his empire and subject himself to the dominion and control of any other power? To which it is obvious to answer that though in the state of nature he has such a right, yet the enjoyment of it is very uncertain and constantly exposed to the invasion of others; for all being kings as much as he, every man his equal, and the greater part no strict observers of equity and justice, the enjoyment of the property he has in this state is very unsafe, very unsecure. This makes him willing to quit a condition which, however free, is full of fears and continual dangers; and it is not without reason that he seeks out and is willing to join in society with others who are already united, or have a mind to unite, for the mutual preservation of their lives, liberties, and estates, which I call by the general name 'property.'

The great and chief end, therefore, of men's uniting into commonwealths and putting themselves under government is the preservation of their property. To which in the state of nature there are many things wanting:

First, there wants an established, settled, known law, received and allowed by common consent to be the standard of right and wrong and the common measure to decide all controversies between them; for though the law of nature be plain and intelligible to all rational creatures, yet men, being biased by their interest as well as ignorant for want of studying it, are not apt to allow of it as a law binding to them in the application of it to their particular cases.

Secondly, in the state of nature there wants a known and indifferent judge with authority to determine all differences according to the established law; for every one in that state being both judge and executioner of the law of nature, men being partial to themselves, passion and revenge is very apt to carry them too far and with too much heat in their own cases, as well as negligence and unconcernedness to make them too remiss in other men's.

Thirdly, in the state of nature there often wants power to back and support the sentence when right, and to give it due execution. They who by any injustice offend will seldom fail, where they are able, by force, to make good their injustice; such resistance many times makes the punishment dangerous and frequently destructive to those who attempt it.

Thus mankind, notwithstanding all the privileges of the state of nature, being but in an ill condition while they remain in it, are quickly driven into society. Hence it comes to pass that we seldom find any number of men live any time together in this state. The inconveniences that they are therein exposed to by the irregular and uncertain exercise of the power every man has of punishing the transgressions of others make them take sanctuary under the established laws of government and therein seek the preservation of their property. It is this makes them so willingly give up every one his single power of punishing, to be exercised by such alone as shall be appointed to it amongst them; and by such rules as the community, or those authorized by them to that purpose, shall agree on. And in this we have the original right of both the legislative and executive power, as well as of the governments and societies themselves.

For in the state of nature, to omit the liberty he has of innocent delights, a man has two powers:

The first is to do whatsoever he thinks fit for the preservation of himself and others within the permission of the law of nature, by which law, common to them all, he and all the rest of mankind are one community, make up one society, distinct from all other creatures. And, were it not for the corruption and viciousness of degenerate men, there would be no need of any other, no necessity that men should separate from this great and natural community and by positive agreements combine into smaller and divided associations.

The other power a man has in the state of nature is the power to punish the crimes committed against that law. Both these he gives up when he joins in a private, if I may so call it, or particular politic society and incorporates into any commonwealth separate from the rest of mankind.

The first power, viz., of doing whatsoever he thought fit for the preservation of himself and the rest of mankind, he gives up to be regulated by laws made by the society, so far forth as the preservation of himself and the rest of that society shall require; which laws of the society in many things confine the liberty he had by the law of nature.

Secondly, the power of punishing he wholly gives up, and engages his natural force—which he might before employ in the execution of the law of nature by his own single authority, as the he thought fit—to assist the executive power of the society, as the law thereof shall require; for being now in a new state, wherein he is to enjoy many conveniences from the labor, assistance, and society of others in the same community as well as protection from its whole strength, he is to part also with as much of his natural liberty, in providing for himself, as the good, prosperity, and safety of the society shall require, which is not only necessary, but just, since the other members of the society do the like.

But though men when they enter into society give up the equality, liberty, and executive power they had in the state of nature into the hands of the society, to be so far disposed of by the legislative as the good of the society shall require, yet it being only with an intention in every one the better to preserve himself, his liberty and property—for no rational creature can be supposed to change his condition with an intention to be worse—the power of the society, or legislative constituted by them, can never be supposed to extend farther than the common good, but is obliged to secure every one's property by providing against those three defects above-mentioned that made the state of nature so unsafe and uneasy. And so whoever has the legislative or supreme power of any commonwealth is bound to govern by established standing laws, promulgated and known to the people, and not by extemporary decrees; by indifferent and upright judges who are to decide controversies by those laws; and to employ the force of the community at home only in the execution of such laws, or abroad to prevent or redress foreign injuries, and secure the community from inroads and invasion. And all this to be directed to no other end but the peace, safety, and public good of the people. . . .

OF THE EXTENT OF THE LEGISLATIVE POWER

The great end of men's entering into society being the enjoyment of their properties in peace and safety, and the great instrument and means of that being the laws established in that society, the first and fundamental positive law of all commonwealths is the establishing of the legislative power; as the first and fundamental natural law which is to govern even the legislative itself is the preservation of the society and, as far as will consist with the public good, of every person in it. This legislative is not only the supreme power of the commonwealth, but sacred and unalterable in the hands where the community have once placed it; nor can any edict of anybody else, in what form soever conceived or by what power soever backed, have the force and obligation of a law which has not its sanction from that legislative which the public has chosen and appointed; for without this the law could not have that which is absolutely necessary to its being a law: the consent of the society over whom nobody can have a power to make laws, but by their own consent and by authority received from them. And therefore all the obedience, which by the most solemn ties any one can be obliged to pay, ultimately terminates in this supreme power and is directed by those laws which it enacts; nor can any oaths to any foreign power whatsoever, or any domestic subordinate power, discharge any member of the society from his obedience to the legislative acting pursuant to their trust, nor oblige him to any obedience contrary to the laws so enacted, or farther than they do allow; it being ridiculous to imagine one can be tied ultimately to obey any power in the society which is not supreme.

Though the legislative, whether placed in one or more, whether it be always in being, or only by intervals, though it be the supreme power in every commonwealth; yet:

First, it is not, nor can possibly be, absolutely arbitrary over the lives and fortunes of the people; for it being but the joint power of every member of the society given up to that person or assembly which is legislator, it can be no more than those persons had in a state of nature before they entered into society and gave up to the community; for nobody can transfer to another more power than he has in himself, and nobody has an absolute arbitrary power over himself or over any other, to destroy his own life or take away the life or property of another. A man, as has been proved, cannot subject himself to the arbitrary power of another; and having in the state of nature no arbitrary power over the life, liberty, or possession of another, but only so much as the law of nature gave him for the preservation of himself and the rest of mankind, this is all he does or can give up to the commonwealth, and by it to the legislative power, so that the legislative can have no more than this. Their power, in the utmost bounds of it, is limited to the public good of the society. It is a power that has no other end but preservation, and therefore can never have a right to destroy, enslave, or designedly to impoverish the subjects. The obligations of the law of nature cease not in society but only in many cases are drawn closer and have by human laws known penalties annexed to them to enforce their observation. Thus the law of nature stands as an eternal rule to all men, legislators as well as others. The rules that they make for other men's actions must, as well as their own and other men's actions, be conformable to the law of nature—i. e., to the will of God, of which that is a declaration—and the fundamental law of nature being the preservation of mankind, no human sanction can be good or valid against it.

Secondly, the legislative or supreme authority cannot assume to itself a power to rule by extemporary, arbitrary decrees, but is bound to dispense justice and to decide the rights of the subject by promulgated, standing laws, and known authorized judges. For the law of nature being unwritten, and so nowhere to be found but in the minds of men, they who through passion or interest shall miscite or misapply it, cannot so easily be convinced of their mistake where there is no established judge; and so it serves not, as it ought, to determine the rights and fence the properties of those that live under it, especially where every one is judge, interpreter, and executioner of it, too, and that in his own case; and he that has right on his side, having ordinarily but his own single strength, has not force enough to defend himself from injuries or to punish delinquents. To avoid these inconveniences which disorder men's properties in the state of nature, men unite into societies that they may have the united strength of the whole society to secure and defend their properties, and may have standing rules to bound it by which every one may know what is his. To this end it is that men give up all their natural power to the society which they enter into, and the community put the legislative power into such hands as they think fit with this trust, that they shall be governed by declared laws, or else their peace, quiet, and property will still be at the same uncertainty as it was in the state of nature.

Absolute arbitrary power or governing without settled standing laws can neither of them consist with the ends of society and government which men would not quit the freedom of the state of nature for, and tie themselves up under, were it not to preserve their lives, liberties, and fortunes, and by stated rules of right and property to secure their peace and quiet. It cannot be supposed that they should intend, had they a power so to do, to give to any one or more an absolute arbitrary power over their persons and estates and put a force into the magistrate's hand to execute his unlimited will arbitrarily upon them. This were to put themselves into a worse condition than the state of nature wherein they had a liberty to defend their right against the injuries of others and were upon equal terms of force to maintain it, whether invaded by a single man or many in combination. Whereas, by supposing they have given up themselves to the absolute arbitrary power and will of a legislator, they have disarmed themselves and armed him to make a prey of them when he pleases, he being in a much worse condition who is exposed to the arbitrary power of one man who has the command of 100,000, than he that is exposed to the arbitrary power of 100,000 single men, nobody being secure that his will, who has such a command, is better than that of other men, though his force be 100,000 times stronger. And, therefore, whatever form the commonwealth is under, the ruling power ought to govern by declared and received laws and not by extemporary dictates and undetermined resolutions; for then mankind will be in a far worse condition than in the state of nature if they shall have armed one or a few men with the joint power of a multitude, to force them to obey at pleasure the exorbitant and unlimited decrees of their sudden thoughts or unrestrained and, till that moment, unknown wills, without having any measures set down which may guide and justify their actions. For all the power the government has, being only for the good of the society, as it ought not to be arbitrary and at pleasure, so it ought to be exercised by established and promulgated laws; that both the people may know their duty and be safe and secure within the limits of the law; and the rulers, too, kept within their bounds, and not be tempted by the power they have in their hands to employ it to such purposes and by such measures as they would not have known, and own not willingly.

Thirdly, the supreme power cannot take from any man part of his property without his own consent; for the preservation of property being the end of government and that for which men enter into society, it necessarily supposes and requires that the people should have property; without which they must be supposed to lose that, by entering into society, which was the end for which they entered into it—too gross an absurdity for any man to own. Men, therefore, in society having property, they have such right to the goods which by the law of the community are theirs, that nobody has a right to take their substance or any part of it from them without their own consent; without this, they have no property at all, for I have truly no property in that which another can by right take from me when he pleases, against my consent. Hence it is a mistake to think that the supreme or legislative power of any commonwealth can do what it will and dispose of the estates of the subject arbitrarily, or take any part of them at pleasure. This is not much to be feared in governments where the legislative consists, wholly or in part, in assemblies which are variable, whose members, upon the dissolution of the assembly, are subjects under the common laws of their country, equally with the rest. But in governments where the legislative is in one lasting assembly, always in being, or in one man, as in absolute monarchies, there is danger still that they will think themselves to have a distinct interest from the rest of the community, and so will be apt to increase their own riches and power by taking what they think fit from the people; for a man's property is not at all secure, though there be good and equitable laws to set the bounds of it between him and his fellow subjects, if he who commands those subjects have power to take from any private man what part he pleases of his property and use and dispose of it as he thinks good. . . .

It is true, governments cannot be supported without great charge, and it is fit every one who enjoys his share of the protection should pay out of his estate his proportion for the maintenace of it. But still it must be with his own consent—i.e., the consent of the majority, giving it either by themselves or their representatives chosen by them. For if any one shall claim a power to lay and levy taxes on the people, by his own authority and without such consent of the people, he thereby invades the fundamental law of property and subverts the end of government; for what property have I in that which another may by right take, when he pleases, to himself?

Fourthly, the legislative cannot transfer the power of making laws to any other hands; for it being but a delegated power from the people, they who have it cannot pass it over to others. The people alone can appoint the form of the commonwealth, which is by constituting the legislative and appointing in whose hands that shall be. And when the people have said, we will submit to rules and be governed by laws made by such men, and in such forms, nobody else can say other men shall make laws for them; nor can the people be bound by any laws but such as are enacted by those whom they have chosen and authorized to make laws for them. The power of the legislative, being derived from the people by a positive voluntary grant and institution, can be no other than what that positive grant conveyed, which being only to make laws, and not to make legislators, the legislative can have no power to transfer their authority of making laws and place it in other hands. . . .

REVOLUTION

There is one way more whereby such a government may be dissolved, and that is when he who has the supreme executive power neglects and abandons that charge, so that the laws already made can no longer be put in execution. This is demonstratively to reduce all to anarchy, and so effectually to dissolve the government; for laws not being made for themselves, but to be by their execution the bonds of the society, to keep every part of the body politic in its due place and function, when that totally ceases, the government visibly ceases, and the people become a confused multitude, without order or connection. Where there is no longer the administration of justice for the securing of men's rights, nor any remaining power within the community to direct the force to provide for the necessities of the public, there certainly is no government left. Where the laws cannot be executed, it is all one as if there were no laws; and a government without laws is, I suppose, a mystery in politics, inconceivable to human capacity and inconsistent with human society.

In these and the like cases, when the government is dissolved, the people are at liberty to provide for themselves by erecting a new legislative, differing from the other by the change of persons or form, or both, as they shall find it most for their safety and good; for the society can never by the fault of another lose the native and original right it has to preserve itself, which can only be done by a settled legislative, and a fair and impartial execution of the laws made by it. But the state of mankind is not so miserable that they are not capable of using this remedy till it be too late to look for any. To tell people they may provide for themselves by erecting a new legislative, when by oppression, artifice, or being delivered over to a foreign power, their old one is gone, is only to tell them they may expect relief when it is too late and the evil is past cure. This is in effect no more than to bid them first be slaves, and then to take care of their liberty; and when their chains are on, tell them they may act like freemen. This, if barely so, is rather mockery than relief; and men can never be secure from tyranny if there be no means to escape it till they are perfectly under it; and therefore it is that they have not only a right to get out of it, but to prevent it.

On Liberty

JOHN STUART MILL

The subject of this essay is not the so-called "liberty of the will," so unfortunately opposed to the misnamed doctrine of philosophical necessity; but civil, or social liberty: the nature and limits of the power which can be legitimately exercised by society over the individual. A question seldom stated, and hardly ever discussed in general terms, but which profoundly influences the practical controversies of the age by its latent presence, and is likely soon to make itself recognized as the vital question of the future. It is so far from being new that, in a certain sense, it has divided mankind almost from the remotest ages; but in the stage of progress into which the more civilized portions of the species have now entered, it presents itself under new conditions and requires a different and more fundamental treatment.

The struggle between liberty and authority is the most conspicuous feature in the portions of history with which we are earliest familiar, particularly in that of Greece, Rome, and England. But in old times this contest was between subjects, or some classes of subjects, and the government. By liberty was meant protection against the tyranny of the political rulers. The rulers were conceived (except in some of the popular governments of Greece) as in a necessarily antagonistic position to the people whom they ruled. They consisted of a governing One, or a governing tribe or caste, who derived their authority from inheritance or conquest, who, at all events, did not hold it at the pleasure of the governed, and whose supremacy men did not venture, perhaps did not desire, to contest, whatever precautions might be taken against its oppressive exercise. Their power was regarded as necessary, but also as highly dangerous; as a weapon which they would attempt to use against their subjects, no less than against external enemies. To prevent the weaker members of the community from being preyed upon by innumerable vultures, it was needful that there should be an animal of prey stronger than the rest, commissioned to keep them down. But as the king of the vultures would be no less bent upon preying on the flock than any of the minor harpies, it was indispensable to be in a perpetual attitude of defense against his beak and claws. The aim, therefore, of patriots was to set limits to the power which the ruler should be suffered to exercise over the community; and this limitation was what they meant by liberty. It was attempted in two ways. First, by obtaining a recognition of certain immunities, called political liberties or rights, which it was to be regarded as a breach of duty in the ruler to infringe, and which if he did infringe, specific resistance or general rebellion was held to be justifiable. A second, and generally a later, expedient was the establishment of constitutional checks by which the consent of the community, or of a body of some sort, supposed to represent its interests, was made a necessary condition to some of the more important acts of the governing power. To the first of these modes of

---

John Stuart Mill (1806-1873) was a prominent British philosopher. He wrote in virtually every area of philosophy.

Excerpted from Mill's *On Liberty* (1859) chapters 1, 2, 3, and 5.

limitation, the ruling power, in most European countries, was compelled, more or less, to submit. It was not so with the second; and, to attain this, or, when already in some degree possessed, to attain it more completely, became everywhere the principal object of the lovers of liberty. And so long as mankind were content to combat one enemy by another, and to be ruled by a master on condition of being guaranteed more or less efficaciously against his tyranny, they did not carry their aspirations beyond this point.

A time, however, came, in the progress of human affairs, when men ceased to think it a necessity of nature that their governors should be an independent power opposed in interest to themselves. It appeared to them much better that the various magistrates of the state should be their tenants or delegates, revocable at their pleasure. In that way alone, it seemed, could they have complete security that the powers of government would never be abused to their disadvantage. By degrees this new demand for elective and temporary rulers became the prominent object of the exertions of the popular party wherever any such party existed, and superseded, to a considerable extent, the previous efforts to limit the power of rulers. As the struggle proceeded for making the ruling power emanate from the periodical choice of the ruled, some persons began to think that too much importance had been attached to the limitation of the power itself. *That* (it might seem) was a resource against rulers whose interests were habitually opposed to those of the people. What was now wanted was that the rulers should be identified with the people, that their interest and will should be the interest and will of the nation. The nation did not need to be protected against its own will. There was no fear of its tyrannizing over itself. Let the rulers be effectually responsible to it, promptly removable by it, and it could afford to trust them with power of which it could itself dictate the use to be made. Their power was but the nation's own power, concentrated and in a form convenient for exercise. This mode of thought, or rather perhaps of feeling, was common among the last generation of European liberalism, in the Continental section of which it still apparently predominates. Those who admit any limit to what a government may do, except in the case of such governments as they think ought not to exist, stand out as brilliant exceptions among the political thinkers of the Continent. A similar tone of sentiment might by this time have been prevalent in our own country if the circumstances which for a time encouraged it had continued unaltered.

But, in political and philosophical theories as well as in persons, success discloses faults and infirmities which failure might have concealed from observation. The notion that the people have no need to limit their power over themselves might seem axiomatic, when popular government was a thing only dreamed about, or read of as having existed at some distant period of the past. Neither was that notion necessarily disturbed by such temporary aberrations as those of the French Revolution, the worst of which were the work of a usurping few, and which, in any case, belonged, not to the permanent working of popular institutions, but to a sudden and convulsive outbreak against monarchical and aristocratic despotism. In time, however, a democratic republic came to occupy a large portion of the earth's surface and made itself felt as one of the most powerful members of the community of nations; and elective and responsible government became subject to the observations and criticisms which wait upon a great existing fact. It was now perceived that such phrases as "self-government," and "the power of the people over themselves," do not express the true state of the case. The "people" who exercise the power are not always the same people with those over whom it is exercised; and the "self-government" spoken of is not the government of each by himself, but of each by all the rest. The will of the people, moreover, practically means the will of the most numerous or the most active *part* of the people—the majority, or those who succeed in making themselves accepted as the majority; the people, consequently, *may* desire to oppress a part of their number, and precautions are as much needed against this as against any other abuse of power. The limitation, therefore, of the power of government over individuals loses none of its importance when the holders of power are regularly accountable to the community, that is, to the strongest party therein. This view of things, recommending itself equally to the intelligence of thinkers and to the inclination of those important classes in European society to whose real or supposed interests democracy is adverse, has had no difficulty in establishing itself; and in political speculations "the tyranny of the majority" is now generally included among the evils against which society requires to be on its guard.

Like other tyrannies, the tyranny of the majority was at first, and is still vulgarly, held in dread, chiefly as operating through the acts of the public authorities. But reflecting persons perceived that when society is itself the tyrant—society collectively over the separate individuals who compose it—its means of tyrannizing are not restricted to the acts which it may do by the hands of its political functionaries. Society can and does execute its own mandates; and if it issues wrong mandates instead of right, or any mandates at all in things with which it ought not to meddle, it practices a social tyranny more formidable than many kinds of political oppression, since, though not usually upheld by such extreme penalties, it leaves fewer means of escape, penetrating much more deeply into the details of life, and enslaving the soul itself. Protection, therefore, against the tyranny of the magistrate is not enough; there needs protection also against the tyranny of the prevailing opinion and feeling, against the tendency of society to impose, by other means than civil penalties, its own ideas and practices as rules of conduct on those who dissent from them; to fetter the development and, if possible, prevent the formation of any individuality not in harmony with its ways, and compel all characters to fashion themselves upon the model of its own. There is a limit to the legitimate interference of collective opinion with individual independence; and to find that limit, and maintain it against encroachment, is as indispensable to a good condition of human affairs as protection against political despotism.

But though this proposition is not likely to be contested in general terms, the practical question where to place the limit—how to make the fitting adjustment between individual independence and social control—is a subject on which nearly everything remains to be done. All that makes existence valuable to anyone depends on the enforcement of restraints upon the actions of other people. Some rules of conduct, therefore, must be imposed—by law in the first place, and by opinion on many things which are not fit subjects for the operation of law. What these rules should be is the principal question in human affairs; but if we except a few of the most obvious cases, it is one of those which least progress has been made in resolving. No two ages, and scarcely any two countries, have decided it alike; and the decision of one age or country is a wonder to another. Yet the people of any given age and country no more suspect any difficulty in it than if it were a subject on which mankind had always been agreed. The rules which obtain among themselves appear to them self-evident and self-justifying. This all but universal illusion is one of the examples of the magical influence of custom, which is not only, as the proverb says, a second nature but is continually mistaken for the first. The effect of custom, in preventing any misgiving respecting the rules of conduct which mankind impose on one another, is all the more complete because the subject is one on which it is not generally considered necessary that reasons should be given, either by one person to others or by each to himself. People are accustomed to believe, and have been encouraged in the belief by some who aspire to the character of philosophers, that their feelings on subjects of this nature are better than reasons and render reasons unnecessary. The practical principle which guides them to their opinions on the regulation of human conduct is the feeling in each person's mind that everybody should be required to act as he, and those with whom he sympathizes, would like them to act. No one, indeed, acknowledges to himself that his standard of judgment is his own liking; but an opinion on a point of conduct, not supported by reasons, can only count as one person's preference; and if the reasons, when given, are a mere appeal to a similar preference felt by other people, it is still only many people's liking instead of one. To an ordinary man, however, his own preference, thus supported, is not only a perfectly satisfactory reason but the only one he generally has for any of his notions of morality, taste, or propriety, which are not expressly written in his religious creed, and his chief guide in the interpretation even of that. Men's opinions, accordingly, on what is laudable or blamable are affected by all the multifarious causes which influence their wishes in regard to the conduct of others, and which are as numerous as those which determine their wishes on any other subject. Sometimes their reason; at other times their prejudices or superstitions; often their social affections, not seldom their antisocial ones, their envy or jealousy, their arrogance or contemptuousness; but most commonly their desires or fears for themselves—their legitimate or illegitimate self-interest. Wherever there is an ascendant class, a large portion of the morality of the country emanates from its class interests and its feelings of class superiority. The morality between Spartans and Helots, between planters and Negroes, between princes and subjects, between nobles and roturiers, between men and women has been for the most part the creation of these class interests and feelings; and the sentiments thus generated react in turn upon the moral feelings of the members of the ascendant class, in their relations among themselves. Where, on the other hand, a class, formerly ascendant, has lost its ascendancy, or where its ascendancy is unpopular, the prevailing moral sentiments frequently bear the impress of an impatient dislike of superiority. Another grand determining principle of the rules of conduct, both in act and forbearance, which have been enforced by law or opinion, has been the servility of mankind toward the supposed preferences or aversions of their temporal masters or of their gods. This servility, though essentially selfish, is not hypocrisy; it gives rise to perfectly genuine sentiments of abhorrence; it made men burn magicians and heretics. Among so many baser influences, the general and obvious interests of society have, of course, had a share, and a large one, in the direction of the moral sentiments; less, however, as a matter of reason, and on their own account, than as a consequence of the sympathies and antipathies which grew out of them; and sympathies and antipathies which had little or nothing to do with the interests of society have made themselves felt in the establishment of moralities with quite as great force.

The likings and dislikings of society, or of some powerful portion of it, are thus the main thing which has practically determined the rules laid down for general observance, under the penalties of law or opinion. And in general, those who have been in advance of society in thought and feeling have left this condition of things unassailed in principle, however they may have come into conflict with it in some of its details. They have occupied themselves rather in inquiring what things society ought to like or dislike than in questioning whether its likings or dislikings should be a law to individuals. They preferred endeavoring to alter the feelings of mankind on the particular points on which they were themselves heretical rather than make common cause in defense of freedom with heretics generally. The only case in which the higher ground has been taken on principle and maintained with consistency, by any but an individual here and there, is that of religious belief: a case instructive in many ways, and not least so as forming a most striking instance of the fallibility of what is called the moral sense; for the *odium theologicum*, in a sincere bigot, is one of the most unequivocal cases of moral feeling. Those who first broke the yoke of what called itself the Universal Church were in general as little willing to permit difference of religious opinion as that church itself. But when the heat of the conflict was over, without giving a complete victory to any party, and each church or sect was reduced to limit its hopes to retaining possession of the ground it already occupied, minorities, seeing that they had no chance of becoming majorities, were under the necessity of pleading to those whom they could not convert for permission to differ. It is accordingly on this battlefield, almost solely, that the rights of the individual against society have been asserted on broad grounds of principle, and the claim of society to exercise authority over dissentients openly controverted. The great writers to whom the world owes what religious liberty it possesses have mostly asserted freedom of conscience as an indefeasible right, and denied absolutely that a human being is accountable to others for his religious belief. Yet so natural to mankind is intolerance in whatever they really care about that religious freedom has hardly anywhere been practically realized, except where religious indifference, which dislikes to have its peace disturbed by theological quarrels, has added its weight to the scale. In the minds of almost all religious persons, even in the most tolerant countries, the duty of toleration is admitted with tacit reserves. One person will bear with dissent in matters of church government, but not of dogma; another can tolerate everybody, short of a Papist or a Unitarian; another, everyone who believes in revealed religion; a few extend their charity a little further, but stop at the belief in a God and in a future state. Wherever the sentiment of the majority is still genuine and intense, it is found to have abated little of its claim to be obeyed.

In England, from the peculiar circumstances of our political history, though the yoke of opinion is perhaps heavier, that of law is lighter than in most other countries of Europe; and there is considerable jealousy of direct interference by the legislative or the executive power with private conduct, not so much from any just regard for the independence of the individual as from the still subsisting habit of looking on the government as representing an opposite interest to the public. The majority have not yet learned to feel the power of the government their power, or its opinions their opinions. When they do so, individual liberty will probably be as much exposed to invasion from the government as it already is from public opinion. But, as yet, there is a considerable amount of feeling ready to be called forth against any attempt of the law to control individuals in things in which they have not hitherto been accustomed to be controlled by it; and this with very little discrimination as to whether the matter is, or is not, within the legitimate sphere of legal control; insomuch that the feeling, highly salutary on the whole, is perhaps quite as often misplaced as well grounded in the particular instances of its application. There is, in fact, no recognized principle by which the propriety or impropriety of government interference is customarily tested. People decide according to their personal preferences. Some, whenever they see any good to be done, or evil to be remedied, would willingly instigate the government to undertake the business, while others prefer to bear almost any amount of social evil rather than add one to the departments of human interests amenable to governmental control. And men range themselves on one or the other side in any particular case, according to this general direction of their sentiments, or according to the degree of interest which they feel in the particular thing which it is proposed that the government should do, or according to the belief they entertain that the government would, or would not, do it in the manner they prefer; but very rarely on account of any opinion to which they consistently adhere, as to what things are fit to be done by a government. And it seems to me that in consequence of this absence of rule or principle, one side is at present as often wrong as the other; the interference of government is, with about equal frequency, improperly invoked and improperly condemned.

The object of this essay is to assert one very simple principle, as entitled to govern absolutely the dealings of society with the individual in the way of compulsion and control, whether the means used be physical force in the form of legal penalties or the moral coercion of public opinion. That principle is that the sole end for which mankind are warranted, individually or collectively, in interfering with the liberty of action of any of their number is self-protection. That the only purpose for which power can be rightfully exercised over any member of a civilized community, against his will, is to prevent harm to others. His own good, either physical or moral, is not a sufficient warrant. He cannot rightfully be compelled to do or forbear because it will be better for him to do so, because it will make him happier, because, in the opinions of others, to do so would be wise or even right. These are good reasons for remonstrating with him, or reasoning with him, or persuading him, or entreating him, but not for compelling him or visiting him with any evil in case he do otherwise. To justify that, the conduct from which it is desired to deter him must be calculated to produce evil to someone else. The only part of the conduct of anyone for which he is amenable to society is that which concerns others. In the part which merely concerns himself, his independence is, of right, absolute. Over himself, over his own body and mind, the individual is sovereign.

It is, perhaps, hardly necessary to say that

this doctrine is meant to apply only to human beings in the maturity of their faculties. We are not speaking of children or of young persons below the age which the law may fix as that of manhood or womanhood. Those who are still in a state to require being taken care of by others must be protected against their own actions as well as against external injury. For the same reason we may leave out of consideration those backward states of society in which the race itself may be considered as in its nonage. The early difficulties in the way of spontaneous progress are so great that there is seldom any choice of means for overcoming them; and a ruler full of the spirit of improvement is warranted in the use of any expedients that will attain an end perhaps otherwise unattainable. Despotism is a legitimate mode of government in dealing with barbarians, provided the end be their improvement and the means justified by actually effecting that end. Liberty, as a principle, has no application to any state of things anterior to the time when mankind have become capable of being improved by free and equal discussion. Until then, there is nothing for them but implicit obedience to an Akbar or a Charlemagne, if they are so fortunate as to find one. But as soon as mankind have attained the capacity of being guided to their own improvement by conviction or persuasion (a period long since reached in all nations with whom we need here concern ourselves), compulsion, either in the direct form or in that of pains and penalties for noncompliance, is no longer admissible as a means to their own good, and justifiable only for the security of others.

It is proper to state that I forego any advantage which could be derived to my argument from the idea of abstract right as a thing independent of utility. I regard utility as the ultimate appeal on all ethical questions; but it must be utility in the largest sense, grounded on the permanent interests of man as a progressive being. Those interests, I contend, authorize the subjection of individual spontaneity to external control only in respect to those actions of each which concern the interest of other people. If anyone does an act hurtful to others, there is a *prima facie* case for punishing him by law or, where legal penalties are not safely applicable, by general disapprobation. There are also many positive acts for the benefit of others which he may rightfully be compelled to perform, such as to give evidence in a court of justice, to bear his fair share in the common defense or in any other joint work necessary to the interest of the society of which he enjoys the protection, and to perform certain acts of individual beneficence, such as saving a fellow creature's life or interposing to protect the defenseless against ill usage—things which whenever it is obviously a man's duty to do he may rightfully be made responsible to society for not doing. A person may cause evil to others not only by his actions but by his inaction, and in either case he is justly accountable to them for the injury. The latter case, it is true, requires a much more cautious exercise of compulsion than the former. To make anyone answerable for doing evil to others is the rule; to make him answerable for not preventing evil is, comparatively speaking, the exception. Yet there are many cases clear enough and grave enough to justify that exception. In all things which regard the external relations of the individual, he is *de jure* amenable to those whose interests are concerned, and, if need be, to society as their protector. There are often good reasons for not holding him to the responsibility; but these reasons must arise from the special expediencies of the case: either because it is a kind of case in which he is on the whole likely to act better when left to his own discretion than when controlled in any way in which society have it in their power to control him; or because the attempt to exercise control would produce other evils, greater than those which it would prevent. When such reasons as these preclude the enforcement of responsibility, the conscience of the agent himself should step into the vacant judgment seat and protect those interests of others which have no external protection; judging himself all the more rigidly, because the case does not admit of his being made accountable to the judgment of his fellow creatures.

But there is a sphere of action in which society, as distinguished from the individual, has, if any, only an indirect interest: comprehending all that portion of a person's life and conduct which affects only himself or, if it also affects others, only with their free, voluntary, and undeceived consent and participation. When I say only himself, I mean directly and in the first instance; for whatever affects himself may affect others through himself; and the objection which may be grounded on this contingency will receive consideration in the sequel. This, then, is the appropriate region of human liberty. It comprises, first, the inward domain of consciousness, demanding liberty of conscience in the most comprehensive sense, liberty of thought and feeling, absolute freedom of opinion and sentiment on all subjects, practical or speculative, scientific, moral, or theological. The liberty of expressing and publishing opinions may seem to fall under a different principle, since it belongs to that part of the conduct of an individual which concerns other people, but, being almost of as much importance as the liberty of thought itself and resting in great part on the same reasons, is practically inseparable from it. Secondly, the principle requires liberty of tastes and pursuits, of framing the plan of our life to suit our own character, of doing as we like, subject to such consequences as may follow, without impediment from our fellow creatures, so long as what we do does not harm them, even though they should think our conduct foolish, perverse, or wrong. Thirdly, from this liberty of each individual fotlows the liberty, within the same limits, of combination among individuals; freedom to unite for any purpose not involving harm to others: the persons combining being supposed to be of full age and not forced or deceived.

No society in which these liberties are not, on the whole, respected is free, whatever may be its form of government; and none is completely free in which they do not exist absolute and unqualified. The only freedom which deserves the name is that of pursuing our own good in our own way, so long as we do not attempt to deprive others of theirs or impede their efforts to obtain it. Each is the proper guardian of his own health, whether bodily *or* mental and spiritual. Mankind are greater gainers by suffering each other to live as seems good to themselves than by compelling each to live as seems good to the rest.

....

OF LIBERTY OF THOUGHT AND DISCUSSION

We have now recognized the necessity to the mental well-being of mankind (on which all their other well-being depends) of freedom of opinion, and freedom of the expression of opinion, on four distinct grounds, which we will now briefly recapitulate:

First, if any opinion is compelled to silence, that opinion may, for aught we can certainly know, be true. To deny this is to assume our own infallibility.

Secondly, though the silenced opinion be an error, it may, and very commonly does, contain a portion of truth; and since the general or prevailing opinion on any subject is rarely or never the whole truth, it is only by the collision of adverse opinions that the remainder of the truth has any chance of being supplied.

Thirdly, even if the received opinion be not only true, but the whole truth; unless it is suffered to be, and actually is, vigorously and earnestly contested, it will, by most of those who receive it, be held in the manner of a prejudice, with little comprehension or feeling of its rational grounds. And not only this, but, fourthly, the meaning of the doctrine itself will be in danger of being lost or enfeebled, and deprived of its vital effect on the character and conduct: the dogma becoming a mere formal profession, inefficacious for good, but cumbering the ground and preventing the growth of any real and heartfelt conviction from reason or personal experience.

Before quitting the subject of freedom of opinion, it is fit to take some notice of those who say that the free expression of all opinions should be permitted on condition that the manner be temperate, and do not pass the bounds of fair discussion. Much might be said on the impossibility of fixing where these supposed bounds are to be placed; for if the test be offense to those whose opinions are attacked, I think experience testifies that this offense is given whenever the attack is telling and powerful, and that every opponent who pushes them hard, and whom they find it difficult to answer, appears to them, if he shows any strong feeling on the subject, an intemperate opponent. But this, though an important consideration in a practical point of view, merges in a more fundamental objection. Undoubtedly, the manner of asserting an opinion, even though it be a true one, may be very objectionable and may justly incur severe censure. But the principal offenses of the kind are such as it is mostly impossible, unless by accidental self-betrayal, to bring home to conviction. The gravest of them is, to argue sophistically, to suppress facts or arguments, to misstate the elements of the case, or misrepresent the opposite opinion. But all this, even to the most aggravated degree, is so continually done in perfect good faith by persons who are not considered, and in many other respects may not deserve to be considered, ignorant or incompetent, that it is rarely possible, on adequate grounds, conscientiously to stamp the misrepresentation as morally culpable, and still less could law presume to interfere with this kind of controversial misconduct. With regard to what is commonly meant by intemperate discussion, namely invective, sarcasm, personality, and the like, the denunciation of these weapons would deserve more sympathy if it were ever proposed to interdict them equally to both sides; but it is only desired to restrain the employment of them against the prevailing opinion; against the unprevailing they may not only be used without general disapproval, but will be likely to obtain for him who uses them the praise of honest zeal and righteous indignation. Yet whatever mischief arises from their use is greatest when they are employed against the comparatively defenseless; and whatever unfair advantage can be derived by any opinion from this mode of asserting it accrues almost exclusively to received opinions. The worst offense of this kind which can be committed by a polemic is to stigmatize those who hold the contrary opinion as bad and immoral men. To calumny of this sort, those who hold any unpopular opinion are peculiarly exposed, because they are in general few and uninfluential, and nobody but themselves feels much interested in seeing justice done them; but this weapon is, from the nature of the case, denied to those who attack a prevailing opinion: they can neither use it with safety to themselves, nor, if they could, would it do anything but recoil on their own cause. In general, opinions contrary to those commonly received can only obtain a hearing by studied moderation of language and the most cautious avoidance of unnecessary offense, from which they hardly ever deviate even in a slight degree without losing ground, while unmeasured vituperation employed on the side of the prevailing opinion really does deter people from professing contrary opinions and from listening to those who profess them. For the interest, therefore, of truth and justice it is far more important to restrain this employment of vituperative language than the other; and, for example, if it were necessary to choose, there would be much more need to discourage offensive attacks on infidelity than on religion. It is, however, obvious that law and authority have no business with restraining either, while opinion ought, in every instance, to determine its verdict by the circumstances of the individual case—condemning everyone, on whichever side of the argument he places himself, in whose mode of advocacy either want of candor, or malignity, bigotry, or intolerance of feeling manifest themselves; but not inferring these vices from the side which a person takes, though it be the contrary side of the question to our own; and giving merited honor to everyone, whatever opinion he may hold, who has calmness to see and honesty to state what his opponents and their opinions really are, exaggerating nothing to their discredit, keeping nothing back which tells, or can be supposed to tell, in their favor. This is the real morality of public discussion; and if often violated, I am happy to think that there are many controversialists who to a great extent observe it, and a still greater number who conscientiously strive toward it.

OF INDIVIDUALITY, AS ONE OF THE ELEMENTS OF WELL-BEING

Such being the reasons which make it imperative that human beings should be free to form opinions and to express their opinions without reserve; and such the baneful consequences to the intellectual, and through that to the moral nature of man, unless this liberty is either conceded or asserted in spite of prohibition; let us next examine whether the same reasons do not require that men should be free to act upon their opinions—to carry these out in their lives without hindrance, either physical or moral, from their fellow men, so long as it is at their own risk and peril. This last proviso is of course indispensable. No one pretends that actions should be as free as opinions. On the contrary, even opinions lose their immunity when the circumstances in which they are expressed are such as to constitute their expression a positive instigation to some mischievous act. An opinion that corn dealers are starvers of the poor, or that private property is robbery, ought to be unmolested when simply circulated through the press, but may justly incur punishment when delivered orally to an excited mob assembled before the house of a corn dealer, or when handed about among the same mob in the form of a placard. Acts, of whatever kind, which without justifiable cause do harm to others may be, and in the more important cases absolutely require to be, controlled by the unfavorable sentiments, and, when needful, by the active interference of mankind. The liberty of the individual must be thus far limited; he must not make himself a nuisance to other people. But if he refrains from molesting others in what concerns them, and merely acts according to his own inclination and judgment in things which concern himself, the same reasons which show that opinion should be free prove also that he should be allowed, without molestation, to carry his opinions into practice at his own cost. That mankind are not infallible; that their truths, for the most part, are only half-truths; that unity of opinion, unless resulting from the fullest and freest comparison of opposite opinions, is not desirable, and diversity not an evil, but a good, until mankind are much more capable than at present of recognizing all sides of the truth, are principles applicable to men's modes of action not less than to their opinions. As it is useful that while mankind are imperfect there should be different opinions, so it is that there should be different experiments of living; that free scope should be given to varieties of character, short of injury to others; and that the worth of different modes of life should be proved practically, when anyone thinks fit to try them. It is desirable, in short, that in things which do not primarily concern others individuality should assert itself. Where not the person's own character but the traditions or customs of other people are the rule of conduct, there is wanting one of the principal ingredients of human happiness, and quite the chief ingredient of individual and social progress.

In maintaining this principle, the greatest difficulty to be encountered does not lie in the appreciation of means toward an acknowledged end, but in the indifference of persons in general to the end itself. If it were felt that the free development of individuality is one of the leading essentials of well-being; that it is not only a co-ordinate element with all that is designated by the terms civilization, instruction, education, culture, but is itself a necessary part and condition of all those things, there would be no danger that liberty should be undervalued, and the adjustment of the boundaries between it and social control would present no extraordinary difficulty. But the evil is that individual spontaneity is hardly recognized by the common modes of thinking as having any intrinsic worth, or deserving any regard on its own account. The majority, being satisfied with the ways of mankind as they now are (for it is they who make them what they are), cannot comprehend why those ways should not be good enough for everybody; and what is more, spontaneity forms no part of the ideal of the majority of moral and social reformers, but is rather looked on with jealousy, as a troublesome and perhaps rebellious obstruction to the general acceptance of what these reformers, in their own judgment, think would be best for mankind.

....

APPLICATIONS

The principles asserted in these pages must be more generally admitted as the basis for discussion of details before a consistent application of them to all the various departments of government and morals can be attempted with any prospect of advantage. The few observations I propose to make on questions of detail are designed to illustrate the principles rather than to follow them out to their consequences. I offer not so much applications as specimens of application, which may serve to bring into greater clearness the meaning and limits of the two maxims which together form the entire doctrine of this essay, and to assist the judgment in holding the balance between them in the cases where it appears doubtful which of them is applicable to the case.

The maxims are, first, that the individual is not accountable to society for his actions in so far as these concern the interests of no person but himself. Advice, instruction, persuasion, and avoidance by other people, if thought necessary by them for their own good, are the only measures by which society can justifiably express its dislike or disapprobation of his conduct. Secondly, that for such actions as are prejudicial to the interests of others, the individual is accountable and may be subjected either to social or to legal punishment if society is of opinion that the one or the other is requisite for its protection.

In the first place, it must by no means be supposed, because damage, or probability of damage, to the interests of others can alone justify the interference of society, that therefore it always does justify such interference. In many cases an individual, in pursuing a legitimate object, necessarily and therefore legitimately causes pain or loss to others, or intercepts a good which they had a reasonable hope of obtaining. Such oppositons of interest between individuals often arise from bad social institutions, but are unavoidable while those institutions last; and some would be unavoidable under any institutions. Whoever succeeds in an overcrowded profession or in a competitive examination, whoever is preferred to another in any contest for an object which both desire, reaps benefit from the loss of others, from their wasted exertion and their disappointment. But it is, by common admission, better for the general interest of mankind that persons should pursue their objects undeterred by this sort of consequences. In other words, society admits no right, either legal or moral, in the disappointed competitors to immunity from this kind of suffering, and feels called on to interfere only when means of success have been employed which it is contrary to the general interest to permit—namely, fraud or treachery, and force.

Alienation

KARL MARX

(XXII) We have begun from the presuppositions of political economy. We have accepted its terminology and its laws. We presupposed private property, the separation of labor, capital and land, as also of wages, profit and rent, the division of labor, competition, the concept of exchange value, etc. From political economy itself, in its own words, we have shown that the worker sinks to the level of a commodity, and to a most miserable commodity; that the misery of the worker increases with the power and volume of his production; that the necessary result of competition is the accumulation of capital in a few hands, and thus a restoration of monopoly in a more terrible form; and finally that the distinction between capitalist and landlord, and between agricultural laborer and industrial worker, must disappear and the whole of society divide into the two classes of property *owners* and propertyless *workers*.

Political economy begins with the fact of private property; it does not explain it. It conceives the *material process* of private property, as this occurs in reality, in general and abstract formulas which then serve it as laws. It does not *comprehend* these laws; that is, it does not show how they arise out of the nature of private property. Political economy provides no explanation of the basis of the distinction of labor from capital, of capital from land. When, for example, the relation of wages to profits is defined, this is explained in terms of the interests of capitalists; in other words, what should be explained is assumed. Similarly, competition is referred to at every point and is explained in terms of external conditions. Political economy tells us nothing about the extent to which these external and apparently accidental conditions are simply the expression of a necessary development. We have seen how exchange itself seems an accidental fact. The only moving forces which political economy recognizes are *avarice* and the *war between the avaricious, competition*.

Just because political economy fails to understand the interconnections within this movement it was possible to oppose the doctrine of competition to that of monopoly, the doctrine of freedom of the crafts to that of the guilds, the doctrine of the division of landed property to that of the great estates; for competition, freedom of crafts, and the division of landed property were conceived only as accidental consequences brought about by will and force, rather than as necessary, inevitable and natural consequences of monopoly, the guild system and feudal property.

Thus we have now to grasp the real connection between this whole system of alienation—private property, acquisitiveness, the separation of labor, capital and land, exchange and competition, value and the devaluation of man, monopoly and competition—and the system of *money*.

Let us not begin our explanation, as does

Karl Marx (1818-1883) made important contributions in every area of social philosophy.

From *Karl Marx: Early Writings*, translated and edited by T. B. Bottomore (London, 1963, C. A. Watts). Reprinted by permission of the publishers. The selection is from *The Economic and Philosophic Manuscripts of 1844*.

the economist, from a legendary primordial condition. Such a primoridal condition does not explain anything; it merely removes the question into a gray and nebulous distance. It asserts as a fact or event what it should deduce, namely, the necessary relation between two things; for example, between the division of labor and exchange. In the same way theology explains the origin of evil by the fall of man; that is, it asserts as a historical fact what it should explain.

We shall begin from a *contemporary* economic fact. The worker becomes poorer the more wealth he produces and the more his production increases in power and extent. The worker becomes an ever cheaper commodity the more goods he creates. The *devaluation* of the human world increases in direct relation with the *increase in value* of the world of things. Labor does not only create goods; it also produces itself and the worker as a *commodity*, and indeed in the same proportion as it produces goods.

This fact simply implies that the object produced by labor, its product, now stands opposed to it as an *alien being*, as a *power independent* of the producer. The product of labor is labor which has been embodied in an object and turned into a physical thing; this product is an *objectification* of labor. The performance of work is at the same time its objectification. The performance of work appears in the sphere of political economy as a *vitiation* of the worker, objectification as a *loss* and as *servitude to the object*, and appropriation as *alienation*.

So much does the performance of work appear as vitiation that the worker is vitiated to the point of starvation. So much does objectification appear as loss of the object that the worker is deprived of the most essential things not only of life but also of work. Labor itself becomes an object which he can acquire only by the greatest effort and with unpredictable interruptions. So much does the appropriation of the object appear as alienation that the more objects the worker produces the fewer he can possess and the more he falls under the domination of his product, of capital.

All these consequences follow from the fact that the worker is related to the *product of his labor* as to an *alien* object. For it is clear on this presupposition that the more the worker expends himself in work the more powerful becomes the world of objects which he creates in face of himself, the poorer he becomes in his inner life, and the less he belongs to himself. It is just the same as in religion. The more of himself man attributes to God the less he has left in himself. The worker puts his life into the object, and his life then belongs no longer to himself but to the object. The greater his activity, therefore, the less he possesses. What is embodied in the product of his labor is no longer his own. The greater this product is, therefore, the more he is diminished. The *alienation* of the worker in his product means not only that his labor becomes an object, assumes an *external* existence, but that it exists independently, *outside himself*, and alien to him, and that it stands opposed to him as an autonomous power. The life which he has given to the object sets itself against him as an alien and hostile force.

(XXIII) Let us now examine more closely the phenomenon of *objectification*, the worker's production and the *alienation* and *loss* of the object it produces, which is involved in it. The worker can create nothing without *nature*, without the *sensuous external world*. The latter is the material in which his labor is realized, in which it is active, out of which and through which it produces things.

But just as nature affords the *means of existence* of labor in the sense that labor cannot *live* without objects upon which it can be exercised, so also it provides the *means of existence* in a narrower sense; namely the means of physical existence for the *worker* himself. Thus, the more the worker *appropriates* the external world of sensuous nature by his labor the more he deprives himself of *means of existence*, in two respects: first, that the sensuous external world becomes progressively less an object belonging to his labor or a means of existence of his labor, and secondly, that it becomes progressively less a means of existence in the direct sense, a means for the physical subsistence of the worker.

In both respects, therefore, the worker becomes a slave of the object; first, in that he receives an *object of work*, i.e., receives *work*, and secondly that he receives *means of subsistence*. Thus the object enables him to exist, first as a *worker* and secondly, as a *physical subject*. The culmination of this enslavement is that he can only maintain himself as a *physical subject* so far as he is a *worker*, and that it is only as a *physical subject* that he is a worker.

(The alienation of the worker in his object is expressed as follows in the laws of political economy: the more the worker produces the less he has to consume; the more value he creates the more worthless he becomes; the more refined his product the more crude and misshapen the worker; the more civilized the product the more barbarous the worker; the more powerful the work the more feeble the worker; the more the work manifests intelligence the more the worker declines in intelligence and becomes a slave of nature.)

Political economy conceals the alienation in the nature of labor insofar as it does not examine the direct relationship between the worker (work) and production. Labor certainly produces marvels for the rich but it produces privation for the worker. It produces palaces, but hovels for the worker. It produces beauty, but deformity for the worker. It replaces labor by machinery, but it casts some of the workers back into a barbarous kind of work and turns the others into machines. It produces intelligence, but also stupidity and cretinism for the workers.

The direct relationship of labor to its products is the relationship of the worker to the objects of his production. The relationship of property owners to the objects of production and to production itself is merely a *consequence* of this first relationship and confirms it. We shall consider this second aspect later.

Thus, when we ask what is the important relationship of labor, we are concerned with the relationship of the *worker* to production.

So far we have considered the alienation of the worker only from one aspect; namely, *his relationship with the products of his labor*. However, alienation appears not only in the result, but also in the *process*, of *production*, within *productive activity* itself. How could the worker stand in an alien relationship to the product of his activity if he did not alienate himself in the act of production itself? The product is indeed only the *résumé* of activity, of production. Consequently, if the product of labor is alienation, production itself must be active alienation—the alienation of activity and the activity of alienation. The alienation of the object of labor merely summarizes the alienation in the work activity itself.

What constitutes the alienation of labor? First, that the work is *external* to the worker, that it is not part of his nature; and that, consequently, he does not fulfill himself in his work but denies himself, has a feeling of misery rather than well being, does not develop freely his mental and physical energies but is physically exhausted and mentally debased. The worker therefore feels himself at home only during his leisure time, whereas at work he feels homeless. His work is not voluntary but imposed, *forced labor*. It is not the satisfaction of a need, but only a *means* for satisfying other needs. Its alien character is clearly shown by the fact that as soon as there is no physical or other compulsion it is avoided like the plague. External labor, labor in which man alienates himself, is a labor of self-sacrifice, of mortification. Finally, the external character of work for the worker is shown by the fact that it is not his own work but work for someone else, that in work he does not belong to himself but to another person.

Just as in religion the spontaneous activity of human fantasy, of the human brain and heart, reacts independently as an alien activity of gods or devils upon the individual, so the activity of the worker is not his own spontaneous activity. It is another's activity and a loss of his own spontaneity.

We arrive at the result that man (the worker) feels himself to be freely active only in his animal functions—eating, drinking and procreating, or at most also in his dwelling and in personal adornment—while in his human functions he is reduced to an animal. The animal becomes human and the human becomes animal.

Eating, drinking and procreating are of course also genuine human functions. But abstractly considered, apart from the environment of other human activities, and turned into final and sole ends, they are animal functions.

We have now considered the act of alienation of practical human activity, labor, from two aspects: (1) the relationship of the worker to the *product of labor* as an alien object which dominates him. This relationship is at the same time the relationship to the sensuous external world, to natural objects, as an alien and hostile world; (2) the relationship of labor to the *act of production* within *labor*. This is the relationship of the worker to his own activity as something alien and not belonging to him, activity as suffering (passivity), strength as powerlessness, creation as emasculation, the *personal* physical and mental energy of the worker, his personal life (for what is life but activity?) as an activity which is directed against himself, independent of him and not belonging to him. This is *self-alienation* as against the above-mentioned alienation of the *thing*.

(XXIV) We have now to infer a third characteristic of *alienated labor* from the two we have considered.

Man is a species-being[1] not only in the sense that he makes the community (his own as well as those of other things) his object both practically and theoretically, but also (and this is simply another expression for the same thing) in the sense that he treats himself as the present, living species, as a *universal* and consequently free being.

Species-life, for man as for animals, has its physical basis in the fact that man (like animals) lives from inorganic nature, and since man is more universal than an animal so the range of inorganic nature from which he lives is more universal. Plants, animals, minerals, air, light, etc. constitute, from the theoretical aspect, a part of human consciousness as objects of natural science and art; they are man's spiritual inorganic nature, his intellectual means of life, which he must first prepare for enjoyment and perpetuation. So also, from the practical aspect they form a part of human life and activity. In practice man lives only from these natural products, whether in the form of food, heating, clothing, housing, etc. The universality of man appears in practice in the universality which makes the whole of nature into his inorganic body: (1) as a direct means of life; and equally (2) as the material object and instrument of his life activity. Nature is the *inorganic body* of man; that is to say, nature excluding the human body itself. To say that man *lives* from nature means that nature is his *body* with which he must remain in a continuous interchange in order not to die. The statement that the physical and mental life of man, and nature, are interdependent means simply that nature is interdependent with itself, for man is a part of nature.

Since alienated labor: (1) alienates nature from man; and (2) alienates man from himself, from his own active function, his life activity; so it alienates him from the species. It makes *species-life* into a means of individual life. In the first place it alienates species-life and individual life, and secondly, it turns the latter, as an abstraction, into the purpose of the former, also in its abstract and alienated form.

For labor, *life activity, productive life*, now appear to man only as *means* for the satisfaction of a need, the need to maintain his physical existence. Productive life is, however, species-life. It is life creating life. In the type of life activity resides the whole character of a species, its species-character; and free, conscious activity is the species-character of human beings. Life itself appears only as a *means of life*.

The animal is one with its life activity. It does not distinguish the activity from itself. It is *its activity*. But man makes his life activity itself an object of his will and consciousness. He has a conscious life activity. It is not a determination with which he is completely identified. Conscious life activity distinguishes man from the life activity of animals. Only for this reason is he a species-being. Or rather, he is only a self-conscious being, i.e. his own life is an object for him, because he is a species-being. Only for this reason is his activity free activity. Alienated labor reverses the relationship, in that man because he is a self-conscious being makes his life activity, his *being*, only a means for his *existence*.

The practical construction of an *objective world*, the *manipulation* of inorganic nature, is the confirmation of man as a conscious species-being, i.e. a being who treats the species as his own being or himself as a species-being. Of course, animals also produce. They construct nests, dwellings, as in the case of bees, beavers, ants, etc. But they only produce what is strictly necessary for themselves or their young. They produce only in a single direction, while man produces universally. They produce only under the compulsion of direct physical need, while man produces when he is free from physical need and only truly produces in freedom from such need. Animals produce only themselves, while man reproduces the whole of nature. The products of animal production belong directly to their physical bodies, while man is free in face of his product. Animals construct only in accordance with the standards and needs of the species to which they belong, while man knows how to produce in accordance with the standards of every species and knows how to apply the appropriate standard to the object. Thus man constructs also in accordance with the laws of beauty.

It is just in his work upon the objective world that man really proves himself as a *species-being*. This production is his active species life. By means of it nature appears as *his* work and his reality. The object of labor is, therefore, the *objectification of man's species life*; for he no longer reproduces himself merely intellectually, as in consciousness, but actively and in a real sense, and he sees his own reflection in a world which he has constructed. While, therefore, alienated labor takes away the object of production from man, it also takes away his *species life*, his real objectivity as a species-being, and changes his advantage over animals into a disadvantage in so far as his inorganic body, nature, is taken from him.

Just as alienated labor transforms free and self-directed activity into a means, so it transforms the species life of man into a means of physical existence.

Consciousness, which man has from his species, is transformed through alienation so that species life becomes only a means for him.

(3) Thus alienated labor turns the *species life of man*, and also nature as his mental species-property, into an *alien* being and into a *means* for his *individual existence*. It alienates from man his own body, external nature, his mental life and his *human* life.

(4) A direct consequence of the alienation of man from the product of his labor, from his life activity and from his species life is that *man* is *alienated* from other *men*. When man confronts himself he also confronts *other* men. What is true of man's relationship to his work, to the product of his work and to himself, is also true of his relationship to other men, to their labor and to the objects of their labor.

In general, the statement that man is alienated from his species life means that each man is alienated from others, and that each of the others is likewise alienated from human life.

Human alienation, and above all the relation of man to himself, is first realized and expressed in the relationship between each man and other men. Thus in the relationship of alienated labor every man regards other men according to the standards and relationships in which he finds himself placed as a worker.

(XXV) We began with an economic fact, the alienation of the worker and his production. We have expressed this fact in conceptual terms as *alienated labor*, and in analyzing the concept we have merely analyzed an economic fact.

Let us now examine further how this concept of alienated labor must express and reveal itself in reality. If the product of labor is alien to me and confronts me as an alien power, to whom does it belong? If my own activity does not belong to me but is an alien, forced activity, to whom does it belong? To a being *other* than myself. And who is this being? The *gods*? It is apparent in the earliest stages of advanced production, e.g., temple building, etc. in Egypt, India, Mexico, and in the service rendered to gods, that the product belonged to the gods. But the gods alone were never the lords of labor. And no more was *nature*. What a contradiction it would be if the more man subjugates nature by his labor, and the more the marvels of the gods are rendered superfluous by the marvels of industry, he should abstain from his joy in producing and his enjoyment of the product for love of these powers.

The *alien* being to whom labor and the product of labor belong, to whose service labor is devoted, and to whose enjoyment the product of labor goes, can only be *man* himself. If the product of labor does not belong to the worker, but confronts him as an alien power, this can only be because it belongs to *a man other than the worker*. If his activity is a torment to him it must be a source of enjoyment and pleasure to another. Not the gods, nor nature, but only man himself can be this alien power over men.

Consider the earlier statement that the relation of man to himself is first realized, objectified, through his relation to other men. If therefore he is related to the product of his labor, his objectified labor, as to an *alien*, hostile, powerful and independent object, he is related in such a way that another alien, hostile, powerful and independent man is the lord of this object. If he is related to his own activity as to unfree activity, then he is related to it as activity in the service, and under the domination, coercion and yoke, of another man.

Every self-alienation of man, from himself and from nature, appears in the relation which he postulates between other men and himself and nature. Thus religious self-alienation is necessarily exemplified in the relation between laity and priest, or, since it is here a question of the spiritual world, between the laity and a mediator. In the real world of practice this self-alienation can only be expressed in the real, practical relation of man to his fellow-men. The medium through which alienation occurs is itself a *practical* one. Through alienated labor, therefore, man not only produces his relation to the object and to the process of production as to alien and hostile men; he also produces the relation of other men to his production and his product, and the relation between himself and other men. Just as he creates his own production as a vitiation, a punishment, and his own product as a loss, as a product which does not belong to him, so he creates the domination of the non-producer over production and its product. As he alienates his own activity, so he bestows upon the stranger an activity which is not his own.

We have so far considered this relation only from the side of the worker, and later on we shall consider it also from the side of the non-worker.

Thus, through alienated labor the worker creates the relation of another man, who does not work and is outside the work process, to this labor. The relation of the worker to work also produces the relation of the capitalist (or whatever one likes to call the lord of labor) to work. *Private property* is therefore the product, the necessary result, of *alienated labor*, of the external relation of the worker to nature and to himself.

Private property is thus derived from the analysis of the concept of *alienated labor*; that is, alienated man, alienated labor, alienated life, and estranged man.

We have, of course, derived the concept of *alienated labor (alienated life)* from political economy, from an analysis of the *movement of private property*. But the analysis of this concept shows that although private property appears to be the basis and cause of alienated labor, it is rather a consequence of the latter, just as the gods are *fundamentally* not the cause but the product of confusions of human reason. At a later stage, however, there is a reciprocal influence.

Only in the final stage of the development of private property is its secret revealed, namely, that it is on one hand the *product* of alienated labor, and on the other hand the *means* by which labor is alienated, the *realization of this alienation*.

This elucidation throws light upon several unresolved controversies:

(1) Political economy begins with labor as the real soul of production and then goes on to attribute nothing to labor and everything to private property. Proudhon, faced by this contradiction, has decided in favor of labor against private property. We perceive, however, that this apparent contradiction is the contradiction of *alienated labor* with itself and that political economy has merely formulated the laws of alienated labor.

We also observe, therefore, that *wages* and *private property* are identical, for wages, like the product or object of labor, labor itself remunerated, are only a necessary consequence of the alienation of labor. In the wage system labor appears not as an end in itself but as the servant of wages. We shall develop this point later on and here only bring out some of the (XXVI) consequences.

An enforced *increase in wages* (disregarding the other difficulties, and especially that such an anomaly could only be maintained by force) would be nothing more than a *better remuneration of slaves*, and would not restore, either to the worker or to the work, their human significance and worth.

Even the *equality of incomes* which Proudhon demands would only change the relation of the present day worker to his work into a relation of all men to work. Society would then be conceived as an abstract capitalist.

(2) From the relation of alienated labor to private property it also follows that the emancipation of society from private property, from servitude, takes the political form of the *emancipation of the workers*; not in the sense that only the latter's emancipation is involved, but because this emancipation includes the emancipation of humanity as a whole. For all human servitude is involved in the relation of the worker to production, and all the types of servitude are only modifications or consequences of this relation.

As we have discovered the concept of *private property* by an *analysis* of the concept of *alienated labor*, so with the aid of these two factors we can evolve all the categories of political economy, and in every category, e.g., trade, competition, capital, money, we shall discover only a particular and developed expression of these fundamental elements.

However, before considering this structure let us attempt to solve two problems.

(1) To determine the general nature of *private property* as it has resulted from alienated labor, in its relation to *genuine human and social property*.

(2) We have taken as a fact and analyzed the *alienation of labor*. How does it happen, we may ask, that *man alienates his labor*? How is this alienation founded in the nature of human development? We have already done much to solve the problem in so far as we have *transformed* the question concerning the *origin of private property* into a question about the relation between *alienated labor* and the process of development of mankind. For in speaking of private property one believes oneself to be dealing with something external to mankind. But in speaking of labor one deals directly with mankind itself. This new formulation of the problem already contains its solution.

ad (1) *The general nature of private property and its relation to genuine human property.*

We have resolved alienated labor into two parts, which mutually determine each other, or rather constitute two different expressions of one and the same relation. *Appropriation* appears as *alienation* and *alienation* as *appropriation*, alienation as genuine acceptance in the community.

We have considered one aspect, *alienated* labor, in its bearing upon the *worker* himself, i.e., *the relation of alienated labor to itself*. And we have found as the necessary consequence of this relation the *property relation* of the *non-worker* to the *worker* and to *labor*. *Private property* as the material summarized expression of alienated labor includes both relations; *the relation of the worker to labor, to the product of his labor and to the non-worker*, and the relation of the *non-worker to the worker and to the product of the latter's labor*.

We have already seen that in relation to the worker, who *appropriates* nature by his labor, appropriation appears as alienation, self-activity as activity for another and of another, living as the sacrifice of life, and production of the object as loss of the object to an alien power, an alien man. Let us now consider the relation of this *alien* man to the worker, to labor, and to the object of labor.

It should be noted first that everything which appears to the worker as an *activity of alienation*, appears to the non-worker as a *condition of alienation*. Secondly, the *real, practical* attitude of the worker in production and to the product (as a state of mind) appears to the non-worker who confronts him as a *theoretical* attitude.

(XXVII) Thirdly, the non-worker does everything against the worker which the latter does against himself, but he does not do against himself what he does against the worker.

Let us examine these three relationships more closely.[2]

NOTES

1. The term "species-being" is taken from Feuerbach's *Das Wesen des Christentums* (The Essence of Christianity). Feuerbach used the notion in making a distinction between consciousness in man and in animals. Man is conscious not merely of himself as an individual but of the human species or "human essence."—*Tr. Note*

2. The manuscript breaks off unfinished at this point.—*Tr. Note*

From *German Ideology*

KARL MARX

The fact is . . . that definite individuals who are productively active in a definite way enter into . . . definite social and political relations. Empirical observation must in each separate instance bring out empirically, and without any mystification and speculation, the connection of the social and political structure with production. The social structure and the State are continually evolving out of the life-process of definite individuals, but individuals, not as they may appear in their own or other people's imagination, but as they really are; i.e., as they are effective, produce materially, and are active under definite material limits, presuppositions and conditions independent of their will.

The production of ideas, of conceptions, of consciousness, is at first directly interwoven with the material activity and the material intercourse of men, the language of real life. Conceiving, thinking, the mental intercourse of men, appear at this stage as the direct efflux of their material behavior. The same applies to mental production as expressed in the language of the politics, laws, morality, religion, metaphysics of a people. Men are the producers of their conceptions, ideas, etc.—real, active men, as they are conditioned by a definite development of their productive forces and of the intercourse corresponding to these, up to its furthest forms. Consciousness can never be anything else than conscious existence, and the existence of men is their actual life-process. If in all ideology men and their circumstances appear upside down as in a *camera obscura*, this phenomenon arises just as much from their historical life-process as the inversion of objects on the retina does from their physical life-process.

In direct contrast to German philosophy which descends from heaven to earth, here we ascend from earth to heaven. That is to say, we do not set out from what men say, imagine, conceive, nor from men as narrated, thought of, imagined, conceived, in order to arrive at men in the flesh. We set out from real, active men, and on the basis of their real life-process we demonstrate the development of the ideological reflexes and echoes of this life-process. The phantoms formed in the human brain are also, necessarily, sublimates of their material life-process, which is empirically verifiable and bound to material premises. Morality, religion, metaphysics, all the rest of ideology and their corresponding forms of consciousness, thus no longer retain the semblance of independence. They have no history, no development; but men, developing their material production and their material intercourse, alter, along with this their real existence, their thinking and the products of their thinking. Life is not determined by consciousness, but consciousness by life. In the first method of approach the starting-point is consciousness taken as the living individual; in the second it is the real living individuals themselves, as they are in actual life, and consciousness is considered solely as *their* consciousness.

This method of approach is not devoid of premises. It starts out from the real premises

From *Karl Marx: Early Writings*, translated and edited by T. B. Bottomore (London, 1963, C. A. Watts). Reprinted by permission of the publishers.

and does not abandon them for a moment. Its premises are men, not in any fantastic isolation or abstract definition, but in their actual, empirically perceptible process of development under definite conditions. As soon as this active life-process is described, history ceases to be a collection of dead facts as it is with the empiricists themselves still abstract), or an imagined activity of imagined subjects, as with the idealists.

Where speculation ends—in real life—there real, positive science begins: the representation of the practical activity, of the practical process of development of men. Empty talk about consciousness ceases, and real knowledge has to take its place. When reality is depicted, philosophy as an independent branch of activity loses its medium of existence. At the best its place can only be taken by a summing-up of the most general results, abstractions which arise from the observation of the historical development of men. Viewed apart from real history, these abstractions have in themselves no value whatsoever. They can only serve to facilitate the arrangement of historical material, to indicate the sequence of its separate strata. But they by no means afford a recipe or schema, as does philosophy, for neatly trimming the epochs of history. On the contrary, our difficulties begin only when we set about the observation and the arrangement—the real depiction—of our historical material, whether of a past epoch or of the present. The removal of these difficulties is governed by premises which it is quite impossible to state here, but which only the study of the actual life-process and the activity of the individuals of each epoch will make evident. We shall select here some of these abstractions, which we use to refute the ideologists, and shall illustrate them by historical examples.

(a) History

Since we are dealing with the Germans, who do not postulate anything, we must begin by stating the first premise of all human existence, and therefore of all history, the premise namely that men must be in a position to live in order to be able to "make history." But life involves before everything else eating and drinking, a habitation, clothing and many other things. The first historical act is thus the production of the means to satisfy these needs, the production of material life itself. And indeed this is an historical act, a fundamental condition of all history, which to-day, as thousands of years ago, must daily and hourly be fulfilled merely in order to sustain human life. Even when the sensuous world is reduced to a minimum, to a stick as with Saint Bruno, it presupposes the action of producing the stick. The first necessity therefore in any theory of history is to observe this fundamental fact in all its significance and all its implications and to accord it its due importance. This, as is notorious, the Germans have never done, and they have never therefore had an earthly basis for history and consequently never a historian. The French and the English, even if they have conceived the relation of this fact with so-called history only in an extremely one-sided fashion, particularly as long as they remained in the toils of political ideology, have nevertheless made the first attempts to give the writing of history a materialistic basis by being the first to write histories of civil society, of commerce and industry.

The second fundamental point is that as soon as a need is satisfied, (which implies the action of satisfying, and the acquisition of an instrument), new needs are made; and this production of new needs is the first historical act. Here we recognize immediately the spiritual ancestry of the great historical wisdom of the Germans who, when they run out of positive material and when they can serve up neither theological nor political nor literary rubbish, do not write history at all, but invent the "prehistoric era." They do not, however, enlighten us as to how we proceed from this nonsensical "pre-history" to history proper; although, on the other hand, in their historical speculation they seize upon this "pre-history" with especial eagerness because they imagine themselves safe there from interference on the part of "crude facts," and, at the same time, because there they can give full rein to their speculative impulse and set up and knock down hypotheses by the thousand.

The third circumstance which, from the

very first, enters into historical development, is that men, who daily remake their own life, begin to make other men, to propagate their kind: the relation between man and wife, parents and children, the *family*. The family which to begin with is the only social relationship, becomes later, when increased needs create new social relations and the increased population new needs, a subordinate one (except in Germany), and must then be treated and analyzed according to the existing empirical data,[1] not according to "the concept of the family," as is the custom in Germany. These three aspects of social activity are not of course to be taken as three different stages, but just, as I have said, as three aspects or, to make it clear to the Germans, three "moments," which have existed simultaneously since the dawn of history and the first men, and still assert themselves in history to-day.

The production of life, both of one's own in labor and of fresh life in procreation, now appears as a double relationship: on the one hand as a natural, on the other as a social relationship. By social we understand the cooperation of several individuals, no matter under what conditions, in which manner and to what end. It follows from this that a certain mode of production, or industrial stage, is always combined with a certain mode of cooperation, or social stage, and this mode of co-operation is itself a "productive force." Further, that the multitude of productive forces accessible to men determines the nature of society, hence that the "history of humanity" must always be studied and treated in relation to the history of industry and exchange. But it is also clear how in Germany it is impossible to write this sort of history, because the Germans lack not only the necessary power of comprehension and the material but also the "evidence of their senses," for across the Rhine you cannot have any experience of these things since history has stopped happening. Thus it is quite obvious from the start that there exists a materialistic connection of men with one another, which is determined by their needs and their mode of production, and which is as old as men themselves. This connection is ever taking on new forms, and thus presents a "history" independently of the existence of any political or religious nonsense which would hold men together on its own.

Only now, after having considered four moments, four aspects of the fundamental historical relationships, do we find that man also possesses "consciousness"; but, even so, not inherent, not "pure" consciousness. From the start the "spirit" is afflicted with the curse of being "burdened" with matter, which here makes its appearance in the form of agitated layers of air, sounds, in short of language. Language is as old as consciousness, language is practical consciousness, as it exists for other men, and for that reason is really beginning to exist for me personally as well; for language, like consciousness only arises from the need, the necessity, of intercourse with other men. Where there exists a relationship, it exists for me: the animal has no "relations" with anything, cannot have any. For the animal, its relation to others does not exist as a relation. Consciousness is therefore from the very beginning a social product, and remains so as long as men exist at all. Consciousness is at first, of course, merely consciousness concerning the immediate sensuous environment and consciousness of the limited connection with other persons and things outside the individual who is growing self-conscious. At the same time it is consciousness of nature, which first appears to men as a completely alien, all-powerful and unassailable force, with which men's relations are purely animal and by which they are overawed like beasts; it is thus a purely animal consciousness of nature (natural religion).

We see here immediately: this natural religion or animal behavior towards nature is determined by the form of society and *vice versa*. Here, as everywhere, the identity of nature and man appears in such a way that the restricted relation of men to nature determines their restricted relation to one another, and their restricted relation to one another determines men's restricted relation to nature, just because nature is as yet hardly modified historically; and, on the other hand, man's consciousness of the necessity of associating with the individuals around him is the beginning of the consciousness that he is living in society at all. This beginning is as animal as social life itself at this stage. It is mere hard-consciousness, and at this point man is only distinguished from sheep by the fact that with him consciousness takes the place of instinct or that his instinct is a conscious one.

This sheep-like or tribal consciousness receives its further development and extension through increased productivity, the increase of needs, and, what is fundamental to both of these, the increase of population. With these there develops the division of labor, which was originally nothing but the division of labor in the sexual act, then that division of labor which develops spontaneously or "naturally" by virtue of natural predisposition (e.g., physical strength), needs, accidents, etc., etc. Division of labor only becomes truly such from the moment when a division of material and mental labor appears. From this moment onwards consciousness *can* really flatter itself that it is something other than consciousness of existing practice, that it is *really* conceiving something without conceiving something *real;* from now on consciousness is in a position to emancipate itself from the world and to proceed to the formation of "pure" theory, theology, philosophy, ethics, etc. But even if this theory, theology, philosophy, ethics, etc. comes into contradiction with the existing relations, this can only occur as a result of the fact that existing social relations have come into contradiction with existing forces of production; this, moreover, can also occur in a particular national sphere of relations through the appearance of the contradiction, not within the national orbit, but between this national consciousness and the practice of other nations, i.e., between the national and the general consciousness of a nation.

Moreover, it is quite immaterial what consciousness starts to do on its own: out of all such muck we get only the one inference that these three moments, the forces of production, the state of society, and consciousness, can and must come into contradiction with one another, because the division of labor implies the possibility, nay the fact that intellectual and material activity—enjoyment and labor, production and consumption—devolve on different individuals, and that the only possibility of their not coming into contradiction lies in the negation in its turn of the division of labor. It is self-evident, moreover, that "spectres," "bonds," "the higher being," "concept," "scruple," are merely the idealistic, spiritual expression, the conception apparently of the isolated individual, the image of very empirical fetters and limitations, within which the mode of production of life, and the form of intercourse coupled with it, move.

With the division of labor, in which all these contradictions are implicit, and which in its turn is based on the natural division of labor in the family and the separation of society into individual families opposed to one another, is given simultaneously the distribution, and indeed the unequal distribution, (both quantitative and qualitative), of labor and its products, hence property: the nucleus, the first form, of which lies in the family, where wife and children are the slaves of the husband. This latent slavery in the family, though still very crude, is the first property, but even at this early stage it corresponds perfectly to the definition of modern economists who call it the power of disposing of the labor-power of others. Division of labor and private property are, moreover, identical expressions: in the one the same thing is affirmed with reference to activity as is affirmed in the other with reference to the product of the activity.

Further, the division of labor implies the contradiction between the interest of the separate individual or the individual family and the communal interest of all individuals who have intercourse with one another. And indeed, this communal interest does not exist merely in the imagination, as "the general good," but first of all in reality, as the mutual interdependence of the individuals among whom the labor is divided. And finally, the division of labor offers us the first example of how, as long as man remains in natural society, that is as long as a cleavage exists between the particular and the common interest, as long therefore as activity is not voluntarily, but naturally, divided, man's own deed becomes an alien power opposed to him, which enslaves him instead of being controlled by him. For as soon as labor is distributed, each man has a particular, exclusive sphere of activity, which is forced upon him and from which he cannot escape. He is a hunter, a fisherman, a shepherd, or a critical critic, and must remain so if he does not want to lose his means of livelihood; while in communist society, where nobody has one exclusive sphere of activity but each can become accomplished in any branch he wishes, society regulates the general production and thus makes it possible for me to do one thing to-day and another to-morrow, to hunt in the morning, fish in the afternoon, rear cattle in the evening, criticize after dinner, just as I have a mind, without ever becoming hunter, fisherman, shepherd or critic.

This crystallization of social activity, this consolidation of what we ourselves produce into an objective power above us, growing out of our control, thwarting our expectations, bringing to naught our calculations, is one of the chief factors in historical development up till now. And out of this very contradiction between the interest of the individual and that of the community the latter takes an independent form as the *State*, divorced from the real interests of individual and community, and at the same time as an illusory communal life, always based, however, on the real ties existing in every family and tribal conglomeration (such as flesh and blood, language, division of labor on a larger scale, and other interests) and especially, as we shall enlarge upon later, on the classes, already determined by the division of labor, which in every such mass of men separate out, and of which one dominates all the others. It follows from this that all struggles within the State, the struggle between democracy, aristocracy and monarchy, the struggle for the franchise, etc., etc., are merely the illusory forms in which the real struggles of the different classes are fought out among one another (of this the German theoreticians have not the faintest inkling, although they have received a sufficient introduction to the subject in *The German-French Annals* and *The Holy Family*).

Further, it follows that every class which is struggling for mastery, even when its domination, as is the case with the proletariat, postulates the abolition of the old form of society in its entirety and of mastery itself, must first conquer for itself political power in order to represent its interest in turn as the general interest, a step to which in the first moment it is forced. Just because individuals seek *only* their particular interest, i.e., that not coinciding with their communal interest (for the "general good" is the illusory form of communal life), the latter will be imposed on them as an interest "alien" to them, and "independent" of them, as in its turn a particular, peculiar "general interest"; or they must meet face to face in this antagonism, as in democracy. On the other hand too, the *practical* struggle of these particular interests, which constantly *really* run counter to the communal and illusory communal interests, make *practical* intervention and control necessary through the illusory "general-interest" in the form of the State. The social power, i.e., the multiplied productive force, which arises through the cooperation of different individuals as it is determined within the division of labor, appears to these individuals, since their co-operation is not voluntary but natural, not as their own united power but as an alien force existing outside them, of the origin and end of which they are ignorant, which they thus cannot control, which on the contrary passes through a peculiar series of phases and stages independent of the will and the action of man, nay even being the prime governor of these.

This "estrangement" (to use a term which will be comprehensible to the philosophers) can, of course, only be abolished given two *practical* premises. For it to become an "intolerable" power, i.e., a power against which men make a revolution, it must necessarily have rendered the great mass of humanity "propertyless," and produced, at the same time, the contradiction of an existing world of wealth and culture, both of which conditions presuppose a great increase in productive power, a high degree of its development. And, on the other hand, this development of produntive forces (which itself implies the actual empirical existence of men in their *world-historical*, instead of local, being) is absolutely necessary as a practical premise: firstly, for the reason that without it only *want* is made general, and with want the struggle for necessities and all the old filthy business would necessarily be reproduced; and secondly, because only with this universal development of productive forces is a *universal* intercourse between men established, which produces in all nations simultaneously the phenomenon of the "propertyless" mass (universal competition), makes each nation dependent on the revolutions of the others, and finally has put *world-historical*, empirically universal individuals in place of local ones. Without this, (1) Communism could only exist as a local event; (2) The forces of intercourse themselves could not have developed as universal, hence intolerable powers: they would have remained home-bred superstitious conditions; and (3) Each extension of intercourse would abolish local communism. Empirically, communism is only possible as the act of the dominant peoples "all at once" or simultaneously, which presupposes the universal development of productive forces and the world-intercourse bound up with them. How otherwise could property have had a history at all, have taken on different forms, and landed property, for instance, according to the different premises given, have proceeded in France from parcellation to centralization in the hands of a few, in England from centralization in the hands of a few to parcellation, as is actually the case today? Or how does it happen that trade, which after all is nothing more than the exchange of products of various individuals and countries, rules the whole world through the relation of supply and demand—a relation which, as an English economist says, hovers over the earth like the Fate of the Ancients, and with invisible hand allots fortune and misfortune to men, sets up empires and overthrows empires, causes nations to rise and to disappear—while with the abolition of the basis of private property, with the communistic regulation of production (and, implicit in this, the destruction of the alien relation between men and what they themselves produce), the power of the relation of supply and demand is dissolved into nothing, and men get exchange, production, the mode of their mutual relation, under their own control again?

Communism is for us not a stable state which is to be established, an *ideal* to which reality will have to adjust itself. We call communism the *real* movement which abolishes the present state of things. The conditions of this movement result from the premises now in existence. Besides, the world market is presupposed by the mass of propertyless workers—labor-power cut off as a mass from capital or from even a limited satisfaction—and therefore no longer by the mere precariousness of labor, which, not giving an assured livelihood, is often lost through competition. The proletariat can thus only exist *world-historically*, just as communism, its movement, can only have a "world-historical" existence. World-historical existence of individuals, i.e., existence of individuals which is directly linked up with world history.

The form of intercourse determined by the existing productive forces at all previous historical stages, and in its turn determining these, is *civil society*. This, as is clear from what we have said above, has as its premises and basis the simple family and the multiple, the so-called tribe, the more precise determinants of which are enumerated in our remarks above. Already here we see how this civil society is the true source and theatre of all history, and how nonsensical is the conception of history held hitherto, which neglects the real relationships and confines itself to high-sounding dramas of princes and states. Civil society embraces the whole material intercourse of individuals within a definite stage of the development of productive forces. It embraces the whole commercial and industrial life of this stage and, in so far, transcends the State and the nation, though, on the other hand again, it must assert itself towards foreign peoples as nationality, and inwardly must organize itself as State. The word "civil society" emerged in the eighteenth century, when property relationships had already extricated themselves from the ancient and medieval communal society. Civil society as such only develops with the bourgeoisie; the social organization evolving directly out of production and commerce, which in all ages forms the basis of the State and of the rest of the idealistic superstructure, has, however, always been designated by the same name. . . .

History is nothing but the succession of the separate generations, each of which exploits the materials, the forms of capital, the productive forces handed down to it by all preceding ones, and thus on the one hand continues the traditional activity in completely changed circumstances and, on the other, modifies the old circumstances with a completely changed activity. This can be speculatively distorted so that later history is made the goal of earlier history, e.g., the goal ascribed to the discovery of America is to further the eruption of the French Revolution. Thereby history receives its own special aims and becomes "a person ranking with other persons" (to wit: "self-consciousness, criticism, the Unique," etc.), while what is designated with the words "destiny," "goal," "germ," or "idea" of earlier history is nothing more than an abstraction formed from later history, from the active influence which earlier history exercises on later history. The further the separate spheres, which interact on one another, extend in the course of this development, the more the original isolation of the separate nationalities is destroyed by the developed mode of production and intercourse and the division of labor naturally brought forth by these, the more history becomes world-history. Thus, for instance, if in England a machine is invented, which in India or China deprives countless workers of bread, and overturns the whole form of existence of these empires, this invention becomes a world-historical fact. Or again, take the case of sugar and coffee which have proved their world-historical importance in the nineteenth century by the fact that the lack of these products occasioned by the Napoleonic Continental system, caused the Germans to rise against Napoleon, and thus became the real basis of the glorious Wars of Liberation of 1813. From this it follows that this transformation of history into world-history is not indeed a mere abstract act on the part of the "self-consciousness," the world-spirit, or of any other metaphysical spectre, but a quite material empirically verifiable act, an act the proof of which every individual furnishes as he comes and goes, eats, drinks and clothes himself.

The ideas of the ruling class are in every epoch the ruling ideas: i.e., the class, which is the ruling material force of society, is at the same time its ruling intellectual force. The class which has the means of material production at its disposal, has control at the same time over the means of mental production, so that thereby, generally speaking, the ideas of those who lack the means of mental production are subject to it. The ruling ideas are nothing more than the ideal expression of the dominant material relationships, the dominant material relationships grasped as ideas; hence of the relationships which make the one class the ruling one, therefore the ideas of its dominance. The individuals composing the ruling class possess among other things consciousness, and therefore think. In so far, therefore, as they rule as a class and determine the extent and compass of an epoch, it is self-evident that they do this in their whole range, hence among other things rule also as thinkers, as producers of ideas, and regulate the production and distribution of the ideas of their age: thus their ideas are the ruling ideas of the epoch. For instance, in an age and in a country where royal power, aristocracy and bourgeoisie are contending for mastery and where, therefore, mastery is shared, the doctrine of the separation of powers proves to be the dominant idea and is expressed as an "eternal law." The division of labor, which we saw above as one of the chief forces of history up till now, manifests itself in the ruling class as the division of mental and material labor, so that inside this class one part appears as the thinkers of the class (its active, conceptive ideologists, who make the perfecting of the illusion of the class about itself their chief source of livelihood), while the others' attitude to these ideas and illusions is more passive and receptive, because they are in reality the active members of this class and have less time to make up illusions and ideas about themselves. Within this class this cleavage can even develop into a certain opposition and hostility between the two parts, which, however, in the case of a practical collision, in which the class itself is endangered, automatically comes to nothing, in which case there also vanishes the semblance that the ruling ideas were not the ideas of the ruling class and had a power distinct from the power of this class. The existence of revolutionary ideas in a particular period presupposes the existence of a revolutionary class; about the premises for the latter sufficient has already been said above.

If now in considering the course of history we detach the ideas of the ruling class from the ruling class itself and attribute to them an independent existence, if we confine ourselves to saying that these or those ideas were dominant, without bothering ourselves about the conditions of production and the producers of these ideas, if we then ignore the individuals and world conditions which are the source of the ideas, we can say, for instance, that during the time that the aristocracy was dominant, the concepts honor, loyalty, etc., were dominant, during the dominance of the bourgeoisie the concepts freedom, equality, etc. The ruling class itself on the whole imagines this to be so. This conception of history, which is common to all historians, particularly since the eighteenth century, will necessarily come up against the phenomenon that increasingly abstract ideas hold sway, i.e., ideas which increasingly take on the form of universality. For each new class which puts itself in the place of one ruling before it, is compelled, merely in order to carry through its aim, to represent its interest as the common interest of all the members of society, put in an ideal form; it will give its ideas the form of universality, and represent them as the only rational, universally valid ones. The class making a revolution appears from the very start, merely because it is opposed to a *class*, not as a class but as the representative of the whole of society; it appears as the whole mass of society confronting the one ruling class. It can do this because, to start with, its interest really is more connected with the common interest of all other non-ruling classes, because under the pressure of conditions its interest has not yet been able to develop as the particular interest of a particular class. Its victory, therefore, benefits also many individuals of the other classes which are not winning a dominant position, but only in so far as it now puts these individuals in a position to raise themselves into the ruling class. When the French bourgeoisie overthrew the power of the aristocracy, it thereby made it possible for many proletarians to raise themselves above the proletariat, but only in so far as they become bourgeois. Every new class, therefore, achieves its hegemony only on a broader basis than that of the class ruling previously, in return for which the opposition of the non-ruling class against the new ruling class later develops all the more sharply and profoundly. Both these things determine the fact that the struggle to be waged against this new ruling class, in its turn, aims at a more decided and radical negation of the previous conditions of society than could all previous classes which sought to rule.

This whole semblance, that the rule of a certain class is only the rule of certain ideas, comes to a natural end, of course, as soon as society ceases at last to be organized in the form of class-rule, that is to say as soon as it is no longer necessary to represent a particular interest as general or "the general interest" as ruling.

Once the ruling ideas have been separated from the ruling individuals and, above all, from the relationships which result from a given stage of the mode of production, and in this way the conclusion has been reached that history is always under the sway of ideas, it is very easy to abstract from these various ideas "the idea," "die Idee," etc., as the dominant force in history, and thus to understand all these separate ideas and concepts as "forms of self-determination" on the part of *the* concept developing in history. It follows then naturally, too, that all the relationships of men can be derived from the concept of man, man as conceived, the essence of man, *man*. This has been done by the speculative philosophers. Hegel himself confesses at the end of *The Philosophy of History* that he "has considered the progress of *the concept* only" and has represented in history "the true theodicy." Now one can go back again to the "producers of the concept," to the theoreticians, ideologists and philosophers, and one comes then to the conclusion that the philosophers, the thinkers as such, have at all times been dominant in history: a conclusion, as we see, already expressed by Hegel. The whole trick of proving the hegemony of the spirit in history (hierarchy, Stirner calls it) is thus confined to the following three tricks.

1. One must separate the ideas of those ruling for empirical reasons, under empirical conditions and as empirical individuals, from these and actual rulers, and thus recognize the rule of ideas or illusions in history.

2. One must bring an order into this rule of ideas, prove a mystical connection among the

successive ruling ideas, which is managed by understanding them as "acts of self-determination on the part of the concept" (this is possible because by virtue of their empirical basis these ideas are really connected with one another and because, conceived as *mere* ideas, they become self-distinctions, distinctions made by thought).

3. To remove the mystical appearance of this "self-determining concept" it is changed into a person—"self-consciousness"—or, to appear thoroughly materialistic, into a series of persons, who represent the "concept" in history, into the "thinkers," the "philosophers" the ideologists, who again are understood as the manufacturers of history, as "the council of guardians," as the rulers. Thus the whole body of materialistic elements has been removed from history and now full rein can be given to the speculative steed.

While in ordinary life every shopkeeper is very well able to distinguish between what somebody professes to be and what really is, our historians have not yet won even this trivial insight. They take every epoch at its word and believe that everything it says and imagines about itself is true.

This historical method which reigned in Germany, (and especially the reason why), must be understood from its connection with the illusion of ideologists in general, e.g., the illusions of the jurists, politicians (of the practical statesmen among them, too), from the dogmatic dreamings and distortions of these fellows; this illusion is explained perfectly easily from their practical position in life, their job, and the division of labor.

NOTES

1. The building of houses. With savages each family has of course its own cave or hut like the separate family tent of the nomads. This separate domestic economy is made only the more necessary by the further development of private property. With the agricultural peoples a communal domestic economy is just as impossible as a communal cultivation of the soil. A great advance was the building of towns. In all previous periods, however, the abolition of individual economy, which is inseparable from the abolition of private property, was impossible for the simple reason that the material conditions governing it were not present. The setting-up of a communal domestic economy presupposes the development of machinery, of the use of natural forces and of many other productive forces—e.g., of water-supplies, of gas-lighting, steam-heating, etc., the removal of the antagonism of town and country. Without these conditions a communal economy would not in itself form a new productive force; lacking any material basis and resting on a purely theoretical foundation, it would be a mere freak and would end in nothing more than a monastic economy.—What was possible can be seen in the formation of towns and the erection of communal buildings for various definite purposes (prisons, barracks, etc.). That the abolition of individual economy is inseparable from the abolition of the family is self-evident.

FURTHER READINGS

Avineri, Shlomo. *The Social and Political Thought of Karl Marx*. London: Cambridge University Press, 1968.

Benn, S. I., and Peters, R. *Social Principles and the Democratic State*. London: Allen and Unwin, 1959.

Edwards, Paul, editor-in-chief. *The Encyclopedia of Philosophy*. New York: Macmillan, 1967.

Feinberg, Joel. *Social Philosophy*. Englewood Cliffs, N. J.: Prentice-Hall, 1973.

McCloskey, H. J. *John Stuart Mill*. London: Macmillan, 1971.

MacPherson, C. B. *The Political Theory of Possessive Individualism*. Oxford: Clarendon Press, 1962.

Peters, R. S. *Hobbes*. Baltimore: Penguin, 1956.

Wolff, R. P. *In Defense of Anarchism*. New York: Harper and Row, 1970.